The Fremont Street Experience, located in the heart of Glitter Gulch, has revitalized downtown Las Vegas and offers a high-tech light-and-laser show. See chapter 7.
© Ken Biggs/Tony Stone Images.

Golf enthusiasts will find a number of challenging courses in the Las Vegas area, including some that host PGA events. See chapter 7. © Sal Maimone/Photophile.

MGM MIRAGE's premiere luxury resort, the adult-oriented Bellagio, features fine dining, a highly regarded art collection, and a dazzling fountain extravaganza. See chapter 5. © Richard Cummins Photography.

Frommer's

Las Vegas 2004

POSTCARDS FROM

The Strip at night, lit up in all its neon glory, is one of the most spectacular sights in the world. © Richard Cummins Photography.

No city in the world features a more diverse group of hotels than that found on the Las Vegas Strip. Watch a "volcano" explode amidst the tropical foliage and waterfalls of the Mirage before heading off to the Roman-themed towers of Caesars. See chapter 1 for our favorite Las Vegas hotels. © *Richard Cummins/Corbis.*

All roads in Vegas lead to casinos, where millions of visitors open their wallets each year in the hopes of winning the Big One. See chapter 8 for our favorite spots to gamble.
© Photophile.

When temperatures soar, many visitors seek relief in a pool, either at their hotel or at The Strip's premier water park, Wet 'n' Wild. See chapter 7. © Mark E. Gibson Photography.

Storm the castle at Excalibur, a kitschy medieval fantasyland where you can take in a joust before you court Lady Luck at the gaming tables. See chapter 5.
© Paul Thompson/International Stock.

The Liberace Museum is a one-of-a-kind attraction; the ultimate shrine to the performer's campy excess. If you have a sense of humor, this is a Las Vegas institution that shouldn't be missed. See chapter 7. © Richard Cummins Photography.

Those seeking respite from the casinos should head for the stunning and unspoiled terrain of Red Rock Canyon, internationally renowned for its magnificent hiking trails. See chapter 11. © *Mark E. Gibson Photography.*

Frommer's

Las Vegas

2004

by Mary Herczog

Here's what the critics say about Frommer's:

"Amazingly easy to use. Very portable, very complete."

—*Booklist*

"Detailed, accurate, and easy-to-read information for all price ranges."
—*Glamour Magazine*

"Hotel information is close to encyclopedic."

—*Des Moines Sunday Register*

"Frommer's Guides have a way of giving you a real feel for a place."
—*Knight Ridder Newspapers*

WILEY

Wiley Publishing, Inc.

About the Author

Mary Herczog lives in Los Angeles and works in the film industry. She is the author of *Frommer's New Orleans*, *California For Dummies*, *Frommer's Portable Las Vegas for Non-Gamblers*, and *Las Vegas For Dummies*, and has contributed to *Frommer's Los Angeles*. She still isn't sure when to hit and when to hold in blackjack.

Published by:

Wiley Publishing, Inc.

111 River St.
Hoboken, NJ 07030

ISBN 0-7645-3888-8
ISSN 1532-0006

Editor: Naomi P. Kraus
Production Editor: Heather Wilcox
Cartographer: Nicholas Trotter
Photo Editor: Richard Fox
Production by Wiley Indianapolis Composition Services

For information on our other products and services or to obtain technical support, please contact our Customer Care Department within the U.S. at 800-762-2974, outside the U.S. at 317-572-3993 or fax 317-572-4002.

Wiley also publishes its books in a variety of electronic formats. Some content that appears in print may not be available in electronic formats.

Manufactured in the United States of America

5 4 3 2 1

Contents

5 Where to Stay 67

6 Where to Dine 122

7 What to See & Do in Las Vegas 173

8 About Casino Gambling 204

List of Maps

Acknowledgments

As always, working for Frommer's and with Naomi Kraus is like hitting 21 a whole bunch of times in a row. Great thanks to Rick Garman for 14 lucky years. Thanks to designated drinkers Arlene and Caroline. Steve Hochman makes me a winner.

—Mary Herczog

The editorial staff at Frommer's also wishes to thank the Las Vegas Convention & Visitors Authority, Brigitte Bélanger and Magdalena Vandenburg at Cirque du Soleil, and Alex Kraus for their assistance in making this book a winner.

An Invitation to the Reader

In researching this book, we discovered many wonderful places—hotels, restaurants, shops, and more. We're sure you'll find others. Please tell us about them, so we can share the information with your fellow travelers in upcoming editions. If you were disappointed with a recommendation, we'd love to know that, too. Please write to:

Frommer's Las Vegas 2004
Wiley Publishing, Inc. • 111 River St. • Hoboken, NJ 07030

An Additional Note

Please be advised that travel information is subject to change at any time—and this is especially true of prices. We therefore suggest that you write or call ahead for confirmation when making your travel plans. The authors, editors, and publisher cannot be held responsible for the experiences of readers while traveling. Your safety is important to us, however, so we encourage you to stay alert and be aware of your surroundings. Keep a close eye on cameras, purses, and wallets, all favorite targets of thieves and pickpockets.

Other Great Guides for Your Trip:

Frommer's Portable Las Vegas
Frommer's Portable Las Vegas for Non-Gamblers
Las Vegas For Dummies
The Unofficial Guide to Las Vegas
Frommer's Irreverent Guide to Las Vegas
Frommer's California
Frommer's Utah
Frommer's Arizona
Frommer's U.S.A

Frommer's Star Ratings, Icons & Abbreviations

Every hotel, restaurant, and attraction listing in this guide has been ranked for quality, value, service, amenities, and special features using a **star-rating system.** In country, state, and regional guides, we also rate towns and regions to help you narrow down your choices and budget your time accordingly. Hotels and restaurants are rated on a scale of zero (recommended) to three stars (exceptional). Attractions, shopping, nightlife, towns, and regions are rated according to the following scale: zero stars (recommended), one star (highly recommended), two stars (very highly recommended), and three stars (must-see).

In addition to the star-rating system, we also use **seven feature icons** that point you to the great deals, in-the-know advice, and unique experiences that separate travelers from tourists. Throughout the book, look for:

Finds	Special finds—those places only insiders know about
Fun Fact	Fun facts—details that make travelers more informed and their trips more fun
Kids	Best bets for kids and advice for the whole family
Moments	Special moments—those experiences that memories are made of
Overrated	Places or experiences not worth your time or money
Tips	Insider tips—great ways to save time and money
Value	Great values—where to get the best deals

The following **abbreviations** are used for credit cards:

AE	American Express	DISC	Discover	V	Visa
DC	Diners Club	MC	MasterCard		

Frommers.com

Now that you have the guidebook to a great trip, visit our website at **www.frommers.com** for travel information on more than 3,000 destinations. With features updated regularly, we give you instant access to the most current trip-planning information available. At Frommers.com, you'll also find the best prices on airfares, accommodations, and car rentals—and you can even book travel online through our travel booking partners. At Frommers.com, you'll also find the following:

- Online updates to our most popular guidebooks
- Vacation sweepstakes and contest giveaways
- Newsletter highlighting the hottest travel trends
- Online travel message boards with featured travel discussions

What's New in Las Vegas

Gee, what *isn't* new in Las Vegas? That they want to take your money and will do so by any means necessary. Cynical? Hardly. That is, after all, why this town was built and don't, for a minute, think anything else.

Otherwise, everything is new in Las Vegas. This town is afflicted with terminal restlessness and must keep finding new ways of attracting visitors who can then be relieved of their money. Heck, by the time we've finished writing this, everything we've written, everything in the whole town, will be outdated, changed, or somehow different.

Perhaps we exaggerate. But really, only a little. Hotels are routinely renovating, upgrading, redecorating their rooms, and changing their themes (because everyone knows that a Spanish theme will bring in more tourist dollars than a Mardi Gras theme—that is, until they decide it's been long enough with the Spanish theme and then switch to an Asian one), and that's only if they aren't blowing up the hotel and starting over from scratch. New restaurants with celebrity chefs and big prices open, and longtime stalwarts with comfort food for the ages close. Shows that have been touted with enormous billboards and bigger budgets close in the blink of an eye. Please remember this and think kindly of us if anything in this book is inaccurate. Because that's why.

So, as we write this, what's new? Or even, what's going to be new?

PLANNING YOUR TRIP The Disneyfication of Vegas is pretty much dead and gone. Do not expect a "family-friendly" place, not at these prices. Vegas is returning to its adult roots, with all that entails, so you should think twice—and then some more—about dragging Junior along with you to Sin City.

Having said that, you might, with some planning, end up spending a little bit less this year than in the most recent past. Vegas experienced a huge loss in revenue after September 11, plus about a 50% drop in tourism, resulting in about 14,000 people being laid off, the largest labor cuts experienced by any one city in the nation following the terrorist attacks.

With the economy in flux, continuing concerns about security during travel, and all sorts of world-shaking events occurring, tourism for Vegas is up and down and up and down, and what you are going to face is unpredictable. Conventions are still coming to town—not as huge, perhaps, as in the past, but enough to make hotel bookings impossible during their staging. The rest of the time, you might well find a bargain. For cost-cutting tips and other useful planning advice, see chapter 2.

ACCOMMODATIONS You'd think that tourism dips would daunt any plans for further expansion, but no, not our fearless Vegas hotel honchos. We shake our heads as reports come in of still another giant Vegas hotel in the planning stages. "Don't they have *enough* hotel rooms by now?"

we wonder, "Don't they *ever* have too many?" Apparently not.

You won't be seeing anything apart from cranes and construction sites until late 2003, when the Weston Spa Resort will open on the site of the former, and not a bit missed, Maxim Hotel. Mandalay Bay and Venetian will both open large new expansions around that same time, with Bellagio following suit in 2004. You will have to wait until 2005 for a new hotel, but it should be worth that wait because it's coming from Steve Wynn, the man responsible for modern-day theme-intensive Vegas. Wynn Las Vegas (originally named Le Reve, but the new one fits so much better!), planned as really tall resort towers, complete with a man-made 150-foot-tall mountain in front, will occupy the place of the demolished **Desert Inn.**

Or you can watch with us as the relatively new Aladdin climbs out of its even newer bankruptcy with the help of a new owner, Planet Hollywood. Watch as the Middle East theme is swiftly replaced by Hollywood memorabilia, and that big globe of theirs goes up on the Strip. Or observe the changes to the Golden Nugget in Downtown now that it has been unloaded by MGM MIRAGE.

This is a town full of self-styled luxury resorts, but the only place with a real claim to such a title is a 30-minute drive away. The brand-new Ritz-Carlton, Lake Las Vegas, is set right on the lake itself, with a dazzling view of the water and mountains. Add to that the kind of service that made the company's name famous—big rooms and lush baths, and a huge list of amenities and recreation activities—and we forget all about the siren lure of the Strip.

Of course, there remain the rumors about still more Titan-sized theme hotels, these paying neon-bedecked homage to San Francisco, London, and water in general. The good news,

of course, is that Vegas isn't the same without such fabulous monsters, though we are equally pleased with talk of a boutique hotel, perhaps a W or something like it, going up next to the Frontier. (Which may happen sooner than you think: There's gossip that the Venetian is partnering with Brad Pitt and George Clooney to build a boutique hotel on the Strip—over a Walgreen's drugstore, no less.)

For complete details on the lodging scene in Las Vegas, see chapter 5.

DINING   If you love sandwiches, then let me put you on to **Canter's,** the popular Los Angeles Jewish deli that just opened a branch at TI (formerly Treasure Island) at the Mirage. Famous for their sourdough rye, piled high with pastrami, corned beef, or whatever, they've also got a lox plate, soups including matzo ball and the "famous" barley bean, and New York cheesecake. For now Canter's is in a temporary space in the casino race book, but a new 125-seat restaurant should be ready by the end of the year. But don't wait: Call me now and I'll join you for a nosh.

For more dining options in Las Vegas, see chapter 6.

ABOUT CASINO GAMBLING
There is a big change quietly happening all over town—and actually, the key word here is "quiet." Like us, perhaps you thrill to that distinct sound of coins dropping, *clinkclinkclinkclinkclink,* as you cash out on your slot (or poker) machine. That sound will always be with us, but very soon it's just going to be a programmed audio track, because all the major casinos (and maybe all of them, period) are changing their machines over to a cashless system, wherein the payouts will come in the form of printed slips you take to exchange at the cages. Gambling will never be the same again.

For tips on maximizing your wins and choosing a casino, see chapter 8.

SHOPPING When Las Vegas Premium Outlets Center opens, near Downtown, in fall 2003, we may be spending so much money there that we won't have any left over for gambling. (Just as well, perhaps.) Can you blame us? It will have 100 stores, including Armani Exchange, Coach, Dolce & Gabbana, Guess, Kenneth Cole, Lacoste, Polo/Ralph Lauren, St. John, and Theory. And it's just what the otherwise moribund (if flashy looking) shopping scene in Vegas needs.

The Forum Shops in Caesars are undergoing yet another huge expansion; this one will have a three-story glass entrance right near the Strip. But don't get your credit cards too ready— it won't be open until late 2004.

LAS VEGAS AFTER DARK It's clear that everyone is open to putting the "sin" back in Sin City, as more adult-oriented shows make a comeback. It's hard to tell the difference these days between the strip bars and the hotel clubs and lounges, when new happening hot spots such as **Rain** (in the Palm), **Bikinis** (in the Rio), and **Risque** (in Paris Las Vegas), among others, have go-go dancers as scantily clad and performing the exact same gyrations as the strippers. Other new joints have names such as **Tabu** (in the MGM Grand). And Cirque du Soleil is opening a new show, *Zumanity,* that will offer glimpses (or more) of bare flesh and is strictly for the 18-and-over set. (Another, regular and nonracy Cirque show is due at the MGM Grand by early 2004.) It's just a matter of time before a hotel opens up its own "gentlemen's club" (read: strip bar), and when that happens, watch the others follow with due haste.

As for real strip clubs, this past year saw the opening of first **Jaguar's,** a 25,000-square-foot extravaganza that is as marbled and over the top as Caesars Palace in its shameless days. But it was quickly eclipsed by **Sapphire's,** which clocks in at 71,000 square feet and so is the largest strip joint in the world.

But it's not all about the nudity; it's also about the big bucks. And that brings us to the return of **Celine Dion** to live performing, thanks to a luxurious new venue built just for her at Caesars, where she performs in a multimillion-dollar extravaganza, accompanied by a giant LED screen, special effects, and many, many Cirque-influenced performers and enigmatic imagery (thanks to the director and producer, who was behind the local productions of *O* and *Mystère*). Thanks to her ticket prices (starting at $88 and going up to $150), the big shows all over town have raised their rates as well.

The long-delayed **Neonopolis,** a $100-million open-air restaurant, shop, and entertainment complex (with an 11-screen movie theater), finally opened right at the Fremont Street Experience, where Fremont Street meets Las Vegas Boulevard South. It includes a serious entertainment area run by Jillian's, a national company, that offers a great arcade, a huge bowling alley, and other fun offerings, making this an alternative to traditional (but age-limited) Vegas entertainment and activities. Best of all, it's open late and it may provide a shot in the arm to the still struggling Downtown.

For the scoop on after-dark activities in Las Vegas, see chapter 10.

1

The Best of Las Vegas

*The point about [Las Vegas], which both its critics and its
admirers overlook, is that it's wonderful and awful simultaneously.
So one loves it and detests it at the same time.*

—David Spanier, *Welcome to the
Pleasure Dome: Inside Las Vegas*

As often as you might have seen it on TV or in a movie, there is nothing that
prepares you for that first sight of Las Vegas. The skyline is hyper-reality, a mélange
of the Statue of Liberty, a giant lion, a pyramid, and a Sphinx, and preternaturally
glittering buildings. At night, it's so bright you can actually get disoriented—and
suffer from a sensory overload that can reduce you to hapless tears or fits of gig-
gles. And that's without setting foot inside a casino, where the shouts from the
craps tables, the crash of coins from the slots, and the general roar combine into
either the greatest adrenaline rush of your life or the 11th pit of hell.

Las Vegas is a true original; there is nothing like it in America or arguably the
world. In other cities, hotels are built near the major attractions. Here, the hotels
are the major attractions. For that matter, what other city has a skyline made up
almost entirely of buildings from other cities' skylines? Instead of historical
codes to follow, builders in Vegas have to worry about the height of the roller
coaster in their hotel.

Once you get to Vegas, you'll want to come back again, if only to make sure
you didn't dream it all. It's not just the casinos with their nonstop action and
sound, the almost-blinding lights, or the buildings that seek to replicate some
other reality (Paris, Venice, New York, and ancient Egypt). It's not the mountains of shrimp at the buffets, the wedding chapels that will gladly unite two
total strangers in holy wedlock, or the promise of free money. It's the whole
package. It's the Megabucks slots. It's Frank and Dino and Sammy. It's Elvis—
the Fat Years. It's volcanoes and white tigers and cocktail waitresses dressed in
Roman togas. It's cheesy and sleazy and artificial and wholly, completely unique.
It's wonderful. It's awful. It's wonderfully awful and awfully wonderful. Love it,
loathe it, or both, no one has ambivalent feelings about Vegas.

Las Vegas can be whatever a visitor wants, and for a few days, a visitor can be
whatever he or she wants. Just be prepared to leave all touchstones with reality
behind. Here, you will rise at noon and gorge on endless amounts of rich food
at 3am. You will watch your money grow or (more likely) shrink. You will watch
a volcano explode and pirates fight sexy showgirls. And after a while, it will all
seem pretty normal. This is not a cultural vacation, okay? Save the thoughts of
museums and historical sights for the real New York, Egypt, Paris, and Venice.
Vegas is about fun. Go have some. Go have too much. It won't be hard.

The Vegas of the Rat Pack years, classic Old Las Vegas, does not exist anymore.
Even as ancient civilizations are replicated, "old" in Vegas terms is anything over a
decade. Indeed, thanks to teardowns and renovations, there is virtually nothing
original left on the Strip. In a way, that is both admirable and ghastly, and also part

Las Vegas & Environs

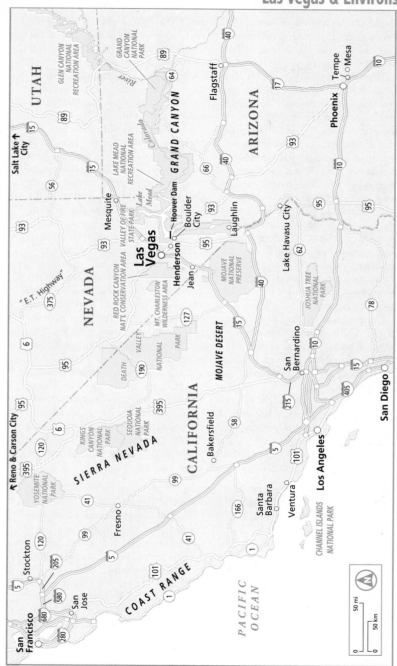

of what makes Vegas so *Vegas*. What other city can completely shed its skin in such a short amount of time?

But as much as one might mourn the loss of such landmarks as the Sands, one has to admit that time marches on, and Vegas has to keep pace. Nostalgia for the vanished does not mean you can't enjoy what turns up in its place. Even as you might sneer at the sheer gaudy tastelessness of it all, you have to admit that what's out there is undeniably remarkable.

And when it's all lit up at night . . . well, even those who have lived here for years agree there is nothing like the sight of the Strip in all its evening glory. "It still takes my breath away, even after all this time," says one long-time resident. Everything is in lights in Vegas: hotels, casinos, 7-Elevens, the airport parking garage. Stand still long enough, and they'll probably cover you in neon.

Oh, the gambling? Yep, there's plenty of that. Which is much like saying there's plenty of sand at the beach. Let's not kid ourselves: Gambling is the main attraction of Vegas. The rest—the buffets, the shows, the cartoonish buildings—is so much window dressing to lure you and your money to the city. But even a nongambler can have a perfectly fine time in Vegas, though the lure of countless slot machines has tempted even the most Puritan of souls in their day.

Unfortunately, the days of an inexpensive Las Vegas vacation are gone. The cheap buffets and meal deals still exist, as do some cut-rate rooms, but both are likely to prove the old adage about getting what you pay for. If all you're looking for is fuel and a place to catch a quick nap, they'll do just fine. Be prepared to pay if you want glamour and fine dining.

However, free drinks are still handed to anyone lurking near a slot, and even if show tickets aren't in your budget, you won't lack for entertainment. Free lounge shows abound, and the people-watching opportunities never disappoint. From the Armani-clad high rollers in the baccarat rooms to the polyester-sporting couples at the nickel slots, Vegas attracts a cross section of America.

Yes, it's noisy and chaotic. Yes, it's gotten more and more like Disneyland for adults. Yes, it's a shrine to greed and the love of filthy lucre. Yes, there is little ambience and even less "culture." Yes, someone lacking self-discipline can come to great grief.

But in its own way, Vegas is every bit as amazing as the nearby Grand Canyon, and every bit as much a must-see. It's one of the Seven Wonders of the Artificial World. And everyone should experience it at least once—you might find yourself coming back for more.

1 Frommer's Favorite Las Vegas Experiences

- **A Stroll on the Strip After Dark:** You haven't really seen Las Vegas until you've seen it at night. This neon wonderland is the world's greatest sound-and-light show. Begin at Luxor and work your way down past the incredible hotels and their attractions. You'll pass the amazing New York–New York on your way, and if your strength holds out, you will end at Circus Circus, where live acrobat acts take place overhead while you gamble. Make plenty of stops en route to take in the new *Sirens* show at Treasure Island, see the Mirage volcano erupt, take a photo of the full moon over the Eiffel Tower, and, most of all, marvel at the choreographed water-fountain ballet at Bellagio.

- **Casino-Hopping on the Strip:** The interior of each lavish new hotel-casino is more outrageous and giggle-inducing than the last. Just when you think they can't possibly top themselves, they do. From Venice to ancient Egypt, from a rainforest to a pirate's lair, from King Arthur's castle to New York City, it is still all, totally, completely, and uniquely Las Vegas.

- **An Evening in Glitter Gulch:** Set aside an evening to tour the Downtown hotels and take in the overhead light show of the **Fremont Street Experience** (p. 179). Unlike the lengthy and exhausting Strip, you can hit 17 casinos in about 5 minutes.

- **Buffets:** They may no longer be the very best of bargains, as the cheaper ones do not provide the quality of the more pricey ones, but there is something about the endless mounds of food that just screams "Vegas" to us. Our choices for the best in town are listed in the dining section later in this chapter.

- **A Creative Adventures Tour:** Char Cruze of **Creative Adventures** (© 702/361-5565) provides personalized tours unlike anything offered by a commercial tour company, full of riveting stories and incredible facts about both natural and artificial local wonders. See p. 197.

- **The Liberace Museum:** It's not the Smithsonian, but then again, the Smithsonian doesn't have rhinestones like these. Only in Vegas. See p. 181.

- **The Dolphins at The Mirage:** Actually, a most un-Vegas experience. Zone out as you watch these gorgeous mammals frolic in their cool, blue pool. If you are really lucky, they'll play ball with you. See p. 184.

- **Playing Penny Slots:** Where even the most budget-conscious traveler can gamble for hours. The Gold Spike in Downtown has them, but so does Bally's on the Strip and any of the Station casinos. See chapter 8.

- **Shop the Big Three Casino Arcades:** Take what Napoleon called "the greatest drawing room in Europe," replicate it, add shops, and you've got the **Grand Canal Shoppes at The Venetian** (p. 239)—it's St. Mark's Square, complete with canals and working gondolas. Then there are the **Forum Shops at Caesars Palace** (p. 237), replicating an ancient Roman streetscape, with classical piazzas and opulent fountains. Don't miss the scary Audio-Animatronic statues as they come to glorious, cheesy life. And not to be outdone, the **Desert Passage at Aladdin** (p. 236) re-creates the ancient trade route through Morocco, complete with a special-effects rainstorm over an indoor harbor (at least until the hotel's new owners take over).

- **Cirque du Soleil's _O_ and _Mystère:_** You haven't really seen Cirque du Soleil until you've seen it performed in a showroom equipped with state-of-the-art sound-and-lighting systems and a seemingly infinite budget for sets, costumes, and high-tech special effects. It's an enchantment. Note that by the time you read this, a new Cirque show, _Zumanity,_ the "intended for adults over 18" risqué show at New York–New York will have opened. Another Cirque production will debut at the MGM Grand in January 2004, though details have yet to be announced. See p. 248 and 249.

- **Your Favorite Headliners:** As soon as you arrive in town, pick up a show guide and see who's playing during your stay. For the top showrooms, see chapter 10.

- **Finding the Worst Lounge Shows:** Some feel this is the ultimate Vegas experience and dedicate many an evening to it. Be sure to watch out for Cook E. Jarr and the Crumbs. See chapter 10 for some ideas.

A Look Back at Vegas: No Tomorrow

Las Vegas is convention central. Orthodontists go there as well as architects. Computer geeks and gynecologists, TV preachers and township clerks, postal workers and pathologists. There's an abundance of good hotel rooms, cheap eats, agreeable weather. Coming and going is reasonably painless. There's golf and gambling and ogling girls—showgirls of unspeakable beauty—and, of course, the mountains and the desert and the sky.

The National Funeral Directors Association advertised its 116th Annual Convention and International Exposition there in the trade press as "A Sure Bet." Debbie Reynolds was talking to the Spouse's Luncheon. Neil Sedaka was singing at the Annual Banquet. There was a golf outing, a new website, the installation of officers. I called the brother and the brother-in-law and said, "Let's get our funeral homes covered and go out to Vegas for the convention." Pat and Mike agreed. All of us are funeral directors. All of us were due for a break. Here's another coincidence: All of our wives are named Mary. The Marys all agreed to come along. They'd heard about the showgirls and high-stakes tables and figured Pat and Mike and I would need looking after. They'd heard about the great malls and the moving statues and the magic shows.

My publisher paid for my airfare and our room at the Hilton. "A Sure Bet" is what they reckoned, too. My book, *The Undertaking—Life Studies from the Dismal Trade,* was being featured in the Marketplace Booth at the exhibit hall. The association would be selling and I'd be signing as many copies as we could for a couple of days. So there I sat, behind a stack of books, glad-handing and autographing, surrounded by caskets and hearses, cremation urns and new computer software, flower stands and funeral flags and embalming supplies. Some things about this enterprise never change—the basic bias toward the horizontal, the general preference for black and blue, the arcane lexicons of loss and wonder. And some are changing every day. Like booksellers and pharmacists and oncologists, many of the small firms are being overtaken by the large consolidators and conglomerates. Custom gives way to convenience. The old becomes old, then new again.

Five thousand undertakers made it to Vegas—the biggest turnout since the last time here, in '74—and 2,300 sales reps and suppliers. It was bigger than Orlando or Kansas City or Chicago, or next year in Boston.

Las Vegas seems perfect for the mortuary crowd—a metaphor for the vexed, late-century American soul that seems these days to run between

2 Best Hotel Bets

- **Best for Conventioneers/Business Travelers:** The **Las Vegas Hilton,** 3000 Paradise Rd. (© **888/732-7117**), adjacent to the Las Vegas Convention Center and the setting for many on-premises conventions, offers extensive facilities that include a full business center—and soon, it will be a stop on the nifty new monorail, making access to the Strip easier than ever. See p. 108.

extremes of fantasy and desolation. Vegas seems just such an oasis: a neon garden of earthly delights amid a moonscape of privations, abundance amid the cacti, indulgence surrounded by thirst and hunger.

Or maybe it's that we undertakers understand these games of chance—the way life is ever asking us to ante up, the way the wager's made before the deal is dealt or dice are tossed, before we pull the lever. Some people play for nickels and dimes, some for dollars, some for keeps. But whatever we play for, we win or lose according to these stakes. We cannot, once winning is certain or losing is sure, change our bet. We cannot play for dollars, then lose in dimes or win in cash when we wager matchsticks. It's much the same with love and grief. They share the same arithmetic and currency. We ante up our hearts in love, we pay our losses off in grief. Baptisms, marriages, funerals—this life's casinos—the games we play for keeps.

Oh, we can play the odds, hedge our bets, count the cards, get a system. I think of Blaise Pascal, the 17th-century French mathematician who bet on heaven thus: "Better to believe in a God who isn't than not to believe in a God who is." Figure the math of that, the odds. Pascal's Wager is what they called it. All of us play a version of this game.

I came downstairs in the middle of the night and lost 200 bucks before it occurred to me that this is how they built this city—on folks like me, on what we'd be willing to lose. The next night my Mary won 800 on one pull of the lever on the slots. They paid her off in crisp C-notes. We laughed and smiled. She tipped the woman who sold her the tokens. She went shopping the next day for a pair of extravagant shoes and came home, as they say, with money in her pockets.

We undertakers understand winners and losers. Our daily lives are lessons in the way love hurts, grief heals, and life—always a game of chance—goes on. In Vegas we get to play the game as if there's no tomorrow. And after a long night of winning or losing, it's good to have a desert close at hand into which we wander, like holy ones of old, to raise our songs of thanks or curse our luck to whatever God there is, or isn't.

—*Thomas Lynch*

Thomas Lynch is a poet and essayist and a funeral director in Milford, Michigan. *The Undertaking—Life Studies from the Dismal Trade* won the Heartland Prize and the American Book Award and was a finalist for the National Book Award. His latest work is *Bodies in Motion and at Rest: On Metaphor and Mortality.*

• **Best Luxury Resort:** There really is only one, and that's the **Ritz-Carlton, Lake Las Vegas,** 1610 Lake Las Vegas Pkwy. (© **800/ 241-3333**), perched on the edge (and over part of) Lake Las Vegas in Henderson. It's the combination of setting (gorgeous, peaceful) and experience (such service!) that wins them the prize. See p. 119. But you might want something that's actually in town, and for that, you must go straight to the **Four Seasons,** 3960 Las Vegas Blvd. S.

(© **877/632-5000**), because experience running luxury resorts around the world makes them the only true claimant to the throne within the Vegas city limits. See p. 73.

- **Best Resort for the Indecisive: Green Valley Ranch,** 2300 Paseo Verde Pkwy. (at I-215), Henderson (© **866/782-9487**), somehow manages to combine the comfort of a Ritz-Carlton with the style of boutique chains such as the W, and makes it all work. Have your cake and eat it too, either in the most comfortable beds in town, or by one of our favorite pools. See p. 121.
- **Best Archetypically Las Vegas Hotel:** As of the end of 2001, there weren't any. Las Vegas hotels are one and all doing such massive face-lifts that the archetype is going to be but a memory. Still, despite some major changes, including a complete exterior face-lift, **Caesars Palace,** 3570 Las Vegas Blvd. S. (© **877/427-7243**), will probably continue to embody the excess and, well, downright silliness that used to characterize Vegas—and to a certain extent still does. See p. 86.
- **Best Swimming Pool:** If you want lushly landscaped areas surrounding amorphously shaped pools with water fountains and slides, plus a rather festive atmosphere, head to **The Mirage,** 3400 Las Vegas Blvd. S. (© **800/627-6667**). See p. 94. But if you've ever longed to swim at Hearst Castle, **Bellagio,** 3600 Las Vegas Blvd. S. (© **888/987-6667**), with six swimming pools in a neoclassical Italian garden setting (and a more hushed, chic ambience), is for you. See p. 85. Then again, the pool at the **Green Valley Ranch Resort** (p. 121), with its foliage, beach, in-water gambling, and everything

else, perhaps has them both beat. But its distant location (in south Las Vegas) takes it out of the running. Only just, though.

- **Best Spa/Health Club:** We only wish our own gym was as handsomely equipped as the one at the Canyon Ranch Spa in **The Venetian** (p. 91), which also has a number of other high-priced amenities on which you can blow your blackjack winnings. A little more affordable is the spa at the **Aladdin,** 3667 Las Vegas Blvd. S. (© **877/333-WISH**); they sent the designers to study the Moorish structures in Morocco, and it shows in the gorgeous detailing of this lush facility. The treatments are wonderful as well. See p. 74. We are also partial to the full compliment of machines at the health club at **The Mirage** (p. 94), probably the best-equipped club of all. Attendants who soothe you with iced towels and drinks, a well-stocked locker room, and comfortable lounges in which to rest up after your workout are other pluses.
- **Best Hotel Dining:** Foodies will work up a good case of gout trying all the haute-cuisine options at **Bellagio** (p. 85), which has branches of Le Cirque, Circo, and Aqua, plus restaurants by Todd English (Olives) and Julian Serrano (Picasso). The hotel has seven James Beard award–winning chefs on staff. **The Venetian** (p. 91) isn't too far behind, with restaurants from Wolfgang Puck, Emeril Lagasse, and Joachim Splichal (Pinot), plus branches of the noted Star Canyon and Lutèce. And the hotel's latest addition is going to feature an entry from Thomas Keller, of Napa Valley's French Laundry, considered perhaps the best restaurant in the country. See chapter 6 for reviews of these restaurants.

- **Best for 20-Somethings to Baby Boomers:** The **Hard Rock Hotel & Casino,** 4455 Paradise Rd. (© **800/473-ROCK**), which bills itself as the world's "first rock 'n' roll hotel and casino" and "Vegas for a new generation." Aficionados of headbanger clubs won't mind the noise level, but we aren't sure about everyone else. See p. 106.

- **Best Interior:** For totally different reasons, it's a tie between **New York–New York Hotel & Casino,** 3790 Las Vegas Blvd. S. (© **800/693-6763**), **The Mirage,** and **The Venetian.** The Mirage's (p. 94) tropical rainforest and massive coral-reef aquarium behind the registration desk may not provide as much relaxation as a Club Med vacation, but they're a welcome change from the general hubbub that is usual for Vegas. Speaking of hubbub, New York–New York (p. 79) has cornered the market on it, but its jaw-dropping interior, with its extraordinary attention to detail (re-creating virtually every significant characteristic of New York City), makes this a tough act to beat (though Big City residents may despise its realism). The Venetian's (p. 91) authentic re-creation of Venice, however, might top it.

- **Best for Families:** The **MGM Grand,** 3799 Las Vegas Blvd. S. (© **800/929-1111**), is still a hit with families, despite backing away from more child-friendly details such as its original Oz theme and eliminating its amusement park. See p. 77. Then there is also the classic choice: **Circus Circus Hotel/Casino,** 2880 Las Vegas Blvd. S. (© **800/444-CIRC**), with ongoing circus acts, a vast video-game arcade, a carnival midway, and a full amusement park. See p. 104. Less aged, and less hectic, **Mandalay Bay,** 3950 Las Vegas

Blvd. S. at Hacienda Ave. (© **877/632-7000**), is a more modern choice, right for families because you can gain access to both the guest rooms and the pool area (itself fun for kids, with a beach, a wave pool, and a lazy river) without trotting through the casino. And grown-ups will find party-fun restaurants, bars, and clubs (including the House of Blues) for their own enjoyment. See p. 75. Those of you with bigger budgets might want to try the **Ritz-Carlton** (p. 119), because not only is it well out of range of Sin City's temptations, it also offers a variety of healthy and fun activities (from hikes to fly-fishing to stargazing).

- **Best Rooms:** Again, we love the **Ritz-Carlton** (p. 119), with its perfect decor, spacious interior, and gorgeous bathrooms, but you'll probably want something closer to town. On the Strip, the 700-square-foot extravaganzas at **The Venetian** (p. 91), with separate sitting and bedroom areas, are full of all sorts of special details. The Grand Tower (but *not* the Emerald Tower) rooms at the **MGM Grand** (p. 77) are the best bet in the lower price range; their modern twist on 1930s curves stands out from the cookie-cutter decor found all around town. Downtown, the rooms at the **Golden Nugget,** 129 E. Fremont St. (© **800/634-3454**), are by far the best. See p. 116.

- **Best Bathrooms:** This honor definitely goes to **Mandalay Bay** (p. 75), where the spacious bathroom setup features copious amounts of glass and marble, plus double sinks and deep soaking tubs—it's a wonder anyone ever leaves them to go to the casino.

- **Best Noncasino Hotel: Four Seasons** (p. 73) wins this category, hands down. Once you've experienced their quiet good taste, superior service and pampering, and the serenity of their noncasino property, it's hard to go back to traditional Vegas hotels. But best of all, should you want the best of both worlds, you need only pass through one door to have access to **Mandalay Bay** (p.75) and all its traditional Vegas hotel accoutrements, including that missing casino.

- **Best Casinos:** Our favorite places to gamble are anywhere we might win. But we also like the casinos in **The Mirage** (lively, beautiful, and not overwhelming; p. 94), **New York–New York** (because of the aforementioned attention to detail—it almost makes losing fun; p. 79), and **Main Street Station,** 200 N. Main St. (© **800/713-8933**), because it's about the most smoke-free casino in town, and because it's pretty. See p. 119.

- **Best Downtown Hotel:** It's a tie. The upscale **Golden Nugget** (p. 116) is exceptionally appealing in every aspect. And **Main Street Station** (p. 119), which has done a terrific job of renovating an older space, now evokes early-20th-century San Francisco, with great Victorian details everywhere, solidly good restaurants, and surprisingly nice rooms for an inexpensive price.

- **Best Views:** From the high-floor rooms at the **Stratosphere Casino Hotel & Tower,** 2000 Las Vegas Blvd. S. (© **800/99-TOWER**), you can see clear to the next county (p. 103), while the Strip-side rooms at **Four Seasons** (p. 73) give you the entire Las Vegas Boulevard panorama from the southernmost end. Higher-up floors at the **Las Vegas Hilton** (p. 108) show you that same panorama from a different perspective.

3 Best Dining Bets

A number of celebrity chefs are cooking in Vegas, awakening us to the opinion that Vegas's rep for lackluster restaurants is no longer deserved. Reviews for all of the restaurants listed below can be found in chapter 6.

- **Best All-Around:** Given our druthers, we are hard-pressed to choose between **Alizé** (© **702/951-7000;** p. 135), at the top of the Palms, where nearly flawless dishes often compete with the sparkling view for sheer delight, and **Rosemary's Restaurant** (© **702/869-2251;** p. 158), a 20-minute drive off the Strip and worth twice as much effort, for some Southern-influenced cooking. Each of these may well put the work of those many high-profile chefs, so prominently featured all over town, to shame. Lastly though, speaking of high-profile

chefs, we never ever turn down a chance to eat what Julian Serrano is making over at **Picasso** (© **702/693-7223;** p. 139), nor what Alex Strada is cooking up at **Renoir** (© **702/791-7223;** p. 140).

- **Best Inexpensive Meal:** The beautiful, fresh, monster submarine sandwiches at **Capriotti's** (© **702/474-0229;** p. 147). They roast their own beef and turkey on the premises and assemble it (or cold cuts, or even vegetables) into delicious well-stuffed submarine sandwiches, ranging in size from 9 to 20 inches, and none of them over $10. We never leave town without one . . . or two.

- **Best Buffet:** On the Strip, it's the **Paris, Le Village Buffet** (© **888/266-5687**), where the stations break from standard form by adhering to regional French food specialties (from places such as Provence, Alsace, and Burgundy) and the results are much better than average. Though not cheap, this is a reasonable substitute for an even more costly fancy meal. See p. 168. **Mirage Buffet** (© **702/791-7111**) remains our favorite midrange choice. The salad bar comes loaded with countless possibilities, including a variety of cold salads (when was the last time you saw gefilte fish on a buffet?). And the gigantic mountain of shrimp is the right sort of decadent touch you want in a Vegas buffet. See p. 169. The **Palms Festival Market Buffet** (© **702/942-7777**) offers the best of the more budget-oriented options, with an array of Middle Eastern goodies and some eccentric additions to the ubiquitous carving stations. See p. 170. Downtown, the **Main Street Station Garden Court,** 200 N. Main St. (© **702/387-1896**), has an incredible buffet: all live-action stations (where the food is made in front of you, sometimes to order); wood-fired brick-oven pizzas; fresh, lovely salsas and guacamole in the Mexican section; and better-than-average desserts. See p. 172.

- **Best Sunday Champagne Brunch:** Head for Bally's, at Mid-Strip, where the lavish **Sterling Sunday Brunch** (© **702/967-7999**) features tables dressed with linen and silver. The buffet itself has everything from caviar and lobster to sushi and sashimi, plus fancy entrees that include the likes of roast duckling with blackcurrant and blueberry sauce. See p. 167.
- **Best Group Budget Meal Deal: Capriotti's** (p. 147) again—a large sandwich can feed two with

leftovers, for about $5 each. Or split a bowl of soup at the **Grand Wok** (© **702/891-7777**) in the MGM. This pan-Asian restaurant offers a variety of soups in such generous portions that four people can make a decent meal out of one serving. See p. 132.

- **Best Bistro:** Actually, we just invented this category to have a way to call **Mon Ami Gabi** (© **702/944-4224**), in the Paris Las Vegas hotel, to your attention. Offering lovely, reasonably priced bistro fare (steak and *pommes frites,* onion soup), it may be our new favorite Vegas restaurant (at least of the noncelebrity-chef variety). See p. 145.
- **Best Restaurant Interiors:** The designers ran amok in the restaurants of **Mandalay Bay.** At **Aureole** (© **702/632-7401**), a four-story wine tower requires that a pretty young thing be hauled up in a harness a la *Peter Pan* to fetch your chosen vintage. See p. 127. The post-Communist party decor at **Red Square** (© **702/632-7407;** p. 129) is topped only by the fire-and-water walls at neighboring **rumjungle** (© **702/632-7408;** p. 270).
- **Best Spot for a Romantic Dinner: Alizé,** at the top of the Palms, has windows on three sides of the dining room, with no other buildings around for many blocks. You get an unobstructed view of all of Vegas, the desert, and the mountains from every part of the restaurant, not just the window seats. Seriously, aren't you in the mood already? See p. 135.
- **Best Spot for a Celebration:** Let's face it, no one parties like the Red Party, so head to **Red Square** in Mandalay Bay, where you can have caviar and vodka in the ultimate capitalist revenge. See p. 129.

Tips **Winning Websites**

Start your online journey to Sin City at **www.vegas4visitors.com**. This small, family-run endeavor is packed full with information; unbiased reviews; contact info; maps; photos; and links to hotels, restaurants, and more.

If you want to pick the brains of the local populace—and who better to ask about life in Las Vegas—head over to **www.lasvegas weekly.com**. You'll find out where locals go for fun, and you can browse through reviews of bars, cafes, nightclubs, restaurants, and amusement parks.

For the most comprehensive Vegas dining resource on the Web, go to **www.nightonthetown.com**. The site arranges its plethora of restaurants by cuisine and location so you can find what you want, where you want it.

If you like your information with a side order of humor, head over to **www.cheapovegas.com**. This fun site offers lots of sassy reviews and unbiased opinions, especially on the Las Vegas casino hotels. There's also a small section on getting freebies while you're in town.

And, finally, for a plethora of information, including trip reports and reviews written by Vegas visitors and locals, try **www.A2Zlas vegas.com**. The site also features ratings for hotels, restaurants, and shows based on their appropriateness for kids, making this a good site for families.

- **Best Free Show at Dinner:** At Treasure Island's **Buccaneer Bay Club** (© **702/894-7223**), everyone rushes to the window when the ship battle begins outside. (Though as we write this, that battle is getting altered, and so is the restaurant. But still.) See p. 136. And then there is the vista offered by the restaurants in Bellagio (**Picasso, Le Cirque, Olives,** and **Circo**), which are grouped to take advantage of the view of the dancing water fountains. See chapter 6 for reviews of all of the Bellagio restaurants.
- **Best Wine List:** It's a competitive market in Vegas for such a title, and with sommeliers switching around, it's hard to guarantee any wine list will retain its quality. Still, you can't go wrong at Mandalay Bay's **Aureole** (© **702/632-7401**),

which has the largest collection of Austrian wines outside of that country, among other surprises. See p. 127.
- **Best Beer List: Rosemary's Restaurant** offers "beer pairings" suggestions with most of its menu options, and includes some curious and fun brands, including fruity Belgian numbers. See p. 158.
- **Best View: Alizé** (p. 135) wins with its floor-to-ceiling window views, but there is something to be said for seeing all of Vegas from the revolving **Top of the World** (© **702/380-7711**), 106 stories off the ground in the Stratosphere Casino Hotel & Tower. See p. 141.
- **Best Seafood:** The Asian-influenced dishes at Bellagio's **Aqua** (© **702/693-7223**) are the only fish dishes consistently worth eating in this desert town—fresh,

light, and beautifully and expertly flavored. See p. 135.

- **Best Italian:** For a Mediterranean angle, head to Todd English's **Onda** (© **702/791-7223**), in The Mirage, which is quietly but swiftly heading to the top of the "locals' favorite" list. See p. 139. For Tuscan cuisine at slightly less dear prices, **Circo** (© **702/693-8150**), in Bellagio, is terrific. See p. 142.

- **Best Deli:** The **Stage Deli** (© **702/ 893-4045**), in Caesars, will give no cause for complaints (your mouth will be too packed with out-of-this-world pastrami to say much of anything). See p. 146.

- **Best New Orleans Cuisine:** **Emeril's New Orleans Fish House** (© **702/891-7374**), in the MGM Grand, and his **Delmonico Steakhouse** (© **702/414-3737**), in The Venetian, bring the celebrity chef's "Bam!" cuisine to the other side of the Mississippi, and we are glad. See p. 128 for Emeril's New Orleans Fish House and p. 136 for his Delmonico Steakhouse.

- **Best Southwestern Cuisine:** We still dream about the huge portions of spicy, amusing food at The Venetian's **Star Canyon** (© **702/ 414-3772**). It's the brainchild of Stephen Pyles, the chef most often credited with inventing Southwestern cuisine. See p. 144.

- **Best Red Meat: Lawry's The Prime Rib,** 4043 Howard Hughes Pkwy. (© **702/893-2223**), has such good prime rib, it's hard to imagine ever having any better. See p. 150.

2

Planning Your Trip to Las Vegas

Before any trip, you need to do a bit of advance planning. You'll need to decide whether a package tour makes sense for you, when to go, and more. In the pages that follow, you'll find everything you need to know to handle the practical details of planning your trip in advance: airlines and area airports, a calendar of events, a list of major conventions you may want to avoid, resources for those of you with special needs, and much more.

We also suggest that you check out chapter 10, "Las Vegas After Dark," before you leave home. If you want to see the most popular shows, it's a good idea to call ahead and order tickets well in advance to avoid disappointment. Ditto if you want to dine in one of the city's top restaurants: Head to chapter 6, "Where to Dine," for full reviews and contact information.

1 Visitor Information

For advance information, call or write the **Las Vegas Convention and Visitors Authority,** 3150 Paradise Rd., Las Vegas, NV 89109 (© **877/VISIT-LV** or 702/892-7575; www.vegasfreedom. com). They can send you a comprehensive packet containing brochures, a map, a show guide, an events calendar, and an attractions list; help you find a hotel that meets your specifications (and even make reservations); and tell you if a major convention is scheduled during the time you would like to visit Las Vegas. Or stop by when you're in town. They're open daily from 8am to 5pm.

Another excellent information source is the **Las Vegas Chamber of Commerce,** 3720 Howard Hughes Pkwy., #100, Las Vegas, NV 89109

(© 702/735-1616; www.lvchamber. com). Ask them to send you their *Visitor's Guide,* which contains extensive information about accommodations, attractions, excursions, children's activities, and more. They can answer all your Las Vegas questions, including those about weddings and divorces. They're open Monday to Friday from 8am to 5pm.

For information on all of Nevada, including Las Vegas, contact the **Nevada Commission on Tourism** (© **800/638-2328;** www.travelnevada. com). They have a comprehensive information packet on Nevada.

There's also lots of great info on the Web. See "Planning Your Trip Online," later in this chapter, which will send you straight to the most useful sites.

2 Money

ATMS
The easiest and best way to get cash away from home is from an ATM (automated teller machine). The **Cirrus** (© **800/424-7787;** www.mastercard.

com) and **PLUS** (© **800/843-7587;** www.visa.com) networks span the globe; look at the back of your bank card to see which network you're on, then call or check online for ATM

Las Vegas Advisor

Professional gambler and longtime Las Vegas resident Anthony Curtis, author of *Bargain City: Booking, Betting, and Beating the New Las Vegas,* knows all the angles for stretching your hotel, restaurant, and, most important, gaming dollar. His 12-page monthly newsletter, the *Las Vegas Advisor,* is chock-full of insider tips on how to maximize your odds on every game, which slot tournaments to enter, casino promotions that represent money-making opportunities for the bettor, where to obtain the best Fun Books (coupon books full of freebies and discounts), which hotel offers a 12-ounce margarita for 99¢ or a steak dinner for $3, what the best buffet and show values in town are, and much, much more.

Subscribers get more than $1,300 worth of coupons for discounts on rooms, meals, show tickets, and car rentals, along with free slot plays, two-for-one bets, and other perks. A subscription is $50 a year, a single issue $5. To subscribe, call ☏ **800/244-2224** or send a check to Las Vegas Advisor, 3687 S. Procyon St., Las Vegas, NV 89103. You can also subscribe through the Las Vegas Advisor website at **www.lasvegasadvisor.com** and get everything except the mailed newsletters and reference guide for $37 per year.

locations at your destination. Be sure you know your personal identification number (PIN) before you leave home and be sure to find out your daily withdrawal limit before you depart. There is an ATM within several feet of you at all times in Las Vegas; no one wants you to find yourself without cash you could lose in a slot! Beware of withdrawal charges, though, which can often run as high as $2 or $3 (the highest charges are usually for commercial machines in convenience stores and hotel lobbies). Also be aware that your own bank may impose a fee every time a card is used at an ATM in a different city or bank. To compare banks' ATM fees within the U.S., use www.bankrate.com.

TRAVELER'S CHECKS

Traveler's checks are something of an anachronism from the days before the ATM made cash accessible at any time. Traveler's checks used to be the only sound alternative to traveling with dangerously large amounts of cash. They were as reliable as currency,

but, unlike cash, could be replaced if lost or stolen.

These days, traveler's checks are less necessary because most cities have 24-hour ATMs that allow you to withdraw small amounts of cash as needed. However, keep in mind that you will likely be charged an ATM withdrawal fee if the bank is not your own, so if you're withdrawing money every day, you might be better off with traveler's checks—provided that you don't mind showing identification every time you want to cash one.

You can get traveler's checks at almost any bank. **American Express** offers denominations of $20, $50, $100, $500, and (for cardholders only) $1,000. You'll pay a service charge ranging from 1% to 4%. You can also get American Express traveler's checks over the phone by calling ☏ **800/221-7282;** Amex gold and platinum cardholders who use this number are exempt from the 1% fee.

Visa offers traveler's checks at Citibank locations nationwide, as well as at several other banks. The service charge ranges between 1.5% and 2%; checks come in denominations of $20, $50, $100, $500, and $1,000. Call ℂ **800/732-1322** for information. **MasterCard** also offers traveler's checks. Call ℂ **800/223-9920** for a location near you.

If you choose to carry traveler's checks, be sure to keep a record of their serial numbers separate from your checks in the event that they are stolen or lost. You'll get a refund faster if you know the numbers.

CREDIT CARDS

Credit cards are safe way to carry money, they provide a convenient record of all your expenses, and they generally offer good exchange rates. You can also withdraw cash advances from your credit cards at banks or ATMs, provided you know your PIN. If you've forgotten yours, or didn't even know you had one, call the number on the back of your credit card and ask the bank to send it to you. It usually takes 5 to 7 business days, though some banks will provide the number over the phone if you tell them your mother's maiden name or some other personal information.

For tips and telephone numbers to call if your wallet is stolen or lost, go to "Lost & Found" in the Fast Facts section of chapter 4.

3 When to Go

Most of a Las Vegas vacation is usually spent indoors, so you can have a good time here year-round. The most pleasant seasons in this area are spring and fall, especially if you want to experience the great outdoors.

Weekdays are slightly less crowded than weekends. Holidays are always a mob scene and come accompanied by high hotel prices. Hotel prices also skyrocket when big conventions and special events are taking place. The slowest times of year are June and July, the week before Christmas, and the week after New Year's.

If a major convention is to be held during your trip, you might want to change your date. Check the box on p. 36 for convention dates, and contact the **Las Vegas Convention and Visitors Authority** (ℂ **877/VISIT-LV** or 702/892-7575; www.vegasfreedom. com), as convention schedules often change.

THE WEATHER

First of all, Vegas isn't always hot, but when it is hot, it's *really* hot. One thing you'll hear again and again is that even though Las Vegas gets very hot, the dry desert heat is not unbearable. This is true. The exception is most of the hotel pool areas because they are surrounded by massive hotels covered in mirrored glass, which acts as a giant magnifying glass, focusing the sun's rays on the antlike people below. Generally the humidity averages a low 22%, and even on very hot days, there's apt to be a breeze. Also, barring the hottest summer days, there's relief at night when temperatures often drop by at least 20°F (−7°C).

(*Fun Fact* **Beating the Odds**

In 1995, Don Harrington entered a satellite event at the World Series of Poker for just $220, won his way into the $10,000 buy for the Championship Event, and went on to win the $1 million prize.

Las Vegas's Average Temperatures (°F/°C) & Precipitation

	Jan	Feb	Mar	Apr	May	June	July	Aug	Sept	Oct	Nov	Dec
Avg. Temp.	47	52	58	66	75	86	91	89	81	69	55	47
	8	11	14	19	24	30	33	32	27	21	13	8
Avg. High Temp.	57	63	69	78	88	99	104	102	94	81	66	57
	14	17	21	26	31	37	40	39	34	27	19	14
Avg. Low Temp.	37	41	47	54	63	72	78	77	69	57	44	37
	3	5	8	12	17	22	26	25	21	14	7	3
Avg. Precip. (in.)	.59	.69	.59	.15	.24	.08	.44	.45	.31	.24	.31	.40
(mm)	1.5	1.8	1.5	.4	.6	.2	1.1	1.1	.8	.6	.8	1.0

For the average, average high, and average low, temperatures are in Fahrenheit on the first line and Celsius on the following line. For the average precipitation measurements, numbers on the first line are in inches, whereas numbers on the second line are in millimeters.

But this is the desert, and it's not hot year-round. It can get quite cold, especially in the winter, when the temperature at night can drop to 30°F (–1°C) and lower. (In the winter of 1998–99, it actually snowed in Vegas, dropping nearly 2 in. on the Strip. For sheer bizarre spectacle, nothing beat the sight of the Luxor's Sphinx blanketed in snow.) The winter breeze can also become a cold, biting, strong wind of up to 40 mph and more. And so, there are entire portions of the year when you won't be using that hotel swimming pool at all (even if you want to—be aware that most of the hotels close huge chunks of those fabulous swimming pool areas for "the season," which can be as long as Labor Day to Memorial Day). If you aren't traveling in the height of summer, bring a wrap. Also, remember your sunscreen and hat—even if it's not all that hot, you can burn very easily and very fast. (You should see all the lobster-red people glowing in the casinos at night.)

LAS VEGAS CALENDAR OF EVENTS

You may be surprised that Las Vegas does not offer as many annual events as most tourist cities. The reason is Las Vegas's very raison d'être: the gaming industry. This town wants its visitors spending their money in the casinos, not at Renaissance fairs and parades.

When in town, check the local paper and call the **Las Vegas Convention and Visitors Authority** (*©* **877/VISIT-LV** or 702/892-7575; www.vegasfreedom.com), or the **Chamber of Commerce** (*©* **702/735-1616**; www.lvchamber.com) to find out about other events scheduled during your visit.

March

NASCAR/Winston Cup. The **Las Vegas Motor Speedway,** 7000 N. Las Vegas Blvd. (*©* **800/644-4444;** www.lvms.com), has become one of the premier facilities in the country, attracting races and racers of all stripes and colors. The biggest of the year are the Sam's Town 300 and UAW–DaimlerChrysler 400 held in early March, often drawing over 100,000 race fans to town.

April

World Series of Poker. This famed 21-day event takes place at **Binion's Horseshoe Casino,** 128 Fremont St. (*©* **702/382-1600;** www.binions. com/worldseries.asp), in late April and early May, with high-stakes gamblers and showbiz personalities competing for six-figure purses. There are daily events with entry stakes ranging from $125 to $5,000. To enter the World Championship Event (purse: $1 million), players must pony up $10,000. It costs nothing to go crowd around the tables and watch the action (which, in 2003, was televised for the first time on The Travel Channel).

June

CineVegas International Film Festival. This annual event, usually held in early June, is growing in popularity and prestige, with film debuts from both independent and major studios, plus lots of celebrities hanging around for the big parties. Call © **800/431-2140** or visit their website at **www.cinevegas.com**.

Las Vegas Jazz Festival. World-class jazz musicians are invited to play at this relatively new but growing festival held at the Fremont Street Experience for 3 days, usually in early June. For details, schedules, and tickets call © **800/249-3559** or visit their website at **www.vegas experience.com**.

September

Oktoberfest. This boisterous autumn holiday is celebrated from mid-September through the end of October at the **Mount Charleston**

Lodge (© **800/955-1314** or 702/872-5408; www.mtcharlestonlodge.com) with music, folk dancers, sing-alongs around a roaring fire, special decorations, and Bavarian cookouts.

International Mariachi Festival. Mandalay Bay, 3950 Las Vegas Blvd. S. (at Hacienda Ave.), started hosting this worldwide Mariachi (Mexican music) festival a few years ago, and it has become one of the city's most eagerly anticipated events. Call Mandalay Bay at © **877/632-7400**. The event is usually held in early September.

October

Invensys Classic. This 5-day championship event (formerly called the PGA Tour Las Vegas Invitational), played on three local courses (the main course is TPC Summerland), is televised by ESPN. For details, call © **702/242-3000**.

Moments New Year's Eve in Las Vegas

Over the last couple of years, more and more people have been choosing Las Vegas as their party destination for New Year's Eve. In fact, some estimates indicate that by the time you read this, there will be more people ringing in the new year in Nevada than in New York City's Times Square.

From experience, we can tell you that there are a lot of people who come here on December 31. We mean a lot of people. Traffic is a nightmare, parking (at least legally) is next to impossible, and there is not 1 square inch of the place that isn't occupied by a human being. Las Vegas doesn't really need a reason to throw a party, but when an event like this comes along, they do it up right.

A major portion of the Strip is closed down, sending the masses and their substantial quantities of alcohol into the street. Each year's celebration is a little different but usually includes a streetside performance by a major celebrity, confetti, the obligatory countdown, and fireworks.

For New Year's 2001, the city launched a massive fireworks extravaganza entitled "America's Party." It involved blasting pyrotechnics from the roofs of 10 different hotels in succession up the Strip, with a grand finale at midnight that rivaled the worldwide millennium celebrations the year before. The event was considered such a success that the city has made it an annual event.

December

National Finals Rodeo. This is the Super Bowl of rodeos, attended by close to 170,000 people each year and offering nearly $5 million in prize money. The top 15 male rodeo stars compete in six different events: calf roping, steer wrestling, bull riding, team roping, saddle bronco riding, and bareback riding. The top 15 women compete in barrel racing. An all-around "Cowboy of the Year" is chosen. In connection with this event, hotels book country stars in their showrooms, and there's even a cowboy shopping opportunity—the **NFR Cowboy Christmas Gift Show,** a trade show for Western gear—at Cashman Field. The NFR runs for 10 days during the first 2 weeks of December at the 17,000-seat Thomas and Mack Center of the University of Nevada, Las Vegas (UNLV). It usually begins on the first Friday in December and lasts through the following Sunday. Order tickets as far in advance as possible (© **702/895-3900**). For more information, see **www.nfrexperience.com**.

Las Vegas Bowl Week. A championship football event in mid-December pits the winners of the Mid-American Conference against the winners of the Big West Conference. The action takes place at the 32,000-seat Sam Boyd Stadium. Call © **702/895-3900** for ticket information.

Western Athletic Conference (WAC) Football Championship. This collegiate championship event takes place the first week in December in Sam Boyd Stadium. Call © **792/731-5595** for ticket information. Ticket prices range from $15 to $100.

New Year's Eve. This is a biggie (reserve your hotel room early). Downtown, on the Fremont Street Experience, there's a big block party with two dramatic countdowns to midnight (the 1st is at 9pm, midnight on the East Coast). The Strip is usually closed to street traffic and hundreds of thousands of people pack the area for the festivities. There are, of course, fireworks.

4 Travel Insurance

Check your existing insurance policies and credit-card coverage before you buy travel insurance. You may already be covered for lost luggage, cancelled tickets, or medical expenses. The cost of travel insurance varies widely, depending on the cost and length of your trip, your age, health, and the type of trip you're taking.

TRIP-CANCELLATION INSURANCE Trip-cancellation insurance helps you get your money back if you have to back out of a trip, if you have to go home early, or if your travel supplier goes bankrupt. Allowed reasons for cancellation can range from sickness to natural disasters to the State Department declaring your destination unsafe for travel. (Insurers usually won't cover vague fears, though, as many travelers discovered who tried to cancel their trips in Oct 2001 because they were wary of flying.) In this unstable world, trip-cancellation insurance is a good buy if you're getting tickets well in advance—who knows what the state of the world, or of your airline, will be in 9 months? Insurance policy details vary, so read the fine print—and especially make sure that your airline or cruise line is on the list of carriers covered in case of bankruptcy. For information, contact one of the following insurers: **Access America** (© 866/807-3982; www.accessamerica.com); **Travel Guard International** (© 800/826-4919; www.travelguard.com); **Travel Insured International** (© 800/243-3174;

www.travelinsured.com); and **Travelex Insurance Services** (℃ 888/457-4602; www.travelex-insurance.com).

MEDICAL INSURANCE Most health insurance policies cover you if you get sick away from home—but check, particularly if you're insured by an HMO. If you require additional medical insurance, try **MEDEX International** (℃ 800/527-0218 or 410/453-6300; www.medexassist. com) or **Travel Assistance International** (℃ 800/821-2828; www.travel assistance.com; for general information on services, call the company's Worldwide Assistance Services Inc. at ℃ **800/777-8710**).

LOST-LUGGAGE INSURANCE On domestic flights, checked baggage is covered up to $2,500 per ticketed passenger. If you plan to check items more valuable than the standard liability, see if your valuables are covered by your homeowner's policy, get baggage insurance as part of your comprehensive travel-insurance package, or buy Travel Guard's "BagTrak" product. Don't buy insurance at the airport, as it's usually overpriced. Be sure to take any valuables or irreplaceable items with you in your carry-on luggage, as many valuables (including books, money, and electronics) aren't covered by airline policies.

If your luggage is lost, immediately file a lost-luggage claim at the airport, detailing the luggage contents. For most airlines, you must report delayed, damaged, or lost baggage within 4 hours of arrival. The airlines are required to deliver luggage, once found, directly to your house or destination free of charge.

5 Health & Safety

THE HEALTHY TRAVELER
It can be hard to find a doctor you can trust when you're in an unfamiliar place. Try to take proper precautions the week before you depart to avoid falling ill while you're away from home. Amid the last-minute frenzy that often precedes a vacation, make an extra effort to eat and sleep well—especially if you feel an illness coming on. It's a drag to be sick on vacation, and a head cold can make a plane flight intolerable.

Limit your exposure to the sun, especially during the first few days of your trip, and from 11am to 2pm every day. Use a sunscreen with a high protection factor and apply it liberally all day, every day, even during the winter. The desert sun can be brutal. Remember that children need more protection than adults do.

WHAT TO DO IF YOU GET SICK AWAY FROM HOME
In most cases, your existing health plan will provide the coverage you need. But double-check; you may want to buy **travel medical insurance** instead. (See the section on insurance, above.) Bring your insurance ID card with you when you travel.

If you suffer from a chronic illness, consult your doctor before your departure. For conditions like epilepsy, diabetes, or heart problems, wear a **Medic Alert Identification Tag** (℃ 800/825-3785; www.medicalert.org), which will immediately alert doctors to your condition and give them access to your records through Medic Alert's 24-hour hot line.

Pack **prescription medications** in your carry-on luggage, and carry prescription medications in their original containers, with pharmacy labels—otherwise they won't make it through airport security. Also bring along copies of your prescriptions in case you lose your pills or run out. Don't forget an extra pair of contact lenses or prescription glasses.

If you do get sick, ask the concierge at your hotel to recommend a local

---

Tips **Quick Luggage I.D.**

Tie a colorful ribbon or piece of yarn around your luggage handle, or slap a distinctive sticker on the side of your bag. This makes it less likely that someone will mistakenly appropriate it. And if your luggage gets lost, it will be easier to find.

---

doctor, even his or her own. See also the "Fast Facts: Las Vegas" at the end of chapter 4, "Getting to Know Las Vegas"; there you'll find listings for hospitals, dental referrals, and even a clinic right on the Strip. For physician referrals, call **Desert Springs Hospital** (© **800/842-5439** or 702/388-4888). Hours are Monday to Friday from 8am to 8pm and Saturday from 9am to 3pm except holidays.

STAYING SAFE

CSI, the nation's top-rated TV show in 2003, may turn up new corpses each week, but the crime rate in real-life Vegas isn't higher than any other major metropolis of its size. Predictably, with all that cash floating around town, pickpockets and thieves are active, so keep an eye on your belongings and store valuables in your in-room safe or a hotel safety-deposit box. And don't flash your cash; it might attract the wrong kind of attention and your big bucks will go bye-bye.

For more information on safety, see "Fast Facts" in chapter 4, and "Safety" in chapter 3. Women should also see "Women Travelers" later in this chapter.

6 Specialized Travel Resources

TRAVELERS WITH DISABILITIES

Most disabilities shouldn't stop anyone from traveling. There are more options and resources out there than ever before.

On the one hand, Las Vegas is fairly well equipped for travelers with disabilities, with virtually every hotel having accessible rooms, ramps, and other requirements. On the other hand, the distance between each hotel (particularly on the Strip) makes a vehicle of some sort virtually mandatory for most people with disabilities, and it may be extremely strenuous and time-consuming to get from place to place (even within a single hotel, because of the crowds). Additionally, the casinos can be quite difficult to maneuver in, particularly for a guest in a wheelchair. The casino floors are crowded, and the machines and tables are often laid out close together, with chairs and such blocking easy access.

You should also consider that it is often a long trek through larger hotels between the entrance and the room elevators (or, for that matter, anywhere in the hotel), and then add a crowded casino to the equation.

The Southern Nevada Center for Independent Living Program, 6039 Eldora St., Suite F, Las Vegas, NV 89146 (© **702/889-4216;** www.sncil. org), can recommend hotels and restaurants that meet your needs, help you find a personal attendant, advise about transportation, and answer all sorts of other questions.

The **Nevada Commission on Tourism** (© **800/638-2328;** www. travelnevada.com) offers a free accommodations guide to Las Vegas hotels that includes access information.

Many travel agencies offer customized tours and itineraries for travelers with disabilities. **Flying Wheels Travel** (© **507/451-5005;** www.flying wheelstravel.com) offers escorted tours and cruises that emphasize sports and private tours in minivans with lifts. **Accessible Journeys** (✆ **800/846-4537** or 610/521-0339; www.disabilitytravel. com) caters specifically to slow walkers and wheelchair travelers and their families and friends.

Wheelchair Getaways (✆ **800/642-2042;** www.wheelchair-getaways.com) rents specialized vans with wheelchair lifts and other features for travelers with disabilities in more than 100 cities across the U.S.

Many of the major car-rental companies now offer hand-controlled cars for drivers with disabilities. **Avis** can provide such a vehicle at any of its locations in the U.S. with 48-hour advance notice; **Hertz** requires between 24 and 72 hours of advance reservations at most of its locations.

Greyhound (✆ **800/229-9424**) allows a person with disabilities to travel with a companion for a single fare. Call at least 72 hours in advance to discuss this and other special needs.

Organizations that offer assistance to travelers with disabilities include the **MossRehab Hospital** (www.moss resourcenet.org), which provides a library of accessible-travel resources online; the **Society for Accessible Travel and Hospitality** (✆ **212/447-7284;** www.sath.org; annual membership fees: $45 adults, $30 seniors and students), which offers a wealth of travel resources for all types of disabilities and informed recommendations on destinations, access guides, travel agents, tour operators, vehicle rentals, and companion services; and the **American Foundation for the Blind** (✆ **800/232-5463;** www.afb.org), which provides information on traveling with Seeing Eye dogs.

For more information specifically targeted to travelers with disabilities, the community website **iCan (www. icanonline.net/channels/travel/index. cfm)** has destination guides and several regular columns on accessible travel. Also check out the quarterly magazine *Emerging Horizons* ($14.95 per year, $19.95 outside the U.S.; www. emerginghorizons.com); **Twin Peaks Press** (✆ **360/694-2462;** http:// disabilitybookshop.virtualave.net/blist8 4.htm), offering travel-related books for travelers with special needs; and *Open World Magazine,* published by the Society for Accessible Travel and Hospitality (see above; subscription: $18 per year, $35 outside the U.S.).

GAY & LESBIAN TRAVELERS

For such a licentious, permissive town, Las Vegas has its conservative side, and is not the most gay-friendly city. This will not manifest itself in any signs of outrage toward open displays of gay affection, but it does mean that the local gay community is largely confined to the bar scene. This may be changing, with local gay pride parades and other activities gathering steam each year, including the first-ever nighttime parade through Downtown, with the mayor in attendance, in 2001. See listings for gay bars in chapter 10, "Las Vegas After Dark."

If you're on the Web, check out Gay Vegas at **http://gayvegas.tripod.com**, which has helpful advice on lodgings, restaurants, and nightlife.

The International Gay & Lesbian Travel Association (IGLTA; ✆ **800/ 448-8550** or 954/776-2626; www. iglta.org) is the trade association for the gay and lesbian travel industry, and offers an online directory of gay- and lesbian-friendly travel businesses; go to their website and click on "Members."

Many agencies offer tours and travel itineraries specifically for gay and lesbian travelers. **Above and Beyond Tours** (✆ **800/397-2681;** www. abovebeyondtours.com) is the exclusive gay and lesbian tour operator for United Airlines. **Now, Voyager**

(© 800/255-6951; www.nowvoyager. com) is a well-known San Francisco–based gay-owned and -operated travel service.

The following travel guides are available at most travel bookstores and gay and lesbian bookstores, or you can order them from **Giovanni's Room** bookstore, 1145 Pine St., Philadelphia, PA 19107 (© 215/923-2960; www. giovannisroom.com): *Out and About* (© 800/929-2268 or 415/644-8044; www.outandabout.com), which offers guidebooks and a newsletter 10 times a year packed with solid information on the global gay and lesbian scene; *Spartacus International Gay Guide* and *Odysseus,* both good, annual English-language guidebooks focused on gay men; the *Damron* guides, with separate, annual books for gay men and lesbians; and *Gay Travel A to Z: The World of Gay & Lesbian Travel Options at Your Fingertips* by Marianne Ferrari (Ferrari Publications; Box 35575, Phoenix, AZ 85069), a very good gay and lesbian guidebook series.

SENIORS

One of the benefits of age is that travel often costs less. Mention the fact that you're a senior citizen when you make travel reservations. Although all of the major U.S. airlines except America West have cancelled their senior discount and coupon book programs, many hotels still offer discounts for seniors. In most cities, people over the age of 60 qualify for reduced admission to theaters, museums, and other attractions, as well as discounted fares on public transportation.

Greyhound (© 800/229-9424; www.greyhound.com) offers seniors travel discounts. **Choice Hotels** (Clarion Hotels, Quality Inns, Comfort Inns, Sleep Inns, Econo Lodges, Friendship Inns, and Rodeway Inns) give 20% to 30% off their published rates to anyone over 60, provided you book your room through their nationwide toll-free reservations number (© 800/4-CHOICE) instead of directly with the hotels or through a travel agent. Those over 50 receive a 10% discount. For a complete list of Choice Hotels, visit **www.hotelchoice.com**.

Members of **AARP** (formerly known as the American Association of Retired Persons), 601 E St. NW, Washington, DC 20049 (© 800/424-3410 or 202/434-2277; www.aarp.org), get discounts on hotels, airfares, and car rentals. AARP offers members a wide range of benefits, including *Modern Maturity* magazine and a monthly newsletter. Anyone over 50 can join.

Many reliable agencies and organizations target the 50-plus market. **Elderhostel** (© 877/426-8056; www.elder hostel.org) arranges study programs for those aged 55 and over (and a spouse or companion of any age) in the U.S. and in more than 80 countries around the world. Most courses last 5 to 7 days, and many include airfare, accommodations in modest inns or hotels, meals, and tuition. Its Las Vegas options include sessions on the city's entertainment and gaming industries.

Recommended publications offering travel resources and discounts for seniors include: the quarterly magazine *Travel 50 & Beyond* (www.travel50 andbeyond.com); *Travel Unlimited: Uncommon Adventures for the Mature Traveler* (Avalon); *101 Tips for Mature Travelers,* available from Grand Circle Travel (© 800/221-2610 or 617/350-7500; www.gct.com); *The 50+ Traveler's Guidebook* (St. Martin's Press); and *Unbelievably Good Deals and Great Adventures That You Absolutely Can't Get Unless You're Over 50* (McGraw Hill).

FAMILY TRAVEL

If you have enough trouble getting your kids out of the house in the morning, dragging them thousands of miles away may seem like an insurmountable challenge. But family travel can be immensely rewarding, giving you new ways of seeing the world through smaller pairs of eyes.

That said, Vegas is hardly an ideal place to bring the kids. For one thing, they're not allowed in casinos at all. Because most hotels are laid out so that you frequently have to walk through their casinos, you can see how this becomes a headache. Some casino hotels will not allow the children of nonguests on the premises after 6pm—and this policy is seriously enforced.

Note also that the Las Vegas Strip is often peppered with people distributing fliers and other information about decidedly adult entertainment options in the city. Sex is everywhere. Just walking down the Strip might give your kids an eyeful of items that you might prefer they avoid. (They don't call it Sin City for nothing!)

On top of everything else, there is a curfew law in Vegas: Kids under 18 are forbidden from being on the Strip without a parent after 9pm on weekends and holidays. In the rest of the county, minors can't be out without parents after 10pm on school nights and midnight on the weekends. If you choose to travel here with the children, see the "Especially for Kids" section in chapter 7, and the "Family-Friendly" boxes in chapters 5, 6, and 10 for suggested hotels, restaurants, and shows.

If you do decide to take your family vacation in Las Vegas, the good news is that children under 12, and in many cases even older, stay free in their parent's rooms in most hotels (we've noted these in chapter 5). You'll definitely want to book a place with a pool. Many hotels also have enormous video arcades and other diversions.

For great tips and suggestions for your Vegas family vacation, we strongly suggest you pick up a copy of *Frommer's Las Vegas with Kids*.

You can find good family-oriented vacation advice on the Internet from sites like the **Family Travel Network** (www.familytravelnetwork.com); **Traveling Internationally with Your Kids** (www.travelwithyourkids.com), a comprehensive site offering sound advice for long-distance and international travel with children; and **Family Travel Files** (www.thefamilytravelfiles.com), which offers an online magazine and a directory of off-the-beaten-path tours and tour operators for families.

How to Take Great Trips with Your Kids (The Harvard Common Press) is full of good general advice that can apply to travel anywhere.

WOMEN TRAVELERS

Las Vegas, thanks to the crowds, is as safe as any other big city for a woman traveling alone. A woman on her own should, of course, take the usual precautions and should be wary of hustlers or drunken businessmen who may mistake her for a "working girl." (Alas, million-dollar proposals a la Robert Redford are a rarity.) Many of the big hotels (all MGM MIRAGE hotels, for example) have security guards stationed at the elevators at night to prevent anyone other than guests from going up to the room floors. Ask when you make your reservation. If you're anxious, ask a security guard to escort you to your room. *Always* double-lock your door *and* deadbolt it to prevent intruders from entering.

Check out the website **Journeywoman** (www.journeywoman.com), a lively travel resource with a free e-mail newsletter; or the travel guide *Safety and Security for Women Who Travel* by Sheila Swan Laufer and Peter Laufer (Travelers' Tales Inc.), offering common-sense advice and tips on safe travel.

7 Planning Your Trip Online

SURFING FOR AIRFARES

The "big three" online travel agencies, **Expedia.com**, **Travelocity.com**, and **Orbitz.com** sell most of the air tickets bought on the Internet. (Canadian travelers should try Expedia.ca and Travelocity.ca; U.K. residents can go for Expedia.co.uk and Opodo.co.uk.) Each has different business deals with the airlines and may offer different fares on the same flights, so it's wise to shop around. Expedia and Travelocity will also send you **e-mail notification** when a cheap fare becomes available to your favorite destination. Of the smaller travel agency websites, **Side-Step** (www.sidestep.com) has gotten the best reviews from Frommer's authors. It's a browser add-on that purports to "search 140 sites at once," but in reality only beats competitors' fares as often as other sites do.

Also remember to check **airline websites,** especially those for low-fare carriers such as Southwest, JetBlue, AirTran, or WestJet whose fares are often misreported or simply missing from travel agency websites. Even with major airlines, you can often shave a few bucks from a fare by booking directly through the airline and avoiding a travel agency's transaction fee. But you'll get these discounts only by **booking online:** Most airlines now offer online-only fares that even their phone agents know nothing about. For the websites of airlines that fly to

and from your destination, go to "Getting There," later in this chapter.

Great **last-minute deals** are available through free weekly e-mail services provided directly by the airlines. Most of these are announced on Tuesday or Wednesday and must be purchased online. Most are only valid for travel that weekend, but some (such as Southwest's) can be booked weeks or months in advance. Sign up for weekly e-mail alerts at airline websites or check megasites that compile comprehensive lists of last-minute specials, such as **Smarter Living** (smarterliving.com). For last-minute trips, **site59.com** in the U.S. and **lastminute.com** in Europe often have better deals than the major-label sites.

If you're willing to give up some control over your flight details, use an **opaque fare service** like **Priceline** (www.priceline.com; www.priceline.co. uk for Europeans) or **Hotwire** (www. hotwire.com). Both offer rock-bottom prices in exchange for travel on a "mystery airline" at a mysterious time of day, often with a mysterious change of planes en route. The mystery airlines are all major, well-known carriers—and the possibility of being sent from Philadelphia to Chicago via Tampa is remote; the airlines' routing computers have gotten a lot better than they used to be. But your chances of getting a 6am or 11pm flight are pretty high. Hotwire tells you flight prices before you buy;

Tips A Web Wonder

A little-known gem, **Travelaxe (www.travelaxe.com)** offers a free, downloadable price comparison program that will make your Las Vegas hotel search infinitely easier. The program searches the hotels (including the major casino hotels' websites) and a host of discount travel websites for the best prices for your travel dates. Click on the price you like and the program will send you straight to the website offering it. And, unlike most websites, Travelaxe prices include hotel tax, so you actually see the total price of the room.

Frommers.com: The Complete Travel Resource

For an excellent travel-planning resource, we highly recommend **Frommers.com** (www.frommers.com). We're a little biased, of course, but we guarantee that you'll find the travel tips, reviews, monthly vacation giveaways, and online-booking capabilities thoroughly indispensable. Among the special features are our popular **Message Boards**, where Frommer's readers post queries and share advice (sometimes even our authors show up to answer questions); **Frommers.com Newsletter**, for the latest travel bargains and insider travel secrets; and **Frommer's Destinations Section**, where you'll get expert travel tips, hotel and dining recommendations, and advice on the sights to see for more than 3,000 destinations around the globe. When your research is done, the **Online Reservations System** (www.frommers.com/book_a_trip) takes you to Frommer's preferred online partners for booking your vacation at affordable prices.

Priceline usually has better deals than Hotwire, but you have to play their "name our price" game. If you're new at this, the helpful folks at **BiddingForTravel** (www.biddingfortravel.com) do a good job of demystifying Priceline's prices. Priceline and Hotwire are great for flights within North America and between the U.S. and Europe. But for flights to other parts of the world, consolidators will almost always beat their fares.

For much more about airfares and savvy air-travel tips and advice, pick up a copy of *Frommer's Fly Safe, Fly Smart* (Wiley Publishing, Inc.).

SURFING FOR HOTELS

Shopping online for hotels is much easier in the U.S., Canada, and certain parts of Europe than it is in the rest of the world. If you try to book a Chinese hotel online, for instance, you'll probably overpay. Also, many smaller hotels and B&Bs—especially outside the U.S.—don't show up on websites at all. Of the "big three" sites, **Expedia** may be the best choice, thanks to its long list of special deals. **Travelocity** runs a close second. Hotel specialist sites **hotels.com** and **hoteldiscounts.com** are also reliable.

Priceline and Hotwire are even better for hotels than for airfares; with both, you're allowed to pick the neighborhood and quality level of your hotel before offering up your money. Priceline's hotel product covers several of the major casino hotels, including the Venetian, the Mirage, and MGM Grand. Be sure to do your research before putting in a bid, however, because their prices aren't always the best available in Vegas. *Note:* Hotwire overrates its hotels by one star—what Hotwire calls a four-star is a three-star anywhere else. Some of Priceline's designations are similarly inflated.

Bidding for Travel (www.biddingfortravel.com) has an excellent Las Vegas board in its hotel section. If you plan on bidding on Priceline, it's a must-stop. It also frequently posts hotel discount codes and available packages.

SURFING FOR RENTAL CARS

For booking rental cars online, the best deals are usually found at rental-car company websites, although all the major online travel agencies also offer rental-car reservations services. Priceline and Hotwire work well for rental cars, too; the only "mystery" is which major rental company you get, and for most travelers the difference between Hertz, Avis, and Budget is negligible.

ONLINE TRAVELER'S TOOLBOX

Following is a selection of online tools to bookmark and use:

- **Visa ATM Locator** (www.visa. com), for locations of Plus ATMs worldwide, or **MasterCard ATM Locator** (www.mastercard.com), for locations of Cirrus ATMs worldwide.
- **Intellicast** (www.intellicast.com) and **Weather.com** (www.weather. com). Give weather forecasts for all 50 states and for cities around the world.
- **Mapquest** (www.mapquest.com). This best of the mapping sites lets you choose a specific address or destination, and in seconds it will return a map and detailed directions.
- **Cybercafes.com** (www.cybercafes. com) or **Net Café Guide** (www.net cafeguide.com/mapindex.htm). Locate Internet cafes at hundreds of locations around the globe. Catch up on your e-mail and log on to the Web for a few dollars per hour.
- **Universal Currency Converter** (www.xe.net/currency). See what your dollar or pound is worth in more than 100 other countries.

8 The 21st-Century Traveler

INTERNET ACCESS AWAY FROM HOME

Travelers have any number of ways to check their e-mail and access the Internet on the road. Of course, using your own laptop—or even a PDA (personal digital assistant) or electronic organizer with a modem—gives you the most flexibility. But even if you don't have a computer, you can still access your e-mail and even your office computer from cybercafes.

WITHOUT YOUR OWN COMPUTER

It's hard nowadays to find a city that *doesn't* have a few cybercafes. Although there's no definitive directory for cybercafes—these are independent businesses, after all—three places to start looking are at **www.cybercaptive.com**, **www.netcafeguide.com**, and **www. cybercafe.com**.

Aside from formal cybercafes, most **youth hostels** nowadays have at least one computer you can get to the Internet on. And most **public libraries** across the world offer Internet access free or for a small charge.

Avoid **hotel business centers,** which often charge exorbitant rates.

Most major airports now have **Internet kiosks** scattered throughout their gates. These kiosks, which you'll also see in shopping malls, hotel lobbies, and tourist information offices around the world, give you basic Web access for a per-minute fee that's usually higher than cybercafe prices. The kiosks' clunkiness and high price means they should be avoided whenever possible.

To retrieve your e-mail, ask your **Internet Service Provider (ISP)** if it has a Web-based interface tied to your existing e-mail account. If your ISP doesn't have such an interface, you can use the free **mail2web** service (www.mail2web.com) to access your home e-mail. For more flexibility, you may want to open a free, Web-based e-mail account with **Yahoo! Mail** (http://mail.yahoo.com) or **Microsoft's Hotmail** (www.hotmail.com). Your home ISP may be able to forward your e-mail to the Web-based account automatically.

If you need to access files on your office computer, look into a service called **GoToMyPC** (www.gotomypc. com). The service provides a Web-based interface for you to access and manipulate a distant PC from anywhere—even a cybercafe—provided your "target" PC is on and has an always-on connection to the Internet (such as with Road Runner cable). The service offers top-quality security, but if you're worried about hackers, use your own laptop rather than a cybercafe to access the GoToMyPC system.

USING A CELLPHONE ACROSS THE U.S.

Just because your cellphone works at home doesn't mean it'll work elsewhere in the country (thanks to our nation's fragmented cellphone system). It's a good bet that your phone will work in major cities. But take a look at your wireless company's coverage map on its website before heading out—T-Mobile, Sprint, and Nextel are particularly weak in rural areas. If you need to stay in touch at a destination where you know your phone won't work, **rent** a phone that does from **InTouch USA** (© **800/872-7626;** www.intouchglobal.com) or a rental-car location, but beware that you'll pay $1 a minute or more for airtime.

If you're venturing deep into national parks, you may want to consider renting a **satellite phone ("satphones")**, which are different from cellphones in that they connect to satellites rather than ground-based towers. A satphone is more costly than a cellphone but works where there's no cellular signal and no towers. Unfortunately, you'll pay at least $2 per minute to use the phone, and it only works where you can see the horizon (that is, usually not indoors). In North America, you can rent Iridium satellite phones from **RoadPost** (© **888/290-1606** or 905/272-5665; www.roadpost.com). InTouch USA (see above) offers a wider range of satphones but at higher rates. As of this writing, satphones were amazingly expensive to buy, so don't even think about it.

If you're not from the U.S., you'll be appalled at the poor reach of our **GSM (Global System for Mobiles) wireless network,** which is used by much of the rest of the world (see below). Your phone will probably work in most major U.S. cities; it definitely won't work in many rural areas. (To see where GSM phones work in the U.S., check out **www. t-mobile.com/coverage/national_ popup.asp**.) And you may or may not be able to send SMS (text messaging) home—something Americans tend not to do anyway, for various cultural and technological reasons. (International budget travelers like to send text messages home because it's much cheaper than making international calls.) Assume nothing—call your wireless provider and get the full scoop. In a worst-case scenario, you can always rent a phone; InTouch USA delivers to hotels.

9 Getting There

BY PLANE

Given the shambles the airline industry is in, writing this section makes us wince. Just be aware that the future of many of the following airlines was in varying degrees of doubt as we went to press.

The following airlines have regularly scheduled flights into Las Vegas

(some of these are regional carriers, so they may not all fly from your point of origin): **AeroMexico** (© 800/237-6639; www.aeromexico.com); **Air Canada** (© 800/776-3000; www.air canada.ca) does not offer direct service but will book on partner airlines, usually with a change in San Francisco; **Alaska Airlines** (© 800/426-0333;

www.alaskaair.com); **Allegiant Air**
(© 877/202-6444; www.allegiant-air.
com) has service only from Fresno,
California; **Aloha Air** (© 800/367-
5250; www.alohaairlines.org); **America West** (© 800/235-9292; www.
americawest.com); **American/Ameri-
can Eagle** (© 800/433-7300; www.aa.
com); **American Trans Air/Comair**
(© 800/435-9282; www.ata.com or
www.fly-comair.com); **Continental**
(© 800/525-0280; www.continental.
com); **Delta/Skywest** (© 800/221-
1212; www.delta.com); **Frontier Airlines** (© 800/432-1359; www.fly
frontier.com); **Hawaiian Airlines**
(© 800/367-5320; www.hawaiianair.
com); **Japan Airlines** (© 800/525-
3663; www.jal.co.jp/en); **JetBlue**
(© 800/538-2583; www.jetblue.com);
Midwest Express (© 800/452-2022;
www.midwestexpress.com); **Northwest** (© 800/225-2525; www.nwa.
com); **Southwest** (© 800/435-9792;
www.iflyswa.com); **United** (© 800/
241-6522; www.ual.com); **US Airways** (© 800/428-4322; www.us
airways.com); and **Virgin Atlantic
Airways** (© 800/862-8621; www.
virgin-atlantic.com).

We've always enjoyed Southwest's
relaxed attitude, and their service
leaves few complaints. However, they
mostly feature first-come, first-served
seating, so if you want to avoid that,
you can't go wrong with United—
assuming, of course, that they are still
in business when you read this.

Then again, now might be the time
to talk about the spiffy new leather
seat/Direct TV wonder that is **Jet
Blue** (© **800/JET-BLUE** or 800/
538-2583; www.jetblue.com). First-
time passengers usually turn into
longtime converts. Currently, they fly
to Vegas from Long Beach, California,
and New York City, and often for very
low prices.

With the federalization of airport
security, security procedures at U.S.

airports are more stable and consistent
than ever. Generally, you'll be fine if
you arrive at the airport **1 hour** before
a domestic flight and **2 hours** before
an international flight; if you show up
late, tell an airline employee and he or
she will probably whisk you to the
front of the line.

Bring a **current, government-
issued photo ID** such as a driver's
license or passport, and if you've got
an e-ticket, print out the **official confirmation page;** you'll need to show
your confirmation at the security
checkpoint, and your ID at the ticket
counter or the gate. (Children under
18 do not need photo IDs for domestic flights, but the adults checking in
with them need them.)

Security lines are getting shorter
than they were during 2001 and 2002,
but some doozies remain. If you have
trouble standing for long periods of
time, tell an airline employee; the airline will provide a wheelchair. Speed
up security by **not wearing metal
objects** such as big belt buckles or
clanky earrings. If you've got metallic
body parts, a note from your doctor
can prevent a long chat with the security screeners. Keep in mind that only
ticketed passengers are allowed past
security, except for folks escorting passengers with disabilities, or children.

Federalization has stabilized **what
you can carry on** and **what you can't.**
The general rule is that sharp things
are out, nail clippers are okay, and
food and beverages must be passed
through the X-ray machine—but that
security screeners can't make you
drink from your coffee cup. Bring
food in your carry-on rather than
checking it, as explosive-detection
machines used on checked luggage
have been known to mistake food
(especially chocolate, for some reason)
for bombs. Travelers in the U.S. are
allowed one carry-on bag, plus a "personal item" such as a purse, briefcase,

or laptop bag. Carry-on hoarders can stuff all sorts of things into a laptop bag; as long as it has a laptop in it, it's still considered a personal item. The Transportation Security Administration (TSA) has issued a list of restricted items; check its website (**www.tsa.gov/public/index.jsp**) for details.

In 2003 the TSA will be phasing out **gate check-in** at all U.S. airports. Passengers with e-tickets and without checked bags can still beat the ticket-counter lines by using **electronic kiosks** or even **online check-in**. Ask your airline which alternatives are available, and if you're using a kiosk, bring the credit card you used to book the ticket. If you're checking bags, you will still be able to use most airlines' kiosks; again call your airline for up-to-date information. **Curbside check-in** is also a good way to avoid lines, although a few airlines still ban curbside check-in entirely; call before you go.

At press time, the TSA is also recommending that you **not lock your checked luggage** so screeners can search it by hand if necessary. The agency says to use plastic "zip ties" instead, which can be bought at hardware stores and can be easily cut off.

FLYING FOR LESS: TIPS FOR GETTING THE BEST AIRFARE

Passengers sharing the same airplane cabin rarely pay the same fare. Travelers who need to purchase tickets at the last minute, change their itinerary at a moment's notice, or fly one-way often get stuck paying the premium rate. Here are some ways to keep your airfare costs down:

 Flying with Film & Video

Never pack film—developed or undeveloped—in checked bags, as the new, more powerful scanners in U.S. airports can fog film. The film you carry with you can be damaged by scanners as well. X-ray damage is cumulative; the slower the film, and the more times you put it through a scanner, the more likely the damage. Film under 800 ASA is usually safe for up to five scans. If you're taking your film through additional scans, U.S. regulations permit you to demand hand inspections. Keep in mind that airports are not the only places where your camera may be scanned: Highly trafficked attractions are X-raying visitors' bags with increasing frequency.

Most photo supply stores sell protective pouches designed to block damaging X-rays. The pouches fit both film and loaded cameras. They should protect your film in checked baggage, but they also may raise alarms and result in a hand inspection.

An organization called **Film Safety for Traveling on Planes (FSTOP;** ⓒ **888/301-2665**; www.f-stop.org), can provide additional tips for traveling with film and equipment.

Carry-on scanners will not damage **videotape** in video cameras, but the magnetic fields emitted by the walk-through security gateways and handheld inspection wands will. Always place your loaded camcorder on the screening conveyor belt or have it hand-inspected. Be sure your batteries are charged, as you will probably be required to turn the device on to ensure that it's what it appears to be.

Travel in the Age of Bankruptcy

At press time, two major U.S. airlines were struggling in bankruptcy court and most of the rest weren't doing very well either. To protect yourself, **buy your tickets with a credit card,** as the Fair Credit Billing Act guarantees that you can get your money back from the credit card company if a travel supplier goes under (and if you request the refund within 60 days of the bankruptcy). **Travel insurance** can also help, but make sure it covers against "carrier default" for your specific travel provider. And be aware that if a U.S. airline goes bust midtrip, a 2001 federal law requires other carriers to take you to your destination (albeit on a space-available basis) for a fee of no more than $25, provided you rebook within 60 days of the cancellation.

- Passengers who can book their ticket **long in advance,** who can **stay over Saturday night,** or who **fly midweek** or **at less-trafficked hours** will pay a fraction of the full fare. If your schedule is flexible, say so, and ask if you can secure a cheaper fare by changing your flight plans.
- You can also save on airfares by keeping an eye out in local newspapers for **promotional specials** or **fare wars,** when airlines lower prices on their most popular routes. You rarely see fare wars offered for peak travel times, but if you can travel in the off-months, you may snag a bargain.
- Search **the Internet** for cheap fares (see "Planning Your Trip Online," earlier in this chapter).
- **Consolidators,** also known as bucket shops, are great sources for international tickets, although they usually can't beat the Internet on fares within North America. Start by looking in Sunday newspaper travel sections; U.S. travelers should focus on the *New York Times, Los Angeles Times,* and *Miami Herald.* For less-developed destinations, small travel agencies that cater to immigrant communities in large cities often have the best deals. *Beware:* Bucket shop tickets are usually nonrefundable or rigged with stiff cancellation penalties, often as high as 50% to 75% of the ticket price, and some put you on charter airlines with questionable safety records. **FlyCheap** (© **800/FLY-CHEAP;** www.1800flycheap.com) is owned by package-holiday megalith MyTravel and so has especially good access to fares for sunny destinations. **Air Tickets Direct** (© **800/778-3447;** www.airtickets direct.com) is based in Montreal and leverages the currently weak Canadian dollar for low fares. And **TravelHub** (www.travelhub.com) represents nearly 1,000 travel agencies, many of whom offer consolidator and discount fares.
- Join **frequent-flier clubs.** Accrue enough miles, and you'll be rewarded with free flights and elite status. It's free, and you'll get the best choice of seats, faster response to phone inquiries, and prompter service if your luggage is stolen, your flight is canceled or delayed, or if you want to change your seat. You don't need to fly to build frequent-flier miles—**frequent-flier credit cards** can provide thousands of miles for doing your everyday shopping.
- For many more tips about air travel, including a rundown of the major frequent-flier credit cards, pick up a copy of *Frommer's Fly Safe, Fly Smart* (Wiley Publishing, Inc.).

> **Tips** **Cancelled Plans**
>
> If your flight is cancelled, don't book a new fare at the ticket counter. Find the nearest phone and call the airline directly to reschedule. You'll be relaxing while other passengers are still standing in line.

BY CAR

The main highway connecting Las Vegas with the rest of the country is I-15; it links Montana, Idaho, and Utah with Southern California. The drive from Los Angeles is quite popular, and thanks to the narrow two-lane highway, can get very crowded on Friday and Sunday afternoons with hopeful weekend gamblers making their way to and from Vegas. (By the way, as soon as you cross the state line, there are three casinos ready to handle your immediate gambling needs, with two more about 20 min. up the road, 30 miles before you get to Las Vegas.)

From the east, take I-70 or I-80 west to Kingman, Arizona, and then U.S. 93 north to downtown Las Vegas (Fremont St.). From the south, take I-10 west to Phoenix and then U.S. 93 north to Las Vegas. From San Francisco, take I-80 east to Reno and then U.S. 95 south to Las Vegas. If you're driving to Las Vegas, be sure to read the driving precautions in "Getting Around" in chapter 4.

Vegas is 286 miles from Phoenix, 759 miles from Denver, 421 miles from Salt Lake City, 269 miles from Los Angeles, and 586 miles from San Francisco.

BY TRAIN

Amtrak (© **800/USA-RAIL;** www.amtrak.com) does not currently offer direct rail service, although plans have been in the works to restore the rails between Los Angeles and Las Vegas for years now. At press time, Amtrak wouldn't confirm a date, but various reports have indicated that by 2004 they will restore service using the **TALGO.** This European-designed "Casino Train" will complete the trip from Los Angeles in about 5½ hours, with a wholesale seat price of $99 round-trip. We've been hearing these reports for so long now they just make us roll our eyes, but believe it, if and when this ever happens, you will have to fight us for a seat.

In the meantime, you can take the train to Los Angeles or Barstow and Amtrak will get you to Vegas by bus.

10 Packages for the Independent Traveler

Before you start your search for the lowest airfare, you may want to consider booking your flight as part of a travel package. Package tours are not the same thing as escorted tours. Package tours are simply a way to buy the airfare, accommodations, and other elements of your trip (such as car rentals, airport transfers, and sometimes even activities) at the same time and often at discounted prices—kind of like one-stop shopping. Packages are sold in bulk to tour operators—who resell them to the public at a cost that usually undercuts standard rates.

Just to give you an example, at press time, **Southwest Airlines** (© **800/435-9792;** www.iflyswa.com) was offering round-trip airfare from Los Angeles with 2 nights at several different hotels complete with ground transportation; per person based on double occupancy, for Bellagio it was $259, and for the Golden Nugget $99 (before taxes and fees), although these prices vary dramatically depending upon when you are traveling.

One good source of package deals is the airlines themselves. Most major airlines offer air/land packages, including **American Airlines Vacations** (© 800/321-2121; www.aavacations.com), **Delta Vacations** (© 800/221-6666; www.deltavacations.com), **Continental Airlines Vacations** (© 800/301-3800; www.coolvacations.com), and **United Vacations** (© 888/854-3899; www.unitedvacations.com).

Another good bet is **Southwest Airlines** (© **888/423-5683;** www.swavacations.com), which has dozens of flights in and out of Las Vegas every day. Sheer volume of flights allows them to offer some relatively inexpensive vacation deals with lots of options in terms of travel time and hotels.

Several big **online travel agencies**—Expedia, Travelocity, Orbitz, Site59, and Lastminute.com—also do a brisk business in packages. **Vacation Together** (© **800/839-9851;** www.vacationtogether.com) allows you to search for and book packages offered by a number of tour operators and airlines.

The **United States Tour Operators Association**'s website (www.ustoa.com) has a search engine that allows you to look for operators that offer packages to a specific destination. Travel packages are also listed in the travel section of your local Sunday newspaper.

Reservations Plus, 2275 A Renaissance Dr., Las Vegas, NV 89119 (© **800/805-9528;** www.resplus.com), runs a free room-reservation service, but they can also arrange packages (including meals, transportation, tours,

show tickets, car rentals, and other features) and group rates.

If you're unsure about the pedigree of a smaller packager, check with the Better Business Bureau in the city where the company is based, or go online to **www.bbb.org.** If a packager won't tell you where it's based, don't fly with them.

Travel packages are also listed in the travel section of your local Sunday newspaper. Or check ads in the national travel magazines such as *Arthur Frommer's Budget Travel Magazine, Travel & Leisure, National Geographic Traveler,* and *Condé Nast Traveler.*

Package tours can vary by leaps and bounds. Some offer a better class of hotels than others. Some offer the same hotels for lower prices. Some offer flights on scheduled airlines, while others book charters. Some limit your choice of accommodations and travel days. You are often required to make a large payment up front. On the plus side, packages can save you money, offering group prices but allowing for independent travel. Some even let you add on a few guided excursions or escorted day trips (also at prices lower than if you booked them yourself) without booking an entirely escorted tour.

Before you invest in a package tour, get some answers. Ask about the **accommodations choices** and prices for each. Then look up the hotels' reviews in a Frommer's guide and check their rates for your specific dates of travel online.

Finally, look for **hidden expenses.** Ask whether airport departure fees and taxes, for example, are included in the total cost.

11 Tips on Accommodations

For information on the various types of accommodations that you'll find in Las Vegas, and suggestions for saving on your hotel costs, see chapter 5, "Where to Stay."

Major Convention Dates for 2004

Listed below are Las Vegas's major annual conventions with projected attendance figures for 2004; believe us, you probably want to avoid the biggies. Since convention schedules frequently change, contact the **Las Vegas Convention and Visitors Authority** (© **800/VISIT-LV** or 702/892-7575; www.vegasfreedom.com) to double-check the latest info before you commit to your travel dates.

Event	Dates	Expected Attendance
ConsumerElectronics Show	Jan 8–11	110,000
National Association of Home Builders	Jan 19–22	75,000
World Floor Covering Associates	Jan 28–30	41,000
Men's Apparel Guild in California (MAGIC)	Feb 23–26	115,000
Associated Surplus Dealers	Mar 7–11	52,000
National Association of Broadcasters (NAB)	Apr 19–22	130,000
National Hardware Show	May 10–12	50,000
Networld/Interop	May 11–13	40,000
JCK Show	June 4–8	50,000
Associated Surplus Dealers	Aug 15–19	52,000
Men's Apparel Guild in California (MAGIC)	Aug 30–Sept 2	115,000
Specialty Equip. Mkt. Assn. (SEMA)	Nov 2–5	88,000
Softbank Comdex	Nov 15–18	125,000

LANDING THE BEST ROOM

Somebody has to get the best room in the house. It might as well be you. You can start by joining the hotel's frequent-guest program, which may make you eligible for upgrades. A hotel-branded credit card usually gives its owner "silver" or "gold" status in frequent-guest programs for free. In the case of Las Vegas, joining a casino hotel's players club may net you upgrade privileges. Always ask about a corner room. They're often larger and quieter, with more windows and light, and they often cost the same as standard rooms. When you make your reservation, ask if the hotel is renovating; if it is, request a room away from the construction. Ask about nonsmoking rooms, rooms with views, rooms with twin, queen- or king-size beds. If you're a light sleeper, request a quiet room away from vending machines, elevators, restaurants, bars, and discos. Ask for one of the rooms that have been most recently renovated or redecorated.

If you aren't happy with your room when you arrive, say so. If another room is available, most lodgings will be willing to accommodate you. And while it may seem hopelessly outdated, the fact is that tipping a desk clerk in Vegas—if you can do it with a straight face—can still sometimes produce results.

In Las Vegas, asking the following questions are also useful before you book a room:

- **What's the view like?** Cost-conscious travelers may be willing to pay less for a back room facing the parking lot, especially if they don't plan to spend much time in their room. A room on a higher floor with a view of the Strip can cost up to $20 a night extra at some hotels. (Paris Las Vegas, for example, charges more for rooms that overlook the Bellagio fountains.)

- **How far is the room from the main entrance, the casino, and other amenities?** We know one exercise fanatic who didn't mind skipping her workouts in Vegas because her room was almost a mile away (or felt like it), one-way, from the hotel's entrance. Most of the world's largest hotels are in Las Vegas, so make sure your room is close to the action if you don't want to hoof it too often.

12 Recommended Reading

If you believe in "reading more about it," here are a select few of our favorites you might turn to:

- Mcmanus, James. *Positively Fifth Street: Murderers, Cheetahs, and Binion's World Series of Poker* (Farrar, 2003). The author went to write about the World Series of Poker, and ended up playing in it, and going farther, and not just in the sense of advancing in the tournament, than he would have thought.
- Hess, Alan. *Viva Las Vegas: After Hours Architecture* (Chronicle Books, 1993). Vegas doesn't have architecture as much as set design, and here you can learn all about how its bizarre skyline is an icon of modern American urban culture.
- McCracken, Robert D. *Las Vegas: The Great American Playground* (University of Nevada Press, 1997). A comprehensive history of Las Vegas.
- Martinez, Andrez. *24/7 Living It Up and Doubling Down in the New Las Vegas* (Villard, 1999).
- Spanier, David. *Welcome to the Pleasure Dome: Inside Las Vegas* (University of Nevada Press, 1992). First-person history and analysis of the Las Vegas phenomenon.
- Thompson, Hunter S. *Fear and Loathing in Las Vegas* (Random House, 1971). A gonzo journalist and his Samoan lawyer head to Sin City for the all-time binge.
- Tronnes, Mike, ed. *Literary Las Vegas* (Henry Holt, 1995). A terrific collection of different essays and excerpts from books about Vegas.

3

For International Visitors

The pervasiveness of American culture around the world may make you feel that you know the United States pretty well, but leaving your own country still requires an additional degree of planning. This chapter will help prepare you for the more common problems you may encounter in Las Vegas.

1 Preparing for Your Trip

ENTRY REQUIREMENTS

Check at any U.S. embassy or consulate for current information and requirements. You can also obtain a visa application and other information online at the **U.S. State Department**'s website, at **www.travel.state.gov**.

VISAS The U.S. State Department has a **Visa Waiver Program** allowing citizens of certain countries to enter the United States without a visa for stays of up to 90 days. At press time these included Andorra, Australia, Austria, Belgium, Brunei, Denmark, Finland, France, Germany, Iceland, Ireland, Italy, Japan, Liechtenstein, Luxembourg, Monaco, the Netherlands, New Zealand, Norway, Portugal, San Marino, Singapore, Slovenia, Spain, Sweden, Switzerland, and the United Kingdom. Citizens of these countries need only a valid passport and a round-trip air or cruise ticket in their possession upon arrival. If they first enter the United States, they may also visit Mexico, Canada, Bermuda, and/or the Caribbean islands and return to the United States without a visa. Further information is available from any U.S. embassy or consulate. Canadian citizens may enter the United States without visas; they need only proof of residence.

Citizens of all other countries must have (1) a valid passport that expires at least 6 months later than the scheduled end of their visit to the United States, and (2) a tourist visa, which may be obtained without charge from any U.S. consulate.

To obtain a visa, the traveler must submit a completed application form (either in person or by mail) with a 1½-inch-square photo, and must demonstrate binding ties to a residence abroad. Usually you can obtain a visa at once or within 24 hours, but it may take longer during the summer rush from June through August. If you cannot go in person, contact the nearest U.S. embassy or consulate for directions on applying by mail. Your travel agent or airline office may also be able to provide you with visa applications and instructions. The U.S. consulate or embassy that issues your visa will determine whether you will be issued a multiple- or single-entry visa and any restrictions regarding the length of your stay.

British subjects can obtain up-to-date visa information by calling the **U.S. Embassy Visa Information Line (© 0891/200-290)** or by visiting the "Consular Services" section of the American Embassy London's website at **www.usembassy.org.uk**.

Irish citizens can obtain up-to-date visa information through the **Embassy of USA Dublin,** 42 Elgin

Rd., Dublin 4, Ireland (℃ **353/1-668-8777**), or by checking the "Consular Services" section of the website at **www.usembassy.ie**.

Australian citizens can obtain up-to-date visa information by contacting the **U.S. Embassy Canberra,** Moonah Place, Yarralumla, ACT 2600 (℃ **02/ 6214-5600**), or by checking the U.S. Diplomatic Mission's website at **http://usembassy-australia.state.gov/ consular**.

Citizens of **New Zealand** can obtain up-to-date visa information by contacting the **U.S. Embassy New Zealand,** 29 Fitzherbert Terrace, Thorndon, Wellington (℃ **644/472-2068**), or get the information directly from the "Services to New Zealanders" section of the website at **http:// usembassy.org.nz**.

MEDICAL REQUIREMENTS Unless you're arriving from an area known to be suffering from an epidemic (particularly cholera or yellow fever), inoculations or vaccinations are not required for entry into the United States. If you have a medical condition that requires **syringe-administered medication,** carry a valid signed prescription from your physician—the Transportation Security Administration (TSA) no longer allows airline passengers to pack syringes in their carry-on baggage without documented proof of medical need. If you have a disease that requires treatment with **narcotics,** you should also carry documented proof with you—smuggling narcotics aboard a plane is a serious offense that carries severe penalties in the U.S.

For **HIV-positive visitors,** requirements for entering the United States are somewhat vague and change frequently. According to the latest publication of *HIV and Immigrants: A Manual for AIDS Service Providers,* the Immigration and Naturalization Service (INS) doesn't require a medical exam for entry into the United States, but INS officials may stop individuals because they look sick or because they are carrying AIDS/HIV medicine.

If an HIV-positive noncitizen applies for a nonimmigrant visa, the question on the application regarding communicable diseases is tricky no matter which way it's answered. If the applicant checks "no," INS may deny the visa on the grounds that the applicant committed fraud. If the applicant checks "yes" or if INS suspects the person is HIV-positive, it will deny the visa unless the applicant asks for a special waiver for visitors. This waiver is for people visiting the United States for a short time, to attend a conference, for instance, to visit close relatives, or to receive medical treatment. It can be a confusing situation. For up-to-the-minute information, contact **AIDSinfo** (℃ **800/448-0440** or 301/519-6616 outside the U.S.; www.aidsinfo.nih.gov) or the **Gay Men's Health Crisis** (℃ **212/367-1000;** www.gmhc.org).

DRIVER'S LICENSES Foreign driver's licenses are mostly recognized in the U.S., although you may want to get an international driver's license if your home license is not written in English.

PASSPORT INFORMATION
FOR RESIDENTS OF CANADA

You can pick up a passport application at one of 28 regional passport offices or most travel agencies. Canadian children who travel must have their own passports. However, if you hold a valid Canadian passport issued before December 11, 2001, that bears the name of your child, the passport remains valid for you and your child until it expires. Passports cost C$85 for those 16 years and older (valid 5 years), C$35 for children 3 to 15 (valid 5 years), and C$20 for children under 3 (valid 3 years). Applications, which must be accompanied by two identical passport-sized photographs and proof of Canadian citizenship, are available at travel agencies throughout Canada or from the central **Passport Office,** Department of Foreign Affairs and International Trade, Ottawa, ON K1A 0G3 (© **800/567-6868;** www. dfait-maeci.gc.ca/passport). Processing takes 5 to 10 days if you apply in person, or about 3 weeks by mail.

FOR RESIDENTS OF THE UNITED KINGDOM

As a member of the European Union, you need only an identity card, not a passport, to travel to other EU countries. However, if you already possess a passport, it's always useful to carry it. To pick up an application for a standard 10-year passport (5-year passport for children under 16), visit the nearest Passport Office, major post office, or travel agency. You can also contact the **United Kingdom Passport Service** at © **0870/571-0410** or visit its website at **www.passport.gov.uk.** Passports are £33 for adults and £19 for children under 16, with an additional £30 fee if you apply in person at a passport office. Processing takes about 2 weeks (1 week if you apply at the passport office).

FOR RESIDENTS OF IRELAND

You can apply for a 10-year passport, costing €57, at the **Passport Office,** Setanta Centre, Molesworth Street, Dublin 2 (© **01/671-1633;** www. irlgov.ie/iveagh). Those under age 18 and over 65 must apply for a €12 3-year passport. You can also apply at 1A South Mall, Cork (© **021/272-525**) or over the counter at most main post offices.

FOR RESIDENTS OF AUSTRALIA

You can pick up an application from your local post office or any branch of Passports Australia, but you must schedule an interview at the passport office to present your application materials. Call the **Australian Passport Information Service** at © **131-232,** or visit the government website at **www.passports.gov.au.** Passports for adults are A$144 and for those under 18 are A$72.

FOR RESIDENTS OF NEW ZEALAND

You can pick up a passport application at any New Zealand Passports Office or download it from their website. Contact the **Passports Office** at © **0800/225-050** in New Zealand or 04/474-8100, or log on to **www.passports. govt.nz.** Passports for adults are NZ$80 and for children under 16, NZ$40.

CUSTOMS
WHAT YOU CAN BRING IN

Every visitor more than 21 years of age may bring in, free of duty, the following: (1) 1 liter of wine or hard liquor; (2) 200 cigarettes, 100 cigars (but not from Cuba), or 3 pounds of smoking tobacco; and (3) $100 worth of gifts. These exemptions are offered to travelers who spend at least 72 hours in the United States and who have not claimed them within the preceding 6 months. It is altogether forbidden to bring into the country foodstuffs (particularly fruit, cooked meats, and canned goods) and plants (vegetables, seeds, tropical plants, and the like). Foreign tourists may bring in or take out up to $10,000 in U.S. or foreign currency with no formalities; larger sums must be declared to U.S. Customs on entering or leaving, which includes filing form CM 4790. For more specific information regarding U.S. Customs, contact your nearest U.S. embassy or consulate, or the **U.S. Customs** office (© **202/927-1770** or www.customs.ustreas.gov).

WHAT YOU CAN TAKE HOME

U.K. citizens returning from a non-EU country have a Customs allowance of: 200 cigarettes; 50 cigars; 250 grams of smoking tobacco; 2 liters of still table wine; 1 liter of spirits or strong liqueurs (over 22% volume); 2 liters of fortified wine, sparkling wine or other liqueurs; 60 cubic centimeters (ml) of perfume; 250 cubic centimeters (ml) of toilet water; and £145 worth of all other goods, including gifts and souvenirs. People under 17 cannot have the tobacco or alcohol allowance. For more information, contact HM Customs & Excise at © **0845/010-9000** (from outside the U.K., 020/8929-0152), or consult their website at **www.hmce.gov.uk.**

For a clear summary of **Canadian** rules, request the booklet *I Declare,* issued by the **Canada Customs and Revenue Agency** (© **800/461-9999** in Canada, or 204/983-3500; www.ccra-adrc.gc.ca). Canada allows its citizens a C$750 exemption, and you're allowed to bring back duty-free one carton of cigarettes, 1 can of tobacco, 40 imperial ounces of liquor, and 50 cigars. In addition, you're allowed to mail gifts to Canada valued at less than C$60 a day, provided they're unsolicited and don't contain alcohol or tobacco (write on the package "Unsolicited gift, under $60 value"). All valuables should be declared on the Y-38 form before departure from Canada, including serial numbers of valuables you

already own, such as expensive foreign cameras. *Note:* The C$750 exemption can only be used once a year and only after an absence of 7 days.

The duty-free allowance in **Australia** is A$400 or, for those under 18, A$200. Citizens age 18 and over can bring in 250 cigarettes or 250 grams of loose tobacco, and 1,125 milliliters of alcohol. If you're returning with valuables you already own, such as foreign-made cameras, you should file form B263. A helpful brochure available from Australian consulates or Customs offices is *Know Before You Go.* For more information, call the **Australian Customs Service** at © **1300/363-263,** or log on to **www.customs.gov.au.**

The duty-free allowance for **New Zealand** is NZ$700. Citizens over 17 can bring in 200 cigarettes, 50 cigars, or 250 grams of tobacco (or a mixture of all three if their combined weight doesn't exceed 250g); plus 4.5 liters of wine and beer, or 1.125 liters of liquor. New Zealand currency does not carry import or export restrictions. Fill out a certificate of export, listing the valuables you are taking out of the country; that way, you can bring them back without paying duty. Most questions are answered in a free pamphlet available at New Zealand consulates and Customs offices: *New Zealand Customs Guide for Travellers, Notice no. 4.* For more information, contact **New Zealand Customs,** The Customhouse, 17–21 Whitmore St., Box 2218, Wellington (© **0800/428-786** or 04/473-6099; www.customs.govt.nz).

Impressions

For the grand debut of Monte Carlo as a resort in 1879 the architect Charles Garnier designed an opera house for the Place du Casino; and Sarah Bernhardt read a symbolic poem. For the debut of Las Vegas as a resort in 1946 Bugsy Siegel hired Abbott and Costello, and there, in a way, you have it all.

—Tom Wolfe

HEALTH INSURANCE

Although it's not required of travelers, health insurance is highly recommended. Unlike many European countries, the United States does not usually offer free or low-cost medical care to its citizens or visitors. Doctors and hospitals are expensive, and in most cases will require advance payment or proof of coverage before they render their services. Policies can cover everything from the loss or theft of your baggage and trip cancellation to the guarantee of bail in case you're arrested. Good policies will also cover the costs of an accident, repatriation, or death. See "Health & Safety" in chapter 2 for more information. Packages such as **Europ Assistance's "Worldwide Healthcare Plan"** are sold by European automobile clubs and travel agencies at attractive rates. **Worldwide Assistance Services Inc.** (© **800/821-2828;** www.worldwide assistance.com) is the agent for Europ Assistance in the United States.

Though lack of health insurance may prevent you from being admitted to a hospital in nonemergencies, don't worry about being left on a street corner to die: The American way is to fix you now and bill the living daylights out of you later.

INSURANCE FOR BRITISH TRAVELERS

Most big travel agents offer their own insurance and will probably try to sell you their package when you book a holiday. Think before you sign. **Britain's Consumers' Association** recommends that you insist on seeing the policy and reading the fine print before buying travel insurance. **The Association of British Insurers** (© **020/7600-3333;** www.abi.org.uk) gives advice by phone and publishes *Holiday Insurance,* a free guide to policy provisions and prices. You might also shop around for better deals: Try **Columbus Direct** (© **020/7375-0011;** www.columbusdirect.net).

INSURANCE FOR CANADIAN TRAVELERS

Canadians should check with their provincial health plan offices or call **Health Canada** (© **613/957-2991;** www.hc-sc.gc.ca) to find out the extent of their coverage and what documentation and receipts they must take home in case they are treated in the United States.

MONEY

CURRENCY The U.S. monetary system is very simple: The most common **bills** are the $1 (colloquially, a "buck"), $5, $10, and $20 denominations. There are also $2 bills (seldom encountered), $50 bills, and $100 bills (the last two are usually not welcome as payment for small purchases). All the paper money was recently redesigned, making the famous faces adorning them disproportionately large. The old-style bills are still legal tender.

There are seven denominations of coins: 1¢ (1 cent, or a penny); 5¢ (5 cents, or a nickel); 10¢ (10 cents, or a dime); 25¢ (25 cents, or a quarter); 50¢ (50 cents, or a half dollar); the new gold "Sacagawea" coin worth $1; and, prized by collectors, the rare, older silver dollar.

Note: The "foreign-exchange bureaus" so common in Europe are rare even at airports in the United States, and nonexistent outside major cities. It's best not to change foreign money (or traveler's checks denominated in a currency other than U.S. dollars) at a small-town bank, or even a branch in a big city; in fact, leave any currency other than U.S. dollars at home—it may prove a greater nuisance to you than it's worth.

TRAVELER'S CHECKS Though traveler's checks are widely accepted, make sure that they're denominated in U.S. dollars, as foreign-currency checks are often difficult to exchange. The three traveler's checks that are most widely recognized—and least likely to be denied—are **Visa, American Express,** and **Thomas Cook.** Be sure to record the numbers of the checks, and keep that information in a separate place in case they get lost or stolen. Most businesses are pretty good about taking traveler's checks, but you're better off cashing them in at a bank (in small amounts, of course) and paying in cash. *Remember:* You'll need identification, such as a driver's license or passport, to change a traveler's check.

CREDIT CARDS & ATMs Credit cards are the most widely used form of payment in the United States: **Visa** (Barclaycard in Britain), **MasterCard** (EuroCard in Europe, Access in Britain, Chargex in Canada), **American Express, Diners Club, Discover,** and **Carte Blanche.** You'll also find that some Vegas vendors may also accept international cards like **enRoute, Euro-Card,** and **JCB,** but not as universally as Amex, MasterCard, or Visa. There are, however, a handful of stores and restaurants that do not take credit cards, so be sure to ask in advance. Most businesses display a sticker near their entrance to let you know which cards they accept. (*Note:* Businesses may require a minimum purchase, usually around $10, to use a credit card.)

It is strongly recommended that you bring at least one major credit card. You must have a credit or charge card to rent a car. Hotels and airlines usually require a credit-card imprint as a deposit against expenses, and in an emergency a credit card can be priceless.

You'll find **automated teller machines (ATMs)** on just about every block—at least in almost every town—across the country. Some ATMs will allow you to draw U.S. currency against your bank and credit cards. Check with your bank before leaving home, and remember that you will need your personal identification number (PIN) to do so. Most accept Visa, MasterCard, and American Express, as well as ATM cards from other U.S. banks. Expect to be charged up to $3 per transaction, however, if you're not using your own bank's ATM.

One way around these fees is to ask for cash back at grocery stores that accept ATM cards and don't charge usage fees. Of course, you'll have to purchase something first.

ATM cards with major credit card backing, known as "debit cards," are now a commonly acceptable form of payment in most stores and restaurants. Debit cards draw money directly from your checking account. Some stores enable you to receive "cash back" on your debit-card purchases as well.

SAFETY

GENERAL SAFETY SUGGESTIONS While tourist areas are generally safe, crime is a national problem, and U.S. urban areas tend to be less safe than those in Europe or Japan. You should always stay alert. It's wise to ask your hotel front-desk staff if you're in doubt about which neighborhoods are safe.

Avoid carrying valuables with you on the street, and don't display expensive cameras or electronic equipment. Hold on to your pocketbook, and place your billfold in an inside pocket. In theaters, restaurants, and other public places, keep your possessions in sight.

Remember also that hotels are open to the public, and in a large hotel, security may not be able to screen everyone entering. Always lock your room door—don't assume that once inside your hotel you are automatically safe and no longer need to be aware of your surroundings. In Las Vegas, many hotels check room keys at the elevators at night, providing some extra security. Many Las Vegas hotels also have in-room safes; if yours doesn't and you're traveling with valuables, put them in a safety-deposit box at the front desk.

SIZE CONVERSION CHART

Women's Clothing

American	4	6	8	10	12	14	16	
French	34	36	38	40	42	44	46	
British	6	8	10	12	14	16	18	

Women's Shoes

American	5	6	7	8	9	10		
French	36	37	38	39	40	41		
British	4	5	6	7	8	9		

Men's Suits

American	34	36	38	40	42	44	46	48
French	44	46	48	50	52	54	56	58
British	34	36	38	40	42	44	46	48

Men's Shirts

American	14½	15	15½	16	16½	17	17½	
French	37	38	39	41	42	43	44	
British	14½	15	15½	16	16½	17	17½	

Men's Shoes

American	7	8	9	10	11	12	13	
French	39½	41	42	43	44½	46	47	
British	6	7	8	9	10	11	12	

Note: The area northeast of Harmon and Koval has had increased gang activity of late and should be avoided or at least approached with caution.

DRIVING SAFETY Driving safety is important too, and carjacking is not unprecedented. Question your rental agency about personal safety and ask for a traveler-safety brochure when you pick up your car. Obtain written directions—or a map with the route clearly marked—from the agency showing how to get to your destination. (Many agencies now offer the option of renting a cellphone for the duration of your car rental; check with the rental agent when you pick up the car. Otherwise, contact **InTouch USA** at © **800/872-7626** or www.intouchusa.com for short-term cellphone rental.) And, if possible, arrive and depart during daylight hours.

If you drive off a highway and end up in a dodgy-looking neighborhood, leave the area as quickly as possible. If you have an accident, even on the highway, stay in your car with the doors locked until you assess the situation or until the police arrive. If you're bumped from behind on the street or are involved in a minor accident with no injuries, and the situation appears to be suspicious, motion to the other driver to follow you. Never get out of your car in such situations. Go directly to the nearest

---

(Tips **Travel-Document Tip**

Be sure to keep a copy of all your travel papers separate from your wallet or purse, and leave a copy with someone at home should you need it faxed in an emergency.

police precinct, well-lit service station, or 24-hour store.

Park in well-lit and well-traveled areas whenever possible—in the casino hotels, take advantage of the free valet parking. Always keep your car doors locked, whether the vehicle is attended or unattended. Never leave any packages or valuables in sight. If someone attempts to rob you or steal your car, don't try to resist the thief/carjacker. Report the incident to the police department immediately by calling ℂ **911.**

2 Getting to the United States

THE MAJOR AIRLINES A number of U.S. airlines offer service from Europe to the United States, though a number of those same airlines are having financial troubles, and may perhaps be in different shape by the time you read this. If they do not have direct flights from Europe to Las Vegas, they can book you straight through on a connecting flight. You can make reservations by calling the following numbers in the United Kingdom: **American** (ℂ **0181/572-5555** in the U.K., 800/433-7300 in the U.S.; www. aa.com), **Continental** (ℂ **01293/776-464** in the U.K., 800/525-0280 in the U.S.; www.continental.com), **Delta** (ℂ **0800/414-767** in the U.K., 800/221-1212 in the U.S.; www.delta. com), and **United** (ℂ **0845/8-444-777** in the U.K., 800/538-2929 in the U.S.; www.ual.com).

And, of course, many international carriers serve LAX and/or San Francisco International Airport. From LAX or San Francisco International Airport, you can take a domestic airline to Las Vegas. Helpful numbers to know include **Virgin Atlantic** (ℂ **01293/747-747** in the U.K., 800/862-8621 in the U.S.; www.virgin-atlantic.com), **British Airways** (ℂ **0345/222-111** in the U.K., 800/AIRWAYS in the U.S.; www.british-airways.com), and **Aer Lingus** (ℂ **01/886-8888** in Dublin, 800/IRISH-AIR in the U.S.; www. aerlingus.ie). **Qantas** (ℂ **13-13-13** in Australia, 800/227-4500 in the U.S.; www.qantas.com.au) has flights from Sydney to Los Angeles and San Francisco; you can also take United from Australia to the West Coast. **Air New Zealand** (ℂ **0800/737-000** in New Zealand, 800/262-1234 in the U.S.; www.airnewzealand.co.nz) also offers service to LAX. Canadian readers can book flights on **Air Canada** (ℂ **800/776-3000;** www.aircanada.ca), which offers direct service from Toronto, Montréal, Calgary, and Vancouver to San Francisco and Los Angeles, and will book your final leg on a partner airline.

JetBlue (ℂ **800/538-2583;** www. jetblue.com) is a highly rated low-cost carrier that operates out of a number of U.S. cities, and just began offering daily direct service to Las Vegas out of New York City.

AIRLINE DISCOUNTS The smart traveler can find numerable ways to reduce the price of a plane ticket simply by taking time to shop around. For example, overseas visitors can take advantage of the APEX (Advance Purchase Excursion) reductions offered by all major U.S. and European carriers. For more money-saving airline advice, see "Getting There" and "Planning Your Trip Online," in chapter 2. For the best rates, compare fares and be flexible with the dates and times of travel.

Operated by the European Travel Network, **www.discount-tickets.com** is a great online source for regular and discounted airfares to Las Vegas and other destinations around the world. You can also use this site to compare rates and book accommodations, car rentals, and tours. Click "Special Offers" for the latest package deals.

Impressions

A few centuries from now archaeologists, studying the ruins of our civilization, will no doubt determine that Las Vegas was an important religious center, boasting dozens of massive temples to which pilgrims from afar brought bountiful offerings.

—Andres Martinez, *24/7: Living It Up While Doubling Down in the New Las Vegas*

IMMIGRATION AND CUSTOMS CLEARANCE Visitors arriving by air, no matter what the port of entry, should cultivate patience and resignation before setting foot on U.S. soil. Getting through immigration control can take as long as 2 hours on some days, especially on summer weekends, so be sure to carry this guidebook or something else to read. This is especially true in the aftermath of the September 11, 2001, terrorist attacks, when security clearances have been considerably beefed up at U.S. airports.

People traveling by air from Canada, Bermuda, and certain countries in the Caribbean can sometimes clear Customs and Immigration at the point of departure, which is much quicker.

3 Getting Around the United States

BY PLANE Some large airlines (for example, Northwest and Delta) offer travelers on their transatlantic or transpacific flights special discount tickets under the name **Visit USA,** allowing mostly one-way travel from one U.S. destination to another at very low prices. These discount tickets are not on sale in the United States and must be purchased abroad in conjunction with your international ticket. This system is the best, easiest, and fastest way to see the United States at low cost. You should obtain information well in advance from your travel agent or the office of the airline concerned, since the conditions attached to these discount tickets can be changed without advance notice.

BY CAR Though you don't necessarily have to rent a car while in Las Vegas, the most cost-effective, convenient, and comfortable way to travel around the United States is by car. The interstate highway system connects cities and towns all over the country; in addition to these high-speed, limited-access roadways, there's an extensive network of federal, state, and local highways and roads. Some of the national car-rental companies include **Alamo** (© 800/462-5266; www.alamo.com), **Avis** (© 800/230-4898; www.avis.com), **Budget** (© 800/527-0700; www.budget.com), **Dollar** (© 800/800-3665; www.dollar.com), **Hertz** (© 800/654-3131; www.hertz.com), **National** (© 800/227-7368; www.nationalcar.com), and **Thrifty** (© 800/847-4389; www.thrifty.com).

If you plan to rent a car in the United States, you probably won't need the services of an additional automobile organization. If you're planning to buy or borrow a car, automobile-association membership is recommended. **AAA, the American Automobile Association** (© 800/222-4357), is the country's largest auto club and supplies its members with maps, insurance, and, most important, emergency road service. The cost of joining runs from $63 for singles to $87 for two members, but if you're a member of a foreign auto club with reciprocal arrangements, you can enjoy free AAA service in America.

See "Getting Around" in chapter 4 for more information on renting a car in Las Vegas.

BY BUS   Although bus travel is often the most economical form of public transit for short hops between U.S. cities, it can also be slow and uncomfortable—certainly not an option for everyone (particularly when Amtrak, which is far more luxurious, offers similar or slightly higher rates). **Greyhound/Trailways** (© **800/231-2222;** www.greyhound.com), the sole nationwide bus line, offers an **International Ameripass** that must be purchased before coming to the United States, or by phone through the Greyhound International Office at the Port Authority Bus Terminal in New York City (© **212/971-0492**). The pass can be obtained from foreign travel agents and costs less than the domestic version. Costs for 2003 passes are as follows: 4 days ($175), 7 days ($224), 10 days ($274), 15 days ($334), 21 days ($384), 30 days ($444), 45 days ($484), or 60 days ($594). You can get more info on the pass at www.greyhound.com, or by calling © **212/971-0492** (2–9pm) or © 402/330-8552 (all other times). Special ticket rates are available for seniors and students. Though bus stations are often located in undesirable neighborhoods, the one in Las Vegas is conveniently located in a safe part of Downtown.

BY TRAIN   Amtrak (© **800/USA-RAIL;** www.amtrak.com) does not currently offer direct rail service, although plans have been in the works to restore the rails between Los Angeles and Las Vegas for years now. At press time, Amtrak wouldn't confirm a date, but various reports have indicated that some time in 2004 they will restore service using the TALGO. This European-designed "Casino Train" completes the trip from Los Angeles in about 5½ hours, with a wholesale seat price of $99 round-trip. (There's some talk that the train's route may continue on to Salt Lake City, but this had not been finalized at press time.) We still don't believe this is going to happen in our lifetime.

Much of the train will be presold to various hotels, so the final price to the traveler will depend on how you get the ticket. High rollers will probably end up with freebies, but the ticket will most likely be $99 if you purchase at the counter. In the meantime, you can take the train to Los Angeles or Barstow and Amtrak will get you to Vegas by bus.

 FAST FACTS: For the International Traveler

Automobile Organizations Auto clubs will supply maps, suggested routes, guidebooks, accident and bail-bond insurance, and emergency road service. The **American Automobile Association (AAA)** is the major auto club in the United States. If you belong to an auto club in your home country, inquire about AAA reciprocity before you leave. You may be able to join AAA even if you're not a member of a reciprocal club; to inquire, call AAA (© **800/222-4357;** www.aaa.com). AAA is actually an organization of regional auto clubs; so look under "AAA Automobile Club" in the White Pages of the telephone directory. AAA has a nationwide emergency road service telephone number (© 800/AAA-HELP).

Business Hours Offices are usually open weekdays from 9am to 5pm. Banks are open weekdays from 9am to 3pm or later, and sometimes on Saturday morning, although there's 24-hour access to the automated teller machines (ATMs) at most banks and other outlets. In Las Vegas, money is also available around the clock at casino cages—and every casino has at least one ATM. Shops, especially those in shopping complexes, tend to stay open late: until about 9pm weekdays and until 6pm weekends (including Sun).

Climate See "When to Go," in chapter 2.

Currency & Currency Exchange See "Money" under "Preparing for Your Trip," earlier in this chapter.

Drinking Laws The legal age for purchase and consumption of alcoholic beverages is 21; proof of age is required and often requested at bars, nightclubs, and restaurants, so it's always a good idea to bring ID when you go out, especially if you look young. Do not carry open containers of alcohol in your car or any public area that isn't zoned for alcohol consumption. The police can fine you on the spot. And nothing will ruin your trip faster than getting arrested for DUI ("driving under the influence"), so don't even think about driving while you're under the influence. Beer, wine, and liquor are all sold in all kinds of stores, pretty much around the clock; trust us, you won't have a hard time finding a drink in this town. It's even legal to have an open container on the Strip.

Electricity Like Canada, the United States uses 110 to 120 volts AC (60 cycles), compared to 220 to 240 volts AC (50 cycles) in most of Europe, Australia, and New Zealand. If your small appliances use 220 to 240 volts, you'll need a 110-volt transformer and a plug adapter with two flat parallel pins to operate them here. Downward converters that change 220–240 volts to 110–120 volts are difficult to find in the United States, so bring one with you.

Embassies & Consulates All embassies are located in the nation's capital, Washington, D.C. Some consulates are located in major U.S. cities, and most nations have a mission to the United Nations in New York City. If your country isn't listed below, call for directory information in Washington, D.C. (© 202/555-1212) or log on to **www.embassy.org/embassies**.

The embassy of **Australia** is at 1601 Massachusetts Ave. NW, Washington, DC 20036 (© **202/797-3000;** www.austemb.org). There are consulates in New York, Honolulu, Houston, Los Angeles, and San Francisco.

The embassy of **Canada** is at 501 Pennsylvania Ave. NW, Washington, DC 20001 (© **202/682-1740;** www.canadianembassy.org). Other Canadian consulates are in Buffalo (N.Y.), Detroit, Los Angeles, New York, and Seattle.

The embassy of **Ireland** is at 2234 Massachusetts Ave. NW, Washington, DC 20008 (© **202/462-3939;** www.irelandemb.org). Irish consulates are in Boston, Chicago, New York, and San Francisco.

The embassy of **Japan** is at 2520 Massachusetts Ave. NW, Washington, DC 20008 (© **202/238-6700;** www.embjapan.org). Japanese consulates are located in Atlanta, Kansas City, San Francisco, and Washington, D.C.

The embassy of **New Zealand** is at 37 Observatory Circle NW, Washington, DC 20008 (© **202/328-4800;** www.nzemb.org). New Zealand consulates are in Los Angeles, Salt Lake City, San Francisco, and Seattle.

The embassy of the **United Kingdom** is at 3100 Massachusetts Ave. NW, Washington, DC 20008 (© **202/462-1340;** www.britainusa.com). British consulates are in Atlanta, Boston, Chicago, Cleveland, Houston, Los Angeles, New York, San Francisco, and Seattle.

Emergencies Call 🕐 **911** to report a fire, call the police, or get an ambulance in Las Vegas. This is a toll-free call (no coins are required at public telephones).

If you have a medical emergency that doesn't require an ambulance, you can walk into a hospital's 24-hour emergency room (usually a separate entrance). For a list of hospitals, see "Fast Facts: Las Vegas" in chapter 4.

If you encounter serious problems, contact **Traveler's Aid International** (🕐 **202/546-1127**; www.travelersaid.org) to help direct you to a local branch. This nationwide, nonprofit, social-service organization geared to helping travelers in difficult straits offers services that might include reuniting families separated while traveling, providing food and/or shelter to people stranded without cash, or even emotional counseling. If you're in trouble, seek them out. In Las Vegas there is an office at **McCarran International Airport** (🕐 **702/798-1742**), which is open daily from 8am to 5pm. Similar services are provided by **Help of Southern Nevada,** 953 E. Sahara Ave., Suite 208, at Maryland Parkway in the Commercial Center on the northeast corner (🕐 **702/369-4357**). Hours are Monday to Friday from 8am to 4pm.

Gasoline (Petrol) Petrol is known as gasoline (or simply "gas") in the United States, and petrol stations are known as both gas stations and service stations. Though prices were volatile and rising sharply throughout the first half of 2003, gasoline costs significantly less here than it does in Europe (about $2 per gallon in Vegas at press time), and taxes are already included in the printed price. One U.S. gallon equals 3.8 liters or .85 Imperial gallons.

Holidays Banks, government offices, post offices, and many stores, restaurants, and museums are closed on the following legal national holidays: January 1 (New Year's Day), the third Monday in January (Martin Luther King Jr. Day), the third Monday in February (Presidents' Day, Washington's Birthday), the last Monday in May (Memorial Day), July 4 (Independence Day), the first Monday in September (Labor Day), the second Monday in October (Columbus Day), November 11 (Veterans Day/Armistice Day), the fourth Thursday in November (Thanksgiving Day), and December 25 (Christmas). Also, the Tuesday following the first Monday in November is Election Day and is a federal government holiday in presidential-election years (held every 4 years, next in 2004).

Legal Aid If you are "pulled over" for a minor infraction (such as speeding), never attempt to pay the fine directly to a police officer; this could be construed as attempted bribery, a much more serious crime. Pay fines by mail, or directly into the hands of the clerk of the court. If accused of a more serious offense, say and do nothing before consulting a lawyer. Here the burden is on the state to prove a person's guilt beyond a reasonable doubt, and everyone has the right to remain silent, whether he or she is suspected of a crime or actually arrested. Once arrested, a person can make one telephone call to a party of his or her choice. Call your embassy or consulate.

Mail If you aren't sure what your address will be in the United States, mail can be sent to you, in your name, c/o General Delivery at the main post office of the city or region where you expect to be. (Call ℭ **800/ 275-8777** for information on the nearest post office.) The addressee must pick up mail in person and must produce proof of identity (driver's license, passport, and so forth). Most post offices will hold your mail for up to 1 month and are open Monday to Friday from 8am to 6pm and Saturday from 9am to 3pm.

Generally found at intersections, mailboxes are blue with a red-and-white stripe and carry the inscription u.s. mail. If your mail is addressed to a U.S. destination, don't forget to add the five-digit postal code (or ZIP code) after the two-letter abbreviation of the state to which the mail is addressed. This is essential to prompt delivery.

At press time, domestic postage rates were 23¢ for a postcard and 37¢ for a letter. For international mail, a first-class letter of up to one-half ounce costs 80¢ (60¢ to Canada and Mexico); a first-class postcard costs 70¢ (50¢ to Canada and Mexico); and a preprinted postal aerogramme costs 70¢. Point your Web browser to **www.usps.gov** for complete U.S. postal information.

In Las Vegas the closest post office to the Strip is behind the Stardust Hotel at 3100 S. Industrial Rd., between Sahara Avenue and Spring Mountain Road (ℭ **800/297-5543**). The **main post office** is at 1001 E. Sunset Rd., same phone number. It's open Monday to Friday from 8:30am to 6pm. You can also mail letters and packages at your hotel, and there's a full-service U.S. Post Office in the Forum Shops in Caesars Palace.

Measurements See the chart on the inside front cover of this book for details on converting metric measurements to U.S. equivalents. See also the "Size Conversion Chart" on p. 43 in this chapter for clothing and shoe-size equivalencies.

Taxes The United States has no value-added tax (VAT) or other indirect tax at the national level. Every state, county, and city has the right to levy its own local tax on all purchases, including hotel and restaurant checks, airline tickets, and so on. These taxes are not refundable and are not included in the price tags you'll see on merchandise. In Clark County (where Las Vegas is located), hotel room tax is 9% and sales tax is 7%.

Telephone, Telegraph, Telex & Fax The telephone system in the United States is run by private corporations, so rates, especially for long-distance service and operator-assisted calls, can vary widely. Generally, hotel surcharges on long-distance and local calls are astronomical, so you're usually better off using a **public pay telephone,** which you'll find clearly marked in most public buildings and private establishments as well as on the street. Convenience grocery stores and gas stations always have them. Many convenience groceries and packaging services sell **prepaid calling cards** in denominations up to $50; these can be the least expensive way to call home. Many public phones at airports now accept American Express, MasterCard, and Visa credit cards. **Local calls** made from public pay phones in most locales cost either 25¢ or 35¢. Pay phones do not accept pennies, and few will take anything larger than a quarter.

You may want to look into leasing a cellphone for the duration of your trip.

Most long-distance and international calls can be dialed directly from any phone. **For calls within the United States and to Canada,** dial 1 followed by the area code and the seven-digit number. **For other international calls,** dial 011 followed by the country code, city code, and the telephone number of the person you are calling.

Calls to area codes **800, 888, 877,** and **866** are toll-free. However, calls to numbers in area codes **700** and **900** (chat lines, bulletin boards, "dating" services, and so on) can be very expensive—usually a charge of 95¢ to $3 or more per minute, and they sometimes have minimum charges that can run as high as $15 or more.

For **reversed-charge or collect calls,** and for person-to-person calls, dial 0 (zero, not the letter O) followed by the area code and number you want; an operator will then come on the line, and you should specify that you are calling collect, or person-to-person, or both. If your operator-assisted call is international, ask for the overseas operator.

For **local directory assistance** ("information"), dial ✆ 411; for long-distance information, dial 1, then the appropriate area code and 555-1212.

Telegraph and telex services are provided primarily by Western Union. You can bring your telegram into the nearest Western Union office (there are hundreds across the country) or dictate it over the phone (✆ **800/ 325-6000**). You can also telegraph money, or have it telegraphed to you, very quickly over the Western Union system, but this service can cost as much as 15% to 20% of the amount sent. You can find a Western Union office at 3250 E. Flamingo Rd. (✆ **702/450-2359**) in the Nevada State Bank.

Most Las Vegas hotels have **fax machines** available for guest use (be sure to ask about the charge to use it, as charges tend to be very expensive), and many hotel rooms are even wired for guests' fax machines. A less-expensive way to send and receive faxes is to do it at stores such as Kinko's, a national chain offering computer and copying services. There is a Kinko's near UNLV at 4440 S. Maryland Pkwy. (✆ **702/735-4402**), and another branch is located Downtown at 830 4th St. (✆ **702/383-7022**).

There are two kinds of telephone directories in the United States. The so-called **White Pages** list private households and business subscribers in alphabetical order. The inside front cover lists emergency numbers for police, fire, ambulance, the Coast Guard, poison-control center, crime-victims hotline, and so on. The first few pages will tell you how to make long-distance and international calls, complete with country codes and area codes. Government numbers are usually printed on blue paper within the White Pages. Printed on yellow paper, the so-called **Yellow Pages** list all local services, businesses, industries, and houses of worship according to activity with an index at the front or back. (Drugstores/ pharmacies and restaurants are also listed by geographic location.) The Yellow Pages also include city plans or detailed area maps, postal ZIP codes, and public transportation routes.

Time The continental United States is divided into four time zones, and Nevada is on **Pacific Standard Time (PST),** which is 3 hours earlier than on the U.S. East Coast. For instance, when it is noon in Las Vegas, it is 3pm in

New York City (EST); 2pm in Chicago (CST), and 1pm in Denver (MST). Nevada, like most of the rest of the United States (but not all of it), observes **daylight savings time** from 1am on the first Sunday in April through 1am on the last Sunday in October. Daylight savings time moves the clock 1 hour ahead of standard time. This results in lovely, long summer evenings, when the sun sets as late as 8:30 or 9pm.

Tipping Tipping is so ingrained in the American way of life that the annual income tax of tip-earning service personnel is based on how much they should have received in light of their employers' gross revenues. Accordingly, they may have to pay tax on a tip you didn't actually give them.

Here are some rules of thumb:

In hotels, tip **bellhops** at least $1 per bag ($2–$3 per bag if you have a lot of luggage) and tip the **chamber staff** $1 to $2 per day (more if you've left a disaster area for him or her to clean up, or if you're traveling with kids and/or pets). Tip the **doorman** or **concierge** only if he or she has provided you with some specific service (for example, calling a cab for you or obtaining difficult-to-get theater tickets). Tip the **valet-parking attendant** $1 every time you get your car.

In restaurants, bars, and nightclubs, tip **service staff** 15% to 20% of the check, tip **bartenders** 10% to 15%, tip **checkroom attendants** $1 per garment, and tip **valet-parking attendants** $1 per vehicle. Tip the **doorman** only if he has provided you with some specific service (such as calling a cab for you). Tipping is not expected in cafeterias and fast-food restaurants.

Tip **cab drivers** 15% of the fare.

As for other service personnel, tip **skycaps** at airports at least $1 per bag ($2–$3 per bag if you have a lot of luggage) and tip **hairdressers** and **barbers** 15% to 20%.

Tipping ushers at movies and theaters, and gas-station attendants, is not expected.

See chapter 10 for details on tipping showroom maitre d's; casino dealers usually get a few dollars if you've had a big win.

Toilets You won't find public toilets or "restrooms" on the streets in most U.S. cities, but they can be found in hotel lobbies, bars, restaurants, museums, department stores, railway and bus stations, and service stations. Large hotels, all of the casino hotels, and fast-food restaurants are probably the best bet for good, clean facilities. If possible, avoid the toilets at parks and beaches, which tend to be dirty; some may be unsafe. Restaurants and bars in resorts or heavily visited areas may reserve their restrooms for patrons. Some establishments display a notice indicating this. You can ignore this sign or, better yet, avoid arguments by paying for a cup of coffee or a soft drink, which will qualify you as a patron.

4

Getting to Know Las Vegas

Located in the southernmost precincts of a wide, pancake-flat valley, Las Vegas is the biggest city in the state of Nevada. Treeless mountains form a scenic backdrop to hotels awash in neon glitter. Although it is one of the fastest-growing cities in America, for tourism purposes, the city is quite compact.

1 Orientation

ARRIVING AT THE LAS VEGAS AIRPORT

Las Vegas is served by **McCarran International Airport,** 5757 Wayne Newton Blvd. (© **702/261-5211,** TDD 702/261-3111; www.mccarran.com), just a few minutes' drive from the southern end of the Strip, where the bulk of casinos and hotels are concentrated. This big, modern airport—with a relatively new $500 million expansion—is rather unique in that it includes several casino areas with more than 1,000 slot machines. Although these are reputed to offer lower paybacks than hotel casinos (the airport has a captive audience and doesn't need to lure repeat customers), it's hard to resist throwing in a few quarters while waiting for the luggage to arrive. We actually know someone who hit a $250 jackpot there on his way out of town, thereby recouping most of his gambling losses at the last possible moment. (He was surprised, too.)

Getting to your hotel from the airport is a cinch. **Bell Trans** (© **702/ 739-7990;** www.bell-trans.com) runs 20-passenger minibuses daily between the airport and all major Las Vegas hotels and motels all day (7:45am–midnight). There are several other companies that run similar ventures—just stand outside on the curb and one will be flagged down for you. Buses from the airport leave about every 10 minutes. When you want to check out of your hotel and head back to the airport, call at least 2 hours in advance to be safe (though often you can just flag down one of the buses outside any major hotel). The cost is $4.25 per person each way to Strip- and Convention Center–area hotels, $5.50 to Downtown or other Off-Strip properties (anyplace north of the Sahara Hotel and west of I-15). Other similarly priced shuttles run 24 hours and can be found in the same place.

Even less expensive are **Citizen's Area Transit (CAT)** buses (© **702/CAT-RIDE**). The no. 108 bus departs from the airport and will take you to the Stratosphere, where you can transfer to the 301, which stops close to most Strip- and Convention Center–area hotels. The no. 109 bus goes from the airport to the Downtown Transportation Center at Casino Center Boulevard and Stewart Avenue. The fares for buses on Strip routes are $2 for adults, 60¢ for seniors and children. *Note:* If you have heavy luggage, you should know that you might have a long walk from the bus stop to the hotel entrance (even if the bus stop is right in front of your hotel). Vans are able to get right up to the entrance, so choose a van if you're lugging lots of baggage.

Tips **Help for Troubled Travelers**

The **Traveler's Aid Society** is a social-service organization geared to helping travelers in difficult straits. Their services might include reuniting families separated while traveling, feeding people stranded without cash, or even emotional counseling. If you're in trouble, seek them out. In Las Vegas there is a Traveler's Aid office at McCarran International Airport (© **702/798-1742**). It's open daily from 8am to 5pm. Similar services are provided by **Help of Southern Nevada,** 953–35B E. Sahara Ave. (Suite 208), at Maryland Parkway in the Commercial Center (© **702/369-4357**). Hours are Monday to Friday from 8am to 4pm.

All of the major car-rental companies are represented in Las Vegas, if you choose to rent a car while you are in town. For a list of agencies and more information on getting a good deal on a rental, see "Getting Around," later in this chapter.

VISITOR INFORMATION

All major Las Vegas hotels provide comprehensive tourist information at their reception and/or sightseeing and show desks.

Other good information sources are: the **Las Vegas Convention and Visitors Authority,** 3150 Paradise Rd., Las Vegas, NV 89109 (© **877/VISIT-LV** or 702/892-7575; www.vegasfreedom.com), open daily from 8am to 5pm; the **Las Vegas Chamber of Commerce,** 3720 Howard Hughes Pkwy., #100, Las Vegas, NV 89109 (© **702/735-1616;** www.lvchamber.com), open Monday to Friday from 8am to 5pm; and, for information on all of Nevada, including Las Vegas, the **Nevada Commission on Tourism** (© **800/638-2328;** www.travelnevada. com), open 24 hours.

CITY LAYOUT

There are two main areas of Las Vegas: the **Strip** and **Downtown.** For many people, that's all there is to Las Vegas. But there is actually more to the town than that: Although maybe not as glitzy and glamorous as the Strip and Down-town—okay, definitely not—Paradise Road and east Las Vegas are home to quite a bit of casino action, Maryland Parkway boasts mainstream and alternative-culture shopping, and there are different restaurant choices all over the city. Confining yourself to the Strip and Downtown is fine for the first-time visitor, but repeat customers (and you will be) should get out there and explore. Las Vegas Boulevard South (the Strip) is the starting point for addresses; any street crossing it will start with 1 East and 1 West (and go up from there) at its intersection with the Strip.

THE STRIP

The Strip is probably the most famous 4-mile stretch of highway in the nation. Officially called Las Vegas Boulevard South, it contains most of the top hotels in town and offers almost all of the major showroom entertainment. First-time visitors will, and probably should, spend the bulk of their time on the Strip. If mobility is a problem, we suggest basing yourself in a South or Mid-Strip location.

For the purposes of organizing this book, we've divided the Strip into three sections. The **South Strip** can be roughly defined as the portion of the Strip south of Harmon Avenue, including the MGM Grand, Mandalay Bay, the Monte Carlo, New York–New York, Luxor, and many more hotels and casinos.

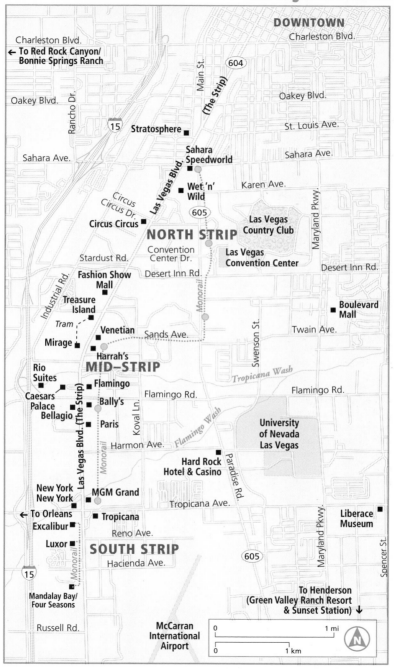

DOWNTOWN

Charleston Blvd.   Charleston Blvd.

← To Red Rock Canyon/
Bonnie Springs Ranch

604

Oakey Blvd.   Oakey Blvd.

Main St.

Rancho Dr.

(The Strip)

15   **Stratosphere** ■   St. Louis Ave.

Sahara Ave.   **Sahara Speedworld**   Sahara Ave.

Las Vegas Blvd.

Wet 'n' Wild ■   Karen Ave.

605

Circus Circus Dr.

Circus Circus ■   **NORTH STRIP**   **Las Vegas Country Club**

Convention Center Dr.   **Las Vegas Convention Center**

Maryland Pkwy.

Stardust Rd.   Desert Inn Rd.   Desert Inn Rd.

Industrial Rd.

Fashion Show Mall

Monorail

Treasure Island

Boulevard Mall

Tram

Venetian ■   Sands Ave.   Twain Ave.

Mirage ■

Swenson St.

Harrah's

MID-STRIP   *Tropicana Wash*

Rio Suites ■

Flamingo ■   Flamingo Rd.   Flamingo Rd.

Caesars Palace

Bally's ■

Koval Ln.

Bellagio ■

Las Vegas Blvd. (The Strip)

Paris ■

Flamingo Wash

Monorail

Harmon Ave.

University of Nevada Las Vegas

Hard Rock Hotel & Casino

Paradise Rd.

New York New York ■

MGM Grand ■

Tropicana Ave.

← To Orleans

Tropicana ■

Excalibur ■

Reno Ave.

Liberace Museum ■

Maryland Pkwy.

Spencer St.

Luxor ■   **SOUTH STRIP**

Hacienda Ave.

605

15

Monorail

Mandalay Bay/ Four Seasons

Russell Rd.

To Henderson (Green Valley Ranch Resort & Sunset Station) ↓

McCarran International Airport

0   1 mi

0   1 km

N

Mid-Strip is a long stretch of the street between Harmon Avenue and Spring Mountain Road, including Bellagio, Caesars, The Mirage and Treasure Island, Bally's, Paris Las Vegas, The Flamingo Las Vegas, and Harrah's, among other hotels and casinos.

The **North Strip** stretches north from Spring Mountain Road all the way to the Stratosphere Casino Hotel & Tower and includes Stardust, Sahara, The Riviera, and Circus Circus, to name a few of the accommodations and attractions.

EAST OF THE STRIP/CONVENTION CENTER

This area has grown up around the Las Vegas Convention Center. Las Vegas is one of the nation's top convention cities, attracting more than 2.9 million conventioneers each year. The major hotel in this section is the Las Vegas Hilton, but in recent years, Marriott has built Residence Inn and Courtyard properties here, and the Hard Rock Hotel has opened. You'll find many excellent smaller hotels and motels southward along Paradise Road. All of these hotels offer close proximity to the Strip.

BETWEEN THE STRIP & DOWNTOWN

The area between the Strip and Downtown is a seedy stretch dotted with tacky wedding chapels, bail-bond operations, pawnshops, and cheap motels.

However, the area known as the **Gateway District** (roughly north and south of Charleston Blvd. to the west of Las Vegas Blvd. S.) is slowly but surely gaining a name for itself as an actual artists' colony. Studios, small cafes, and other signs of life are springing up, and we hope this movement will last.

DOWNTOWN

Also known as **"Glitter Gulch"** (narrower streets make the neon seem brighter), downtown Las Vegas, which is centered on Fremont Street between Main and 9th streets, was the first section of the city to develop hotels and casinos. With the exception of the Golden Nugget, which looks like it belongs in Monte Carlo, this area has traditionally been more casual than the Strip. But with the advent of the **Fremont Street Experience** (p. 179), Downtown has experienced a revitalization. The area is clean, the crowds are low-key and friendly, and the light show overhead is as ostentatious as anything on the Strip. Don't overlook this area. Las Vegas Boulevard runs all the way into Fremont Street Downtown.

2 Getting Around

It shouldn't be too hard to navigate your way around. But remember, between huge hotel acreage, increased and very slow traffic, and lots and lots of people trying to explore like you, getting around takes a lot longer than you might think. Heck, it can take 15 to 20 minutes to get from your room to another part of your hotel! Always allow for plenty of time to get from point A to point B.

A warning note: The Las Vegas monorail is under construction. This upcoming transport system will surely alter Vegas traffic flow in the best of all possible ways, as the monorail will run from the Sahara Hotel, zigzag out to the Hilton and the Convention Center, and then come back down the east side of the Strip, making several stops along its 4-mile journey before ending at the MGM Grand and turning around for a return trip. A fabulous idea, and we can't wait. And it won't be too much longer now—the monorail is scheduled to open in January 2004. For $2.50 per person one-way, you will get to ride in comfort, in deluxe modern cars on these driverless trains, complete with roving attendants to answer your questions. Look for stations at MGM Grand, Bally's/Paris, the

Flamingo, Venetian/Harrah's, the Convention Center, a separate stop at the LV Hilton, and the Sahara. There will be a spur that will connect Circus Circus and the Stardust in 2006 and the Downtown link is scheduled for 2007. An extension to the airport is in the works for after that.

So if you do get caught in some of the resulting construction traffic mess, just remind yourself, it's all for a good cause—and swear never to use a car again once the monorail is up and humming.

BY CAR

We highly recommend that visitors rent a car. The Strip is too spread out for walking (and Las Vegas is often too hot or too cold to make strolls pleasant), Downtown is too far away for a cheap cab ride, and public transportation is often ineffective in getting you from point A to point B. Plus, return visits call for exploration in more remote parts of the city, and a car brings freedom (especially if you want to do any side trips—bus tours are available, but a car lets you explore at your own pace rather than according to a tour schedule).

You should note that places with addresses some 60 blocks east or west from the Strip are actually less than a 10-minute drive—provided there is no traffic.

That said, if you plan to confine yourself to one part of the Strip or to Downtown, your feet will suffice.

Having advocated renting a car, we should warn you that the growing population means a proportionate increase in the number of cars. Traffic is getting worse, and it's harder and harder to get around town with any certain swiftness. We've included a list of particular traffic danger zones in the "Chopper Tom's Traffic Tips" box below, but a general rule of thumb is to avoid driving on the Strip whenever you can, and avoid driving at all during peak rush hours (8–9:30am and 4:30–6pm), especially if you have to make a show curtain.

Parking is usually a pleasure, because all casino hotels offer free valet service. That means that for a mere $1 to $2 tip, you can park right at the door, though the valet usually fills up on busy nights. In those cases, you can use the gigantic self-parking lot that all hotels have.

RENTING A CAR

National companies with outlets in Las Vegas include **Alamo** (© 877/227-8367; www.goalamo.com), **Avis** (© 800/230-4898; www.avis.com), **Budget** (© 800/527-0700; https://rent.drivebudget.com/Home.jsp), **Dollar** (© 800/800-3665; www.dollar.com), **Enterprise** (© 800/736-8227; www.enterprise.com), **Hertz** (© 800/654-3131; www.hertz.com), **National** (© 800/227-7368; www.national car.com), **Payless** (© 800/729-5377; www.paylesscarrental.com), and **Thrifty** (© 800/847-4389; www.thrifty.com).

Car-rental rates vary even more than airline fares. The price you pay will depend on the size of the car, where and when you pick it up and drop it off, the length of the rental period, where and how far you drive it, whether you purchase insurance, and a host of other factors. A few key questions could save you hundreds of dollars:

- Are weekend rates lower than weekday rates? Ask if the rate is the same for pickup Friday morning, for instance, as it is for Thursday night.
- Is a weekly rate cheaper than the daily rate? Even if you need the car for only 4 days, it may be cheaper to keep it for 5.
- Does the agency assess a drop-off charge if you don't return the car to the same location where you picked it up? Is it cheaper to pick up the car at the airport compared to a Downtown location?

(Tips) **Chopper Tom's Traffic Tips**

"Chopper" Tom Hawley has watched Las Vegas grow since he was a little kid catching lizards in the desert back in the '60s. A self-described "traffic geek," Tom reports from the helicopter and from the studio most mornings and afternoons in Las Vegas on KVBC-TV/Channel 3. For further information on the following projects, tips, and much more, stop by Channel 3's website at **www.kvbc.com** and click "Traffic."

- **Monorail Mania:** After decades of abandoned plans and false starts, a commuter monorail serving the Strip is finally a reality! This 4-mile system is a larger, faster, and more modern version of the Disney hand-me-down that used to run between the MGM and Bally's. The new Las Vegas Monorail will start life with seven stations sprinkled from the MGM to the Sahara, and is set to begin passenger service in early 2004 at a fare of $2.50 per trip.
- **People Movers Galore:** Las Vegas has a greater variety of independent people-mover systems than any other city in the world, and they're a great way to get around without having to get into your car. In addition to the people movers at McCarran Airport, a variety of trains will take you from hotel to hotel. The **Doppelmayr Cable Liner Shuttle** whisks you from the Tropicana Walkways to the Excalibur, Luxor, and Mandalay Bay hotels. Smaller shuttles operate between the Mirage and Treasure Island, and between the Circus Circus Big Top and East Tower. *Note:* A shuttle between the Bellagio and Monte Carlo is down for maintenance until 2005.
- **Spaghetti Bowl:** The "Spaghetti Bowl" is what locals call the mess where I-15 intersects U.S. 95. The whole thing was reconstructed in 2000, but some studies indicate that it's already carrying more traffic than it was designed for, so don't expect a congestion-free ride.
- **U.S. 95 Widening:** The west leg of U.S. 95 was designed in the early '70s, when growth at the turn of the 21st century was expected to be about one-third of what it actually turned out to be. A massive widening project is underway with a projected 2006 completion. For now, this stretch of U.S. 95 (called the **Oran K. Gragson Expressway,** after a former Las Vegas mayor) is bulging at the seams. During rush hours, surface streets like Charleston and Lake Mead Boulevard are your best alternate routes.
- **Keep Your Feet off the Streets:** Local engineers have been trying to improve traffic on the Strip by separating the cars from the pedestrians. The first overhead pedestrian walkways opened at Tropicana Avenue in 1995; similar bridges were completed at Flamingo Avenue by 2000. Another bridge connects The Venetian and Treasure Island,

---

- Are special promotional rates available? If you see an advertised price in your local newspaper, be sure to ask for that specific rate; otherwise, you may be charged the standard cost. Terms change constantly, and reservations agents are notorious for not mentioning available discounts unless you ask.

and three more broke ground at Spring Mountain in the summer of 2003 and are scheduled for completion in August 2004.

- **Do D.I. Direct:** Most visitors seem to get a lot of mileage out of the Strip and I-15. But if you're checking out the local scene, you can bypass both of those using Desert Inn Road, which, after a recent addition, is now one of the longest streets running from one side of the valley to the other. Plus, the 2-mile "Superarterial" section between Valley View and Paradise zips you nonstop over the Interstate and under the Strip. The biggest thrill ride this side of the New York–New York roller coaster!
- **Grin and Bear It:** Yes, there are ways to avoid traffic jams on the Strip. But at least these traffic jams are entertaining! If you have the time and patience, go ahead and take a ride along the Strip from Hacienda to Sahara. The 4-mile drive might take an hour, but while you're grinding along, you might see a Sphinx, an active volcano, a water ballet, and some uniquely Vegas architecture.
- **Industrial Age:** Had enough of the glamour? Just want to sneak in the back door of your favorite hotel? Industrial Road may be the way to go. After a widening and face-lift a few years ago from Russell to Oakey, Industrial is a nice alternative to congestion on the Strip and I-15. Industrial provides rear-entrance access to most hotels between Caesars Palace and Circus Circus. Eventually it will tie in with Frank Sinatra Drive, another frontage road that now provides rear access to hotels from the Mandalay Bay to Monte Carlo.
- **Beltway Bypass:** Starting in December 2003, a 53-mile beltway (I-215) will wrap around the valley, allowing for easy access to the outskirts and to bypass the city. The "ultimate facility" of six-lane, limited-access divided highway won't be complete for another decade, but the southern section is a full freeway, and a few dozen more miles of interim roads are now open as frontage roads and four-lane highways.
- **Catch the CAT:** Some locals complain about Citizens Area Transit (CAT) bus service in certain neighborhoods. But the Strip routes are frequent and well serviced, running 'round the clock from the South Strip Transfer Terminal to the Downtown Transportation Center in the north. The 301 runs every 10 minutes during busy hours, and there's also a limited-stop express bus (no. 302) every 15 minutes. Other routes go for $1.25, but the 301 and 302 are the CAT's gravy trains and will run you $2. Exact change, please.

- Are discounts available for members of AARP, AAA, frequent-flier programs, or trade unions? If you belong to any of these organizations, you may be entitled to discounts of up to 30%.
- How much tax will be added to the rental bill? Local tax? State use tax?

- What is the cost of adding an additional driver's name to the contract?
- How many free miles are included in the price? Free mileage is often negotiable, depending on the length of your rental.
- How much does the rental company charge to refill your gas tank if you return with the tank less than full? Though most rental companies claim these prices are "competitive," fuel is almost always cheaper in town. Try to allow enough time to refuel the car yourself before returning it.

Some companies offer "refueling packages," in which you pay for an entire tank of gas up front. The price is usually fairly competitive with local gas prices, but you don't get credit for any gas remaining in the tank. If a stop at a gas station on the way to the airport will make you miss your plane, then by all means take advantage of the fuel purchase option. Otherwise, skip it.

Many packages are available that include airfare, accommodations, and a rental car with unlimited mileage. Compare these prices with the cost of booking airline tickets and renting a car separately to see if these offers are good deals. See "Money-Saving Package Deals," in chapter 2, for details on packages and where to find them.

Internet resources can make comparison-shopping easier. See "Planning Your Trip Online," in chapter 2, for tips on the best sites.

Demystifying Renter's Insurance

Before you drive off in a rental car, be sure you're insured. Hasty assumptions about your personal auto insurance or a rental agency's additional coverage could end up costing you tens of thousands of dollars—even if you are involved in an accident that was clearly the fault of another driver.

If you already hold a **private auto insurance** policy, you are most likely covered in the United States for loss of or damage to a rental car and liability in case of injury to any other party involved in an accident. Be sure to find out whether you are covered in the area you are visiting, whether your policy extends to all persons who will be driving the rental car, how much liability is covered in case an outside party is injured in an accident, and whether the type of vehicle you are renting is included under your contract. (Rental trucks, sport utility vehicles, and luxury vehicles such as the Jaguar may not be covered.) There is also another area—"loss," as in "loss of income," as in the loss of the income that rental car would have made for the rental-car company. Many insurers don't cover this.

Most **major credit cards** provide some degree of coverage as well—provided they were used to pay for the rental. Terms vary widely, however, so be sure to call your credit-card company directly before you rent.

If you are **uninsured,** your credit card may provide primary coverage as long as you decline the rental agency's insurance. This means that the credit card will cover damage or theft of a rental car for the full cost of the vehicle. If you already have insurance, your credit card may provide secondary coverage—which basically covers your deductible. *Credit cards will not cover liability,* or the cost of injury to an outside party and/or damage to an outside party's vehicle. If you do not hold an insurance policy, you may seriously want to consider purchasing additional liability insurance from your rental company. Be sure to check the terms, however: Some rental agencies cover liability only if the renter is not at fault; even then, the rental company's obligation varies from state to state. Bear in mind that each credit-card company has its own peculiarities; call your own credit-card company for details before relying on a card for coverage.

The basic insurance coverage offered by most car-rental companies, known as the **Loss/Damage Waiver (LDW)** or **Collision Damage Waiver (CDW),** can cost as much as $20 per day. The former should cover everything, including loss: It usually covers the full value of the vehicle with no deductible if an outside party causes an accident or other damage to the rental car. In all states but California, you will probably be covered in case of theft as well. Liability coverage varies according to the company policy and state law, but the minimum is usually at least $15,000. If you are at fault in an accident, however, you will be covered for the full replacement value of the car but not for liability. In Nevada, you can buy additional liability coverage for such cases. Most rental companies will require a police report in order to process any claims you file, but your private insurer will not be notified of the accident. Check your own policies and credit cards before you shell out money on this extra insurance, because you may already be covered.

DRIVING SAFETY

Because driving on the outskirts of Las Vegas—for example, coming from California—involves desert driving, you must take certain precautions. It's a good idea to check your tires, water, and oil before leaving. Take at least 5 gallons of water in a clean container that can be used for either drinking or the radiator. Pay attention to road signs that suggest when to turn off your car's air conditioner. And don't push your luck with gas—it may be 35 miles or more between stations. If your car overheats, do not remove the radiator cap until the engine has cooled, and then remove it very slowly. Add water to within an inch of the top of the radiator.

BY TAXI

Since cabs line up in front of all major hotels, an easy way to get around town is by taxi. Cabs charge $2.70 at the meter drop and 20¢ for each additional ⅑ mile, plus an additional $1.20 fee for being picked up at the airport. A taxi from

---

Fun Fact **Did You Know?**

- Las Vegas (Sin City) has more churches per capita than any other city in America.
- Illusionists Siegfried & Roy have sawed a woman in half more times than anyone else.
- Visitors on a trail ride once brought a horse into the crowded casino of the Thunderbird Hotel. They put a pair of dice between his lips at the craps table and he threw a natural 7.
- In January a Las Vegas visitor can ski the snowy slopes of Mount Charleston and water-ski on Lake Mead in the same day.
- Former president Ronald Reagan performed at the Last Frontier in 1954. Those who saw him said he was a pretty good song-and-dance man.
- Bandleader Xavier Cugat and Spanish bombshell singer Charo were the first couple to exchange vows at Caesars Palace, 2 days after its 1966 opening.

> **Tips** **Safety Alert**
>
> The area northeast of Harmon and Koval has had increased gang activity of late and should be avoided or at least approached with caution.

the airport to the Strip will run you $10 to $15, from the airport to Downtown $15 to $20, and between the Strip and Downtown about $10 to $12. You can often save money by sharing a cab with someone going to the same destination (up to five people can ride for the same fare).

If you want to call a taxi, any of the following companies can provide one: **Desert Cab Company** (© 702/386-9102), **Whittlesea Blue Cab** (© 702/384-6111), and **Yellow/Checker Cab/Star Company** (© 702/873-2000).

BY PUBLIC TRANSPORTATION

The no. 301 bus operated by **Citizens Area Transit** (© 702/CAT-RIDE) plies a route between the Downtown Transportation Center (at Casino Center Blvd. and Stewart Ave.) and a few miles beyond the southern end of the Strip. The fare is $2 for adults, 60¢ for seniors 62 and older and children 5 to 17, and free for those under 5. CAT buses run 24 hours a day and are wheelchair-accessible. Exact change is required, but dollar bills are accepted.

Or you can hop aboard a classic streetcar replica run by **Las Vegas Strip Trolley** (© 702/382-1404). These old-fashioned, dark-green vehicles have interior oak paneling and are comfortably air-conditioned. Like the buses, they run northward from Hacienda Avenue, stopping at all major hotels en route to the Sahara, and then loop back from the Las Vegas Hilton. They do not, however, go to the Stratosphere Casino Hotel & Tower or Downtown. Trolleys run about every 15 minutes daily between 9:30am and 2am. The fare is $1.65 (free for children under age 5), and exact change is required.

There are also a number of free transportation services, courtesy of the casinos. A free monorail connects Mandalay Bay with Luxor and Excalibur, another connects Bellagio with the Monte Carlo (though it's out of commission for all of 2004 due to renovations), still another runs between the MGM and Bally's (currently closed because of work on the Las Vegas monorail and scheduled to reopen in winter 2004), and a free tram shuttles between The Mirage and Treasure Island. Given how far apart even neighboring hotels can be, thanks to their size, and how they seem even farther apart on really hot days, these are blessed additions—and the more tourists who take them, the less traffic there might be on the Strip.

 FAST FACTS: **Las Vegas**

American Express There are about a dozen offices in town, but the closest one to the Strip is located inside the MGM Grand Hotel at 3799 Las Vegas Blvd. S. (corner of Tropicana; © 702/739-8474).

Area Codes The area code for Las Vegas is **702**.

Babysitters Contact **Around the Clock Child Care** (© 800/798-6768 or 702/365-1040). In business since 1987, this reputable company clears its sitters with the health department, the sheriff, and the FBI, and carefully screens references. Charges are $46 for 4 hours for one or two children,

$9.50 for each additional hour, with surcharges for additional children and on holidays. Sitters are on call 7 days a week, 24 hours a day, and they will come to your hotel. Call at least 3 hours in advance.

Banks Banks are generally open from 9 or 10am to 5 and sometimes 6pm, and most have Saturday hours. ATMs are plentiful all around town. See also "Cash & Credit" below.

Car Rentals See "Renting a Car" under "Getting Around," earlier in this chapter.

Cash & Credit It's extremely easy, too easy, to obtain cash in Las Vegas. Most casino cashiers will cash personal checks and can exchange foreign currency, and just about every casino has a machine that will provide cash on a wide variety of credit cards.

Conventions Las Vegas is one of America's top convention destinations. Much of the action takes place at the **Las Vegas Convention Center,** 3150 Paradise Rd., Las Vegas, NV 89109 (© **702/892-7575**), which is the largest single-level convention center in the world. Its 1.3 million square feet includes 89 meeting rooms. And this immense facility is augmented by the **Cashman Field Center,** 850 Las Vegas Blvd. N., Las Vegas, NV 89101 (© **702/ 386-7100**). Under the same auspices, Cashman provides another 98,100 square feet of convention space. Additionally, there are massive convention facilities at many of the big hotels, including the MGM Grand, The Mirage, Mandalay Bay, The Venetian, and more.

Dentists & Doctors Hotels usually have lists of dentists and doctors should you need one. In addition, they are listed in the Centel Yellow Pages. See also "Hospitals," below.

For dentist referrals, you can also call the **Clark County Dental Society** (© **702/255-7873**), weekdays from 9am to noon and 1 to 5pm; when the office is closed, a recording will tell you who to call for emergency service.

For physician referrals, call the **Desert Springs Hospital** (© **800/842-5439** or 702/733-6875). Hours are Monday to Friday from 8am to 5pm.

Drugstores See "Pharmacies," below.

Dry Cleaners Things spill, and silk is easily stained. When in need, go to **Steiner Cleaners,** 1131 E. Tropicana Ave., corner of Maryland Parkway, in the Vons Shopping Center (© **702/736-7474**), open Monday to Friday from 7am to 6:30pm, Saturday 8am to 6pm. Not only did they clean all the costumes for the movie *Casino,* but they were Liberace's personal dry cleaner for years.

Emergencies Dial © **911** to contact the police or fire department or to call an ambulance.

Highway Conditions For recorded information, call © **702/486-3116.** You can also tune in 970 AM for traffic news or 1610 AM for highway reports.

Hospitals Emergency services are available 24 hours a day at **University Medical Center,** 1800 W. Charleston Blvd., at Shadow Lane (© **702/383-2000**); the emergency-room entrance is on the corner of Hastings and Rose streets. **Sunrise Hospital and Medical Center,** 3186 Maryland Pkwy., between Desert Inn Road and Sahara Avenue (© **702/731-8080**), also has a 24-hour emergency room.

For more minor problems, if you are on the Strip, the Imperial Palace has a 24-hour urgent-care facility, the **Nevada Resort Medical Center,** an independently run facility on the eighth floor, with doctors and X-ray machines. It's located at 3535 Las Vegas Blvd. S., between the Sands and The Flamingo (© **702/893-6767**).

Hot Lines Emergency hot lines include the **Rape Crisis Center** (© **702/ 366-1640**), **Suicide Prevention** (© **702/731-2990**), and **Poison Emergencies** (© **800/446-6179**).

Liquor & Gambling Laws You must be 21 to drink or gamble; proof of age is required and often requested at bars, nightclubs, and restaurants, so it's always a good idea to bring ID when you go out, especially if you look young. There are no closing hours in Las Vegas for the sale or consumption of alcohol, even on Sunday. Don't even think about driving while you're under the influence, or having an open container of alcohol in your car. Beer, wine, and liquor are all sold in all kinds of stores pretty much around the clock; trust us, you won't have a hard time finding a drink in this town. It's even legal to have an open container while walking on the Strip.

Lost & Found Be sure to tell all of your credit-card companies the minute you discover your wallet has been lost or stolen and file a report at the nearest police precinct. Your credit-card company or insurer may require a police report number or record of the loss. Most credit-card companies have an emergency toll-free number to call if your card is lost or stolen; they may be able to wire you a cash advance immediately or deliver an emergency credit card in a day or two. **Visa**'s U.S. emergency number is © **800/847-2911** or 410/581-9994. **American Express** cardholders and traveler's check holders should call © **800/221-7282**. **MasterCard** holders should call © **800/307- 7309** or 636/722-7111. For other credit cards, call the toll-free number directory at © **800/555-1212**.

If you need emergency cash over the weekend when all banks and American Express offices are closed, you can have money wired to you via **Western Union** (© **800/325-6000**; www.westernunion.com).

Identity theft or fraud are potential complications of losing your wallet, especially if you've lost your driver's license along with your cash and credit cards. Notify the major credit-reporting bureaus immediately; placing a fraud alert on your records may protect you against liability for criminal activity. The three major U.S. credit-reporting agencies are **Equifax** (© **800/ 766-0008**; www.equifax.com), **Experian** (© **888/397-3742**; www.experian. com), and **TransUnion** (© **800/680-7289**; www.transunion.com). Finally, if you've lost all forms of photo ID, call your airline and explain the situation: They might allow you to board the plane if you have a copy of your passport or birth certificate and a copy of the police report you've filed.

Newspapers & Periodicals There are two Las Vegas dailies: the *Las Vegas Review Journal* and the *Las Vegas Sun*. The *Review Journal*'s Friday edition has a helpful "Weekend" section with a comprehensive guide to shows and buffets. There are two free alternative papers, with club listings and many unbiased restaurant and bar reviews. Both *City Life* and *Las Vegas Weekly* are published weekly. And at every hotel desk, you'll find dozens of free local magazines, such as *Vegas Visitor, What's On in Las Vegas,*

Showbiz Weekly, and *Where to Go in Las Vegas,* that are chock-full of helpful information—although probably of the sort that comes from paid advertising.

Parking Free valet parking is one of the great pleasures of Las Vegas and well worth the dollar tip (given when the car is returned) to save walking a city block from the far reaches of a hotel parking lot, particularly when the temperature is over 100°F (38°C). Another summer plus: The valet will turn on your air-conditioning so that you don't have to get into an "oven on wheels."

Pharmacies There's a 24-hour **Walgreen's** (which also has 1-hr. photo processing) at 3763 Las Vegas Blvd. S. (✆ **702/739-9638**), almost directly across from the Monte Carlo. **Sav-On** is a large 24-hour drugstore and pharmacy close to the Strip at 1360 E. Flamingo Rd., at Maryland Parkway (✆ **702/731-5373** for the pharmacy, 702/737-0595 for general merchandise). **White Cross Drugs,** 1700 Las Vegas Blvd. S. (✆ **702/382-1733**), open daily from 7am to 1am, will make pharmacy deliveries to your hotel during the day.

Police For nonemergencies, call ✆ **702/795-3111.** For emergencies, call ✆ **911.**

Post Office The most convenient post office is immediately behind the Stardust hotel at 3100 Industrial Rd., between Sahara Avenue and Spring Mountain Road (✆ **800/297-5543**). It's open Monday to Friday from 8:30am to 5pm. You can also mail letters and packages at your hotel, and there's a full-service U.S. Post Office in the Forum Shops in Caesars Palace.

Safety In Las Vegas vast amounts of money are always on display, and criminals find many easy marks. Don't be one of them. At gaming tables and slot machines, men should keep wallets well concealed and out of the reach of pickpockets, and women should keep handbags in plain sight (on laps). If you win a big jackpot, ask the pit boss or slot attendant to cut you a check rather than give you cash—the cash may look nice, but flashing it can attract the wrong kind of attention. Outside casinos, popular spots for pickpockets and thieves are restaurants and outdoor shows, such as the volcano at The Mirage or the fountains at Bellagio. Stay alert. Unless your hotel room has an in-room safe, check your valuables in a safe-deposit box at the front desk.

Show Tickets See chapter 10 for details on obtaining show tickets.

Taxes Clark County hotel room tax is 9%, and in Henderson it's 10%; the sales tax is 7%.

Time Zone Las Vegas is in the Pacific time zone, 3 hours earlier than the East Coast, 2 hours earlier than the Midwest. For exact local time, call ✆ **702/248-4800.**

Veterinarian If Fido or Fluffy gets sick while traveling, go to the **West Flamingo Animal Hospital,** 5445 W. Flamingo Rd., near Decatur Boulevard (✆ **702/876-2111**). They're open 24 hours and they take Discover, MasterCard, and Visa, and have an ATM.

Weather See "When to Go" in chapter 2. For local weather information, call ✆ **702/248-4800.** The radio station 970 FM does weather reports.

Weddings Las Vegas is one of the easiest places in the world to tie the knot. There's no blood test or waiting period, the ceremony and license are inexpensive, chapels are open around the clock, and your honeymoon destination is right at hand. More than 101,000 marriages are performed here each year. Get a license Downtown at the **Clark County Marriage License Bureau,** 200 S. 3rd St., at Bridger Avenue (℃ **702/455-4415**), which is open Monday to Thursday from 8am to midnight, and from 8am Friday through midnight Sunday. On legal holidays, they're open 24 hours. The cost of a marriage license is $55; the cost of the ceremony varies depending on where you go to have it done. See "Getting Married" in chapter 7 for details on the local wedding chapels.

5

Where to Stay

If there's one thing Vegas has, it's hotels. Big hotels. And lots of them. You'll find the 10 largest hotels in the United States—9 of the top 10 in the world—right here. And you'll find a whole lot of rooms: 132,000 rooms, to be exact—or at least exact as of this writing. Every 5 minutes, or so it seems, someone is putting up a new giant hotel, or adding another 1,000 rooms to an existing one. So finding a place to stay in Vegas should be the least of your worries.

Or should it?

When a convention, a fight, or some other big event is happening—and these things are always happening—darn near all of those 132,000 rooms are going to be sold out. (Over the course of a regular year—one not affected by the Sept 11, 2001, terrorist attacks—the occupancy rate for hotel rooms in Las Vegas runs at about 90%.) A last-minute Vegas vacation can turn into a housing nightmare. If possible, plan in advance so that you can have your choice: Ancient Egypt or Ancient Rome? New York or New Orleans? Strip or Downtown? Luxury or economy? Vegas has all that and way too much more.

The bottom line is that with a few, mostly subtle differences, a hotel room is a hotel room is a hotel room. After you factor in location, price, and whether you have a pirate-loving kid, there isn't that much difference between rooms, except for perhaps size and the quality of their surprisingly similar furnishings.

Hotel prices in Vegas are anything but fixed, so you will notice wild price ranges. The same room can routinely go for anywhere from $60 to $250, depending on demand, and even that range is negotiable if it's a slow time (though such times are less and less common thanks to the influx of conventions). So use our price categories with a grain of salt, and don't rule out a hotel just because it's listed as "Very Expensive"—on any given day, you might get a great deal on a room in a pricey hotel. Just ask.

Yes, if you pay more, you'll probably (but not certainly) get a "nicer" establishment and clientele to match (perhaps not so many loud drunks in the elevators). On the other hand, if a convention is in town, the drunks will be there no matter how upscale the hotel—they'll just be wearing business suits and/or funny hats. And frankly, the big hotels, no matter how fine, have mass-produced rooms; at 3,000 rooms or more, they are the equivalent of '60s tract housing. Consequently, even in the nicest hotels, you can (and probably will) encounter plumbing noises, overhear conversations from other rooms, or get woken by the maids as they knock on the doors next to yours that don't have the DO NOT DISTURB sign up.

1 Coming Attractions

Part of the reason that we patiently tell people they haven't really been to Vegas, even if they have, is because if they haven't been by in the last, oh, week—okay, let's say 2 or 3 years—they might find several surprises awaiting them on the Strip. And if it's been more than a decade, well, forget it. All of the classic old hotels are either gone (Sands, Hacienda) or renovated virtually beyond recognition (Caesars, The Flamingo). In their place rise bigger and better and trendier resort hotels, changing the landscape and altering the welcome that Vegas visitors receive.

The new era of Vegas hotels was ushered in by The Mirage, and since then, everyone has been trying to up the ante. The year 1997 began with the opening of New York–New York, which set yet another level of stupendous excess that remained unmatched for, oh, at least 18 months.

The fall of 1998 saw the official beginning of the new era of Vegas luxury resorts (many with themes), with the opening of the opulent Bellagio, followed by Mandalay Bay and Four Seasons. And then these took a back seat (sort of) to The Venetian, which combines the jaw-dropping detail and extravagance of New York–New York (complete with canals and gondolas) with the luxury of Bellagio. Could anything top it? Possibly—hot on its heels was Paris, themed as you can imagine, and just a few months later, the new and improved Aladdin, with its desert-fantasy decor.

For a change, 2003 seemed rather quiet in terms of new things to see and do. Sure, Caesars opened its Roman Colosseum replica, built just to house Celine Dion's new show, but other than that, no grand new hotels or major expansions arrived, unless you count (and we sure do) the arrival of a true luxury resort, the Ritz-Carlton, Lake Las Vegas, over in nearby Henderson.

On the other hand, 2004 will kick off another wave of new construction. Look for 1,000 new rooms and other new goodies at Mandalay Bay; 1,000 more rooms at The Venetian, along with several new restaurants, and 900 new rooms (and restaurants and spa) for the Bellagio. Caesars is gearing up for another 700 rooms themselves. And hotels that aren't building are changing hands: Look for the Aladdin to get a cinematic makeover, care of its new owner Planet Holly-wood, and for likely renovations at the Golden Nugget by its new owners. Look also for the brand-new Westin Spa Resort to open on the totally gutted remains of the Maxim Hotel, by the end of 2003 or so. It was only beams when we went to press, but given the reputation of the company, this could finally be the classy boutique hotel we've been hoping someone would open in town. (And, if not, the local scuttlebutt says that *Ocean's 11* stars Brad Pitt and George Clooney are in talks to open a boutique hotel on the Strip in partnership with the Venetian.)

And then 2005 will bring the eagerly awaited Wynn Las Vegas, the latest hotel concept from Steve Wynn, the man behind Mirage Corp., at a mere cost of $2 billion. Wynn Las Vegas (formerly billed as Le Reve after a Picasso painting that Wynn owns but whose title had zero name recognition—a marketing no-no in Vegas) is going up on the hallowed grounds once occupied by the Desert Inn. Look for a new expensive art collection, a 150-foot-tall man-made mountain that will block the hotel from the Strip, a state-of-the-art $100 million domed showroom, a new golf course, many fantastic restaurants, and much more. Just as The Mirage set off an explosion of development, so too may Wynn Las Vegas, with continued rumors of the New Frontier being replaced by a San Fran-cisco–themed resort and an $800 million hotel/casino next door, a London-themed resort just north of The Riviera, a boutique hotel (maybe a W?) next to the Frontier, and possible wrecking balls in store for the Stardust and the Tropi-cana. Of course, another economic downturn of even the slightest size could prevent all of it. Stay tuned.

2 Three Questions to Ask Before You Book a Room

WHERE SHOULD I STAY?

Your two main choices for location are the Strip and Downtown. The Strip, home to many of the most dazzling hotels and casinos in Vegas, is undeniably the winner, especially for first-timers, if only because of the sheer, overwhelming force of its "Vegas-ness." On the other hand, it is crowded, confining, and strangely claustrophobic. We say "strangely claustrophobic" because the hotels only *look* close together: In reality, they are situated on large properties, and it's a long (and often very hot or very cold) walk from one place to the next.

Contrast that with Downtown, which is nowhere near as striking, but more easily navigated on foot. Within 5 minutes you can reach about 17 different casinos. The Fremont Street upgrade and the brand-new Neonopolis entertainment-and-shopping complex have turned a rapidly declining area into a very pleasant place to be, and the crowds reflect that: They seem nicer and more relaxed, and a calmer atmosphere pervades. Since it's only a 5-minute ride by car between Downtown and Strip hotels (the Convention Center is more or less in between), there's no such thing as a bad location if you have access to a car. If money is no object, a $10 cab ride separates the Strip from Downtown.

For those of you depending on public transportation: While the bus ride between Downtown and the Strip is short in distance, it can be long in time if you get stuck in traffic. You should also be aware that the buses become quite crowded once they reach the Strip and may bypass a bus stop if no one signals to get out and the driver does not wish to take on more passengers. Without a car, your ease of movement between different areas of town is limited.

 Reservations Services

If you get harried when you have to haggle, use a free service offered by **Reservations Plus**, 2275 A Renaissance Dr., Las Vegas, NV 89119 (© **800/805-9528**; fax 702/795-3999; www.reservationsplus.com). They'll find you a hotel room in your price range that meets your specific requirements. Because they book rooms in volume, they are able to get discounted rates. Not only can they book rooms, but they can arrange packages (including meals, transportation, tours, show tickets, car rentals, and other features) and group rates.

The **Las Vegas Convention and Visitors Authority** also runs a room-reservations hot line (© **877/VISIT-LV**) that can be helpful. They can apprise you of room availability, quote rates, contact a hotel for you, and tell you when major conventions will be in town.

Other reputable online reservation services that book rooms in Las Vegas are listed in "Planning Your Trip Online" in chapter 2.

A couple words of warning: Make sure they don't try to book you into a hotel you've never heard of. Try to stick with the hotels listed in this book. Always get your information in writing and then make some phone calls just to confirm that you really have the reservations that they say they've made for you.

Frankly, for first-timers, there probably isn't any point to staying anywhere but the Strip—you're going to spend most (if not all) of your time there anyway. For future visits, however, we'd strongly advise you to consider Downtown.

But the Strip vs. Downtown location isn't the end of the debate; there is also the issue of where to stay on the Strip. Staying on the **South Strip** end means an easy trip (sometimes in the air-conditioned comfort of covered walkways or monorail) to Mandalay Bay, MGM Grand, New York–New York, Tropicana, Luxor, and Excalibur—all virtually on one corner. **Mid-Strip** has Caesars, The Mirage, Bellagio, Treasure Island, Paris, The Venetian, Bally's, The Flamingo, Harrah's, and so forth. The **North Strip** gets you The Riviera, Sahara, Stardust, and Circus Circus, though with a bit more of a walk between them. For this reason, if mobility is a problem and you want to see more than just your own hotel casino, the South and Mid-Strip locations are probably the best bets.

WHAT AM I LOOKING FOR IN A HOTEL?

If gambling is not your priority, what are you doing in Vegas? Just kidding. But not 100% kidding. Vegas's new identity as a luxury resort destination means there are several brand-spanking-new hotels that promise to offer you all sorts of alternatives to gambling—lush pool areas, fabulous spas, incredible restaurants, lavish shopping. But if you look closely, much of this is Vegas bait and switch; the pools are often chilly (and often partially closed during nonsummer months), and it will be years before there is more foliage than concrete in these newly landscaped environments. The spas cost extra (sometimes a whole lot extra); the best restaurants are rarely cheap; and the stores are often the kinds of places where average mortals can't even afford the oxygen. So what does that leave you with? Why, that's right—gambling.

The other problem with these self-proclaimed luxury hotels is their size. True luxury hotels do not have 3,000 rooms—they have a couple of hundred at best, because you simply can't provide first-class service and Egyptian-cotton sheets in mass quantity. But while Bellagio, The Venetian, and, to a lesser extent, Mandalay Bay have done their best to offer sterling service and to make their rooms more attractive and luxurious than those at other Vegas hotels, there's only so much that any place that big can do. Don't get us wrong—these places are absolutely several steps up in quality from other large hotels, and compared to them, even the better older hotels really look shabby. But they are still sprawling, frequently noisy complexes.

Sadly, it's relatively easy for both you and us to make a mistake about a hotel; either of us may experience a particular room or two in a 1,000-plus-room hotel, and from there conclude that a place is nicer than it is or more of a dump than it is. Maintenance, even in the best of hotels, can sometimes be running a bit behind, so if there is something wrong with your room, don't hesitate to ask for another. Of course, if it's one of those busy weekends, there may not be another room to be had, but at least this way you've registered a complaint, perhaps letting a busy hotel know that a certain room needs attention. And who knows? If you are gracious and persistent enough, you may be rewarded with a deal for some future stay.

If you want a true luxury-resort hotel, there are only two options: On the Strip it's the Four Seasons, and off, way off, in nearby Henderson, it's the Ritz-Carlton. Both offer, in addition to that same service and level of comfort only found at a smaller hotel, those extra goodies that pile on the hidden charges at other hotels—health club, poolside cabanas, and so on—as part of the total

---

Tips **Who Kept the Kids Out?**

Some hotels—notably Bellagio, which started the practice—ban children who are not staying onsite from stepping foot on the hotel premises. Child-free adults love the ban, but families who travel to Vegas (can we say yet again that this is not a family destination?) may be seriously inconvenienced by it. The policy doesn't appear to be uniformly enforced (hotels don't want to offend parents with plenty of dough to gamble, after all), but we've seen families and teenagers get turned away from a hotel because they couldn't produce a room key. If you're traveling with your kids, or want to be free of someone else's, your best bet is to call your chosen hotel and ask what its policy is.

---

package, meaning that their slightly higher prices may be more of a bargain than you'd think.

Still, if you want peace and quiet and don't land in the tax bracket that Four Seasons/Ritz caters to, there are other, less high-profile hotels without a casino. Make certain the hotel has a pool, however, especially if you need some recreation. There is nothing as boring as a noncasino, nonpool Vegas hotel—particularly if you have kids.

Casino hotels, by the way, are not always a nice place for children. It used to be that the casino was a separate section in the hotel and children were not allowed inside (we have fond memories of standing just outside the casino line, watching our dads put quarters in a slot machine "for us"). But in almost all the new hotels, you have to walk through the casino to get anywhere—the lobby, the restaurants, the outside world. This makes sense from the hotel's point of view; it gives you many opportunities to stop and drop a quarter or $10 into a slot. But this often long, crowded trek gets wearying for adults—and it's far worse for kids. The rule is that kids can walk through the casinos, but they can't stop, even to gawk for a second at someone hitting a jackpot nearby. The casino officials who will immediately hustle the child away are just doing their job, but, boy, it's annoying.

So, take this (and what a hotel offers that kids might like) into consideration when booking a room. Note also that those gorgeous hotel pools are often cold (and again, sometimes closed altogether) and not very deep. They look like places you would want to linger, but often (from a kid's point of view) they are not. Plus, the pools close early. Hotels want you inside gambling, not outside swimming.

Ultimately, though, if it's a busy time, you'll have to nab any room you can, especially if you get a price you like. How much time are you going to spend in the room, anyway?

WHAT WILL I HAVE TO PAY?

The rack rate is the maximum rate that a hotel charges for a room. It's the rate you'd get if you walked in off the street and asked for a room for the night. Hardly anybody pays these prices, however, especially in Vegas, where prices fluctuate wildly with demand and there are many ways around rack rates. Here are some tips for landing a low rate:

- **Don't be afraid to bargain.** Get in the habit of asking for a lower price than the first one quoted. Always ask politely whether a less expensive room is available than the first one mentioned, or whether any special rates apply to you. If you belong to one of the players clubs at a hotel casino, you may be able to secure a better deal on a hotel room. Of course, you will also be expected to spend a certain amount of time, and money, gambling there. See below for more details on players clubs.

- **Rely on a qualified professional.** Certain hotels give travel agents discounts in exchange for steering business their way, so if you're shy about bargaining, an agent may be better equipped to negotiate discounts for you.
- **Dial direct.** When booking a room in a chain hotel (The Flamingo, for example), call the hotel's local line, as well as the toll-free number, and see where you get the best deal. A hotel makes nothing on a room that stays empty. The clerk who runs the place is more likely to know about vacancies and will often grant deep discounts in order to fill up.
- **Remember the law of supply and demand.** Las Vegas hotels are most crowded and therefore most expensive on weekends. So the best deals are offered midweek, when prices can drop dramatically. If possible, go then. You can also call the **Las Vegas Convention and Visitors Authority** (© 877/ VISIT-LV) to find out if an important convention is scheduled at the time of your planned visit; if so, you might want to change your date. Some of the most popular conventions are listed under "When to Go" in chapter 2. Remember also that planning your vacation just a week before or after official peak season can mean big savings.
- **Look into group or long-stay discounts.** If you come as part of a large group, you should be able to negotiate a bargain, since the hotel can then guarantee occupancy in a number of rooms. Likewise, when you're planning a long stay in town (usually from 5 days to a week), you'll usually qualify for a discount.
- **Avoid excess phone charges.** When you book a room, find out before you dial whether your hotel imposes a surcharge on local or long-distance calls. A pay phone, however inconvenient, may save you money.
- **Beware of hidden extras.** Almost all of the major hotels (Four Seasons is one notable exception) charge extra for things that are always free in other destinations, like health-club privileges. Expect to pay anywhere from $15 to $30 to use almost any hotel spa/health club. (We've noted these charges in the listings that follow so that you won't be taken by surprise.)
- **Watch for coupons and advertised discounts.** Scan ads in your local Sunday travel section, an excellent source for up-to-the-minute hotel deals. "The Fun Book," available from the Las Vegas Convention and Visitors Authority (see above), offers some discounts on lodging.
- **Consider a suite.** If you are traveling with your family or another couple, you can pack more people into a suite (which usually comes with a sofa bed), and thereby reduce your per-person rate. Remember that some places charge for extra guests and some don't.
- **Investigate reservation services.** These outfits usually work as consolidators, buying up or reserving rooms in bulk and then dealing them out to customers at a profit. Most of them offer online reservation services as well. See the box on "Reservations Services," above, for outfits that operate in the Las Vegas area.

As far as prices go, keep in mind that our price categories are rough guidelines at best. If you see a hotel that appeals to you, even if it seems out of your price range, give them a call anyway. They might be having a special, a slow week, or some kind of promotion, or they may just like the sound of your voice (we have no other explanation for it). You could end up with a hotel in the "expensive" category offering you a room for $35 a night. (Even Bellagio, which insists they will never fall below a certain three-figure price, has been quietly offering rooms for as low as $80 on certain nights.) Since it's a toll-free call, it's worth a try.

Consider also, even if you think from the outset that this is your one and only trip to Vegas, joining a hotel players club—or possibly every hotel's players club. This costs you nothing, and players/members often get nifty offers in the mail for heavily discounted, and occasionally even free, rooms (plus meals, shows, and so on). Players clubs reward you with freebies and discounts when you play in their casinos, regardless of whether you win or not. Even as one luxury hotel was firmly insisting their prices would never, ever fall below about $149 per night, players club members were receiving invitations to stay for $89. How much you have to play to get these deals varies, but if you are going to gamble anyway, why not make it work more to your advantage?

We've classified all our hotel recommendations based on the average rack rate that you can expect to be quoted for a double room on an average night (not when the Consumer Electronics Show is in town, and not on New Year's Eve). Expect to pay a little less than this if you stay only Sunday to Thursday and a little more than this if you stay Friday and Saturday.

Of course, you can expect significant savings if you book a money-saving package deal, like those described in chapter 2. And on any given night when business is slow, you might be able to stay at a "very expensive" hotel for a "moderate" price.

Note: All the casinos for the major hotels on the strip and Downtown (and a few other ones) are reviewed in chapter 8.

3 South Strip

VERY EXPENSIVE

Four Seasons Hotel Las Vegas ★★★ *Kids*   Various mammoth Vegas hotels attempt to position themselves as luxury resorts, insisting that service and fine cotton sheets can be done on a mass scale. But there is only one true luxury resort—in some people's eyes, *the* luxury resort—in town (see later in this chapter for two more in Henderson!), located, on the top five floors of Mandalay Bay, though in many ways, the Four Seasons is light-years away. A separate driveway and portico entrance, plus an entire registration area, sets you up immediately. This is the one fancy hotel in town where you are not greeted, even at a distance, with the clash and clang of slots, and the general hubbub that is the soundtrack to Vegas.

Inside the hotel, all is calm and quiet. But it's really the best of both worlds—all you have to do is walk through a door and instantly you are in Mandalay Bay, with access to a casino, nightlife, and, yes, general hubbub. The difference is quite shocking, and frankly, once you've experienced Vegas this way, it's kind of hard to go back to the constant sensory overload. So let's scurry quickly back to the womblike comfort of Four Seasons.

The rooms don't look like much at first—slightly bland but in good taste—but when you sink down into the furniture, you appreciate the fine quality. Here at last is a Vegas hotel where they really don't care if you ever leave your room, so the beds have feather pillows and down comforters, robes are plush, and amenities (such as safes, irons, voice mail, hair dryers, and VCRs) are really, really nice. Since Four Seasons has the southernmost location on the Strip, its

Strip-view rooms (the most expensive units) give you the whole incredible panorama.

Service is superb (if they say 20 min. for room service, you can expect your food in 19½ min.). Your needs are anticipated so quickly that you're tempted to sink to the floor in the lobby because you know someone will have a chair under your rear before you land. Children are encouraged and spoiled with welcome gifts of toys and goodies, rooms are childproofed in advance, and the list of comforts available for the asking is a yard long. Once you factor in all the freebies (gym/spa access, pool cabanas, various other amenities), not to mention the service and the blessed peace, the difference in price between Four Seasons and Bellagio (with all its hidden charges) is nothing.

3960 Las Vegas Blvd. S., Las Vegas, NV 89119. © **877/632-5000** or 702/632-5000. Fax 702/632-5195. www. fourseasons.com. 424 units. $200–$500 double; from $400 suite. Extra person $30. Children 17 and under stay free in parent's room. AE, DC, DISC, MC, V. Free self- and valet parking. **Amenities:** 2 restaurants; heated outdoor pool with free cabanas and other luxury perks; elegant health club (free to guests) and spa; concierge; car-rental desk; courtesy car; full 24-hr. business center with faxing, delivery, and secretarial service; 24-hr. room service; in-room massage; babysitting; overnight laundry/dry-cleaning service; nonsmoking rooms; executive-level rooms. *In room:* A/C, TV w/pay movies, dataport, minibar, fridge, coffeemaker, hair dryer, iron and board, safe.

EXPENSIVE

Aladdin Resort & Casino ✦ ***Note:*** As we were going to press, the beleaguered and bankrupt Aladdin had just been bought by Planet Hollywood, which, as of now, intends to rename, remodel, and restyle the property. This process may or may not be under way by the time you read this, but at least you won't be confused if there is a big blue globe out front, a new name, and lots of cast-off clothes and props from various Hollywood movies enshrined inside.

It's a bit of a pity, because the new Aladdin, rising on the ashes of the old Vegas stalwart, which was desperately out of date, is a handsome building both inside and out. The theme is a generic Middle East theme—you know, the sort that pretends there is no significant difference between Egypt, Morocco, and Turkey, which may be news to Egyptians, Moroccans, and Turks—best characterized by one observer as "the Sahara with a billion dollars thrown at it." Details that indicate considerable thought went into the design are everywhere—what other casino has actual tile work (clearly Moroccan in origin) throughout? But all that work came at a price, hence a $700 million bankruptcy—the largest in Nevada history.

That petty detail aside, this is already what a sexy, but distinctly Vegas, hotel ought to be: a little bit of kitsch, a little bit of class, and all of it playful. And we hope that the new owners will concentrate on maintaining and building on these aspects. The rooms are not distinctive, but they are pleasing (except for the beds; the money must have run out before buying the mattresses, which are some of the most uncomfortable we've slept on), and the bathrooms can be quite large, with a deep tub and separate glass shower, plus little Aladdin-lamp-shaped faucets and exotic spice-scented amenities. Another plus is that the hotel is constructed so that guests need to see little of the casino (a plus for you, a drag for needed gambling revenue, and likely one of the first things the new owners will change), while the pool area is decent but nothing spectacular.

And then there is the **Desert Passage** shopping area (p. 236), another one to rival the capitalist ventures over at Caesars and The Venetian. This one is Arabian Nights themed, all Casbah this and Sultan that. It's impressive, to be sure, and better still for the live-action touches such as jugglers, acrobats, and belly dancers who

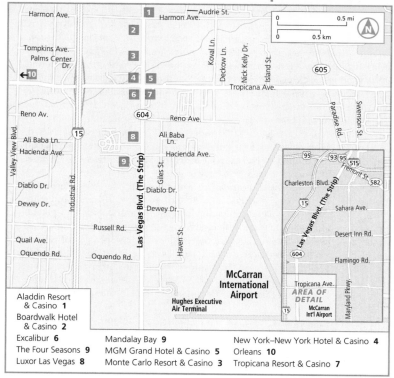

Harmon Ave. · **1** · Audrie St. · Harmon Ave.
2
Tompkins Ave. Palms Center Dr. · **3**
←**10**
4 **5** · Tropicana Ave.
6 **7**
Reno Av. · 604 · Reno Ave.
15
Ali Baba Ln. · **8** · Ali Baba Ln.
Hacienda Ave. · Hacienda Ave.
9
Diablo Dr. · Diablo Dr.
Dewey Dr. · Dewey Dr.
Russell Rd.
Quail Ave.
Oquendo Rd. · Oquendo Rd.

Koval Ln. · Deckow Ln. · Nick Kelly Dr. · Island St. · 605
Paradise Rd. · Swenson St.
95 · 93 95 · 515
Charleston Blvd. · Fremont St. · 582
15 · Sahara Ave.
Desert Inn Rd.
604 · Flamingo Rd.

0 — 0.5 mi
0 — 0.5 km

McCarran International Airport
Hughes Executive Air Terminal
Tropicana Ave. *AREA OF DETAIL*
15 · McCarran Int'l Airport
Maryland Pkwy.

Aladdin Resort & Casino **1**
Boardwalk Hotel & Casino **2**
Excalibur **6**
The Four Seasons **9**
Luxor Las Vegas **8**

Mandalay Bay **9**
MGM Grand Hotel & Casino **5**
Monte Carlo Resort & Casino **3**

New York–New York Hotel & Casino **4**
Orleans **10**
Tropicana Resort & Casino **7**

pop up regularly to entertain shoppers and add that hectic souk feel to the experience. Inside the Desert Passage are a number of terrific restaurants, including a branch of New Orleans's venerated **Commander's Palace** (p. 128). The hotel also has its own arena, the **Center for the Performing Arts,** which is attracting big names back to Vegas. Finally, there is the **Elemis spa** ★★★, maybe aesthetically our hands-down local favorite; the owners (who also run Elemis in London) sent their designers to Morocco for ideas, and it shows in this Medina-flavored facility; just looking at it is pampering, and that's before one of their people puts you in a wrap and "dry float" (a womblike water bed–style cradle).

All in all, the place teeters on the brink of a higher rating, and all we can hope is that the new owners help push it over the hump, rather than in the other direction. The place deserves it.

3667 Las Vegas Blvd. S., Las Vegas, NV 89109. © **877/333-WISH** (333-9474) or 702/785-5555. Fax 702/785-5558. www.aladdincasino.com. 2,567 units. $99 and up double. Extra person $30, no discount for children. AE, DC, DISC, MC, V. Free self- and valet parking. **Amenities:** Casino; performing-arts center; showroom; 15 restaurants; 7 bars/lounges; 2 outdoor pools; health club and spa; Jacuzzi; sauna; concierge; tour desk; car-rental desk; business center; shopping arcade; 24-hr. room service; in-room massage; babysitting; laundry/dry-cleaning service; nonsmoking rooms; executive-level rooms. *In room:* A/C, TV w/pay movies, dataport, high-speed Internet access (for a fee), hair dryer, iron and board, safe.

Mandalay Bay ★★   Let's hope the extreme southern Strip location doesn't make you overlook Mandalay Bay, as it's one of our favorite hotels. Why? Well, we love that the lobby (impossibly high ceilings, calm, gleaming with marble, and housing a large aquarium) and the other public areas really do make this seem more like an actual resort hotel than just a Vegas version of one. You don't have to walk through the casino to get to any of these public areas or the guest-room elevators, the pool area is spiffy, and the whole complex is marginally less confusing and certainly less overwhelming than some of the neighboring behemoths.

We wouldn't say it really evokes colonial Southeast Asia—oh, maybe around the edges, if you squint, thanks to the odd bit of foliage or Balinese carving. This may well keep out the gawkers, who are looking for bigger visual thrills, but we find a place whose theme doesn't bop you over the head refreshing.

Note that a new tower with 1,000 rooms is set to open sometime in 2004. Good news, especially because the complex has also opened a huge convention center, which is reported to be entirely booked for the upcoming year. If true, rooms will likely cost more and be harder to get.

The rooms are among the most desirable on the Strip (king rooms are more attractive than doubles), spacious and subdued in decor. Tropical influence seems to be limited to faux leopard-skin chairs by the worktables, and plantation shutter doors to closets and the bathroom (unfortunately, the bathroom's shutter doors seem to not entirely join together, leaving an open gap of varying size). King beds have large, carved headboard posts and firm mattresses. The bathrooms are the crowning glory, probably the best on the Strip; they're downright large, with impressive, slightly sunken tubs, glassed-in showers, double sinks, and separate water closets, plus fab amenities and lots of them. (Bathrobes are available on request.)

Service overall is pretty good, and those pool-area employees are the tops in Vegas, though there were no security guards at the guest elevators. A monorail system connects the hotel with Luxor and Excalibur, which are located in the heart of the Strip action, and this should more than help you get over any feelings of isolation.

The restaurants in Mandalay Bay feature some of the most innovative interiors in Vegas, each one more whimsical and imaginative than the last. Even if you don't eat at the hotel, drop in and poke around the restaurants. **Aureole,** a branch of Charlie Palmer's renowned New York City restaurant, the **Border Grill, Red Square,** and the **buffet** are reviewed in chapter 6. And then there's **rumjungle,** which features a dramatically skewered, all-you-can-eat, multi-course Brazilian feast, which you'll enjoy while listening to world-beat drums, surrounded by walls of fire and water and other striking visual features. More casual food can be found at the **House of Blues,** whose Southern delicacies are often quite palate pleasing; HOB is probably the best place in town to see rock bands. Mandalay Bay has a showroom and a separate arena, which was inaugurated by none other than Luciano Pavarotti, and currently offers *Mamma Mia,* the Broadway musical of ABBA songs. See chapter 10 for details on the hotel's major nightlife offerings. There's also a big, comfortable casino, airier and less claustrophobic than most, plus three bars, often featuring live music (including rock impersonator acts) at night.

There are no fewer than four pools (entering this area is like going to a water park, thanks to upgraded security—*all* guests, regardless of age, must show a room key—and general size), including the touted wave pool, which is unfortunately a classic example of Vegas bait-and-switch. It was supposed to feature waves of various sizes, from "Barely There" to "Stun," breaking on a sand-covered beach. But it turned out that the waves couldn't be turned on full force, as the pool was too short and surfers went crashing into the concrete lip at the end. Still, bobbing in the miniwaves is delightful, as is floating happily in the lazy river (tubes available for rental—we say, save some bucks and share a tube with friends, taking turns using it). All in all, this area alone makes this resort a top choice for families. What doesn't is the new topless swimming area that opened in 2003.

The health club is sufficiently stocked to give you a good workout (it should be, as they charge guests $22 per day to use it). The spa area proper—featuring hot and warm pools, plus a cold plunge—is exotically designed, as close to those found in the Turkish spas in Eastern Europe as we've come across, though without the patina (read: weathered decay) of decades or centuries, which can be a good thing. Load up on that rich moisturizer when dressing—it costs $17 a bottle in the store outside the door.

3950 Las Vegas Blvd. S. (at Hacienda Ave.), Las Vegas, NV 89119. © **877/632-7000** or 702/632-7000. Fax 702/632-7228. www.mandalaybay.com. 3,309 units. From $99 standard double; from $149 suite; from $149 House of Blues Signature Rooms. Extra person $35, no discount for children. AE, DC, DISC, MC, V. Free self- and valet parking. **Amenities:** Casino; 12,000-seat events center; 1,700-seat performing-arts theater; 13 restaurants; 4 outdoor pools; health club and spa; Jacuzzi; sauna; watersports equipment/rental; concierge; tour desk; business center; 24-hr. room service; in-room massage; babysitting; laundry service; dry cleaning; nonsmoking rooms; executive-level rooms. In room: A/C, TV w/pay movies, dataport, hair dryer, iron and board, safe.

MGM Grand Hotel & Casino ★★ Kids   Vegas goes back and forth on its position on whether size does matter, and the MGM Grand is a perfect example of that. When it first opened, the massive glaring green behemoth was the largest hotel in town, with a casino to match—and its owners were mighty proud of it, boasting still further of their family-appropriateness, as typified by the theme park that was originally in the back. But times and emphasis change, and with everyone else in Vegas moving away from the pseudo-family-friendly direction to the whole luxury-resort persona, the MGM Grand had no choice but to follow. So if you book here thinking your kids are still welcome, you should think again. The amusement park in the back is gone, and so is the Wizard of Oz theme that originally gave the hotel its identity. Instead, there are striptease shows and a lounge called Tabu. That sort of thing certainly sends a message.

Consider also the place's size. The hotel management now downplays the once touted hugeness, trying to pretend that the really big casino is actually several medium-big casinos. Whatever. Despite plenty of signage, it is still a lengthy, confusing schlep from anywhere to anywhere. The 80 42-inch TV monitors (apprising registering guests of hotel happenings) in the otherwise lovely and vast white-marble lobby only add to the chaotic confusion a guest might feel—all the worse if you are toting kids. (At least the lobby is now immediately accessible from the outside world.)

On the absolute plus side, we are just knocked out by the Grand Tower rooms. No cookie-cutter, generic, upscale-but-forgettably-bland furniture here—instead, it's a modern-day homage to 1930s moderne, all clean, curvy lines, good wood, and a fun palette of colors, plus black-and-white movie-star glamour photos. The results are some of the most distinctive rooms on the Strip—and even if there are a heck of a lot of them, they are the best choice in town in their price range. The Emerald Tower rooms (about 700 of the hotel's total rooms) are a whole lot less grand. The remnants of the old Marina Hotel, these rooms are plainer (and smaller by about 100 sq. ft.) and more run of the mill (though the windows have shutters, which is semi-nifty). The expanded pool area is another victory, with several choices for dunking including a lazy river (though we wish portions of it weren't closed off for nonsummer months). Overall, report guests, the staff couldn't be more friendly and helpful.

MGM houses a prestigious assemblage of dining rooms, among them the **Wolfgang Puck Café,** Emeril Lagasse's **New Orleans Fish House,** and Mark Miller's **Coyote Cafe.** These, along with buffet offerings and the **Rainforest Cafe,** are reviewed in chapter 6.

As befits a behemoth of this size, there's an appropriately gigantic casino. The family-friendly *EFX Alive!* has closed, and a new (as yet unnamed) Cirque du Soleil show is due to open in 2004. Plus, there's *La Femme,* a very adult topless show; a hot new lounge, **Tabu;** nightclub **Studio 54;** a headliner showroom; and a larger events arena that hosts sporting events and bigger concerts. See chapter 10 for details on all the nightlife options.

The **Lion Habitat** is reviewed on p. 183.

The MGM Grand's spa is a Zen-Asian minimalist wonder, all natural stone and aged wood. The services offered are quite marvelous—for a romantic outing or a Mother's Day treat, try the half-day full services and private room (it's a mere $400, but for what you get, it might be worth the price). The state-of-the-art health club is larger than most, with some serious machines, including ones equipped with fancy computer video monitors (it'll cost you $25 to work up a sweat here most of the day, but you can use the gym facilities only, without the whirlpools and other amenities of the spa, for only $10 after 6pm).

The swimming pool area is a rousing success. The 6.6 acres of landscaped grounds feature five pools, including the longest lazy river in town.

It's not a family-friendly hotel anymore, but it still offers the **MGM Grand Youth Center,** a first-rate facility for children ages 3 to 16, which has separate areas for different age groups. The center has a playhouse and tumbling mats for toddlers, a game room, extensive arts-and-crafts equipment, video games, a dining area, and a large-screen TV/VCR for children's movies. Call ✆ **702/891-3200** for details and prices.

3799 Las Vegas Blvd. S. (at Tropicana Ave.), Las Vegas, NV 89109. ✆ **800/929-1111** or 702/891-7777. Fax 702/891-1030. www.mgmgrand.com. 5,034 units. $69–$329 standard double; $99–$2,500 suite. Extra person $25. Children under 13 stay free in parent's room. AE, DC, DISC, MC, V. Free self- and valet parking. **Amenities:** Casino; events arena; showroom; cabaret theater; 2 wedding chapels; 14 restaurants; outdoor pool; health club and spa; Jacuzzi; sauna; youth center; game room/video arcade; concierge; tour desk; car-rental desk; business center; 24-hr. room service; in-room massage; babysitting; laundry service; dry cleaning; nonsmoking rooms; executive-level rooms. *In room:* A/C, TV w/pay movies, dataport, hair dryer, iron and board, safe.

Monte Carlo Resort & Casino ✪ When it was built, the massive Monte Carlo was the world's seventh-largest hotel. It's now considerably overshadowed by its high-profile, more theme-intensive brethren. Entering it is still nice, as it comes off more as a European casino hotel alternative (before Bellagio usurped that position), replete with Corinthian colonnades, triumphal arches and big and busy statuary, with an entranceway opening onto a bustling casino. A separate entrance in the rear of the hotel leads to a splendid marble-floored, crystal-chandeliered lobby evocative of a European grand hotel. We love that the guest rooms are accessible without going through the casino, but we hate that said rooms are somewhat dingy and badly in need of a makeover, with dinky bathrooms. The pool area, once the very last word in local pool fun, is now put to shame by better versions (including superior lazy rivers) over at Mandalay Bay and the MGM Grand. It does have a number of child/family/budget-friendly restaurants. All in all, just about last on our list of second-choice hotels, but a serious room redo, plus some work on the pool area, could move it up fast.

The Monte Carlo's **Pub & Brewery** and **Dragon Noodle Co.** are described in chapter 6. In addition, there is a highly recommended branch of the classic

Downtown French restaurant **Andre's** (p. 163). There's a large and overly ornate casino, plus a lavish showroom that currently hosts the recommended show by magician **Lance Burton** (p. 253).

Monte Carlo's health club and spa is nothing special, but then again, it's $17 for 1 day's access, which is cheaper than the fee at most other hotels.

3770 Las Vegas Blvd. S. (between Flamingo Rd. and Tropicana Ave.), Las Vegas, NV 89109. © **800/311-8999** or 702/730-7777. Fax 702/730-7250. www.monte-carlo.com. 3,002 units. Sun–Thurs $59–$179 double, Fri–Sat $109–$269 double; $149–$339 suite. Extra person $25, no discount for children. AE, DC, DISC, MC, V. Free self- and valet parking. **Amenities:** Casino; showroom; wedding chapel; 7 restaurants; large wave pool with lazy-river ride and separate kiddie pool; 3 night-lit tennis courts with full services and equipment rental; health club and spa; Jacuzzi; sauna; watersports equipment/rental; video arcade; concierge; tour desk; business center; 24-hr. room service; in-room massage; babysitting; laundry service; dry cleaning; nonsmoking rooms; executive-level rooms. *In room:* A/C, TV w/pay movies, dataport, hair dryer, iron and board.

New York–New York Hotel & Casino ★★ *(Kids)*   Isn't this exactly the kind of hotel you think about—or dream about or fear—when you think "Las Vegas"? There it is, a jumbled pile mock-up of the venerable Manhattan skyline, the Empire State Building, the Chrysler Building, the Public Library, all crammed together, along with the 150-foot Statue of Liberty and Ellis Island, all built to approximately one-third scale. And as if that weren't enough, they threw in a roller coaster running around the outside and into the hotel and casino itself.

And inside, it all gets better. There are details everywhere—so many, in fact, that the typical expression on the face of casino-goers is slack-jawed wonder. If you enter the casino via the Brooklyn Bridge (the walkway from the Strip), you'll find yourself in a replica of Greenwich Village, down to the cobblestones, the manhole covers, the tenement-style buildings, and the graffiti. (Yes, they even re-created that. You should see the subway station.) The reception area and lobby are done in an Art Deco, golden-age-of-Manhattan style; you'll feel like breaking into a 1930s musical number while standing there. It's a *wow!* all right. The word *subtle* was obviously not in the lexicon of the designers. We will leave it to you to decide, based on your own aesthetic values, if all this is a good or bad thing. Let's just say that to us, it's very, very good indeed. Because this is exactly what we come to Vegas for—unbridled, unrepentant, theme-gone-wild.

Upstairs—oh, yes, there's much more—is the arcade, which is Coney Island–themed (naturally), and just as crowded as the real thing. Kids play boardwalk games in the hopes of winning tickets redeemable for cheap prizes. (You're never too young to start learning about gambling.) The line for the roller coaster (lengthy at this writing) starts here. There are many restaurants, all housed in buildings that fit the theme of whatever New York neighborhood is represented in that particular part of the hotel.

Rooms are housed in different towers, each with a New York–inspired name. Truthfully, the place is so massive and mazelike that finding your way to your room can take a while. There are 64 different styles of rooms, and most are quite smashing (oddly, the style diminishes in inverse proportion to the size of the room). Essentially, each is done up in Art Deco style: various shades of inlaid wood, rounded tops on the armoires and headboards, brown and wood colors dominating. Some of the rooms are downright tiny (just like New York again!), however, and in those rooms all this massively detailed decoration can be overwhelming, if not suffocating. The bathrooms are also small, but have black-marble-topped sinks, which again lend a glamorous '20s feel. The toiletries come in bottles shaped like the New York City skyline—these are the sorts of goodies you'll want to stash in your suitcase to take home! Light sleepers should request a room away from the roller coaster.

Cranks would have us note that coming here is not like going to the real New York. On the other hand, given how crowded it is (everyone wants to come check it out and stays to play) and how noisy, it kind of is just like being in New York. Especially with the all-too-realistic traffic and parking nightmares.

Note: There are a few visual references to the World Trade Center at the resort—it was not a part of the faux skyline, luckily, but at this writing it pops up in photos, paintings and murals. Movingly, locals and visitors started an impromptu memorial to September 11 by leaving notes and flowers on the fence surrounding the property. The hotel decided to make it permanent, placing a glass box featuring a rotating exhibit of those same tributes. It's at the corner of Tropicana and the Strip.

There's a small health club and spa, and the mediocre pool is right next to the parking lot.

In addition to a number of more-than-decent restaurants, including reliable Italian chain Il Fornaio, there are several festive and beautifully decorated bars throughout the property. **Hamilton's** is a sophisticated cigar bar, owned by perennially tanned and good-natured actor George Hamilton. It's a clubby, Art Deco, seriously priced smoking den that would not be out of place in the real New York City. **Coyote Ugly** is a party-hearty bar where dancing on furniture is encouraged, and the female bartenders are hired just to be sassy. At the **Bar at Times Square,** a lighted ball drops every night at midnight to re-create the famous New Year's Eve event in the real location. New Year's Eve every night: A terrific promotion, or hell on earth? In August 2003, a new—topless and adults-only—Cirque du Soleil production, *Zumanity,* opened to acclaim. See chapter 10 for more on the hotel's nightlife.

The main casino area is done as Central Park, complete with trees, babbling brooks, streetlamps, and footbridges. The change carts are little yellow cabs.

3790 Las Vegas Blvd. S. (at Tropicana Ave.), Las Vegas, NV 89109. ℂ **800/693-6763** or 702/740-6969. Fax 702/740-6920. www.nynyhotelcasino.com. 2,033 units. Sun–Thurs from $59 double, Fri–Sat from $109 double. Extra person $20, no discount for children. AE, DC, DISC, MC, V. Free self- and valet parking. **Amenities:** Casino; showrooms; 10 restaurants; outdoor pool; small health club and spa; Jacuzzi; sauna; video arcade with carnival midway games; concierge; tour desk; 24-hr. room service; laundry service; dry cleaning; nonsmoking rooms; executive-level rooms. *In room:* A/C, TV w/pay movies, dataport, high-speed Internet access (for a fee), hair dryer, iron and board, safe.

Tropicana Resort & Casino ⚘   As we go to press, the Trop's future remains in doubt. No formal announcement will be made before the end of 2003, but the hotel has, at this point, stopped taking bookings past April 2004, which may or may not tell you something. The rumors are it will be torn down and in its place will be erected two miniresorts of 2,000 rooms each. We'd like to say we are sorry—and in a nostalgic way we are, but really, the Trop has seen better days. Once known for its lavish tropical resort stylings, it's now more than a little worn around the edges, especially when compared with its splashy neighbors. The birds and other wildlife are gone, which makes things a little less messy, but the tacky "Garden rooms" are still around and ought to be demolished ASAP. Gone also is the outside light show.

Rooms—well, think a clean '70's motel room, but a little bit nicer. Unless you're a Jimmy Buffet fan, you are better off staying in the Paradise tower, where the rooms are slightly bigger and much easier on the eyes—mock provincial, to be sure (check out the plaster molding and ceiling cornices—a curious and welcome little

Kids Family-Friendly Hotels

We've said it before, and we'll say it again: Vegas is simply not a good place to bring your kids. Most of the major hotels are backing away from being perceived as places for families. But if you want to make it a family trip, here are our recommendations, based, if not on overall kid-friendly attitude, at least on elements that make it appealing for families.

In addition to the suggestions below, you might consider choosing a noncasino hotel, particularly a reliable chain, and a place with kitchenettes. See "East of the Strip," later in this chapter, for details on several such choices.

- **Circus Circus Hotel/Casino** (p. 104)   Centrally located on the Strip, this is our first choice if you're traveling with the kids. The hotel's mezzanine level offers ongoing circus acts daily from 11am to midnight, dozens of carnival games, and an arcade with more than 300 video and pinball games. And behind the hotel is a full amusement park.
- **Excalibur** (p. 82)   Owned by the Mandalay Bay Resort Group, Excalibur features a whole floor of midway games, a large video-game arcade, free shows for kids (puppets, jugglers, and magicians), and thrill cinemas. It also has child-oriented eateries and shows.
- **Four Seasons** (p. 73)   For free goodies, service, and general child-pampering, the costly Four Seasons is probably worth the dough (your kids will be spoiled!).
- **Luxor Las Vegas** (p. 83)   Another Mandalay Bay Resort Group property. Kids will enjoy the Games of the Gods Arcade, an 18,000-square-foot video-game arcade that showcases Sega's latest game technologies. Another big attraction here is the "Secrets of the Luxor Pyramid," a high-tech adventure/thrill ride using motion simulators and IMAX film.
- **MGM Grand Hotel & Casino** (p. 77)   This resort houses a state-of-the-art video-game arcade and carnival midway. A unique offering here is a youth center for hotel guests ages 3 to 16, with separate sections for different age groups. Its facilities range from a playhouse and tumbling mats for toddlers to extensive arts-and-crafts materials for the older kids. There is also a terrific pool area. The whole property is a perennial favorite with families.
- **New York–New York** (p. 79)   Over-stimulating and hectic, for sure, but between the roller coaster and the Coney Island–style Midway, not to mention just looking around, this has many options for children (though going almost anywhere requires walking through the casino).
- **Ritz-Carlton, Lake Las Vegas** (p. 119)   Like the Four Seasons, it's costly, but with so many recreational activities, and the Lake Las Vegas setting (well out of the way of the path of Sin City—although parents can make nighttime getaways thanks to the hotel's babysitting services), it offers a lot over the regular Vegas resorts.

touch), but it all appears less shabby and more fresh. Bathrooms are also bigger here, but dull, except for the ones with Jacuzzi tubs. Even without the wildlife, the pool area is among the best around and is the place's biggest draw. Note, however, that their touted swim-up blackjack is seasonal (read: summer only).

Calypsos (p. 134), the 24-hour coffee shop, is a good value, as are the Trop's **buffet** (p. 166) offerings. There's a good-looking casino, and the **Casino Legends Hall of Fame** (p. 178) has the largest collection of gaming chips in the world, along with other gambling doodads and ephemera. The showroom currently hosts the **Folies Bergère** revue (p. 251).

3801 Las Vegas Blvd. S. (at Tropicana Ave.), Las Vegas, NV 89109. ℂ **888/826-8767** or 702/739-2222. Fax 702/739-2469. www.tropicanalv.com. 1,878 units. $79–$229 double. Extra person $20. Children under 18 stay free in parent's room. AE, DC, DISC, MC, V. Free self- and valet parking. **Amenities:** Casino; showrooms; wedding chapel; 8 restaurants; 3 outdoor pools; small health club and spa; video arcade; concierge; tour desk; car-rental desk; 24-hr. room service; laundry service; dry cleaning; nonsmoking rooms; executive-level rooms. *In room:* A/C, TV w/pay movies, dataport; minifridge in some rooms, hair dryer, iron and board, safes.

MODERATE

Boardwalk Hotel & Casino   This is just like a Holiday Inn—in fact, up until recently, it *was* a Holiday Inn, but in Vegas you gotta have a theme, and the hotel underwent an extensive renovation to give it a more attractive Coney Island and Boardwalk flavor, inside and especially out. The facade is kind of fun, with clowns and games and mannequins dressed in turn-of-the-last-century clothes. Of course, all this is completely eclipsed by New York–New York, which is just a few doors (in Strip terms) down. After all, the roller coaster on the outside of this hotel is just a facade, while New York–New York's coaster is real. The whole property is now owned by the MGM MIRAGE Corp, which hasn't done anything special to the place, but does mean a certain amount of quality control.

You don't have to walk through the casino to get to the lobby, which is a plus, as is the hotel's coveted Strip location. On the other hand, it's a bit pricey for what you get—standard Holiday Inn hotel rooms.

3750 Las Vegas Blvd. S. (between Harmon and Tropicana aves.), Las Vegas, NV 89109. ℂ **800/635-4581** or 702/735-2400. Fax 702/730-3166. www.hiboardwalk.com. 653 units. $39–$139 double; $295–$495 1-bedroom suite; $495–$895 2-bedroom suite. Extra person $15. Children under 13 stay free in parent's room. AE, DC, DISC, MC, V. Free self- and valet parking. **Amenities:** Casino; showroom; 4 restaurants; outdoor pool; small exercise room; tour desk; car-rental desk; 24-hr. room service; coin-op washers and laundry service; dry cleaning; nonsmoking rooms. *In room:* A/C, TV w/pay movies, dataport, coffeemaker, hair dryer, iron and board.

Excalibur ⭐ (Kids)   Now *this* is kitsch. One of the largest resort hotels in the world, Excalibur (aka "the Realm") is a gleaming white, turreted castle complete with moat, drawbridge, battlements, and lofty towers. And it's huger than huge.

You know, as much as we might publicly stand in favor of quiet good taste, there is a part of our soul that is secretly thrilled by overblown fantasy locations—it's so authentically Vegas. And so we just pray that the Lords of Taste never touch Excalibur, and it is allowed to forever run amok with sword and sorcery imagery. Actually, the decorating fairies have already made some quiet changes (the deep reds in the public areas have been switched to creams), but nothing that really sullies the silliness. (Have fun by having the hotel page you and your friends: "Lady Doe to the white courtesy phone" or "Sir Jones to the house phone." Really, they do this.) There are some ominous rumblings in keeping with the rest of Vegas's careening away from the "family-friendly" image—gone is the Animatronic dragon and wizard show out front, and inside, where a nice horse show used to be, there is a male stripper act, *Thunder from Down Under*. The hotel remains big and chaotic, thanks to a sprawling casino full of families and small-time gamblers, which is located smack dab in the middle of everything, including, naturally, the path between you and the elevators to your room.

Rooms are done in neutrals (a little too much brown for our tastes). They have vague heraldic overtones and, given the price, are perhaps the best bet on the Strip for the budget-minded. Note that none of the bathrooms have tubs, just showers. Guests who have stayed in Tower 2 have complained about the noise from the roller coaster across the street at New York–New York. (It runs till 11pm, so early birds should probably stay in a different part of the hotel.) Frankly, we prefer stopping in for a visit rather than actually settling in here, but we know others who love the price and the authentic Vegas-tacky atmosphere.

The second floor holds the Medieval Village, where Excalibur's restaurants and shops are peppered along winding streets and alleyways, a sort of permanent Renaissance Faire, which could be reason enough to stay away (or to come). On the Village's "Jester's Stage," jugglers, puppeteers, and magicians amuse guests with free 20-minute performances throughout the day. Up here you can access the enclosed, air-conditioned, moving sidewalk that connects with the Luxor. There are plenty of restaurants, including the **buffet** (p. 167). Excalibur won our hearts forever by installing a branch of **Krispy Kreme** doughnuts on the second level, on the way to the Luxor walkway. The *Tournament of Kings* (p. 256) is a medieval-style dinner show, and there's a very loud, claustrophobic casino.

3850 Las Vegas Blvd. S. (at Tropicana Ave.), Las Vegas, NV 89109. (C) **800/937-7777** or 702/597-7777. Fax 702/597-7163. www.excaliburlasvegas.com. 4,008 units. $49 and up double. Extra person $15. Children under 13 stay free in parent's room. AE, DC, DISC, MC, V. Free self- and valet parking. **Amenities:** Casino; showrooms; wedding chapel; 11 restaurants; outdoor pool; video arcade; concierge; tour desk; car-rental desk; shopping arcade; 24-hr. room service; laundry service; dry cleaning; nonsmoking rooms. *In room:* A/C, TV w/pay movies, dataport, hair dryer.

Luxor Las Vegas ★★ (*Kids*)   Another hotel that thrills us to our very kitsch-worshipping souls. How happy you, who share our aesthetic taste—or lack thereof—will be when you behold the main hotel, a 30-story onyx-hued pyramid, complete with a really tall 315,000-watt light beam at the top. (The Luxor says that's because the Egyptians believed their souls would travel up to heaven in a beam of light. We think it's really because it gives them something to brag about: "The most powerful beam on earth!") You'll be giddy when you spy replicas of Cleopatra's Needle and the Sphinx gracing the outside. And when you get inside, and see the towering statues of Ramses and overhear the talking Animatronic camels, well, you might not care that the lobby tries also to be classy, vaguely Art Deco (influenced by Egyptian Revival, remember) marble and cherrywood. You will just want to ride the 39-degree high-speed "inclinators"—that's what an elevator is when it works inside a pyramid. (Really, they are part conveyance, part thrill ride—check out that jolt when they come to a halt!) Great fun, the Luxor, you can gather. Not as impressive as the real landmarks in the real Egypt, of course. But you knew that.

Once you stop laughing (or screaming) at what greets you, you should be quite pleased with this hotel. Rooms in the pyramid open onto the vast center that contains the casino—indeed, ground-level rooms open more or less right into the action (though many of these have been turned into offices), so if you want only a short drunken stumble back to your room, these are for you. Otherwise, ask for a room higher up. The pyramid rooms cross Egyptian kitsch with Art Deco stylings, including gleaming inlaid wood furniture and a hilarious hieroglyphic bedspread. Marvelous views are offered through the slanted windows (the higher up the better, of course), but the bathrooms are shower-only, no tubs. Tower rooms (an expansion put additional rooms in a tower rather than another pyramid. Drat!) are even heavier on the Egyptian motif (with huge armoires housing the TVs and closet space), pleasing in a campy way but not as aesthetically successful. The bathrooms, however, including deep tubs, are better, so it might be a worthwhile tradeoff. Regardless of which room you get, these are some of the few rooms in Las Vegas that stand out. You know you are in the Luxor when you find yourself surrounded by unique, charming room design, as opposed to the cookie-cutter room decor usually found elsewhere in town. Especially desirable is a group of suites with glamorous Art Deco elements, private sitting rooms, refrigerators, and, notably, whirlpools by the window (enabling you to soak under the stars at night). And we would love to meet the person who rents the 4,000-square-foot luxury suite at the top of the tower.

The Luxor's **Pharaoh's Pheast** buffet (p. 167) offers a cool archaeological-dig atmosphere. The hotel's high-tech nightclub **Ra** (p. 269) is a happening nightspot. Two notable attractions here are **King Tut's Tomb & Museum** (p. 180) and the **Luxor IMAX Theater** (p. 182).

3900 Las Vegas Blvd. S. (between Reno and Hacienda aves.), Las Vegas, NV 81119. © **800/288-1000** or 702/ 262-4000. Fax 702/262-4478. www.luxor.com. 4,400 units. Sun–Thurs $49 and up double, Fri–Sat $99 and up double; $149 and up whirlpool suite, $249–$800 other suites. Extra person $25. Children under 12 stay free in parent's room. AE, DC, DISC, MC, V. Free self- and valet parking. **Amenities:** Casino; showrooms; 10 restaurants; 5 outdoor pools; health club and spa; 18,000-sq.-ft. video arcade with the latest Sega games and more; concierge; tour desk; car-rental desk; business center; shopping arcade; 24-hr. room service; dry cleaning; non-smoking rooms; executive-level rooms. *In room:* A/C, TV w/pay movies, dataports, hair dryer, iron and board.

INEXPENSIVE

Orleans ☆ *Value*   The Orleans is owned by the same company that owns the Barbary Coast and Gold Coast casinos. It's a little out of the way, and there is virtually nothing around it, but with a 12-screen movie complex, complete with a food court and day-care center, a bowling alley, plus a new 9,000-seat arena for a minor-league hockey team (but also available for concerts and the like), this is a reasonable alternative to staying on the hectic Strip. Plus, there is a shuttle that runs continuously to the Barbary Coast on the Strip. The facade is aggressively fake New Orleans, more reminiscent of Disneyland than the actual Big Easy. Inside it's much of the same. But a bright casino (complete with Cajun and zydeco music over the loudspeakers) and a policy of handing out Mardi Gras beads at all the restaurants and bars (ask if you haven't gotten yours) make for a pleasantly festive atmosphere.

If the prices hold true (as always, they can vary), this hotel is one of the best bargains in town, despite the location, though the staff can be rotten, which can seriously sour a bargain experience. The rooms are nice enough and you'll find the largest standard rooms in town, or so the hotel claims. They all have a definite New Orleans–French feel. Each is L-shaped, with a seating alcove by the windows, and comes complete with an old-fashioned overstuffed chair and sofa. The beds have brass headboards, the lamps (including some funky iron floor lamps) look antique, and lace curtains flutter at the windows. The one drawback is that all these furnishings, and the busy floral decorating theme, make the room seem crowded (particularly down by the seating area in front of the bathrooms). Still, it's meant to evoke a cozy, warm Victorian parlor, which traditionally is very over-crowded, so maybe it's successful after all. There are 1,400 brand-new rooms in a newly built tower, and these hold to the same surprisingly nice standard.

The hotel has your basic Vegas-type places to eat. Worth noting is the moderately priced Italian **Sazio** (p. 132), Big Al's Oyster Bar, a not unauthentic Creole/Cajun-themed restaurant, and **Don Miguel's,** a basic but satisfying

Mexican restaurant that makes its own tortillas while you watch. There are several bars, including one with live music at night. The **Orleans Showroom** is an 827-seat theater featuring live entertainment, and, of course, there's a casino.

4500 W. Tropicana Ave. (west of the Strip and I-15), Las Vegas, NV 89103. © **800/ORLEANS** (675-3267) or 702/365-7111. Fax 702/365-7505. www.orleanscasino.com. 840 units. $39 and up standard double; $175–$225 1-bedroom suite. Extra person $10. Children under 15 stay free in parent's room. AE, DC, DISC, MC, V. Free self- and valet parking. **Amenities:** Casino; showroom; 12 restaurants; 2 outdoor pools; health club; 70-lane bowling center; 12 movie theaters; Kids Tyme children's center offering amusements and day care for kids 12 and under; video arcade; concierge; tour desk; car-rental desk; airport shuttle; 24-hr. room service; laundry service; dry cleaning; nonsmoking rooms; executive-level rooms. *In room:* A/C, TV w/pay movies, dataport, hair dryer, iron and board.

4 Mid-Strip

VERY EXPENSIVE

Bellagio ★★   The $1.6 billion luxury resort that ushered in the new post-Vegas-is-for-families elegance epoch. What do you get for that money? Well, for starters, though it is named for a charming Lake Como village, Bellagio is not, thankfully, as theme-intensive as some of its nearest competition. There is an 8-acre Lake Como stand-in out front, complete with a dazzling choreographed water-ballet extravaganza, plus a representation of an Italian lakeside village, while the pool area is sort of Hearst Castle Romanesque, but that's about it. Just as well. This is not much like a getaway to a peaceful, romantic Italian village. But it is exactly like going to a big, grand, state-of-the-art Vegas hotel. To expect more probably isn't fair, but then again, they tried to set the tone with dreamy, soft-focus TV ads aired when the hotel debuted. Nothing with a casino stuck in the middle of it can be that serene and restful.

But does it work as a luxury hotel? Sort of. It certainly is much closer to a European casino hotel than a Vegas one. Fabulous touches abound, including a lobby that's unlike any other in Vegas. It's not just grand, with marble and a gaudy blown-glass flower sculpture on the ceiling (the largest of its kind in the world), but it's also brave with plants, natural lighting, and actual seating. There's also a downright lovely conservatory, complete with a 100-year-old fountain and stuffed full of gorgeous, brightly colored flowers and plants, preposterously (and delightfully) changed every few weeks to go with the season (yellows and whites for Easter, for example)—it's one of the sweetest spots in all of Vegas.

On the down side, you still can't avoid a walk through the casino to get just about anywhere (with the inevitable ruckus shattering your blissful state every time you exit the elevators from your room). At least the casino is laid out in an easy-to-navigate grid with wide aisles. (*Tip:* Black carpets indicate the main casino paths.) There are hidden charges galore (a pricey fee for the spa, another one for poolside cabanas). The rooms are nice—nicer than The Mirage even—but maybe not quite nice enough for the price. Furnishings are plush (good beds with quality linens, comfy chairs), the roomy bathrooms even more so (marble and glass plus good-smelling soap and hair dryers—it works every time), but it's all just a busier and slightly more luxurious variation on what's found over at The Mirage. Strip-side rooms, while featuring a much-desired view of the water fountains, don't quite muffle the booms that said fountains make as they explode. Still, service is top-notch, despite the size of the place; the staff is eager to please and nonpatronizing.

Meanwhile, just about all the best new restaurants are found in Bellagio. Full reviews of **Picasso, Le Cirque, Circo, Aqua,** and **Olives** are found in chapter 6, as is a review of the buffet. And the man who brought us a free pirate show and a volcano explosion now brings us a **water ballet** ★★★, courtesy of a dancing fountain with jets timed to a rotating list of nine songs (everything from pop to Sinatra to Broadway to opera). This sounds cheesy, but it absolutely is not. It's really quite delightful and even witty (no, really), and is the best free show in Vegas. Hotel guests should try to stay on the Strip side so that they can watch from their windows (although there are some booms as the fountains explode, we didn't find it annoying). Note that a channel on the TV will play the songs as the fountains dance because you can't quite hear the music from your room.

Bellagio also features an upscale casino, and *O* (p. 249), perhaps the most incredible show from Cirque du Soleil.

The hotel's pool area has skidded to the top of our favorites list; it boasts six swimming pools (two heated year-round and two with fountains) geometrically set in a neoclassical Roman garden, with flowered, trellised archways and Italian opera piped in over the sound system. The Grand Patio could have come right off a movie set (pillars, domes, you get the idea). Arguably a more sophisticated environment than the tropical party over at The Mirage (our other favorite), it is sure to be the place where thonged model types hang out with moneyed Euro-trash—it comes off as *that* chic.

The spa and health club are marvelous, but at $25 a pop, it's pretty pricey if all you want is a simple session on a treadmill (though with your fee, you are allowed to return throughout the day for additional soakings/steamings/work-outs). The gym has the latest in cardio and weight machines, but can get very crowded. Attendants ply you with iced towels and drinks. The spa offers a full range of pricey treatments and has a serene soaking area, with sumptuous plunge pools ranging in temperature from icy to boiling. In addition to drinks and snacks, smoothies are often offered—take one.

The shopping area, called **Via Bellagio,** features all the stores that advertise in color in glossy magazines: Tiffany, Armani, Gucci, Prada, Hermès, and the like. And there's also an **art gallery** (p. 176) that boasts enough highly regarded works to draw some million visitors a year.

What does all this add up to? The ultimate in the new Vegas luxury resort experience, certainly. If it doesn't quite work, that's probably more the fault of the initial concept than the hotel itself. And in 2004, look for a new tower with 900 additional rooms, a second spa, and more shopping and restaurants.

3600 Las Vegas Blvd. S. (at the corner of Flamingo Rd.), Las Vegas, NV 89109. © **888/987-6667** or 702/693-7111. Fax 702/693-8546. www.bellagio.com. 3,005 units. $139–$499 double. Extra person $35, no discount for children. AE, DC, DISC, MC, V. Free self- and valet parking. **Amenities:** Casino; showrooms; wedding chapel; 16 restaurants; 6 outdoor pools; health club and spa; concierge; tour desk; car-rental desk; business center; 24-hr. room service; in-room massage; laundry service; dry cleaning; nonsmoking rooms; executive-level rooms. *In room:* A/C, TV w/pay movies, dataport, high-speed Internet access for a fee, hair dryer, iron and board, safe.

Caesars Palace ★★　Since 1966, Caesars has stood simultaneously as the ultimate in Vegas luxury and the nadir (or pinnacle, depending on your values) of Las Vegas cheese. It's the most Vegas-style hotel you'll find, covering all the bases from the tacky fabulous cheese of the recent past to the current trend in high-end luxury. And it's moving ever on, with the most over-the-top showroom in town, specially built for Miss Thang herself, Celine Dion, and yet another expansion to the Forum Shops, the first themed shopping experience on the Strip.

When Caesars was originally built to reflect Roman decadence, its designers probably had no idea how guffaw-inducing this would be some years later. It's

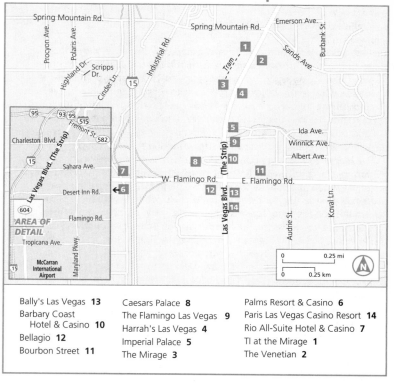

Bally's Las Vegas **13**
Barbary Coast
   Hotel & Casino **10**
Bellagio **12**
Bourbon Street **11**

Caesars Palace **8**
The Flamingo Las Vegas **9**
Harrah's Las Vegas **4**
Imperial Palace **5**
The Mirage **3**

Palms Resort & Casino **6**
Paris Las Vegas Casino Resort **14**
Rio All-Suite Hotel & Casino **7**
TI at the Mirage **1**
The Venetian **2**

the level of kitsch all should aspire to: Roman colonnades, Roman pillars, gigantic faux-marble Roman statues, staff attired in gladiator outfits—it's splendidly ridiculous. It's what Vegas ought to be.

But all things change, and Caesars had been outshined over the years by more modern glamour. And frankly, that facade was looking dated 2 decades ago. Never one to rest on any kind of laurels, Roman or otherwise, Caesars gave itself a massive face-lift, and keeps on building and expanding. Never fear, the Roman statues still remain, as do the toga-clad cocktail waitresses, and so does Caesars's giggle factor (it's still pretty campy). But the hotel is also getting a bit too big for its own britches. The layout has become ever more confusing and hard to negotiate, and it takes forever to get anywhere—especially out to the Strip.

Past or future, Caesars remains spectacular. From the Roman temples, heroic arches, golden charioteers, and 50-foot Italian cypresses at its entrance, to the impressive interiors, it's the spectacle a good Vegas hotel should be. However, all of this makes for a very haphazard layout; this is one of the more confusing and hard-to-navigate hotels in town. Sometimes you feel like just surrendering and staying in, which isn't necessarily a bad thing. Caesars is also known for its luxurious rooms and service. (Long lines at the reservations desk are sometimes relieved by gratis champagne.)

Accommodations occupy four towers, and there are too many decorating schemes to describe here. Art in the rooms keeps to the Greco-Roman theme (some have classical sculptures in niches); furnishings tend to neoclassic styles;

Tips **Staying off the Strip**

First-time visitors, and even second-timers, will prefer, as they should, to stay on the Strip or Downtown, hang the cost (most of the time anyway). But if you can't get a room price to your liking, or you are a three-peater (or more), you might want to consider some alternatives. Each of the following is out of the way, relatively speaking, but each makes up for it with rack rates you just aren't going to get—well, not that often—on the Strip. We're talking as low as $49 a night. Maybe lower. The rooms aren't anything to write home about, which is why we didn't bother writing much about them, but they are clean, comfortable, and sufficiently (in some cases) easy on the eyes. And several of the hotels, particularly those that are part of the Station chain, have so many extras to offer that they really could compete with some of the big boys on the Strip. However, you trade away location; for the most part, once you leave the hotel property, you enter a vast nothingness. So what? Get in that rental car—or take the shuttle that many of the hotels provide—and drive 15 minutes to the big boys' free parking lots, and use the money you saved to see *O,* or to eat at a fancy restaurant, or to gamble. But hey, even gambling is cheaper out here in the vast nothingness!

Northwest Las Vegas
JW Marriott *⚐,* 221 N. Rampart, Las Vegas, NV 89128 (*©* **877/869-8777** or 702/869-8777), was the Resort at Summerlin but was recently bought out by the Marriott chain. With a handsome Spanish Mission–style building, fabulously landscaped grounds, and tricked-out rooms, this is much more of a true resort property than any Strip destination. But then again, what you gain there you lose in location—with traffic, it could take 40 minutes to get to the Strip.

Roman columns, pilasters, and pediments are common. Many rooms have four-poster beds with mirrored ceilings. The newest rooms are handsome, if not as giggle-inducingly overwhelming as the classic ones, and have floor-to-ceiling windows that offer a hypnotizing panoramic view. You'll likely enjoy a lavish bathroom with marble floor, European fixtures, and oversize marble tubs (about half are whirlpools). Some of the rooms have lavish tubs in the middle of the room, which can be uncomfortable if you wish to shower and don't want your shower to turn into a spectator sport.

Caesars has a well-deserved reputation for superior in-house restaurants. There are nine in the hotel, plus dining facilities in the Forum shopping area. All are highly recommended. The hotel's sushi restaurant, **Hyakumi,** is described in chapter 6, as are the hotel's food court and buffets. Restaurants in the Forum Shops arcade include **Spago, The Palm,** and the **Stage Deli**—all discussed in chapter 6. In the new Atlantis section, there is a **Caviartorium**—a place to sample high-priced fish eggs, and a **Cheesecake Factory.** See also **Cleopatra's Barge Nightclub** on p. 268.

Texas Station, 2102 Texas Star Lane, Las Vegas, NV 89130 (© **800/654-8888** or 702/631-1000), features a bowling alley, movie theaters, a dozen restaurants, child care, and a huge casino. The **Fiesta Rancho,** 2400 N. Rancho Dr., Las Vegas, NV 89130 (© **800/731-7333** or 702/631-7000), has a friendly local touch that used to be found in Downtown but is rarely seen there these days, plus a performance venue that frequently has some decent names, and a Mexican restaurant with over 300 different kinds of margaritas. **Palace Station,** 2411 W. Sahara Ave., Las Vegas, NV 89102 (© **800/634-3101** or 702/367-2411), has long been a favorite with locals for gambling. While not quite as crammed with diversions as some of the others, it makes up for it with extra friendliness.

Henderson & Boulder Highway

Boulder Station, 4111 Boulder Hwy., Las Vegas, NV 89121 (© **800/683-7777** or 702/432-7777), has an 11-screen movie theater, tons of cheap eateries, nifty child-care facilities, and a lot more—consequently, it's not always as cheap as some of the others. **Sunset Station,** 1301 W. Sunset Rd., Henderson, NV 89014 (© **888/SUNSET-9**), is more of the same, plus there's an outdoor performance space that features a lot of retro (read: has-been) performers and a microbrew pub. It's really more of an entertainment complex than hotel, and even has a mall across the street, so it isn't so totally isolated. **Arizona Charlie's East,** 4575 Boulder Hwy., Las Vegas, NV 89121 (© **800/362-4040** or 702/951-5900), is relatively new and consequently most spiffy. It has very low limits in the casino, a cheap and reliable coffee shop, and a buffet priced like buffets used to be. The Mexican pueblo–themed **Fiesta Henderson,** 777 W. Lake Mead Dr., Henderson, NV 89015 (© **888/899-7770** or 702/558-7000), has fewer facilities than some of the other options, and may be a better choice for people visiting family in the neighborhood than folks looking for fun.

Yet another thing to take advantage of is the **Race for Atlantis IMAX 3-D Ride** (p. 183).

Having spent over $100 million renovating its **Garden of the Gods,** Caesars has created a tasteful, undeniably "Caesar-esque" masterpiece. With three pools measuring a total of 22,000 square feet, there is plenty of space for frolicking in the hot sun. Inspired by the healing Baths of Caracalla in Rome, each of the pools is adorned with griffins or sea horses and inlaid with classic granite-and-marble mosaics. To feel even more regal, snatch one of the 16 shaded cabanas that offer phones, TV, and air-conditioning for $150 a day (reserve them early). Several amenities are also available by the pool area, including massage, two whirlpools, three tennis courts, the Neptune Bar, and of course, a Snackus Maximus.

The **Caesars Spa** is another gorgeous facility, offering full salon services (a large range of facials, massages, wraps, and other beauty treatments). While we can't say we've tried every masseuse or facialist in town, we have tried a lot, and what we got at Caesars was the best so far. The spa also offers saunas, steam rooms, and whirlpool tubs, plus an incredibly well-supplied health club with state-of-the-art machinery, a rock-climbing wall, personal trainers, and more (it's a whopping $24 per day just to work out, though). Go work off some of that Caesars indulgence and then get a little pampered.

The **Forum Shops** (p. 237) are in the grandest mall you can imagine (think of the *La Dolce Vita* walk on the Via Veneto), and are about to get grander. A massive addition should roughly double the size of the existing shopping areas, and is due to open in 2004.

Not content to stop paying contractors, Caesars recently opened a new 4,000-seat Colosseum, a replica of the original building in Rome. This was built for one purpose only—to give diva Celine Dion a place to play. No kidding. She's supposed to appear 200 nights a year, in a ridiculously expensive production created just to showcase her vocal talents, and featuring Cirque du Soleil–type visuals. See p. 248 for a review of the production.

3570 Las Vegas Blvd. S. (just north of Flamingo Rd.), Las Vegas, NV 89109. ⓒ 877/427-7243 or 702/731-7110. Fax 702/731-6636. www.caesars.com. 2,471 units. From $99 standard double, $109–$500 "run-of-house deluxe" double; $549–$1,000 suite. Extra person $20. Children under 18 stay free in parent's room. AE, DC, DISC, MC, V. Free self- and valet parking. **Amenities:** Casino; wedding chapel; 23 restaurants; 3 outdoor pools; health club and spa; concierge; tour desk; car-rental desk; business center; shopping arcade; 24-hr. room service; laundry service; dry cleaning; nonsmoking rooms; executive-level rooms. *In room:* A/C, TV w/pay movies, dataport, hair dryer, iron and board, safe.

Paris Las Vegas Casino Resort ⚝ *Sacre bleu!* The City of Light comes to Sin City in this, the most recent fantasy hotel to hit the Strip. It's theme-run-amok time again, and we are so happy about it. The outside reproduces various Parisian landmarks (amusing anyone familiar with Paris, as the Hotel de Ville is crammed on top of the Louvre), complete with a half-scale perfect replica of the Eiffel Tower. The interior puts you in the middle of a dollhouse version of the city. You can stroll down a mini–Rue de la Paix, ride an elevator to the top of the Eiffel Tower, stop at an overpriced bakery for a baguette, and take your photo by several very nice fountains.

You'll find signage employing the kind of dubious use of the French language that makes genuine Frenchmen really cross ("le car rental" and so forth), while all the employees are forced to dust off their high school French ("Bonjour, Madame! Merci beaucoup!") when dealing with the public. Don't worry, it's all not quite enough to make you sick to "le stomach."

Quel dommage, this attention to detail does not extend to the rooms, which are nice enough but disappointingly uninteresting, with furniture that only hints at mock French Regency. Bathrooms are small but pretty, with deep tubs. Try to get a Strip-facing room so that you can see Bellagio's fountains across the street; note also that north-facing rooms give you nice Peeping-Tom views right into neighboring Bally's. Overall, not a bad place to stay but a great place to visit—*quel hoot!*

The hotel has eight more-or-less French-themed restaurants, including a highly lauded **buffet,** the **Eiffel Tower restaurant** (located guess where), and bistro **Mon Ami Gabi,** all of which are covered in chapter 6. The bread for all these restaurants is made fresh on-site at the bakery. You can buy delicious, if pricey, loaves of it at the bakery, and we have to admit, that's kinda fun. There are also five lounges.

The **Eiffel Tower** attraction is covered on p. 178, and the hotel's new nightclub, **Risque,** is reviewed on p. 265.

3655 Las Vegas Blvd. S., Las Vegas, NV 89109. ⓒ 888/BONJOUR (266-5687) or 702/946-7000. Fax 702/967-3836. www.parislv.com. 2,916 units. $119–$269 double; $350 and up suites. Extra person $30. Children under

18 stay free in parent's room. AE, DC, DISC, MC. V. Free self- and valet parking. **Amenities:** Casino; showrooms; 2 wedding chapels; 11 restaurants; outdoor pool; health club and spa; concierge; tour desk; business center; shopping arcade; 24-hr. room service; laundry service; dry cleaning; nonsmoking rooms; executive-level rooms. *In room:* A/C, TV w/pay movies, dataport, hair dryer, iron and board, safe.

The Venetian ★★   One of the most elaborate hotel spectacles in town, The Venetian falls squarely between an outright adult Disneyland experience and the luxury resort experience that many of the other recently renovated Vegas hotels offer. Its exterior, which re-creates most of the top landmarks of Venice (the Campanile, a portion of St. Mark's Square, part of the Doge's Palace, a canal or two), ranks right up there with New York–New York as a must-see, and since you can wander freely through the "sights," it even has a slight edge over New York–New York. (This may be the only hotel in Vegas where it seems inviting to wander around outside in the front.) As stern as we get about re-creations *not* being a substitute for the real thing, we have to admit that the attention to detail here is impressive indeed. Stone is aged for that weathered look, statues and tiles are exact copies of their Italian counterparts, security guards wear Venetian police uniforms—all that's missing is the smell from the canals, but we are happy to let that one slide.

Inside, it's more of the same, particularly in the lobby area and the entrance to the extraordinary shops, as ceilings are covered with hand-painted re-creations of Venetian art. With plenty of marble, soaring ceilings, and impressive pillars and archways, it's less kitschy than Caesars but more theme park than Bellagio. The lobby says classy hotel. The lobby, casino, and shops can all be accessed from outside through individual entrances, which helps avoid that irritating circuitous maneuvering required by most other locations. This is all the more appreciated because the casino seems to have a most confusing layout, with poor signage; perhaps it's just our problem with spatial navigation, but we consistently got lost on the way to the guest elevators.

The rooms are the largest and probably the most handsome in town, with a flair that's more European than Vegas. They are all "suites," with a good-size bedroom giving way to a sunken living area, complete with pullout sofa bed. The decor features just one too many patterns, but it manages to work, and nice touches abound. Rooms have somewhat stately furniture, including painted, scallop-topped armoires; thickly draped half canopies over the beds; and crown moldings on ceilings. The marbled bathrooms rocketed virtually to the top of our list of favorites, in a tie for second place with those at Bellagio. (Mandalay Bay's are the best.) Glassed-in showers, deep soaking tubs (though your feet can easily kick the plug out), double sinks, fluffy towels, and lots of space—that does it for us every time. Devices for the hearing-impaired (ranging from door-knock lights to vibrating alarm clocks and telecaption decoders) are available upon request.

Despite the niceties, there is a certain amount of price gouging at this hotel that unpleasantly reminds one of the real Venice. There is a charge for that in-room faxing and printing, and the minibar is automated so that if you so much as rearrange items inside, you are charged for it.

There are many celebrity chefs and high-profile restaurants in residence at The Venetian. Reviews of **Star Canyon, Delmonico Steakhouse, Canaletto, Valentino, Lutèce,** and **Pinot Brasserie** can be found in chapter 6. Also worth noting is that **Zeffirino's** chef Paolo Belloni has cooked for some of the most eminent judges of Italian food: the Pope and Sinatra. And, of course, there is an elegant but confusingly laid-out casino.

The Venetian has five pools and whirlpools, but so far its pool area is disappointing—sterile and bland. Pools are neoclassical (think rectangles with the corners lopped off), and the fourth-floor location probably means that more dense foliage is not going to be forthcoming.

The **Canyon Ranch SpaClub** is run by a branch of arguably the finest getaway spa in America. This is an unbelievably lavish facility, certainly the finest hotel spa in town. From the Bed Head and Bumble & Bumble products on sale in the shop to the nutritionists, physical therapists, and acupuncturists on the staff, to the vibrating massage chairs that you rest in during pedicures—geez, what more could you want? Well, we want our own home gym to be as nice as the one here, with ample equipment, racks of big TVs, and a staff eager to help you with advice and bring you bottled water. The $30-a-day fee is high, but it does include a full day's worth of classes ranging from regular aerobics to yoga, Pilates, and dance. Did we mention the rock-climbing wall?

The **Grand Canal Shoppes** rank with Caesars's shops as an absolute mustsee. Like Caesars, the area is a mock Italian village with a blue, cloud-studded, painted sky overhead. But down the middle runs a canal, complete with singing gondoliers. (The 10-min. ride costs about $12, which seems steep, but trust us, it's a *lot* more in the real Venice.) The whole thing finishes up at a small re-creation of St. Mark's Square, which features glass blowers, traveling musicians, flower sellers, and the like. Expect to run into famous Venetians such as a flirty Casanova and a travel-weary Marco Polo. It's ambitious and a big step up from Animatronic figures. Oh, and the stores are also probably worth a look—a decent mixture of high-end fashion and more affordable shops.

And let's not forget that this is the only hotel in town with a branch of the famed Guggenheim Museum, called the **Guggenheim-Hermitage** (p. 180).

Note: Summer 2003 saw the opening of a new $250 million Venezia tower with 1,013 rooms (reportedly even more luxurious than the current ones), making the Venetian the third-largest hotel in the world. Also inside the tower are several new restaurants, including the first restaurant outside of Napa Valley by Thomas Keller, arguably the finest chef in America.

3355 Las Vegas Blvd. S., Las Vegas, NV 89109. (©) **888/2-VENICE** (283-6423) or 702/414-1000. Fax 702/414-4805. www.venetian.com. 3,354 units. $125–$399 double. Extra person $35. Kids under 13 stay free in parent's room. AE, DC, DISC, MC, V. Free self- and valet parking. **Amenities:** Casino; wedding chapel; showroom; 17 restaurants; 5 outdoor pools; health club and spa; video arcade; concierge; tour desk; car-rental desk; business center; shopping arcade; 24-hr. room service; laundry service; dry cleaning; nonsmoking rooms; executive-level rooms. *In room:* A/C, TV w/pay movies, fax, dataport, fridge, hair dryer, iron and board, safe.

EXPENSIVE

Bally's Las Vegas (✦)   With all the fancy-pants new hotels in town, it's so hard to keep up with the Joneses, or the Wynns as the case may be. And here's poor Bally's, with a perfect location, and it's got no big fountain or Eiffel Tower or anything to make a passerby think "right, gotta go gamble there," much less a tourist booking long distance to think "right, gotta stay there." And we aren't really going to make you change your mind, though lately, we might give you a reason to consider it. After all, you can get a room for a ridiculously low rate these days, and those rooms, which are larger than average, have recently been redone to an admirable degree, with some swell touches including modern curvy couches, big TVs, wireless Internet access, and marble this and that. The public areas still feel dark and dated, but the hotel is connected to its sister property, Paris Las Vegas, which is swanky and modern enough. Also, it will be a stop on the new monorail system, so you'll be able to go just about everywhere by foot or by swift train, and, thanks to those nice new rooms, you've got someplace pleasant to return to.

Bally's has the usual range of dining choices and is justly renowned for its **Sterling Sunday Brunch** (p. 167). The casino is large, well lit, and colorful, and there's also a headliner showroom and the splashy *Jubilee!* revue (p. 251).

3645 Las Vegas Blvd. S. (at Flamingo Rd.), Las Vegas, NV 89109. ⓒ **800/634-3434** or 702/739-4111. Fax 702/967-3890. www.ballyslv.com. 2,814 units. $69 and up double, $35–$60 more concierge floor (including breakfast); $300 and up suite. Extra person $30. Children under 18 stay free in parent's room. AE, DC, MC, V. Free self- and valet parking. **Amenities:** Casino; showrooms; 14 restaurants; outdoor pool; 8 night-lit tennis courts; health club and spa; video arcade; concierge; tour desk; car-rental desk; business center; shopping arcade; 24-hr. room service; laundry service; dry cleaning; nonsmoking rooms; executive-level rooms. *In room:* A/C, TV w/pay movies, iron and board.

The Flamingo Las Vegas ⭐

The Flamingo is the Strip's senior citizen, boasting a colorful history. It's changed a great deal since Bugsy Siegel opened his 105-room oasis "in the middle of nowhere" in 1946. It was so luxurious for its time that even the janitors wore tuxedos. Jimmy Durante was the opening headliner, and the wealthy and famous flocked to the tropical paradise of swaying palms, lagoons, and waterfalls. A fresh, new look, enhanced by a recent $130 million renovation and expansion, has made Siegel's "real class joint" better than ever—including making it somewhat easier to reach the outside world, which in the past was often difficult. As we write this, several of the restaurants in the front of the building are being taken out and replaced by singer Jimmy Buffett's Margaritaville nightclub, with a *Baywatch*-themed nightclub going in by the pool. So let's see how these additions continue to keep the old girl going.

Rooms occupy six towers and are variously decorated. Some are done up in soft blues and peach, and enhanced by pretty fabrics, light painted-wood furnishings, and watercolors of tropical scenes, lending a resort look. Others use soft earth tones, forest green, or coral. The **Flamingo's Paradise Garden Buffet** (p. 169) is a decent choice. There are also several bars, plus a huge casino and the **Second City Improv** production show (p. 254).

For those planning some leisure time outside the casino, The Flamingo's exceptional pool area, spa, and tennis courts are a big draw. Five gorgeous swimming pools, two whirlpools, water slides, and a kiddie pool are located in a 15-acre Caribbean landscape amid lagoons, meandering streams, fountains, waterfalls, a rose garden, and islands of live flamingos and African penguins. Ponds have ducks, swans, and koi, and a grove of 2,000 palms graces an expanse of lawn. Although the water can be a little chilly, kids should be able to spend hours in the pool area.

A health club ($20 fee per day) offers a variety of Universal weight machines, treadmills, stair machines, free weights, sauna, steam, a TV lounge, and hot and cold whirlpools. Exercise tapes are available, and spa services include massage, soap rub, salt glow, tanning beds, and oxygen pep-up.

3555 Las Vegas Blvd. S. (between Sands Ave. and Flamingo Rd.), Las Vegas, NV 89109. ⓒ **800/732-2111** or 702/733-3111. Fax 702/733-3353. www.flamingolv.com. 3,999 units. $69–$299 double; $250–$580 suite. Extra person $20. Children under 18 stay free in parent's room. Inquire about packages and timeshare suites. AE, DC, DISC, MC, V. Free self- and valet parking. **Amenities:** Casino; showrooms; 11 restaurants; 5 outdoor pools; 4 night-lit tennis courts; health club and spa; small video arcade; tour desk; car-rental desk; business center; shopping arcade; 24-hr. room service; in-room massage; babysitting; laundry service; dry cleaning; nonsmoking rooms; executive-level rooms. *In room:* A/C, TV w/pay movies, dataport, hair dryer, iron and board, safe.

Harrah's Las Vegas ⭐

Here's another property that is doing its best to keep up with the pace in Vegas, to no great success. Though parts of Harrah's benefited from a reworking of the place a few years ago, the rest of it evokes old

Las Vegas in the way The Riviera does—as in, dark, dated, and claustrophobic. Still, there is much to like here, and occasional quite good rates might make the so-so bits worth overlooking. Certainly, they want to be the fun and convivial place we wish more of Vegas was (instead of pretty much catering to high rollers and simply tolerating the rest of us with normal budgets).

Guest rooms were slowly being refurbished at press time—just in time, as guests were complaining. All the rooms are larger than average; the points that emerge from both the old and the new tower wings translate inside into an extra triangle of space for a couch and table. Some rooms also contain a kitchen. Spacious minisuites in this section, offering large sofas and comfortable armchairs, are especially desirable.

The Range (p. 140) steakhouse is one of the few hotel restaurants that overlooks the Strip, and the hotel's **buffet** (p. 169) isn't bad. The casino has a fun, festive atmosphere, complete with "party pits." Harrah's showroom was hosting singer **Clint Holmes** (p. 250) and his 12-piece band at press time. An improv comedy show, comedy cabaret, and Greg Thompson's late-night revue *Skintight* are also on the docket here, as is weekend happy-hour karaoke time in the La Playa lounge.

Carnaval Court (p. 238) is a festive, palm-fringed shopping plaza where strolling entertainers perform. It's notable because it's right on the Strip, but entirely outdoors; similar ventures at other hotels are inside artificial environments. Note that lounge singer legend Cook E. Jarr plays here late on Friday and Saturday nights (p. 244).

Harrah's has an Olympic-size swimming pool and sun-deck area with waterfall and trellised garden areas, a whirlpool, and a kids' wading pool. It's a pretty underwhelming pool by Vegas standards.

The hotel's health club is one of the better facilities on the Strip with a full-range spa and a gym with Lifecycles, treadmills, stair machines, rowing machines, lots of Universal equipment, free weights, and two TVs and a VCR for which aerobic exercise tapes are available. Its $20-a-day access charge is more reasonable than the fees in other hotels.

3475 Las Vegas Blvd. S. (between Flamingo and Spring Mountain roads), Las Vegas, NV 89109. ℭ **800/ HARRAHS** (427-7247) or 702/369-5000. Fax 702/369-6014. www.harrahs.com. 2,700 units. $65–$195 standard "deluxe" double, $85–$250 standard "superior" double; $195–$1,000 suite. Extra person $20, no discount for children. AE, DC, DISC, MC, V. Free self- and valet parking. **Amenities:** Casino; showrooms; 8 restaurants; outdoor pool; health club and spa; concierge; tour desk; car-rental desk; business center; shopping arcade; 24-hr. room service; laundry service; dry cleaning; nonsmoking rooms; executive-level rooms. *In room:* A/C, TV w/pay movies, dataport, hair dryer, iron and board, safe.

The Mirage ☆☆ Even though it has gotten somewhat eclipsed by the very hotels whose presence it made possible, we still really like this place. From the moment you walk in and breathe the faintly tropically perfumed air (we think it's vanilla) and enter the lush rainforest, it's just a different experience from most Vegas hotels.

The Mirage was Steve Wynn's first project built from the ground up. It seems funny now, but back in 1989, this was considered a complete gamble that was sure to be a failure. That was before the hotel opened, mind you. On opening day, the crowds nearly tore the place down getting inside, and The Mirage soon made its money back. Now it is the model upon which all recent hotels have been based.

Occupying 102 acres, The Mirage is fronted by more than a city block of cascading waterfalls and tropical foliage centering on a "volcano," which, after dark,

> ## *Tips* So Your Trip Goes Swimmingly . . .
>
> Part of the delight of the Vegas resort complexes is the gorgeous pools—what could be better for beating the summer heat? But there are pools and there are *pools,* so you'll need to keep several things in mind when searching for the right one for you.
>
> During the winter, it's often too cold or windy to do much lounging, and even if the weather is amenable, the hotels often close part of their pool areas during winter and early spring. The pools are also not heated for the most part, but in fairness, they largely don't need to be.
>
> Most hotel pools are shallow, chest-high at best, only about 3-feet deep in many spots (the hotels want you gambling, not swimming). Diving is impossible—not that a single pool allows it anyway.
>
> And finally, during those hot days, be warned that sitting by pools next to heavily windowed buildings such as The Mirage and Treasure Island will allow you to experience the same thing a bug does under a magnifying glass with a sun ray directed on it. Regardless of time of year, be sure to slather on the sunscreen; there's a reason you see so many unhappy lobster-red people roaming the streets. Many pool areas don't offer much in the way of shade. On the other hand, if your tan line is important to you, head for Caesars or Mandalay Bay, which both have topless sunbathing areas where you can toast even more flesh than at the other hotels.
>
> At any of the pools, you can rent cabanas (which often include TVs, special lounge chairs, and even better poolside service), but these should be reserved as far in advance as possible, and with the exception of the Four Seasons, where they are complimentary, most cost a hefty fee. If you are staying at a chain hotel, you will most likely find an average pool, but if you want to spend some time at a better one, be aware that most of the casino-hotel pool attendants will ask to see your room key. If they are busy, you might be able to sneak in, or at least, blend in with a group ahead of you.

erupts every 15 minutes, spewing fire 100 feet above the lagoons below. To be honest, it's not very volcano-like; if you've seen any of the lava-saturated volcano movies, you'll be disappointed. Instead of lava flow, expect a really neat light show, and you won't mind a bit. (In passing, that volcano cost $30 million, which is equal to the entire original construction cost for Caesars next door.) The lobby is dominated by a 53-foot, 20,000-gallon simulated coral-reef aquarium stocked with more than 1,000 colorful tropical fish. This gives you something to look at while waiting (never for long) for check-in.

Next, you'll walk through the rainforest, which occupies a 90-foot domed atrium—a path meanders through palms, banana trees, waterfalls, and serene pools. If we must find a complaint with The Mirage, it's with the next bit, as you have to negotiate 8 miles (or so it seems) of casino mayhem to get to your room, the pool, food, or the outside world. It gets old, fast. (On the other hand, the sundries shop is located right next to the guest-room elevators, so if you forgot toothpaste, you don't have to travel miles to get more.)

The rooms have recently been redone to a strong color palette that is oddly similar to the rooms' original tropical decor scheme. Frankly, it's here most of all where The Mirage isn't holding up its end; the rooms are nice, but there are nicer—and larger—ones all over town now, and the bathrooms are a little too cramped for a what's supposed to be a swanky hotel.

Off the casino is a habitat for Siegfried and Roy's white tigers, a plaster enclosure that allows for photo-taking and "aaaahhhs." Behind the pool is the **Dolphin Habitat** and Siegfried and Roy's **Secret Garden,** which has a separate admission (p. 184).

The superb Italian food at **Onda** and the **Mirage Buffet** are detailed in chapter 6.

The highly prominent production shows by **Siegfried & Roy** and **Danny Gans** are reviewed in chapter 10, and The Mirage has one of our favorite casinos.

Out back is the pool, one of the nicest in Vegas, with a ¼-mile shoreline, a tropical paradise of waterfalls and trees, water slides, and so forth. It looks inviting, but truth be told, it's sometimes on the chilly side and isn't very deep. But it's so pretty you'll hardly care. Free swimming lessons and water-aerobics classes take place daily at the pool. The **Mirage Day Spa** teems with friendly staff anxious to pamper you, bringing you iced towels to cool you during your workout and refreshing juices and smoothies afterward. The gym is one of the largest and best stocked on the Strip.

3400 Las Vegas Blvd. S. (between Flamingo Rd. and Sands Ave.), Las Vegas, NV 89109. ℂ **800/627-6667** or 702/791-7111. Fax 702/791-7446. www.mirage.com. 3,323 units. Sun–Thurs $79–$399 double, Fri–Sat and holidays $159–$399 double; $250–$3,000 suite. Extra person $30, no discount for children. AE, DC, DISC, MC, V. Free self- and valet parking. **Amenities:** Casino; showrooms; 14 restaurants; beautiful outdoor pool; health club and spa; concierge; tour desk; car-rental desk; business center; shopping arcade; 24-hr. room service; laundry service; dry cleaning; nonsmoking rooms; executive-level rooms. *In room:* A/C, TV w/pay movies, dataport, hair dryer, iron and board, safes.

Palms Resort & Casino ✪

The latest Vegas hotel wonder, though maybe "wonder" is a bit of a stretch. In keeping with the tropical-foliage name, it's more or less Miami-themed (but without the pastels), with a strange aversion toward straight lines (really, check out all those curves). Inside a bland building is a pretty nice complex—which we say only because it's a puzzle, but as we write this, the Palms is hands down the hottest hotel in town. That's mostly due to the nightlife options—both **Ghost Bar** and the nightclub **Rain** have lines of people every night the facilities are open, offering to sell their firstborn sons for a chance to go inside. Why did those two places catch on so? Not really sure (though you can read our speculations about both in chapter 10), but you need to know that the entrances to them stand right by the elevators to your hotel room, which means on a busy weekend night, there can be upwards of 4,000 gorgeous and antsy (if not angry) people standing between you and access to your hotel room. If you are a Hilton Sister, or wish to see if one will date you, this could be heaven, but if encountering the beautifully dressed and coifed, with 0% body fat and sullen expressions of entitlement, and the 19-year-olds who seek to become all of that (and usually affect a thuggish demeanor) makes you, like us, itch, this might not be the most comfortable place to stay.

Impressions

Supercalifragilisticexpialidocious!
　　　　　—Governor Bob Miller's reaction upon first visiting The Mirage

---

Having said all that, note that The Palms has perhaps some of the most comfortable beds in Vegas, thanks to fluffy pillows and duvets that make one reluctant to rise, plus big TVs and huge bathrooms. The main pool is oddly cheap looking—it's really a posing spot rather than a splash, while a second pool has a bar and mermaids swimming in the water at night. Also on the property is **Alizé** (p. 135), in competition for the title Best Restaurant in Town (and owner of the title Most Gorgeous and Romantic Restaurant), a cheap and hearty **buffet** (p. 170), movies theaters, a McDonald's, and other reliable cheap chain eateries.

4321 W. Flamingo Rd. (at I-15), Las Vegas, NV 89103. ✆ 866/942-7777 or 702/942-7777. Fax 702/942-6859. www.palms.com. 400 units. Sun–Thurs $79 and up double, Fri–Sat $119 and up double. Extra person $12, no discount for children. AE, DC, DISC, MC, V. Free self- and valet parking. **Amenities:** Casino; nightclub/showroom; 8 restaurants; outdoor pool; health club and spa; Jacuzzi; sauna; concierge; business center; 24-hr. room service; in-room massage; laundry service; dry cleaning; nonsmoking rooms; executive-level rooms. *In room:* A/C, TV w/pay movies, dataport, high-speed Internet access (for a fee), coffeemaker, hair dryer, iron and board, safe.

Rio All-Suite Hotel & Casino ✦

Rio pushes itself as a "carnival" atmosphere hotel, which in this case means hectic, crowded, and noisy, and the recent edict requiring the already Most Scantily Clad Waitresses in town to burst into song and dance in between delivering beers. The newer section, the Masquerade Village, is actually pretty pleasant, with a very high ceiling, but the older section's low ceilings only seem to accentuate how crowded the area is in both the number of people and the amount of stuff (slot machines, gaming tables, and so on). All this party atmosphere, by the way, is strictly for adults; the hotel actively discourages guests from bringing children.

The rooms are touted because of their size. Every one is a "suite," which does not mean two separate rooms, but rather one large room with a sectional, corner sofa, and coffee table at one end. The dressing areas are certainly larger than average and feature a number of extra amenities, such as refrigerators (unusual for a Vegas hotel room) and small snacks. Windows, running the whole length of the room, are floor to ceiling, with a pretty impressive view of The Strip, Vegas, or the mountains (depending on which way you're facing). The furniture doesn't feel like hotel-room standard, but otherwise the decor is fairly bland.

Rosemary's at the Rio, a new version of one of our favorite restaurants in town, **Fiore,** and the hotel's first-rate buffet are described in chapter 6. You might consider checking out the **Wine Cellar Tasting Room,** which bills itself as "the world's largest and most extensive collection of fine wines" and hyperbole aside, it's certainly impressive and a must-do for any wine aficionado.

Penn & Teller, the smartest show in town, is reviewed in chapter 10, as are the **Voodoo Lounge, Bikinis,** and **Club Rio.** The missable Scintas also do a regular act while we adore the unpredictable antics produced by the improv dinner show *Tony & Tina's Wedding.* The casino, alas, is dark and claustrophobic. In case you missed the party/carnival theme, there is a rather bizarre live-action show called *The Masquerade Show in the Sky.* It is presented Thursday through Tuesday at 3:30, 4:30, 5:30, 7, 8, 9, and 10pm. Sets modeled after Mardi Gras floats (sort of) move on grids set in the ceiling, filled with costumed performers who lip-sync to music designed to rev up the crowd but not continue the theme (swing selections, for example). These floats are best viewed from the second floor of the village. Down below, dancers do their thing on a stage, while even stranger costumes (ostriches, dragons, and so on) prance next to them. Guests can also don costumes and ride a float, but you have to pay for the privilege.

Out back is a pool with a sandy beach, and two new pools in imaginative fish and shell shapes that seem inviting until you get up close and see how small they are. It could be especially disappointing after you have braved the long, cluttered walk (particularly from the new tower rooms) to get there. Three whirlpool spas nestle amid rocks and foliage, there are two sand-volleyball courts, and blue-and-white-striped cabanas (equipped with rafts and misting coolers) can be rented for $100 and up per day. The 18-hole championship **Rio Secco golf course** was designed by Rees Jones.

3700 W. Flamingo Rd. (at I-15), Las Vegas, NV 89103. ☎ **888/752-9746** or 702/777-7777. Fax 702/777-7611. www.playrio.com. 2,582 units. Sun–Thurs $90 and up double-occupancy suite, Fri–Sat $140 and up double-occupancy suite. Extra person $30, no discount for children. Inquire about golf packages. AE, DC, MC, V. Free self- and valet parking. **Amenities:** Casino; showrooms; 13 restaurants; 4 outdoor pools; golf course; health club and spa; Jacuzzi; sauna; video arcade; concierge; car-rental desk; business center; shopping arcade; 24-hr. room service; in-room massage; laundry service; dry cleaning; nonsmoking rooms; executive-level rooms. *In room:* A/C, TV w/pay movies, fridge, coffeemaker, hair dryer, iron and board, safe.

TI at The Mirage ★★   Huh? What happened to Treasure Island? What happened to the pirates? Why, Vegas grew up, that's what. Or, rather, it wants the kids it once actively tried to court to grow up, or at least, not come around until they are able to drink and gamble properly.

Originally the most modern family-friendly hotel, the former Treasure Island was a blown-up version of Disneyland's Pirates of the Caribbean. But that's all behind them now, and the name change is there to make sure you understand this is a grown-up, sophisticated resort. There might still be the odd pirate element here and there, but only because someone absent-mindedly missed it in a recent ruthless purging of the last remnants. The latest victim is the pirate stunt show out front; as we write this, it was being shut down, reconceived, and will, by the time you read this, have reopened with the addition of, and we did not make this up, "sexy dancers" who will "battle the pirates." Right.

To be fair, none of this matters a whit, unless, like us, you got a kick out of the skulls and crossbones, and treasure chests bursting with jewels and gold, that originally decorated the place. What remains, after they stripped the pirate gilt, is such a nice place to stay that in some ways, it even outranks its older sister, The Mirage. The well-sized rooms pretty much follow the pattern of The Mirage—modified French Regency with a mélange of patterns, but the monochromatic color (many shades of gold) tones it down, and overall, while not distinctive, per se, they are much nicer than most in their price range. Good bathrooms feature a large soaking tub—a bather's delight. Best of all, Strip-side rooms have a view of the pirate battle (however it's going to end up looking)—views are best from the sixth floor on up.

The hotel's premier restaurant, the **Buccaneer Bay Club,** is described in chapter 6, as are the hotel's **buffet** offerings. And we're incredibly enthusiastic about the new branch of Los Angeles's Canter's deli that opened as this book went to press. The **Battle Bar,** in the casino near the race and sports book, airs athletic events on TV monitors overhead and offers live music Tuesday through Sunday nights. More importantly, it provides patio seating overlooking Buccaneer Bay; for the best possible view of what's now going to be called "The Sirens of TI," arrive at least 45 minutes before the show and snag a table by the railing. Treasure Island is home to **Cirque du Soleil's** *Mystère* (p. 248), one of the best shows in town.

A free tram travels between Treasure Island and The Mirage almost around the clock. For a good photo op, sit in the front of the first car: As you leave the loading dock, note how The Mirage, palm trees, and a bit of the New York–New York skyline are framed in an attractive, and surreal, manner.

There's a full-service spa and health club with a complement of machines, plus sauna, steam, whirlpool, massage, on-site trainers, TVs and stereos with headsets, and anything else you might need (including a full line of Sebastian grooming products in the women's locker rooms). There's a $20-per-day fee to use the facilities.

The pool is not that memorable, with none of the massive foliage and other details that make the one at The Mirage stand out (so blah is it that the staff didn't even bother to check room keys when last we swam here). It's a large, free-form swimming pool with a 230-foot loop slide and a nicely landscaped sun-deck area. It's often crawling with kids, so if that's a turn-off, go elsewhere.

3300 Las Vegas Blvd. S. (at Spring Mountain Rd.), Las Vegas, NV 89109. ℂ 800/944-7444 or 702/894-7111. Fax 702/894-7446. www.treasureisland.com. 2,891 units. From $69 double; from $109 suite. Extra person $25, no discount for children. Inquire about packages. AE, DC, DISC, MC, V. Free self- and valet parking. **Amenities:** Casino; showrooms; 11 restaurants; outdoor pool; health club and spa; very well-equipped game and video arcade; concierge; tour desk; car-rental desk; business center; shopping arcade; 24-hr. room service; laundry service; dry cleaning; nonsmoking rooms; executive-level rooms. *In room:* A/C, TV w/pay movies, fax, dataport, hair dryer, iron and board, safe.

MODERATE

Barbary Coast Hotel & Casino   You can't fault the location of this hotel. It's right on the busiest corner of the Strip, smack in the middle of the action. With all the hotel business (the itty-bitty reception desk and tiny sundries/gift shop counter) set on the fringes of the small, dark, cluttered casino, this is very old Vegas, which is sort of a good thing; but unfortunately, it's becoming harder to wrap one's mind around it in these days of megacasino complexes. Nevertheless, a small hotel is a rare thing in this town, and a face-lift would make the Barbary Coast a nice boutique hotel. Let's encourage them in that direction.

Rooms have not-precisely-inviting dark tones (think bordello burgundy) and little sitting areas separated by curtains. King rooms are more spacious. Bathrooms are dinky but not dreary, mattresses are new and thick. *Beware:* The very loud intersection outside can make rooms noisy.

Drai's, an upscale restaurant, is covered in detail in chapter 6. **Michael's** is the hotel's premier restaurant, with only two seatings a night in an intimate, old-fashioned room. The food gets raves, but the menu is completely dated (chops and the like), so it's best for those with deep pockets who mistrust nouvelle cuisine. Two bars serve the cheerful and ornate casino.

3595 Las Vegas Blvd. S. (at Flamingo Rd.), Las Vegas, NV 89109. ℂ 800/634-6755 or 702/737-7111. Fax 702/894-9954. www.barbarycoastcasino.com. 200 units. Sun–Thurs $39 and up double; Fri–Sat and holidays $89 and up double. Extra person $10. Children under 15 stay free in parent's room. AE, DC, DISC, MC, V. Free self- and valet parking. **Amenities:** Casino; 4 restaurants; tour desk; car-rental desk; 24-hr. room service; dry cleaning; nonsmoking rooms. *In room:* A/C, TV w/pay movies, dataport, hair dryers, iron and board.

Bourbon Street *Value*   Just a few steps (well, okay, more than a few, but not by much) down from the main Strip action, Bourbon Street is a bargain. It looks like a dump, but it's not. Adequately sized rooms, while hardly comparable to those in the luxe establishments on the Strip, are surprisingly nice—brighter, cleaner, and more cheerful than you would expect, with small but sweetly attended-to bathrooms (including some nice grooming amenities). Given price and location, it's a heck of a deal overall.

120 E. Flamingo Rd. (between the Strip and Koval Lane), Las Vegas, NV 89109. ℂ 800/634-6956 or 702/ 737-7200. Fax 702/794-3490. www.bourbonstreethotel.com. 167 units. $39 and up standard double; $59 and up minisuite; $69 and up executive suite. Extra person $10. Children under 12 stay free in parent's room. AE, DC, DISC, MC, V. Free self- and valet parking. **Amenities:** Small casino; restaurant; dry cleaning; nonsmoking rooms. *In room:* A/C, TV w/pay movies, safe.

Tips **Is There a Doctor in the House?**

The Imperial Palace hotel has a well-appointed 24-hour urgent-care clinic, which is open to the public. Given its location, right in the middle of the action, it's well worth knowing about.

Imperial Palace *Value*   Location, location, location. And price, price, price. That's what the IP has going for it—don't think anything else. It's smack in the middle of the Strip—it doesn't get any more centrally located than this—and on a weekend night when rooms at nicer hotels are running $400 (that's for a regular room) lodgings can be had here for under $60. What you get in exchange is an older, darker hotel that looks sort of sleazy in spots, but really isn't. Not much, anyway. It just seems like it in comparison to the gleaming hulks across and down the street. We actually know types who prefer this, a more classic Vegas feel, to the airy new upstairs. We aren't among those, we have to admit, and you may not be as well. The standard rooms are just that (remodeling is in the works, which is a good thing), but they all have balconies, which is exceedingly rare in Vegas. A perfect Vegas hoot, the "luv tub" rooms are some of the best deals on the Strip, especially if you can get them for the cheapest end of the price range; you'll get a larger bedroom (with a mirror over the bed!) and a larger-than-usual bathroom that features a 300-gallon sunken "luv tub" (with still more mirrors).

From April to October, the hotel holds "luaus" at the pool, with a Polynesian revue and buffet. Expect tiki torches.

The hotel is also home to the long-running *Legends in Concert* impersonator show (p. 253). The casino has relatively low (for the Strip) table limits.

A unique feature is the **Auto Collections at Imperial Palace** (p. 176), displaying more than 800 antique, classic, and special-interest vehicles spanning a century of automotive history.

3535 Las Vegas Blvd. S. (between Sands Ave. and Flamingo Rd.), Las Vegas, NV 89109. *(C)* **800/634-6441** or 702/731-3311. Fax 702/735-8578. www.imperialpalace.com. 2,700 units. $49 and up double; $79 and up "luv tub" suite, $159 and up other suites. Extra person $19. Children under 6 stay free in parent's room. Inquire about packages. AE, DC, DISC, MC, V. Free self- and valet parking. **Amenities:** Casino; showrooms; wedding chapel; 9 restaurants; outdoor pool; health club and spa; video arcade; concierge; tour desk; car-rental desk; shopping arcade; 24-hr. room service; laundry service; dry cleaning; nonsmoking rooms; executive-level rooms. *In room:* A/C, TV w/pay movies, hair dryer, irons and boards.

5 North Strip

EXPENSIVE

The Riviera Hotel & Casino *Overrated*   Its best days long past, this former Strip star is looking awfully dumpy these days (and there are rumors, thanks to its part-ownership by development-happy Donald Trump, that it will soon be knocked down anyway). Between that and its promotion as an "alternative for grown-ups" and an "adult-oriented hotel," you should probably only stay here if you can get a deal and simply must be on the Strip. You certainly shouldn't bring the kids, who are actively discouraged as guests.

Opened in 1955 (Liberace cut the ribbon and Joan Crawford was the official hostess of opening ceremonies), The Riviera was the first "high-rise" on the Strip, at nine stories. Today, it tries to evoke the Vegas of the good old days—"come drink, gamble, and see a show"—and while it is appropriately dark and

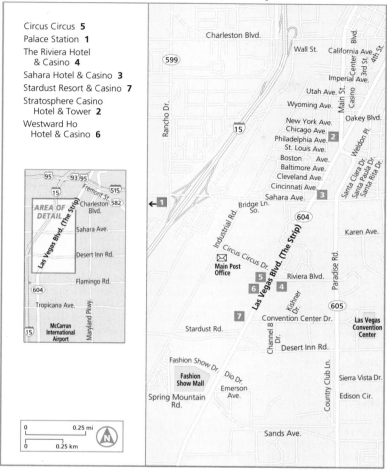

Circus Circus **5**
Palace Station **1**
The Riviera Hotel
& Casino **4**
Sahara Hotel & Casino **3**
Stardust Resort & Casino **7**
Stratosphere Casino
Hotel & Tower **2**
Westward Ho
Hotel & Casino **6**

glitzy, it's also very crowded and has a confusing layout. Don't miss your chance to take your photo with the bronze memorial to the Crazy Girls (their premier, largely nekkid, show), and their butts, outside on the Strip. There is a pool here, but it's very dull.

Rooms are blah and not likely to improve. Half the rooms offer pool views. There is the predictable assortment of dining choices—though an excellent choice for families, ironically, is the **Mardi Gras Food Court,** which, unlike most of its genre, is extremely attractive. White-canvas umbrella tables and Toulouse-Lautrec-style murals create a comfortable, French cafe ambience. Food choices are wide-ranging, including burgers, pizza, gyros, falafel, and Chinese fare. The Riviera's enormous **casino** is one of the world's largest; see chapter 10 for reviews of its production shows, **_An Evening at La Cage_** (female impersonators), **_Crazy Girls_** (sexy Las Vegas–style revue), and **_Splash_** (aquatic revue).

2901 Las Vegas Blvd. S. (at Riviera Blvd.), Las Vegas, NV 89109. ✆ **800/634-6753** or 702/734-5110. Fax 702/794-9451. www.theriviera.com. 2,136 units. $59 and up double; $125 and up suite. Extra person $20 (all ages—no discount for children). AE, DC, MC, V. Free self- and valet parking. **Amenities:** Casino; wedding chapel; showrooms; 6 restaurants; outdoor pool; 2 night-lit tennis courts; health club and spa; concierge; tour desk; car-rental desk; business center; shopping arcade; 24-hr. room service; laundry service; dry cleaning; nonsmoking rooms; executive-level rooms. *In room:* A/C, TV w/pay movies, hair dryer (deluxe rooms only), iron and board (deluxe rooms only), safe.

MODERATE

Sahara Hotel & Casino *Value*   One of the few venerable old casino hotels still standing in Vegas (it's come a long way since it opened in 1952 on the site of the old Club Bingo), the Sahara completed a major face-lift in 1999. Alas, that included the loss of the landmark sign, once the tallest in Vegas. (The new one, featuring a camel, is frankly going to look just as dated even more quickly.) The point was not only to keep up with the Joneses (as the newer, glitzy hotels make the old ones seem not just quaint but shabby), but also to attempt to unify the theme of the hotel. This meant trying to make everything more Moroccan, though in reality, the hotel seems to feature details from all over North Africa. A new entrance showcases an arched neon dome with Moroccan detail, plenty of marble and chandeliers, plus small tiles and other Arabian Nights decorations. This entrance is quite a hike from the actual registration area—be sure to bring your camel. And then to top it all off, they added a roller coaster around the outside (quite a good ride, enthusiasts assure us).

Unfortunately, none of this really adds up to a nice hotel experience. Recent guests had found the place, renovations notwithstanding, just a bit dreary and maybe even shabby. Again, this may simply be in comparison to the gleaming new kids in town, a comparison suffered by most of the older hotels. It should be noted that the Sahara feels they are not as well equipped as other hotels for children and discourages you from bringing yours—and yet, they added a roller coaster. Go figure.

The room decor suffers from overkill, with stars and stripes assaulting the eyes and not looking terribly Moroccan. The boldly striped bedspreads on the otherwise comfortable beds are a particular mistake. The windows open, which is unusual for Vegas.

The hotel has just remodeled their **Sahara Buffet.** The casino is there, of course, and there's a headliner showroom as well.

2535 Las Vegas Blvd. S. (at E. Sahara Ave.), Las Vegas, NV 89109. © **888/696-2121** or 702/737-2111. Fax 702/791-2027. www.saharavegas.com. 1,720 units. $39 and up double. Extra person $15, no discount for children. AE, DC, DISC, MC, V. Free self- and valet parking. **Amenities:** Casino; showrooms; 6 restaurants; 2 outdoor pools (including 1 Olympic-size monster unfortunately located at the foot of a parking garage); Jacuzzi; tour desk; car-rental desk; business center; shopping arcade; limited room service; laundry service; dry cleaning; nonsmoking rooms; executive-level rooms. *In room:* A/C, TV w/pay movies, minifridge on request (free but limited availability), hair dryer, iron and board.

Stardust Resort & Casino *☆*   Opened in 1958, the Stardust is a longtime resident of the Strip, and its 188-foot starry sign is one of America's most recognized landmarks. Don't get too used to it: The owners (Boyd Gaming) have been vocal about wanting to get rid of it, either through a sale or a teardown/do-over. It's a pity, in a way; it is a likable hotel, offering on-Strip accommodations at cheap rates, but it has no personality, despite being the only star of the movie *Showgirls.* (It was probably chosen for its oh-so-Vegas light bulb–intensive facade, which turns up in just about every location-establishing shot for Vegas called for by commercials, TV, or movies. The movie *Swingers* also shot a number of scenes here.)

Rooms in the Towers are perfectly adequate, nice even, but forgettable. If you must know more, the 32-story West Tower rooms are decorated in earth tones while East Tower rooms go the floral route. You can rent an adjoining parlor room with a sofa bed, whirlpool, refrigerator, and wet bar—a good choice for families. Also quite nice are Villa rooms in two-story buildings surrounding a large swimming pool. Decorated in soft Southwestern pastels, they have private shaded patios overlooking the pool.

Mr. Wayne Newton himself has taken up residence at the Stardust, performing regularly in its showroom.

3000 Las Vegas Blvd. S. (at Convention Center Dr.), Las Vegas, NV 89109. © **800/634-6757** or 702/732-6111. Fax 702/732-6257. www.stardustlv.com. 1,552 units. From $60 standard double; from $250 suite. Extra person $20. Children under 13 stay free in parent's room. AE, DC, DISC, MC, V. Free self- and valet parking. **Amenities:** Casino; showrooms; 5 restaurants; 2 outdoor pools; small exercise room; Jacuzzi; video arcade; concierge; tour desk; car-rental desk; shopping arcade; 24-hr. room service; dry cleaning; nonsmoking rooms; executive-level rooms. *In room:* A/C, TV w/pay movies, dataport, safe.

Stratosphere Casino Hotel & Tower ★

A really neat idea, in that Vegas way, in a really bad location. At 1,149 feet, it's the tallest building west of the Mississippi. In theory, this should have provided yet another attraction for visitors: Climb (okay, elevator) to the top and gaze at the stunning view. But despite being on the Strip, it's a healthy walk from anywhere—the nearest casino is the Sahara, which is 5 very long blocks away. This, and possibly the hefty price charged for the privilege of going up to the top of the tower, may have conspired to keep the crowds away.

And while the crowds might have been justified before, they—and by "they," we mean "you"—might reconsider, especially if you are looking for a friendly place to hang your hat, but nothing more. The smaller-size rooms here are basically motel rooms—really nice motel rooms, but with that level of comfort and style. Then again, you can often get such a room for around $29 a night. (And do join the casino's players club—they tend to offer free rooms with more or less minimal play.) Perfect if you are coming to Vegas with no plans to spend time in your room except to sleep (if even that).

Which isn't to say there aren't other elements to like here, including the aforementioned casino, a Midway area with kiddie-oriented rides, a pool with a view and some of the friendliest, most accommodating staff in town. You can still ride the incredible thrill rides (provided the wind isn't blowing too hard that day) on top of the Tower: The world's highest roller coaster—aka the **High Roller**—(it careens around the outer rim of the Tower 909 ft., 108 stories, above ground) and the **Big Shot,** a fabulous free-fall ride that thrusts passengers up and down the Tower at speeds of up to 45 mph. (See p. 186 for a review of these two adrenaline pumpers.) Indoor and outdoor observation decks offer the most stunning city views you will ever see, especially at night. For the price, this might be the right place for you. Just remember you need a rental car or a lot of cash for cabs to get to the true thrills down the Strip.

In addition to the casino, the hotel also sports two productions shows: *American Superstars* (an impression-filled production show) and *Viva Las Vegas* (Las Vegas–style revue), which are reviewed in chapter 10.

2000 Las Vegas Blvd. S. (between St. Louis St. and Baltimore Ave.), Las Vegas, NV 89104. © **800/99-TOWER** (998-6937) or 702/380-7777. Fax 702/383-5334. www.stratospherehotel.com. 2,500 units. Sun–Thurs $39 and up double, Fri–Sat $59 and up double; $69 and up suite. Extra person $15. Children under 13 stay free in parent's room. AE, DC, DISC, MC, V. Free self- and valet parking. **Amenities:** Casino; showrooms; wedding chapel; 11 restaurants; large new pool area with great views of the Strip; children's rides and games located at the base of the Tower; concierge; tour desk; car-rental desk; shopping arcade; 24-hr. room service; laundry service; dry cleaning; nonsmoking rooms; executive-level rooms. *In room:* A/C, TV w/pay movies, dataport, hair dryer, iron and board, safe.

INEXPENSIVE

Circus Circus Hotel/Casino ⭐ *Kids*   The last bastion of family-friendly Las Vegas—indeed, for years, the only hotel with such an open mind. But even it isn't what it ought to be, thanks to a reconfiguring a few years ago that took the pervasive (and for some, nightmare inducing) Jumbo the Clown decorating scheme and turned it into somewhat more tasteful, more commedia dell'arte harlequins. Like everyone else, even the venerable Circus Circus, once the epitome of kitsch, is trying to be taken more seriously.

Which is not to say this is an adult atmosphere; the circus theme remains and the kid appeal along with it. (Which is also not to say that you should confuse this with a theme park hotel. All the circus fun is still built around a busy casino.) The midway level features dozens of carnival games, a large arcade (more than 300 video and pinball games), trick mirrors, and ongoing circus acts under the big top from 11am to midnight daily. The world's largest permanent circus (according to the *Guinness Book of World Records*), it features renowned trapeze artists, stunt cyclists, jugglers, magicians, acrobats, and high-wire daredevils. Spectators can view the action from much of the midway or get up close and comfy on benches in the performance arena. There's a "be-a-clown" booth where kids can be made up with washable clown makeup and red foam-rubber noses. They can grab a bite to eat in McDonald's (also on this level), and since the mezzanine overlooks the casino action, they can also look down and wave to Mom and Dad—or more to the point, Mom and Dad can look up and wave to the kids without having to stray too far away from the blackjack table. Circus clowns wander the midway creating balloon animals and cutting up in various ways.

The thousands of rooms here occupy sufficient acreage to warrant a free Disney World–style aerial shuttle (another kid pleaser) and minibuses connecting its many components. Tower rooms have newish, just slightly better-than-average furnishings, and offer safes and TVs with in-house information and gaming-instruction stations. The Manor section comprises five white three-story buildings out back, fronted by rows of cypresses. Manor guests can park at their doors, and a gate to the complex that can be opened only with a room key assures security. These rooms are usually among the least expensive in town, but we've said it before and we'll say it again: You get what you pay for. A renovation of these rooms added a coat of paint and some new photos on the wall, but not much else. All sections of this vast property have their own swimming pools; additional casinos serve the main tower and Skyrise buildings; and both towers provide covered parking garages.

Adjacent to the hotel is **Circusland RV Park,** with 384 full-utility spaces and up to 50-amp hookups. It has its own 24-hour convenience store, swimming pools, saunas, whirlpools, kiddie playground, fenced pet runs, video-game arcade, and community room. The rate is $17 and up Sunday to Thursday, $19 and up Friday and Saturday.

(*Value* **Joining the Club**

It's worth noting that joining the players clubs at the "older hotels"— **Bally's,** the **Trop, The Flamingo, Sahara,** and **The Riviera,** among others— is something smart tourists simply must do. Watch how after rather minimal play, your mailbox is suddenly flooded with offers for $19-a-night, midweek room rates.

The very reasonably priced **Pink Pony** is Circus Circus's cheerful bubble-gum-pink-and-bright-red 24-hour eatery, with big paintings of clowns on the walls and pink pony carpeting. It offers a wide array of coffee-shop fare, including a number of specially marked "heart-smart" (low-fat, low-cholesterol) items. For gorging, there's always the **Circus Circus Buffet** (p. 170).

In addition to the ongoing circus acts, there's also the upgraded **Adventure-dome** (p. 195) indoor theme park out back. There are three full-size casinos, all crowded and noisy, where you can gamble while trapeze acts take place overhead.

2880 Las Vegas Blvd. S. (between Circus Circus Dr. and Convention Center Dr.), Las Vegas, NV 89109. © **800/444-CIRC** (444-2472), 800/634-3450, or 702/734-0410. Fax 702/734-5897. www.circuscircus.com. 3,744 units. Sun–Thurs $39 and up double, Fri–Sat $59 and up double. Extra person $12. Children under 17 stay free in parent's room. AE, DC, DISC, MC, V. Free self- and valet parking. **Amenities:** Casino; circus acts; wedding chapel; 8 restaurants; 2 outdoor pools; midway-style carnival games; video arcade; tour desk; car-rental desk; 24-hr. room service; shopping arcade; laundry service; dry cleaning; nonsmoking rooms; executive-level rooms. *In room:* A/C, TV w/pay movies, hair dryer, safe.

Westward Ho Hotel & Casino   We know we referred to the Stratosphere as having motel rooms, but we did emphasize that those were nice motel rooms. These are just plain basic motel rooms, because this is, after all, a motel. Which means that it just doesn't have the facilities and other doodads that a true resort, even the Strat, offers. But the price lures. Located next door to Circus Circus, the Westward Ho is fronted by a vast casino, with rooms in two-story buildings that extend out back for several city blocks. In fact, the property is so large that a free bus shuttles regularly between the rooms and the casino 24 hours a day. Plans are in the works for a new casino and a gas station/convenience store in the back of the property. A good buy here are the two-bedroom suites with 1½ bathrooms, living rooms with sofa beds, and refrigerators. Suites sleep up to six people.

2900 Las Vegas Blvd. S. (between Circus Circus Dr. and Convention Center Dr.), Las Vegas, NV 89109. © **800/634-6803** or 702/731-2900. www.westwardho.com. 777 units. $37 and up double; $76 and up suite. Extra person $15, no discount for children. MC, V. Free parking at your room door. **Amenities:** Casino; restaurant; 3 outdoor pools; tour desk; car-rental desk; nonsmoking rooms. *In room:* A/C, TV w/pay movies.

6 East of the Strip

In this section we've covered hotels near the Convention Center, along with those farther south on Paradise Road, Flamingo Road, and Tropicana Avenue. Note that in the area around Paradise, there are over a dozen chain-style hotels—various Marriotts (Courtyard, Residence Inn), a Budget Suites, and many others—any one of which is going to provide comfortable, reliable, utterly undistinguished lodging, all of which often go for more money than they ought to. We've singled out a few here, but they are really very interchangeable. Do some searching around online, and don't hesitate to try to play them off each other in an attempt to get a deal.

VERY EXPENSIVE

Courtyard by Marriott ⭐   A complex of three-story terra cotta–roofed stucco buildings in an attractively landscaped setting of trees, shrubbery, and flower beds, the Courtyard is a welcome link in the Marriott chain. Although the services are limited, don't picture a no-frills establishment. This is a good-looking hotel (in a chain-establishment kind of way), with a pleasant, plant-filled lobby and very nice rooms indeed. Public areas and rooms still look spanking new. Most rooms have king-size beds, and all have balconies or patios.

3275 Paradise Rd. (between Convention Center Dr. and Desert Inn Rd.), Las Vegas, NV 89109. © **800/321-2211** or 702/791-3600. Fax 702/796-7981. www.courtyard.com. 159 units. Sun–Thurs $109 and up double,

Fri–Sat $119 and up double; $119 and up suite. No charge for extra person above double occupancy. AE, DC, DISC, MC, V. Free parking at your room door. **Amenities:** Restaurant; outdoor pool; small exercise room; Jacuzzi; business center; limited room service; coin-op washers and laundry service; dry cleaning; nonsmoking rooms; executive-level rooms. *In room:* A/C, TV w/pay movies, dataport; coffeemaker, hair dryer, iron and board.

Crowne Plaza ✦ An upscale sister of the Holiday Inn chain, this business-oriented hotel is right next to the Hard Rock, but is hardly a Gen-X destination. Each room is technically a suite, but apparently after building its five-story atrium, the hotel didn't have a lot of space left for the rooms, and so each is on the small side, made more so by the sheer amount of stuff crammed into them. Expect a wet bar, a sitting area complete with convertible sofa bed, a fridge, and a desk. Summertime can find calypso bands playing by the pool, making it a party spot for the many flight crews who regularly stay here.

4255 Paradise Rd. (just north of Harmon Ave.), Las Vegas, NV 89109. ✆ **800/2-CROWNE** (227-6963) or 702/369-4400. Fax 702/369-3770. $125 and up for up to 5 in the room. AE, DC, DISC, MC, V. Free self-parking. No valet parking. **Amenities:** Restaurant; outdoor pool; small exercise room with Nautilus, weights, and treadmills; Jacuzzi; sauna; concierge; airport shuttle; business center; limited room service; dry cleaning; nonsmoking rooms; executive-level rooms. *In room:* A/C, TV w/pay movies, dataport, minibar, fridge, coffeemaker, hair dryer, iron and board.

Hard Rock Hotel & Casino ✦✦ As soon as you check out the Hard Rock clientele, you'll know you are in a Vegas hotel that's like no other. The body-fat percentage (and median age) plummets; the percentage of black clothing skyrockets. Yep, the hip—from Hollywood and the music industry, among others—flock to the Hard Rock, drawn by the cool 'n' rockin' ambience and the goodies offered by a boutique hotel (657 rooms could be considered a "boutique hotel" only in Vegas). Our problem is that we are not famous pop stars and we do not look enough like Pamela Anderson to warrant the kind of attention that the staff seems to reserve for those types.

It's that Boomer-meets-Gen-X sensibility that finds tacky-chic so very hip. Luckily, the "no-tell motel" look of the older rooms has been updated to more closely match the decor of the rooms in the new addition. We still aren't crazy about the decor scheme in any of them—even the newer section is too '60s-futuristic hip to come off as posh, and all of it is showing more wear than it ought to. Bathrooms are a big step forward—bigger, brighter, and shinier; though in the older section, they can be cramped, space-wise, in suites. On a high note, the beds have feather pillows, and mattresses are surprisingly comfortable. Uncharacteristically large 27-inch TVs (most hotel sets are smaller, since they want you in the casino, not staring at the tube) offer special music channels.

The lobby borders on the casino (you can see how that immediately plunges you into the action, like it or not), which takes the center position in the round public area you immediately enter when arriving. On the perimeter is a collection of rock memorabilia, ranging from sad (a Kurt Cobain tribute) to cool (various guitars and outfits) to useless (various other guitars and outfits). The Hard Rock now has a permanent, if unwelcome and sad, bit of rock memorabilia for its collection—John Entwistle, bassist for the Who, died in one of its rooms on the eve of the start of a tour with the band.

There are several fine restaurants, including **AJ's Steakhouse,** a tribute to owner Peter Morton's dad, who brought us the legendary Morton's. You'll also find **Nobu,** a branch of highly famed chef Nobu Matsuhisa's wildly popular Japanese restaurant. Kicky and funky Mexican food can be had at lunch and dinner in the Mexican, folk-art-filled **Cantina Pink Taco,** while three diner-type meals a day are served at the 22-seat **Counter.** The Hard Rock's premier restaurant, **Mortoni's,** is

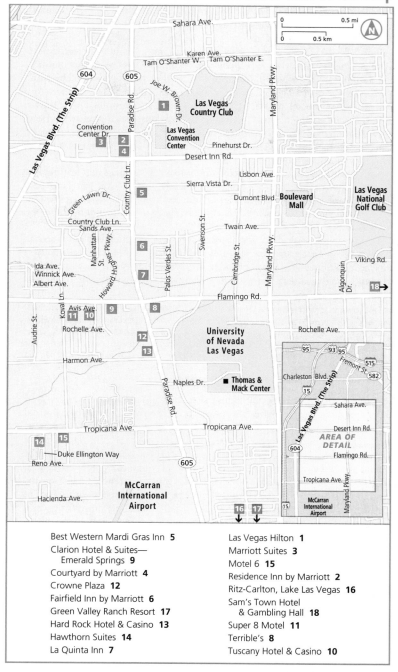

Sahara Ave.

0   0.5 mi

0   0.5 km

Karen Ave.
Tam O'Shanter W.   Tam O'Shanter E.

604   605

Joe W. Brown Dr.

Maryland Pkwy.

1   Las Vegas
Country Club

Paradise Rd.

Las Vegas Blvd. (The Strip)

Convention
Center Dr.

3   2   Las Vegas
Convention
4   Center   Pinehurst Dr.

Desert Inn Rd.

Lisbon Ave.

Sierra Vista Dr.

Green Lawn Dr.   5   Dumont Blvd.   Boulevard
Mall   Las Vegas
National
Golf Club

Country Club Ln.

Country Club Ln.
Sands Ave.

Twain Ave.

Manhattan St.

Swenson St.

6   Viking Rd.

Ida Ave.
Winnick Ave.   7   Palos Verdes St.

Albert Ave.   Cambridge St.   Maryland Pkwy.   Algonquin Dr.

Howard Hughes Pkwy.   Flamingo Rd.   18 →

Koval Ln.   Avis Ave.   9   8

Audrie St.   11   10

Rochelle Ave.   Rochelle Ave.

12   95   93 95   515

13   Fremont St.   582

University
of Nevada
Las Vegas   Charleston Blvd.

Harmon Ave.   15

Paradise Rd.   Las Vegas Blvd. (The Strip)

Naples Dr.   ■ Thomas &
Mack Center   Sahara Ave.

Tropicana Ave.   Tropicana Ave.   Desert Inn Rd.

14   15   AREA OF
DETAIL

Duke Ellington Way   604   Flamingo Rd.

Reno Ave.   605

Tropicana Ave.

Hacienda Ave.   McCarran
International
Airport   McCarran
International
Airport

Maryland Pkwy.

15

16   17

a beauty that serves vast portions of Italian fare. **Mr. Lucky's 24/7** is the hotel's round-the-clock coffee shop, displaying rock memorabilia and old Las Vegas hotel signs. And the **Hard Rock Cafe** (p. 131) is adjacent to the hotel.

Baby's (p. 267) is the hot nightspot offering from L.A. club impresario Sean MacPherson, but its velvet-rope policy may keep the likes of us out of there. The casino itself has a playful decor but an unbelievable noise level. **The Joint** (p. 258) is a major showroom that often hosts big-name rock musicians.

If you've ever dreamed of being in a beach party movie, or on the set of one of those MTV summer beach-house shows, the reconstructed pool at the Hard Rock is for you. Multiple pools are joined by a lazy river, and fringed in spots by actual sand beaches. You won't get much swimming done—the water is largely so shallow that it won't hit your knees—but there is swim-up blackjack (they give you little plastic pouches to hold your money), and a stage that features live music in the summer and is fronted by a sandy area, so you can make like Frankie, Annette, and Erik Von Zipper and do the Watusi. Or just pose in a thong bikini and new breasts. Whichever. On warm days and nights, this is *the* hangout scene.

The newly refurbished spa is smaller than its Strip counterparts but is soothing in its posh Space Age Zen way, and the health club is plenty large and well equipped, offering a full complement of Cybex equipment, stair machines, treadmills, massage, and steam rooms. There's an $18 per day fee to use the health-club facilities.

4455 Paradise Rd. (at Harmon Ave.), Las Vegas, NV 89109. ℂ **800/473-ROCK** (473-7625) or 702/693-5000. Fax 702/693-5588. www.hardrockhotel.com. 657 units. Sun–Thurs $79 and up double, Fri–Sat $145 and up double; from $250 suite. Extra person $35. Children under 13 stay free in parent's room. AE, DC, MC, V. Free self- and valet parking. **Amenities:** Casino; showroom; 6 restaurants; 2 outdoor pools with a lazy-river ride and sandy beach bottom; small health club and spa; concierge; tour desk; 24-hr. room service; laundry and dry-cleaning service; nonsmoking rooms; executive-level rooms. *In room:* A/C, TV w/pay movies, high-speed Internet access (for a fee), dataport, irons and boards, hair dryer.

Las Vegas Hilton ✦   It's easy for us to overlook this dinosaur—look, we even called it a dinosaur. Totally unfair. It's one of the last of the dying breed of old Vegas hotels, but unlike many of its peers, it's still offering fine accommodations and even a bit more than that. Consider it even if you don't fall into either of those demographics, and don't be put off by the distance from the Strip; the Monorail will be stopping here once it opens, making access there easier than ever. When you consider that on nights when you can't touch a room on the Strip for less than $175, the Hilton will put in you a nice room with plenty of marble (including large bathtubs) and clean, well-maintained furnishings for a decent price, then it seems silly to not make the Hilton a top choice more often. The clientele mix is between the business travelers who know a good deal and Trekkers lured in by the Spacequest Casino and *Star Trek: The Experience.* There are quite a few terrific restaurants, plus the largest hotel convention and meeting facilities in the world.

Those very same facilities, however, mean that even a small convention can sometimes drive the prices up at odd times—then again, since conventions are often booked for weekdays, that can also mean atypical drops in price on weekends. Just call.

Note: As we went to press, the Hilton was for sale. Be aware that by the time you read this, some of the information contained herein may have changed.

The Hilton has a strong showing of restaurants, including a **Benihana** and a **buffet** that's reviewed in chapter 6. *Note:* Children 12 and under can dine in any

Hilton restaurant for half the listed menu prices, making this a great option for budget-conscious families.

The **Nightclub,** a first-rate casino lounge, has live entertainment nightly. It's a great place to hang out in the evening and features regular sets by local cover bands. One of Elvis's sequined jumpsuits is enshrined in a glass case in the front, near the entrance to the lobby/casino (he played 837 sold-out shows here). In addition, Colonel Tom Parker's memorial service was held here in the hotel. There's also a major **headliner showroom** (see chapter 10).

There are also a number of shops, plus *Star Trek: The Experience* (p. 186), the themed attraction, with its accompanying space-themed casino. At press time, we received word that a new multimedia show, *Borg Invasion 4D,* featuring a 3-D film and lots of special effects will be added to the attraction in spring 2004.

The casino is especially well designed, with some fun gimmicks.

The third-floor roof comprises a beautifully landscaped 8-acre recreation deck with a large swimming pool, a 24-seat whirlpool spa, six Har-Tru tennis courts lit for night play, Ping-Pong, and a putting green. Also on this level is a luxurious 17,000-square-foot state-of-the-art health club offering Nautilus equipment, Lifecycles, treadmills, rowing machines, three whirlpool spas, steam, sauna, massage, and tanning beds. There's a $15-per-day fee to use the facilities, but guests are totally pampered: All toiletries are provided; there are comfortable TV lounges; complimentary bottled waters and juices are served in the canteen; and treatments include facials and oxygen pep-ups (you inhale pure oxygen).

3000 Paradise Rd. (at Riviera Blvd.), Las Vegas, NV 89109. (*C*) **888/732-7117** or 702/732-5111. Fax 702/732-5805. www.lvhilton.com. 3,174 units. $49 and up double. Extra person $30. Children under 18 stay free in parent's room. AE, DC, DISC, MC, V. Free self- and valet parking. **Amenities:** Casino; showrooms; 13 restaurants; outdoor pool; golf course adjacent; 6 tennis courts (4 night-lit); health club and spa; Jacuzzi; car-rental desk; business center; shopping arcade; 24-hr. room service; laundry service; dry cleaning; nonsmoking rooms; executive-level rooms. *In room:* A/C, TV w/pay movies, dataport, hair dryer, iron and board.

Marriott Suites ✯   Oh sure, you don't lack for Marriotts in Las Vegas, but it is a reliable chain (if a tad overpriced), and you can't fault the location of this one. It's just 3 blocks off the Strip (a 10-min. walk at most, though in 100°F/38°C heat, that may be too far) and not much farther from the Convention Center. This is a solid choice for business travelers, but families might also like the lack of casino and accompanying mayhem, not to mention the extra-large, quite comfortable rooms. Each suite has a sitting area separated from the bedroom by French doors. And there are gorgeous prints on the walls—far, far better than you would expect in a hotel, much less in one of the chain variety.

325 Convention Center Dr., Las Vegas, NV 89109. (*C*) **800/228-9290** or 702/650-2000. Fax 702/650-9466. www.marriott.com. 278 units. $159 and up suites (up to 4 people). AE, DC, DISC, MC, V. Free outdoor parking. **Amenities:** Restaurant; outdoor pool; small exercise room; Jacuzzi; tour desk; car-rental desk; business center; 24-hr. room service; coin-op washers available at Residence Inn next door; laundry service; dry cleaning; nonsmoking rooms; executive-level rooms. *In room:* A/C, TV w/pay movies, dataport, minifridge, coffeemaker, hair dryer, iron and board, safe.

EXPENSIVE

La Quinta Inn ✯   This is a tranquil and immediately visually appealing (within the limited range of chains) alternative to the Strip's hubbub, featuring courtyards, rustic benches, attractive pools, barbecue grills, and picnic tables. The staff is terrific—friendly and incredibly helpful. The rooms are immaculate and attractive. Executive rooms feature one queen-size bed, a small refrigerator, a wet bar, and a microwave oven—spend the extra money for it. Double queens are larger but have no kitchen facilities. And two-bedroom suites are not just spacious, they are really full apartments, with large living rooms (some with sofa beds), dining areas, and full kitchens. Ground-floor accommodations have patios, and all accommodations feature bathrooms with oversize whirlpool tubs.

3970 Paradise Rd. (between Twain Ave. and Flamingo Rd.), Las Vegas, NV 89109. © **800/531-5900** or 702/ 796-9000. Fax 702/796-3537. www.laquinta.com. 251 units. $79 and up standard double, $89 and up executive queen; $115 and up suite. Rates include continental breakfast. Inquire about seasonal discounts. AE, DC, DISC, MC, V. Free self-parking. **Amenities:** Outdoor pool; Jacuzzi; tour desk; car-rental desk; free airport/Strip shuttle; coin-op washers; nonsmoking rooms. *In room:* A/C, TV w/pay movies, dataport, kitchens in executive rooms and suites, coffeemaker, hair dryer, iron and board.

Residence Inn by Marriott ⋇   Staying here is like having your own apartment in Las Vegas. The property occupies 7 acres of perfectly manicured lawns with tropical foliage and neat flower beds. It's a great choice for families and business travelers.

Accommodations, most with working fireplaces, are housed in condolike, two-story wood-and-stucco buildings fronted by little gardens. Studios have adjoining sitting rooms with sofas and armchairs, dressing areas, and fully equipped eat-in kitchens complete with dishwashers. Every guest receives a welcome basket of microwave popcorn and coffee. TVs have VCRs (you can rent movies nearby), and all rooms have balconies or patios. Duplex penthouses, some with cathedral ceilings, add an upstairs bedroom (with its own bathroom, phone, TV, and radio) and a full dining room.

3225 Paradise Rd. (between Desert Inn Rd. and Convention Center Dr.), Las Vegas, NV 89109. © **800/331-3131** or 702/796-9300. www.marriott.com. 192 units. $119 and up studio; $149 and up penthouse. Rates include continental breakfast and free breakfast buffet, offered in lobby lounge. AE, DC, DISC, MC, V. Free self-parking. **Amenities:** Outdoor pool; guests have access to small exercise room next door at the Marriott Suites; Jacuzzi; coin-op washers; nonsmoking rooms. *In room:* A/C, TV/VCR w/pay movies, dataport, kitchenette, coffeemaker, hair dryer, iron and board.

MODERATE

Best Western Mardi Gras Inn *Value*   This well-run little casino hotel has a lot to offer. A block from the Convention Center and close to major properties, its three-story building sits on nicely landscaped grounds. There's a gazebo out back where guests can enjoy a picnic lunch.

Accommodations are all spacious, queen-bedded minisuites with sofa-bedded living-room areas and eat-in kitchens, the latter equipped with wet bars, refrigerators, and coffeemakers. All are midlevel motel okay, but they were recently redone so the furnishings and so forth should be fresh. Staying here is like having your own little Las Vegas apartment. A pleasant restaurant/bar off the lobby, open from 6:30am to 11pm daily, serves typical coffee-shop fare; a 12-ounce prime rib dinner here is just $9.

3500 Paradise Rd. (between Sands Ave. and Desert Inn Rd.), Las Vegas, NV 89109. © **800/634-6501** or 702/731-2020. Fax 702/731-4005. www.mardigrasinn.com. 314 units. $59 and up double. Extra person $8. Rates include free continental breakfast. Children under 18 stay free in parent's room. AE, DC, DISC, MC, V. Free parking at your room door. **Amenities:** Small casino; restaurant; outdoor pool; Jacuzzi; tour desk; car-rental desk; business center; free airport shuttle; limited room service; coin-op washers; nonsmoking rooms. *In room:* A/C, TV w/pay movies, dataport, kitchenette, fridge, coffeemaker, iron and board.

Clarion Hotel & Suites—Emerald Springs ⋇ *Value*   Recently switched from the Holiday Inn brand to Clarion, we aren't sure if over time that will make an ounce of difference. We hope that if it does, it's not for the negative. Housed in three peach stucco buildings, the Emerald Springs offers a friendly, low-key alternative to the usual glitz and glitter of Vegas accommodations. You'll enter via a charming marble-floored lobby with a waterfall fountain and lush, faux tropical plantings under a domed skylight. Off the lobby is a comfortably furnished lounge with a large-screen TV and working fireplace. Typical of the inn's hospitality, there is a bowl of apples for the taking at the front desk (something we usually only see in more expensive hotels—why is that? It's not like the fruit is expensive). Although your surroundings here are serene, you're only 3 blocks from the heart of the Strip.

Public areas and rooms here are notably clean and spiffy. Pristine hallways are hung with nice abstract paintings and have small seating areas on every level, and rooms are nicely decorated with bleached-oak furnishings. Even the smallest accommodations (studios) offer small sofas, desks, and armchairs with hassocks.

325 E. Flamingo Rd. (between Koval Lane and Paradise Rd.), Las Vegas, NV 89109. (C) **800/732-7889** or 702/732-9100. Fax 702/731-9784. www.clarionlasvegas.com. 150 units. $69 and up studio; $99 and up whirlpool suite, $129 and up hospitality suite. Extra person $15. Children under 19 stay free in parent's room. AE, DC, DISC, MC, V. Free self-parking. **Amenities:** Restaurant; outdoor pool; small exercise room; Jacuzzi; concierge; tour desk; car-rental desk; courtesy limo to airport or Strip; nonsmoking rooms; executive-level rooms. *In room:* A/C, TV w/pay movies, dataport, kitchenette or minibar with fridge, coffeemaker, hair dryer, iron and board.

Fairfield Inn by Marriott (Value)

This pristine property is a pleasant place to stay. It has a comfortable lobby with sofas and armchairs, where coffee, tea, and hot chocolate are provided free all day. Rooms are cheerful. Units with king-size beds have convertible sofas, and all accommodations offer well-lit work areas with desks; TVs have free movie channels as well as pay-movie options. Local calls are free. Breakfast pastries, fresh fruit, juice, and yogurt are served free in the lobby each morning, and many restaurants are within easy walking distance.

3850 Paradise Rd. (between Twain Ave. and Flamingo Rd.), Las Vegas, NV 89109. (C) **800/228-2800** or 702/791-0899. Fax 702/791-2705. www.fairfieldinn.com. 129 units. $62 and up (up to 5 people). Rates include continental breakfast. AE, DC, DISC, MC, V. Free self-parking. **Amenities:** Outdoor pool; small exercise room; Jacuzzi; tour desk; car-rental desk; airport shuttle; dry cleaning; nonsmoking rooms. *In room:* A/C, TV w/pay movies, dataport, iron and board.

Hawthorn Suites ★★

This "all-suite" hotel has plenty of extras, making it stand out from its brethren, and is extremely appealing to families. Sure, the suites themselves are bland, but they have full kitchens (perfect for families seeking to save some money) and actual balconies, a huge relief in stuffy Vegas where the windows usually don't open. There is a full free breakfast buffet, and an evening happy hour with snacks. The pool is large, and they've got courts for basketball and volleyball. And they take pets! All this, just a block from the corner of the Strip and Trop! This is really a lifesaver for families looking for a nice place not too far off the beaten path (especially if said family is using Vegas as a stopping point during a family vacation with Fido)—think of the savings with the free breakfast, the snacks, and that full kitchen for other meals.

5051 Duke Ellington Way, Las Vegas, NV 89119. (C) **800/811-2450** or 702/739-7000. Fax 702/739-9350. www.hawthorn.com. 280 units. $79–$109 1-bedroom suite (up to 4 people), $109–$169 2-bedroom suite (up to 6 people). Cribs free, no rollaways. Rates include complimentary breakfast. AE, DC, DISC, MC, V. Free outdoor parking. Pets accepted. **Amenities:** Outdoor pool; Jacuzzi; small exercise room; coin-op washers; laundry service; dry cleaning; nonsmoking rooms. *In room:* A/C, TV w/pay movies, dataport, full kitchen, hair dryer, iron and board.

Sam's Town Hotel & Gambling Hall ★

Just 5 miles from the Strip (which means it's not precisely near anything, but if you have a car, it's also not far), Western-themed Sam's Town is immensely popular with locals and tourists alike. This unexpectedly pleasing resort is well worth considering for the price. Off the beaten track though it may be, regular (if not exactly frequent), free shuttles to the Strip and Downtown may help you with any feelings of isolation. The addition of a new entertainment complex (including an 18-screen movie theater and a child-care center) makes it an even more positive option, particularly for families.

Sam's Town's main draw is its centerpiece atrium, a high-rising edifice that is part park, part Western vista. With living trees and splashing fountains, plus silly Animatronic animals, it's kind of goofy, but also a nice, albeit artificial (as if that's unusual for Vegas) place to wander through and sit in, which is a rare thing for this town. And if it's a bit noisy, well, we'll take the splashing sounds of the water over the ca-chinging of slots any day. The other public areas, including the casino, have gotten a face-lift. If it isn't up to the impossible standards set by the new Strip hotels, everything is certainly less dated and dark.

Rooms are adequately sized if a tad dim, thanks to the Western/Native American–themed decor, but they are clean and fine, especially for the price. All either have mountain views (higher up is much better) or inside-atrium views, which are great fun.

And bless it, having completed an end-to-end remodel, the hotel is now starting a whole new remodeling. And while we love it when a place does not rest on its laurels but constantly seeks the improvements of change, that also means that every time we come here, there is some wall up indicating that construction is going on, and every place within the hotel is subject to the whims of fortune and decor. The point being, don't totally count on anything we've mentioned above being here forever—after all, they took out a diner with the best burger in town and a large country-and-western dance hall of considerable tradition.

Sam's Town Firelight Buffet is described on p. 171. There's a variety of other dining options, including a cart in the atrium that serves homemade ice cream.

Roxy's Saloon, 1 of 13 bars on the premises, offers live entertainment (country and western) for dancing, daily from noon to the wee hours. There's also a deli in the race-and-sports-book area, a bowling alley snack bar, a food court, an ice-cream parlor, and the aforementioned 18-screen movie theater and entertainment complex, complete with child-care facility.

The **Sunset Stampede** is a laser-and-water show that takes place four times daily (at 2, 6, 8, and 10pm) in the Mystic Falls Park. It begins with a howl from an Animatronic wolf atop the waterfall, and then water spurts in sync with orchestral themes, as lasers fire pretty colors around the room. As a 10-minute show, it's not long enough or special enough to be worth the drive from the Strip (though there are free buses to transport you—call for details). But if you happen to be around, grab a seat at the bar early. This is particularly important for kids, as it gets pretty crowded, and it's tough to see the show unless you are close up.

The enormous, three-floor casino has a friendly, casual atmosphere.

5111 Boulder Hwy. (at Flamingo Rd.), Las Vegas, NV 89122. © **800/634-6371** or 702/456-7777. Fax 702/454-8014. www.samstownlv.com. 650 units. $50 and up double; $140 and up suite. Extra person $10. Children under 16 stay free in parent's room. AE, DC, DISC, MC, V. Free self- and valet parking. **Amenities:** Huge casino; showrooms; 12 restaurants; outdoor pool; day-care center for children 3–12 (charges apply); video arcade; tour desk; car-rental desk; shuttle to airport, Strip, and Downtown; laundry service; nonsmoking rooms. *In room:* A/C, TV w/pay movies, dataport.

Tuscany Hotel & Casino 🟊   This may be the right kind of hybrid between chain hotel and fancier resort—not as lush as the latter, but not anywhere near as expensive, either, with far more personal detail and indulgent touches than you can find at chains. It's another "all-suite" hotel, and another where "suite" really means "very big room." The rooms aren't memorable, just like the chain rooms, but they are brand-spanking new, and smart enough so that you won't get depressed like you might when you see some of the rooms in similarly priced

Tips **Cheap Hotel Alternatives**

If you're determined to come to Vegas during a particularly busy season and you find yourself shut out of the prominent hotels, here's a list of moderate to very inexpensive alternatives.

On or Near the Strip
Budget Suites of America, 1500 Stardust Rd.; ☎ 702/732-1500
Budget Suites of America, 4205 W. Tropicana Ave.; ☎ 702/889-1700
Budget Suites of America, 3655 W. Tropicana Ave.; ☎ 702/739-1000
Econo Lodge, 211 E. Flamingo Rd.; ☎ 800/221-2222
Travelodge, 3735 Las Vegas Blvd. S.; ☎ 800/578-7878

Paradise Road & Vicinity
Budget Suites of America, 3684 Paradise Rd.; ☎ 702/699-7000

Downtown & Vicinity
Budget Inn, 301 S. Main St.; ☎ 800/959-9062
Econo Lodge, 1150 S. Las Vegas Blvd.; ☎ 800/553-2666

East Las Vegas & Vicinity
Budget Suites of America, 4625 Boulder Hwy.; ☎ 702/454-4625
Budget Suites of America, 4855 Boulder Hwy.; ☎ 702/433-3644
Motel 6 Boulder Highway, 4125 Boulder Hwy.; ☎ 800/466-8356
Super 8 Motel, 5288 Boulder Hwy.; ☎ 800/825-0880

West Las Vegas & Vicinity
Motel 6, 5085 Industrial Rd. (South Las Vegas); ☎ 800/466-8356
Parkfield Motel, 5201 S. Industrial Rd. (South Las Vegas); ☎ 800/32-MOTEL

hotels. The large complex (27 acres, complete with a winding pool) isn't so much Italian as it is vaguely evoking the idea of Italian architecture, but it, too, is more stylish than most of the chains in town. And, unlike those other chains, this one comes with a large casino, roped off in such a way that this is still an appropriate place for families who want the best of all worlds (price, looks, family-friendly atmosphere, and gambling), especially as the rooms come with a separate dining area, a kitchenette, and large TVs, plus convertible couches on request. (And while the kids play, there is a large soaking tub for their folks to relax in.) There's a good Italian restaurant on the premises, plus a lounge.

255 E. Flamingo Rd., Las Vegas, NV 89109. ☎ 877/887-2261 or 702/893-8933. www.tuscanylasvegas.com. 700 units. $69–$110 suite. AE, MC, V. **Amenities:** Restaurant; lounge; fitness center; casino; swimming pool; concierge; car rental; business center; room service; dry cleaning/laundry. *In room:* A/C, TV, dataport, Nintendo, fridge, coffeemaker, hair dryer, iron and ironing board, safe.

INEXPENSIVE

Motel 6   Fronted by a big neon sign, Las Vegas's Motel 6 is the largest in the country, and it happens to be a great budget choice. Most Motel 6 properties are a little out of the way, but this one is quite close to major Strip casino hotels (the MGM is nearby). It has a big, pleasant lobby, and the rooms, in two-story, cream-stucco buildings, are clean and attractively decorated. Some rooms have showers only; others have tub and shower bathrooms. Local calls are free.

195 E. Tropicana Ave. (at Koval Lane), Las Vegas, NV 89109. ⓒ 800/4-MOTEL-6 (466-8356) or 702/798-0728. Fax 702/798-5657. 602 units. Sun–Thurs $35 and up single, Fri–Sat $58 and up single. Extra person $6. Children under 17 stay free in parent's room. AE, DC, DISC, MC, V. Free parking at your room door. **Amenities:** 2 outdoor pools; Jacuzzi; tour desk; coin-op washers; nonsmoking rooms. *In room:* A/C, TV w/pay movies.

Super 8 Motel   Billing itself as "the world's largest Super 8 Motel," this friendly property occupies a vaguely Tudor-style stone-and-stucco building. Free coffee is served in a pleasant little lobby furnished with comfortable sofas and wing chairs. Rooms are clean and well maintained.

The nautically themed **Ellis Island Restaurant,** open 24 hours, offers typical coffee-shop fare at reasonable prices. In the adjoining bar—a library-like setting with shelves of books and green marble tables—sporting events are aired on TV monitors. The **Ellis Island casino** (actually located next door) has a race book and 50 slot/poker/21 machines; a bar here has a karaoke machine.

4250 Koval Lane (just south of Flamingo Rd.), Las Vegas, NV 89109. ⓒ 800/800-8000 or 702/794-0888. 290 units. Sun–Thurs $41 and up double, Fri–Sat $56 and up double. Extra person $8. Children under 13 stay free in parent's room. AE, DC, DISC, MC, V. Pets $8 per night (1 pet only). Free self-parking. **Amenities:** Casino next door; restaurant; outdoor pool; Jacuzzi; tour desk; car-rental desk; airport shuttle; coin-op washers; nonsmoking rooms. *In room:* A/C, TV w/pay movies.

Terrible's ★ *Finds*   First of all, this place isn't terrible at all (the owner is Ed "Terrible" Herbst, who operates a chain of convenience stores and gas stations). Second, it isn't a bit like the hotel it took over, the rattrap known as the Continental. The Continental is gone, and good riddance. In its place is an unexpected bargain, a hotel with ridiculously low prices offered frequently. Try this on for size: $29 a night! Near the Strip! Near a bunch of really good restaurants! Hot diggity! So what are we getting? Well, don't expect much in the way of memorable rooms; they are as basic as can be (despite some sweet attempts with artwork depicting European idylls), and some have views of a wall (though even those get plenty of natural light). Some, however, are considerably larger than others, so ask. The pool area is a surprise; it looks like what you might find in a nice apartment complex (which, actually, is what Terrible's resembles on the outside), with plenty of palms and other foliage. There's a small but thoroughly stocked casino (not to mention penny slots, continuing the budget theme) plus a very good 24-hour coffee shop. How could you want for anything more? Did we mention price and location? Plus a free airport shuttle? Okay, so we all wish they had used a bit more imagination with the rooms.

4100 Paradise Rd. (at Flamingo Rd.), Las Vegas, NV 89109 ⓒ 800/640-9777 or 702/733-7000. Fax 702/765-5109. www.terribleherbst.com/casinos/terriblescasinolasvegas. 374 units. Sun–Thurs $29 and up double, Fri–Sat $59 and up double. Extra person $10. Children under 13 stay free in parent's room. AE, DC, DISC, MC, V. Free self- and valet parking. **Amenities:** 3 restaurants; outdoor pool; 24-hr. room service; laundry service; nonsmoking rooms. *In room:* A/C, TV w/pay movies, dataport, pay-per-use Nintendo, coffeemaker, hair dryer.

7 Downtown
EXPENSIVE

Castaways ★   Close to neither the Strip nor Downtown, this nearly 50-year-old hotel has gone through a few incarnations, but none quite so significant as the latest, which saw a name and theme change. In other words, if you are looking for the venerable Showboat, it's here, under the Tom Hanks movie title name. Gone is the most recent Mardi Gras theme and in its place is a tropical/Polynesian atmosphere; nothing this town doesn't have bigger and better elsewhere, but the public areas do look improved with their foliage (real and

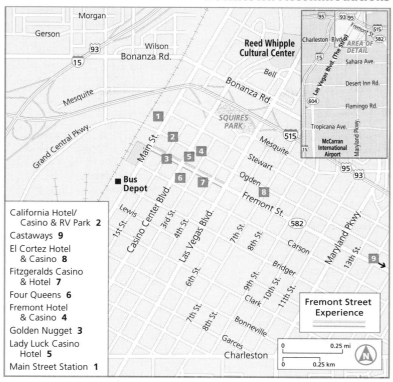

Morgan

Gerson

93
15

Wilson
Bonanza Rd.

Mesquite

Grand Central Pkwy.

Bonanza Rd.

Bell

Reed Whipple
Cultural Center

SQUIRES
PARK

**Bus
Depot**

Main St.

Casino Center Blvd.

Lewis

1st St.

3rd St.

4th St.

6th St.

7th St.

8th St.

Las Vegas Blvd.

Mesquite

Stewart

Ogden

Fremont St.

582

7th St.

8th St.

9th St.

10th St.

11th St.

Carson

Bridger

Clark

Bonneville

Garces

Charleston

515

Maryland Pkwy.

13th St.

**Fremont Street
Experience**

95

93

9

AREA OF
DETAIL

Charleston Blvd.

Fremont St.

95   93 95
515
582

Las Vegas Blvd. (The Strip)

15   Sahara Ave.

Desert Inn Rd.

604   Flamingo Rd.

Tropicana Ave.

**McCarran
International
Airport**

15

Maryland Pkwy.

0   0.25 mi
0   0.25 km

N

California Hotel/
   Casino & RV Park **2**

Castaways **9**

El Cortez Hotel
   & Casino **8**

Fitzgeralds Casino
   & Hotel **7**

Four Queens **6**

Fremont Hotel
   & Casino **4**

Golden Nugget **3**

Lady Luck Casino
   Hotel **5**

Main Street Station **1**

---

faux), stone, and woodwork. It was already a good-looking, if low-profile hotel, and the changes have made it even more attractive. Rates here can be quite low, so if you don't mind the out-of-the-immediate-action location (nothing having a car can't easily handle—5 min. to Downtown, 10-plus to the Strip), this can be a decent budget alternative. The rooms have not yet had the benefit of a remodeling, and given the new owners' recent financial woes, it may be some-time before that happens. Currently, rooms are adequately good-looking and comfortable, though the rooms in the three-story motel building around the pool can be dark (this is alleviated somewhat by sliding glass doors and small patios in first-floor rooms). RV travelers may want to take advantage of the 84-space park with full hook-ups, private showers, a dog run, and a live-in manager.

The casino is popular with locals. And the hotel was the first to offer buffet meals and bingo, not to mention a bowling alley. The bowling alley, North America's largest, used to host major PBA tournaments, and the new owners are attempting to bring them back again. The Windjammer lounge by the main casino offers free entertainment (not even a drink minimum at the tables, which most, if not all, of the other hotel lounges do), including bands such as the Coasters and the Drifters (pretty good free stuff, if you ask us). The hotel is also doing a big promotion with local golf courses, with packages including cheap rooms and special greens fees and the like. This might be a nice enticement if you are going to golf and not gamble.

Note: At press time, Castaways had filed for Chapter 11 bankruptcy and, though it is still in operation, its prospects—including a transformation into a Holiday Inn property—had dimmed considerably.

2800 Fremont St. (between Charleston Blvd. and Mojave Rd.), Las Vegas, NV 89104. © **800/826-2800** or 702/385-9123. Fax 702/383-9238. www.castaways-lv.com. 447 units. $129 and up double; $149 and up 1-bedroom suite, $195 and up 2-bedroom suite. Extra person $10. Children under 12 stay free in parent's room. Inquire about golf packages. AE, DC, DISC, MC, V. Free self- and valet parking. **Amenities:** Casino; 4 restaurants; outdoor pool; tour desk; car-rental desk; limited room service; in-room massage; laundry service; dry cleaning; nonsmoking rooms. *In room:* A/C, TV w/pay movies, coffeemaker.

Golden Nugget ★★   The Golden Nugget opened in 1946 as the first building in Las Vegas constructed specifically for casino gambling. Steve Wynn, who is basically responsible for the "new" Vegas hotel look, took the Golden Nugget over as his first major project in Vegas in 1973. He gradually transformed the Old West/Victorian interiors (typical for Downtown) into something more high rent; marble and brass gleam, and the whole package seems considerably more resortlike and genuinely luxurious, especially for downtown Vegas. The sunny interior spaces are a welcome change from the Las Vegas tradition of dim artificial lighting. Don't forget their mascot (well, it ought to be): the world's largest gold nugget. The *Hand of Faith* nugget weighs in at 61 pounds, 11 ounces, and is on display for all to see.

If the decor of The Mirage sounds appealing to you and you want to stay Downtown, come here, because the same people own them and the rooms look almost identical—in fact, when The Mirage redid their rooms from a beige palette to a more vividly hued one, the Golden Nugget had the exact same remodel. In the North Tower, the rooms are slightly larger than in the South (and also slightly larger than at The Mirage). You don't have to walk through the casino to get to your room, but you do have to walk a distance to get to the pool. During the winter, they put up a pavilion over part of the pool-deck space to allow for more interior space. The presence of the pool, and general overall quality, makes this the best hotel Downtown for families; the other Downtowners seem geared toward the much older set and/or the single-minded gambler set.

The Nugget's superb buffets and Sunday brunch are described in chapter 6. Oh, and yes, there is a casino (don't think they'd forget that!).

The Nugget's top-rated health club ($15-per-day fee to use the facilities) offers a full line of Universal equipment, Lifecycles, stair machines, treadmills, rowing machines, free weights, steam sauna, tanning beds, and massage. Salon treatments include everything from leg waxing to seaweed-mask facials. Free Sebastian products are available for sprucing up afterward. The spa's opulent Palladian-mirrored foyer is modeled after a room in New York's Frick Museum.

Note: As this book went to press, MGM MIRAGE sold the Golden Nugget and its sister hotel in Laughlin to two Internet entrepreneurs for $215 million. Though some changes are likely to be made in 2004—it's rumored that the new owners want to turn the Nugget into a modern version of "Old Vegas"— specifics are still unavailable.

129 E. Fremont St. (at Casino Center Blvd.), Las Vegas, NV 89101. © **800/634-3454** or 702/385-7111. Fax 702/ 386-8362. www.goldennugget.com. 1,907 units. $59 and up double; $275 and up suite. Extra person $20. AE, DC, DISC, MC, V. Free self- and valet parking. **Amenities:** Casino; showroom; 4 restaurants; outdoor pool; health club and spa; concierge; tour desk; car-rental desk; 24-hr. room service; laundry service; dry cleaning; nonsmoking rooms; executive-level rooms. *In room:* A/C, TV w/pay movies, dataport, hair dryer, iron and board, safe.

MODERATE

Fitzgeralds Casino & Hotel ★   Fitzgeralds recently got a new owner, the first African-American to own a Vegas casino, an interesting bit of trivia. At this writing, a few changes had already been made: Mr. O'Lucky, the hotel's longtime mascot, is already gone; the check-in area has been redone; and a new outdoor pool—open until the unheard of (in Vegas) hour of 9pm—opened in summer 2003. More renovation work and upgrading is scheduled to take place throughout 2004. Right now, you can expect a sort of Irish country-village walkway, complete with giant fake trees, leading to the room elevators. Fitzgeralds has the only balcony in Downtown from which you can watch the Fremont Street Experience. You can also sit in its McDonald's and gawk at the light show through the atrium windows.

The rooms are clean and comfortable, featuring standard hotel-room decor done in shades of green. Because this is the tallest building in Downtown (34 stories), you get excellent views: snowcapped mountains, Downtown lights, or the Strip. Whirlpool-tub rooms are $20 more and are slightly larger, offering wraparound windows.

301 Fremont St. (at 3rd St.), Las Vegas, NV 89101. © **800/274-LUCK** (274-5825) or 702/388-2400. Fax 702/388-2181. www.fitzgeralds.com. 638 units. $36 and up double; $60 and up suite. Extra person $10. Children under 19 stay free in parent's room. AE, DC, DISC, MC, V. Free self- and valet parking. **Amenities:** Casino; 5 restaurants; lounge; outdoor pool; concierge; tour desk; car-rental desk; courtesy car or limo; business center; 24-hr. room service; laundry service; dry cleaning; nonsmoking rooms. *In room:* A/C, TV w/pay movies, dataport, iron and board, safe.

Four Queens ✪   Opened in 1966 with a mere 120 rooms, the Four Queens (named for the owner's four daughters) has evolved over the decades into a major Downtown property occupying an entire city block. This property gets sold so often we think it's being used as a stake in some ongoing card game—it was just sold again, so the usual warnings about potential change still hold. The lobby is small but elegant—in a slightly faded, slightly dated way (with mirrors and huge chandeliers). In the Four Queens, you just know you're in Old Las Vegas. And you are glad. As the staff says, this is the place to stay if you just want to gamble—or if you want to experience the *real* old Las Vegas, and we don't just mean the clientele (though that, too; most are 50-plus and have been coming here for years). Another draw is the consistently helpful and friendly staff.

Rooms aren't going to blow you away, but note that the ones in the South Tower are a shade larger than the others, though we wouldn't hold any multiperson slumber parties in either. In most cases, rooms in the North Tower offer views of the Fremont Street Experience. The restaurant, **Hugo's Cellar** (p. 163), has a cozy lounge with a working fireplace, and two bars serve the casino.

202 Fremont St. (at Casino Center Blvd.), Las Vegas, NV 89101. © **800/634-6045** or 702/385-4011. Fax 702/387-5122. www.fourqueens.com. 690 units. $29 and up double; $119 and up suite. Extra person $15. AE, DC, DISC, MC, V. Free self- and valet parking. **Amenities:** Casino; 2 restaurants; small exercise room; limited room service; laundry service; dry cleaning; nonsmoking rooms. *In room:* A/C, TV w/pay movies, coffeemaker, hair dryer, iron and board, safe.

INEXPENSIVE

California Hotel/Casino & RV Park   This is a hotel with a unique personality. California-themed, it markets mostly in Hawaii, and since 85% of its guests are from the Aloha State, it offers Hawaiian entrees in several of its restaurants and even has an on-premises store specializing in Hawaiian foodstuffs. You'll also notice that dealers are wearing colorful Hawaiian shirts. The rooms, however, reflect neither California nor Hawaii; they have mahogany furnishings and attractive marble bathrooms.

12 Ogden Ave. (at 1st St.), Las Vegas, NV 89101. © **800/634-6255** or 702/385-1222. Fax 702/388-2660. www.thecal.com. 781 units. Sun–Thurs $50 and up double, Fri–Sat $60 and up double, holidays $70 and up double. Extra person $5. Children under 13 stay free in parent's room. AE, DC, DISC, MC, V. Free self- and valet

parking. **Amenities:** Casino; 4 restaurants; small rooftop pool; video arcade; tour desk; shopping arcade; limited room service; laundry service; dry cleaning; nonsmoking rooms. *In room:* A/C, TV w/pay movies, safe.

El Cortez Hotel & Casino   This small hotel is popular with locals for its casual, oh, and let's just admit it, dated Downtown atmosphere. Rooms offer nothing except a place to rest your head and not get lice. And there is no room to swing a cat, dead or otherwise, in the bathrooms. But on the other hand, said rooms supposedly do not cost more than $40 a night, so really, whaddaya want for next to nothing (by Vegas prices)? The nicest accommodations are the enormous minisuites in the 14-story tower. Some are exceptionally large king-bedded rooms with sofas; others have separate sitting areas with sofas, armchairs, and tables. Local calls are just 25¢. Note that although this place is but 2 blocks from Fremont Street, these are probably not 2 blocks you want to walk at night. Rumor has it that the company that bought the other hotels from the family who still owns the El Cortez has an option on it as well, and that all of them are destined for the wrecking ball.

Under the same ownership is **Ogden House,** just across the street, with rooms that go for just $18 a night. And that's everything you need to know right there.

600 Fremont St. (between 6th and 7th sts.), Las Vegas, NV 89101. ℂ **800/634-6703** or 702/385-5200. Fax 702/474-3626. www.elcortez.net. 428 units. $25 and up double; $40 minisuite. Extra person $5. AE, DISC, MC, V. Free self- and valet parking. **Amenities:** Casino; 2 restaurants; nonsmoking rooms. *In room:* A/C, TV.

Fremont Hotel & Casino   When it opened in 1956, the Fremont was the first high-rise in downtown Las Vegas. Wayne Newton got his start here, singing in the now-defunct Carousel Showroom. Step just outside the front door and there you are, in the Fremont Street Experience. Rooms are larger, more comfortable, and more peaceful than you might expect. (Though up until midnight you can hear, sometimes all too well, music and noise from the Fremont St. Experience show. But then again, if you are in bed before midnight in Vegas, it's your own fault.) The hotel encourages environmental awareness by changing linens only every other day; upon request, it can be more often, but why not help out the earth a bit? For that matter, why not help out your wallet a bit and stay here?

The Fremont boasts an Art Deco restaurant called the **Second Street Grill,** which is reviewed in chapter 6 along with the buffet. Guests can use the swimming pool and RV park at the nearby California Hotel, another Sam Boyd enterprise.

200 E. Fremont St. (between Casino Center Blvd. and 3rd St.), Las Vegas, NV 89101. ℂ **800/634-6182** or 702/385-3232. Fax 702/385-6229. www.fremontcasino.com. 452 units. $35 and up double. Extra person $8. Children under 12 stay free in parent's room. AE, DC, DISC, MC, V. Free valet parking; no self-parking. **Amenities:** Casino; 5 restaurants; tour desk; car-rental desk; free shuttle to Sam's Town; limited room service; laundry service; dry cleaning; nonsmoking rooms. *In room:* A/C, TV w/pay movies, fridge, coffeemaker, hair dryer, iron and board.

Lady Luck Casino Hotel   Today's Lady Luck opened in 1964 as Honest John's, a 2,000-square-foot casino with five employees, five pinball machines, and 17 slots. Today, that casino occupies 30,000 square feet, and the hotel, including sleek 17- and 25-story towers, is a major Downtown player, taking up an entire city block. What it retains from earlier times is a friendly atmosphere, one that has kept customers coming back for decades. Eighty percent of Lady Luck's clientele is repeat business.

A ton of dough was recently dumped into this venerable facility (by a national riverboat-owning chain), which means that while it doesn't look shockingly different, it has been given a face-lift that makes it, like a 60-year-old showgirl, a significant bit fresher. Nothing is special, but with these prices, it's well worth considering as a Downtown alternative. However, that same riverboat-owning chain has, at this writing, put the old gal up for sale (is there no end to the indignities of time and age?), and so who knows what her fate will be by the time you read this. Until then, Garden rooms are small and basic with nice motel-style furnishings, while tower rooms (the newer ones) have fresh carpeting and furnishings, and all are clean and comfy. In other words, it's good enough even before you get to the econo-prices.

206 N. 3rd St. (at Ogden Ave.), Las Vegas, NV 89101. ℭ **800/523-9582** or 702/477-3000. Fax 702/382-2346. www.ladyluckLv.com. 792 units. $40 and up double; Sun–Thurs $55 and up junior suite, Fri–Sat $70 and up junior suite. Extra person $8. AE, DC, DISC, MC, V. Free self- and valet parking. **Amenities:** Casino; small showroom; 3 restaurants; outdoor pool; tour desk; car-rental desk; free airport shuttle; limited room service; laundry service; dry cleaning; nonsmoking rooms. *In room:* A/C, TV w/pay movies, fridge, coffeemaker.

Main Street Station ★★ *Finds*   Though not actually on Fremont Street, the Main Street Station is just 2 short blocks away, barely a 3-minute walk. Considering how terrific it is, this is hardly an inconvenience. Having taken over an abandoned hotel space, the Main Street Station reopened in November 1996 to become, in our opinion, one of the nicest hotels in Downtown and one of the best bargains in the city.

The overall look here, typical of Downtown, is early-20th-century San Francisco. However, unlike everywhere else, the details here are outstanding, resulting in a beautiful hotel by any measure. Outside, gas lamps flicker on wrought-iron railings and stained-glass windows. Inside, you'll find hammered-tin ceilings, ornate antique-style chandeliers, and lazy ceiling fans. The small lobby is filled with wood panels, long wooden benches, and a front desk straight out of the Old West with an old-time key cabinet with beveled-glass windows. (Check out the painting of a Victorian gambling scene to the left of the front desk.) Even the cashier cages look like antique brass bank tellers' cages. It's all very appealing and just plain pretty. An enclosed bridge connects the hotel with the California across the street, where you will find shopping and a kids' arcade.

The long and narrow rooms are possibly the largest in Downtown, though the ornate decorating downstairs does not extend up here. White-painted, wooded plantation shutters replace the usual curtains; each room has a very large gilt-framed mirror; and the simple but not unattractive furniture is vaguely French Provincial. It's all clean and in good taste. The bathrooms are small but well appointed. Rooms on the north side overlook the freeway, and the railroad track is nearby. The soundproofing seems quite strong—we couldn't hear anything when inside, but then again, we're from L.A. A few guests have complained about noise in these rooms, but the majority haven't had any problems. If you're concerned, request a room on the south side.

The **Pullman Grille** is the steak-and-seafood place, and is much more reasonably priced than similar (and considerably less pretty) places in town. The stylish **Triple 7 Brew Pub** is described in detail in chapter 10. The excellent buffet is described in chapter 6. And the casino, thanks to some high ceilings, is one of the most smoke-free around.

200 N. Main St. (between Fremont St. and I-95), Las Vegas, NV 89101. ℭ **800/465-0711** or 702/387-1896. Fax 702/386-4466. www.mainstreetcasino.com 452 units. $45–$175 standard double. AE, DC, DISC, MC, V. Free self- and valet parking. **Amenities:** Casino; 3 restaurants; outdoor pool next door at California Hotel; car-rental desk; dry cleaning; nonsmoking rooms. *In room:* A/C, TV w/pay movies.

8 Henderson

VERY EXPENSIVE

Ritz-Carlton, Lake Las Vegas ★★★ *Kids*   Vegas prides itself, these days, on offering all sorts of "luxury resorts." Vegas exaggerates—in some cases, by a lot.

Truth be told, this is the *only* luxury resort (Four Seasons Las Vegas is a luxury hotel more than anything else, because of its set-up), and it's not even in Las Vegas. It's on the outskirts of next-door suburb Henderson, on the shores of Lake Las Vegas. Which means a 30-minute or so drive from the Strip.

Why on earth are we recommending it? Because to come here is to come to a gobsmackingly beautiful resort—between the sparkling water and the crisp mountains, all the better in the early evening with a warm breeze blowing, this is the serene oasis everyone dreams of when they come to the desert. Plus, it has all the pampering bells and whistles you could want. Here's the thing you have to remember: Those Strip "resorts" aren't in the hotel business, they are in the casino business. The hotel is just a sideline. Ritz-Carlton is a proper hotelier and you are the beneficiary. Certainly, the price is not cheap (though watch the web-site for some *great* deals) but once you realize what's included—all manner of treats that Strip "resorts" will charge you for as extras, plus impeccable service and a setting that's a dream—it's not a bad deal. Come here for a true getaway, and treat Vegas as a nearby attraction, an additional perk for your vacation.

Set right on the shores of the man-made (but so's Lake Mead and we've gotten over it) Lake Las Vegas, and styled like an Italian lakeside resort, this property couldn't be more handsome, from the lobby to the cool-palette rooms, with plump beds, comforters and Frette linens. All bathrooms are large and fully mar-bled (not tile, but real marble), with deep long soaking tubs and amenities for miles. Most of the rooms have water views (make sure you get one of those) either of the serpentine lake (our favorite) or of the little bay that abuts the property. Some have balconies, and all have windows that open (keep an eye on the lake for sights of the big fish that occasionally cruise just below the surface).

The health club is the sort where all machines have flat-screen TVs, and the spa offers hot and cold plunge pools, plus a 360-degree Vichy shower. There is one basic pool and one "sandy beach" little dipping area. And the overall service? We felt like if we sneezed, three people would have rushed at us with tissues, and four would have called doctors, just to make sure we were okay. It's also quiet, a great change from the hurly-burly found at most Strip hotels. And yet, it's not at all stuffy; no one minds if you run around in a bathing suit and bare feet.

The activities are the best around, from a large array of desert and mountain hikes, both on your own and guided (including a restful evening one that includes a round of tai chi), to stargazing (you are far enough from city lights so the looking is good), to boating on the lake, to honest to gosh fly-fishing. Daily yoga sessions and other physical fitness classes are also offered. And the hotel has access to three high-level golf courses.

Parents in particular should note that the Club Level rooms offer, for an extra $100 a night, access to a lounge (complete with its own concierge and even more fabulous service), with nearly round-the-clock free "snacks," generous (and most of the time, rather fancy) enough to cover all your meal needs—that, plus free drinks, alcoholic and otherwise, makes this option a bargain. (Think how much you spend on meals and drinks, and tell us that it doesn't routinely go over an extra $100 a day.) Right next door is a charming faux Italian village with nearly 40 shops and restaurants (so you need not rely on the hotel's restaurant, though it is excellent), plus a large, if borderline dull, casino, if you want that kind of action but don't want to drive to the Strip. There are regular shuttles to the Strip until 2am, never fear, though why anyone would leave here is beyond us.

1610 Lake Las Vegas Pkwy., Henderson, NV 89011. (℃ **800/241-3333** or 702/567-4700. Fax 702/567-4777. www.ritzcarlton.com. 349 units. $229–$259 (additional charge for rollaway bed). AE, DC, DISC, MC, V. Pets

accepted. **Amenities:** Restaurant; bar; concierge; 2 pools; health club and spa; business center; shuttle to Strip; water taxis to nearby attractions; some free exercise classes; 24-hr. room service; in-room massage; babysitting; laundry and dry cleaning; nonsmoking rooms; Club-level rooms. *In room:* A/C, TV w/pay movies, Nintendo, dataport, high-speed Internet access (for a fee), minibar, hair dryers, irons and ironing boards, safe.

EXPENSIVE

Green Valley Ranch Resort ★★ Now, for all our heartfelt rhapsodizing above about the Ritz, do not think that we love Green Valley any less. It's not fair to this flat-out fabulous resort to compare the two—they can't quite compete on the same playing field, because it doesn't have the same level of pedigree as the Ritz, nor does it have the knockout physical positioning on the lake. But it makes up for that with earnest efforts and lower prices (plus it's about half the distance back to the Strip, which is visible from the pool area), and if you can't stay at the one, you won't be unhappy staying at the other. Two different experiences, but each will make you feel like a resort should. Anyway, it seems that Green Valley's designers took careful notes on places like the Ritz-Carlton when coming up with their design—the interiors, rooms and public spaces both, feel completely influenced by same, while the exterior pool area borrowed much from hip hotel concepts such as the Standard and the W. This sounds like a potentially risky combination, but it works smashingly. You can stay here with your parents or your kids and every age group should be happy.

Inside all is posh and stately, a dignified classy lobby, large rooms with the most comfortable beds in town (high-thread-count linens, feather beds, plump down comforters) and luxe marble bathrooms. Outside is the hippest pool area this side of the aforementioned Hard Rock; part lagoon, part geometric, with shallow places for reading and canoodling, and your choice of poolside lounging equipment, ranging from teak lounge chairs to thick mattresses strewn with pillows, plus drinks served from the trendy Whiskey Beach. The tiny health club is free, and the spa is also modern and hip. At night, you can hang out at the ultra-trendy Whiskey Sky as more mattresses and pillows get strewn about, all the better to attract the most beautiful bodies in town (desperate souls try to get past the velvet rope—you can pass with ease because you are staying here), or you can head over to the entirely separate (as in, an adjoining building) casino area, which offers a disappointingly old school–looking gambling area, plus a variety of restaurants, from a Pancake House to a small Stage Deli to fine steaks and fried goodies at kicky BullShrimp. There is also a multiscreen movie theater.

2300 Paseo Verde Pkwy. (at I-215), Henderson, NV 89052. (✆ **866/782-9487** or 702/782-9487. Fax 702/617-6885. www.greenvalleyranchresort.com. 200 units. Sun–Thurs $109 and up double, Fri–Sat $159 and up double. Extra person $12. Children under 12 stay free in parent's room. AE, DC, DISC, MC, V. Free self- and valet parking. **Amenities:** Casino; lounge; 10 restaurants; outdoor pool; health club and spa; Jacuzzi; sauna; concierge; business center; 24-hr. room service; in-room massage; laundry service; dry cleaning; non-smoking rooms; executive-level rooms. *In room:* A/C, TV w/pay movies, high-speed Internet access (for a fee), dataport, coffeemaker, hair dryer, iron and board, safe.

6

Where to Dine

Among the many images that come to mind when people think of Las Vegas are cheap food deals, bargains so good the food is practically free. They think of the buffets—all a small country can eat—for only $3.99!

All that is true, but frankly, eating in Las Vegas is no longer something you don't have to worry about budgeting for. The buffets are certainly there—no good hotel would be without one—as are the cheap meal deals, but you get what you pay for. Some of the cheaper buffets, and even some of the more moderately priced ones, are mediocre at best, ghastly and inedible at worst. And we don't even want to *think* about those 69¢ beef stew specials.

However, there is some good, indeed, almost unheard-of news on the Vegas food scene. Virtually overnight, there has been an explosion of new restaurants that are actually of high quality. For this, we can thank those new luxury-resort hotels, whose management realized that food today is a major indulgence and obsession, and thus a significant part of the vacation experience. All of a sudden, Vegas can hold its head up alongside other big cities as a legitimate foodie destination.

Look at this partial list: Celebrity chefs Wolfgang Puck and Emeril Lagasse have half a dozen restaurants in town between them; deservedly famed chef Julian Serrano has set up shop at Bellagio's **Picasso;** and branches of L.A., New York, San Francisco, and Boston high-profile names such as **Pinot, Le Cirque, Aqua, Aureole, Olives, Star Canyon, Lutèce, Border Grill, Nobu,** and others have all rolled into town.

Unfortunately, this boom has affected only the very highest end of the price category. In other words, boy, can you eat well, as long as you have a trust fund. Even as dedicated foodies, we can't in good conscience tell you to eat only at places that will require taking out a small bank loan—except we just don't really have any other options. For the moment, with a few exceptions, it's hard to eat extremely well in Vegas (especially on the Strip) for a down-to-earth price. The buffets remain, certainly, but they're not the bargains they once were; the midprice-range food is, by and large, pretty forgettable; and the really low-end food found in the hotels—well, we try not to think of it as anything but fuel. Of course, this may not bother you as much as it bothers us.

If you get off the Strip, however, you can find some cheaper, more interesting alternatives, which we have listed below. If you're staying on the Strip and you don't have the mobility of a car, your food options will be severely limited. Getting outside of those enormous hotel resorts is a major proposition (and don't think that's not done on purpose), which is why visitors often settle for what the hotel has to offer—long lines and diminished quality. Walking to another hotel—on the Strip, yet another major investment of time—means probably encountering much of the same thing. But not always.

Once, when faced with dismal breakfast choices, we went from The Mirage
over to Caesars, landing in their
Forum Shops where the Stage Deli
stood, largely empty and with considerably better munchie options.

OUR BEST LAS VEGAS RESTAURANT ADVICE

GETTING IN   There are tricks to surviving dining in Vegas. If you can, make
reservations in advance, particularly for the better restaurants (you might get to
town, planning to check out some of the better spots, only to find they are totally
booked throughout your stay). Eat during off-hours when you can. Know that
noon to, say, 1:30 or 2pm is going to be prime time for lunch, and 5:30 to
8:30pm (and just after the early shows get out) for dinner. Speaking of time, give
yourself plenty of it, particularly if you have to catch a show. We once tried to
grab a quick bite in The Riviera before running up to *La Cage*. The only choice
was the food court, where long lines in front of all the stands (fast-food chains
only) left us with about 5 minutes to gobble something decidedly unhealthy.

STAYING HEALTHY   *Unhealthy* is the watchword here; if you don't care
about your heart or your waistline, you will do just fine in Vegas. (And really,
what says "vacation" more than cream sauce?) But slowly, salads are making their
way onto the menus, and some more health-conscious restaurants are opening.
You just have to look for them. And we certainly don't mean to take away any
enjoyment of those extravagant buffets; heck, that's a major part of the fun of
Vegas! Excess is the other watchword here, and what better symbol is there than
mounds of shrimp and unlimited prime rib?

SAVING MONEY   So you want to sample the creations of a celebrity chef, but
you took a beating at the craps table? Check our listings to see which of the
high-profile restaurants are open for lunch. Sure, sometimes the more interesting and exotic items are found at dinner, but the midday meal is usually no
slouch and can be as much as two-thirds cheaper.

Or skip that high-falutin' stuff all together. The late-night specials—a complete
steak meal for just a couple dollars—are also an important part of a good, decadent Vegas experience (and a huge boon for insomniacs). And having complained
about how prices are going up, we'll also tell you that you still can eat cheaply and
decently (particularly if you are looking upon food only as fuel) all over town. The
locals repeatedly say that they almost never cook, because in Vegas it is always
cheaper to eat out. To locate budget fare, check local newspapers (especially Fri
editions) and free magazines (such as *Vegas Visitor* and *What's On in Las Vegas*),

---

Tips **Hot Off the Presses**

September 2003 will see the opening of **Bouchon** (in the Venetian), a
branch of Thomas Keller's bistro in Napa Valley. Keller is best known for
The French Laundry, considered perhaps the best restaurant in the United
States. Bouchon in Napa offers what you might expect from a French
bistro—not just frites and paté, but divine *boudin blanc* (sausage made
with pork and rice) and other wonderful dishes. The chef on the premises
will be Michael Deimers, who worked at Rio's Napa under Jean Louis Pallidin and briefly at Alizé, and as both of those restaurants were/are among
the finest Vegas has ever seen, we can only imagine what working for
Keller is going to mean. You will see us there a lot.

which are given away at hotel reception desks (sometimes these sources also yield money-saving coupons).

ABOUT PRICE CATEGORIES The restaurants in this chapter are arranged first by location, then by the following price categories (based on the average cost of a dinner entree): **Very Expensive,** more than $20; **Expensive,** $15 to $20; **Moderate,** $10 to $15; **Inexpensive,** under $10 (sometimes well under). In expensive and very expensive restaurants, expect to spend no less than twice the price of the average entree for your entire meal with a tip; you can usually get by on a bit less in moderate and inexpensive restaurants. Buffets and Sunday brunches are gathered in a separate section at the end of this chapter.

A FINAL WORD As welcome as the influx of designer chefs is—and good lord, is it welcome—you can't help but notice that the majority are simply re-creating their best work from elsewhere, rather than producing something new. So the Vegas food scene remains, like its architecture, a copy of something from somewhere else. And as happy as we are to encourage you to throw money at these guys, please don't forget the mom and pop places, which struggle not to disappear into the maw of the big hotel machines, and who produce what comes the closest to true local quality. If you can, get in your car and check out some of the options listed below that are a bit off the beaten track. Show Vegas you aren't content—you want a meal you can brag about *and* afford, now!

1 Restaurants by Cuisine

AMERICAN

Buccaneer Bay Club ★ (Mid-Strip, $$$$, p. 136)

Carson Street Café (Downtown, $, p. 165)

Hard Rock Cafe ★ (East of the Strip, $$, p. 131)

Harley Davidson Cafe ★ (South Strip, $$, p. 131)

Rainforest Cafe ★ (South Strip, $$, p. 131)

Spago ★ (Mid-Strip, $$$$, p. 141)

Top of the World (North Strip, $$$$, p. 141)

ASIAN

Dragon Noodle Co. ★★ (South Strip, $$, p. 132)

Grand Wok and Sushi Bar ★★ (South Strip, $$, p. 132)

Spago ★ (Mid-Strip, $$$$, p. 141)

BAGELS

Einstein Bros. Bagels ★ (East of the Strip, $, p. 156)

BARBECUE

Memphis Championship Barbecue ★★ (East of the Strip, $$, p. 154)

BISTRO

Mon Ami Gabi ★★ (Mid-Strip, $$, p. 145)

Pinot Brasserie ★★ (Mid-Strip, $$$, p. 143)

BUFFETS/BRUNCHES

Bally's Big Kitchen Buffet (Mid-Strip, $$, p. 169)

Bally's Sterling Sunday Brunch ★★ (Mid-Strip, $$$$, p. 167)

Bellagio Buffet ★★ (Mid-Strip, $$$, p. 168)

The Buffet at the Las Vegas Hilton ★ (East of the Strip, $$, p. 171)

Circus Circus Buffet (North Strip, $, p. 170)

Excalibur's Round Table Buffet ★ (South Strip, $, p. 167)

Flamingo Paradise Garden Buffet ★ (Mid-Strip, $, p. 169)

Fremont Paradise Buffet ★ (Downtown, $, p. 171)

Key to Abbreviations: $$$$ = Very Expensive $$$ = Expensive $$ = Moderate $ = Inexpensive

Golden Nugget Buffet ★★
(Downtown, $$, p. 171)

Harrah's Fresh Market Buffet ★
(Mid-Strip, $$, p. 169)

Luxor's Pharaoh's Pheast Buffet ★★
(South Strip, $, p. 167)

Main Street Station Garden
Court ★★★ (Downtown,
$, p. 172)

Mandalay Bay's Bay Side Buffet ★
(South Strip, $$, p. 166)

MGM Grand Buffet ★ (South
Strip, $, p. 167)

Mirage Buffet ★★ (Mid-Strip,
$$, p. 169)

Monte Carlo Buffet ★ (South
Strip, $, p. 167)

Palms Festival Market Buffet ★★
(Mid-Strip, $, p. 170)

Paris, Le Village Buffet ★★★
(Mid-Strip, $$$, p. 168)

Rio's Carnival World Buffet ★★
(Mid-Strip, $, p. 170)

Sam's Town Firelight Buffet ★
(East of the Strip, $, p. 171)

Spice Market Buffet ★ (South
Strip, $$, p. 166)

Treasure Island Buffet ★
(Mid-Strip, $, p. 170)

Tropicana Island Buffet ★ (South
Strip, $$, p. 166)

CALIFORNIA

Gordon-Biersch Brewing
Company ★ (East of the Strip,
$$, p. 153)

Spago ★ (Mid-Strip, $$$$, p. 141)

Wolfgang Puck Café ★★ (South
Strip, $$, p. 133)

CHINESE

Cathay House (West Las Vegas,
$$, p. 160)

Chang's of Las Vegas ★ (North
Strip, $, p. 147)

COFFEE SHOP

Bougainvillea ★★ (East of the
Strip, $, p. 155)

CONTEMPORARY CREOLE

Delmonico Steakhouse ★★ (Mid-
Strip, $$$$, p. 136)

Emeril's New Orleans Fish House
★★ (South Strip, $$$$, p. 128)

CONTINENTAL

Buccaneer Bay Club ★ (Mid-Strip,
$$$$, p. 136)

Cafe Nicolle ★ (West Las Vegas,
$$$, p. 158)

Red Square ★★ (South Strip,
$$$$, p. 129)

Top of the World (North Strip,
$$$$, p. 141)

CREOLE

Commander's Palace ★★ (South
Strip, $$$$, p. 128)

CUBAN

Rincon Criollo (North Strip,
$, p. 149)

DELI

Leo's Deli ★ (East of the Strip,
$, p. 155)

Stage Deli ★★ (Mid-Strip,
$$, p. 146)

DESSERTS

Freed's Bakery (East of the Strip,
$, p. 162)

Luv-It Frozen Custard (North
Strip, $, p. 162)

DINER

Calypsos ★ (South Strip,
$, p. 134)

Liberty Cafe at the White Cross
Pharmacy ★★ (North Strip,
$, p. 148)

DONUTS

Krispy Kreme Donuts (West Las
Vegas, $, p. 162)

Ronald's Donuts (West Las Vegas,
$, p. 162)

FOOD COURT

Cypress Street Marketplace ★★
(Mid-Strip, $$, p. 145)

FRENCH

Alizé ★★★ (Mid-Strip,
$$$$, p. 135)

Andre's ★★ (Downtown,
$$$$, p. 163)

Le Cirque ⭐ (Mid-Strip,
  $$$$, p. 138)
Lutèce ⭐⭐ (Mid-Strip,
  $$$$, p. 138)
Pamplemousse ⭐ (East of the
  Strip, $$$$, p. 152)
Picasso ⭐⭐⭐ (Mid-Strip,
  $$$$, p. 139)

GERMAN
Cafe Heidelberg German Deli and
  Restaurant ⭐ (North Strip,
  $$, p. 147)

HUNGARIAN
Goulash Pot ⭐ (West Las Vegas,
  $, p. 161)

INDIAN
Shalimar (East of the Strip,
  $$, p. 154)

INTERNATIONAL
Hugo's Cellar ⭐ (Downtown,
  $$$$, p. 163)
Second Street Grill ⭐⭐ (Down-
  town, $$$, p. 164)

ITALIAN
Canaletto ⭐⭐ (Mid-Strip,
  $$$, p. 142)
Carluccio's Tivoli Gardens ⭐ (East
  of the Strip, $$, p. 153)
Circo ⭐⭐ (Mid-Strip,
  $$$, p. 142)
Fiore ⭐ (Mid-Strip, $$$$, p. 138)
Olives ⭐⭐ (Mid-Strip, $$, p. 146)
Onda ⭐⭐ (Mid-Strip,
  $$$$, p. 139)
Sazio ⭐ (South Strip, $$, p. 132)
Valentino ⭐ (Mid-Strip,
  $$$$, p. 142)

JAPANESE
Kabuki (East of the Strip,
  $$, p. 153)
Mizuno's ⭐⭐ (South Strip,
  $$$, p. 131)

MEDITERRANEAN
Mediterranean Café & Market ⭐
  (East of the Strip, $, p. 157)
Olives ⭐⭐ (Mid-Strip, $$, p. 146)

MEXICAN
Border Grill ⭐⭐⭐ (South Strip,
  $$$, p. 131)
Dona Maria Tamales ⭐⭐ (North
  Strip, $, p. 148)
El Sombrero Cafe ⭐⭐ (Down-
  town, $, p. 165)
Pink Taco ⭐ (East of the Strip,
  $$, p. 154)
Toto's ⭐⭐ (East of the Strip,
  $, p. 157)
Viva Mercados ⭐⭐ (West Las
  Vegas, $$, p. 161)

NOUVELLE AMERICAN
Aureole ⭐ (South Strip,
  $$$$, p. 127)
Rosemary's Restaurant ⭐⭐⭐
  (West Las Vegas, $$$, p. 158)

NOUVELLE ITALIAN
Renoir ⭐⭐ (Mid-Strip,
  $$$$, p.140)

PACIFIC RIM
Second Street Grill ⭐⭐ (Down-
  town, $$$, p. 164)

PROVENÇAL
Fiore ⭐ (Mid-Strip, $$$$, p. 138)

PUB FARE
Monte Carlo Pub & Brewery ⭐⭐⭐
  (South Strip, $, p. 134)

RUSSIAN
Red Square ⭐⭐ (South Strip,
  $$$$, p. 129)

SANDWICHES
Capriotti's ⭐⭐⭐ (North Strip,
  $, p. 147)

SEAFOOD
Aqua ⭐⭐ (Mid-Strip,
  $$$$, p. 135)
Austins Steakhouse ⭐⭐ (West Las
  Vegas, $$$, p. 157)
Drai's (Mid-Strip, $$$$, p. 137)
Lawry's The Prime Rib ⭐⭐⭐ (East
  of the Strip, $$$$, p. 150)
Limericks ⭐ (Downtown,
  $$$, p. 164)

Morton's of Chicago ⭐ (East of
the Strip, $$$$, p. 150)
The Palm ⭐⭐ (Mid-Strip,
$$$$, p. 139)
The Tillerman ⭐ (East of the
Strip, $$$$, p. 152)

SOUTHERN
House of Blues ⭐⭐ (South Strip,
$$$, p. 130)

SOUTHWESTERN
Coyote Cafe ⭐ (South Strip,
$$$$, p. 128)
Star Canyon ⭐ (Mid-Strip,
$$$, p. 144)

STEAK
Austins Steakhouse ⭐⭐ (West Las
Vegas, $$$, p. 157)
Delmonico Steakhouse ⭐⭐ (Mid-
Strip, $$$$, p. 136)
Drai's (Mid-Strip, $$$$, p. 137)
Lawry's The Prime Rib ⭐⭐⭐ (East
of the Strip, $$$$, p. 150)
Limericks ⭐ (Downtown,
$$$, p. 164)

Morton's of Chicago ⭐ (East of
the Strip, $$$$, p. 150)
The Palm ⭐⭐ (Mid-Strip,
$$$$, p. 139)
The Range ⭐⭐ (Mid-Strip,
$$$$, p. 140)
The Tillerman ⭐ (East of the
Strip, $$$$, p. 152)

SUSHI
Dragon Sushi (West Las Vegas,
$, p. 161)
Hyakumi ⭐ (Mid-Strip,
$$$, p. 143)

TEX-MEX
Z Tejas Grill ⭐ (East of the Strip,
$$, p. 155)

THAI
Komol (East of the Strip,
$$, p. 153)
Lotus of Siam ⭐⭐⭐ (East of the
Strip, $, p. 156)
Thai Spice (West Las Vegas,
$$, p. 161)

2 South Strip

Note: In addition to the restaurants listed in this section, the Monte Carlo has
a branch of Andre's, the French restaurant that has long been a favorite in
Downtown (p. 163). The South Strip branch is just as highly recommended for
fabulous food and attentive, not intimidating, service.

VERY EXPENSIVE

Aureole ⭐ *Overrated* NOUVELLE AMERICAN This branch of a New York
City fave (it's pronounced are-ree-*all*), run by Charlie Palmer, is noted locally for its
glass wine tower. Four stories of carefully chosen bottles (including the largest collection of Austrian wines outside of Austria, which are well worth trying for a new
wine experience) are plucked from their perches by comely, cat-suited lasses who fly
up and down via pulleys. It's quite the show, and folks come in just to watch.

Should you come for the food? Perhaps. Certainly the Asian-influenced
fusion is solid, but it's more consistently good than outstanding, and since it's
currently a fixed-price three-course meal, it may simply not be worth the price.
A recent visit found the duck foie gras mousse served with a sweet balsamic
sauce to be creamy, and the smoked capon ravioli very smoky indeed, but the
pasta casing was a little tough. A pepper-seared tuna entree with green-onion
risotto produced some sharp flavors, while the pan-roasted lobster was sweet,
and there was a hint of cinnamon in the caramelized fennel side. Desserts are
dainty but pale when compared to others around town.

In Mandalay Bay, 3950 Las Vegas Blvd. S. ℂ **702/632-7401**. Reservations required. Fixed-price dinner $55,
$75, or $95 for a tasting menu. AE, DISC, MC, V. Daily 6–11pm.

Commander's Palace ★★ CREOLE This is an offshoot of the famous New Orleans restaurant, which is considered the best in that town, and sometimes even the best in the country. We did not expect quite that high a level of, well, anything, from this branch, but we did expect a lot, and they came through. It doesn't look precisely like the one in New Orleans, so it wasn't the huge shock to the system we expected (what city are we in now?), but it does have that classic handsome old New Orleans restaurant wood paneling, big chandeliers, and that sort of thing. Service is nearly as good as at the original; no group of waiters hovering to fulfill every whim and remove every crumb, but we hardly felt neglected. And the food was, if not yet as spectacular as that of its elder cousin's, just about the best we've had in Vegas yet, with not one thing, from appetizer to dessert, that disappointed our palates. On the other hand, it's interesting to see how portions shrink and prices rise when exposed to the Vegas area code. You might be best off getting the $39 three-course Creole favorite, featuring Commander's justly legendary turtle soup with sherry, Louisiana pecan-crusted fish, and signature bread pudding soufflé, three things they do very, very well indeed. Shrimp rémoulade, though, is another fine starter, and the Chocolate Sheba is one of our top desserts. Overall, this is a really nice restaurant run by people who really care about the restaurant business.

3663 Las Vegas Blvd. S. (in the Desert Passage in the Aladdin hotel). © **702/892-8272.** www.commanders palace.com. Reservations suggested. Lunch $16–$28, dinner $25–$39. AE, DISC, MC, V. Daily 11:30am– 3:30pm and 6–10pm.

Coyote Cafe ★ SOUTHWESTERN Mark Miller was one of the first celebrity chefs to hit Vegas, way back before the current boom of trendy restaurants. His robust regional cuisine combines elements of traditional Mexican, Native American, Creole, and Cajun cookery. The Grill Room menu changes monthly, but on a recent visit we enjoyed a bibb-lettuce salad with a lovely, light lemon dressing and some fine, spicy pork chops. Desserts include a chocolate-banana torte served on banana crème anglaise and topped with a scoop of vanilla ice cream. The wine list includes many by-the-glass selections, including champagnes and sparkling wines, which nicely complement spicy Southwestern fare; Brazilian daiquiris are a house specialty.

The Cafe menu offers similar but somewhat lighter fare. Southwestern breakfasts ($6–$9.50) range from huevos rancheros to blue-corn pancakes with toasted pine nuts, honey butter, and real maple syrup.

In the MGM Grand, 3799 Las Vegas Blvd. S. © **702/891-7349.** Reservations recommended for the Grill Room, not accepted for the Cafe. Grill Room main courses $15–$32. Cafe main courses $7.50–$18 (many under $10). AE, DC, DISC, MC, V. Grill Room daily 5:30–10pm; cafe daily 8:30am–11pm.

Emeril's New Orleans Fish House ★★ CONTEMPORARY CREOLE Chef Emeril Lagasse, a ubiquitous presence on cable's Food Network, is becoming nearly as common in Vegas as in his adopted hometown of New Orleans. Seafood is the specialty here, flown in from Louisiana or from anywhere else that he finds the quality of the ingredients to be the very finest. Be sure to start off with one of Lagasse's savory "cheesecakes": a lobster cheesecake with tomato-tarragon sauce, topped with a dollop of succulent Louisiana choupique fish caviar. It's a heady, rich appetizer that may be completely unlike anything you've ever had. Oysters on the half shell are also a favorite, served with two tangy dipping sauces. And try the barbecued shrimp, which come in a garlic-and-herb butter sauce that will have you mopping your plate with bread. For an entree, try one of Lagasse's sauce-enhanced fish dishes. Meat eaters will also be very happy with

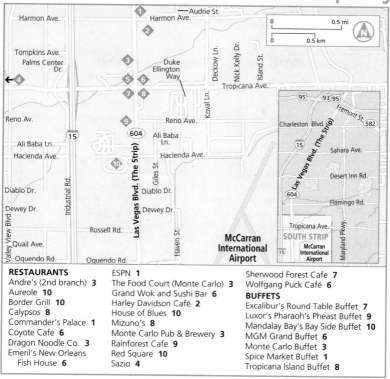

RESTAURANTS
Andre's (2nd branch) **3**
Aureole **10**
Border Grill **10**
Calypsos **8**
Commander's Palace **1**
Coyote Cafe **6**
Dragon Noodle Co. **3**
Emeril's New Orleans
  Fish House **6**

ESPN **1**
The Food Court (Monte Carlo) **3**
Grand Wok and Sushi Bar **6**
Harley Davidson Café **2**
House of Blues **10**
Mizuno's **8**
Monte Carlo Pub & Brewery **3**
Rainforest Cafe **9**
Red Square **10**
Sazio **4**

Sherwood Forest Cafe **7**
Wolfgang Puck Café **6**
BUFFETS
Excalibur's Round Table Buffet **7**
Luxor's Pharaoh's Pheast Buffet **9**
Mandalay Bay's Bay Side Buffet **10**
MGM Grand Buffet **6**
Monte Carlo Buffet **3**
Spice Market Buffet **1**
Tropicana Island Buffet **8**

the utterly tender and flavorful filet of beef with *tasso* (Louisiana Cajun dried ham), hollandaise sauce, and homemade Worcestershire.

It's difficult to recommend one particular dessert from the vast menu, but a slice of the banana-cream pie with banana crust and caramel drizzle is one of the finest desserts you will ever have.

In the MGM Grand, 3799 Las Vegas Blvd. S. ✆ **702/891-7374.** Reservations required. Main courses $12–$18 at lunch, $18–$38 at dinner (more for lobster). AE, DC, DISC, MC, V. Daily 11am–2:30pm and 5:30–10:30pm.

Red Square ✧✧ CONTINENTAL/RUSSIAN   The beheaded and pigeon-dropping-adorned statue of Lenin outside Red Square only hints at the near-profane delights on the interior. Inside you will find decayed posters that once glorified the Worker, cheek by jowl with a patchwork mix of remnants of Czarist trappings, as pillaged from toppled Bolsheviks and Stalinists. It is disconcerting to see the hammer and sickle so blithely and irreverently displayed, but then again, what better way to drain it of its power than to exploit it in a palace of capitalistic decadence? And then there's the ice-covered bar—all the better to keep your drinks nicely chilled. After all, they have 150 different kinds of vodka, perhaps the largest collection in the world. It's all just one big post-Communist party. (Sorry, we had to say it.)

Anyway, if you can tear your eyes away from the theme-run-amok, you might notice the menu is quite good, one of our favorites around. Blow your expense

You Gotta Have a Theme

It shouldn't be too surprising to learn that a town devoted to themes (what hotel worth its salt doesn't have one, at this point?) has one of virtually every theme restaurant there is. Almost all have prominent celebrity co-owners and tons of "memorabilia" on the walls, which in virtually every case means throwaway items from blockbuster movies, or some article of clothing a celeb wore once (if that) on stage or on the playing field. Almost all have virtually identical menus and have gift shops full of logo items.

This sounds cynical, and it is—but not without reason. Theme restaurants are for the most part noisy, cluttered, overpriced places that are strictly tourist traps, and, though some have their devotees, if you eat at one of these places, you've eaten at them all. We don't want to be total killjoys. Fans should have a good time checking out the stuff on the walls of the appropriate restaurant. And while the food won't be the most memorable ever, it probably won't be bad (and will be moderately priced). But that's not really what you go for.

The **House of Blues** ★★, in Mandalay Bay, 3950 Las Vegas Blvd. S. (🕿 **702/632-7607**; open daily 8am–1am on event nights and 'til midnight on nonevent nights), is, for our money, food and theme-wise, the best of the theme restaurants. The food is really pretty good (if a little more costly than it ought to be in a theme restaurant), and the mock Delta/New Orleans look works well, even if it is unavoidably commercial. You can dine here without committing to seeing whatever band is playing, as the dining room is separate from the club (note, though, that HOB gets very good bookings from nationally known acts). The gospel brunch might also be worth checking out (the food is good, but

account on some caviar (we found we liked nutty Osetra better than stronger Beluga), properly chilled in ice, served with the correct pearl spoon. Or try some steak tartare, mixed (with egg, onion, crème fraîche, and so forth) at your table, but if you don't like food with a generous kick to it, ask them to go lighter on the mustard sauce. Or, more affordably, nosh on Siberian nachos—smoked salmon, citron caviar, and crème fraîche. Arugula and spinach salad has slivers of pears, a bit of Stilton, and apple cider vinaigrette. The chef's special is a Roquefort-crusted, tender filet mignon, with some soft caramelized garlic and a fine reduction sauce; it's a grand piece of meat, one of the best in town and more cheaply priced than similarly ranked places. We also very much liked the pan-seared halibut with a roasted beet vinaigrette and basil oil on a mushroom risotto. Try a silly-themed drink, such as the "Cuban Missile Crisis," which is rain vodka, dark rum, sugarcane syrup, and lime juice, or better still, take advantage of that vodka menu and try a tasting flight of four kinds, joined by theme (in our case, the "Ultimate Flight" paired Polish, Russian, Scottish, and Estonian vodkas). Desserts are not as clever but are worth saving room for, especially the warm chocolate cake with a liquid center and the strawberries Romanoff.

In Mandalay Bay, 3950 Las Vegas Blvd. S. 🕿 702/632-7407. Reservations recommended. Main courses $17–$31. AE, DC, MC, V. Daily 5:30pm–midnight.

there's too much of it), but be warned: It's served inside the actual club, which is miked very loudly, and it can be unbelievably loud, so bring earplugs (we left with splitting headaches).

Presumably filling the hole left by the demise of the All Star Café, so that you sports fans won't feel left out in the theme restaurant race, **ESPN,** in New York–New York, 3790 Las Vegas Blvd. S. (© **702/933-3776;** open Mon–Thurs 11:30am–11pm, Fri 11am–midnight, Sat 9am–midnight, and Sun 9am–11pm), is a gigantic facility featuring rather wacky and entertaining sports memorabilia (such as Evel Knievel set up as the old "Operation" game, displaying his many broken bones), plus additions such as a rock-climbing wall/machine. It's pretty fun, actually, and the food, in a couch-potato-junk-food-junkie way, is not bad either, especially when you're sitting in one of the La-Z-Boy recliners, ordering delights such as three Krispy Kreme donuts topped with ice cream, whipped cream, and syrup, and watching sports.

There are those who rave about the warm Tollhouse-cookie pie at the **Harley Davidson Cafe** ⭐, 3725 Las Vegas Blvd. S. at Harmon Avenue (© **702/740-4555;** open Sun–Thurs 11am–11pm, Fri–Sat 11am–midnight).

The **Hard Rock Cafe** ⭐, 4475 Paradise Rd. at Harmon Avenue (© **702/ 733-8400;** open Sun–Thurs 11am–11:30pm, Fri–Sat 11am–1am), has decent burgers. The serious hipster quotient at the adjacent hotel means that the people-watching opportunities are best here.

Visually, the **Rainforest Cafe** ⭐, in the MGM Grand, 3799 Las Vegas Blvd. S. (© **702/891-8580;** open Sun–Thurs 8am–midnight, Fri–Sat 8am– 1am), with its jungle interior, complete with sound effects and Animatronic animals, is the best of the bunch.

EXPENSIVE

Border Grill ⭐⭐⭐ MEXICAN   For our money, here's the best Mexican food in town. This big, cheerful space (like a Romper Room for adults) houses a branch of the much-lauded L.A. restaurant, conceived and run by the Food Network's "Two Hot Tamales," Mary Sue Milliken and Susan Feniger. This is truly authentic Mexican home cooking—the Tamales learned their craft from the real McCoy south of the border—but with a nuevo twist. So don't expect precisely the same dishes you'd encounter in your favorite corner joint, but do expect fresh and fabulous food, sitting as brightly on the plates as the decor on the walls. Stay away from the occasionally bland fish and head right toward rich and cheesy dishes like chiles rellenos (with perfect black beans) and chicken *chilaquiles* (a sister to the taco), or try nuevo items such as mushroom empanadas. Don't miss the dense but fluffy Mexican chocolate-cream pie (with a meringue crust).

In Mandalay Bay, 3950 Las Vegas Blvd. S. © **702/632-7403.** Reservations recommended. Main courses $15–$20. AE, DC, DISC, MC, V. Sun–Thurs 11:30am–10pm; Fri–Sat 11:30am–11pm.

Mizuno's ⭐⭐ JAPANESE   Mizuno's has long had a strong reputation in town for terrific Japanese food, and while it seems like a gimmicky place, there is a good reason for those perpetually good reviews. Anyone who has eaten at a Benihana isn't going to find the concept here novel—you are seated at a grill and your own chef cooks in front of you—but we do note that the crowd is often predominantly Asian, so from that we can gather they are doing things right, gimmick or no. Yes indeedy, from our standpoint they are definitely doing things right; we told the chef what we wanted, what we didn't, and he followed instructions—with a great show, all clinging and clanging and flying utensils and even flashing Vegas strobe lights. It's hilarious even if it is schlock—and we loved everything he did for us. What we ate recently (but hey, don't limit yourself to our choices—he's *your* personal chef, remember!): crunchy and crispy deep-fried pork pot stickers *(gyoza)*, filet mignon with fried rice cooked to order, and teppanyaki vegetables featuring perfectly spiced enormous onions. The menu options are either the Samurai dinners (one entree with all the fixings, including miso soup and salad) or the Shogun combo (all of the above but with two entrees). This is a good choice for a group or even a celebration, since it's such a giddy dining experience.

In Tropicana Resort & Casino, 3801 Las Vegas Blvd. S. ✆ **702/739-2713.** Reservations recommended. Full Samurai dinners mostly $15–$20, Shogun combination dinners $25–$45. AE, DC, DISC, MC, V. Daily 5–10:45pm.

MODERATE

See also the listing for **Coyote Cafe** (p. 128), an expensive restaurant fronted by a more moderately priced cafe.

Dragon Noodle Co. ★★ ASIAN   A strong choice for a reasonably priced meal, Dragon Noodle is one of the better Chinese restaurants in town. We were glad to see that in addition to the usual suspects, there are some other interesting (if not radically less commonplace) choices on the menu. Note also the many Asian clients (part of our criteria for the authenticity of a place) and that the restaurant can handle large groups. Food is served family-style and prepared in an open kitchen, so you know it's fresh. Be sure to try the very smooth house green tea. You might let your waiter choose your meal for you, but try the crispy Peking pork, the sweet pungent shrimp, the pot stickers, and perhaps the generous seafood soup. We were a little disappointed by the popular sizzling black-pepper chicken, but you may not be, so don't let us stop you. And they now have a sushi bar!

In the Monte Carlo Resort & Casino, 3770 Las Vegas Blvd. S. (between Flamingo Rd. and Tropicana Ave.). ✆ **702/ 730-7965.** Main courses $5.50–$17 (many under $10). AE, DC, DISC, MC, V. Sun–Thurs 11am–11pm; Fri–Sat 11am–midnight.

Grand Wok and Sushi Bar ★★ *Value* ASIAN   A pan-Asian restaurant runs the risk of attempting to be a jack-of-all-trades and master of none, but somehow this new MGM eatery pulls it off. We didn't try every cuisine offered (Japanese, Chinese, Korean, Vietnamese, and maybe more!), but a random sampling (including lovely fresh sushi, fat dumplings, and a huge Vietnamese combo soup that was full of noodles and different kinds of meat) produced really superb and delicately prepared food. Hotel Asian restaurants are often a bit dubious, especially if they try to have too much variety, but this one really is marvelous—and the primarily Asian clientele clearly agrees. Note that soup portions are most generous; four people could easily split one order and have a nice and very cheap lunch, one of the best bargain meals in town.

In the MGM Grand, 3799 Las Vegas Blvd. S. ✆ **702/891-7777.** Reservations not accepted. Main courses $8.95–$14, sushi rolls and pieces $4.50–$9.50. AE, DC, DISC, MC, V. Restaurant Sun–Thurs 11am–10pm, Fri–Sat 11am–midnight; sushi bar Sun–Thurs 5–10pm, Fri–Sat 11am–midnight.

Sazio ★ ITALIAN   We're happy to have a place like this to recommend, because this area of town is kind of shy on decent dining joints. For this spot, you have Gustav Mauler, who originally set up all the restaurants in The Mirage, to thank. He's out on his own now, creating kicky little restaurants all over town. For our tastes, his food isn't quite interesting enough, and can be hit or miss, but when Sazio is on, the food's delicious. The menu is full of traditional Italian dishes—no, it's not just spaghetti with meat sauce, but don't look for any froufrou nouveau cuisine here. Having said that, it's a heck of a lot better than most Vegas hotels' generic Italian food, and portions are sized either for one person or in "grandioso," which is meant to feed two people and easily does so, with likely leftovers. It's great fun to come in a group, order a few of the larger portions, plop 'em in the center of the table, and have a feeding frenzy. Desserts include a knockout cheesecake. And they do takeout!

4500 W. Tropicana Ave. (in the Orleans Hotel). (✆ **702/948-9500**. www.saziolasvegas.com. Reservations not accepted except for private parties. Lunch mostly under $10; dinner entrees single portion $7.95–$15, "Grandioso" (feeds 2 or more) $13–$19. AE, DC, DISC, MC, V. Mon–Thurs 11:30am–10pm; Fri–Sat 4–10:30pm; Sun 4–10pm.

Wolfgang Puck Café ★★ CALIFORNIA   A brightly colored riot of mosaic tiles and other experiments in geometric design, the Wolfgang Puck Café stands out in the MGM Grand. It's more or less Spago (Puck's famous L.A. restaurant) Lite: downscaled salads, pizzas, and pastas, all showing the Puck hand. While perhaps a little pricier than what you'd find at your average cafe, the food is comparably better, if sometimes not that special. It's all very fresh nouvelle cuisine, however, which makes a nice change of pace. There does tend to be a line to get in, particularly after shows let out just across the casino.

The specialty pizzas are fun; constructed on crusts topped with fontina and mozzarella cheeses, they're brushed with pesto and layered with embellishments such as spicy jalapeño-marinated sautéed chicken, leeks, and cilantro. (And no, it's not just like eating the Puck brand sold in the frozen-food section of your grocery store.) It's always a thrill to get a good salad in Vegas, and there are quite

---

Value Great Meal Deals

We've already alluded to the rock-bottom budget meals and graveyard specials available at casino hotel restaurants. Quality not assured and Pepto-Bismol not provided. As prices and deals can change with no notice, we don't want to list examples (though Castaway's had an 18 oz. T-bone steak and two beers for $6.50, last we checked, and the San Remo was offering a prime rib special for $4.95, both round the clock).

Your best bet is to keep your eyes open as you travel through town, as hotels tend to advertise their specials on their marquees. Or you can go to **www.lasvegasweekly.com** and click **"dining"** and then **"dining bargains,"** though the tips and prices may be similarly somewhat out of date. Two particularly noteworthy places for late-night munchies are the **Bay City Diner** at the Golden Gate Casino in Downtown; get the grilled cheddar-and-bacon sandwich, or the **"777"**—a 16-ounce porterhouse steak, plus salad and potato, for $7.77. It's available around the clock, but you have to ask for it, as it's not on the menu. And **Mr. Lucky's 24/7** at the Hard Rock Hotel is a particularly good coffee shop, with particularly good people-watching. Check out the blonde eating the messy nachos, and the scruffy guy eating an especially good steak. Pamela and Kid Rock? Finally, the buffet at the **Boardwalk Holiday Inn** is the only one open 24 hours, and they start serving breakfast at 11pm.

a few on this menu. Worth noting is the signature "Chinois" chicken salad tossed with crispy fried wontons, julienne carrots, cabbage, and green onions in a Chinese honey-mustard sauce.

In the MGM Grand, 3799 Las Vegas Blvd. S. ℭ 702/891-3019. Reservations not accepted. Main courses $9–$15. AE, DC, MC, V. Sun–Thurs 8am–11pm; Fri–Sat 8am–1am.

INEXPENSIVE

Calypsos ⭐ *Value* DINER   Here's a solid, reasonably priced place to eat, which is pretty rare on the Strip. Honestly, it's kind of like a Denny's, but its traditional coffee-shop choices (including a "create your own burger") are somewhat better than you might expect. There are some eccentric items such as a chopped Mediterranean shrimp salad, a smoked salmon plate, a rosemary-chicken sandwich on onion focaccia bread, and a strawberry cream puff swan for dessert. Note also a very good (and low-fat!) Thai shrimp satay, loaded with vegetables, which is listed under "classic American" dishes. We were amused by the fruit plate, which is actually melons and such atop a pound cake. It's a dessert masquerading as a salad!

In Tropicana Resort & Casino, 3801 Las Vegas Blvd. S. ℭ 702/739-2222. Reservations not accepted. Main courses $5.95–$17. AE, MC, V. Daily 24 hr.

Monte Carlo Pub & Brewery ⭐⭐⭐ *Kids* *Finds* PUB FARE   Lest you think we are big, fat foodie snobs who can't appreciate a meal unless it comes drenched in truffles and caviar, we hasten to direct you to this lively, working microbrewery (with a sort of rustic factory appearance) and its hearty, not-so-high-falutin' food. No fancy French frills, and best of all, no inflated prices. Combine the general high quality with generous portions—a nachos appetizer could probably feed eight (though it was not the best nachos appetizer ever)—and this may be a better deal than most buffets. It's not, however, the place for a quiet rendezvous, with about 40 TVs spread throughout (a sports fan's dream) and music blaring.

Earning recent raves were the short ribs in a fine barbecue sauce, cooked just right; the excellent appetizer of chicken fingers and shrimp fried in beer; the garlic pizza with mounds of our favorite aromatic herb; the pizza topped with lamb, grilled eggplant, and goat cheese (well, maybe that has more frills than we promised); and the avocado-and-shrimp salad. We also highly enjoyed the double-chocolate-fudge suicide brownie, though really, what's not to love about something like that? After 9pm, only pizza is served, and dueling pianos provide dance music and entertainment.

In the Monte Carlo Resort & Casino, 3770 Las Vegas Blvd. S. (between Flamingo Rd. and Tropicana Ave.). ℭ 702/730-7777. Reservations not accepted. Main courses $6–$15. AE, DC, DISC, MC, V. Sun–Thurs 11am–2am; Fri–Sat 11am–4am.

(*Value* Quick Bites

Food courts are a dime a dozen in Vegas, but the one in the **Monte Carlo,** 3770 Las Vegas Blvd. S., between Flamingo Road and Tropicana Avenue (ℭ 702/730-7777), has some surprisingly good options. Sure, there's the always-reliable **McDonald's,** and for sweets there is **Häagen-Dazs,** but they also have a branch of **Nathan's Hot Dogs,** New York's finest. **Golden Bagel** offers another New York staple, big and tasty enough to satisfy even picky natives. **Sbarro** offers enticing pizza slices. If you want a good, cheap meal on the Strip and wish to avoid some of those dubious night-owl specials, come here. It's open daily from 6am to 3am.

3 Mid-Strip

Note: The Rio has a branch of Rosemary's (p. 158), one of our favorite restaurants in town. The Rio branch has a somewhat different menu than the original, but both are highly recommended.

VERY EXPENSIVE

Alizé ★★★ FRENCH   Just a perfect restaurant, thanks to a combination of the most divine dining room and view in Vegas (situated at the top of the Palms Hotel, with three sides of full length windows that allow a panoramic view of the night lights of Vegas; obviously, window-side tables are best, but even seats in the center of the room have a good view), and one of the best chefs in a town where many great chefs have restaurants but are rarely in their kitchens (Emeril and Wolfgang, we love them, but they can't be in 25 different places at once). Overseen by Andre, he of the eponymous (and excellent) restaurants in Downtown and the Monte Carlo, the executive chef is Jacques Van Staden, who trained with one of the world's greatest chefs, Jean-Louis Pallidin. The menu changes seasonally, but anything you order will be heavenly.

On our last visit, we had perhaps 14 different courses, and not a single one disappointed. In the appetizer department, the marinated jumbo lump crabmeat and avocado salad with heirloom tomato consommé and basil oil was a riot of freshness, while the gnocchi with sautéed wild mushrooms, black truffle, and mushroom emulsion was the kind of dish clearly created by someone thoughtful and clever. A phyllo-wrapped baked pear and Roquefort cheese with a vinegar and port reduction was less salad (as it was billed) and more hot appetizer. The foie gras comes in a pink-grapefruit–and-citrus-honey reduction, a tangy combination. Fish can be a little dry here, so we suggest either the stunning New York steak with summer truffle jus and potato herb pancakes, or the meltingly tender lamb chops with some shredded lamb shank wrapped in a crispy fried crepe. Desserts are similarly outstanding, and often of great frivolity, such as sorbet in a case of browned marshmallow, floating in raspberry soup. Yeah, we're going over the top on this one, but we bet you won't think we're wrong.

In the Palms Hotel, 4321 W. Flamingo Rd. ⓒ **702/951-7000.** Fax 702/951-7002. www.alizelv.com. Reservations strongly recommended. Entrees $28–$37. AE, MC, V. Sun–Thurs 5–10pm; Fri–Sat 5–10:30pm.

Aqua ★★ SEAFOOD   Fish fans should certainly head quickly over to Aqua, a branch of a highly respected San Francisco restaurant. And even fish-phobes might reconsider their position when they try Aqua's slightly Asian-influenced pleasures. Stylistically, the restaurant's Japanese tearoom/Frank Lloyd Wright–craftsman decor is more Melrose Avenue power restaurant than Vegas fish house, and the clientele seem to be local businessmen in search of a health-conscious, client-impressing dinner. Service is quite sensitive and solicitous. Our waiter recalled that the folks at the table next to us had been in some months prior; he also remembered which dessert they liked best, making sure they got a portion of it along with their actual dessert order.

You can start your meal with a nonseafood choice such as Hudson Valley foie gras, which comes with a warm apple Charlotte, a cinnamon-baked apple compote that tastes a bit like something you might eat at breakfast—though foie gras is hardly a breakfast meat. The mixed-seasonal-greens salad looks like a flower, and is a light, amiable mix of flavors. For a main course, go straight to the vaguely Japanese miso-glazed Chilean sea bass in a rich, but not heavy, shellfish consommé. More timid fish eaters might try the robust Hawaiian swordfish au poivre, though its side of pancetta-wrapped shrimp dumplings (think fancy bacon-wrapped shrimp) is not as successful. Also winning raves is the potato-crusted John Dory. The lobster potpie is cooked in a pot, then brought to the table and disassembled with great ceremony, as 1½ pounds of lobster is laid out, a creamy sauce with veggies is poured over it, and it's all topped with the crust. Do try some of their dainty and clever desserts, particularly their signature root-beer float—no, really. It's got root-beer sorbet, sarsaparilla ice cream, a chocolate straw, and warm cookies right out of the oven.

In Bellagio, 3600 Las Vegas Blvd. S. © 702/693-7223. Reservations recommended. Main courses $29–$34 (lobster and whole foie gras higher). AE, DISC, MC, V. Daily 5:30–10pm.

Buccaneer Bay Club ★ _Finds_ AMERICAN/CONTINENTAL   This is a good middle-of-the-road choice—a little bit of adventure for those who don't usually take dining risks, but not so much that the truly timid will find nothing to eat. As we write this, however, the restaurant, originally built as a place to watch TI's Pirate Battle, is getting an overhaul—perhaps to tone down the pirate imagery, since said Pirate Battle is turning into a showcase for scantily clad dancers. It's going to be more fun than ever to watch fellow diners drop their forks and race to the windows when the cry "Pirates are on!" goes up.

Appetizers come in both hot (jerk-style shrimp Jamaica and escargot brioche) and cold (shrimp cocktail and Parma prosciutto) varieties. The savory celery-root flan and the quail are the true stars of the appetizer menu. (The quail wasn't on the menu, so be sure to ask about specials.) Entrees range from poultry to beef to seafood. Consider the Colorado buffalo prime rib, which is roasted and grilled over mesquite wood and served with creamy horseradish potatoes. If you haven't tried buffalo before, check it out. Desserts include apple beignets, white-chocolate cheesecake with raspberry sauce, and the house specialty, apricot or harlequin (Grand Marnier and white and dark chocolate) mini soufflés.

In Treasure Island, 3300 Las Vegas Blvd. S. © 702/894-7223. Reservations recommended. Main courses $20–$35. AE, DC, DISC, MC, V. Daily 5–10:30pm.

Delmonico Steakhouse ★★ CONTEMPORARY CREOLE/STEAK Watching the Food Network, you might well feel that Emeril Lagasse is omnipresent. Slowly but surely, he's becoming as ubiquitous here in Vegas (though he has a long way to go to match Puck) as he is in New Orleans, as he brings variations on his Big Easy brand-name eateries to town. This latest is a steakhouse version of his hard-core classic Creole restaurant; this ever-so-slight twist is just enough to make it a superior choice over the more disappointing New Orleans locale. It's set in two dining rooms (the left-hand one is '70s-den ugly—choose instead the Neutra/Schindler–influenced right-hand side).

You can try Emeril's concoctions, plus fabulous cuts of red meat. You can't go wrong with most appetizers, especially the superbly rich smoked mushrooms with homemade tasso ham over pasta—it's enough for a meal in and of itself. The same advice holds for any of the specials, or the gumbo, particularly if it's the hearty, near-homemade country selection. If you want to experiment, defi-nitely do it with the appetizers; you're better off steering clear of complex entrees, no matter how intriguing they sound (such as a 1-night special of foie gras–stuffed ahi tuna). We've found the entree specials to be generally disap-pointing, while the more deceptively simple choices are more successful. The bone-in rib steak is rightly recommended (skip the gummy béarnaise sauce in favor of the fabulous homemade Worcester or the A.O.K. sauce). Sides are hit or miss—the creamed spinach was too salty, but a sweet-potato purée (a special,

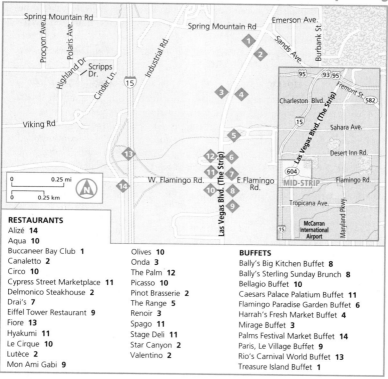

RESTAURANTS

Alizé **14**
Aqua **10**
Buccaneer Bay Club **1**
Canaletto **2**
Circo **10**
Cypress Street Marketplace **11**
Delmonico Steakhouse **2**
Drai's **7**
Eiffel Tower Restaurant **9**
Fiore **13**
Hyakumi **11**
Le Cirque **10**
Lutèce **10**
Mon Ami Gabi **9**

Olives **10**
Onda **3**
The Palm **12**
Picasso **10**
Pinot Brasserie **2**
The Range **5**
Renoir **3**
Spago **11**
Stage Deli **11**
Star Canyon **2**
Valentino **2**

BUFFETS

Bally's Big Kitchen Buffet **8**
Bally's Sterling Sunday Brunch **8**
Bellagio Buffet **10**
Caesars Palace Palatium Buffet **11**
Flamingo Paradise Garden Buffet **6**
Harrah's Fresh Market Buffet **4**
Mirage Buffet **3**
Palms Festival Market Buffet **14**
Paris, Le Village Buffet **9**
Rio's Carnival World Buffet **13**
Treasure Island Buffet **1**

but maybe they'll serve you a side if you ask sweetly) is most definitely a winner. Too full for dessert? No, you aren't. Have a chocolate soufflé, a bananas-Foster cream pie, a chocolate Sheba (a sort of dense chocolate mousse), or the lemon icebox pie, a chunk of curd that blasts tart lemon through your mouth.

In The Venetian, 3355 Las Vegas Blvd. S. ℂ **702/414-3737**. Reservations strongly recommended for dinner. Main courses $21–$36. AE, DC, DISC, MC, V. Daily 11:30am–2pm; Sun–Thurs 5:30–10:30pm; Fri–Sat 5:30–11pm.

Drai's STEAK/SEAFOOD   It's a famous Los Angeles restaurant and the place that young Hollywood execs flock to when out for a Vegas jaunt, but we can't help but notice that the food is very ordinary. It's not bad, but it may not justify the high prices. There are multiple dining rooms done in dark wood—very L.A. '70s mellow bar—with leopard prints on the menus and plates, and too-loud jazz music blaring throughout.

Peculiarly, the most expensive menu item is Dover sole with mashed potatoes—a cheap fish and a cheap accompaniment. The menu boasts that none of their soups is made with dairy products. But they might want to reconsider that policy, because the potato-leek soup was flat and dull—it really needed cream or butter. Lake Superior whitefish in phyllo dough (a flaky, thin dough) with onion marmalade will please those who don't mind their appetizers on the sweet side. On the plus side, the duck was crispy and not dry. The crab cakes were also tasty, with shredded—not puréed—crab, and were served with a stiff but nice and cheesy risotto (though the lemon-caper sauce had no flavor). And it would be worth going to Drai's just for the chocolate-mousse dessert—light and delectable, and not overly sweet.

In the Barbary Coast Hotel & Casino, 3595 Las Vegas Blvd. S. ℰ **702/737-7111.** Reservations recommended. Main courses $22–$28. AE, MC, V. Daily 5pm–midnight.

Fiore ✪ ITALIAN/PROVENÇAL   This is a worthwhile dining choice with a very attentive staff. Try to get a seat on the patio; outdoor dining is rare in Vegas, so it's worth taking advantage of. You can't go wrong with a perfectly done rack of lamb with roasted garlic sauce, or the appetizer of pancetta-wrapped shrimp with port-wine glaze (sure, it's just a more tony version of bacon-wrapped shrimp, but it's good!). Skip the disappointingly overdone Chilean sea bass. Save room for a cheese plate and, especially, the gooey chocolate desserts—Fiore has a very talented pastry chef.

In the Rio All-Suite Hotel & Casino, 3700 W. Flamingo Rd. (at I-15). ℰ **702/252-7777.** Reservations recommended. Main courses $26–$48. AE, DC, DISC, MC, V. Daily 5–11pm.

Le Cirque ✪ FRENCH   The influx of haute-cuisine, high-profile restaurants in Vegas means there are ever so many places now where you may feel like you have to take out a bank loan in order to eat—and you may wonder why you ought to. Though generally we always feel free to spend your money for you, we actually are going to suggest that you hold on to it in the case of Le Cirque, unless someone else is doing the buying. It's not that the food is bad—quite the contrary—but it's not the very best in town, and it is among the most expensive. And remember what we said about most of Vegas being quite casual? Here, forget it. If you didn't bring your nicest black, you are going to feel very uncomfortable.

The surprisingly small dining room (you may be virtually rubbing elbows with your neighbor, so keep inflammatory secrets out of the conversation) is decorated with murals of quaint bygone circus themes and a ceiling draped with gay fabric meant to evoke the Big Top. The busy decor does add to the cramped feeling. The menu changes seasonally, but you can expect genuine French cuisine—heavy, with lots of butter, though a recent visit brought a duo of cold cucumber and heirloom tomato soups that were so refreshing, every restaurant in this desert town ought to serve them. The lobster salad is sweet and tender, with a perfect black truffle dressing; risotto is French-style, almost soupy, perfect with fresh morels (in season) and Parmesan. The filet mignon is, oddly, not as good a cut as served elsewhere, but it does come with a generous portion of foie gras. For dessert, we loved the white chocolate cream (solid, but not overwhelming), layered with banana and wrapped in phyllo, along with a milk chocolate dome with crème brûlée espresso.

In Bellagio, 3600 Las Vegas Blvd. S. ℰ **702/693-8100.** www.lecirque.com. Reservations required. Jacket/tie required for men. Main courses $29–$39. AE, DC, DISC, MC, V. Daily 5:30–10:30pm.

Lutèce ✪✪ FRENCH   A branch of the highly esteemed New York City restaurant, Lutèce is yet another example of how, if you want to dine well in Vegas, you've got to pay for it. The minimalist decor is relieved by a modern industrial look that extends to the cutlery and bathrooms (have a look!). It's full of style, style, style. It's genuinely chic, which is unusual for Vegas, but it's not threatening or cavernous—it's New York all the way. A self-aware, self-confident place, this may prove to be one of our favorite dining spots in Vegas. Try to get a table in the little nook area that looks out at the Strip—it's more romantic than it sounds.

The presentation of the French cuisine is just lovely. The menu will probably change periodically, but on a recent visit, we enjoyed the appetizer of smoked codfish with white-truffle oil and arugula, a combo that works surprisingly well. For a main course, we loved the crisp black bass with lobster sauce and herb noodles, and the turbot poached in tarragon broth with baby veggies.

In The Venetian, 3355 Las Vegas Blvd. S. © **702/414-2220.** Reservations strongly recommended for dinner. Main courses $26–$38. AE, DC, DISC, MC, V. Daily 5:30–10:30pm.

Onda ★★ ITALIAN   Onda is anything but a run-of-the-mill hotel restaurant. Chef Todd English, whose Olives cafe over at Bellagio is also well worth your dining time, offers a Mediterranean slant on Italian cooking, coming up with a menu that's full of pleasant thrills, putting most other Italian joints in town to shame. Vegetables are flown in especially for Onda, so we encourage you toward menu choices that feature them. The restaurant itself is pretty and comfortable (dress is casual chic), with a particularly good vibe later in the evening (after 9pm, say)—for some reason, the staff doesn't tire but is still ready to take care of your every wish, allowing you to linger as much as you like.

Begin with that basket of varied breads, making sure that the Gorgonzola-laced breadsticks are among them. Move on to antipasti with polenta, truffles, fresh mozzarella, onions, stuffed zucchini, roasted peppers, and goodness knows what else. Soup is good food, in particular the fine baby-sweet-spring-pea purée with a dollop of mascarpone cheese. A foil-wrapped veggie packet (slit at the table for you) includes porcini mushrooms good enough to make even non–mushroom fans fall to their knees, reconsidering their previous conviction. Gnocchi in sauce are light and wonderful. By now you don't need a heavy dessert, but the chocolate-mousse cake is highly recommended if you can handle it, as is the sorbet sampler (featuring flavors such as champagne grape and caramelized grape) if you can't.

In The Mirage, 3400 Las Vegas Blvd. S. © **702/791-7223.** Reservations recommended. Main course $17–$35. AE, DC, DISC, MC, V. Daily 5:30–10pm.

The Palm ★★ STEAK/SEAFOOD   A branch of the venerable New York eatery, which has been branching ever farther afield recently, this place attracts a star-studded clientele fond of the reliable and hearty, if not terribly exciting, bill of fare. (The famous may also be hoping to find their faces among the many caricatures that cover the walls.) This is plain but filling food—at manly prices. Red-meat lovers will be happy with the high-quality steaks found here, though those on a budget will shudder in horror. The tendency is to give them a good charring, so if you don't like your meat blackened, start with it less well done and send it back for more if necessary. If you've hit a jackpot, your money will be well spent on one of The Palm's Buick-size lobsters. They're utterly succulent and outrageously priced, but given their size—they start at 3 pounds—they can easily be shared. If you're worried that all this won't be enough, add one of the delicious appetizers (plump but high-priced shrimp cocktails or a perfect prosciutto with melon) or toss in a side of crispy deep-fried onions. Desserts are similarly heavy and unspectacular.

In Caesars Palace Forum Shops, 3570 Las Vegas Blvd. S. © **702/732-7256.** Reservations recommended. Main courses $8.50–$14 at lunch, $15–$35 at dinner. AE, DC, MC, V. Daily 11:30am–10pm.

Picasso ★★★ FRENCH   A Spanish chef who cooks French cuisine in an Italian-themed hotel in Vegas? Trust us, it works. This may well be the best restaurant in Vegas, and given the sudden serious competition for such a title, that says a lot. Steve Wynn spent months trying to talk Madrid-born chef Julian Serrano (whose Masa was considered the finest French restaurant in San Francisco) into coming to Bellagio. His bulldog tenacity paid off, and we should all thank him. This is an extraordinary dining experience, including the thrill of having $30 million worth of Picassos gaze down over your shoulders while you eat. It's not like dining in a stuffy museum, however—the water fountains going off outside every 15 minutes (with staid diners rushing to the windows to check it out) pretty much take care of that. Many of the furnishings were designed by one of Picasso's sons, and even the paintings themselves are challenged for beauty by the exceptional floral arrangements.

Needless to say, Serrano's cooking is a work of art that can proudly stand next to the masterpieces. The menu changes nightly and is always a choice between a four- or five-course fixed-price dinner or a tasting menu. The night we ate there, we were bowled over by roasted Maine lobster with a "trio" of corn—kernels, sauce, and a corn flan that was like eating slightly solid sunshine. Hudson Valley foie gras was crusted in truffles and went down most smoothly. A filet of roasted sea bass came with a light saffron sauce and dots of cauliflower purée. And finally, pray that they're serving the lamb rôti—it was an outstanding piece of lamb, perfectly done, tender, and crusted with truffles. Portions are dainty, but so rich that you'll have plenty to eat without groaning and feeling heavy when you leave. Desserts are powerful, yet prettily constructed. A molten chocolate cake leaves any other you may have tried in the dust, and comes with ice cream made with imported European chocolate. A crisp banana tart with coconut ice cream is a fine nonchocolate (foolish you) choice, while a passion-fruit flan in a citrus-soup sauce is perfect if you don't have much room left. Everything is delivered by an attentive staff that makes you feel quite pampered. Can we go back soon and try it all again?

In Bellagio, 3600 Las Vegas Blvd. S. ✆ **702/693-7223**. Reservations recommended. Fixed-price 4-course dinner $80, 5-course degustation $90. AE, DC, DISC, MC, V. Thurs–Tues 6–9:30pm.

The Range ★★ STEAK   This place is worth visiting if only for the spectacular view of the Strip (few Strip restaurants take advantage of this view, oddly enough) from 40-foot-high wraparound windows. Muted copper and wood tones make for a formal but not intimidating environment and a fine-looking room. The small menu features the usual steakhouse offerings—various cuts of beef and some chicken dishes plus a few salads—but at a high-medium price. That said, the quality is better than we've found at the usual Vegas steakhouse suspects. We particularly liked the filet mignon on a Gorgonzola-onion croustade. All entrees come with family-style side dishes (they change nightly, but can include such items as marinated mushrooms or horseradish mashed potatoes). Appetizers are also worth noting. The five-onion soup is thick, heavy, creamy, and served in a giant, hollowed-out onion. It's delicious, as was a smoked chicken quesadilla. Don't miss the bread, which comes with a sweet and savory apricot-and-basil butter.

In Harrah's, 3475 Las Vegas Blvd. S. ✆ **702/369-5084**. Reservations highly recommended. Main courses $19–$27. AE, DC, DISC, MC, V. Daily 5:30–11:30pm.

Renoir ★★ NOUVELLE ITALIAN   Executive Chef Alessandro Stratta was named one of "America's 10 Best Chefs" by *Food & Wine,* and has several serious culinary awards including the 1998 "Best Chef in the Southwest" by the James Beard Foundation. Though surely both of these awards paled in comparison to Stratta's being named one of the four Iron Chefs on the American version of the beloved, campy cooking show.

Moments **A Dining Room, or Two, with a View**

As we keep noting, the Strip at night is a dazzling sight, which is why hotel rooms with Strip views come at such a premium. Regardless of whether you were able to get the proverbial room with a view, consider dining at either the chic **Eiffel Tower** restaurant, in Paris Las Vegas, 3655 Las Vegas Blvd. S. (© 702/948-6937; open Sun–Thurs 5:30–10pm, Fri–Sat 5:30–10:30pm), located on the 11th floor of said Mid-Strip hotel, or the **Stratosphere's Top of the World**, in the Stratosphere Casino Hotel & Tower, 2000 Las Vegas Blvd. S. (© 702/380-7711; open daily 11am–3pm; Sun–Thurs 6–11pm, Fri–Sat 6pm–midnight), which is almost at the top of the North Strip's Stratosphere Tower, the tallest structure west of the Mississippi. Both offer fantastic views. The latter even revolves 360 degrees, while the former also looks down on the Bellagio fountains. Both, however, also match sky-high views with sky-high prices, and, unfortunately, neither has food worth the price. Go for a special night out, or see if you can get away with just ordering appetizers and dessert (which are both superior to the entrees, anyway). You can also just have a drink at their respective bars, though each is set back far enough from the windows that drinkers have less-choice views than diners.

Kidding aside, Stratta's cooking has given Renoir the distinction of five Mobil stars (as of 2000). While the space itself is less inspired than Picasso (the Renoirs on the walls seem an afterthought), it does have a tad more intimacy, thanks to some banquettes and a more hushed atmosphere, plus less obtrusive and less intimidating service, and cunning touches such as stools for the ladies' handbags. (And yet, the bathrooms are out in the casino.)

Nightly, there are two tasting menus, including one focused solely on vegetables, but items from each can be interchanged with some from the a la carte menu. Standouts include downy pillows of potato gnocchi with black truffles—so good it seems like a pity when the dish is finished—and a combo of Maine lobster and sweet-corn ravioli, an always-welcome pairing of flavors. Also enjoyable, but grudgingly portioned, are the cannelloni of red-wine-braised duck (with creamed leeks), and the Napoleon of ahi tuna and yellowtail with Gazpacho vegetables and a dollop of Osetra caviar. If you are looking to conserve money, note that the appetizer of terrine of foie gras (with Waldorf salad and toasted currant bread) is generously sized and would be fine as an entree. This is also the place for a cheese plate: One night it featured St. Andre, Vacheron, Comte, Tellagio, and Roquefort, all at perfect temperature. And thanks to a thoughtfully priced wine list, even the average person can try something as rare as Chateau D'Yquem—they offer a 1-ounce glass for $25.

3400 Las Vegas Blvd. S. (in The Mirage). © 702/791-7223. Reservations recommended. Entrees $36–$44. AE, DC, DISC, MC, V. Daily 5:30–9:30pm.

Spago ⭐ AMERICAN/ASIAN/CALIFORNIA   With Wolfgang Puck showing up in a different incarnation at every hotel in town these days (or so it seems), his original creation might get lost in the shuffle. Certainly, it's no longer what it used to be—the only foodie game in town—and you get the feeling that it was so far ahead of the pack for so long that it has gotten a bit complacent.

Which is not to say that Spago is not worth the expense—it just means that others have caught up with, and in some cases surpassed, it.

When Nomi Malone, Elizabeth Berkley's character in the film *Showgirls*, came to eat at the cafe, she peevishly said that she didn't "know what any of this stuff is." She must not get out much: The cafe menu features such familiar items as meatloaf and pizza, although glamorized versions—this isn't Country Kitchen, and so this pizza features smoked salmon, not to mention crème fraîche. It sounds like an unholy hybrid of Italian and deli, but it's sublime. It's not on the menu, so be sure to ask for this "Jewish pizza." Other cafe specialties include Puck's signature Chinese chicken salad and a superb mesquite-fried salmon served with a tangy toss of soba noodles and cashews in a coconut-sesame-chile paste vinaigrette nuanced with lime juice and Szechuan mustard. The inside menu changes seasonally, but the signature dish is a Chinese-style duck, moist but with a perfectly crispy skin. It's about as good as duck gets, served with a doughy, steamed bun and Chinese vegetables. Desserts range from fresh-fruit sorbets in surprising flavors (cantaloupe, honeydew), to a luscious brownie topped with homemade chocolate, whipped cream, and ice cream. The wine list is impressive, but the house wine was a disappointment and possibly not worth the cost.

In Caesars Palace, 3570 Las Vegas Blvd. S. ✆ **702/369-6300.** Reservations recommended for the dining room, not accepted at the cafe. Dining room main courses $14–$31; cafe main courses $9.50–$23. AE, DC, DISC, MC, V. Dining room daily 6–10pm; cafe Sun–Thurs 11am–11pm, Fri–Sat 11am–midnight.

Valentino ⭐ ITALIAN   Valentino was long considered the best Italian restaurant in L.A., and even the best in America (per *Bon Appetit*, who we suppose oughta know). But this branch (with generic nice restaurant decor) isn't quite as successful as its Southern California counterpart, with complicated offerings that too often just miss the mark. Quail stuffed with snails and served with white-and-yellow polenta, for example, or house-smoked shrimp with crispy veggies and an apple-balsamic sauce—they're all interesting, but the combinations don't quite work. Working entirely well, however, are the four-cheese ravioli with truffle-cream sauce and fresh truffle shavings—we shamelessly mopped our plate with our bread—and the wild-rabbit loin in rhubarb-encrusted prosciutto.

In The Venetian, 3355 Las Vegas Blvd. S. ✆ **702/414-3000.** Reservations strongly recommended. Main courses $15–$37. AE, DC, DISC, MC, V. Daily 5:30–10pm.

EXPENSIVE

Canaletto ⭐⭐ ITALIAN   Come here for solid, true Italian fare—and that means less sauce-intensive than the red-checked-tablecloth establishments of our American youths. Here, the emphasis is on the pasta, not the accompaniments. This place is all the more enjoyable for being perched on the faux St. Mark's Square; in theory, you can pretend you are sitting on the edge of the real thing, a fantasy we don't mind admitting we briefly indulged in. A risotto of porcini, sausage, and white-truffle oil was full of strong flavors, while the wood-fired roast chicken was perfectly moist. You know, a properly roasted chicken should be a much-celebrated thing, and that alone may be a reason to come here.

In The Venetian Grand Canal Shoppes, 3377 Las Vegas Blvd. S. ✆ **702/733-0070.** Reservations recommended for dinner. Main courses $12–$29. AE, DC, MC, V. Sun–Thurs 11:30am–11pm; Fri–Sat 11:30am—midnight.

Circo ⭐⭐ ITALIAN   Yes, this is the less-expensive offering from the same family that brings you Le Cirque, but going to one does not excuse you from going to the other. (By the way, "less-expensive" is a relative term. While dinner prices for entrees other than pasta and pizza fall into our "very expensive" category, lunch prices are less high, and there are, as you will see, ways to make this fall into the "moderate" category. So we decided to split the difference and list this as "expensive." Just thought you'd like to know.)

Le Cirque's gourmet French haute cuisine does not prepare you for what to expect from Circo, or for that matter, vice versa. Ignore the bright primary-color scheme, meant to evoke the circus but instead sadly recalling outdated hotel buffets (albeit with expensive wood grain), in favor of watching the dancing fountains outside. And then order the *mista di Campo,* a lovely little salad, both visually and in terms of taste; it's a creative construction of vegetables bound with cucumber and topped with a fab balsamic vinaigrette. Or you could start with the antipasto appetizer sampler of Tuscan sheep's-milk cheese, marinated veggies, prosciutto, and Italian pastrami. Follow that with a perfect tagliatelle with rock shrimp—it comes loaded with various crustacean bits in a light sauce. Note that appetizer portions of pastas are plenty filling and cheaper than full-size servings. Nighttime brings more elaborate dishes, such as breast of Muscovy duck with dried organic fruit in port-wine sauce. Save room for desserts such as *panna cotta* (Italian cream-filled donuts), or *tutto cioccolato,* consisting of chocolate mousse, ice cream, and crumb cake.

In Bellagio, 3600 Las Vegas Blvd. S. ⓒ 702/693-8150. Reservations recommended for dinner. Main courses $17–$24 at lunch (pizza $12–$19), $20–$32 at dinner (pizza and pasta $12–$22). AE, DC, DISC, MC, V. Wed–Sun 11:30am–2:30pm and 5:30–10:30pm.

Hyakumi ✦ SUSHI   Hyakumi (say "Yah-*koo*-me") is a quaint little oasis in the midst of a bustling casino. Tastefully decorated with hardwood floors in a tea-garden atmosphere, it is a relaxing respite from the madness of Vegas, as kimono-clad waitresses cater to your every need with a never-ending cup of particularly good green tea, plus hot towels, to put you in a Zen-like state.

But the setting, as serene and beautiful as it is, is not the reason for a visit to Hyakumi; it's the sushi. Supervised by executive chef Hiroji Obayashi, famed for his award-winning Hirozen Gourmet Restaurant in Los Angeles, Hyakumi offers some of the best sushi in town. It's not the cheapest, but it is well worth the extra cost. From the toro to the salmon roll, every bite melts in your mouth. The fish is shipped in daily and is prepared by friendly sushi chefs who obviously love what they do. If sushi isn't your thing, there is also a restaurant serving up traditional (but very expensive) Japanese fare in a lovely garden setting.

In Caesars Palace, 3570 Las Vegas Blvd. S. ⓒ 702/731-7731. Reservations recommended. Sushi $6–$7 per roll or piece, main courses $25–$60. AE, DC, DISC, MC, V. Restaurant and sushi bar daily 11am–4pm for lunch and 6pm–11pm for dinner.

Pinot Brasserie ✦✦ BISTRO   This is the latest incarnation of a series of well-regarded Los Angeles restaurants whose mother ship, Patina, regularly tops "Best of" lists among City of Angels foodies. While the more innovative cooking is going on back in L.A., Pinot reliably delivers French and American favorites that are thoughtfully conceived and generally delicious. It's an excellent choice if you want a special meal that is neither stratospherically expensive nor too complex. And the space is highly attractive, with various props culled from French auctions and flea markets forming the archetypal, clubby bistro feel. (We particularly like the small room off the bar to the right, just perfect for a tête-à-tête.)

Salads are possibly fresher and more generous than other similar starters in town (thank that California influence), and they can come paired with various toppings for *crostini* (toasted slices of French bread) such as herbed goat cheese.

Kids Family-Friendly Restaurants

Buffets   Cheap meals for the whole family. The kids can choose what they like, and there are sometimes make-your-own sundae machines. Section 8 of this chapter reviews all the buffets and notes which ones have reduced prices for kids.

Rainforest Cafe (p. 131)   This is like eating in the Jungle Book Ride at Disneyland. Animals howl, thunder wails, everywhere there is something to marvel at. There is a decent kids' menu, and they might even learn a little bit about ecology and the environment.

Hard Rock Cafe (p. 131)   Kids adore this restaurant, which throbs with excitement and is filled with rock memorabilia.

Pink Pony   This bubble-gum-pink, circus-motif, 24-hour coffee shop at Circus Circus will appeal to kids. Mom and Dad can linger while the kids race upstairs to watch circus acts and play carnival games.

Sherwood Forest Cafe   Kids love to climb on the lavender dragons fronting this 24-hour coffee shop at Excalibur, and they can also enjoy numerous child-oriented activities while you're on the premises.

Toto's (p. 157)   This Mexican restaurant that features enormous portions served family-style is a casual place favored by locals.

The Monte Carlo Pub & Brewery (p. 134)   Despite the "pub" part of the name, this noisy place in the Monte Carlo hotel has many TVs to distract short-attention kids and brooding teenagers, all of whom will like the BBQ, pizza, and chicken fingers. Parents will be pleased with the low prices.

Cypress Street Marketplace (p. 145)   Caesars Palace's food court (stylish enough to offer real plates and cloth napkins) offers a range of food (from very good hot dogs to wrap sandwiches to Vietnamese noodles) wide enough to ensure bottomless-pit teenagers, picky grade-schoolers and health-conscious parents will all find something that appeals, at affordable prices.

Word is that they might add Patina's delightful butternut-squash soup to the menu here, and if so, you should try it. The signature dish, beloved by many, is a roasted chicken accompanied by heaping mounds of garlic fries; but if you wish to get a little more elaborate (and yet rather light), thin slices of smoked salmon with celery rémoulade could be a way to go. Desserts are lovely, and the ice cream is homemade—the chocolate alone should make you wish you'd never eaten at 31 Flavors, because it was wasted calories compared to this. *Note:* It's easy to graze through this menu and have a less costly meal here than at most other high-end places, and the constant operating hours mean you can also pop in for a nosh at times when other fine-dining options are closed.

In The Venetian, 3355 Las Vegas Blvd. S. © **702/735-8888.** Reservations recommended for dinner. Main courses $12–$18 at lunch, $19–$30 at dinner. AE, DISC, MC, V. Daily 11:30am–10:30pm.

Star Canyon ⭐ SOUTHWESTERN   Texas-based chef Stephen Pyles is more or less credited with inventing Southwestern cuisine, and this new branch of his highly touted Dallas restaurant not only gives Coyote Cafe a serious run for the title of Best Southwestern Restaurant in Vegas, but it might just be the Best American Restaurant. Not the place for intimate romantic encounters, this is decidedly the fun high-end restaurant in town, lively and playful, with a menu to match. If you thought Texas cuisine was limited to just barbecue, you're wrong. Here's a menu that mixes the haute and nouvelle with the down home, and the results should leave you pleased.

For this reason, we urge you to take some chances with appetizers—we'd go a bit more plain, though with equal satisfaction, with the main courses. All dishes use classic Southwestern flavors, and more importantly, spices, and combine them with just the right nouvelle cuisine influences. A tamale pie's spicy crust is cooled by its filling of roast-garlic custard topped with crabmeat, while that gourmand's delight, seared foie gras, is most happily paired with a more humble corn cake, itself dressed up with pineapple salsa. Molasses-coated quail is dainty and sweet tasting atop arugula, poached pear, and a bit of cambazola cheese. Be sure to try the hearty, serious, chewy breads, which can come in such flavors as pesto and chipotle. While you may justly feel tempted to make a meal of appetizers, don't. For then you would miss the signature dish, a bone-in rib-eye, served cowboy-style (think Western spices), an utterly tender, flavorful dish (topped with a mile-high tower of crispy onions) that makes it hard to imagine a better piece of meat. Desserts are perhaps not quite as joy producing. The noted Heaven and Hell cake (alternating layers of devil's food, angel food, and peanut-butter mousse covered in chocolate ganache) reads better than it tastes, though the chocolate bread pudding is more like a heavy soufflé than a boring basic bread pudding.

In The Venetian, 3355 Las Vegas Blvd. S. ✆ **702/414-3772**. Reservations recommended for dinner. Main courses $10–$17 at lunch, $21–$30 at dinner. AE, MC, V. Daily 8am–10pm.

MODERATE

See also the listing for **Spago** (p. 141), an expensive restaurant fronted by a more moderately priced cafe.

Cypress Street Marketplace ★★ *Kids* FOOD COURT   Often when we go to a Vegas buffet (and we are not alone in this), we sigh over all the choices, all those different kinds of pretty good, if not better, cuisines, there for the taking, but of course, we can't possibly try everything. And yet, in some of the higher priced venues, we are charged as if we can. Here, in this modern version of the classic food court, it's sort of like being at a well-stocked buffet; there's darn fine BBQ (including North Carolina influenced pulled pork), wrap sandwiches (grilled shrimp for one example), Asian (including pot stickers and Vietnamese noodles), decent NY pizza, plump Chicago hot dogs, peel-and-eat shrimp and lobster chowder, a bargain-priced build your own salad bar, plus pastries and even wine. You get a card when you enter, and it's swiped whenever you choose something, and then you pay the one price after you eat (on real plates with real napkins and forks). It's slightly more convenient than the traditional pay-as-you-go food court, certainly more efficient than a cafeteria, and a better value (especially given how large the portions are) than many a buffet. And with the range of food, an entire family with very different tastes will all find something satisfactory.

3570 Las Vegas Blvd. S. (in Caesars Palace). ✆ **702/731-7110**. Everything under $10. AE, MC, V. Mon–Thurs 11am–11pm; Fri–Sat 11am–midnight.

Mon Ami Gabi ★★ BISTRO   This charming bistro is our new favorite local restaurant. It has it all: a delightful setting, better-than-average food, and affordable prices. Sure, it goes overboard in trying to replicate a classic Parisian bistro, but the results are less cheesy than most Vegas attempts at atmosphere, and the patio seating on the Strip (no reservations taken there—first-come, first-served, but a recent addition of 70 more seats probably helps matters) actually makes you feel like you're in a real, not a pre-fab, city. You can be budget-conscious and order just the very fine onion soup, or you can eat like a real French person and order classic steak (the filet mignon is probably the best cut, if not the cheapest) and *pommes frites* (french fries). There are plenty of cheaper options (which is why we listed this place in the "moderate" category, by the way), especially at lunch. Yes, they have snails, and we loved 'em. Desserts, by the way, are massive and should be shared (another way to save). The baseball-size profiteroles (three or four to an order) filled with fine vanilla ice cream and the football-size bananas-Foster crepe are particularly recommended. Ooh, la la!

In Paris Las Vegas, 3655 Las Vegas Blvd. S. ℂ 702/944-GABI (944-4224). Reservations recommended. Main courses $8.95–$27. AE, DC, DISC, MC, V. Sun–Thurs 11:30am–11pm; Fri–Sat 11:30am–midnight.

Olives ★★ ITALIAN/MEDITERRANEAN   If there was an Olives cafe in our neighborhood, we would eat there regularly. The less-expensive relative of The Mirage's Onda (as well as a branch of Todd English's original Boston-based restaurant), Olives is a strong choice for a light lunch that need not be as expensive as you might think. Here's how to enjoy a moderately priced meal here: munch on the focaccia bread, olives, and excellent tapenade they give you at the start, have a lovely salad (maybe of bibb lettuce, Maytag bleu cheese and walnut dressing) and then split a flatbread. Think pizza with an ultrathin crust (like a slightly limp cracker), topped with delicious combinations such as the highly recommended Moroccan spiced lamb, eggplant purée, and feta cheese, or our other favorite, fig, prosciutto, and Gorgonzola. They are rich and wonderful—split one between two people, and you have an affordable and terrific lunch. Or try a pasta; we were steered toward the simple but marvelous spaghettini with roasted tomatoes, garlic, and Parmesan, and were happy with it. The Cuban sandwich was basic but huge enough for another split option. The constructed, but not too fussy, food gets more complicated and costly at night, adding an array of meats and chickens, plus pastas such as butternut squash with brown butter and sage.

In Bellagio, 3600 Las Vegas Blvd. S. ℂ 702/693-7223. Reservations recommended. Main courses $15–$19 at lunch, $20–$34 at dinner; flatbreads $10–$15. AE, DC, DISC, MC, V. Daily 11am–2:30pm and 5–10:30pm.

Stage Deli ★★ DELI   New York City's Stage Deli—a legendary hangout for comedians, athletes, and politicians—has been slapping pastrami on rye for more than half a century. Its Las Vegas branch retains the Stage's brightly lit, Big Apple essence. Walls are embellished with subway graffiti and hung with Broadway theater posters, bowls of pickles grace the white Formica tables, and, in the New York tradition, comics and celebrities such as Buddy Hackett and Arnold Schwarzenegger drop by whenever they're in town.

The deli is often not crowded. In addition to being handy for Caesars guests, it's easy to pop over if you're staying next door at The Mirage, making it a satisfying breakfast alternative to the often overcrowded, overpriced, and not very good hotel breakfast joints in the area. The huge (we mean it) menu means it's easy to find something for even the pickiest of eaters.

Most of the fare—including fresh-baked pumpernickel and rye, meats, chewy bagels, lox, spicy deli mustard, and pickles—comes in daily from New York. The Stage dishes up authentic 5-inch-high sandwiches stuffed with pastrami, corned beef, brisket, or chopped liver. Maybe "overstuffed" is a better description. Unless you have a hearty appetite, are feeding two, or have a fridge in your room for leftovers, you might want to try the half sandwich and soup or salad combos.

Other specialties here include matzo ball soup, knishes, kasha varnishkes, cheese blintzes, kreplach, pirogen, and smoked-fish platters accompanied by bagels and cream cheese. Or you might prefer a full meal consisting of pot roast and gravy, salad, homemade dinner rolls, potato pancakes, and fresh vegetables. Desserts run the gamut from rugelach cheesecake to Hungarian-style apple strudel, and available beverages include wine and beer, milkshakes, Dr. Brown's sodas, and chocolate egg creams.

In the Forum Shops at Caesars, 3570 Las Vegas Blvd. S. ℂ 702/893-4045. Reservations accepted for large parties only. Main courses $10–$14; sandwiches $6–$14. AE, DC, DISC, MC, V. Sun–Thurs 8:30am–10:30pm; Fri–Sat 7:30am–11:30pm.

4 North Strip

MODERATE

Cafe Heidelberg German Deli and Restaurant ✦ GERMAN   A once-ponderous and dated German restaurant has been transformed into a German cafe already well packed (admittedly, with only six booths, not hard to do) with locals. Certainly, it's not a Vegas type of place, and because it's close enough to the Strip, it's a good place for refuge. The food is better than fine, though certainly not "lite" fare by any means. You should feel full but not heavy when you leave; you will be moaning and holding your stomach in sorrow only if you don't share those huge portions. Recommended is the sausage sampler platter, so you can finally learn the difference between knockwurst and bratwurst, and the schnitzel sandwich of delicious breaded veal. Wash it down with a vast choice of imported beer. As you munch, enjoy traditional (or, at times, not so) accordion music and note that the entire staff is German. This is also a full-service deli and German market, so it's a good place to pick up a picnic for sightseeing outside of the city.

604 E. Sahara. ℂ 702/731-5310. Reservations highly recommended for Fri–Sat nights. Main courses under $10 at lunch, $15–$20 at dinner. AE, DC, DISC, MC, V. Mon 11am–7pm; Tues–Thurs 11am–9pm; Fri–Sat 11am–10pm.

INEXPENSIVE

Capriotti's ✦✦✦ *Finds* SANDWICHES   It looks like a dump, but there's a reason that Capriotti's is one of the fastest-growing businesses in town. They roast their own beef and turkeys on the premises and stuff them (or Italian cold cuts, or whatever) into sandwiches mislabeled "small," "medium," and "large"—the latter clocks in at 20 inches, easily feeding two for under $10 total. And deliciously so; the "Bobby" (turkey, dressing, and cranberry sauce, like Thanksgiving dinner in sandwich form) would be our favorite sandwich in the world had we not tried their "Slaw B Joe"—roast beef, coleslaw, and Russian dressing. But other combos, such as the aforementioned Italian cold cuts, have their fans too, and they even have veggie varieties. There are outlets throughout the city, but this one is not only right off the Strip, but right by the freeway. When we say Vegas needs more true budget fare, with both taste and a mom and pop background (as opposed to a generic chain), we mean places like Capriotti's. We never leave town without a stop here, and you shouldn't, either.

324 W. Sahara Ave. (at Las Vegas Blvd. S.). ℂ 702/474-0229. Most sandwiches under $10. No credit cards. Daily 10am–7pm.

Chang's of Las Vegas ✦ CHINESE   Dim sum are little Chinese nibbles, most often spiced and diced bits of meat and shellfish stuffed into buns or wrapped with dough, then steamed or deep-fried. The menu lists the options

but doesn't explain what the heck anything is (here's one, just to help you out—
hai gow are steamed balls of dough-wrapped shrimp). Don't bother ordering
from the menu; instead, wait as steam carts are pushed around the room and
toward you, and the cart pusher pulls the lids off the many little pots, exposing
various tasties within. (Dim sum service stops at 3pm except by special order.)
You could ask for identification, but the answers might scare you—and scare
you off something quite marvelous. (We first tried chicken feet—yep—
to impress a mainland-born Chinese friend, and liked it very much indeed.) So
be brave and just point at something that looks good. Find out what you ate
later. Or never. Sometimes it's just better that way.

This strip-mall, cheerful, family-friendly (but possibly smoky) restaurant is a
good place to experiment, and is usually full of local and visiting Asians, which
is a stamp of authenticity. Highly recommended are the rice-noodle-wrapped
shrimp, and anything in a dumpling, particularly the pan-fried ones stuffed with
vegetables. For such seemingly small portions, dim sum can be quite filling, so
it works as both a snack and a potentially cheap meal. For some reason probably
having to do with quantum physics, we've noticed that whenever we eat dim
sum, alone, in a pair, or in a group of 12, the bill always works out to approximately $9 a person. Go figure.

In Gold Key Shopping Center, 3055 Las Vegas Blvd. S. ℭ **702/731-3388**. Dim sum $1.80–$5; main courses
$9.95–$17. AE, MC, V. Daily 10am–11pm (dim sum 10am–3pm).

Dona Maria Tamales ★★ MEXICAN   Decorated with Tijuana-style quilt
work and calendars, this quintessential Mexican diner is convenient to both the
north end of the Strip and Downtown. The cooks use lots of lard, lots of cheese,
and lots of sauce. As a result, the food is really good—and really fattening. Yep, the
folks who did those health reports showing how bad Mexican food can be for
your heart probably did some research here. The fat just makes it all the better,
in our opinion. Locals apparently agree; even at lunchtime the place is crowded.

You will start off with homemade chips and a spicy salsa served in a mortar.
Meals are so large that it shouldn't be a problem getting full just ordering off the
sides, which can make this even more of a budget option. Naturally, the specialty
is the fantastic tamales, which come in red, green, cheese, or sweet. They also
serve up excellent enchiladas, chiles rellenos, burritos, and fajitas. All dinners
include rice, beans, tortillas, and soup or salad. Sauces are heavy but oh-so-good.
For dessert, they have flan, fried ice cream, and Mexican-style pumpkin pie.

910 Las Vegas Blvd. S. (corner of Charleston Blvd.). ℭ **702/382-6538**. Main courses $5.45–$8 breakfast,
$6–$13 lunch or dinner. AE, MC, V. Daily 8am–10pm.

Liberty Cafe at the White Cross Pharmacy ★★ *Value* DINER   You can go
to any number of retro soda-fountain replicas (such as Johnny Rockets) and
theme restaurants that pretend to be cheap diners, but why bother when the real
thing is just past the end of the Strip? The decidedly unflashy soda fountain/
lunch counter at the White Cross Pharmacy was Las Vegas's first 24-hour restaurant, and it has been going strong for 60 years. Plunk down at the counter and
watch the cooks go nuts trying to keep up with the orders. The menu is basic
comfort food: standard grill items (meatloaf, ground round steak, chops, and so
on), fluffy cream pies, and classic breakfasts served "anytime"—try the biscuits
and cream gravy at 3am. They also serve gyros and the like. But the best bet is
a ⅓-pound burger and "thick, creamy shake," both the way they were meant to
be and about as good as they get. At around $5, this is half what you would pay
for a comparable meal at the Hard Rock Cafe. And as waitress Beverly says,

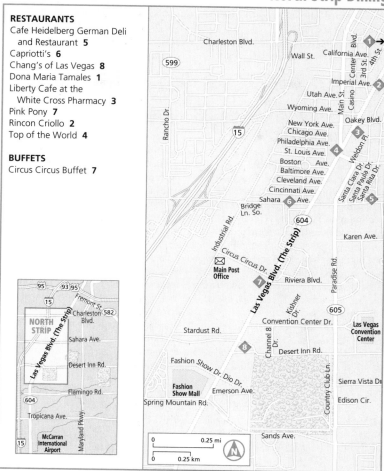

RESTAURANTS

Cafe Heidelberg German Deli
  and Restaurant **5**
Capriotti's **6**
Chang's of Las Vegas **8**
Dona Maria Tamales **1**
Liberty Cafe at the
  White Cross Pharmacy **3**
Pink Pony **7**
Rincon Criollo **2**
Top of the World **4**

BUFFETS

Circus Circus Buffet **7**

"This is really real." Places like this are a vanishing species—it's worth the short walk from the Stratosphere. Note, however, that the neighborhood remains stubbornly rough in appearance, full of litter and dubious-looking people, and that can be a turnoff. Keep alert if you come here at night.

1700 Las Vegas Blvd. S. ℂ **702/383-0196**. Reservations not accepted. Most items under $7. No credit cards. Daily 24 hr.

Rincon Criollo CUBAN   Located beyond the wedding chapels on Las Vegas Boulevard, Rincon Criollo has all the right details for a good, cheap ethnic joint: It's full of locals and empty of frills. It's not the best Cuban food ever, but it gets the job done. The main courses (featuring Cuban pork and chicken specialties) are hit or miss; try the marinated pork leg or, better still, ask your server for a recommendation. Paella is offered, but only for parties of three or more (and starts at $20). The side-course *chorizo* (a spicy sausage) is excellent, and the Cuban sandwich (roast pork, ham, and cheese on bread, which is then pressed and flattened out) is huge and tasty. For only $3.50, the latter makes a fine change-of-pace meal.

1145 Las Vegas Blvd. S. 🕿 **702/388-1906.** Reservations not accepted. Main courses $6.50–$10, paella (for 3) $20. AE, DISC, MC, V. Tues–Sun 11am–9:30pm.

5 East of the Strip

In this section, we cover restaurants close to the Convention Center, along with those farther south on Paradise Road, Flamingo Road, and Tropicana Avenue.

VERY EXPENSIVE

Lawry's The Prime Rib ★★★ STEAK/SEAFOOD   If you love prime rib, come here. If you could take or leave prime rib, Lawry's will turn you into a believer. Lawry's does one thing, and it does it better than anyone else. Lawry's first opened in Los Angeles in 1938 and remains a popular tradition. Over the years, they have added three branches; the most recent landed in Las Vegas at the beginning of 1997. Yes, you can get prime rib all over town for under $5. But, to mix a food metaphor, that's a tuna sandwich when you can have caviar at Lawry's.

Eating at Lawry's is a ceremony, with all the parts played the same way for the last 60 years. Waitresses in brown-and-white English-maid uniforms, complete with starched white cap, take your order—for side dishes, that is. The real decision, what cut of rib you are going to have, comes later. Actually, that's the only part of the tradition that has changed. Originally, all Lawry's offered was prime rib, which they did perfectly and with tremendous style. Now they have added fresh fish (halibut, salmon, or swordfish, depending on the evening) to the menu. Anyway, you tell the waitress what side dishes you might want (sublime creamed spinach, baked potato, and so on) for an extra price. Later, she returns with a spinning salad bowl (think of salad preparation as a Busby Berkeley musical number). The bowl, resting on crushed ice, spins as she pours Lawry's special dressing in a stream from high over her head. Tomatoes garnish. Applause follows. Eventually, giant metal carving carts come to your table, bearing the meat. You name your cut (the regular Lawry's, the extra-large Diamond Jim Brady for serious carnivores, and the wimpy thin English cut) and specify how you'd like it cooked. It comes with terrific Yorkshire pudding, nicely browned and not soggy, and some creamed horseradish that is combined with fluffy whipped cream, simultaneously sweet and tart.

Flavorful, tender, perfectly cooked, and lightly seasoned, this will be the best prime rib you will ever have. Okay, maybe that's going too far, but the rest is accurate, honest. It just has to be tasted to be believed. You can finish off with a rich dessert (English trifle is highly recommended), but it almost seems pointless. Incidentally, the other Lawry's are decorated English-manor style, but the Vegas branch has instead tried to re-create a 1930s restaurant, with Art Deco touches all around and big-band music on the sound system.

4043 Howard Hughes Pkwy. (at Flamingo Rd., between Paradise Rd. and Koval Lane). 🕿 **702/893-2223.** Reservations recommended. Main courses $20–$30. AE, DC, DISC, MC, V. Sun–Thurs 5–10pm; Fri–Sat 5–11pm.

Morton's of Chicago ★ STEAK/SEAFOOD   A venerable steakhouse with branches throughout the U.S.—in fact, Mr. Morton is the proud papa of Peter Morton, he of the Hard Rock Hotel over yonder. Like The Palm (p. 139), this place serves "boy food"—steaks, really good steaks—and we are not prepared to say which (The Palm or Morton's) has the better hunk o' red meat because frankly, after a while, these subtle distinctions elude us. Anyway, this is an old-time Vegas

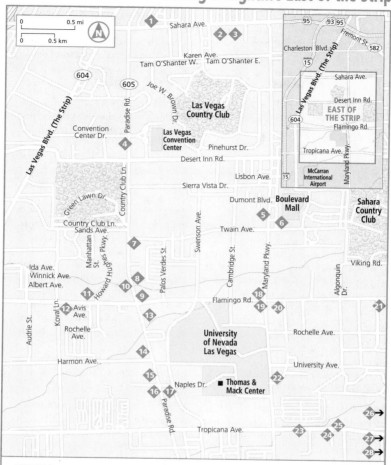

RESTAURANTS

Bougainvillea **13**
Carluccio's Tivoli Gardens **23**
Einstein Bros. Bagels **22**
Gordon-Biersch Brewing
  Company **10**
Hard Rock Cafe **14**
Kabuki **6**
Komol **3**
Lawry's The Prime Rib **11**
Leo's Deli **18**
Lotus of Siam **2**
Mediterranean Café
  & Market **19**
Memphis Championship
  Barbecue **28**

Mr. Lucky's 24/7 **14**
Morton's of Chicago **9**
Pamplemousse **1**
Pink Taco **14**
Shalimar **8**
The Tillerman **21**
Toto's **24**
Z Tejas Grill **7**

BUFFETS

The Buffet at the Las
  Vegas Hilton **7**
Sam's Town Firelight
  Buffet **21**

NIGHTLIFE

Icon **16**
Baby's **14**
The Beach **4**
The Buffalo **17**
Champagnes Cafe **5**
Club Monaco **20**
The Dispensary **24**
Double Down Saloon **17**
The Eagle **26**
Ellis Island Casino—
  Karaoke **12**
Gipsy **15**
Good Times **25**
Jazzed Cafe & Vinoteca **27**

hangout (because most actual old-time Vegas hangouts have closed), even in its relatively new off-Strip location. In addition to your cut of beef, suggested sides include flavorfully fresh al dente asparagus served with hollandaise or hash browns. And it's a good place to hang around, post-dinner, drink Scotch, and smoke.

400 E. Flamingo Rd. (at Paradise Rd.). ✆ **702/893-0703**. Reservations recommended. Main courses $18–$30. AE, DC, MC, V. Sun–Thurs 5:30–11pm; Fri–Sat 5–11:30pm.

Pamplemousse ✸ FRENCH   A little bit off the beaten path, Pamplemousse is a long-established Vegas restaurant that shouldn't be overlooked in the crush of new high-profile eateries. Evoking a cozy French-countryside inn (at least, on the interior), it's a catacomb of low-ceilinged rooms and intimate dining nooks with rough-hewn beams. It's all very charming and un-Vegasy. There's additional seating in a small garden sheltered by a striped tent. The restaurant's name, which means grapefruit in French, was suggested by the late singer Bobby Darin, one of the many celebrity pals of owner Georges La Forge.

The menu, which changes nightly, is recited by your waiter. The meal always begins with a large, complimentary basket of crudités (about 10 different crisp, fresh vegetables), a big bowl of olives, and, in a nice country touch, a basket of hard-boiled eggs. Recent menu offerings have included out-of-this-world soups (such as French onion and cream of asparagus), and such appetizers as shrimp in cognac-cream sauce or Maryland crab cakes with a macadamia-nut crust. Recommended entrees include a sterling veal with mushrooms and a Dijon sauce, and an even-better rack of lamb with a pistachio-nut crust and a rosemary-cream sauce (all sauces, by the way, are made with whatever the chef has on hand that evening in the kitchen). That's not to mention fabulous desserts such as homemade ice cream in a hard chocolate shell.

400 E. Sahara Ave. (between Santa Paula and Santa Rita drives, just east of Paradise Rd.). ✆ **702/733-2066**. Reservations required. Main courses $18–$26. AE, DC, DISC, MC, V. Tues–Sat 6–10:30pm; closed Mon except during major conventions and holidays.

The Tillerman ✸ STEAK/SEAFOOD   The Tillerman is on any number of locals' "best of Vegas" lists, and while we agree the food is terrific, the high prices and somewhat snooty attitude make us feel we can spend our money better elsewhere.

Of the four main dining rooms, the center one is the best; it's filled with plants and trees, and has high ceilings and a huge circular stained-glass window. There's additional seating on the mezzanine level, where diners enjoy treetop views. The meal begins with a relish tray and a basket of delicious oven-fresh breads. Also complimentary is a Lazy Susan salad bar served at your table with a choice of homemade dressings, including a memorable chunky blue cheese. Portions are immense, so appetizers are really not necessary, but then again, they're too good to pass up. Especially notable: crab cake garnished with carrot chips, superb filet medallions in a spicy red sauce, and yellowfin tuna blackened on the outside and almost rare on the inside, served in a spicy mustard sauce. For entrees, regulars often order the crab legs, which are excellent. The swordfish and halibut are wonderful too, as is the shrimp in garlic-cream sauce. The wine list is huge but expensive; the cheapest glass is $8. After such a large meal, a lighter dessert such as the Bavarian crème with strawberries might be in order. Skip the carrot cake in favor of the divine chocolate éclair.

2245 E. Flamingo Rd. (at Channel 10 Dr., just west of Eastern Ave.). ✆ **702/731-4036**. Reservations recommended. Main courses $20–$39. AE, DC, DISC, MC, V. Mon–Fri 5–10pm; Sat–Sun 5–10:30pm; bar/lounge until midnight daily.

MODERATE

Carluccio's Tivoli Gardens ⭐ *Finds* ITALIAN   A bit of a drive, but well worth it for those seeking an authentic (read: dining in a restaurant that's been around more than 10 years) Vegas experience. This joint used to be owned by none other than the Rhinestone King himself, Liberace. See, it's formerly Liberace's Tivoli Gardens, and he designed the interior himself, so you know what that looks like (it was reopened a few years after his death and they kept the decor pretty much intact). This kind of history is more and more rare in this town with no memory, plus it's right next door to the Liberace Museum, no coincidence, so go pay your giggling respects in the late afternoon and then stop here for dinner. Expect traditional Italian food (pasta, pasta, pasta, and scampi).

1775 E. Tropicana Blvd. (at Spencer). ✆ 702/795-3236. Reservations recommended. Main courses $10–$25. AE, DC, DISC, MC, V. Tues–Sun 4:30–10pm.

Gordon-Biersch Brewing Company ⭐ CALIFORNIA   This is a traditional brewpub (exposed piping and ducts, but still comfortable and casual), but it's worth going to for a meal as well. The menu is pub fare meets California cuisine (kids will probably find the food too complicated), and naturally, there are a lot of beers (German-style lagers) to choose from. Appetizers include satays (marinated meat on skewers served with spicy peanut sauce), pot stickers, calamari, baby back ribs, delicious beer-battered onion rings, and amazing garlic-encrusted fries. A wood-burning pizza oven turns out pies with California-type toppings: eggplant, shrimp, and so forth. For lunch, there are various pastas, stir-fries, sandwiches, and salads. The dinner menu eliminates the sandwiches and adds rosemary chicken, steaks, fish items, and, just in case you forgot it was a brewpub-type joint, beer everything: beer-glazed ham, beer meatloaf, and beer-barbecued glazed ribs. Doesn't that make you want to order a glass of milk?

3987 Paradise Rd. (just north of Flamingo Rd.). ✆ 702/312-5247. Main courses $11–$16. AE, DISC, MC, V. Sun–Thurs 11am–10pm; Fri–Sat 11:30am–11pm; bar open until 2am daily.

Kabuki JAPANESE   Primarily catering to a Japanese clientele, the Kabuki is a real taste of Japan. Rice paper covers the windows of this tastefully converted diner, while various paintings of Japanese kabuki actors grace the walls. The service is excellent, starting your meal off with a warm towel and green tea. Yes, they do have a small sushi bar, but the locals (who voted this their favorite Japanese restaurant in a recent *Las Vegas Review-Journal* poll) come back for the other Japanese dishes. *Negi ma,* a teriyaki-marinated beef rolled with onions, and *yaki gyoza* (pot stickers) are both amazing starters. For the main course, try *zarusoba* (cold Japanese buckwheat noodles), beef and chicken teriyaki, or *tatsuta age* (marinated chicken). They have plenty of sushi specials, including yellowtail, shrimp, and calamari, but there are other sushi places in town that do sushi better (admittedly in some cases for a higher price).

3949 S. Maryland Pkwy. ✆ 702/733-0066. Reservations required on weekend nights. Main courses $7–$17. AE, DC, DISC, MC, V. Mon–Sat 11:30am–2:30pm and 5:30–11pm.

Komol THAI   This is a hole-in-the-wall dive, like most good ethnic places. The menu is pretty large, divided into different sections for poultry, beef, and pork, plus a separate section for vegetarian dishes, plus many rice and noodle selections. They'll spice the food to your specifications. Unless you know your spicy Asian food, it might be best to play it on the safe side. (While we don't want things bland, too much heat can overwhelm all other flavors. The mild to medium packs enough of a kick for most people.)

Among the items tried during a recent visit were a vegetarian green curry and the *pud-kee-mao* (flat rice noodles stir-fried with ground chicken, mint, garlic, and hot peppers). *Nam sod* is ground pork with a hot-and-sour sauce, ginger, and peanuts, all of which you wrap up in lettuce leaves—sort of an Asian burrito. Sort of. The Thai iced tea was particularly good—just the right amount of sweetness and tea taste for a drink that is often served overly sweet.

Worth noting: The Commercial Center also has any number of other ethnic (mostly Asian) restaurants, including Korean barbecue.

In the Commercial Center, 953 E. Sahara. ℭ 702/731-6542. Reservations accepted. Main courses $5.60–$11. AE, DISC, MC, V. Mon–Sat 11am–10pm; Sun noon–10pm.

Memphis Championship Barbecue ★★ BARBECUE   Okay, we refuse, simply refuse, to get into the debate about Texas vs. Kansas City vs. Mississippi barbecue (and if you've got another state with the best dang barbecue, we really don't want to hear about it). But we can say that if you aren't physically in those places, you gotta take what you can get—and luckily for Vegas visitors, eating at Memphis Championship Barbecue is hardly settling. Its vinegar-based sauce is sweet but has a kick. Food is cooked over mesquite applewood, and the meat falls off the bone just the way you want it to. They have hot links, baked beans, everything you would want and hope for. Standouts include a pulled-barbecue-chicken sandwich, onion straws, and delicious mac and cheese. Note this special: a $50 feast includes a rack of baby back ribs, three-fourths of a pork shoulder, ¾ pound of beef brisket, ½ pound of hot links, a whole chicken, baked beans, coleslaw, rolls, cream corn, and fries. It feeds four; we think even if two of those four are teenage boys, you might have leftovers.

2250 E. Warm Springs Rd. (near 215 Fwy.). ℭ 702/260-6909. Reservations not required. Entrees $8–$17. Special barbecue dinner $50 for 4 people. AE, DC, DISC, MC, V. Sun–Thurs 11am–10pm; Fri–Sat 11am–11pm.

Pink Taco ★ MEXICAN   A mega-hip Mexican cantina, this folk-art-bedecked spot is a scene just waiting to happen, or rather, it's already happened. There are no surprises in terms of the food—you know the drill, tacos, burritos, quesadillas—but it's all tasty and filling, and some of it comes with some surprising accompaniments, like *tapenade* (an olive-based spread), along with the usual guacamole and sour cream. This is hip Mexican as opposed to a mom and pop joint, and it's a good place to eat on this side of town.

In the Hard Rock Hotel & Casino, 4455 Paradise Rd. ℭ 702/693-5525. Reservations not accepted. Main course $7.50–$13. AE, DC, DISC, MC, V. Sun–Thurs 11:30–10pm, Fri–Sun 11:30am–midnight.

Shalimar INDIAN   In a town full of buffet deals, it's hard to get excited about another one, but on the other hand, all those other buffet deals offer pretty much identical food: carving stations, various cafeteria hot dishes, and so forth. Here at Shalimar, a lunch buffet means about two dozen different North Indian–style dishes, all for about $7.50. It's not as colorful or huge (in fact, it's just a table covered with steam trays) as those buffets up the street, but it is far more interesting. It's also a great deal and one of the first places to run to if you're sick of Strip food. Just ask the locals, who voted it their favorite ethnic restaurant in the *Las Vegas Review-Journal's* annual poll.

The buffet usually includes *tandoori* (chicken marinated in spiced yogurt and cooked in a clay oven), *masala* (tandoori in a curry sauce), *naan* (the flat Indian bread), and various vegetable dishes. Vegetarians will find plenty to eat here—they offer special veggie dishes daily. One standout at a recent visit was the *ben-gan bharta* (eggplant diced fine and cooked with onions, tomatoes, and spices).

There was also a yellow-squash curry that was outrageously good. The tandoori chicken was perfect, tender, and moist. (Tandoori, by the way, is a very low-fat way of preparing chicken.) In the evening, there is a full Indian menu, with *vindaloo* (an especially hot curry where the meat is marinated in vinegar), flavored naans (try the garlic or onion), and other Indian specialties offered a la carte. They will spice to order: mild, medium, hot, or very hot. If you make a mistake, you can always order *raita* (yogurt mixed with mild spices and cucumber); it cools your mouth nicely.

The restaurant has managed to spruce up its strip-mall corner nicely, thanks to some Indian-style metal hanging lamps and peaked archways.

In the Citibank Plaza, 3900 S. Paradise Rd. ℂ **702/796-0302**. Reservations recommended. Lunch buffet $7.50, main courses $11–$16 at dinner. AE, DISC, MC, V. Mon–Fri 11:30am–2:30pm; daily 5:30–10:30pm.

Z Tejas Grill ★ TEX-MEX   This Austin, Texas–based restaurant's rather odd name came about because its original chef, a Frenchman, kept referring to it as "zee" Tejas Grill. Featuring self-proclaimed "South by Southwestern" cuisine, it recently got a handsome makeover, lining the interior with streamlined warm woods and black accents. There is a vine-covered patio for outdoor dining, rare for Vegas, with misters for summer and a fireplace and heaters for winter. For some reason, traffic noise does not permeate from the nearby street.

You might also consider downing some large and excellent margaritas at the newly enlarged, very lively bar, particularly on weeknights, when happy hour (4–7pm) finds all starters half price. Given the size of said starters, this would be a very cheap meal option. In particular, we like the generously portioned grilled-fish tacos, which come wrapped in fresh tortillas, stuffed with all kinds of veggies, and served with a spicy Japanese sauce. Not your usual drippy, fattening tacos. Less of a bargain, but mighty tasty, is the tender and piquant black-sesame tuna, with a black-peppercorn vinaigrette and a soy-mustard sauce. (There's a larger version of this found under the entrees; it's called "Voodoo Tuna," and it's not quite as good.) A better main course would be the spicy grilled Jamaican-jerk chicken, nuanced with lime and served with peanut sauce and rum-spiked coconut-banana ketchup; it comes with two side dishes—when we were there, garlic mashed potatoes and a corn-casserole soufflé.

3824 Paradise Rd. (between Twain Ave. and Corporate Dr.). ℂ **702/732-1660**. Reservations recommended. Main courses $7.25–$12 at lunch, $8.75–$17 at dinner. AE, DC, DISC, MC, V. Daily 11am–10pm.

INEXPENSIVE

Bougainvillea ★★ (Value COFFEE SHOP   Oh, how we love a Vegas coffee shop. You got your all-day breakfasts, your graveyard-shift specials (10pm–8am, New York Steak and eggs for $4.99), your prime rib, and, of course, your full Chinese menu. And it's all hearty and well priced; we're talkin' build your own three-egg, three-ingredient omelet for $4.99. You can get a full dinner entree, or a nice light lunch of a large half a sandwich and soup, also for $4.99 (is that someone's lucky number?). And 24-hour specials, which include a slab of meat, plus potato or rice, veggies, soup or salad, and a 12-ounce draft beer, run between $7.99 and $12.99. Yep. That's the ticket.

4100 Paradise Rd. (in Terrible's hotel). ℂ **702/733-7000**. Entrees $1.99–$12.99. AE, MC, V. Daily 24 hr.

Leo's Deli ★ (Finds DELI   Under new ownership, this is a basic, solid New York deli, though lacking the mammoth portions of the Stage Deli (though perhaps that's a good thing), but it also doesn't charge the occasionally mammoth prices that the Stage does. It also does not require navigating the Strip and the

Caesars Forum Shops (which means it's more convenient for those staying at accommodations east of the Strip). And in many ways, it's more authentic, from its revolving pastry case to the middle-aged waitresses with thick foundation and thick ankles who shout your order back to the kitchen. The clientele are classic Vegas characters, of an age to have been fans of the youthful Paul Anka. If you are lucky, you might sit next to a table full of dealers swapping war stories about their pit bosses.

As mentioned, these are not the monster portions of modern-day chain delis, but you won't go hungry. Don't look for anything vegetarian here; instead, you got your pastrami on rye, your matzo-ball soup, your chopped liver, your tongue, your meatloaf, your lox and bagel, and so on. Desserts are a bit sparse for a deli, but you can't go wrong with the black-and-white cookies. Go ahead—have a nosh.

4055 S. Maryland Pkwy. (at Flamingo Rd.). ℂ **702/733-7827**. Reservations not accepted. Main courses $7–$12. AE, MC, V. Mon–Sat 9am–8pm; Sun 9am–4pm.

Einstein Bros. Bagels ✿ BAGELS   You may not like digging into an enormous buffet first thing in the morning, and the continental breakfast in most hotels is a rip-off. A welcome alternative is a fresh-baked bagel, of which there are 15 varieties here—everything from onion to wild blueberry. Cream cheeses also come in many flavors, anything from sun-dried tomato to vegetable and jalapeño. Einstein's is a pleasant place for a morning meal, with both indoor seating and outdoor tables cooled by misters. Service is friendly, and four special-blend coffees are available each day.

Note: Bagel buffs might also want to check out the nearby **Bagelmania** at 855 Twain Ave. (ℂ **702/369-3322**). The bagels are sometimes chilled for freshness, which is heresy. Avoid this problem by catching them early in the morning, when their extensive selection is hot and fresh.

In the University Gardens Shopping Center, 4626 S. Maryland Pkwy. (between Harmon and Tropicana aves.). ℂ **702/795-7800**. All items under $6. MC, V. Mon–Fri 6am–7pm; Sat 6am–6pm; Sun 6:30am–5pm.

Lotus of Siam ✿✿✿ *(Finds)* THAI   So we drag you out to a strip mall in the east end of nowhere and you wonder why? Because here is what critic Jonathan Gold of *Gourmet* magazine called no less than the best Thai restaurant in North America.

What makes this place so darn special? First of all, in addition to all the usual beloved Thai favorites, they have a separate menu featuring lesser-known dishes from northern Thailand—they don't routinely hand this one out (since most of the customers are there for the more pedestrian, if still excellent, $5.99 lunch buffet). Second, the owner drives at least twice a week back to Los Angeles (where his original venue, Renu Na Korn, is still operating under another family member) to pick up the freshest herbs and other ingredients needed for his dishes' authenticity. That's dedication that should be rewarded with superlatives.

You might be best off letting them know you are interested in northern food (with dried chiles and more pork, it's not un-Cajun-like, says the owner) and letting them guide you through, though you must assure them that you aren't of faint heart or palate (some customers complain the heat isn't enough, even with "well spiced" dishes, though others find even medium spice sufficient). Standouts include the Issan sausage (a grilled sour pork number), the *nam kao tod* (that same sausage, ground up with lime, green onion, fresh chile, and ginger, served with crispy rice), *nam sod* (ground pork mixed with ginger, green onion, and lime juice, served with sticky rice), jackfruit *larb* (spicy ground meat), and *sua rong hai* ("weeping tiger"), a dish of soft, sliced, grilled, marinated beef. If you insist on more conventional Thai, that's okay, in that it's unlikely you are going to have better *mee krob* noodles or *tom kah kai* (that beloved soup can also be served northern style, if asked, which is without the coconut milk). If in season, finish with mango with sticky rice, or if not, coconut ice cream with sticky rice, something you would find at many a street stall in Thailand.

953 E. Sahara Ave. #A-5. (C) 702/735-3033. Reservations strongly suggested for dinner. Lunch buffet $5.99, other dishes $3.95–$14. AE, MC, V. Daily 11:30am–2:30pm and 5–9:30pm.

Mediterranean Café & Market ★ MEDITERRANEAN The emphasis on safe mainstream food for the masses, to say nothing of the basic economy involved in running a Vegas restaurant (take your pick, either pay costly rent to a Strip hotel, or get less tourist traffic with an off-Strip site), means that the kind of eateries other big cities take for granted—you know, cheap holes-in-the-wall, or charming little quirky joints, or the kind of ethnic places the chowhound folks brag about discovering—are rare indeed. And when you do find them, they are always, but always, in a strip mall.

The Mediterranean Café is no exception, and its main dining room has no decor worth mentioning. But it gets extra points for having a courtyard seating area full of Middle Eastern touches and an honest-to-goodness hookah lounge—it's a good break from an otherwise often stifled, insulating time in Sin City.

Plus, it's just so darn nice to find ethnic food in this town. Kebobs take, the menu warns, 25 minutes, so order an appetizer plate with various dips to while away the time. Hummus is too reminiscent of its chickpea origins, but baba ghanouj is properly smoky, and the falafel has the right crunch. Gyros may not be the most adventurous thing to order, but who cares about that when you've got a well-stuffed pocket of pita, gloopy with sweet yogurt sauce. *Fresenjan* is a dish of falling-apart chicken, swimming in a tangy pomegranate sauce; ask them to ensure that the ratio of sauce to chicken is greater than 10:1.

4147 S. Maryland Pkwy. (at Flamingo Rd., in the Tiffany Sq. strip mall). (C) 702/731-6030. Reservations not accepted. Main courses $8–$16 (all sandwiches under $8). AE, DISC, MC, V. Restaurant Mon–Sat 11am–9pm, Sun 11am–5pm; lounge Tues–Thurs 5pm–midnight, Fri–Sat 5pm–2am.

Toto's ★★ *Kids* *Value* MEXICAN A family-style Mexican restaurant favored by locals, with enormous portions and quick service, this is good value for your money. With all that food, you could probably split portions and still be satisfied. There are no surprises on the menu, though there are quite a few seafood dishes. Everything is quite tasty, and they don't skimp on the cheese. The non-greasy chips come with fresh salsa, and the nachos are terrific. Chicken tamales got a thumbs-up, while the veggie burrito was happily received by non–meat eaters (although it's not especially healthy, all the ingredients were fresh, with huge slices of zucchini and roasted bell peppers). The operative word here is *huge;* the burritos are almost the size of your arm. The generous portions continue with dessert—a piece of flan was practically pie-size. The Sunday margarita brunch is quite fun, and the drinks are large (naturally) and yummy.

2055 E. Tropicana Ave. (C) 702/895-7923. Main courses $6.25–$14. AE, DISC, MC, V. Mon–Thurs 10am–10pm; Fri–Sat 11am–11pm; Sun 9am–10pm.

6 West Las Vegas

EXPENSIVE

Austins Steakhouse ★★ *Finds* STEAK/SEAFOOD Now, understand that we don't send you out to nether regions such as Texas Station lightly. We do so here because, improbably, Austins Steakhouse has gained a reputation for the best steak in town. Really. Even the snooty critics at the *Las Vegas Review-Journal* agree with the hubbub about this place. And here's what has everyone, including us, raving: a 24-ounce rib-eye—yes, we know, just split it—aged and marinated, cooked over mesquite applewood, then rubbed with peppercorns and pan-seared in garlic, butter, and cilantro. A massive chunk of meat with a smoky, garlicky flavor like no other steak we can think of. Most of the dishes have a Southern twist, like the fried green tomatoes with a rémoulade dipping sauce, and for those not watching their cholesterol, or at least only watching it go up, the shrimp sautéed in garlic butter sauce, dipped in cheese and wrapped in bacon. The Maui onion soup is also a standout, as is, over in the desserts, the chocolate decadence cake, which actually has a molten center, sort of a semi-soufflé. Note that a comparable meal on the Strip would cost $10 to $20 more per person—yet another reason to head out to the hinterlands.

In Texas Station, 2101 Texas Star Lane. © **702/631-1000.** Reservations recommended. Main courses $15–$30. AE, DC, DISC, MC, V. Sun–Thurs 5–10pm; Fri–Sat 5–11pm.

Cafe Nicolle ★ CONTINENTAL   Cafe Nicolle is a local favorite, a place to go for either a special occasion (we noted at least one pre-prom couple) or just to hang out on the lovely patio, which features a cooling mist on hot summer nights. (Patio dining is a rarity in Vegas, and the space is just charming.) Even the waitstaff eats here on their off nights, which is a mighty fine recommendation. Inside, it's airy, though unimaginatively decorated ('80s black lacquer), with tables set far enough apart for a pleasant buzz but not enough for your neighbor to eavesdrop.

There are no surprises on the menu—pastas, crepes, chicken, and veal—but everything is beautifully prepared and served attractively with generous portions. They have extremely good, fresh fish, presented very simply, so the fish's own flavor is able to shine, as opposed to being overwhelmed by sauces. The Florentine crepe is made with lots of fresh spinach and not too much cheese in the sauce. Be sure to dip your fresh bread in the excellent garlic-and-rosemary olive oil found on the table.

Cafe Nicolle is not all that different from restaurants found on the Strip, but if you need a break from the hubbub and the sometimes suffocating crush of people there, or just want a chance to dine in a restaurant with windows and breathe some fresh air, this is worth the short drive.

In the Sahara Pavilion, 4760 W. Sahara Blvd. (at Decatur Blvd.). © **702/870-7675.** Reservations recommended for large parties. Main courses $7–$15 at lunch, $16–$25 at dinner. AE, DC, MC, V. Mon–Sat 11am–10pm.

Rosemary's Restaurant ★★★ *Finds* NOUVELLE AMERICAN   No visitor would be blamed for never leaving the Vegas Strip—it's the raison d'être of any Vegas tourist—but a true foodie should make a point of finding the nearest moving vehicle that can get them to Rosemary's Restaurant. A 15-minute (or so) drive down Sahara (hardly anything) is all it takes to eat what may well be the best food in Las Vegas (certainly, it is consistently voted the best food in the *Las Vegas Review-Journal*'s annual poll, by food critics and readers alike).

The brainchild of Michael and Wendy Jordan, both veterans of the New Orleans food scene (Michael actually opened Emeril's Seafood here in Vegas), Rosemary's Restaurant (named for Michael's mother) shows more than a few NOLA touches, from the food to the service, in a room that's warmer and

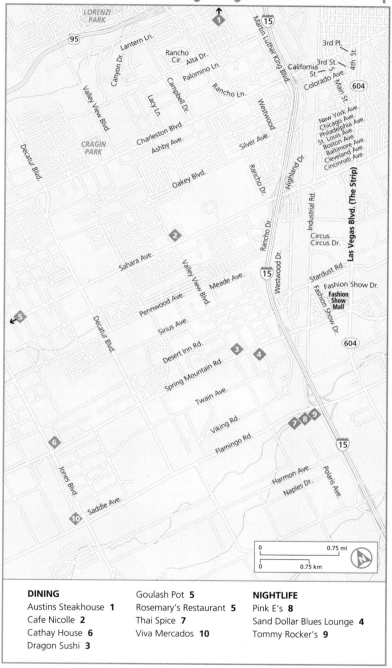

DINING

Austins Steakhouse **1**
Cafe Nicolle **2**
Cathay House **6**
Dragon Sushi **3**

Goulash Pot **5**
Rosemary's Restaurant **5**
Thai Spice **7**
Viva Mercados **10**

NIGHTLIFE

Pink E's **8**
Sand Dollar Blues Lounge **4**
Tommy Rocker's **9**

more inviting than most others in Vegas. Note that you can get seats at the bar overlooking the open kitchen, great fun for foodie interaction and not a bad choice for singles, or for couples looking for an unusual romantic evening.

The cuisine covers most regions of the U.S., though Southern influences dominate. But the Northern California–Alice Waters example has not been lost; 50 local farmers help supply products. Seared foie gras with peach coulis, candied walnuts, and vanilla bean–scented arugula is like a quilt, with distinct flavors that all hang together nicely. Interesting sides include ultra-rich bleu-cheese slaw, slightly spicy crispy fried tortilla strips, and perfect cornmeal jalapeño hush puppies, to say nothing of "Grandma's pickled cucumbers." A recent visit found the crispy striped bass fighting it out with the pan-seared honey-glazed salmon for "best fish dish I've ever had." Desserts are similarly Southern—lemon icebox pie!—and most pleasant.

There is a nice little wine list with a broad range, especially when it comes to half-price bottles. They also specialize, unusually, in beer suggestions to pair with courses, including some fruity Belgian numbers; this is such a rare treat, if you drink, you must try some of their suggestions.

Note: Rosemary's Restaurant has a second location, Rosemary's at the Rio (© **702/777-2300**), in the former Napa space at the Rio hotel. More convenient for most of you, but also slightly higher priced and with less directly American classic influenced dishes and more flights of culinary fancy such as goat cheese stuffed squash blossoms and roasted elk loin.

8125 W. Sahara. © **702/869-2251.** Reservations strongly suggested. Lunch $12–$16, dinner $18–$29. AE, MC, V. Mon–Fri 11:30am–2:30pm and nightly 5:30–10:30pm for dinner.

MODERATE

Cathay House CHINESE   Las Vegas actually has a Chinatown—a very large strip mall (naturally) on Spring Mountain Road near Wynn. There are several Asian restaurants there, but ask locals who look like they know, and they will send you instead farther up Spring Mountain Road to the Cathay House (on the opposite side of the street). This only looks far from the Strip on a map; it's really about a 7-minute drive from Treasure Island.

Ordering dim sum, for those of you who haven't experienced it, is sort of like being at a Chinese sushi bar, in that you order many individual, tasty little dishes. Of course, dim sum itself is nothing like sushi. Rather, it's a range of pot stickers, pan-fried dumplings, *baos* (soft, doughy buns filled with such meat as barbecued pork), translucent rice noodles wrapped around shrimp, sticky rice in lotus leaves, chicken feet, and so forth. Some of it is steamed; some is fried—for that extra-good grease! You can make your own dipping sauce by combining soy sauce, vinegar, and hot-pepper oil. The waitstaff pushes steam carts filled with little dishes; point, and they'll attempt to tell you what each one is. Better, just blindly order a bunch and dig in. Each dish ranges from approximately $1 to $3; each server makes a note of what you just received, and the total is tallied at the end. (For some reason, it almost always works out to about $9 per person.) Dim sum is usually available only until midafternoon.

The standout at the Cathay House was a vegetable *bao* that included Chinese glass noodles. Lightly browned and not overly doughy like many baos, it was slightly sweet and utterly delicious. The shrimp wrapped in rice noodles were big and plump, while anything that was fried was so good we decided to ignore our arteries for a while. Cathay House (which features quite a good view through the windows on one side) also has a full dinner menu, which includes the strawberry chicken invented by Chin's; it's considerably cheaper here.

In Spring Valley, 5300 W. Spring Mountain Rd. ℂ **702/876-3838**. Reservations recommended. Main courses $6.75–$19. AE, DC, DISC, MC, V. Daily 10:30am–10pm.

Thai Spice *(Value* THAI   Just off the Strip and across from the Rio hotel, this modern-looking, nonglitzy Thai restaurant offers decent food at reasonable prices. The subdued ambience (okay, it's a little boring, but not everything can be flashy, even in Vegas), quick service, and good food make it a local favorite. The menu is extensive and offers an array of Thai dishes and even some Chinese fare. For appetizers, the *tom kah kai* soup and pork or chicken satay (served on skewers with a spicy peanut sauce) are excellent. Skip the terrible *moo goo gai pan* in favor of terrific pad Thai and tasty lemon chicken. Lunch specials are $5.95 and include spring rolls, salad, soup, and steamed rice. Make sure you tell the waitress how spicy you want your food.

4433 W. Flamingo Rd. (at I-15). ℂ **702/362-5308**. Main courses $5.95 at lunch, $8–$15 at dinner. AE, DISC, MC, V. Mon–Thurs 11am–10pm; Fri–Sat 11am–11pm.

Viva Mercados *★★* MEXICAN   Ask any local about Mexican food in Vegas and almost certainly they will point to Viva Mercados as the best in town. That recommendation, plus the restaurant's health-conscious attitude, makes this worth the roughly 10-minute drive from the Strip.

Given all those warnings lately about Mexican food and its heart-attack-inducing properties, the approach at Viva Mercados is nothing to be sniffed at. No dish is prepared with or cooked in any kind of animal fat. Nope, the lard so dear to Mexican cooking is not found here. The oil used is an artery-friendly canola. This makes the place particularly appealing to vegetarians, who will also be pleased by the regular veggie specials. Everything is quite fresh, and they do particularly amazing things with seafood. Try the *Maresco Vallarta,* which is orange roughy, shrimp, and scallops cooked in a coconut tomato sauce, with capers and olives. They have all sorts of noteworthy shrimp dishes, and 11 different salsas, ranked 1 to 10 for degree of spice. (Ask for advice first.) The staff is friendly (try to chat with owner Bobby Mercado) and the portions hearty.

6182 W. Flamingo Rd. (at Jones Blvd.). ℂ **702/871-8826**. Reservations accepted only for large parties. Main courses $8–$17. AE, DISC, MC, V. Sun–Thurs 11am–9:30pm; Fri–Sat 11am–10:30pm.

INEXPENSIVE

Dragon Sushi SUSHI   Those used to really extraordinary sushi need to remember that you are in the middle of the desert, and so there is no way the fish you are going to eat here were swimming the ocean all that recently. This also results in less than generously sized pieces. That said, they do pretty good sushi here, with rolls that pack a wallop, such as the Tuna Tuna Roll (spicy tuna with fresh tuna wrapped around it, and, unless we miss our guess, some kind of chili oil for good measure). Don't say we didn't warn you about the Hell Roll. If the incongruously named sushi chef Bruce is working, let this morose and talented man do his work for you. Better still, let him make all your choices.

4115 Spring Mountain Rd. (at Valley View Blvd.). ℂ **702/368-4336**. Sushi $3.50–$5.50 per portion, main courses all under $20. AE, MC, V. Sun–Thurs 11:30am–10:30pm; Fri–Sat 11:30am–midnight.

Goulash Pot *★ (Finds* HUNGARIAN   Here's a sign that Vegas might really be developing a culture of its own, as contradictory as that sounds. When the local immigrant culture is moving beyond the basic Asian and South-of-the-Border entries and starts showing representatives from, say, the Balkans and Eastern Europe, the local personality is all the better. This (naturally) strip mall–located spot serves absolutely authentic Hungarian food—we've eaten paprikash and

Sweet Sensations

Plenty of opportunities exist in Vegas for satisfying your sweet tooth, but for the discriminating, here are four spots that you may have to make a detour for. We think they're worth it.

There aren't lots of doughnut places around town, and most of the ones you'll find are of the chain variety—fine if you have a yen on the spot, but in reality, you might as well be eating frosted foam rubber. If you're a connoisseur with a car or happen to be checking out the restaurants in the Chinatown area on Spring Mountain Road, go to **Ronald's Donuts,** 4600 Spring Mountain Rd., at Decatur (② **702/873-1032**). Hours are Monday to Saturday from 4am to 5pm, Sunday from 4am to 2pm. Some have called these doughnuts celestial. You decide.

Do a comparison taste test with **Krispy Kreme Donuts,** just a few more minutes down the road at 7015 W. Spring Mountain Rd., at Rainbow Boulevard (② **702/222-2320**). There are more convenient but more crowded (and higher-priced) Krispy Kreme locations in the Palace Station, Texas Station, Boulder Station, Treasure Island, and Excalibur, as well. Krispy Kreme prompts rabid devotion in its fans— like us, who on our first visit ate two of their famous glazed (don't bother with any of the other varieties) before we even cleared the drive-through. These are better hot, or at least nearly, and the "hot donuts" sign flashes from 5 to 11am and 5 to 11pm. Dine-in 5am to 11pm, drive-through Sunday through Thursday between 5am and 11pm, Friday and Saturday between 5am and 1am.

Another favorite is **Freed's Bakery,** 4780 S. Eastern Ave., at Tropicana Boulevard (② **702/456-7762**), open Monday through Saturday from 7am to 6pm. If you've got a serious sugar craving, this is worth making the 15-minute drive from the Strip. Despite the minimalist setting, it's like walking into Grandma's kitchen (provided you had an old-fashioned granny who felt pastries should not be fancy but should definitely be gooey, chocolaty, and buttery). The chocolate coffee cake is especially good. They also have fresh bread, napoleons, strawberry cheesecake, cream puffs, hamantaschen, sweet rolls, Danishes, and doughnuts. Some may find the goodies too heavy and rich, but for those of us with a powerful sweet tooth, this place hits the spot.

Hot Vegas days call for cool desserts, and frozen custard (softer than regular ice cream, but harder than soft serve) is a fine way to go. Head for **Luv-It Frozen Custard,** 505 E. Oakey, at the Strip (② **702/384-6452**), open Monday to Thursday from 11am to 10pm, Friday from 11am to 11pm, Saturday from noon to 11pm, and Sunday from 1 to 10pm. Since it has less fat and sugar than premium ice cream, from which it also differs slightly in taste and texture, you can even fool yourself into thinking this is somewhat healthy (hah!). Made every few hours using fresh cream and eggs, Luv-It Frozen Custard has basic flavors available for cup or cone, but more exotic ones (maple walnut, apple spice, and more) in tubs.

goulash (remember, real goulash is a soup, not a stew; you want a *porkolt* for that) exactly the same in Budapest and smaller towns. Which is to say the portions aren't huge (unless you get the sample platter of various meats and sausages), but they are hearty, complete with the traditional tiny dumplings and good-quality bread. Try the sweet-vinegar cucumber salad or the Hungarian crepes for dessert. On a recent visit, the place was full of homesick expats (who knew?), including one woman on the phone with her ailing Hungarian mother, whom she was just about to visit in Colorado. Mom was placing an order. It's comfort food for her, for us, and maybe for you. And when you are done, drop by the next-door Crown International Market, run by the same folks, for all your deli and other import-grocery wants, or get a fabulous Hungarian salami sandwich to go.

6135 W. Sahara. ℂ **702/253-7378.** Everything under $12. AE, MC, V. Daily 11am–9pm.

7 Downtown

VERY EXPENSIVE

Andre's ✦✦ FRENCH   Andre's has long been the bastion of gourmet dining in Vegas, but with all the new big boys crowding the Strip, it runs the risk of getting overlooked. It shouldn't—Andre may not have a show on the Food Network, but he ought to be a household name. Besides, his first restaurant still dominates Downtown. (This is also a celebrity haunt where you're likely to see Strip headliners. One night, Tom Hanks, Steven Spielberg, and James Spader were all spotted joining some pals for a bachelor party. The staff played it cool, though.) In a small, converted 1930s house, you'll find an elegant French provincial atmosphere, overseen by owner-chef Andre, who brings over 40 years of experience to the table. Much of the waitstaff is also French, and they will happily lavish attention on you and guide you through the menu.

The food presentation is exquisite, and choices change seasonally. On a recent visit, an appetizer of Northwest smoked salmon *mille feuille* with cucumber salad and sevruga caviar was especially enjoyed, as was a main course of grilled veal tournedos with chive sauce accompanied by a mushroom and foie gras crepe. You get the idea. Desserts are similarly lovely, an exotic array of rich delights. An extensive wine list (more than 900 labels) is international in scope and includes many rare vintages; consult the sommelier.

Note: An additional branch of Andre's is in the **Monte Carlo Hotel & Casino,** 3775 Las Vegas Blvd. S. (ℂ **702/798-7151**), and is also highly recommended, as is their slightly different take, **Alizé** (p. 135), in the new Palms hotel.

401 S. 6th St. (at Lewis St., 3 blocks south of Fremont St.). ℂ **702/385-5016.** Reservations required. Main courses $25–$38. AE, DC, MC, V. Sun–Thurs 5:30–9:30pm; Fri–Sat 5:30–10:30pm.

Hugo's Cellar ✦ INTERNATIONAL   Hugo's Cellar is indeed in a cellar, or at least below street level in the Four Queens hotel. No, they aren't ashamed of it—quite the opposite. This is a gourmet restaurant, and it is highly regarded by the locals. Each female guest is given a red rose when she enters the restaurant—the first of a series of nice touches. The restaurant proper is dimly lit, lined with dark wood and brick. It's fairly intimate, but if you really want to be cozy, ask for one of the curtained booths against the wall.

The meal is full of ceremony, perfectly delivered by a well-trained and cordial waitstaff. Salads, included in the price, are prepared at your table, from a cart full of choices. (In Vegas style, though, most choices are on the calorie-intensive side.) A tiny cup with a palate-cleansing sorbet prepares you for the main course.

Unfortunately, despite the high regard, the main courses are not all that novel (various cuts of meat, seafood, and chicken prepared different ways) and can be disappointing. Promising choices include the chicken "Hugo" (with basil and pine nuts prepared in a cream sauce), and the rack of lamb with Indonesian spices. Vegetables are included, as is a finish of chocolate-dipped fruits with cream.

The service is impeccable (you have little-to-no wait between courses), and it really makes you feel pampered. The fact that salad, the small dessert, and so forth are included makes an initially hefty-seeming price tag appear a bit more reasonable, especially when compared to Strip establishments that aren't much better and can cost nearly twice as much. While the main courses aren't spectacular, the salads and desserts are fine. It's not worth going out of your way for the food, but perhaps it is for the whole package.

In the Four Queens hotel, 202 Fremont St. (at Casino Center Blvd.). ℂ **702/385-4011**. Reservations required. Main courses $26–$42. AE, DC, DISC, MC, V. Daily 5:30–11pm.

EXPENSIVE

Limericks ⭐ STEAK/SEAFOOD   Decorated in the classic Olde English gentlemen's club style, Limericks is meant to be an oasis of gracious dining away from hectic casino life, and the overall effect is comforting and moderately womblike, particularly in the cozy booths at the back. Unfortunately, casino "cachings" still creep in, but it's not overly bothersome. The menu is classic, upscale steakhouse: beef, chops, some lobster, and chicken. The portions are Vegas-size (the small prime rib was 14 oz.), so bring an appetite (and a love of red meat), or take your leftovers back to the room to feed the kids for a couple days. The filet mignon was tender enough to cut with a fork, and the lamb chops came with a pecan-mustard glaze. Patrons who don't eat red meat might want to try the apricot chicken. Appetizers are mostly seafood, though there is a fine-sounding baked brie with strawberry preserves. "Chef's choice" desserts change nightly, and the wine list is both good and extensive.

In Fitzgeralds Casino Holiday Inn, 301 Fremont St. (at 3rd St.). ℂ **702/388-2400**. Reservations recommended. Main courses $18–$40. AE, DISC, MC, V. Thurs–Mon 5pm–1am.

Second Street Grill ⭐⭐ *Finds* INTERNATIONAL/PACIFIC RIM   One of the better-kept secrets of Las Vegas, this is a Downtown jewel, a lovely bit of romantic, cozy class tucked away inside the Fremont Hotel, with excellent food to boot. There is hardly a misstep on the menu, from taste to beautiful presentation. To call this food Hawaiian-influenced would be accurate, but don't think of the "Polynesian" craze of the '60s and '70s (in other words, forget flaming whatevers and sickly sweet-and-sour sauce). This is more like what you would find in a top-flight restaurant on the Big Island. You begin with warm sourdough bread accompanied by garlic-eggplant-and-olive-oil dipping sauce. For starters, try the unusual lemon-chicken pot stickers and the duck confit. Entrees include lobster, ahi tuna, and filet mignon, but the whole fish (*opaka paka* on a recent visit), served in a bowl with a giant tealeaf lid, is the best bet. It comes with sautéed mushrooms that will melt in your mouth. Other notable side dishes include some fabulous pesto mashed potatoes. Tiramisu fans should be pleased with the Grill's version of that ubiquitous dessert; it's light on the alcohol and more like an airy tiramisu cheesecake. But don't skip the Chocolate Explosion: a piece of chocolate cake topped with chocolate mousse and covered with a rich chocolate shell.

In the Fremont Hotel & Casino, 200 E. Fremont St. ℂ **702/385-3232**. Reservations recommended. Main courses $17–$23. AE, DC, DISC, MC, V. Sun–Mon and Thurs 6–10pm; Fri–Sat 5–11pm.

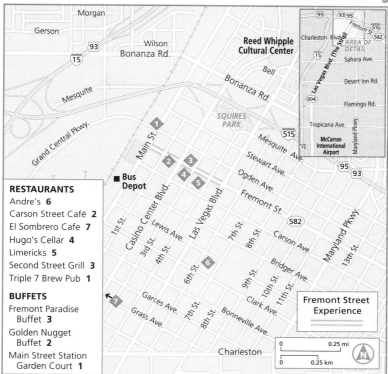

RESTAURANTS
Andre's **6**
Carson Street Café **2**
El Sombrero Cafe **7**
Hugo's Cellar **4**
Limericks **5**
Second Street Grill **3**
Triple 7 Brew Pub **1**

BUFFETS
Fremont Paradise
   Buffet **3**
Golden Nugget
   Buffet **2**
Main Street Station
   Garden Court **1**

INEXPENSIVE

Carson Street Café AMERICAN   Here's a slightly better-than-adequate hotel coffee shop, though it's a mixed bag in terms of quality of food. Sandwiches are better than ribs, burgers, and fries, all of which are merely just filling. On the other hand, the linguine with shrimp is surprisingly good, while desserts, especially pecan pie a la mode and the famous bread pudding (former Golden Nugget owner Steve Wynn's mom's own recipe and a heavily guarded secret) more than earn their rep.

In the Golden Nugget, 129 E. Fremont St. (between 1st St. and Casino Center Blvd.). ☎ **702/385-7111.** Reservations not accepted. Main courses $6–$15. AE, DC, DISC, MC, V. Daily 24 hr.

El Sombrero Cafe ★★ MEXICAN   This kind of hole-in-the-wall Mexican joint can be found all over California but not always so readily elsewhere. It's also the kind of family-run (since 1950) place increasingly forced out of Vegas by giant hotel conglomerates, making it even more worth your time (it's becoming harder and harder, particularly in Downtown, to find budget options that serve food that is more than just mere fuel). Mexican-food fans in particular should seek out this friendly place, though it's not in an attractive part of town. Portions are generous, better than average, and unexpectedly spicy. They also cater to special requests—changing the beef burrito to a chicken one (an option that comes highly recommended), for example, without batting an eyelash. The enchilada and taco combo also won raves.

807 S. Main St. ☎ **702/382-9234.** Everything under $10. AE, MC, V. Mon–Sat 11am–9:30pm.

8 Buffets & Sunday Brunches

Lavish, low-priced buffets are a Las Vegas tradition, designed to lure you to the gaming tables, and to make you feel that you got such a bargain for your meal that you can afford to drop more money. They're gimmicks, and we love them. Something about filling up on too much prime rib and shrimp just says "Vegas" to us. Of course, there is quite a range. Some are just perfunctory steam-table displays and salad bars that are heavy on the iceberg lettuce, while others are unbelievably opulent spreads with caviar and free-flowing champagne. Some are quite beautifully presented, as well. Some of the food is awful, some of it is decent, and some of it is memorable.

No trip to Las Vegas is complete without trying one or two buffets. Of the dozens, the most noteworthy are described below. Mind you, almost all buffets have some things in common. Unless otherwise noted, every one listed below will have a carving station, a salad bar (quality differs), and hot main courses and side dishes. We will try to point out only when a buffet has something original or notable.

Also, at press time, Sahara and Stratosphere had completely remodeled their buffets. While new reviews were not to be had in time for this edition, neither was a particular standout buffet and the new decor probably won't change that.

Note: Buffet meals are extremely popular, and reservations are usually not taken (we've indicated when they are accepted, and in all those cases, they are highly recommended). Arrive early (before opening) or late to avoid a long line, especially on weekends.

SOUTH STRIP
MODERATE
Mandalay Bay's Bay Side Buffet ✮ BUFFET   This is a particularly pretty, not overly large buffet. Actual windows, floor to ceiling, no less, overlooking the beach part of the elaborate pool area, make it less stuffy and eliminate that closed-in feeling that so many of the other buffets in town have. The buffet itself is adequately arranged but features nothing particularly special, though there are some nice cold salads, hearty meats, and a larger and better-than-average dessert bar (they make their own desserts, and it shows).

3950 Las Vegas Blvd. S. ☎ 702/632-7402. Breakfast $13, lunch $15, dinner $23, Sun brunch $23. AE, DC, DISC, MC, V. Daily 7am–10pm.

Spice Market Buffet ✮ BUFFET   A particularly good buffet, if not perhaps quite good enough to justify the price (though the range of food was large enough to please just about anyone). Come for lunch, as a more affordable compromise, and you can take advantage of the better-than-average salads (they had one with white balsamic vinegar on our last visit that was quite good), plus an especially notable Mexican station, Middle Eastern specialties, and other fun goodies.

In the Aladdin, 3667 Las Vegas Blvd. S. ☎ 702/785-9005. Breakfast $11.99, lunch $13.99, dinner $19.99, champagne brunch $17.99. AE, DC, DISC, MC, V. Mon–Fri 8–10:30am, 11am–2pm, 4–9:30pm; Sat–Sun brunch 8:30am–2:30pm and 4–9:30pm.

Tropicana Island Buffet ✮ BUFFET   This buffet is served in a large and delightful dining room, lushly decorated with tropical flowers and foliage. There are coral-reef aquariums at the entrance, and the appealing interior keeps to the island theme. Big semicircular booths backed by mirrored walls are separated by bead curtains, and, on the lower level, floor-to-ceiling windows overlook the

Trop's stunning palm-fringed pool. Dinners here feature an extensive salad bar and peel-and-eat shrimp.

3801 Las Vegas Blvd. S. © 702/739-2222. Brunch $8.95, dinner $13, weekend champagne brunch $13. AE, DC, DISC, MC, V. Daily 7:30am–1:30pm brunch; 4–10pm dinner.

INEXPENSIVE

Excalibur's Round Table Buffet ⭐ BUFFET   This one strikes the perfect balance of cheap prices, forgettable decor, and adequate food. It's what you want in a cheap Vegas buffet. But they don't always have mashed potatoes or macaroni salad, which are essential for an archetypal buffet. The plates are large, so you don't have to make as many trips to the buffet tables.

3850 Las Vegas Blvd. S. © 702/597-7777. Breakfast $8.99, lunch $9.99, dinner $11.49, Sun champagne brunch $9.99. AE, DC, DISC, MC, V. Daily 6:30am–10pm (Fri–Sat until 11pm).

Luxor's Pharaoh's Pheast Buffet ⭐⭐ BUFFET   Located on the lower level, where the Luxor showroom used to be, this huge buffet looks like it was set in the middle of an archaeological dig, complete with wood braces holding up the ceiling, pot shards, papyrus, and servers dressed in khaki-dig outfits. It's a unique and fun decor—be sure to avoid tripping on the mummies and their sarcophagi sticking half up out of the ground. The food is the best in its price range, and one of the top ones in town. There's a Mexican station with some genuinely spicy food, a Chinese stir-fry station, and different Italian pastas. Desserts were disappointing, though they do offer a pretty large selection of diabetic-friendly options. A beer and wine cart makes the rounds. Word has probably gotten out, unfortunately, because the lines are always enormous.

3900 Las Vegas Blvd. S. © 702/262-4000. Breakfast $9.49, lunch $9.99, dinner $15.99. AE, DC, DISC, MC, V. Daily 6:30am–11pm.

MGM Grand Buffet ⭐ BUFFET   This rather average buffet does feature a fresh Belgian waffle station at breakfast. Dinner also has an all-you-can-eat shrimp and prime-rib option. Also available: low-fat, sugar-free desserts! And at all meals, you get a full pot of coffee on your table.

3799 Las Vegas Blvd. S. © 702/891-7777. Breakfast $9.99, lunch $10.99, dinner $17.99; reduced prices for children under 10, free for children under 4. AE, DC, DISC, MC, V. Daily 7am–10pm.

Monte Carlo Buffet ⭐ BUFFET   A "courtyard" under a painted sky, the Monte Carlo's buffet room has a Moroccan market theme, with murals of Arab scenes, Moorish archways, Oriental carpets, and walls hung with photographs of, and artifacts from, Morocco. Dinner includes a rotisserie (for chicken and pork loin, or London broil), a Chinese food station, a taco/fajita bar, a baked potato bar, numerous salads, and more than a dozen desserts, plus frozen yogurt and ice-cream machines. Lunches are similar. At breakfast, the expected fare is supplemented by an omelet station, and choices include crepes, blintzes, and corned-beef hash. Fresh-baked New York–style bagels are a plus.

3770 Las Vegas Blvd. S. © 702/730-7777. Breakfast $9.49, lunch $9.99, dinner $14, Sun brunch $15. AE, DC, DISC, MC, V. Daily 7am–10pm.

MID-STRIP
VERY EXPENSIVE

Bally's Sterling Sunday Brunch ⭐⭐ BUFFET   Now, the admittedly high cost of this brunch seems antithetical to the original purpose of a buffet, which was a lot of food for minimal money. However, if you're a dedicated buffet fan, this is probably a better spree than one of the many new high-priced restaurants.

It works out to less money in the long run, and you will get, for your purposes, more bang for your buck. It's a fancy deal—linen and silver-bedecked tables, waiters to assist you if you choose—and while the variety of food isn't as massive as at regular buffets, the quality is much higher in terms of both content and execution. We're talking unlimited champagne, broiled lobster, caviar, sushi, and rotating dishes of the day (items such as monkfish with pomegranate essence, tenderloin wrapped in porcini mushroom mousse, and even ostrich). No French toast that's been sitting out for days here! Perfect for a wedding breakfast or business brunch or just a big treat; stay a long time and eat as much as you can.

3645 Las Vegas Blvd. S. ✆ **702/967-7999.** Reservations recommended. Brunch $53. AE, DC, MC, V. Sun 9:30am–2:30pm.

EXPENSIVE

Bellagio Buffet ★★ BUFFET   Though even pricier than its counterpart over at The Mirage, the Bellagio buffet gets nearly as high marks. The array of food is fabulous, with one ethnic cuisine after another (Japanese, Chinese that includes unexpected buffet fare like dim sum, build-it-yourself Mexican items, and so on). There are elaborate pastas and semitraditional Italian-style pizza from a wood-fired oven. The cold fish appetizers at each end of the line are not to be missed—scallops, smoked salmon, crab claws, shrimp, oysters, and assorted condiments. Other specialties include breast of duck and game hens. There is no carving station, but you can get the meat precarved. The salad bar is more ordinary, though prepared salads have some fine surprises, such as the eggplant-tofu salad and an exceptional Chinese chicken salad. Desserts, unfortunately, look better than they actually are.

3600 Las Vegas Blvd. S. ✆ **888/987-6667.** Breakfast $13, lunch $16, dinner Sun–Thurs $25, dinner Fri–Sat $32, Sat–Sun brunch $22. AE, DC, DISC, MC, V. Breakfast Mon–Fri 8–10:30am; lunch Mon–Fri 11am–3:30pm; dinner Mon–Thurs 4–10pm, Fri–Sat 4–11pm, Sun 4:30–10pm; brunch Sat–Sun 8am–4pm.

Paris, Le Village Buffet ★★★ BUFFET   One of the more ambitious buffets, with a price hike to match—still, you do get, even at the higher-priced dinner, a fine assortment of food, and more value for the dollar than you are likely to find anywhere else (unless it's another buffet).

Plus, the Paris buffet is housed in the most pleasing room of the buffet bunch. It's a Disneylandesque two-thirds replica of your classic French village clichés; it's either a charming respite from Vegas lights or it's sickening, depending on your tolerance level for such things. Buffet stations are grouped according to French regions, and though in theory entrees change daily, there do seem to be some constants, including most of the following dishes: In Brittany, you'll find things like made-to-order crepes, surprisingly good roasted duck with green peppercorn and peaches, and steamed mussels with butter and shallots. In Normandy, there's quiche and some dry bay scallops with honey cider. The carving station shows up in Burgundy, but distinguishes itself by adding options of chateaubriand sauce and cherry sauce Escoffier. Lamb stew is a possibility for Alsace, while Provence has pasta to order and a solidly good braised beef. The salad station isn't strong on flavors, but the veggies are fresh, and there is even some domestic (darn it) cheese.

You can skip the dessert station in favor of heading back to Brittany for some made-to-order crepes, but you might want to try the bananas Foster.

3665 Las Vegas Blvd. S. ✆ **888/266-5687.** Breakfast $12, lunch $17, dinner $22, Sun brunch $22. AE, DC, DISC, MC, V. Sun–Thurs 7am–10pm, Fri–Sat 7am–11pm.

MODERATE

Bally's Big Kitchen Buffet *(Overrated* BUFFET   Buffet buffs give the breakfast and brunch offered here a thumbs down, feeling that while there is quite a variety of food on display, breakfast features some fairly cheap stuff, and brunch only has a single item—a pretty decent prime rib—worth mentioning. Dinner fares somewhat better (it could be seafood casserole in a creamy dill sauce, baked red snapper, pork chops sautéed in Cajun spices, barbecued chicken, or broiled steak in peppercorn sauce), but overall, this is a disappointing choice for the Strip.
3645 Las Vegas Blvd. S. ℂ **702/739-4111**. Breakfast $11, brunch $13, dinner $18. AE, DC, MC, V. Daily 7am–2:30pm and 4–10pm.

Harrah's Fresh Market Buffet ⚹ BUFFET   The theme here is farmers market, which means lots of big sculptures of fresh fruits and vegetables, if not actual fresh fruits and vegetables. It follows the new trend of various food stations, as opposed to one long buffet. You'll find seafood, pasta, Mexican, Asian, and American specialties ranging from meatloaf to Cajun entrees. Above-average food combined with an extremely friendly staff makes this one of the better buffet choices.
3475 Las Vegas Blvd. S. ℂ **702/369-5000**. Breakfast $8.99, lunch $9.99, brunch $15, dinner $14.99, Sat–Sun champagne brunch $14.99. AE, DC, DISC, MC, V. Daily 7am–10pm.

Mirage Buffet ⚹⚹ BUFFET   We've said it before and we'll say it again: Nothing says Vegas excess like endless mounds of shrimp and prime rib. Until recently, The Mirage's buffet was one of the higher priced in town, but also one of the most reliable in terms of food quality. It's been eclipsed in the former category, but still holds true in the latter. Like most local buffets, flavors tend toward the middle-of-the-road—but at least here the road is a broader one. The ubiquitous carving station is complimented by a fajita station, an Asian station, and a pasta station. The pasta station features made-to-order sauces, starting with either a cream or tomato base. Note the standout salad bar, which features surprises like hummus, baba ghanouj, and couscous, plus a variety of veggie-intensive dishes. And there's gefilte fish, which is not something commonly seen on a Vegas buffet. Put your plate-loading emphasis on the salad bar, with some selections from the aforementioned special stations. Desserts are also better than the foam-rubber average, including bread pudding, chewy peanut-butter cookies, and an unexpectedly intense chocolate mousse.
3400 Las Vegas Blvd. S. ℂ **702/791-7111**. Breakfast $9.50, lunch $11, dinner $15, Sun brunch $15; reduced prices for children ages 5–10, free for children under 5. AE, DC, DISC, MC, V. Daily 7am–10pm.

INEXPENSIVE

Flamingo Paradise Garden Buffet ⚹ BUFFET   The buffet here occupies a vast room, with floor-to-ceiling windows overlooking a verdant tropical landscape of cascading waterfalls and koi ponds. The interior, formerly one of the most pleasant in Las Vegas, is clean and tidy but showing some wear. At dinner, there is an extensive international food station (which changes monthly) presenting French, Chinese, Mexican, German, or Italian specialties. A large salad bar, fresh fruits, pastas, vegetables, potato dishes, and a vast dessert display round out the offerings. Lunch is similar, featuring a mix of international cuisines as well as a stir-fry station and a soup/salad/pasta bar. At breakfast, you'll find all the expected fare, including a made-to-order omelet station and fresh-baked breads. The seafood is dry and tough, and desserts uninspired. Drinks are unlimited, of course, but are served in small glasses, so expect to call your server for many refills.

3555 Las Vegas Blvd. S. (*C*) **702/733-3111.** Champagne breakfast/brunch $8.75, lunch/dinner $9.95. Prices may be higher on holidays. AE, DC, DISC, MC, V. Daily breakfast 6–11:30am; lunch 11:30am–2:30pm; dinner 4:30–10pm.

Palms Festival Market Buffet ★★ *Finds* BUFFET   As a rule, you are better off fulfilling your buffet desires (unless you demand the cheapest of prices) at one of the newer hotels, and the Palms's entry in the buffet sweepstakes bears this adage out. Not only does it look rather swell, but since the owners of the hotel are from a Middle Eastern background, that translates into some fresher concepts at the stations, most notably an emphasis on Middle Eastern fare such as gyros with warm pita bread, hummus, baba ghanouj, and kebabs of every variety. Plus there's a huge Chinese station complete with dumplings, a Mongolian barbecue section (where they toss all your chosen ingredients in one stir-fry vat), some "Jewish" foods (knishes and kugel), an ambitious carving station with ribs and pastrami, and desserts that, as usual, aren't much of anything. And actually, this comes for close-to-classic-buffet budget prices—while still supplying food that can be described as better than "merely edible."

4321 W. Flamingo Rd. (*C*) **702/942-7777.** Breakfast $5.99, lunch $6.99, dinner $10.99, Sun brunch $10.99. AE, DC, DISC, MC, V. Daily 8am–10pm.

Rio's Carnival World Buffet ★★ BUFFET   This buffet has often been voted by locals as the best in town. We don't agree—it's possible that it's been riding on its reputation for a couple of years—but it is still a cut and more above basic buffet offerings. The buffet looks like an upscale food court, with stir-fries, Mexican taco fixings and accompaniments, Chinese fare, a Japanese sushi bar and teppanyaki grill, a Brazilian mixed grill, Italian pasta and antipasto, and fish and chips. There's even a diner setup for hot dogs, burgers, fries, and milkshakes. All this is in addition to the usual offerings of most Las Vegas buffets. An array of oven-fresh cakes, pies, and pastries (including sugar-free and low-fat desserts) is arranged in a palm-fringed circular display area, and there's also a make-your-own sundae bar.

3700 W. Flamingo Rd. (*C*) **702/252-7777.** Breakfast $9.99, lunch $11.99, dinner $16.99, Sat–Sun champagne brunch $16.99. AE, DC, MC, V. Daily 7am–10pm.

Treasure Island Buffet ★ BUFFET   This buffet is served in two internationally themed rooms. The American room, under a central rough-hewn beamed canopy hung with the flags of the 13 colonies, re-creates New Orleans during the era of Jean Lafitte. And the Italian room, modeled after a Tuscan villa overlooking a bustling piazza, has strings of festival lights overhead and food displays under a striped awning. Both rooms are filled with antiques and artifacts typical of their locales and time periods. And both serve identical fare, including extensive American breakfasts. Dinners offer a Chinese food station, peel-and-eat shrimp, a salad bar, potato and rice side dishes, cheeses and cold cuts, fresh fruits and vegetables, breads, and a large choice of desserts. Lunch is similar, and Sunday brunch includes unlimited champagne.

3300 Las Vegas Blvd. S. (*C*) **702/894-7111.** Breakfast $7.99, lunch $8.99, dinner $12.99, Sun brunch $12.99. AE, DC, DISC, MC, V. Daily 7am–10pm.

NORTH STRIP
INEXPENSIVE

Circus Circus Buffet BUFFET   Here's a tradeoff: It's just about the cheapest buffet on the Strip but also the worst buffet food in town. Here you'll find

50 items of typical cafeteria fare, and none of them are all that good. Kids love it; some adults find it inedible. If food is strictly fuel for you, you can't go wrong here. Otherwise, trundle off to another buffet.

2880 Las Vegas Blvd. S. ☎ **702/734-0410.** Breakfast and lunch $6.99, Sat–Sun brunch $7.99, dinner $8.99. AE, DC, DISC, MC, V. Mon–Fri 7–11:30am, noon–4pm, and 4:30–10pm; Sat–Sun 7am–4pm and 4:30–11pm.

EAST OF THE STRIP
MODERATE

The Buffet at the Las Vegas Hilton ⊛ BUFFET   The buffet space at the Hilton was renovated just a bit ago and is now a surprisingly stylish looking room, with the usual suspects (salad bar, bagel bar, desserts) and a good selection of Chinese food (including Peking duck). The fare is fresh and delicious, with special mention going to the prime rib and the outstanding cream puffs and superior rice pudding (it's hard to find good desserts at Vegas buffets). Dinner additionally features all-you-can-eat crab and shrimp. The Friday-night seafood selection is particularly large and palatable.

3000 Paradise Rd. ☎ **702/732-5111.** Breakfast $8.99, lunch $9.99, dinner $13.99, weekend brunch $12.99 (includes unlimited champagne); half price for children age 12 and under. DC, DISC, MC, V. Mon–Fri 7am–2:30pm and 5–10pm; Sat–Sun 8am–2:30pm and 5–10pm.

INEXPENSIVE

Sam's Town Firelight Buffet ⊛ BUFFET   This former buffet is back with a new name and a new, nicer room, with actual natural lighting, and a big wall of flames—hence, firelight, plus lighting that changes throughout the day according to mood requirements, and a view of the water and laser light show in the atrium of the hotel (kind of alfresco dining, in a Vegas artificial way). The buffet now has international stations (Chinese, Mexican), a bar, and a dessert station with hand-scooped ice cream. The food is fine—for a buffet anyway.

5111 Boulder Hwy. ☎ **702/456-7777.** Lunch $6.99, dinner $9.99, Sat–Sun brunch $8.99, theme dinner nights (seafood, barbecue, and so forth) $6.99–$15.99; discount prices for children 4–8, free for children under 4. AE, DC, DISC, MC, V. Mon–Fri 11am–3pm and 4–9pm; Sat–Sun 10am–3pm and 4–9pm.

DOWNTOWN
MODERATE

Golden Nugget Buffet ⊛⊛ BUFFET   This buffet has often been voted number one in Las Vegas. Most of the seating is in plush booths. The buffet tables are laden with an extensive salad bar (about 50 items), fresh fruit, and marvelous desserts, including the famous bread pudding made from the secret recipe of Zelma Wynn (Steve's mom). Fresh seafood is featured every night. Most lavish is the all-day Sunday champagne brunch, which adds such dishes as eggs Benedict, blintzes, pancakes, creamed herring, and smoked fish with bagels and cream cheese.

129 E. Fremont St. ☎ **702/385-7111.** Breakfast $6.75, lunch $7.75, dinner $12, Sun brunch $13. AE, DC, DISC, MC, V. Mon–Sat 7am–3pm and 4–10pm; Sun 7am–10pm.

INEXPENSIVE

Fremont Paradise Buffet ⊛ BUFFET   This buffet is served in a tropically themed room. Diners sit in spacious booths amid lots of jungle foliage—birds of paradise, palms, and bright tropical blooms.

On Sunday, Tuesday, and Friday nights, the buffet is renamed the Seafood Fantasy, and food tables, adorned with beautiful ice sculptures, are laden with lobster claws, crab legs, shrimp, raw oysters, smoked salmon, clams, and entrees such as steamed mussels, shrimp scampi, and scallops Provençale—all in addition to the usual meat-carving stations and a few nonseafood entrees. It's great! And finally, the Fremont has a delightful champagne Sunday brunch served by "island girls" in colorful Polynesian garb. It includes not only unlimited champagne, but a full carving station, lox with bagels and cream cheese, an omelet station, and desserts.

200 E. Fremont St. © **702/385-3232.** Breakfast $5, lunch $6.50, dinner $10, Seafood Fantasy $15, Sun brunch $9. AE, DC, DISC, MC, V. Mon–Sat 7–10:30am and 11am–3pm; Mon and Wed–Thurs 4–10pm; Fri–Sat 4–11pm; Sun 7am–3pm; Seafood Fantasy Sun and Tues 4–10pm.

Main Street Station Garden Court ★★★ *Finds* BUFFET   Set in what is truly one of the prettiest buffet spaces in town (and certainly in Downtown), with very high ceilings and tall windows bringing in much-needed natural light, the Main Street Station Garden Court buffet is one of the best in town, let alone Downtown. It features nine live-action stations (meaning you can watch your food being prepared), including a wood-fired, brick-oven pizza (delicious); many fresh salsas at the Mexican station; a barbecue rotisserie; fresh sausage at the carving station; Chinese, Hawaiian, and Southern specialties (soul food and the like); and so many more we lost count. On Friday night they have all this plus nearly infinite varieties of seafood all the way up to lobster. We ate ourselves into a stupor and didn't regret it.

200 N. Main St. © **702/387-1896.** Breakfast $5, lunch $7, dinner $10, Fri seafood buffet $14, Sat–Sun champagne brunch $9; free for children 3 and under. AE, DC, DISC, MC, V. Daily 7–10:30am, 11am–3pm, 4–10pm.

7

What to See & Do in Las Vegas

You aren't going to lack for things to do in Las Vegas. More than likely you've come here for the gambling, which should keep you pretty busy (we say that with some understatement). But you can't sit at a slot machine forever. (Or maybe you can.) In any event, it shouldn't be too hard to find ways to fill your time between poker hands.

Just walking on the Strip and gazing at the gaudy, garish, absurd wonder of it all can occupy quite a lot of time. This is the number-one activity we recommend in Vegas; at night, it is a mind-boggling sight. And, of course, there are shows and plenty of other nighttime entertainment. But if you need something else to do beyond resting up at your hotel's pool, or if you are trying to amuse yourself while the rest of your party gambles away, this chapter will guide you.

Don't forget to check out the **free hotel attractions,** such as Bellagio's water-fountain ballet, The Mirage's volcano and white-tiger exhibit, and the masquerade show at the Rio. *Note:* Treasure Island's pirate show, alas, has walked the plank and will be replaced with another "sexier" (but still free) outdoor production, *The Sirens of TI,* in fall 2003.

You could also consider using a spa at a major hotel; they seem too pricey (as high as $25 a day) to fill in for your daily gym visit if you are just going to use a few machines, but spending a couple of hours working out, sweating out Vegas toxins in the steam room, and generally pampering yourself will leave you feeling relaxed, refreshed, and ready to go all night again.

There are also plenty of out-of-town sightseeing options, like **Hoover Dam** (a major tourist destination), **Red Rock Canyon,** and nexus-of-all-conspiracy-theories **Area 51,** along with excursions to the Grand Canyon. We've listed the best of these in chapter 11.

SUGGESTED ITINERARIES

The itineraries outlined here are for adults. If you're traveling with kids, incorporate some of the suggestions from "Especially for Kids," listed later in this chapter. The activities mentioned briefly here are described more fully later in this chapter.

If You Have 1 Day

Spend most of the day **casino-hopping.** These are buildings like no other (thank goodness). Each grandiose interior tops the last. Be sure to see The Venetian, Bellagio, The Mirage (including the white tigers), Treasure Island, Paris, Caesars Palace (including the Forum Shops and the talking statues), New York–New York, MGM Grand, Luxor, and Excalibur. Then at night, take a drive (if you can) down **the Strip.** As amazing as all this is during the day, you just can't believe it at night. Aside from just the Strip itself, there are Bellagio's **water fountains,** which "perform" to various musical numbers, the **pirate battle** at Treasure Island

Sin City Inverted

If you want to get away from the glitz and kitsch or just go where most of the tourists don't go, here are several "un-Vegasy" things to do, kindly supplied by James P. Reza, Geoff Carter, and the editors of the *Las Vegas Weekly*.

- **Double Down Saloon** (p. 264). Sin City's coolest bar, hands down. Enjoy cocktails, plug songs into the world's wildest jukebox, admire the bizarre mural work by Vegas artists, or just mingle with local characters and the occasional celebrity.
- **Utopia** (p. 271). This two-story discotheque is not only the best nightclub in town, but may also have a lock on the entire Southwest. Dance to techno, rave, acid jazz, and rare groove while watching people feel each other up.
- **West Sahara Library Fine Arts Museum,** 9600 W. Sahara Ave. (© 702/507-3630). Don't laugh. Las Vegas has its very own gala art museum, ensconced in the most impressive building built in the valley since Wayne Newton set up residence. Built to Smithsonian specs, the museum is one of the few urban buildings in Vegas that lends a sense of space and quality to the surrounding stucco. Hours are Monday through Thursday from 9am to 9pm, Saturday from 9am to 5pm, and Sunday from 1 to 5pm.
- **The Arts Factory** (see below). Las Vegas's premier artist collective maintains a gallery inside the "Arts Factory" art compound. The CAC's unique vision of this town is too good to miss. Open Monday, Tuesday, Thursday, and Friday from noon to 5pm.
- **Jazzed Cafe & Vinoteca** (p. 260). Run by professional dancers Kirk Offerle and Connie Chambers, this tiny, elegant bistro stays open until the wee hours, lit by candles and the brilliance of the clientele. Great java, terrific wine list.
- **Floyd Lamb State Park,** I-95 North; exit at Durango. This huge former working ranch once served as a forerunner of those trendy "desert spas" so popular in Scottsdale. Today you'll find acres and acres of grassy picnic areas; walking, hiking, biking, and horse trails; huge shade trees; and two lakes. Wanna be a true native? Always call it "Tule Springs."
- **Chinatown Mall,** 4255 Spring Mountain Rd. The Occident meets the Orient in a big way. A prodigious meeting of great restaurants, interesting shops, and unique amenities, all with roots buried deep in the Far East.

(consider watching it from the Battle Bar), and the **volcano explosion** next door at The Mirage. Eat at a buffet (details in chapter 6) and have a drink at the top of the Stratosphere, goggling at the view from the tallest building west of the Mississippi. Oh, and maybe you should gamble a little too.

If You Have 2 Days
Do more of the above since you may not have covered it all. Then do something really Vegasy and visit

the **Liberace Museum.** The **Dolphin Habitat** at The Mirage is also worth a look. At night, take in a show. We think *O* and *Mystère,* the productions from the avant-garde **Cirque du Soleil,** are the finest in Vegas, but there are plenty to choose from. Though buffets are still the most Vegas-appropriate food experience, genuine haute cuisine by celebrity chefs has invaded the town and you should take advantage of it. Le Cirque, Renoir, and Picasso are our top choices, but you can't go wrong with anything by Emeril Lagasse, plus there are branches of Onda, Olives, Aqua, Circo, Pinot, Star Canyon, and the Border Grill. Be sure to leave some time to go Downtown to check out the casinos in the classic Glitter Gulch and to visit the **Fremont Street Experience** light show.

If You Have 3 Days

By now you've spent 2 days gambling and gawking. So take a break and drive out to **Red Rock Canyon.** The panoramic 13-mile Scenic Loop Drive is best seen early in the morning when there's little traffic. If you're so inclined, spend some time hiking here. If you want to spend the whole day out, have lunch at nearby **Bonnie Springs Ranch.** After lunch, enjoy a guided trail ride into the desert wilderness or enjoy the silliness at **Old Nevada** (see chapter 11 for details).

If You Have 4 Days or More

Plan a tour to **Hoover Dam.** Leave early in the morning, returning to Las Vegas after lunch via **Valley of Fire State Park,** stopping at the **Lost City Museum** in Overton en route (see chapter 11 for details). Alternatively, you can rest up by spending the day by the hotel pool or going to the hotel spa. At night, presumably refreshed and toxins purged, hit the casinos and/or catch another show. If you aren't tired of magic, **Lance Burton** is a wonderful show for a reasonable price, or there is the arty weirdness of the **Blue Man Group** at Luxor, or *Jubilee!* if your trip won't be complete without a topless revue. You can also feast at dinner, since you certainly haven't tried all there is. If you want a good dinner with a great free show, go to Treasure Island's **Buccaneer Bay Club,** which overlooks that hotel's new *Sirens of TI* production.

As you plan any additional days, consider excursions to other nearby attractions such as **Lake Mead,** the **Grand Canyon,** or even **Area 51.** Inquire about interesting tours at your hotel sightseeing desk.

1 The Top Attractions

See also the listings for theme parks and other fun stuff in section 4, "Especially for Kids."

The Arts Factory ★★ *Finds*   Believe it or not, Las Vegas has a burgeoning art scene (what some would consider soul-crushing is what others consider inspirational), and this complex, located in the Gateway district, is the place to find proof. It features a few galleries and a number of workspaces for local artists. Several of the spaces are closed to the public. On the first Friday of each month, they have a party event (unimaginatively named "First Friday") showcasing local artists and arts-oriented businesses, with live music, street performances, and other entertainment and activities. Go to their website for further details.

101–109 E. Charleston Blvd. ℂ **702/676-1111.** www.theartsfactory.com. Mon–Tues and Thurs–Fri noon–5pm and by appointment.

Auto Collections at Imperial Palace ★★ Even if you're not a car person, don't assume you won't be interested in this premier collection of antique, classic, and special-interest vehicles. Check out the graceful lines and handsome sculpture of one of the many Model J Duesenbergs (one of which Elvis Presley drove in the movie *Spinout*). The craftsmanship and attention to detail make these cars, and others here, true works of art.

Note that the vehicles on display change regularly, so there's no telling what you may see when you visit. However, the last time we were here we saw a great deal of history. Down President's Row we saw JFK's 1962 "bubbletop" Lincoln Continental, Lyndon Johnson's 1964 Cadillac, Eisenhower's 1952 Chrysler Imperial 20-foot-long parade car, Truman's 1950 Lincoln Cosmopolitan with gold-plated interior, FDR's unrestored 1936 V-16 Cadillac, and Herbert Hoover's 1929 Cadillac. There's also a 1964 Chaika that belonged to Soviet leader Nikita Krushchev.

Commercial vehicles of bygone days include antique buses, military transports, taxis (among them, the 1908 French model that appeared in the movie version of *My Fair Lady*), gasoline trucks, fire engines, delivery trucks and vans, dump trucks, and pickup trucks. Other highlights are the 1959 Cadillac Fleetwood Special 60 driven by Marilyn Monroe in *The Misfits;* Al Capone's 1930 V-16 Cadillac; a 1954 Mercedes-Benz 220 Cabriolet currently owned by Wayne Newton; the 1967 Ford Mustang Fastback driven by Nicolas Cage in *Gone in 60 Seconds;* Howard Hughes's 1954 Chrysler (because of his phobia about germs, Hughes installed a special air-purification system that cost more than the car itself!); and a 1933 Pierce Arrow Silver, one of only three still in existence today.

In the Imperial Palace hotel, 3535 Las Vegas Blvd. S. ✆ **702/794-3174.** www.autocollections.com. Admission $6.95 adults, $3 seniors and children under 12, free for children under 4 and AAA members. Check website for free-admission coupon. Daily 9:30am–9:30pm.

Bellagio Art Gallery ★ Everyone—ourselves not nearly least among them—scoffed when then-Bellagio owner Steve Wynn opened an art gallery on his fabulous property. Sure, Wynn's been a serious and respected fine-art collector for years, and consequently there was good stuff on display (though there are no masterpieces, there certainly are serious works by masters), but who would go see *art* in Las Vegas? Tons of tourists, as it happens, so many that they had to almost immediately relocate the gallery to a larger space.

When the MGM MIRAGE company bought Wynn's empire, the future of the gallery, which did rely on his collection (he took most of it with him), was in doubt. Surprise again, you scoffers (and that again includes us). The gallery is not only open again, it's getting written up by real art critics, thanks in part to such well-chosen shows as an exhibit from the collection of none other than Steve Martin—yes, we mean the stand-up-comedian-turned-actor-turned-playwright/author. See, he's a longtime well-respected collector too, and consequently there were real live reviewers, hushed with happy reverence, who took the whole show most seriously indeed.

Now, will there be as interesting a show up when you go? Beats us. (When we wrote this, it was an acclaimed exhibit of European masterpieces, silver, gold, jewelry, furniture, and rare books on loan from England's famous Chatsworth manor.) Then there's that ticket price: Do let us point out that the Louvre and the Vatican art collections, both of which are, needless to say, quite a bit larger and both of which, one can safely say, do have some notable works, cost around $9.

In Bellagio, 3600 Las Vegas Blvd. S. ✆ **702/693-7871.** Reservations suggested, but walk-ins taken every 15 min. Admission $15 adults, $12 seniors, students with ID, and Nevada residents. Daily 9am–9pm.

Las Vegas Attractions

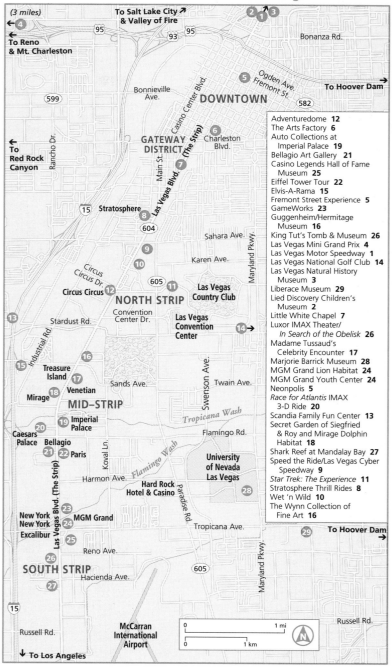

(3 miles)

To Salt Lake City ↗
& Valley of Fire

95   93   95

To Reno
& Mt. Charleston

Bonanza Rd.

599

Bonnieville
Ave.

Ogden Ave.
Fremont St.

DOWNTOWN

To Hoover Dam →

582

To
Red Rock
Canyon

Rancho Dr.

Casino Center Blvd.

GATEWAY
DISTRICT

Las Vegas Blvd. (The Strip)

Charleston
Blvd.

Main St.

15   Stratosphere

604

Sahara Ave.

Maryland Pkwy.

Karen Ave.

Circus
Circus Dr.

605

Las Vegas
Country Club

Circus Circus

NORTH STRIP

Convention
Center Dr.

Stardust Rd.

Industrial Rd.

Las Vegas
Convention
Center

Treasure
Island

Venetian

Mirage

MID-STRIP

Sands Ave.

Swenson Ave.

Twain Ave.

Tropicana Wash

Imperial
Palace

Caesars
Palace   Bellagio

Paris

Koval Ln.

Flamingo Rd.

Las Vegas Blvd. (The Strip)

Harmon Ave.

Flamingo Wash

Hard Rock
Hotel & Casino

University
of Nevada
Las Vegas

Paradise Rd.

New York
New York   MGM Grand

Excalibur

Tropicana Ave.

To Hoover Dam →

Reno Ave.

SOUTH STRIP

Hacienda Ave.

605

Maryland Pkwy.

15

Russell Rd.

McCarran
International
Airport

0   1 mi
0   1 km

Russell Rd.

N

↓ To Los Angeles

Attractions list:

Adventuredome **12**
The Arts Factory **6**
Auto Collections at
   Imperial Palace **19**
Bellagio Art Gallery **21**
Casino Legends Hall of Fame
   Museum **25**
Eiffel Tower Tour **22**
Elvis-A-Rama **15**
Fremont Street Experience **5**
GameWorks **23**
Guggenheim/Hermitage
   Museum **16**
King Tut's Tomb & Museum **26**
Las Vegas Mini Grand Prix **4**
Las Vegas Motor Speedway **1**
Las Vegas National Golf Club **14**
Las Vegas Natural History
   Museum **3**
Liberace Museum **29**
Lied Discovery Children's
   Museum **2**
Little White Chapel **7**
Luxor IMAX Theater/
   In Search of the Obelisk **26**
Madame Tussaud's
   Celebrity Encounter **17**
Marjorie Barrick Museum **28**
MGM Grand Lion Habitat **24**
MGM Grand Youth Center **24**
Neonpolis **5**
Race for Atlantis IMAX
   3-D Ride **20**
Scandia Family Fun Center **13**
Secret Garden of Siegfried
   & Roy and Mirage Dolphin
   Habitat **18**
Shark Reef at Mandalay Bay **27**
Speed the Ride/Las Vegas Cyber
   Speedway **9**
Star Trek: The Experience **11**
Stratosphere Thrill Rides **8**
Wet 'n Wild **10**
The Wynn Collection of
   Fine Art **16**

Casino Legends Hall of Fame Museum ⭐ *Finds*   A substantial and fascinating collection of gaming memorabilia (chips, cards, dice, even swizzle sticks, from long-gone and current hotels), photographs (the original Flamingo surrounded by nothing but desert, for example), videos, displays, and minitributes to the people and professions that made and make Las Vegas what it is. Over 150,000 items make this the largest collection of its kind in the world. Provided that this kind of history interests you, this shouldn't be missed. It's well worth the time and small admission charge, though you can sometimes avoid even that, courtesy of the hotel's free slot-pull area, and local magazines, both of which often offer free passes. A large gift shop is attached where you can buy all sorts of collectibles—even slot machines. *Note:* With the hotel's future in jeopardy, so is this collection's. Let's hope that if it has to close here, it gets picked up elsewhere.

In the Tropicana, 3801 Las Vegas Blvd. S. 🕐 702/739-5444. Admission $6.95, seniors $5.95. You must be 18 to enter. Daily 9am–9pm.

Eiffel Tower Tour *Overrated*   Whether this is worth the dough depends on how much you like views. An elevator operator (we refuse to call them guides) delivers a few facts about this Eiffel Tower (this is a half-size exact replica down to the paint color of the original) during the minute or so ride to the uppermost platform, where you are welcome to stand around and look out for as long as you want, which probably isn't 2 hours, the length of the average movie, which also costs $9. Nice view, though.

In Paris Las Vegas, 3655 Las Vegas Blvd. S. 🕐 702/946-7000. Admission Mon–Thurs $9 adults, $7 seniors over 65 and children 6–12, free for children under 6; Fri–Sun $12 adults, $9 seniors over 65 and children 6–12. Daily 10am–midnight, weather permitting.

Elvis-A-Rama ⭐   Three million dollars worth of Elvis memorabilia—we thought surely this place would give our beloved Liberace museum a run for its top spot in our camp-lovin' hearts. But alas, while this is a must for the Elvis faithful (and admittedly, they are legion) looking to view holy relics, it's not the place for a novice to start.

The amount of cool stuff is amazing: Elvis ephemera ranging from his Social Security card (a $14,000 auction purchase) to his "little black book" (entries not divulged, darn it!), his Army uniform, a love letter to his hometown girlfriend, fan-club souvenirs (Elvis lipstick!), and on and on it goes. But alas, these precious (and discarded) possessions are exhibited in cases that, as of this writing, are lacking much-needed labels and identification, so all too often you have no idea what you're looking at, much less its significance. The displays also don't precisely give you a good view of the King's life; it assumes you already know the highlights (Momma's boy, the Colonel, 'Scilla), and it's hardly complete. Despite our morbid hopes for prescription-pill bottles, there was nary a mention of Dr. Nick nor even The Death. There is, however, a whole case displaying what amounts to the contents of Vernon Presley's wallet. It's also all a little too straight-faced and reverent, though the gift shop makes up for it a bit. And they do have various Elvis impersonator shows, ranging in price from around $15 to $20. All in all, best for fans thinking, "You know, I really *should* brush up on my Elvis-iania."

⸢ *Fun Fact* **When Downtown Ruled**

Fremont Street was the hub of Las Vegas for almost 4 decades before the first casino hotel, El Rancho, opened on the Strip in 1941.

3401 Industrial Rd. (C) **702/309-7200.** www.elvisarama.com. Admission $9.95 adults, $7.95 seniors, students with ID, and Nevada residents; free for kids under 12. Daily 10am–6pm. Call for free shuttle bus.

Fremont Street Experience ★★   For some years, downtown Vegas has been losing ground to the Strip. But thanks to a $70 million revitalization project, that's starting to change. Fremont Street, the heart of "Glitter Gulch," has been closed off and turned into a pedestrian mall. The Fremont Street Experience is a 5-block open-air pedestrian mall, a landscaped strip of outdoor cafes, vendor carts, and colorful kiosks purveying food and merchandise. Overhead is a 90-foot-high steel-mesh "celestial vault"; at night, it is the **Sky Parade,** a high-tech light-and-laser show (the canopy is equipped with more than 2.1 million lights) enhanced by a concert-hall-quality sound system, which takes place four times nightly. But there's music between shows, as well. Not only does the canopy provide shade, it cools the area through a misting system in summer and warms you with radiant heaters in winter. The difference this makes cannot be overemphasized; what was once a ghost town of tacky, rapidly aging buildings, in an area with more undesirables than not, is now a bustling (at least at night), friendly, safe place (they have private security guards who hustle said undesirables away). It's a place where you can stroll, eat, or even dance to the music under the lights. The crowd it attracts is more upscale than in years past, and of course, it's a lot less crowded than the hectic Strip. Some rightly mourn the passing of cruising Glitter Gulch, gawking at the original lights. It does indeed mean the end of classic Las Vegas, but on the other hand, classic Las Vegas was dead and nearly buried anyway. This has given a second life to a deserving neighborhood.

> **Tips Insider Info**
>
> A good place to view the Sky Parade light show is from the balcony at Fitzgeralds Hotel & Casino.

And in a further effort to retain as much of classic Las Vegas as possible, the **Neon Museum** is installing vintage hotel and casino signs along the promenade. The first installation is the horse and rider from the old Hacienda, which presently rides the sky over the intersection of Fremont and Las Vegas Boulevard. Eventually, the Neon Museum hopes to have an indoor installation a couple of blocks from the Fremont Street Experience to showcase some of the smaller signs they have collected. It's uncertain when it will open, but in the meantime the Neon Graveyard is there and it's amusing to see the (unlit, of course) old signs languishing away until they once again get lit up in their glittery glory.

Fremont St. (between Main St. and Las Vegas Blvd.), Downtown. www.vegasexperience.com. Free admission. Shows nightly every hour on the hour after dark.

GameWorks ★★   What do you get when Steven Spielberg and his Dream-Works team get in on the arcade video-game action? Grown-up state-of-the-art fun. High-tech movie magic has taken over all sorts of traditional arcade games and turned them interactive, from a virtual-reality batting cage to a *Jurassic Park* game that lets you hunt dinosaurs. There are motion-simulator rides galore and even actual-motion activities like rock climbing. But classic games, from Pac-Man to pool tables, are here too, though sometimes with surprising twists, such as air hockey where multiple pucks occasionally shoot out at once.

All this doesn't exactly come cheap. There are two routes to pricing. First is the standard version where $15 gets you $15 in game play, $20 gets you $25, or

$25 gets you $35. Alternatively, you can purchase a block of time ($20 for 1 hr., $25 for 2 hr., $27 for 3 hr.; or if you get there at opening or closing you get 2 hr. for $20), which goes on a debit card that you then insert into the various machines to activate them. But you do get value for your money, which makes this a viable alternative to casinos, particularly if you have children (though it's clearly geared toward a college-age-and-older demographic). Children probably should be 10 years old and up—any younger and parents will need to stand over them, rather than go off and have considerable fun on their own. *Note:* If you don't like crowds, come here earlier rather than later when it can get packed.

In the Showcase Mall, 3785 Las Vegas Blvd. S. ⓒ **702/432-GAME**. www.gameworks.com. See game prices listed above in the review. Sun–Thurs 10am–midnight; Fri–Sat 10am–2am. Hours may vary.

Guggenheim/Hermitage Museum ★★   When two branches of the famous Guggenheim opened in Vegas, it was seen as a sure sign that Vegas was on its way, or at least had an actual chance, of becoming a real city with real culture, and not just a glittery tourist trap. No one has said much now that the first branch, the one built for special exhibits, closed after just one show. The second, and perhaps ultimately better reviewed and regarded, remains in operation, so maybe there is hope yet for Vegas's cultural significance. That museum, the Guggenheim/Hermitage, is the first co-venture between the Guggenheim and the State Hermitage Museum in St. Petersburg. The State Hermitage in St. Petersburg has one of the finest encyclopedic collections in the world, but few have had a chance to experience any of it. Unfortunately, the exhibit here at press time was of American pop icons. We're not really sure how the Hermitage collection figures into that, fond as we are of that particular moment in modern art, so we do rather hope that future exhibits feature more of those masterworks rarely, if ever, seen outside of Russia. After all, price-wise too, we note again that both the Louvre and the Vatican come considerably cheaper (well, once you pay to fly there) and offer quite a bit more.

In The Venetian, 3355 Las Vegas Blvd. S. ⓒ **866/484-4849**. $15 adults, $12 seniors and Nevada residents, $11 students with ID, $7 children 6–12, free for children under 6. Daily 9:30am–8:30pm.

King Tut's Tomb & Museum ★   This full-scale reproduction of King Tutankhamen's tomb includes the antechamber, annex, burial chamber, and treasury housing replicas of the glittering inventory discovered by archaeologists Howard Carter and Lord Carnarvon in the Valley of Kings at Luxor in 1922. It was all handcrafted in Egypt by artisans using historically correct gold leaf and linens, pigments, tools, and ancient methods, and all items have been meticulously positioned according to Carter's records. It's hardly like seeing the real thing, but if you aren't going to Egypt anytime soon, perhaps checking out reproductions isn't a bad idea—and for a Vegas fake, it's surprisingly enjoyable. A 4-minute introductory film precedes a 15-minute audio tour (available in English, French, Spanish, and Japanese).

In Luxor Las Vegas, 3900 Las Vegas Blvd. S. ⓒ **702/262-4000**. Admission $5. Sun–Thurs 9am–11pm; Fri–Sat 9am–midnight.

Las Vegas Mini Grand Prix ★★ *Kids*   Finally, after all our yammering about how Vegas isn't for families and how most of the remaining options are really overpriced tourist traps, we can whole-heartedly recommend an actual family-appropriate entertainment option. Part arcade, part go-kart racetrack, this is exactly what you want to help your kids (and maybe yourselves) work their ya-ya's out. The arcade is well stocked, with a better quality of prizes than one often finds, but we suggest not spending too much time in there, and instead hustling outside to the slide, the little roller coaster, and best of all, the four go-kart tracks. Each offers a different thrill, from the longest road track in Vegas, full of twists and turns as you try to out-race other drivers (be a sport, let the little kids win occasionally), to a high-banked oval built just so you can try to make other drivers take spills on to the grass, to, best of all, a timed course. The latter requires a driver's license, so it's for you rather than your kids (but the wee ones will find the 4th course is just for them), and here you can live out your Le Mans or Police Chase fantasies, as you blast through twisting runs, one kart at a time, trying to beat your personal best. A good kind of adrenaline rush, believe us. The staff is utterly friendly, and the pizzas at the food court are triple the size and half the price of those found in your hotel. The one drawback: It's far away from main Strip action—here's where you'll need that rental car, for sure. *Note:* Kids have to be at least 36 inches tall to ride any of the attractions.

1401 N. Rainbow Rd., just off US 95 N. ℂ 702/259-7000. www.lvmgp.com. Ride tickets $4.95 each, $23 for 5. Sun–Thurs 10am–10pm, Fri–Sat 10am–11pm.

Las Vegas Motor Speedway ★★   This 107,000-seat facility was the first new super-speedway to be built in the Southwest in over 2 decades. A $100 million state-of-the-art motor-sports entertainment complex, it includes a 1½-mile super-speedway, a 2½-mile FIA-approved road course, paved and dirt short-track ovals, and a 4,000-foot drag strip. Also on the property are facilities for Go-Kart, Legends Car, Sand Drag, and Motocross competition. The new speedway is accessible via shuttle buses to and from the Imperial Palace hotel, though some of the other major hotels have their own shuttles to the speedway.

7000 Las Vegas Blvd. N., directly across from Nellis Air Force base (take I-15 north to Speedway exit 54). ℂ 702/644-4443 for ticket information. www.lvms.com. Tickets $10–$75 (higher prices for major events).

Liberace Museum ★★★ *Moments*   You can keep your Louvres and Vaticans and Smithsonians: *This* is a museum. Housed, like everything else in Vegas, in a strip mall, this is a shrine to the glory and excess that was the art project known as Liberace. You've got your costumes (bejeweled), your many cars (bejeweled), your many pianos (bejeweled), and many jewels (also bejeweled). Also, the entrance itself is a giant jewel. It just shows what can be bought with lots of money and no taste.

The thing is, Liberace was in on the joke (we think). The people who come here largely aren't. Many of these guests would not have liked him living next door to them if his name was, say, Bruce Smith, but they idolize the-man-the-myth. Not found here is any reference to AIDS or chauffeurs who had plastic surgery to look more like him. But you will find a Czar Nicholas uniform with 22-karat-gold braiding and a blue-velvet cape styled after the coronation robes of King George V and covered with $60,000 worth of rare chinchilla. Not to mention a 50.6-pound rhinestone costing $50,000, the world's largest, presented to him by the grateful (we bet they were) Austrian firm that supplied all his costume stones.

The museum is now better than ever thanks to a costly renovation that turned what was once a too-low-key exhibition (especially given the subject matter) into something much more gaudy and over the top—and, better still, properly enshrined. Expect a ridiculously outrageous entrance (three words: giant pink piano) into rooms with various exhibits that finally give detailed attention to facts and figures. Admission has been cranked up, probably to pay for the renovations, but we don't mind—this is a one-of-a-kind place. Unless you have a severely underdeveloped appreciation for camp or take your museum-going very seriously, you shouldn't miss it. The museum is 2½ miles east of the Strip on your right.

1775 E. Tropicana Ave. (at Spencer St.). ℂ **702/798-5595.** www.liberace.org. Admission $12 adults, $8 seniors over 64 and students, free for children under 6. Mon–Sat 10am–5pm; Sun noon–4pm. Closed Thanksgiving, Dec 25, and Jan 1.

Luxor IMAX Theater/*In Search of the Obelisk* ⭐ *(Kids*   This is a state-of-the-art theater that offers both motion-simulator films and IMAX projects, some in standard two dimensions, and one in 3-D. The glasses for the latter are really cool headsets that include built-in speakers, bringing certain sounds right into your head (though they're a little too heavy for comfort). The movies change periodically but always include some extraordinary special effects. If you have a fear of heights, make sure to ask for a seat on one of the lower levels.

In Search of the Obelisk is a motion-simulator ride encompassing an action adventure involving a chase sequence inside a pyramid. Two other less-Egyptian-theme-tie-in simulator rides that also play at the Luxor are *Fun House Express* and *Dracula's Haunted Castle*.

In Luxor Las Vegas, 3900 Las Vegas Blvd. S. ℂ **702/262-4000.** Admission $8.95 and up, prices vary depending on the movie; $7 for *In Search of the Obelisk*; $6 for IMAX Ridefilm (both episodes). Can be purchased as part of an all-attractions package for $24. Sun–Thurs 9am–11pm; Fri–Sat 9am–midnight. IMAX show times vary depending on the length of the film.

Madame Tussaud's Celebrity Encounter ⭐ *(Kids*   Madame Tussaud's waxworks exhibition has been the top London attraction for nearly 2 centuries, so even if you aren't a fan of wax museums, this, its sole branch west of the Mississippi, is probably worth a stop—if you can stomach the price. Figures here are state-of-the-art, painstakingly constructed to perfectly match the original person. (Truth be told, though some are nearly identical to their living counterparts—Brad Pitt gave us a start—others look about as much like the celebrity in question as a department-store mannequin.) There's no Chamber of Horrors, but the exhibit makes up for it, since all the waxworks are free-standing, allowing, and indeed encouraging, guests to get up close and personal. (Go ahead, lay your cheek next to Elvis's or Sinatra's and have your photo taken. You know you want to.) The emphasis here is on film, television, music, and sports celebrities, plus some Vegas icons, who are housed in five themed rooms ("Sports Arena," for example). There's also a behind-the-scenes look at the lengthy process involved in creating just one of these figures.

3355 Las Vegas Blvd. S. ℂ **702/990-3530.** Admission $19 adults, $14 seniors and Nevada residents, $9.95 children 6–12, children 5 and under free. Daily 10am–10pm, hours vary seasonally.

Marjorie Barrick Museum ⭐   Formerly known as the Natural History Museum (as opposed to the existing Las Vegas Natural History Museum, and now you can see why they changed the name), here's a cool place to beat the heat and noise of Vegas, while examining some attractive, if not overly imaginative, displays on Native American craftwork and Las Vegas history. Crafts include 19th-century Mexican religious folk art, a variety of colorful dance masks of Mexico, and Native American pottery. The first part of the hall is often the highlight, with impressive traveling art exhibits. Children won't find much that's entertaining other than some glass cases containing examples of local, usually poisonous reptiles (who, if you are lucky—or unlucky, depending on your view—will be dining on mice when you drop by). Outside is a pretty garden demonstrating how attractive more desert-appropriate plants (in other words, those requiring little water) can be. You just wish the local casinos, with their lush and wasteful lawns, would take notice.

On the UNLV campus, 4505 Maryland Pkwy. ℂ **702/895-3381.** Free admission. Mon–Fri 8am–4:45pm; Sat 10am–2pm.

MGM Grand Lion Habitat ⭐⭐ (Kids)   Hit this attraction at the right time and it's one of the best freebies in town. It's a large, multilevel glass enclosure, in which various lions frolic during various times of day. In addition to regular viewing spots, you can walk through a glass tunnel and get a worm's-eye view of the underside of a lion (provided one is in position); note how very big Kitty's paws are. Multiple lions share show duties (about 6 hr. on, and then 2 days off at a ranch for some free-range activity, so they're never cooped up here for long). So you could see any combo from one giant male to a pack of five females who have grown from cub to near adult-size during their MGM time. Each comes with a trainer or three, who are there to keep the lions busy with play, so they don't act like the big cats they are and sleep the whole time. But obviously, photo ops are more likely to occur as the more frisky younger set tussles, so what you observe is definitely going to depend on who is in residence when you drop by. (And of course, actually seeing anything depends on how many other people think this is a two-star attraction; hordes of tourists are often pressed against the glass, preventing you, not to mention your kids, from doing the same.)

In the MGM Grand, 3799 Las Vegas Blvd. S. ℂ **702/891-7777.** Free admission. Daily 11am–10pm.

Neonopolis ⭐⭐   It's hard to get visitors Downtown, but if you are genuinely looking for activities that do not have to do with gambling, this $100 million open-air restaurant, shop, and entertainment complex (with an 11-screen movie theater) provides plenty of motivation. Located right at the Fremont Street Experience, where Fremont Street meets Las Vegas Boulevard South, it's basically a big, open-air mall, but one that is powered by Jillian's, a national chain that specializes in creating little urban entertainment centers (they are behind the similar Metreon in San Francisco), with a state-of-the-art arcade (as well stocked, from air hockey to virtual-reality games, as we've ever seen), bowling alley, billiards, two bars, a nightclub, and a restaurant all in one tidy package. It's not a 24-hour joint, but the hours are long enough that nongamblers can amuse themselves here while the gamblers in their party are doing their thing. The cafe has an extensive menu (from hamburgers to jambalaya) with most items in the $4-to-$10 range and as tasty as you could want from such a place. It's too close to the Fremont Street Experience not to go and has too much to offer not to stay, but it is too noisy, thanks to happy kids and teenagers, to want to stay too long, depending on where you fit in those demographics.

450 Fremont St. (at Las Vegas Blvd.). ℂ **702/678-5777.** Sun–Thurs 11am–1am; Fri–Sat 11am–3am.

Race for Atlantis IMAX 3-D Ride ⭐ (Kids)   Following the trend of virtual-reality theme-park rides, Caesars Palace joined forces with IMAX to create the Race for Atlantis. If you've never been on a virtual-reality ride, you will enjoy it, but the production values pale when compared to *Star Trek: The Experience* (but then again, that's also twice as expensive).

This experience begins as you walk past a giant statue of Neptune and his chariot drawn by wild-looking sea serpents. The stone hallway appears to lead into an underwater palace. As the line twists around, a sci-fi fantasy world unfolds, with mists clouding the multicolored lights of the legendary city of Atlantis. Once inside the ride, you are treated to a 3-D visor (which has a tendency to slip, putting unpleasant pressure on one's nose, so hang on tight) and a silly safety rap sung by Neptune's cowardly secretary. The ride itself is a 3-D motion simulator, which uses computer animation to create the lost city and the racecourse. The goal is to get to the ring before the evil demon god gets there. If you like a bumpy ride, be sure to sit in the very front or very back. During the 4-minute race, your chariot is impeded by flying shrapnel, the evil god, and even by Neptune's own inept secretary. With the 3-D glasses, all of these sharp objects flying at you can get pretty intense. Eventually, the ring is saved, and the famed city of Atlantis survives. Not for the weak of stomach.

In Caesars Palace Forum Shops, 3570 Las Vegas Blvd. S. Admission $10 adults; $9 Nevada residents, seniors, and students; $7 children under 12. Sun–Thurs 10am–11pm; Fri–Sat 10am–midnight.

Secret Garden of Siegfried & Roy and Mirage Dolphin Habitat ★★★ *Kids*

Siegfried & Roy's famous white tigers have long had a free exhibit in The Mirage. They still do, but now they have an additional space, the **Secret Garden** ★, a gorgeous area behind the dolphin exhibit. Here, white lions, Bengal tigers, an Asian elephant, a panther, and a snow leopard join the white tigers. (Many of these are bred by Siegfried & Roy and are also in their nightly show.) It's really just a glorified zoo, featuring only the big-ticket animals; however, it is a very pretty place, with plenty of foliage and some bits of Indian- and Asian-themed architecture. Zoo purists will be horrified at the smallish spaces the animals occupy, but all the animals are rotated between here and their more lavish digs at the illusionist team's home. What this does allow you to do is get very close up to a tiger, which is quite a thrill—those paws are massive indeed. Visitors are given little portable phonelike objects on which they can play a series of programs, listening to Roy and former Mirage owner Steve Wynn discuss conservation or the attributes of each animal, and deliver anecdotes.

The **Dolphin Habitat** ★★★ is more satisfying. It was designed to provide a healthy and nurturing environment and to educate the public about marine mammals and their role in the ecosystem. Specialists worldwide were consulted in creating the habitat, which was designed to serve as a model of a quality, man-made environment. The pool is more than eight times larger than government regulations require, and its 2.5 million gallons of man-made seawater are cycled and cleaned once every 2 hours. It must be working, as the adult dolphins here are breeding regularly. The Mirage displays only dolphins already in captivity—no dolphins will be taken from the wild. You can watch the dolphins frolic both above and below ground through viewing windows, in three different pools. (There is nothing quite like the kick you get from seeing a baby dolphin play.) The knowledgeable staff, who surely have the best jobs in Vegas, will answer questions. If they aren't doing it already, ask them to play ball with the dolphins; they toss large beach balls into the pools, and the dolphins hit them out with their noses, leaping out of the water, cackling with dolphin glee. You catch the ball, getting nicely wet, and toss it back to them. If you have never played ball with a dolphin, shove that happy child next to you out of the way and go for it. There is also a video of a resident dolphin (Duchess) giving birth underwater; her fourth calf (30 lb. and 3 ft. long) was born just before Mother's Day in 2003 (in the spirit of Vegas, at press time The Mirage was holding an employee contest to name the newest arrival). You can stay as long as you like, which might just be hours.

Siegfried & Roy's House

When they aren't on stage, they are just plain (okay, nothing is plain with them) Siegfried Fischbacher and Roy Horn. And they live in a house at 1639 Valley on the corner of Vegas Drive (right across from the golf course). We aren't giving much away; if you want to be anonymous, you don't put a big gold "SR" on all your gates, which by the way are huge and gilt. White lions top the massive white-stucco wall that lines the property. You can't see any of the fabulous wonders inside, but you can see bits of the vaguely Spanish mission–style dwelling peeking over the top of the walls. (If you're dying of curiosity, check out the book that's on sale at The Mirage, complete with many photos of their house, overdecorated and stuffed within an inch of its life with objects from around the world, and with tigers roaming freely.) Across the street are much smaller houses, also sporting the gold "SR" on their gates. These have been purchased by the Austrian magicians as guesthouses, turning the whole block into a sort of compound. Drive by with the windows down and maybe you can hear lions and tigers (and bears) roar.

In The Mirage, 3400 Las Vegas Blvd. S. © 702/791-7111. Admission $10, free for children under 10 if accompanied by an adult. On Wed, when only Dolphin Habitat is open, admission $5. Secret Garden Mon–Tues and Thurs–Fri 11am–5pm, Sat–Sun 10am–5pm; Dolphin Habitat Mon–Fri 11am–7pm, Sat–Sun 10am–7pm. Hours subject to change and vary by season.

Shark Reef at Mandalay Bay ✦ Given that watching fish can lower your blood pressure, it's practically a public service for Mandalay Bay to provide this facility in a city where craps tables and other gaming areas can bring your excitement level to dangerous heights. Unfortunately, it's just a big giant aquarium (though we admire the style—it's built to look like a sunken temple), which, hey, we like, but gee, not at these prices. (Though standing in the all-glass tunnel, surrounded by sharks and finny friends, was kinda cool.) Note also that it is *waaay* off in a remote part of Mandalay Bay, which might be a hassle for those with mobility problems.

In Mandalay Bay, 3950 Las Vegas Blvd. S. © 702/632-7000. Admission $15 adults, $9.95 children 5–12, free for children under 5. Daily 10am–11pm.

Speed: The Ride/Las Vegas Cyber Speedway ✦✦ Auto racing is the fastest-growing spectator sport in America, so it's no surprise that these two attractions at the Sahara are a popular stop. The first is an 8-minute virtual-reality ride, **Cyber Speedway** ✦✦, featuring a three-quarter-size replica of a NASCAR race car. Hop aboard for an animated, simulated ride—either the Las Vegas Motor Speedway or a race around the streets of Las Vegas (start with the Strip, with all the hotels flashing by, and then through the Forum Shops—whoops! There goes Versace!—and so forth). Press the gas and you lean back and feel the rush of speed; hit a bump and you go flying. Should your car get in a crash, off you go to a pit stop. At the end, a computer-generated report tells you your average speed, how many laps you made, how you did racing against the others next to you, and so forth. It's a pretty remarkable experience.

In a separate **3-D motion theater** ✦, you'll don goggles to view a film that puts you right inside another race car for yet another stomach-churning ride (even more dizzying than the virtual-reality portion). Speed junkies and race-car buffs will be in heaven here, though those with tender stomachs should consider shopping at the well-stocked theme gift shop instead.

Speed: The Ride ✦✦ is a roller coaster that blasts riders out through a hole in the wall by the new NASCAR Cafe, then through a loop, under the sidewalk, through the hotel's marquee, and finally straight up a 250-foot tower. At the peak, you feel a moment of weightlessness, and then you do the whole thing backwards! Not for the faint of heart.

In the Sahara hotel & casino, 2535 Las Vegas Blvd. S. ℭ 702/737-2111. $15 for 1 ride on each attraction, $18 for all-day pass for all attractions. Stock-car simulator only $10 (you must be at least 48 in. tall to ride), Speed: The Ride (roller coaster) $10 for all-day pass. Opens daily at 10am; closing hours vary seasonally, but usually it's 10pm.

Star Trek: The Experience ✦   It goes without saying that hard-core Trekkers (note use of correct term) will be delighted. On the other hand, normal, sensible fans, and those who couldn't care less about *Star Trek,* may find themselves saying, "I spent $25 and 2 hours in line for this?"

This is the undisputed champ in the Vegas motion-simulator ride category. You can't fault the setup and interior design; after a walk through a space-themed casino (check out those light-beam-activated slot machines!), your long wait in line will be somewhat entertaining, thanks to memorabilia (displayed as if this were the stuff of fact, not fiction) and TVs showing various *Trek* clips. As you make your way to the ride proper, you encounter actors dressed in *Trek* gear, who let you know that you've crossed the line into the *Trek* future.

There is a story line, but we won't spoil it for you. Suffice to say it involves time travel and evil doings by the Borg, and if all doesn't work out, the very history of *Star Trek* could be affected. Do expect to be beamed aboard the *Enterprise* (that's really kind of cool), and know that if you have a sensitive stomach, you can skip the actual motion-simulator part, a wild and sometimes headache-inducing chase through space. In addition to the often-lengthy wait (on average, 20 min.; best shot at a slight lull would be noon–1pm on weekdays), the quality of your experience can vary depending on the quality of those *Trek*-garbed actors, whose line delivery can be awfully stilted. On the way out, through the shops selling everything *Trek*- and space-related (go ahead, get that Tribble you've always wanted), don't miss the TV showing a "news report" about some of the very things you just experienced. ***Note:*** In spring 2004, a new, "edgier" attraction will be added to *Star Trek: The Experience. Borg Invasion 4D* will feature a 3D film starring several *Star Trek Voyager* cast members, as well as numerous sensory and special effects. There's no word yet on what the ticket prices—we'd bet on astronomical—will be.

In the Las Vegas Hilton, 3000 Paradise Rd. ℭ 888/GO-BOLDLY. www.startrekexp.com. Admission $25 for an all-day pass. Daily 11am–11pm.

Stratosphere Thrill Rides ✦✦ *(Kids)*   Atop the 1,149-foot Stratosphere Tower are two marvelous thrill rides. The **High Roller** ✦✦ (the world's highest roller coaster) was recently revamped to go at even faster speeds as it zooms around a hilly track that is seemingly suspended in midair. Even more fun is the **Big Shot** ✦✦, a breathtaking free-fall ride that thrusts you 160 feet in the air along a 228-foot spire at the top of the tower, then plummets back down again. Sitting in an open car, you seem to be dangling in space over Las Vegas. We have one relative, a thrill-ride enthusiast, who said he never felt more scared than when he rode the Big Shot. After surviving, he promptly put his kids on it; they loved it. ***Note:*** The rides are shut down in inclement weather and high winds.

Atop the Stratosphere Casino Hotel & Tower, 2000 Las Vegas Blvd. S. ✆ **702/380-7777**. Admission for Big Shot $8; for roller coaster $5; $5 per reride, plus $7 to ascend the Tower (if you dine in the buffet room or Top of the World, there's no charge to go up to the Tower). Multiride packages also available for varying costs. Sun–Thurs 10am–midnight; Fri–Sat 10am–1am. Hours vary seasonally. Minimum height requirement for both rides is 48 in.

The Wynn Collection of Fine Art ★ So MGM took over Steve Wynn's resort empire, and along with it, much of the art he (trailblazingly) showcased at Bellagio. Wynn then turned around, bought the Desert Inn, blew it up, and is building a new extraordinary resort on the property. But meanwhile, he's put his art on exhibit again. Only a double handful of paintings is currently on exhibit, but that number could go up and down (Wynn is a ferocious collector with a keen appreciation, who just set some art-purchasing records while acquiring a couple of costly masterpieces). At this writing, among the pieces exhibited are Picasso's *Le Reve* (for which his new resort will be named) and Matisse's *The Persian Robe*. Perhaps not enough to go out of your way for, but then again, what an alternative to slots . . .

3145 S. Las Vegas Blvd. ✆ **702/733-4100**. Admission $10 adults, $6 children 6–12. Daily 10am–5pm.

2 Getting Married

This is one of the most popular things to do in Las Vegas. Why? It's very easy to get married here. Too easy. See that total stranger standing next to you? Grab him or her and head down to the **Clark Country Marriage License Bureau,** 200 S. 3rd St., at Briger Avenue (✆ **702/455-3156;** open daily 8am–midnight, 24 hr. legal holidays), to get your license. Find a wedding chapel (not hard, as there are about 50 of them in town; they line the north end of the Strip, and most hotels have one) and tie the knot. Just like that. No blood test, no waiting period—heck, not even an awkward dating period.

Even if you have actually known your intended for some time, Las Vegas is a great place to get married. The ease is the primary attraction, but there are a number of other appealing reasons. You can have any kind of wedding you want, from a big, traditional production number to a small, intimate affair; from a spur-of-the-moment "just-the-happy-couple-in-blue-jeans" kind of thing to an "Elvis-in-a-pink-Cadillac-at-a-drive-through-window" kind of thing. (Oh, yes. More on that later.) The wedding chapels take care of everything; usually they'll even provide a limo to take you to the license bureau and back. Most offer all the accessories, from rings to flowers to a videotaped record of the event.

We personally know several very happy couples who opted for the Vegas route. Motivations differed, with the ease factor heading the list (though the Vegas-ness of the whole thing came in a close second), but one and all reported having great fun. Really, is there a more romantic way to start off your life together than in gales of laughter?

In any event, the more than 100,000 couples who yearly take advantage of all this can't be wrong. If you want to follow in the footsteps of Elvis and Priscilla (at the first incarnation of the Aladdin Hotel), Michael Jordan, Joan Collins, Bruce Willis and Demi Moore, and, of course, Dennis Rodman and Carmen Electra, you'll want to peruse the following list of the most notable wedding chapels on or near the Strip. There are many more in town, and almost all the

---

Fun Fact **An Elvis Impersonator's Top 10 Reasons
to Get Married in Las Vegas**

Jesse Garon has appeared in numerous Las Vegas productions as "Young Elvis." He arrives at any special event in a 1955 pink, neon-lit Cadillac, and does weddings, receptions, birthdays, conventions, grand openings, and so on. For all your Elvis impersonator needs, call © 877/ ELVIS-35 or visit his website at www.elvis-vegas.com.

1. It's the only place in the world where Elvis will marry you, at a drive-up window, in a pink Cadillac—24 hours a day.
2. Chances are you'll never forget your anniversary.
3. Where else can you treat all your guests to a wedding buffet for only 99¢ a head?
4. Four words: One helluva bachelor party.
5. On wedding night, show spouse that new "watch me disappear" act you learned from Siegfried & Roy.
6. Show your parents who's boss—have your wedding your way.
7. Wedding bells ring for you everywhere you go. They just sound like slot machines.
8. You can throw dice instead of rice.
9. Easy to lie about age on the marriage certificate—just like Joan Collins did!
10. With all the money you save, it's dice clocks for everyone!

---

major hotels offer a chapel as well; though the latter are cleaner and less tacky than some of the Strip chapels, they do tend to be without any personality at all. (One exception might be the chapel at the Excalibur Hotel, where you can dress in medieval costumes, and the lovely chapel at Bellagio, which has personal wedding coordinators and a high level of customer service, holding only 8–10 weddings a day—seems like a lot, but it's nothing compared to the volume on the Strip.)

With regard to decor, there isn't a radical difference between the major places (hence, no star ratings here), though some are decidedly spiffier and less sad than others. Attitude certainly makes a difference with several and varies radically depending on who's working at any given time. Given how important your wedding is—or should be—we encourage you to give yourself time to comparison-shop, and spurn anyone who doesn't seem eager enough for your business. (**Passing note:** Standing outside a wedding chapel for a couple of hours makes for interesting people-watching, as you see brides in full white gowns accompanied by a whole retinue, pregnant brides in ordinary dresses, or happy couples wearing sweats, all ready to march down that aisle.)

You can also call **Las Vegas Weddings and Rooms** (© 800/488-MATE), which offers one-stop shopping for wedding services. They'll find a chapel or outdoor garden that suits your taste (not to mention such only-in-Vegas venues as the former mansions of Elvis Presley and Liberace); book you into a hotel for the honeymoon; arrange the ceremony; and provide flowers, a photographer (or videographer), a wedding cake, a limo, car rental, music, champagne, balloons, and a garter for the bride. Basically, they can arrange anything you like. Theme weddings are a specialty. They even have a New Age minister on call who can perform a Native American ceremony. And yes, you can get married by an Elvis impersonator. Las Vegas Weddings can also arrange your honeymoon stay, complete with sightseeing tours, show tickets, and meals.

Weddings can be very cheap in Vegas: A license is about $55, and a basic service not much more. Even a full-blown shebang package—photos, music, some flowers, video, cake, and other doodads—will run only about $500 total. We haven't quoted any prices here, as the ultimate cost depends entirely on how much you want to spend. Go cheap, and the whole thing will set you back maybe $100, including the license (maybe even somewhat less); go elaborate, and the price is still reasonable by today's wedding-price standards. Be sure to remember that there are often hidden charges, such as expected gratuities for the minister (about $25 should do; no real need to tip anyone else), and so forth. If you're penny-pinching, you'll want to keep those in mind.

Be aware that Valentine's Day is a very popular day to get married in Vegas. Some of the chapels perform as many as 80 services on February 14.

But remember, you also don't have to plan ahead. Just show up, get your paperwork, close your eyes, and pick a chapel. And above all, have fun. Good luck and best wishes to you both.

Chapel of Love This is a friendly place largely run by women (men take the photos and are the limo drivers), featuring four different chapels. Good news came when the Divine Madness fantasy wedding chapel closed and brought all of their many costumes and props over here—along with their silly sensibility. The chapels herein have been remodeled as well, and while you won't get, say, fantasy hotel level set-design, this is the spot for Fun Weddings, for those who want Renaissance or Egyptian-themed nuptials (to say nothing of Gangster, Tarzan & Jane or Adam & Eve). None of the rooms are very big; and again, if they say "jungle," you should think "plastic plants." It's a hoot, anyway. There is also a reception room for a cold buffet or hot hors d'oeuvres. Their packages are quite reasonable, and they put all the "hidden" charges (such as suggested gratuities for the minister and so forth) right in their brochure, so there are no surprises. 1431 Las Vegas Blvd. S. ℭ **800/922-5683** or 702/387-0155. www.chapelsoflove.com. Mon–Thurs 8am–10pm; Fri–Sat 8am–midnight; Sun 9am–9pm.

Chapel of the Bells Sporting perhaps the largest and gaudiest sign on the Strip, this chapel also shares a parking lot with the bright pink Fun City Motel. We won't make any jokes. It is also probably the least helpful, most cranky of the wedding chapels we've dealt with—on such a special day, who needs it? The chapel has wood paneling, sage carpeting, and gilt trim up by the pulpit. Electric candles light the walls. It seats only about 25. They prefer advance booking but can do same-day ceremonies if called to. 2233 Las Vegas Blvd. S. ℭ **800/233-2391** or 702/735-6803. www.vegas.com/weddings/chapelofthebells. Mon–Thurs 9am–9pm; Fri–Sat 9am–midnight. They stay open as late as they need to on holidays.

Cupid's Wedding Chapel "The little chapel with the big heart." Well, it just might be. The manager explains that, unlike other chapels on the Strip, they schedule weddings an hour apart; this gives them time for the full production number. The folks at Cupid's pride themselves on offering "a traditional church wedding at a chapel price." This includes a bridal processional, dimmed lights as the minister introduces the happy couple, and then a tape of the couple's favorite song, so they can have their first dance right there at the pulpit after their "first" kiss. They also offer family weddings for those couples blending pre-existing families; the children become a part of the service, and as their parents exchange rings with each other, the kids are given their own small token, to let them know the parents are marrying them as well. The chapel is pleasantly low-frills and down to earth, with white walls and pews, and modern stained glass with doves and roses. (Kitsch-phobes will be pleased to know that the cupids are only in the lobby.) It seats 60 to 70. They recently added a classic banquet hall (and by that we mean, think New Jersey banquet hall) so you can have your reception and wedding all in one place. And, yes, if they don't have something already scheduled, they will take walk-ups.

827 Las Vegas Blvd. S. (C) **800/543-2933** or 702/598-4444. www.cupidswedding.com. Sun–Thurs 10am–10pm; Fri–Sat 10am–1am.

Graceland Wedding Chapel

Housed in a landmark building that's one of the oldest wedding chapels in Vegas, the Graceland bills itself as "the proverbial mom and pop outfit. We offer friendly, courteous service, and are willing to go that extra step." No, Elvis never slept here (one of the owners was friends with Elvis and asked his permission to use the name). This is a tiny New England church building with a small bridge and white picket fence out front. Inside is a 33-seat chapel; the walls are burgundy and white, with a large, modern stained-glass window of doves and roses behind the pulpit. The pews are dark blond wood. It's not the nicest of the chapels, but Catherine Oxenberg and Caspar Van Diem got married here. Jon Bon Jovi and Lorenzo Lamas did also, though not to each other.

619 Las Vegas Blvd. S. (C) **800/824-5732** or 702/382-0091. www.gracelandchapel.com. Sun–Thurs 9am–9pm; Fri–Sat 9am–midnight.

Little Chapel of the Flowers

Their current claim to fame is that Dennis Rodman and Carmen Electra exchanged their deathless vows here. Given that fact, it doesn't look the way you might think. This is actually the spiffiest wed-ding operation on the Strip, with another miniature old-fashioned church build-ing with a very tiny garden and gazebo. They have two chapels off their pretty and comfortable lobby (mock-antique look). The Victorian chapel, which holds only 30, has white walls and dark-wood pews and doesn't look very Victorian at all, but is the nicest of the lot. The Heritage Chapel holds 70 and adds rose-colored drapes and electric-candle chandeliers. They also offer a medium-size reception room and live organ music upon request. It's a pretty, friendly place that somehow manages to act as if every one of the many daily weddings they do is special. They do not allow rice or confetti throwing.

1717 Las Vegas Blvd. S. (C) **800/843-2410** or 702/735-4331. www.littlechapel.com. Mon–Thurs 9am–10pm; Fri–Sat 9am–11pm.

Little White Chapel

This is arguably the most famous of the chapels on the Strip, maybe because they have the big sign saying Michael Jordan and Joan Collins were married here (again, not to each other), maybe because they were the first to do the drive-up window. It is indeed little and white. However, there is a factory-line atmosphere, processing wedding after wedding after wedding, 24 hours a day. Move 'em in, and move 'em out. (No wonder they put in that drive-up window!) The staff, dressed in hot-pink smocks, is brusque, hasty, and has a bit of an attitude (though we know one couple who got married here and had no complaints). They do offer full wedding ceremonies, complete with can-dlelight service and traditional music. There are two chapels, the smaller of which has a large photo of a forest stream. They also have a gazebo for outdoor services, but since it's right on the Strip, it's not as nice as it sounds. If you want something special, there are probably better choices, but for a true Vegas wedding experience, this is Kitsch Wedding Central.

1301 Las Vegas Blvd. S. © **800/545-8111** or 702/382-5943. www.alittlewhitechapel.com. Open 24 hr.

San Francisco Sally's Victorian Chapel *Finds* This is an extremely tiny wedding chapel bursting at the seams with Victorian frills (fringed lamps, swags of lace curtains). They basically offer "an Olde Tyme Parlor Wedding." This is perfect if you want a very intimate wedding—like you, your intended, and someone to officiate. It literally can't hold more than six people. (And the space at the back of the room opens for an even tinier reception area—it can barely fit the cake!) But if you love Victoriana, or you want to play dress-up at your wedding, this is the place. The shop rents out dresses and costumes, so you can wear a Scarlett O'Hara antebellum outfit or some other period number for your big day. (It's all fantasy anyway, so why not go whole hog?) They specialize in extras without extra charges, like altering and whatnot. The women who run it refer to themselves as "a bunch of mother hens"; they're delightful and will pamper you to within an inch of your life. (One couple drops in every year just to say "hi.") Some may find it a bit cutesy, but it really is quite charming and has its own distinct personality, unlike most of the other chapels in the area (where the interiors all start to blur together after a while). This is a decidedly special place that, depending on your wedding desires and fantasies, might be just right.

1304 Las Vegas Blvd. S. © **800/658-8677** or 702/385-7777 Mon–Sat 10am–6pm; Sun 10am–4pm.

A Special Memory Wedding Chapel This is a very nice wedding chapel, particularly when compared to the rather tired facades of the classics on the Strip. This is absolutely the place to go if you want a traditional, big-production wedding; you won't feel in the least bit tacky. It's a New England church–style building, complete with steeple. The interior looks like a proper church (well, a plain one—don't think ornate Gothic cathedral) with a peaked roof, pews with padded red seats, modern stained-glass windows of doves and flowers, and lots of dark wood. It's all very clean and new and seats about 87 comfortably. There is a short staircase leading to an actual bride's room; she can make an entrance coming down it or through the double doors at the back. The area outside the chapel is like a minimall of bridal paraphernalia stores. Should all this just be too darn nice and proper for you, they also offer a drive-up window (where they do about 300 weddings a month!). It'll cost you $25—just ring the buzzer for service. They have a photo studio on-site and will do a small cake, cold cuts, and champagne receptions. There is a gazebo for outside weddings, and they sell T-shirts!

800 S. 4th St. (at Gass Ave.). © **800/962-7798** or 702/384-2211. www.aspecialmemory.com. Sun–Thurs 8am–10pm; Fri–Sat 8am–midnight.

Wee Kirk O' the Heather This is the oldest wedding chapel in Las Vegas (it's been here since 1940) and the one at the very end of the Strip, right before Downtown (and thus even closer to the license bureau). It would be declared a historic landmark, except some renovations in the past moved just enough of the interior walls to alter it sufficiently and keep it from being official. A recent renovation isn't all that impressive and seems to feature a great deal of bright lavender. They have an organ as well.

231 Las Vegas Blvd. S. © **702/382-9830.** Daily 10am–midnight.

3 Attractions in Nearby Henderson

About 6 miles from the Strip in the town of Henderson are two factories that offer free tours (there used to be more, but they recently closed), and if that's your kind of thing, well, you won't be entirely alone. It's best to see them on a weekday when they're fully operative.

To get to Henderson, drive east on Tropicana Avenue, make a right on Mountain Vista, then go 2 miles to Sunset Way; turn left into Green Valley Business Park. You will soon see Ethel M Chocolates, a good place to begin. Use the map in this section to find your way to the other facility.

Ethel M Chocolates ⋆ This tourist attraction draws about 2,000 visitors a day. Ethel Mars began making fine chocolates in a little candy kitchen around the early 20th century. Her small enterprise evolved to produce not only dozens of varieties of superb boxed chocolates, but some of the world's most famous candies: M&Ms, Milky Way, 3 Musketeers, Snickers, and Mars bars.

Alas, the tour lasts only about 10 minutes and consists entirely of viewing stations with an audiotape explaining the chocolate-baking process. You learn very little. But the place does look like a bakery, rather than a factory, which is nice, as no one wants to see their chocolates handled without love. Even more sadly, you get only one small chocolate as a sample—delicious, but hardly satisfying. (Surely, this is by design; now overwhelmingly in the mood for sugar, you are more likely to buy some of their expensive chocolate.) ***Note:*** Come before 2:30pm, which is when the workers start to pack up and go home.

What's really worth seeing is outside: a lovely and extensive **2½-acre garden** ⋆ displaying 350 species of rare and exotic cacti with signs provided for self-guided tours. It's best appreciated in spring, when the cacti are in full bloom. There's a little gazebo in which to sit and enjoy the garden, which would be quite peaceful were it not for the busloads of tourists in the area. Behind the garden, also with a self-guided tour, is Ethel M's "Living Machine," a natural wastewater treatment and recycling plant that consists of aerated tanks, ecological fluid beds, a constructed wetlands, reed beds, and a storage pond.

2 Cactus Garden Dr. (just off Mountain Vista and Sunset Way in the Green Valley Business Park). (℃ **702/433-2500** for recorded information, or 702/458-8864. www.ethelm.com. Free admission. Daily 8:30am–7pm. Closed Dec 25.

Ron Lee's World of Clowns It's easy to give this one a miss, but you're here, so what the heck. This factory manufactures clown figurines (and other types, most notably Disney figures). The tour itself consists of simply looking in windows as people mold and paint. The real attraction (aside from a beautiful carousel) is the gift shop, with a nearly limitless amount of high-quality figurines, primarily with a clown motif.

330 Carousel Pkwy., Henderson. (℃ **800/829-3928** or 702/434-3920. Free admission. Mon–Fri 8:30am–4:30pm; Sat 10am–4pm.

4 Especially for Kids

Like much of the rest of the world, you may be under the impression that Las Vegas has evolved from an adults-only fantasyland into a vacation destination suitable for the entire family. The only explanation for this myth is that Las Vegas was referred to as "Disneyland for adults" by so many and for so long that the town became momentarily confused and decided it actually *was* Disneyland. Some of the gargantuan hotels then spent small fortunes on redecorating in an

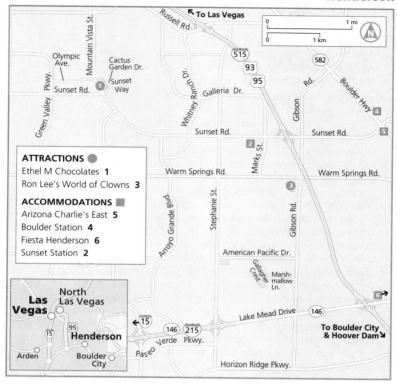

attempt to lure families with vast quantities of junk food and a lot of hype. They now vehemently deny that any such notion ever crossed their collective minds, and, no, they don't know how that roller coaster got into the parking lot.

To put things simply, Las Vegas makes money—lots and lots of money—by promoting gambling, drinking, and sex. These are all fine pursuits if you happen to be an adult, but if you haven't reached the magical age of 21, you really don't count in this town. In any case, the casinos and even the Strip itself are simply too stimulating, noisy, and smoky for young kids.

Older progeny may have a tolerance for crowds and the incessant pinging of the slot machines, but they will be thoroughly annoyed with you when casino security chastises them if they so much as stop to tie their shoelaces anywhere near the gaming tables. Since you can't get from your hotel room to the parking lot without ambling through a casino, you can't reasonably expect a teenager to be in a good mood once you stagger outside. And those amusement parks and video halls that haven't yet been purged are very expensive places to park your kids for an afternoon or evening, assuming they are old enough to be left unsupervised.

Nevertheless, you may have a perfectly legitimate reason for bringing your children to Las Vegas (like Grandma was busy, or you were just stopping off on your way from somewhere else), so here are some places to take the children both on and off the Strip.

Going Vegas

If you're looking for a quintessential Las Vegas experience, try these suggestions from James P. Reza, Geoff Carter, and the editors of *Scope* magazine (now the *Las Vegas Weekly*).

- **Peppermill's Fireside Lounge** (p. 264). This lounge is so evocative of the Me Decade, it's impossible not to love it. Dark, cozy, sexy, and somewhat kitschy, it's a great place for romantic encounters. Try to sit by the year-round fire pit, if you can stand the heat.
- **GameWorks**, 3785 Las Vegas Blvd. S. (© 702/432-4263). This multi-level entertainment center gives visitors a chance to wreak digitized havoc on the latest video-game creations. A few brave souls try the 75-foot climbing wall; most just hang in the lounge and shoot pool.
- **Cheetah's** (p. 271). How could you possibly visit Sin City and not sample the ubiquitous lap dance? Couples are welcome at Cheetah's, the site of Paul Verhoven's laughably overdone film *Showgirls*. More quality, less silicone, and a VIP lounge that has hosted lap dances for Wilt Chamberlain, Sting, and Drew Barrymore.
- **The Forum Shops at Caesars Palace** (p. 237). The most unique shopping experience in the world. Take Rodeo Drive, marry it to Rome, douse the whole thing in Spielberg, and you're still nowhere near this elegant retail space.
- **The Sky Lounge at the Polo Towers** (p. 266). Hidden on the 19th floor of a timeshare condominium complex, this lounge offers a far more engaging view than the Stratosphere Tower, absolutely free of charge. Watch out for kamikaze tour groups.
- **The Hard Rock Hotel & Casino** (p. 106). Everything about this hotel/casino—the bars, the Joint showroom, Mr. Lucky's 24/7—manages to evoke classic Vegas, a city that was built for young hipsters, not fanny-pack-wielding families.
- **Love Shack** (check local listings for various locations). Our vote for Sin City's best lounge act. Covering the music of the '70s and '80s with tenacious fervor, Love Shack is nothing short of a funky riot in 6-inch heels and mascara.
- **Red Rock Canyon** (p. 285). Providing needed respite from the neon jungle, Red Rock is as beautiful as the desert gets. This haven for hikers and rock climbers gets a bit overrun at times, but it is still worth the trip. *Note:* Don't feed the wild burros. Unlike the entertainers at Cheetah's, they bite.

Circus Circus (p. 104) has ongoing circus acts throughout the day, a vast video-game-and-pinball arcade, and dozens of carnival games on its mezzanine level. Behind the hotel is the **Adventuredome,** detailed below.

Excalibur (p. 82) also offers video and carnival games, plus thrill cinemas and free shows (jugglers, puppets, and so on).

At **Caesars Palace** (p. 86), the Race for Atlantis IMAX ride is a thrill for everyone in the family. Animated talking statues in the **Forum Shops** are also a kick, while kids should also be wowed by clamoring around inside the giant moving Trojan horse outside FAO Schwarz. They may also like to poke around in the shops and marvel at the Atlantis fountain show.

Star Trek: The Experience (p. 186) deserves to draw families to the **Las Vegas Hilton,** but it may be a bit much for younger children.

The ship battle in front of **Treasure Island** (p. 98) is sure to please, as will the erupting volcano and the Secret Garden of Siegfried & Roy and Dolphin Habitat at **The Mirage** (p. 184), and the new **Shark Reef at Mandalay Bay** (p. 185). Ditto the various attractions at **Luxor Las Vegas** (the IMAX Theater, p. 182; King Tut's Tomb, p. 180; and simulator ride, p. 182) and **Cyber Speedway** and **Speed: The Ride** (p. 185) at the **Sahara.**

Children 10 and up will love the many options for play (from high-tech to low-tech, from video wonders to actual physical activity) offered at **GameWorks** (p. 179), as will their parents.

Of moderate interest to youngsters are the **factory tours in Henderson** (p. 192), especially Ethel M Chocolates, though they will like the free sweets best. More educational is the **Marjorie Barrick Museum** at UNLV (p. 182), but only the reptile exhibit will really interest kids.

Appropriate shows for kids include *Tournament of Kings* at Excalibur, **Siegfried & Roy** at The Mirage, **Lance Burton** at the Monte Carlo, and Cirque du Soleil's *Mystère* at Treasure Island. As a general rule, early shows are less racy than late-night shows. All of these productions are reviewed in detail in chapter 10.

Beyond the city limits (see chapter 11 for details on all of these) is **Bonnie Springs Ranch/Old Nevada,** with trail and stagecoach rides, a petting zoo, old-fashioned melodramas, stunt shootouts, a Nevada-themed wax museum, crafts demonstrations, and more. **Lake Mead** has great recreational facilities for family vacations. Finally, organized tours (see the next section of this chapter) to the Grand Canyon and other interesting sights in southern Nevada and neighboring states can be fun family activities. Check with your hotel sightseeing desk. Kids should also be entertained by the personalized tours offered by **Creative Adventures** (© **702/361-5565**); see p. 197.

Specifically kid-pleasing attractions are described below.

Adventuredome ★★ This isn't a half-bad place to spend a hot afternoon, especially now that Circus Circus, the casino/hotel that built this indoor amusement park, has undergone a face-lift. The glass dome that towers overhead lets in natural light, a solace to those of us who look peaked under the glow of the artificial kind. A double-loop roller coaster careens around the simulated Grand Canyon, and there's the requisite water flume, a laser-tag area, and a modest number of other rides for kids of all ages. A dinosaur-bone excavation area will provide a good time for preschoolers, and a place to rest for the supervising adults. Video games and an arcade are separate from the attractions, cutting down just a tad on the noise level. Jugglers and magicians provide impromptu entertainment. Our only suggestion is not to leave kids here alone; they could easily get lost.

2880 Las Vegas Blvd. S. (behind Circus Circus). © 702/794-3939. Free admission; pay per ride $3–$5; daily pass $20 adults, $14 children 33–47 in. AE, DC, DISC, MC, V. Park hours vary seasonally but are usually Mon–Thurs 10am–6pm, Fri–Sat 10am–midnight, Sun 10am–8pm.

Las Vegas Natural History Museum ★ Conveniently located across the street from the Lied Discovery Children's Museum (described below), this humble temple of taxidermy harkens back to elementary-school field trips circa

1965, when stuffed elk and brown bears forever protecting their kill were as close as most of us got to exotic animals. Worn around the edges but very sweet and relaxed, the museum is enlivened by a hands-on activity room and two life-size dinosaurs that roar at one another intermittently. A small boy was observed leaping toward his dad upon watching this display, so you might want to warn any sensitive little ones that the big tyrannosaurs aren't going anywhere. Surprisingly, the gift shop here is particularly well stocked with neat items you won't too terribly mind buying for the kids.

900 Las Vegas Blvd. N. (at Washington). ℂ 702/384-3466. http://vegaswebworld.com/lvnathistory. Admission $5.50 adults; $4.50 seniors, students, and military; $3 children 4–12; free for children under 4. Daily 9am–4pm.

Lied Discovery Children's Museum ⭐⭐ *Finds* A hands-on science museum designed for curious kids, the bright, airy, two-story Lied makes an ideal outing for toddlers and young children. With lots of interactive exhibits to examine, including a miniature grocery store, a tube for encasing oneself inside a soap bubble, a radio station, and music and drawing areas, you'll soon forget your video-poker losses. Clever, thought-inducing exhibits are everywhere. Learn how it feels to be handicapped by playing basketball from a wheelchair. Feed a wooden "sandwich" to a cutout of a snake and to a human cutout, and see how much nutrition each receives. See how much sunscreen their giant stuffed mascot needs to keep from burning. On weekend afternoons from 1 to 3pm, free drop-in art classes are offered, giving you a bit of time to ramble around the gift store or read the fine print on the exhibit placards. The Lied also shares space with a city library branch, so after the kids run around, you can calm them back down with a story or two.

833 Las Vegas Blvd. N. (½ block south of Washington, across the street from Cashman Field). ℂ 702/382-5437. www.ldcm.org. Admission $6 adults, $5 seniors and children 1–17. Tues–Sun 10am–5pm.

MGM Grand Youth Center This is the sole child-care center on the Strip, and according to the genial manager, it's booked solid during summers and on holidays. MGM Grand hotel guests get first priority to leave their youngsters in this warren of brightly decorated and well-supervised, albeit windowless, rooms. Arts and crafts compete with Nintendo and videos for kids' attention, and there are no organized activities (although they do serve meals). If we were children and our parents left us here on a family vacation, we'd never let them forget it.

In the MGM Grand Hotel, 3799 Las Vegas Blvd. S. ℂ 702/891-3200. For children 3–12 (no diaper wearers). Daily 11am–11pm. Costs vary, depending on season and whether you are a guest of the hotel (call ahead to get more information).

Scandia Family Fun Center ⭐⭐ This family-amusement center, located just a few blocks off the Strip, is still the most viable alternative for those who need to amuse children not quite old enough for GameWorks, or for those on a tighter budget. Certainly it's where local families come for outings, and they keep the batting cages hopping ($1.25 for 25 pitches). The arcade is a bit warm and stinky, and other parts (including miniature-car racing and bumper boats, $4 per ride; small children ride free with an adult) are a bit worn, but the miniature-golf course (three 18-hole courses, $5.50 per game, free for children under 6) is quite cute. Still, we do have to wonder about those round-the-clock weekend hours; we certainly hope those playing miniature golf at 4am are not parents occupied by children.

2900 Sirius Ave. (at Rancho Dr. just south of Sahara Ave.). ℂ 702/364-0070. Free admission, but there's a fee for each game or activity. Super Saver Pass $12 (includes 1 round of miniature golf, 2 rides, and 5 game tokens); Unlimited Wristband Package $17 (includes unlimited bumper-boat and car rides, unlimited minia-ture golf, and 10 tokens for batting cages or arcade games). Mar–Oct daily 24 hr.; Nov–Feb Sun–Thurs 10am–11pm, Fri–Sat 24 hr.

Wet 'n Wild ★★   Before we begin, a warning: At press time, it seemed that Wet 'n Wild was facing imminent doom—it was due to be torn down to make way for a (appropriately) water-themed resort called Voyagers. We hope they get through at least one more summer. When temperatures soar, head for this 26-acre water park right in the heart of the Strip and cool off while jumping waves, careen-ing down steep flumes, and running rapids. There are a variety of slides and rides, plus a lazy river and a beach for those looking for more sedentary activities. The noise level can be extraordinarily high (people have to shout to be heard over the rushing water) so don't think of this as relaxing—but when it's 108°F (42°C) in the shade, who cares? Also, be on the lookout for discount coupons. Many Las Vegas packages include a free admission (sometimes partial-day).

2601 Las Vegas Blvd. S. (just south of Sahara Ave.). © **702/871-7811**. www.wetnwildlv.com. Admission $27 adults, $16 seniors over 55, $21 children under 48 in., free for children under 3. Early May to Sept 30 daily 10am–6 or 8pm (sometimes later). Season and hours vary somewhat from year to year, so call ahead.

5 Organized Tours

Just about every hotel in town has a sightseeing desk offering a seemingly infi-nite number of tours in and around Las Vegas. You're sure to find a tour com-pany that will take you where you want to go.

Coach USA (© **888/COACHUSA;** www.coachusa.com) offers a rather com-prehensive roster, including:

- Several 3½-hour **city tours,** with various itineraries including visits to Ethel M Chocolates, the Liberace Museum, Tropicana Legends Museum, and the Fremont Street Experience.
- Half-day excursions to **Hoover Dam, Mount Charleston,** and **Red Rock Canyon** (see chapter 11 for details).
- A full-day excursion to **Valley of Fire** and **Lake Mead.**
- A 13-hour **Grand Canyon excursion.**

Call for details or inquire at your hotel's sightseeing desk, where you'll also find free magazines with coupons for discounts on these tours.

GRAND CANYON TOURS

Generally, tourists visiting Las Vegas don't drive 300 miles to Arizona to see the Grand Canyon, but there are dozens of sightseeing tours departing from the city daily. In addition to the Coach USA tours described above, the major operator, **Scenic Airlines** (© **800/634-6801** or 702/638-3300; www.scenic.com), runs deluxe, full-day guided air-ground tours starting at $219 per person ($189 for children 2–11); the price includes a bus excursion through the national park, a flight over the canyon, and lunch. All scenic tours include flightseeing. The company also offers both full-day and overnight tours with hiking.

Scenic also offers tours to other points of interest and national parks, includ-ing Bryce Canyon and Monument Valley. Ask for details when you call.

UNIQUE DESERT TOURS

A totally different type of tour is offered by Char Cruze of **Creative Adven-tures** ★★★ (© **702/361-5565**). Char, a charming fourth-generation Las Vegan (she was at the opening of The Flamingo), spent her childhood riding horseback through the mesquite and cottonwoods of the Mojave Desert, discovering

Mayor Oscar B. Goodman's Top 10 Places to Recapture Old Las Vegas

1. The proposed "Mob" Museum in the old U.S. Courthouse and Post Office (300 E. Stewart Ave.)
2. "Bugsy" Suite at the Flamingo Hotel & Casino
3. Bob Taylor's Ranch House on 6250 Rio Vista (where the old timers went)
4. Fellini's Restaurant on 5555 W. Charleston (ambience of yore)
5. Piero's Italian Cuisine on 355 Convention Center Dr. (characters eating pasta)
6. 200 feet at bottom of Lake Mead
7. 6 feet in desert near the state line
8. Howard Hughes's Bungalow behind Channel 8
9. WELCOME TO LAS VEGAS sign south of the Strip
10. The Huntridge Theater on 1208 E. Charleston

Oscar B. Goodman is the Mayor of Las Vegas.

magical places you'd never find on your own or on a commercial tour. Char is a lecturer and storyteller as well as a tour guide. She has extensively studied southern Nevada's geology and desert wildlife, its regional history, and its Native American cultures. Her personalized tours, enhanced by fascinating stories about everything from miners to mobsters, visit haunted mines, sacred Paiute grounds, ghost towns, canyons, and ancient petroglyphs. She also has many things to entertain and educate children, and carries a tote bag full of visual aids, like a board covered in labeled rocks to better illustrate a lecture on local geology. Char has certain structured tours, but she loves to do individual tours tailored to the group. This is absolutely worth the money—you are definitely going to get something different than you would on a conventional tour, while Char herself is most accommodating, thoughtful, knowledgeable, and prompt. Char rents transport according to the size of the group and can handle clients with disabilities.

Depending on your itinerary, the cost is about $100 a day if you use your own car (more, depending on the number of people, if rental transportation is required; however, it's even more of a bargain with a larger group). It's a good idea to make arrangements with her prior to leaving home.

6 Fore! Great Desert Golf

In addition to the listings below, there are dozens of local courses, including some very challenging ones that have hosted PGA tournaments. *Note:* Greens fees vary radically depending on time of day and year. Also, call for opening and closing times as these change frequently.

If you're a serious golfer, you may want to contact **American Golf** ((C) **800/468-7918**), a nationwide reservations service that's based in Arizona. They can help you arrange golf packages and book hard-to-get tee times.

Note also that the **Rio All-Suite Hotel** (p. 97) has an affiliated golf course.

Angel Park Golf Club   This 36-hole, par-70/71 public course is a local favorite. Arnold Palmer originally designed the Mountain and Palm courses (the

Palm Course was redesigned several years later by Bob Cupp). Players call this a great escape from the casinos, claiming that no matter how many times they play it, they never get tired of it. The Palm Course has gently rolling fairways that offer golfers of all abilities a challenging yet forgiving layout. The Mountain Course has rolling natural terrain and gorgeous panoramic views. In addition to these two challenging 18-hole courses, Angel Park offers a night-lit Cloud 9 Course (12 holes for daylight play, 9 at night), where each hole is patterned after a famous par-3. You can reserve tee times up to 60 days in advance with a credit-card guarantee.

Yardage: Palm Course 6,525 championship and 5,438 resort; Mountain Course 6,722 championship and 5,164 resort.

Facilities: Pro shop, night-lit driving range, 18-hole putting course, restaurant, snack bar, cocktail bar, and beverage cart.

100 S. Rampart Blvd. (between Summerlin Pkwy. and Alta St.; 20 min. NW of the Strip). ℂ 888/629-3929 or 702/254-0566. www.angelpark.com. Greens fees $65–$160. Discounted twilight rates available.

Bali Hai Golf Club   One of the newest and most exclusive golf addresses belongs to this multimillion-dollar course built in 2000 on the Strip just south of Mandalay Bay. Done in a wild South Seas theme, the par-71 course features over 7 acres of water hazards, plus an island green, palm trees, and tropical foliage everywhere you look. Not impressed yet? How about the fact that all of its golf carts are equipped with Global Positioning Satellite (GPS) tracking systems. Or that celeb chef Wolfgang Puck chose to open his newest Vegas eatery here. Okay, if that doesn't convince you of the upscale nature of the joint, check out the greens fees.

Even at those prices, tee times are often booked 6 months in advance.

Yardage: 7,002 championship.

Facilities: Pro shop, putting green, gourmet restaurant, grill, and lounge.

5150 Las Vegas Blvd. S. ℂ 888/397-2499. www.waltersgolf.com. Greens fees $155–$325.

Black Mountain Golf & Country Club   Two new greens have recently been added to this 27-hole, par-72 semiprivate course, which requires reservations 4 days in advance. It's considered a great old course, with lots of wildlife, including roadrunners. However, unpredictable winds may affect your game.

Yardage: 6,550 championship, 6,223 regular, and 5,518 ladies.

Facilities: Pro shop, putting green, driving range, restaurant, snack bar, and cocktail lounge.

In nearby Henderson, 500 Greenway Rd. ℂ 702/565-7933. Greens fees $40–$100.

Craig Ranch Golf Club *Value*   This is a flat 18-hole, par-70 public course with many trees and bunkers; both narrow and open fairways feature Bermuda turf. The greens fees are a bargain, and you can reserve tee times 7 days in advance.

Yardage: 6,001 regular and 5,221 ladies.

Facilities: Driving range, pro shop, PGA teaching pro, putting green, and snack bar.

628 W. Craig Rd. (between Losee Rd. and Martin Luther King Blvd.). ℂ 702/642-9700. Greens fees $19 walking, $29 in golf cart.

Desert Rose Golf Club   This is an 18-hole, par-71 public course built in 1963 and designed by Dick Wilson/Joe Lee. Narrow fairways feature Bermuda turf. You can reserve tee times up to 7 days in advance.

Yardage: 6,511 championship, 6,135 regular, and 5,458 ladies.

Facilities: Driving range, putting and chipping greens, PGA teaching pro, pro shop, restaurant, and cocktail lounge.

5483 Clubhouse Dr. (3 blocks west of Nellis Blvd., off Sahara Ave.). © **702/431-4653**. Greens fees $33–$79; some packages include cart rentals.

Las Vegas National Golf Club   This is an 18-hole (about eight with water on them), par-71 public course, and a classic layout (not the desert layout you'd expect). If you play from the back tees, it can really be a challenge. The 1996 Las Vegas Invitational, won by Tiger Woods, was held here. Discounted tee times are often available. Reservations are taken up to 60 days in advance; a $5 to $7 fee applies.

Yardage: 6,815 championship, 6,418 regular, and 5,741 ladies.

Facilities: Pro shop, golf school, driving range, restaurant, and cocktail lounge.

1911 Desert Inn Rd. (between Maryland Pkwy. and Eastern Ave.). © **702/734-1796**. Greens fees $135–$175, some including cart rental.

Royal Links Golf Club *(Finds*   More than just greens and water traps, Royal Links is an 18-hole, par-72 course designed to simulate play on some of the greatest courses in the British Open tour. St. Andrews Road Hole, the Postage Stamp at the Royal Troon in Scotland, and a dozen others are all faithfully re-created here for a unique game and an interesting history lesson.

Also fun is the clubhouse, designed (of course) to resemble a medieval castle, complete with an English pub inside.

Yardage: 7,029 championship, 6,602 regular, and 5,864 ladies.

Facilities: Pro shop, golf school, driving range, restaurant, and cocktail lounge.

5995 E. Vegas Valley Rd. (east of Boulder Hwy., between Flamingo and Sahara). © **702/450-8000**. Greens fees $135–$275.

7 Staying Active

You need not be a slot-hypnotized slug when you come to Vegas. The city and surrounding areas offer plenty of opportunities for active sports. In addition to many highly rated golf courses (described above), just about every hotel has a large swimming pool and health club, and tennis courts abound. All types of watersports are offered at Lake Mead National Recreation Area; there's rafting on the Colorado, horseback riding at Mount Charleston and Bonnie Springs, great hiking in the canyons, and much, much more. Do plan to get out of those smoke-filled casinos and into the fresh air once in a while. It's good for your health and your finances.

Note: When choosing a hotel, check out its recreational facilities, all listed in chapter 5.

BOWLING   The **Castaways Hotel & Casino,** 2800 E. Fremont St. (© **702/385-9123**), is famous for housing the largest bowling center in North America (106 lanes) and for being the oldest stop on the Professional Bowlers Tour. A recent renovation has made its premises bright and spiffy. Open 24 hours.

Gold Coast Hotel, 4000 W. Flamingo Rd. (at Valley View; © **702/367-7111**), has a 72-lane bowling center open 24 hours a day.

The **Orleans,** 4500 W. Tropicana Ave. (© **702/365-7111**), has 70 lanes, a pro shop, lockers, meeting rooms, and more. Open 24 hours.

Out on the east side of town, you'll find 56 lanes at **Sam's Town,** 5111 Boulder Hwy. (© **702/456-7777**), plus a snack shop, cocktail lounge, video arcade, day-care center, pro shop, and more. Open 24 hours.

Suncoast, 9090 Alta Dr., in Summerlin (© **702/636-7111**), offers one of the newer facilities in town with 64 lanes divided by a unique center aisle. The high-tech center with touch-screen scoring has become a regular stop on the Pro Bowlers tours. Open 24 hours.

BUNGEE JUMPING   If you want to take a *real* gamble, this is the place to do it—the odds are stacked in your favor, but the thrill is nearly immeasurable. **A. J. Hackett Bungy,** 810 Circus Circus Dr., between Las Vegas Boulevard South and Industrial Road (© **702/385-4321**), is a worldwide chain; they've done more than one million jumps and they haven't lost anyone yet. The instructors are enthusiastic and do much to make you feel comfortable. Expect about an hour wait (there is a bar with a TV and pool table to keep you occupied), but given how meticulous and careful they are with each jumper, you'll be glad they aren't rushing people through.

An elevator in the shape of a rocket takes you to the top of a 175-foot tower, the base for an exhilarating plunge toward a large swimming pool below. During the ride up, you will receive your instructions (which basically amount to "stick your toes over the edge, arms out in front, and dive"). Our guinea pig needed a gentle shove. The whole jump lasts perhaps 3 minutes, but you will have enough adrenaline pumping through your veins to keep you up all night. (And then go gamble!) Dive at night, and you sail right into the lights of Vegas. The price is $54 for your first jump, including a membership and T-shirt ($15 additional for a videotape of your jump), $25 for each subsequent jump. Students and military with ID should inquire about discounts. If you're under 18, you must be accompanied by a parent. Call for hours.

HORSEBACK RIDING   **Cowboy Trail Rides** ✦ (© **702/948-7061;** www. cowboytrailrides.com) offers a variety of rides and trails in Red Rock Canyon and on Mount Charleston (at the 12-mile marker), ranging in price from $89 to $139. The high end is for a Red Rock Canyon sunset trail ride; it's about 2 hours, with the canyon providing a glorious backdrop for the sunset. Riders then return to camp for a barbecue dinner (including a 16-oz. T-bone steak), joined by the cowboys for singalongs and marshmallow roasting. They also offer hourly rates of $25 and buses from the Excalibur hotel. Riding stables at **Bonnie Springs Ranch** (© **702/875-4191;** www.bonniesprings.com) also offer guided trail rides daily. Rates start at $25 per person for a 1-hour ride and go up to $135 for dinner rides.

ROCK CLIMBING   **Red Rock Canyon,** just 19 miles west of Las Vegas, is one of the world's most popular rock-climbing areas. In addition to awe-inspiring natural beauty, it offers everything from boulders to big walls. If you'd like to join the bighorn sheep, Red Rock has more than 1,000 routes to inaugurate beginners and challenge accomplished climbers. Experienced climbers can contact the **visitor center** (© **702/363-1921**) for information.

If you're interested in learning or improving your skills, an excellent rock-climbing school and guide service called **Sky's the Limit** (© **800/733-7597** or 702/363-4533; www.skysthelimit.com) offers programs for beginning, intermediate, and advanced climbers. No experience is needed. The school is accredited by the American Mountain Guides Association.

Tips **Desert Hiking Advice**

Except in summer, when temperatures can reach 120°F (49°C) in the shade, the Las Vegas area is great for hiking. The best hiking season is November to March. Great locales include the incredibly scenic Red Rock Canyon and Valley of Fire State Park (see chapter 11 for details on both).

Hiking in the desert is exceptionally rewarding, but it can be dangerous. Here are some safety tips:

1. Don't hike alone.
2. Carry plenty of water and drink it often. Don't assume spring waters are safe to drink. A gallon of water per person per day is recommended for hikers.
3. Be alert for signs of heat exhaustion (headache; nausea; dizziness; fatigue; and cool, damp, pale, or red skin).
4. Gauge your fitness accurately. Desert hiking may involve rough or steep terrain. Don't take on more than you can handle.
5. Check weather forecasts before starting out. Thunderstorms can turn into raging flash floods, which are extremely hazardous to hikers.
6. Dress properly. Wear sturdy walking shoes for rock scrambling, long pants (to protect yourself from rocks and cacti), a hat, sunscreen, and sunglasses.
7. Carry a small first-aid kit.
8. Be careful when climbing on sandstone, which can be surprisingly soft and crumbly.
9. Don't feed or play with animals, such as the wild burros in Red Rock Canyon. (It's actually illegal to approach them.)
10. Be alert for snakes and insects. Though they're rarely encountered, you'll want to look into a crevice before putting your hand into it.
11. Visit park or other information offices before you start out and acquaint yourself with rules and regulations and any possible hazards. It's also a good idea to tell the staff where you're going, when you'll return, how many are in your party, and so on. Some park offices offer hiker-registration programs.
12. Follow the hiker's rule of thumb: Take only photographs and leave only footprints.

TENNIS   Tennis buffs should choose one of the many hotels in town that have tennis courts.

Bally's (© 702/967-3380) has eight night-lit hard courts. Fees per hour range from $10 to $15 for guests, $15 to $20 for nonguests. Facilities include a pro shop. Hours vary seasonally. Reservations are advised.

The Flamingo Las Vegas (© 702/733-3444) has four outdoor hard courts (all lit for night play) and a pro shop. It's open to the public daily from 7am to 7pm. Rates are $20 per hour for nonguests, $12 for guests. Lessons are available. Reservations are required.

Monte Carlo (℃ **702/730-7777**) has three night-lit courts available to the public for $15 per hour.

In addition to hotels, the **University of Nevada, Las Vegas (UNLV),** Harmon Avenue just east of Swenson Street (℃ **702/895-0844**), has a dozen courts (all lit for night play) that are open weekdays from 6am to 9:45pm, weekends 8am to 9pm. Rates are $5 per person per day. You should call before going to find out if a court is available.

8 Spectator Sports

Las Vegas isn't known for its sports teams. Except for minor-league baseball and hockey, the only consistent spectator sports are those at UNLV. The **Las Vegas Motor Speedway** (p. 181) is a main venue for car racing and should draw major events to Las Vegas.

But since the city has several top-notch sporting arenas, there are important annual events that take place in Las Vegas, details for which can be found in the "Las Vegas Calendar of Events" in chapter 2. The **PGA Tour's Las Vegas Senior Classic** is held each April in nearby Summerlin, and the **Las Vegas Invitational** takes place in Las Vegas each October. The **National Finals Rodeo** is held in UNLV's Thomas and Mack Center each December. From time to time, you'll find NBA exhibition games, professional ice-skating competitions, or gymnastics exhibitions. Then there are the only-in-Vegas spectaculars, such as Evel Knievel's ill-fated attempt to jump the fountains in front of Caesars.

Finally, Las Vegas is well known as a major location for **boxing matches.** These are held in several Strip hotels, most often at Caesars or the MGM Grand, but sometimes at The Mirage. Tickets are hard to come by and quite expensive.

Tickets to sporting events at hotels are available either through **Ticketmaster** (℃ **702/893-3000;** www.ticketmaster.com) or through the hotels themselves (why pay Ticketmaster's exorbitant service charges?).

MAJOR SPORTS VENUES IN HOTELS

Caesars Palace (℃ **800/634-6698** or 702/731-7110) has a long tradition of hosting sporting events, from Evel Knievel's attempted motorcycle jump over its fountains in 1967 to Grand Prix auto races. Mary Lou Retton has tumbled in gymnastic events at Caesars, and Olympians Brian Boitano and Katarina Witt have taken to the ice, as has Wayne Gretzky. And well over 100 world-championship boxing contests have taken place here since the hotel opened. In the spirit of ancient Rome, Caesars awards riches and honors to the "gladiators" who compete in its arenas.

The **MGM Grand's Garden Events Arena** (℃ **800/929-1111** or 702/891-7777) is a major venue for professional boxing matches, rodeos, tennis, ice-skating shows, World Figure Skating Championships, and more.

Mandalay Bay (℃ **877/632-7400**) has been hosting a number of boxing matches in its 12,000-seat Events Center.

The Mirage (℃ **800/627-6667** or 702/791-7111) also features occasional championship boxing matches.

8

About Casino Gambling

What? You didn't come to Las Vegas for the Liberace Museum? We are shocked. Shocked.

Yes, there are gambling opportunities in Vegas. We've noticed this. You will too. The tip-off will be the slot machines in the airport as soon as you step off the plane. Or the slot machines in the convenience stores as soon as you drive across the state line. Let's not kid ourselves, gambling is what Vegas is about. The bright lights, the shows, the showgirls, the food—it's all there just to lure you in and make you open your wallet. (The free drinks certainly help ease the latter as well.)

You can disappoint them if you want, but what would be the point? *This is Las Vegas.* You don't have to be a high roller. You would not believe how much fun you can have with a nickel slot machine. You won't get rich, but neither will most of those guys playing the $5 slots, either.

Of course, that's not going to stop anyone from trying. Almost everyone plays in Vegas with the hopes of winning The Big One. That only a few ever do win doesn't stop them from trying again and again and again. That's how the casinos make their money, by the way.

It's not that the odds are stacked so incredibly high in their favor—though the odds *are* in their favor, and don't ever think otherwise. Rather, it's that if there is one constant in this world, it's human greed. Look around in any casino, and you'll see countless souls who, having doubled their winnings, are now trying to quadruple

them, and are losing it all and then trying to recoup their initial bankroll and losing still more in the process. See that chandelier up there? Enjoy it—you paid for it.

Which is not meant to dissuade you from gambling. Just be sure to look at it as recreation and entertainment, *not* as an investment or moneymaking opportunity. Spend only as much as you can afford to lose and not a penny more. It doesn't matter if that's $10 or $100,000. You can have just as good a time with either. (Though if you can afford to lose $100,000, we would like to meet you.)

Remember also that there is no system that's sure to help you win. We all have our own systems and our own ideas. Reading books and listening to others at the tables will help you pick up some tips, but if there were a sure-fire way to win, the casinos would have taken care of it (and we will leave you to imagine just what that might entail). Try to have the courage to walk away when your bankroll is up, not down. Remember, your children's college fund is just that, and not a gambling-budget supplement.

The first part of this chapter is a contribution from James Randi, a master magician, who looks at the four major fallacies people bring with them to the gaming tables in Las Vegas; it's fascinating, and we thank him for this contribution.

The second part tells you the basics of betting. Knowing how to play the games not only improves your odds but also makes playing more enjoyable. In

Impressions

Stilled forever is the click of the roulette wheel, the rattle of dice, and the swish of cards.

—Shortsighted editorial in the *Nevada State Journal* after gambling was outlawed in 1910

addition to the instructions below, you'll find dozens of books on how to gamble at all casino hotel gift shops, and many casinos offer free gaming lessons on the premises.

The third part of this chapter describes all the major casinos in town. Remember that gambling is supposed to be entertainment. Picking a gaming table where the other players are laughing, slapping each other on the back, and generally enjoying themselves tends to make for considerable more fun than a table where everyone is sitting around in stony silence, morosely staring at their cards. Unless you really need to concentrate, pick a table where everyone seems to be enjoying themselves, and you will too, even if you don't win. Maybe.

1 The Four Most Pervasive Myths About Gambling

by James Randi

James Randi is a world-class magician (the Amazing Randi), now involved in examining supernatural, paranormal, and occult claims. He is the author of 11 books on these subjects, and is the president of the James Randi Educational Foundation in Fort Lauderdale, Florida. The JREF offers a prize of $1.1 million to any person who can produce a demonstration of any paranormal activity. His website is www.randi.org, where details of the offer can be found.

Most of us know little, if anything, about statistics. It's a never-never land we can live without, something for those guys in white coats and thick glasses to mumble over. And because we don't bother to learn the basics of this rather interesting field of study, we sometimes find ourselves unable to deal with the realities that the gambling process produces.

I often present my audiences with a puzzle. Suppose that a mathematician, a gambler, and a magician are walking together on Broadway and come upon a small cluster of people who are observing a chap standing at a small table set up on the sidewalk. They are told that this fellow has just tossed a quarter into the air and allowed it to fall onto the table, nine times. And that has produced nine "tails" in a row. Now the crowd is being asked to bet on what the next toss of the coin will bring. The question: How will each of these three observers place their bets?

The mathematician will reason that each toss of the coin is independent of the last toss, so the chances are still exactly 50/50 for heads or tails. He'll say that either bet is okay, and that it doesn't make any difference which decision is made.

The gambler will go one of two ways; either he'll reason that there's a "run" taking place here—and that a bet on another tail will be the better choice—or he'll opine that it's time for the head to come up, and he'll put his wager on that likelihood.

The magician? He has the best chance of winning, because he knows that there is only 1 chance in 512 that a coin will come up tails nine times in a row— *unless there's something wrong with that coin!* He'll bet tails and he'll win!

The reasoning of the mathematician is quite correct, that of the gambler is quite wrong (in either one of his scenarios), but just as long as that isn't a double-tailed coin. The point of view taken by the magician is highly specialized, but human nature being what it is, that view is probably the correct one.

In professional gambling centers such as Las Vegas, great care is taken to ensure that there are no two-tailed quarters or other purposeful anomalies that enable cheating to take place. The casinos make their percentages on the built-in mathematical advantage, which is clearly stated and available to any who ask, and though that is a very tiny "edge," it's enough to pay for the razzle-dazzle that lures in the customers. It's volume that supports the business. The scrutiny that is applied to each and every procedure in Vegas is evident everywhere.

So, **Fallacy Number One** is: Cheating of some sort is necessary for an operation to prosper. It isn't.

Fallacy Number Two: Some people just have "hunches" and "visions" that enable them to win at the slots and tables. Sorry folks, it just ain't so. The science of parapsychology, which has studied such claims for many decades now, has never come up with evidence that any form of clairvoyance ("clear-seeing," the supposed ability to know hidden data, such as the next card to come up in a deal or the next face on the dice) or telepathy ("mind reading") actually exists. It's remarkably easy for us to imagine that we have a hot streak going, or that the cards are falling our way, but the inexorable laws of chance prevail and always will.

Fallacy Number Three: There are folks who can give us systems for winning. Now, judicious bet placing is possible, and there are mathematical methods of minimizing losses, it's true. But the investment and base capital needed to follow through with these methods makes them a rather poor investment. The return percentage can be earned much more easily by almost any other form of endeavor, at less risk and less expenditure of boring hours following complicated charts and equations. The best observation we can make on the "systems" is: Why would the inventors of the "systems" sell something that they themselves could use to get rich, which is what they say you can do with it? Think about that!

Of course, the simplest of all the systems is bet doubling. It sounds great in theory, but an hour spent tossing coins in your hotel room, or at the gaming tables, will convince you that theory and practice are quite different matters. Bet doubling, as applied to heads or tails (on a fair coin!), consists of placing a unit bet on the first coin toss, then pocketing the proceeds if you win, but doubling your bet on the next toss if you lose. If you get a lose, lose, win sequence, that means you will have lost three units (one plus two) and won four. You're up one unit. You start again. If you get a lose, lose, lose, win sequence, you've put out 15 units and brought in 16. Again, you're only up one unit. And no matter how long your sequences go, you'll always be up only one unit at the end of a sequence. It requires you to make that "unit" somewhat sizable if you want to have any significant winnings at all, and that may mean going bankrupt by simply running out of capital before a sequence ends—and if you hang on, you'll only have been able to end up one unit ahead, in any case. Not a good investment at all.

Fallacy Number Four: Studying the results of the roulette wheels will provide the bettor with useful data. We're peculiar animals in that we constantly search for meaning in all sets of observations. That's how subjects of Rorschach tests find weird faces, figures, and creatures in inkblots that are actually random patterns with single symmetry. Similarly, any sets of roulette results are, essentially, random numbers; there are no patterns to be found there that can give indications of probable future spins of the wheels. Bearing in mind that those wheels are carefully monitored to detect any biases or defects, we should conclude that finding clues in past performances is futile.

I recall that when I worked in Wiesbaden, Germany, just after World War II, I stuck around late one night after closing at the "Spielbank" and watched as an elderly gentleman removed all the rotors of the 12 wheels they had in operation, wrote out the numbers 1 to 12 on separate scraps of paper, and reassembled the wheels according to the random order in which he drew each slip of paper from a bowl. He was ensuring that any inconsistencies in the wheels would be essentially nullified. Yet, as he told me, the front desk at the casino continued to sell booklets setting out the results of each of the wheels, because patrons insisted on having them, and persisted in believing that there just had to be a pattern there, if only it could be found.

We're only human. We can't escape certain defects in our thinking mechanism, but we can resist reacting to them. When we see Penn and Teller, Ayala, Siegfried & Roy, or Lance Burton doing their wonders, we smile smugly and assure ourselves that those miracles are only illusions. But if we haven't solved those illusions, and we haven't, how can we assume that we aren't being fooled by our own self-created delusions? Let's get a grip on reality and enjoy Las Vegas for what it really is: a grand illusion, a fairyland, a let's-pretend project, but not one in which the laws of nature are suspended or can be ignored.

Enjoy!

2 The Games

by Alex Kraus

Alex Kraus is a freelance writer and tournament-level card player.
The former Las Vegas resident currently lives in New York City.

As you walk through the labyrinthine twists and turns of a casino floor, your attention will likely be dragged to the various games and, your interest piqued, your fingers may begin to twitch in anticipation of hitting it big. Before you put your money on the line, it's imperative to know the rules of the game you want to play. Most casinos offer free gambling lessons at scheduled times on weekdays. This provides a risk-free environment for you to learn the games that tickle your fancy. Some casinos follow their lessons with low-stakes game play, enabling you to put your newfound knowledge to the test at small risk. During those instructional sessions, and even when playing on your own, dealers in most casinos will be more than happy to answer any questions you might have. Remember, the casino doesn't need to trick you into losing your money . . . the odds are already in their favor across the board; that's why it's called gambling. Another rule of thumb: Take a few minutes to watch a game being played in order to familiarize yourself with the motions and lingo. Then go back and reread this section—things will make a lot more sense at that point Good luck!

BACCARAT

The ancient game of baccarat, or *chemin de fer,* is played with eight decks of cards. Firm rules apply, and there is no skill involved other than deciding whether to bet on the bank or the player. No, really—that's all you have to do. The dealer does all the other work. You can essentially stop reading here. Oh, all right, carry on.

Any beginner can play, but check the betting minimum before you sit down, as this tends to be a high-stakes game. The cards are shuffled by the croupier and

---

⌐Tips **Size Counts . . . Sort of**

For those who desire a more informal environment in which to play baccarat, casinos offer minibaccarat, played on a normal-size table no larger than a blackjack table. There is no substantive difference between baccarat and its little brother. It's simply a matter of size and speed; the size of your bankroll and the speed with which you may build it (or lose it). Table stakes in minibaccarat tend to be lower, and the hands proceed at a much faster pace.

---

then placed in a box called the "shoe." Players may wager on "bank" or "player" at any time. Two cards are dealt from the shoe and given to the player who has the largest wager against the bank, and two cards are dealt to the croupier, acting as banker. If the rules call for a third card, the player or banker, or both, must take the third card. In the event of a tie, the hand is dealt over. *Note:* The guidelines that determine if a third card must be drawn (by the player or banker) are provided at the baccarat table upon request.

The object of the game is to come as close as possible to the number 9. To score the hands, the cards of each hand are totaled and the *last digit* is used. All cards have face value. For example: 10 plus 5 equals 15 (score is 5); 10 plus 4 plus 9 equals 23 (score is 3); 4 plus 3 plus 3 equals 10 (score is 0); and 4 plus 3 plus 2 equals 9 (score is 9). The closest hand to 9 wins.

Each player has a chance to deal the cards. The shoe passes to the player on the right each time the bank loses. If the player wishes, he or she may pass the shoe at any time.

Note: When you bet on the bank and the bank wins, you are charged a 5% commission. This must be paid at the start of a new game or when you leave the table.

BIG SIX

Big Six provides pleasant recreation and involves no study or effort. The wheel has 56 positions on it, 54 of them marked by bills from $1 to $20. The other two spots are jokers, and each pays 40 to 1 if the wheel stops in that position. All other stops pay at face value. Those marked with $20 bills pay 20 to 1; the $5 bills pay 5 to 1; and so forth. The idea behind the game is to predict (or just blindly guess) what spot the wheel will stop at and place a bet accordingly.

BLACKJACK

The dealer starts the game by dealing each player two cards. In some casinos, they're dealt to the player faceup, in others facedown, but the dealer always gets one card up and one card down. Everybody plays against the dealer. The object is to get a total that is higher than that of the dealer without exceeding 21. All face cards count as 10; all other number cards, except aces, are counted at their face value. An ace may be counted as 1 or 11, whichever you choose it to be.

Starting at his or her left, the dealer gives additional cards to the players who wish to draw (be "hit") or none to a player who wishes to "stand" or "hold." If your count is nearer to 21 than the dealer's, you win. If it's under the dealer's, you lose. Ties are a push and nobody wins. After all the players are satisfied with their counts, the dealer exposes his or her facedown card. If his or her two cards total 16 or less, the dealer must "hit" (draw an additional card) until reaching

17 or over. If the dealer's total exceeds 21, he or she must pay all the players whose hands have not gone "bust." It is important to note here that the black-jack dealer has no choice as to whether he or she should stay or draw. A dealer's decisions are predetermined and known to all the players at the table.

If you're a novice or just rusty, do yourself a favor and buy one of the small laminated cards available in shops all over town that illustrate proper play for every possible hand in blackjack. Even longtime players have been known to pull them out every now and then, and they can save you from making costly errors.

HOW TO PLAY

Here are eight "rules" for blackjack:

1. Place the number of chips that you want to bet on the betting space on your table.

2. Look at the first two cards the dealer starts you with. If you wish to "stand" then wave your hand over your cards, palm down (watch your fellow play-ers), indicating that you don't wish any additional cards. If you elect to draw an additional card, you tell the dealer to "hit" you by tapping the table with a finger (watch your fellow players).

3. If your count goes over 21, you are "bust" and lose, even if the dealer also goes "bust" afterward.

4. If you make 21 in your first two cards (any picture card or 10 with an ace), you've got blackjack. You will be paid 1½ times your bet, provided the dealer does not have blackjack too, in which case it's a push and nobody wins.

5. If you find a "pair" in your first two cards (say, two 8s or two aces), you may "split" the pair into two hands and treat each card as the first card dealt in two separate hands. You will need to place an additional bet, equal to your original bet, on the table. The dealer will then deal you a new *second* card to the first split card and play commences as described above. This will be done for the second split card as well. *Note:* When you split aces you will receive only one additional card per ace and must "stand."

6. After seeing your two starting cards, you have the option to "double down." You place an amount equal to your original bet on the table and you receive only one more card. Doubling down is a strategy to capitalize on a poten-tially strong hand against the dealer's weaker hand. *Tip:* You may double down for less than your original bet, but never for more.

7. Anytime the dealer deals himself or herself an ace for the "up" card, you may insure your hand against the possibility that the hole card is a 10 or face card, which would give him or her an automatic blackjack. To insure, you

---

Tips **Look, but Don't Touch!**

1. *Never* touch your cards (or anyone else's), unless it's specifically stated at the table that you may. While you'll only receive a verbal slap on the wrist if you violate this rule, you *really* don't want to get one.

2. Players must use hand signals to indicate their wishes to the dealer. All verbal directions by players will be politely ignored by the dealer, who will remind players to use hand signals. The reason for this is the "Eye in the Sky," the casino's security system, which focuses an "eye" on every table, and must record players' decisions to avoid accusa-tions of misconduct or collusion.

place an amount up to one half of your bet on the "insurance" line. If the dealer does have a blackjack you get paid 2 to 1 on the insurance money while losing your original bet: You break even. If the dealer does not have a blackjack, he or she takes your insurance money and play continues in the normal fashion.

8. *Remember:* The dealer must stand on 17 or more and must hit a hand of 16 or less.

PROFESSIONAL TIPS

Advice of the experts in playing blackjack is as follows:

1. *Do not* ask for an extra card if you have a count of 17 or higher, *ever.*
2. *Do not* ask for an extra card when you have a total of 12 or more if the dealer has a 2 through 6 showing in his or her "up" card.
3. *Ask* for an extra card or more when you have a count of 12 through 16 in your hand if the dealer's "up" card is a 7, 8, 9, 10, or ace.

There's a lot more to blackjack strategy than the above, of course. So consider this merely as the bare bones of the game. Blackjack is played with a single deck or with multiple decks; if you're looking for a single-deck game, your best bet is to head to a Downtown casino.

A final tip: Avoid insurance bets; they're sucker bait!

CRAPS

The most exciting casino action is usually found at the craps tables. Betting is frenetic, play fast-paced, and groups quickly bond while yelling and screaming in response to the action.

THE POSSIBLE BETS

The craps table is divided into marked areas (Pass, Come, Field, Big 6, Big 8, and so on), where you place your chips to bet. The following are a few simple directions.

PASS LINE   A "Pass Line" bet pays even money. If the first roll of the dice adds up to 7 or 11, you win your bet; if the first roll adds up to 2, 3, or 12, you lose your bet. If any other number comes up, it's your "point." If you roll your point again, you win, but if a 7 comes up again before your point is rolled, you lose.

DON'T PASS LINE   Betting on the "Don't Pass" is the opposite of betting on the "Pass Line." This time, you lose if a 7 or an 11 is thrown on the first roll, and you win if a 2 or a 3 is thrown on the first roll.

If the first roll is 12, however, it's a push (standoff), and nobody wins. If none of these numbers is thrown and you have a point instead, in order to win, a 7

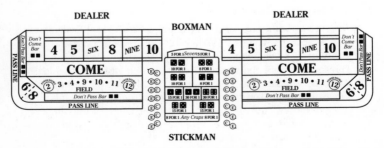

A typical craps table.

Dice Probabilities

Number	Possible Combinations	Actual Odds	Percentage Probability
2	1	35:1	2.8%
3	2	17:1	5.6%
4	3	11:1	8.3%
5	4	8:1	11.1%
6	5	6.2:1	13.9%
7	6	5:1	16.7%
8	5	6.2:1	13.9%
9	4	8:1	11.1%
10	3	11:1	8.3%
11	2	17:1	5.6%
12	1	35:1	2.8%

will have to be thrown before the point comes up again. A "Don't Pass" bet also pays even money.

COME Betting on "Come" is the same as betting on the Pass Line, but you must bet after the first roll or on any following roll. Again, you'll win on 7 or 11 and lose on 2, 3, or 12. Any other number is your point, and you win if your point comes up again before a 7.

DON'T COME This is the opposite of a "Come" bet. Again, you wait until after the first roll to bet. A 7 or an 11 means you lose; a 2 or a 3 means you win; 12 is a push, and nobody wins. You win if 7 comes up before the point. (The point, you'll recall, was the first number rolled if it was none of the above.)

FIELD This is a bet for one roll only. The "Field" consists of seven numbers: 2, 3, 4, 9, 10, 11, and 12. If any of these numbers is thrown on the next roll, you win even money, except on 2 and 12, which pay 2 to 1 (at some casinos 3 to 1).

BIG 6 AND 8 A "Big 6 and 8" bet pays even money. You win if either a 6 or an 8 is rolled before a 7. Mathematically this is a sucker's bet.

ANY 7 An "Any 7" bet pays the winner 5 for 1. If a 7 is thrown on the first roll after you bet, you win.

"HARD WAY" BETS In the middle of a craps table are pictures of several possible dice combinations together with the odds the casino will pay you if you bet and win on any of those combinations being thrown. For example, if double 3s or 4s are rolled and you had bet on them, you will be paid 7 to 1. If double 2s or 5s are rolled and you had bet on them, you will be paid 9 to 1. If either a 7 is rolled or if the number you bet on was rolled any way other than the "Hard Way," then the bet is lost. In-the-know gamblers tend to avoid "Hard Way" bets as an easy way to lose their money.

ANY CRAPS Here you're lucky if the dice "crap out"—if they show 2, 3, or 12 on the first roll after you bet. If this happens, the bank pays 7 to 1. Any other number is a loser.

PLACE BETS You can make a "Place Bet" on any of the following numbers: 4, 5, 6, 8, 9, and 10. You're betting that the number you choose will be thrown before a 7 is thrown. If you win, the payoff is as follows: 4 or 10 pays at the rate of 9 to 5; 5 or 9 pays at the rate of 7 to 5; 6 or 8 pays at the rate of 7 to 6. "Place Bets" can be removed at any time before a roll.

SOME PROBABILITIES

The probability of a certain number being rolled at the craps table is not a mystery. As there are only 36 possible outcomes when the dice are rolled, the probability for each number being rolled is easily ascertained. See the "Dice Probabilities" chart in this section to help you in case you decided it was more fun to pass notes or sleep during your Math classes.

So 7 has an advantage over all other combinations, which, over the long run, is in favor of the casino. You can't beat the law of averages, but if you can't beat 'em, join 'em. (Play the "Don't Pass" bet.)

KENO

Originating in China, this is one of the oldest games of chance. Legend has it that funds acquired from the game were used to finance construction of the Great Wall of China.

Chinese railroad construction workers first introduced keno into the United States in the 1800s. Easy to play, and offering a chance to sit down and converse between bets, it is one of the most popular games in town—despite the fact that *the house percentage is greater than that of any other casino game!*

To play, you must first obtain a keno form, available at the counter in the keno lounge and in most Las Vegas coffee shops. In the latter, you'll usually find blank keno forms and thick black crayons on your table. Fill yours out, and a

		PRICE PER WAY	PRICE PER GAME
$50,000.00 LIMIT TO AGGREGATE PLAYERS EACH GAME			
MARK NUMBER OF SPOTS OR WAYS PLAYED		NO. OF GAMES	TOTAL PRICE

WINNING TICKETS MUST BE COLLECTED IMMEDIATELY AFTER EACH KENO GAME IS CALLED.

1	2	3	4	5	6	7	8	9	10
11	12	13	14	15	16	17	18	19	20
21	22	23	24	25	26	27	28	29	30
31	32	33	34	35	36	37	38	39	40

WE PAY ON MACHINE ISSUED TICKETS - TICKETS WITH ERRORS NOT CORRECTED BEFORE START OF GAME WILL BE ACCEPTED AS ISSUED.

41	42	43	44	45	46	47	48	49	50
51	52	53	54	55	56	57	58	59	60
61	62	63	64	65	66	67	68	69	70
71	72	73	74	75	76	77	78	79	80

WE ARE NOT RESPONSIBLE FOR KENO RUNNERS TICKETS NOT VALIDATED BEFORE START OF NEXT GAME.

A sample keno ticket.

miniskirted keno runner will come and collect it. After the game is over, she'll return with your winning or losing ticket. If you've won, it's customary to offer a tip, depending on your winnings.

For those of you with state lotteries, this game will appear very familiar. You can select from 1 to 15 numbers (out of a total of 80) and if all of your numbers come up, you win. Depending on how many numbers you've selected, you can win smaller amounts if less than all of your numbers have come up. For example, if you bet a "3 spot" (selecting a total of three numbers) and two come up, you'll win something but not as much as if all three had shown up. A one-number mark is known as a 1-spot, a two-number selection is a 2-spot, and so on. After you have selected the number of spots you wish to play, write the amount you want to wager on the ticket, in the right-hand corner where indicated. The more you bet, the more you can win if your numbers come up. Before the game starts, you have to give the completed form to a keno runner, or hand it in at the keno lounge desk, and pay for your bet. You'll get back a duplicate form with the number of the game you're playing on it. Then the game begins. As numbers appear on the keno board, compare them to the numbers you've marked on your ticket. After 20 numbers have appeared on the board, the game is over, and if you've won, turn in your ticket to collect your winnings.

The more numbers on the board matching the numbers on your ticket, the more you win (in some cases, you get paid if *none* of your numbers come up). If you want to keep playing the same numbers over and over, you can replay a ticket by handing in your duplicate to the keno runner; you don't have to keep rewriting it.

In addition to the straight bets described above, you can split your ticket, betting various amounts on two or more groups of numbers. It does get a little complex, as combination-betting options are almost infinite. Helpful casino personnel in the keno lounge can assist you with combination betting.

POKER

Poker is the game of the Old West. There's at least one sequence in every Western where the hero faces off against the villain over a poker hand. In Las Vegas, poker is a tradition, although it isn't played at every casino.

There are lots of variations on the basic game, but one of the most popular is **Hold 'Em.** Two cards are dealt facedown to the players. After a betting round, five community cards (everyone can use them) are dealt faceup on the table. The player makes the best five-card hand, using their own cards and the "board" (the community cards), and the best hand wins. The house dealer takes care of the shuffling and the dealing and moves a marker around the table to alternate the start of the deal. The house rakes 1% to 5% (it depends on the casino) from each pot. Most casinos also provide tables for playing Seven-Card Stud, Omaha High and Omaha Hi-Low. A few will even have Seven-Card Stud hi-lo split. To learn how these variations are played, either read a book or take lessons.

Warning: If you don't know how to play poker, don't attempt to learn at a table. Card sharks are not a rare species in Vegas; they will gladly feast on fresh meat (you!). Find a casino that provides free gaming lessons and learn, to paraphrase Kenny Rogers, when to hold 'em, and when to fold 'em.

PAI GOW POKER

Pai gow poker (a variation on poker) has become increasingly popular. The game is played with a traditional deck plus one joker. The joker is a wild card that can be used as an ace or to complete a straight, a flush, a straight flush, or a royal flush. Each player is dealt seven cards to arrange into two hands: a two-card hand and a five-card hand. As in standard poker, the highest two-card hand is two aces, and the highest five-card hand is a royal flush. The five-card hand *must* be higher than the two-card hand (if the two-card hand is a pair of sixes, for example, the five-card hand must be a pair of sevens or better). Any player's hand that is set incorrectly is an automatic loser. The object of the game is for both of the players' hands to rank higher than both of the banker's hands. Should one hand rank exactly the same as the banker's hand, this is a tie (called a "copy"), *and the banker wins all tie hands.* If the player wins one hand but loses the other, this is a "push," and no money changes hands. The house dealer or any player may be the banker. The bank is offered to each player, and each player may accept or pass. Winning hands are paid even money, less a 5% commission.

CARIBBEAN STUD POKER

Caribbean stud poker is yet another variation of poker that is gaining in popularity. Players put in a single ante bet and are dealt five cards facedown from a single deck; they play solely against the dealer, who receives five cards, one of them faceup. Players are then given the option of folding, or may call by making an additional bet that is double their original ante. After all player bets have been made, the dealer's cards are revealed. If the dealer doesn't qualify with *at least an ace/king combination,* players are paid even money on their ante and their call bets are returned. If the dealer does qualify, each player's hand is compared to the dealer's. On winning hands, players receive even money on their ante bets, and call bets are paid out on a scale according to the value of their hands. The scale ranges from even money for a pair, to 100 to 1 on a royal flush, although there is usually a cap on the maximum payoff that varies from casino to casino.

An additional feature of Caribbean stud is the inclusion of a progressive jackpot. For an additional side bet of $1, a player may qualify for a payoff from a progressive jackpot. The jackpot bet pays off only on a flush or better, but you can win on this bet even if the dealer ends up with a better hand than you do. Dream all you want of getting that royal flush and taking home the jackpot, but the odds of it happening are astronomical, so don't be so quick to turn in your resignation letter. Most veteran gamblers will tell you this a bad bet, but considering that Caribbean stud already has a house advantage that is even larger than the one in roulette, if you're going to play, you might as well toss in the buck and pray.

LET IT RIDE

Let It Ride is another popular game that involves poker hands. You place three bets at the outset and are dealt three cards. The dealer is dealt two cards that act as community cards (you're not playing against the dealer). Once you've seen your cards, you can choose to pull the first of your three bets back, or "Let It Ride." The object of this game is to get a pair of 10s or better by combining your cards with the dealer's. If you're holding a pair of 10s or better in your first three cards, you want to let your bets ride the whole way through. Once you've decided whether or not to let your first bet ride, the dealer exposes one of his or her two cards. Once again you must make a decision to take back your middle bet or keep on going. Then the dealer exposes the last of his or her cards; your third bet must stay. The dealer then turns over the hands of the players and determines if you've won or not. Winning bets are paid on a scale, ranging from even money for a single pair up to 1,000 to 1 for a royal flush. These payouts are for each bet you have in play. Like Caribbean Stud, Let It Ride has a progressive jackpot that you can win for high hands if you cough up an additional dollar per hand, but be advised that the house advantage on that $1 is obscene. But hey, that's why it's called gambling.

ROULETTE

Roulette is an extremely easy game to play, and it's really quite colorful and exciting to watch. The wheel spins and the little ball bounces around, finally dropping into one of the slots, numbered 1 to 36, plus 0 and 00. You can place bets "Inside" the table and "Outside" the table. Inside bets are bets placed on a particular number or a set of numbers. Outside bets are those placed in the boxes

Roulette Chart Key	Odds	Type of Bet
		Straight Bets
A	35 to 1	*Straight-up:* All numbers, plus 0 and 00.
B	2 to 1	*Column Bet:* Pays off on any number in that horizontal column
C	2 to 1	*First Dozen:* Pays off on any number 1 through 12. Same for second and third dozen.
D	Even money	
		Combination Bets
E	17 to 1	*Split:* Pays off on 11 or 12.
F	11 to 1	Pays off on 28, 29, or 30.
G	8 to 1	*Corner:* Pays off on 17, 18, 20, or 21.
H	6 to 1	Pays off on 0, 00, 1, 2, or 3.
I	5 to 1	Pays off on 22, 23, 24, 25, 26, or 27.

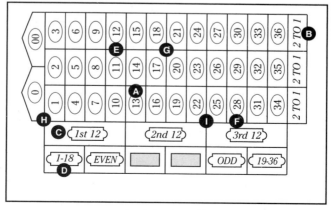

A typical roulette table.

Players Clubs

If you play slots or video poker, or, indeed, just gamble quite a bit, or even just gamble, it definitely pays to join a players club. These so-called clubs are designed to attract and keep customers in a given casino by providing incentives: meals, shows, discounts on rooms, gifts, tournament invitations, discounts at hotel shops, VIP treatment, and (more and more) cash rebates. Join a players club, and soon you too will be getting those great hotel-rate offers—$20-a-night rooms, affordable rooms at the luxury resorts, even free rooms. (This is one way to beat the high hotel rates.) Of course, your rewards are often greater if you play just in one casino, but your mobility is limited.

When you join a players club (inquire at the casino desk), you're given something that looks like a credit card, which you must insert into an ATM-like device whenever you play. Yes, many casinos even have them for the tables as well as the machines. (Don't forget to retrieve your card when you leave the machine, as we sometimes do—though that may work in your favor if someone comes along and plays the machine without removing it.) The device tracks your play and computes bonus points.

Which players club should you join? Actually, you should join one at any casino where you play, because even the act of joining usually entitles you to some benefits. It's convenient to concentrate play where you're staying; if you play a great deal, a casino hotel's players-club benefits may be a factor in your accommodations choice. Consider, though, particularly if you aren't a high roller, the players clubs Downtown. You get more bang for your buck, because you don't have to spend as much to start raking in the goodies.

surrounding the number table (see picture above). If you bet on a specific number and it comes up, you'll be paid 35 to 1 on your bet. Bear in mind, however, that the odds of a particular number coming up are actually 38 to 1 (don't forget that 0 and 00!) so the house has an advantage the moment you place an Inside bet. For payoffs on Outside bets, such as Red/Black, Odd/Even, and so forth, see the table below. The methods of placing single-number bets, column bets, and others are fairly obvious. The dealer will be happy to show you how make many interesting betting combinations, such as betting on six numbers at once. Each player is given different-colored chips so that it's easy to follow the numbers you've bet on.

Some typical bets are indicated by means of letters on the roulette layout depicted here. The winning odds for each of these sample bets are listed. These bets can be made on any corresponding combinations of numbers.

SLOTS

You put the coin in the slot and pull the handle. What, you thought there was a trick to this?

Actually, there is a bit more to it. But first, some background. Old-timers will tell you slots were invented to give wives something to do while their husbands gambled. Slots used to be stuck at the edges of the casino and could be counted

Another advantage is to join a players club that covers many hotels under the same corporate umbrella. Park Place runs Caesars, The Flamingo Las Vegas, Paris, Bally's, and more, and their players club offers discounts and point awards at all of their properties. The same goes for the aforementioned Harrah's hotels, those in the MGM MIRAGE stable (The Mirage, Bellagio, MGM Grand, and so on), the locals' favorite Station Casinos (Palace, Sunset, Texas, and more), and the Carl Icahn properties, which include Stratosphere Casino Hotel & Tower and Arizona Charlie's.

We're particularly fond of the latter. In 2000 and 2001, Stratosphere offered a guaranteed payback for new members, and offers of free rooms, slot tournaments, meals, and more are common.

One way to judge a players club is by the quality of service when you enroll. Personnel should politely answer all your questions (for instance, is nickel play included, and is there a time limit for earning required points?) and be able to tell you exactly how many points you need for various bonuses.

Maximizing your players club profits and choosing the club that's best for you is a complex business. If you want to get into it in depth, order a copy of Jeffrey Compton's *The Las Vegas Advisor Guide to Slot Clubs* ($9.95 plus shipping), which examines just about every facet of the situation (© 800/244-2224). Compton gives high ratings to the clubs at Caesars Palace, The Mirage, Treasure Island, The Flamingo Las Vegas, Rio, Sahara, Sam's Town, Four Queens, Golden Nugget, and Lady Luck.

on one hand, maybe two. But now they *are* the casino. The casinos make more from slots than from craps, blackjack, and roulette combined. There are 115,000 slot machines (not including video poker) in the county. Some of these are at the airport, steps from you as you deplane. It's just a matter of time before the planes flying into Vegas feature slots that pop up as soon as you cross the state line.

But in order to keep up with the increasing competition, the plain old machine, where reels just spin, has become nearly obsolete. Now, they are all computerized and have added buttons to push, so you can avoid getting carpal tunnel syndrome from yanking the handle all night. (The handles are still there on many of them.) Many don't even have reels any more, but are entirely video screens, which offer a number of little bonus extras that have nothing to do with actual play. The idea is still simple: Get three (sometimes four) cherries (clowns, sevens, dinosaurs, whatever) in a row and you win something. Each machine has its own combination. Some will pay you something with just one symbol showing; on most, the more combinations there are, the more opportunities for loot. Some will even pay if you get three blanks. Study each machine to learn what it does. *Note:* The **payback** goes up considerably if you bet the limit (from 2 to as many as 45 coins).

Progressive slots are groups of linked machines (sometimes spread over several casinos) where the jackpot gets bigger every few moments (just as lottery
jackpots build up). Bigger and better games keep showing up; for example, there's
Anchor Gaming's much-imitated **Wheel of Gold,** wherein if you get the right
symbol, you get to spin a roulette wheel, which guarantees you a win of a serious
number of coins. **Totem Pole** is the Godzilla of slot machines, a behemoth that
allows you to spin up to three reels at once (provided you put in the limit).

Other gimmick machines include the popular **Wheel of Fortune** machines,
slots that have a gorilla attempt to climb the Empire State Building, heading up as
you win, and machines with themes like Elvis or the Three Stooges. And, of
course, there are always those **giant slot machines,** gimmicky devices found in
almost every casino. They may not win as often as regular slots (though there is
no definite word on it one way or the other), but not only are they just plain fun
to spin, they often turn into audience-participation gambling, as watchers gather
to cheer you on to victory.

Nickel slots, which for a long time had been overlooked, regulated to a lonely
spot somewhere by a back wall because they were not as profitable for the casinos as quarter and dollar slots, are making a comeback. Many machines now offer
a 45-nickel maximum (meaning a larger bet on those machines than on the five-
quarter-maximum slots), and gamblers have been flocking to them. As a result,
more cash is pocketed by the casino (which keeps a higher percentage of cash off
nickel slots than it does off of quarter slots), which is happy to accommodate this
trend by offering up more and more nickel slots. (See how this all works? Are you
paying attention?)

The biggest trend in Vegas, though, is the use of cashless machines. When
gambling with these machines, players insert their money, they play, and when
they cash out, they get—instead of the comforting sound of coins cascading out
into the tray—a little paper ticket with their total winnings on it. (Those of us
who find the sound of the coins pouring out a comfort are only slightly pleased
to learn that that noise plays, as a computer generated audio effect, when the
ticket is disgorged.) It's not nearly as viscerally satisfying, but it is the wave of the
future; many of the casinos are already entirely cashless, and the rest are on their
way. Why take this cheap thrill from us? Because it saves gambling time (instead
of waiting for the flow of coins to stop, you can grab your ticket and pop it into
another machine), maintenance time (keeping the machines stocked with
coins), and the casinos no longer need worry about having enough quarters on
hand. We are not pleased about this.

Are there surefire ways to win on a slot machine? No. But you can lose more
slowly. The slot machines use minicomputers known as Random Number Gen-
erators (RNG) to determine the winning combinations on a machine; depending on how many numbers have been programmed into the RNG, some
machines are going to be "looser" than others. A bank of empty slots probably
(but not certainly) means the machines are tight. Go find a line where lots of
people are sitting around with trays full of money. (Of course, yours will be the

one that doesn't hit.) A good rule of thumb is that if your slot doesn't hit something in four or five pulls, leave it and go find another. It's not as though you won't have some choice in the matter. Also, each casino has some bank of slots that they advertise as more loose or with a bigger payback. Try these. It's what they want you to do, but what the heck.

SPORTS BOOKS

Most of the larger hotels in Las Vegas have sports-book operations, which look a lot like commodities-futures trading boards. In some, almost as large as theaters, you can sit comfortably, occasionally in recliners and sometimes with your own video screen, and watch ball games, fights, and, at some casinos, horse races on huge TV screens. To add to your enjoyment, there's usually a deli/bar nearby that serves sandwiches, hot dogs, soft drinks, and beer. As a matter of fact, some of the best sandwiches in Las Vegas are served next to the sports books. Sports books take bets on virtually every sport (and not just who'll win, but what the final score will be, who'll be first to hit a home run, who'll be MVP, who'll wear red shoes, you name it). They are best during important playoff games or big horse races, when everyone in the place is watching the same event, shrieking, shouting, and moaning sometimes in unison. Joining in with a cheap bet (so you feel like you too have a personal stake in the matter) makes for bargain entertainment.

VIDEO POKER

Rapidly coming up on slots in popularity, video poker works the same way as regular poker, except you play against the machine. You are dealt a hand, you pick which cards to keep and which to discard, and then get your new hand. And, it is hoped, you collect your winnings. This is somewhat more of a challenge and more active than slots because you have some control (or at least the illusion of control) over your fate, and it's easier than playing actual poker with a table full of folks who probably take it very seriously.

There are a number of varieties of this machine, with **Jacks or Better, Deuces Wild,** and so forth. Be sure to study your machine before you sit down. (The best returns are offered on the **Bonus Poker** machines; the payback for a pair of Jacks or better is two times your bet, and three times for three of a kind.) The Holy Grail of video-poker machines is the 9/6 (it pays nine coins for a full house, six coins for a flush), but you'll need to pray a lot before you find one in town. Some machines offer **double down:** After you have won, you get a chance to draw cards against the machine, with the higher card the winner. If you win, your money is doubled and you are offered a chance to go again. Your money can increase nicely during this time, and you can also lose it all very quickly, which is most annoying.

Technology is catching up with video poker, too. Now they even have touch screens, which offer a variety of different poker games, blackjack, and video slots—just touch your screen and choose your poison.

3 The Casinos

Casino choice is a personal thing. Some like to find their lucky place and stick with it, while others love to take advantage of the nearly endless choices that Vegas offers. Everyone should casino-hop at least once to marvel (or get dizzy) at the decor/spectacle and the sheer excess of it all. But beyond decoration, there isn't too much difference. You've got your slot machines, your gaming tables, and your big chandeliers.

Virtually all casinos make sure they have no clocks or windows—they do not want you to interrupt your losing streak by realizing how much time has passed. Of course, we've all heard the legend that Vegas casinos pump in fresh oxygen to keep the players from getting tired and wanting to pack it in. The veracity of this is hard to confirm, but we can only hope it's true, especially when we think of that time we looked up after a long stretch of gambling and discovered it was Thursday.

Don't be a snob, and don't be overly dazzled by the fancy casinos. Sometimes you can have a better time at one of the older places Downtown, where stakes are lower, pretensions are nonexistent, and the clientele is often friendlier. Frankly, real gamblers—and by that we don't necessarily mean high rollers, but those who play to win regardless of the amount of said win—head straight for Downtown (and most often, straight for Binion's) for these precise reasons, caring not a whit about glitz and glamour. Even if you don't take your gambling as seriously as that, you may well want to follow their example. After all, it's getting harder and harder to find cheap tables (where you can play a hand of blackjack, for example, for less than $10) on the Strip—so take your hard-earned money to where you can lose it more slowly!

We would also call your attention to less glamorous, less readily accessible casinos, such as local favorites Sunset Station, Texas Station, Cannery, Fiesta Rancho & Henderson and Santa Fe, where payoffs are often higher than on the Strip, and the limits are lower.

You can expect to find in every casino the usual and expected assortment of games—slot machines, of course, video poker, blackjack, table poker (though less and less these days), a race and sports book, a keno lounge, a poker room, baccarat, minibaccarat, Caribbean stud, Let It Ride, craps, roulette, pai gow poker, and more, more, more. If you want a particular game, and it's not one of the most obvious, you might want to call before heading over to a particular casino, just to make sure.

What follows is a description of most of the major casinos in Vegas, including their level of claustrophobia, whether they have a giant slot machine (it's a sucker bet, but we love them), and a completely arbitrary assessment based on whether we won there.

SOUTH STRIP

Excalibur   As you might expect, the Excalibur casino is replete with suits of armor, stained-glass panels, knights, dragons, and velvet and satin heraldic banners, with gaming action taking place beneath vast iron-and-gold chandeliers fit for a medieval castle fortress. This all makes it fine for kitsch-seekers, but anyone who hates crowds or is sensitive to noise will hate it. The overall effect is less like a castle and more like a dungeon. One of us won a lot of money here and refused to share it with the other, so our final judgment about the casino is, well, mixed. Excalibur is now part of Mandalay Resorts' "One Club" slot-reward program, which is also valid at Luxor, Mandalay Bay, Circus Circus, and others. 3850 Las Vegas Blvd. S. ✆ 702/597-7777.

Luxor Las Vegas   More accessible than ever thanks to the air-conditioned people-mover from Excalibur and the monorail from Mandalay Bay, Luxor has been

---

Impressions

Tip Number 3: Win a bunch of money. I can't recommend this too highly. If it hasn't occurred to you, win $1,200 and see for yourself. It's very energizing and really adds to your Vegas fun.

—Merrill Markoe, *Viva Las Wine Goddesses!*

completely remodeled and, in our opinion, improved immeasurably. You enter through a giant temple gateway flanked by massive statues of Ramses. Gone is the space-wasting central area that used to contain the bathrooms, cashiers, and casino offices. This additional space gives the casino a much more airy feel, which produces a low claustrophobia level—in parts, you can see all the way up the inside of the pyramid. King Tut heads and sphinxes adorn slot areas. The "One Club," a Mandalay Resorts slot-players club, also valid at sister properties such as Excalibur, Mandalay Bay, Circus Circus, and others, offers rewards of cash, merchandise, meals, and special services to slot and table players. Sports action unfolds on 17 large-screen TVs and 128 personalized monitors in Luxor's race and sports book. We already felt inclined to like this casino thanks to a good run at blackjack, but the redesign has made it even more inviting. 3900 Las Vegas Blvd. S. ✆ 702/262-4000.

Mandalay Bay   You'll find "elegant" gaming in a pre-fab, deliberate way, with a very high ceiling that produces a very low claustrophobia factor. It's definitely the right place to gamble if you're looking for less hectic, less gimmick-filled play. The layout makes it look airy, and it's marginally less confusing and certainly less overwhelming than many other casinos. Because it is so far down the Strip, there are fewer walk-in players, but the presence of the House of Blues and the increasing popularity of the rumjungle nightclub can mean a late-night influx of customers. There's a big, ultracomfortable sports book (complete with armchairs that could well encourage a relaxed gambler to fall asleep), including a live daily sports-radio show. Players can sign up for the One Club, a Mandalay Resorts player-reward system also valid at sister properties like Luxor, Excalibur, Circus Circus, and others. 3950 Las Vegas Blvd. S. ✆ 702/632-7777.

MGM Grand   Las Vegas's largest casino at 171,500 square feet—we've been to countries that were smaller!—is divided into four themed areas, in a futile attempt to make it seem smaller. Most of the *Wizard of Oz* decorations have been removed, but spend an hour in here and you may feel like Dorothy after she was whisked away by the twister. You will get lost at least once. One section features a high-roller slot area with machines that operate on coins valued at $100 and $500! The sports casino houses a big poker room, a state-of-the-art race and sports book, and the Turf Club Lounge. And the French Riviera–themed Monte Carlo casino has a luxurious marble-columned and gold-draped private high-end gaming area. Carousels of progressive slots unique to the MGM Grand include the very popular Majestic Lions high-frequency $1 slot machines that pay out more than $1 million daily, and the Lion's Share $1 slots, which are capable of jackpots exceeding $1 million each at any time. This hotel takes part in the MGM MIRAGE Players Club, which is also valid at sister properties like The Mirage, New York–New York, and others. 3799 Las Vegas Blvd. S. ✆ 702/891-7777.

The Monte Carlo   This place is all huge ceilings and white-light interior: Obviously, they're trying to evoke gambling in Monaco. While the decor shows lots of attention, it perhaps had too much attention. Bulbs line the ceiling, and everywhere you look is some detail or other. It's busy on both your eyes and your ears. So despite the effort put in, it's not a pleasant place to gamble. However, there is a large and comfortable race and sports-book area, with its own cocktail lounge. This casino takes part in the One Club player-reward system, also valid at Mandalay Bay, Luxor, and others. 3770 Las Vegas Blvd. S. ✆ 702/730-7777.

New York–New York   Another theme-run-wild place: tuxes on the backs of gaming chairs, change carts that look like yellow cabs, and so forth, all set in a miniature New York City. It's all fabulous fun, but despite a low claustrophobia

Memories of a Longtime Dealer

Lou has been a part of the gaming industry for 40 years, the first 20 of which he spent as a dealer in Las Vegas.

"My favorite places were The Flamingo, the Sands, and the Desert Inn. That's when the corporations weren't there. That's when the other folks were in. The mob guys—I never knew it, but that's what they were. I was just a kid. Bugsy had just gotten killed when I went to work at The Flamingo. The Sands was my very first favorite. That was the hotel of all hotels. They had the very best management team. They took care of their help. Their benefits were better than any union. It was the place.

"Years ago, you had great entertainment. You could go to a lounge and catch better acts than in the showroom. Major stars were in the lounges, or they would come in and sit in with the acts after the showroom closed. Don Rickles: Sinatra would get up with him once in a while. Sinatra gave me my first $100 tip. He was playing blackjack. Then he said, 'Do you want to play it or keep it?' I wanted to be polite, so I said, 'Bet it.' And he lost. In those days when the star would appear on stage, between shows they would come out into the casinos. Sinatra and Sammy would deal. They would blow money, but the casinos didn't care. It was a fun, fun place.

"The casinos were run the way they were supposed to be run—for the customer, not so corporate-minded. In those days, you could go to Vegas, get your room very reasonable, your food was practically free, your shows were practically free, you would spend $500 in the casino, but you would come back and be happy because gaming was a form of entertainment. When they ran the casinos, you would have a ball, come home, and be happy. They were very happy if the restaurants and shows lost money—you still lost that $500. Now it would cost you $100 to stay

level (thanks to an unusually high ceiling), it is a major case of sensory overload. This may prove distracting. On the other hand, we won here, so we love it. And in places, it is, if one can say this about anything in Vegas with a straight face, quite beautiful—or at least dazzling. Serious gamblers understandably may sniff at it all and prefer to take their business to a more seemly casino, but everyone else should have about the most Vegasy time they can. NY–NY participates in the MGM MIRAGE Player's Club, also valid at sister properties like the MGM Grand and The Mirage. 3790 Las Vegas Blvd. S. © **702/740-6969.**

Orleans   This is not a particularly special gambling space, though it does have a low claustrophobia level. Another plus is that they sometimes play Cajun and zydeco music over the sound system, so you can two-step while you gamble, which can make losing somewhat less painful. It has all the needed tables—blackjack, craps, and so forth—plus plenty of slots, including the popular Wheel of Fortune machine, which works like those other roulette-wheel slots, but in this case, actually plays the theme song from the TV show. It will even applaud for you if you win. Since Orleans is popular with locals, there are lots of video-poker options. And because it's not on the Strip, you'll find better odds for craps, and cheaper table minimums. 4500 W. Tropicana Ave. © **702/365-7111.**

at a hotel, and food is much more expensive, and to get a ticket to one of these shows is ridiculous. Now you gamble only $150 and you aren't as happy when you come home, because you don't feel like you've been treated to anything. It all goes into the same pocket—what difference does it make? It gives the customer the same hours and more fun. They don't understand that. It's not the same industry as when they ran it. And it shows."

LOU THE DEALER'S GAMING TIPS

If you are a **craps** shooter, just look around at the tables where they have the most chips. Find the guy with the most chips, and do what he does. Follow him along.

For **blackjack,** everybody will tell you in all your books to try to play single and double decks. I don't agree with that, and I never will. The average player goes in to enjoy himself and to win a few dollars. So he is not a professional card counter. Play a shoe. If that shoe is going bad and you catch a run, you will make a lot more money than with a single deck.

Look at gaming as a form of entertainment. Look at that $100 that you might have spent on dinner or a club, where we laughed and had a few drinks and had a good time. Think of it that way.

If you double your money, quit. Not quit gambling, but quit that table. Go have a sandwich or watch a show. And *then* come back. The odds aren't that tremendously in favor of the casinos. How they make their money is through greed; gamblers doubling their money then trying to quadruple it and losing it all, and more.

Try to survive. Don't try to win the hotel. Just try to win a few dollars. Then stop and enjoy it.

Tropicana   Not quite as good looking as it once was, and, yes, highly tropical, with gaming tables situated beneath a massive stained-glass archway and Art Nouveau lighting fixtures. In summer it offers something totally unique: swim-up blackjack tables located in the hotel's 5-acre tropical garden and pool area. Slot and table-game players can earn bonus points toward rooms, shows, and meals by obtaining an Island Winners Club card in the casino. A luxurious high-end slot area has machines that take up to $100 on a single pull. Numerous tournaments take place here, and free gaming lessons are offered weekdays. 3801 Las Vegas Blvd. S. ✆ 702/739-2222.

MID-STRIP

Aladdin   The newest big casino on the Strip and we've grown to like it a lot, but perhaps that's because the sight of actual Moroccan tile (and other *Arabian Nights* touches) makes us happy. It's just good and tacky, that's all. It's big, with high ceilings that help the claustrophobia index, but it's also confusingly laid out, though a recent revamping of the floor has helped alleviate the problem some. Still, we won with the giant slot machine, and one of our moms won there, so, hey, no complaints. Also, the big problem, from the hotel's standpoint, though not really from ours, is that it was planned so that one was not required

---

Tips A Breath of Fresh Air

Las Vegas is one of the few cities in America that welcomes smokers with open arms. Smoking doesn't just exist in the casino hotels, it runs rampant. (Would you like some air with your smoke?) Which is why we were pleasantly shocked when Bellagio's poker room and The Mirage's keno lounge and poker room went completely smoke free. It seems the hotels are doing their darnedest to attract those most rabid of anti-smokers—Californians. (Right across the border, California is one of Sin City's biggest markets.)

---

to walk through it to get to other Aladdin goodies, but what that does mean is that, in some ways, it's kind of hard to find—which is not good for business. That may change, maybe even by the time you read this, as there are plans in the works to restructure the outside to make casino passage virtually mandatory. A bigger potential change to keep in mind is that as this book went to press, Planet Hollywood had just bought the Aladdin and was planning to remake the casino in its own image (what that means is hard to say, but we can all probably look to the Hard Rock for ideas). Do notice the European-style gaming salon that is operated by famed London Clubs International. It has its own private entrance and elevator, a gourmet restaurant, and 24-hour butler service in addition to the high-stakes tables and slots. Too rich for our blood, but perhaps not for yours. 3667 Las Vegas Blvd. S. ☎ 702/736-0111.

Bally's Las Vegas   Bally's casino is large (the size of a football field), with lots of colorful signage. The big ceiling makes for a low claustrophobia level. There's Park Place Connection, a players club valid at sister properties like Caesars Palace and Paris, offering members cash rebates, room discounts, free meals and show tickets, and invitations to special events, among other perks. The casino hosts frequent slot tournaments, and free gaming lessons are offered. 3645 Las Vegas Blvd. S. ☎ 702/739-4111.

Barbary Coast   The Barbary Coast is an 1890s-style casino ornately decorated with $2 million worth of gorgeous stained-glass skylights and signs, as well as immense crystal-dangling globe chandeliers over the gaming tables. It's kind of small, dark, and cluttered, but it's also old Las Vegas (and we mean "old" loosely), and small is rare on the Strip. The casino has a free Fun Club for slot players; participants earn points toward cash and prizes. 3595 Las Vegas Blvd. S. ☎ 702/737-7111.

Bellagio   The slot machines here are mostly encased in marble and fine woods. How's that for upping the ante on classy? In all fairness, Bellagio comes the closest to re-creating the feel of gambling in Monte Carlo (the country, not the next-door casino), but its relentless good taste means that this is one pretty forgettable casino. After all, we are suckers for a wacky theme that screams "Vegas," and European class just doesn't cut it. Sure, there are good touches— we always like a high ceiling to reduce the claustrophobia index, and the place is laid out in an easy-to-navigate grid with ultrawide aisles, so walking through doesn't seem like such a crowded collision-course maze. (*Tip:* The main casino path is identified with black carpets.) And we won big here, so there's that. Anyway, the cozy sports book has individual TVs and entirely denlike leather chairs—quite, quite comfortable. 3600 Las Vegas Blvd. S. ☎ 888/987-6667.

Caesars Palace   Caesars's casino is simultaneously the ultimate in gambling luxury and the ultimate in Vegas kitsch. Cocktail waitresses in togas parade about, as you gamble under the watchful gaze of faux-marble Roman statues. The very high ceiling in certain areas of the casino makes for a very low claustrophobia level, especially thanks to the recent face-lift, which has lightened up the paint and made the area much brighter. Unfortunately, some spots in the casino are dark and entirely too claustrophobic. Although we love it, the casino has become somewhat confusing and unmanageable because of its size and meandering layout, like Caesars itself.

A notable facility is the state-of-the-art **Race and Sports Book,** with huge electronic display boards and giant video screens. (Caesars pioneered computer-generated wagering data that can be communicated in less than half a second, and has sophisticated satellite equipment that can pick up the broadcast of virtually any sporting event in the world.) The domed VIP slot arena of the Forum Casino (minimum bet is $5, but you can wager up to $1,500 on a single pull!) is a plush, crystal-chandeliered precinct with seating in roomy, adjustable chairs. Gamblers can accumulate bonus points toward cash back, gifts, gratis show tickets, meals, and rooms by joining the Park Place Connection, a players club also valid at sister properties like Bally's and Paris. Club membership also lets you in on grand-prize drawings, tournaments, and parties.

The most upscale of the Caesars gaming rooms is the intimate, European-style casino adjoining the **Palace Court** restaurant. It's a gorgeous and elegant place to gamble, but we've never won there, so we hate it. 3570 Las Vegas Blvd. S. ⓒ 702/731-7110.

The Flamingo Las Vegas   If you've seen the movie *Bugsy*, you won't recognize this as Mr. Siegel's baby. We can't say for sure what their seemingly years-long casino renovation actually did. It all looks pretty much the same, but it might be marginally less confusing and tortuous a layout (trust us, anything is an improvement) with better, and most welcome, access to the street (before, you needed a trail of breadcrumbs and a lot of stamina to find your way out). Still, the claustrophobia factor is moderately high. We have to say that of all the casinos that qualify as older, this is the most pleasant one in which to play. Unfortunately, the gambler seems to be paying for it; no more daytime $3 blackjack. One of our favorite slot machines is here, but we won't tell you which one, to save it for ourselves. Sorry. The Flamingo takes part in the Park Place Connection, a players-reward club also valid at sister properties such as Caesars and Paris. 3555 Las Vegas Blvd. S. ⓒ 702/733-3111.

Gold Coast   Adjacent to the Rio, this casino is not only well lit, but totally unique in Vegas: It has windows! It's a little thing, but it made us really excited. They also had a higher ratio of video-poker machines to slot machines, rather than the other way around. A remodeling made it much bigger, with high ceilings, and very bright overall. Nice job. 4000 W. Flamingo Rd. ⓒ 702/367-7111.

Harrah's   A mixed bag of a casino, one that is both dated (low ceilings, old lighting, stuffy) and fun (parts have high enough ceilings, and there are special attractions we will detail in a moment). The main reason to come here are the "party pits," gaming-table areas where dealers are encouraged to wear funny hats, celebrate wins, and otherwise break the usual stern dealer facade. Singing, dancing, and the handing out of party favors have all been known to erupt. (Gambling is supposed to be fun, so enjoy it!) Slot and table-game players can earn bonus points toward complimentary rooms, meals, and show tickets by joining Harrah's Total Rewards in the casino, which is also valid at sister hotel Rio. There are nonsmoking areas (fat lot of good that did, the place reeks of smoke), and free gaming lessons are offered on weekdays. 3475 Las Vegas Blvd. S. ⓒ 702/369-5000.

Imperial Palace   The 75,000-square-foot casino here reflects the hotel's pagoda-roofed Asian exterior with a dragon-motif ceiling and giant wind-chime chandeliers. There is a Breathalyzer for voluntary alcohol-limit checks on your way to the parking lot (useful, since there are nine bars on the casino premises). The Imperial Palace boasts a 230-seat race and sports book, attractively decorated with oil murals of sporting events; the room is tiered like a grandstand, and every seat has its own color monitor. One giant slot machine is red, white, and blue; try singing the National Anthem to it, and see if you win more money. One kitsch feature of note is the casino's Legends Pit, where, on weekends after 6pm, celebrity impersonators aping everyone from Elvis to Madonna deal blackjack. This is also one of the few places on this part of the Strip where you might be able to find $5 table minimums. 3535 Las Vegas Blvd. S. ℂ 702/731-3311.

The Mirage   Gamble in a Polynesian village in one of the prettiest casinos in town. It has a meandering layout, and the low ceiling makes for a medium claus-trophobia level, but neither of these aspects is overwhelming. This remains one of our favorite places to gamble. Facilities include a plush European-style *salon privé* for high rollers at baccarat, blackjack, and roulette; an elegant dining room serves catered meals to gamblers there. Slot and table players can join the MGM MIRAGE Players Club, also valid at sister hotels such as Treasure Island and MGM Grand, and work toward bonus points for cash rebates, special room rates, complimentary meals and/or show tickets, and other benefits. The elabo-rate race and sports book offers theater stereo sound and a movie-theater-size screen. It's one of the most pleasant and popular casinos in town, so it's crowded more often than not. 3400 Las Vegas Blvd. S. ℂ 702/791-7111.

Palms Resort & Casino   Here's where this Desperately-Seeking-the-Hip hotel has a bit of an identity crisis, because it also wants to be a place where locals feel comfortable gambling. You know, like Palace and Texas Station. Huh? That's right, the Palm wants to mirror those hotels off the Strip that offer loose slots and other incentives to make the locals feel at home. This rarely makes for a chic play-ing area (because locals don't want to have to get glammed up to go out and play some slots). On the other hand, the area is, especially on weekend nights, ringed with the beautiful and slender and aloof, desperate to get into Ghost Bar and Rain. If they aren't inside, they are surly about it. Let's hope everyone just keeps getting along. The gaming area covers most of the ground floor (it recently had part of its bulk diminished, in response to complaints that it was too crowded with tables and machines), and is replete with Miami-tropical-inspired details. 4321 W. Flamingo Rd. ℂ 702/942-7777.

Paris Las Vegas Casino   Surrounded by a rather Disneyesque one-third-scale replica of the streets of Paris, this 83,000-square-foot casino is a very pleasant place to gamble, in that Vegas-gimmick kind of way. It's one of those kitschy places that "real" gamblers are appalled by. To heck with them, we say. A tall ceiling gives the illusion that you are trying to bust the bank while strolling outside, and results in an airy effect. The place doesn't feel all that large, thanks to a meandering layout. There are over 2,000 slot machines and over 100 table games. A state-of-the-art race and sports book features live satellite feeds of sporting events from around the world. The Park Place Connection is the Paris's players' club, under the umbrella of Park Place Entertainment—owners of Paris, Bally's, Caesars, The Flamingo, and the Las Vegas Hilton—so you can rack up points at one casino and redeem them at any in the family. 3655 Las Vegas Blvd. S. ℂ 702/946-7000.

The Rio All Suite Hotel & Casino This Brazilian-themed resort's 85,000-square-foot casino is, despite the presence of plenty of glitter and neon, very dark. It has about the highest claustrophobia rating of the major casinos and seems very dated these days. Its sports book feels a little grimy. The waitresses wear scanty costumes (particularly in the back), probably in an effort to distract you and throw your game off (all the more now that they are adding "Bev-entertainment"—those poor waitresses are going to have to burst into song and/or dance in between delivering your beer). Do not let them. The part of the casino in the Masquerade Village is considerably more pleasant (the very high ceilings help), though still crowded, and the loud live show here adds even more noise. In the high-end slot area ($5–$100 a pull), guests enjoy a private lounge and gratis champagne. There are nonsmoking slot and gaming table areas. The Rio participates in the Harrah's Total Rewards players club, allowing gamers to earn points toward meals, cash back, rooms, and more that can be used at any Harrah's-owned casino. 3700 W. Flamingo Rd. ℂ **702/252-7777.**

TI at the Mirage We really loved it when this place was a casino set in Disneyland's Pirates of the Caribbean—or so it seemed. It doesn't seem like a big deal, the loss of those pirate chests dripping gold, jewels, and skulls with eye patches, but with the removal of the theme, this is now just a very nice casino. But it is that, so you should come here. Players Club members can earn points toward meals, services, show tickets, and cash rebates at any of the MGM MIRAGE hotels, including The Mirage, MGM Grand, and more.

There are nonsmoking gaming tables in each pit. A race and sports book boasts state-of-the-art electronic information boards and TV monitors at every seat, as well as numerous large-screen monitors. 3300 Las Vegas Blvd. S. ℂ **702/894-7111.**

The Venetian "Tasteful" is the watchword in these days of classy Vegas gaming, and consequently, with the exception of more hand-painted Venetian art re-creations on parts of the ceiling, The Venetian's casino is interchangeable with those found at Mandalay Bay, the Monte Carlo, and to a certain extent, Bellagio. All that gleaming marble, columns, and such is very nice, but after a while it's also a bit ho-hum. Besides, this is Vegas, and we want our tacky theme elements, by gosh. The lack thereof, combined with poor signage, may be why this casino is so hard to get around—every part looks exactly the same. It's not precisely claustrophobic, but it can be confusing. Plus, there is no (at this writing) giant slot machine. On the other hand, we made a killing at blackjack and my editor struck it rich at the slots, so we have to love the place for those reasons. Another (less personal) plus is that you can access the casino directly from the St. Mark's Square re-creation out front. The smoke-sensitive report that the ventilation system here seems to be tops. 3355 Las Vegas Blvd. S. ℂ **702/414-1000.**

NORTH STRIP

Circus Circus This vast property has three full-size casinos that, combined, comprise one of the largest gaming operations in Nevada (more than 100,000 sq. ft.). More importantly, they have an entire circus midway set up throughout, so you are literally gambling with trapeze stunts going on over your head. The other great gimmick is the slot machine carousel—yep, it turns while you spin the reels. The Mandalay Resorts "One Club" offers slot/video-poker and table players the opportunity to earn points redeemable for cash, discounted rooms and meals, and other benefits at Circus or any of the sister properties such as

Mandalay Bay or Luxor. The Circus Bucks progressive slot machines here build from a jackpot base of $500,000, which players can win on a $2 pull. Gaming facilities include a 10,000-square-foot race and sports book with 30 video monitors ranging from 13 to 52 inches, 40-seat and 89-seat keno lounges. Unfortunately, the casino is crowded and noisy, and there are lots of children passing through (making it more crowded and noisy). That, plus some low ceilings (not in the Big Top, obviously), makes for a very high claustrophobia rating, though the current commedia dell'arte clown motif (as opposed to the old garish circus motif) has upgraded the decor. 2880 Las Vegas Blvd. S. *©* **702/734-0410.**

The Riviera   The Riviera's 100,000-square-foot casino, once one of the largest in the world, offers plenty of opportunities to get lost and cranky. A wall of windows lets daylight stream in (most unusual), but as the hotel gets shabbier, every inch of the casino smells like smoke and age. The casino's Slot and Gold (seniors) clubs allow slot players to earn bonus points toward free meals, rooms, and show tickets. Nickeltown is just that—nothin' but nickel slots and video poker. The race and sports book here offers individual monitors at each of its 250 seats, and this is one of the few places in town where you can play the ancient Chinese game of *sic bo*. 2901 Las Vegas Blvd. S. *©* **702/734-5110.**

Sahara   This is one place where there seem to be more tables than slots and video-poker machines. It's also one of the few Strip casinos that offers low-rollers good deals such as $1 craps and blackjack. But belligerent drunks and other fun-killing folks are often found at these $1 tables. When we were last there, they had a whole row of Piggy Bankin' machines that were all paying off, so we were happy. The Sahara runs frequent slot tournaments and other events, and its slot club, Club Sahara, offers cash rebates and other perks. *Note:* This is the only Strip casino that offers pan, a card game. 2535 Las Vegas Blvd. S. *©* **702/737-2111.**

Stardust   This once-popular casino features 90,000 square feet of lively gaming action, including a 250-seat race and sports book with a sophisticated satellite system and more than 50 TV monitors airing sporting events and horse-racing results around the clock. Adjacent to it is a sports handicapper's library offering comprehensive statistical information on current sporting events. Stardust Slot Club members win cash rebates, with credit piling up even on nickel machines; free rooms, shows, meals, and invitations to special events are also possible bonuses. We usually do well here, so even though it's a little loud, we like it. Check out those $1 slots just inside the front door—they've been very good to us. 3000 Las Vegas Blvd. S. *©* **702/732-6111.**

Stratosphere Casino Hotel & Tower   Originally set up to evoke a world's fair but ending up more like a circus, Stratosphere redid its whole casino area to make it more appealing to the many adults who were staying away in droves. This should lure many of you, because it is a nicer, and less crowded, place to play. They heavily advertise their high payback on certain slots and video poker: 98% payback on dollar slots and 100% payback on quarter video poker (if you bet the maximum on each). We can't say we noticed a difference, but other people around us were winning like crazy. There's a test area for new slot games, a Harley slot area with motorcycle-seat stools, and a high-roller slot room ($5 minimum bet) where chairs move up and down and can vibrate to give you a back massage while you play. The Stratosphere Players Club sponsors frequent tournaments, and its members can earn points toward gifts, VIP perks, discounted room rates, meals, and cash rebates—just a bit of play here, and you may be getting more free-room offers than you know what to do with. 2000 Las Vegas Blvd. S. *©* **702/380-7777.**

Westward Ho Hotel & Casino   This small but centrally located Strip casino hosts many slot tournaments, and slot players who obtain Preferred Customer cards can amass credits toward complimentary rooms, meals, and shows, among other benefits. 2900 Las Vegas Blvd. S. ℂ 702/731-2900.

EAST OF THE STRIP

Green Valley Ranch Resort   Probably too far for the average traveler to drive—after all, when there is a casino just steps (or floors) away from your hotel room (and between you and anywhere in the world apart from your hotel room), to say nothing of several dozen more within a few blocks of your hotel room, you may be disinclined to drive out to one that is isolated from many other decent casinos. But given that this is a swank resort (or at least, trying to be), that it's smallish and elegant, that it's got a happening, decadent bar with girls prancing in go-go boots right in the center, and that more bars attracting the young and beautiful and well-heeled are opening here, you might want to make a visit, just to see the scene. And they have penny slots. Go figure. 2300 Paseo Verde Dr. (at I-215), Henderson. ℂ 702/617-7777.

Hard Rock Hotel & Casino   Where Gen X goes to gamble. The Hard Rock has certainly taken casino decor to a whole new level. The attention to detail and the resulting playfulness is admirable, if not incredible. Gaming tables have piano keyboards at one end; some slots have Fender guitar fret boards as arms; gaming chips have band names and/or pictures on them; slot machines are similarly rock-themed (check out the Jimi Hendrix machine!); and so it goes. The whole thing is set in the middle of a circular room, around the outskirts of which are various rock memorabilia in glass cases. Rock blares over the sound system, allowing boomers to boogie while they gamble.

A bank of slots makes gambling an act of charity: Environmentally committed owner Peter Morton (the Hard Rock's motto is "Save the Planet") donates profits from specified slots to organizations dedicated to saving the rainforests. A Back Stage Pass allows patrons to rack up discounts on meals, lodging, and gift-shop items while playing slots and table games. The race and sports book here provides comfortable seating in leather-upholstered reclining armchairs. All this is genuinely amazing, but the noise level is above even that of a normal casino and we just hated it. We are in the minority, though; most people love it, so assume you will be one of them. 4455 Paradise Rd. ℂ 702/693-5000.

Las Vegas Hilton   The casino has two parts, thanks to the space-themed portion adjacent to *Star Trek: The Experience*. In an area designed to look like a spaceport, you find space-themed slot machines, many of which have no handles—just pass your hand through a light beam to activate. You'll find other gimmicks throughout the casino (though already some have been dropped since the opening), including urinals that give you an instant "urinalysis"—usually suggesting this is your lucky day to gamble. We do like a well-designed space in which to lose our money.

Over in the original casino section, Austrian-crystal chandeliers add a strong touch of class. The casino is actually medium-size, but it does have an enormous sports book—at 30,500 square feet, it's the world's largest race and sports book facility. It, too, is a luxurious precinct equipped with the most advanced audio, video, and computer technology available, including 46 TV monitors, some as large as 15 feet across. In fact, its video wall is second in size only to NASA's. The casino is adjacent to the lobby but is neither especially loud nor frantic. Especially plush are the vast 6,900-square-foot baccarat room—with gorgeous crystal chandeliers, silk-covered walls, and velvet-upholstered furnishings—and the VIP slot area where personnel are attired in tuxedos. Both areas offer gracious service to players.

Because so many conventioneers stay here, the crowd is more changeable than at most casinos. By joining the Park Place Connection, a players club, you can amass bonus points toward cash prizes, gifts, and complimentary rooms, meals, and show tickets at any of the company's hotels including Paris and Bally's. 3000 Paradise Rd. ⓒ 702/732-7111.

Sam's Town   On its two immense floors of gaming action (153,083 sq. ft., 2nd only to the MGM Grand in size), Sam's Town maintains the friendly, just-folks ambience that characterizes the entire property. The casino is adorned with Old West paraphernalia (horseshoes, Winchester rifles, holsters, and saddlebags) and is looking a bit less dated thanks to some recent sprucing up (it's subtle, but believe us, it's better). Sam's Town claims its friendliness extends to looser slots. Join the Sam's Town Slot Club to earn points toward rooms, meals, and cash rebates. Free gaming lessons are offered weekdays from 11am to 4pm, with poker lessons at other times. 5111 Boulder Hwy. (at Nellis Blvd.). ⓒ 702/456-7777.

DOWNTOWN

Binion's Horseshoe *Finds*   Professionals in the know say that "for the serious player, the Binions are this town." Benny Binion could neither read nor write, but boy did he know how to run a casino. His venerable establishment has been eclipsed over the years, but it claims the highest betting limits in Las Vegas on all games (probably in the entire world, according to a spokesperson). It offers single-deck blackjack and $2 minimums, 10-times odds on craps, and high progressive jackpots. Real gamblers won't consider going anywhere else.

We especially like the older part of the casino here, which—with its flocked wallpaper, fancy lighting fixtures, and gold-tasseled burgundy velvet drapes—looks like an Old West bordello. Unfortunately, all this adds up to a very high claustrophobia level. They do, however, have a giant slot machine, which has been very, very good to us. 128 E. Fremont St. (between Casino Center Blvd. and 1st St.). ⓒ 702/382-1600.

The California Hotel/Casino   The California is a festive place filled with Hawaiian shirts and balloons. This friendly facility actually provides sofas and armchairs in the casino area—an unheard-of luxury in this town. Players can join the Cal Slot Club and amass points toward gifts and cash prizes, or participate in daily slot tournaments. This is the first place we found our favorite Piggy Bankin' machines. 12 Ogden Ave. (at 1st St.). ⓒ 702/385-1222.

Castaways   The former Showboat traded in its Mardi Gras/Showboat gambling theme for a Polynesian one. It's a big casino, nearly as big as the ones on the Strip, but over time has been portioned off into deceptively small rooms and other sections. It's not the most elaborate in town, but it is certainly clean, friendly, and comfortable. At night, various bands play from an open lounge. Castaways' enormous 24-hour bingo parlor is a facility noted for high payouts.

Impressions

I am, after all, the best hold 'em player alive. I'm forced to play this tournament, you understand, to demonstrate this fact.

—Once and future casino owner Bob Stupak on why he entered Binion's Horseshoe World Series of Poker

The World Series, Las Vegas–Style

Binion's Horseshoe is internationally known as the home of the World Series of Poker. It was "Nick the Greek" Dondolos who first approached Benny Binion in 1949 with the idea for a high-stakes poker marathon between top players. Binion agreed, with the stipulation that the game be open to public viewing. The competition, between Dondolos and the legendary Johnny Moss, lasted 5 months with breaks only for sleep. Moss ultimately won about $2 million. As Dondolos lost his last pot, he rose from his chair, bowed politely, and said, "Mr. Moss, I have to let you go."

In 1970, Binion decided to re-create the battle of poker giants, which evolved into the annual World Series of Poker. Johnny Moss won the first year, and went on to snag the championship again in 1971 and 1974. Thomas "Amarillo Slim" Preston won the event in 1972 and popularized it on the talk-show circuit. In 2002, there were more than 7,595 entrants from over 22 countries, each ponying up the $10,000 entrance fee, and total winnings were in excess of $19 million (the tournament was also televised on ESPN). During one memorable year, the participants included actors Matt Damon and Edward Norton, fresh from *Rounders,* a movie in which they played a couple of card sharks. They decided to try out their newly acquired moves against the pros, who were unhappy that these kids were barging in on their action, and so, rumor has it, offered a separate, large bounty to whatever player took them out. Both actors got knocked out on the first day but took it with good grace and apparently had a blast.

Slot players can join a club to accumulate bonus points toward free meals, rooms, gifts, and cash prizes. And if you're traveling with kids ages 2 to 7, you can leave them at an in-house babysitting facility free for 3 hours while you gamble. 2800 Fremont St. (between Charleston Blvd. and Mojave Rd.). *©* **702/385-9123.**

El Cortez   This casino is one of the last shreds of pre-1980s Las Vegas, which is either wonderful or horrible depending on your view. It features frequent big-prize drawings (up to $50,000) based on your Social Security number. It's also popular for low limits (10¢ roulette and 25¢ craps). 600 Fremont St. (between 6th and 7th sts.). *©* **702/385-5200.**

Fitzgeralds   This casino is done up in greens and golds, and the overall effect is not quite as tacky as you might expect. In fact, it's rather friendly and with a medium to low claustrophobia level. The casino actually has two levels: From the upstairs part, you can access a balcony from which you get an up-close view of the Fremont Street Experience.

Blackjack, craps, and keno tournaments are frequent events here. Slot machines that paid back over 100% the previous week are marked with a Mr. Lucky sign. The Fitzgerald Card offers slot players gifts, meals, and other perks for accumulated points. Several slot machines have cars as prizes, fun books provide two-for-one gaming coupons, and there are $1-minimum blackjack tables. 301 Fremont St. (at 3rd St.). *©* **702/388-2400.**

The Four Queens   The Four Queens is New Orleans–themed, with late-19th-century-style globe chandeliers, which make for good lighting and a low claustrophobia level. It's small, but the dealers are helpful, which is one of the pluses of gambling in the more manageably sized casinos.

The facility boasts the world's largest slot machine: More than 9 feet high and almost 20 feet long, six people can play it at one time! It's the Mother of all giant slot machines, and frankly, it intimidates even us. Here is also the world's largest blackjack table (it seats 12 players). The Reel Winners Club offers slot players bonus points toward cash rebates. Slot, blackjack, and craps tournaments are frequent events, and there are major poker tournaments every January and September. The casino also offers exciting multiple-action blackjack (it's like playing three hands at once with separate wagers on each). 202 Fremont St. (at Casino Center Blvd.). ✆ 702/385-4011.

Fremont Hotel & Casino   This 32,000-square-foot casino offers a relaxed atmosphere and low gambling limits ($2 blackjack, 25¢ roulette). It's also surprisingly open and bright for a Downtown casino. Just 50¢ could win you a Cadillac or Ford Mustang here, plus a progressive cash jackpot. Casino guests can accumulate bonus points redeemable toward cash by joining the Five Star Slot Club, and take part in frequent slot and keno tournaments. No giant slot machine, though. 200 E. Fremont St. (between Casino Center Blvd. and 3rd St.). ✆ 702/385-3232.

The Golden Gate   This is one of the oldest casinos in Downtown, and though its age is showing, it's still fun to go there. As you might expect from the name, old San Francisco (think earthquake time) artifacts and decor abound. At one end of the narrow casino is the bar, where a piano player performs ragtime jazz, which is better than the homogenized pop offered in most casino lounges. Unfortunately, the low ceiling, dark period wallpaper, and small dimensions give this a high claustrophobia level. 1 Fremont St. ✆ 702/382-3510.

Golden Nugget   Frankly, this is not the standout that other casino properties developed by Steve Wynn (and recently sold by MGM MIRAGE to Internet entrepreneurs Thomas Breitling and Timothy Poster) are. It goes for luxury, of course, but there's too much crammed into too little space. And compared to most other Downtown properties, this is the most like the Strip. Despite the overcrowding, it has a much cleaner and fresher feeling than many of the dingy, time-forgotten spaces of Downtown. There's no word on what the new owners plan to do to the casino, but they've promised to bring back "Old Vegas" style to Downtown. Stay tuned. 129 E. Fremont St. (at Casino Center Blvd.). ✆ 702/385-7111.

The Gold Spike   Despite an updating (after a serious fire), the Gold Spike remains deliciously, or frighteningly (depending on your aesthetic views and desires) dated; it may no longer have that '70s-era shag carpeting and wood panels, but it has the 2002 spiritual equivalent. It's still one of those dingy, forgotten Downtown spaces that we usually criticize. So what? Here, everyone is equal, and everyone is having a good time, or at least they can sincerely join you in your misery. Best of all, they have penny slots! (Not very many, to be sure, and getting a seat at one can require patience.) Hey tightwads, take a buck and spend a few hours. 400 Ogden Ave. (at Las Vegas Blvd.). ✆ 702/384-8444.

Jackie Gaughan's Plaza Hotel/Casino   This is old Vegas, with an attempt at '60s glamour (think women in white go-go boots). Now it's worn. Cautious bettors will appreciate the $1 blackjack tables and penny slots here. 1 Main St. (at Fremont St.). ✆ 702/386-2110.

Lady Luck   A complete remodeling didn't do too much to change this old gal, who is still a bit more smoky and crowded than we prefer, but that doesn't mean she's not good for a few go-rounds. Plus, its liberal game rules are attractive to gamblers. You can play "fast-action hold 'em" here—a combination of 21, poker, and pai gow poker. 206 N. 3rd St. (at Ogden Ave.). ℂ **702/477-3000.**

Main Street Station *(Finds*   This is the best of the Downtown casinos, at least in terms of comfort and a pleasant environment. Even the Golden Nugget, nice as it is, has more noise and distractions. The decor here is, again, classic Vegas/old-timey (Victorian-era) San Francisco, but with extra touches (check out the old-fashioned fans above the truly beautiful bar) that make it work much better than other attempts at the same decor. Strangely, it seems just about smoke-free, perhaps thanks in part to a very high ceiling. The claustrophobia level is zero. 200 N. Main St. (between Fremont St. and I-95). ℂ **800/713-8933** or 702/387-1896.

9

Shopping

Shopping in Vegas—Nirvana or an endless Sisyphean repetition of every mall you've ever been to? Depends on your viewpoint. If you are looking for quaint, clever, unique stores, this isn't the town for you (with a few notable exceptions, most of which will require you to drive some blocks off the Strip). But if you are looking for general shop-till-you-drop fun, this is your kind of town. In addition to some extensive (and recently revamped) malls, many hotels have comprehensive, and sometimes highly themed, shopping arcades. The most notable of the arcades are in Caesars Palace, Aladdin, and The Venetian (details below).

In addition to exploring the malls, outlets, and shops listed below, you might consider driving **Maryland Parkway,** which runs parallel to the Strip on the east and has just about one of everything: Target, Toys "R" Us, several major department stores, Tower Records, major drugstores (in case you forgot your shampoo and don't want to spend $8 on a new bottle in your hotel sundry shop), some alternative-culture stores (tattoo parlors and hip clothing stores), and so forth. It goes on for blocks.

1 The Malls

Boulevard Mall   The Boulevard is the largest mall in Las Vegas—at least until the remodeled Fashion Show Mall trumps it in late 2003. Its 144-plus stores and restaurants are arranged in arcade fashion on a single floor occupying 1.2 million square feet. Geared to the average consumer, it has anchors like Sears, JCPenney, Macy's, Dillard's, and Marshalls. There's a wide variety of shops offering all sorts of items—moderately priced shoes and clothing for the entire family, books and gifts, jewelry, and home furnishings. There are also more than a dozen fast-food eateries. In short, you can find just about anything you need here. And there's free valet parking. The mall is open Monday through Saturday from 10am to 9pm and Sunday from 11am to 6pm. 3528 S. Maryland Pkwy. (between Twain Ave. and Desert Inn Rd.). ✆ 702/732-8949. www.blvdmall.com.

Fashion Show Mall   What was a nondescript, if large, mall has now been revamped with a *yowsa* exterior much more fitting Las Vegas. It's capped by a giant . . . well . . . they call it a "Cloud" but we call it "that weird thingy that looks like a spaceport for UFOs, what in the heck were they thinking?" Inside, you will find the city's first Nordstrom, a Bloomingdale's, Saks Fifth Avenue, a Macy's and eventually a Lord & Taylor. Construction on the $300 million expansion should be completed in late 2003. The mall presently comprises more than 130 shops, restaurants, and services. And the Cloud/Alien Spaceport Thingy will have giant LED screens, music, and other distractions—again, much more fitting for Vegas, where even the malls have to light up. Valet parking is available, and you can even arrange to have your car hand-washed while you shop. The Fashion Show is open Monday through Friday from 10am to 9pm, Saturday from 10am to 7pm, and

Sunday from noon until 6pm. 3200 Las Vegas Blvd. S. (at the corner of Spring Mountain Rd.). ℂ **702/369-0704.** www.thefashionshow.com.

The Galleria at Sunset   This is a 1-million-square-foot Southwestern-themed shopping center, 9 miles southeast of downtown Las Vegas. Anchored by four department stores (Dillard's, JCPenney, Mervyn's California, and Robinsons-May), the Galleria's 110 emporia include branches of The Disney Store, Gap/Gap Kids/Baby Gap, The Limited Too, Eddie Bauer, Ann Taylor, bebe, Caché, Lane Bryant, Lerner New York, Victoria's Secret, The Body Shop, B. Dalton, and Sam Goody. In addition to shoes and clothing for the entire family, you'll find electronics, eyewear, gifts, books, home furnishings, jewelry, and luggage here. Dining facilities include an extensive food court and two restaurants. Open Monday through Saturday from 10am to 9pm and Sunday from 11am to 6pm. In nearby Henderson, 1300 W. Sunset Rd. (at Stephanie St., just off I-515). ℂ **702/434-0202.** www.galleria atsunset.com.

The Meadows   Another immense mall, The Meadows is made up of more than 140 shops, services, and eateries, anchored by four department stores: Macy's, Dillard's, Sears, and JCPenney. In addition, there are 15 shoe stores, a full array of apparel for the entire family (including maternity wear, petites, and large sizes), an extensive food court, and shops purveying toys, books, CDs and tapes, luggage, gifts, jewelry, home furnishings (The Bombay Company, among others), accessories, and so on. Fountains and trees enhance The Meadows's ultramodern, high-ceilinged interior, and there are a few comfortable seating areas for resting your feet a moment. The Meadows Mall is open Monday through Saturday from 10am to 9pm and Sunday from 10am to 6pm. 4300 Meadows Lane (at the intersection of Valley View and U.S. 95). ℂ **702/878-3331.** www.themeadowsmall.com.

Showcase Mall   Less traditional mall than an entertainment center, it has plenty of both shopping and fun—we rarely miss a chance to drop by M&M World, to say nothing of Sephora. Other occupants include GameWorks, the World of Coca Cola store, Grand Canyon Experience, and the United Artist Cinemas—the only regular movie theater complex on the Strip. Hours vary by store. 3785 S. Las Vegas Blvd (right next to the MGM Grand). ℂ **702/597-3122.**

2 Factory Outlets

Las Vegas has a big factory-outlet center just a few miles past the southern end of the Strip (see below). If you don't have a car, you can take a no. 301 CAT bus from anywhere on the Strip and change at Vacation Village to a no. 303. You can see from the review below that it doesn't do much for us, which is why we usually head to Primm to drop more money than we do at the tables (Williams-Sonoma outlet, how we love you). That's why we anxiously await the opening of the $80 million, 435,000 square-foot "high-end" Las Vegas Premium Outlets Center near Downtown. It will have 100 stores, a food court, and other stuff. Announced stores include Armani Exchange, Coach, Dolce & Gabbana, Guess, Kenneth Cole, Lacoste, Polo/Ralph Lauren, St. John, Tahari, and Theory. It's due to open in August of 2003 right where the 15 and 93 come together behind the Plaza hotel.

Belz Factory Outlet World   Belz houses more than 150 air-conditioned outlets, including a few dozen clothing stores and shoe stores. It offers a range of merchandise, but even given our understanding of the hit-and-miss nature of outlets, we've never bought a thing here and feel nothing but apathy for the center. Among other stores (which you will perhaps find less disappointing than we have), you'll find Casual Corner, Liz Claiborne, Perry Ellis, Calvin Klein, Levi's, Nike, Dress Barn, Oshkosh B'Gosh, Leggs/Hanes/Bali, Esprit, Carter's, Reebok, Spiegel, Jockey, Oneida, Springmaid, Bose (electronics), Danskin, Van Heusen, Tommy Hilfiger, Burlington, Royal Doulton, Waterford (crystal), Black & Decker (tools), and Geoffrey Beene. There is also a carousel and a food court. Open Monday through Saturday from 10am to 9pm, Sunday from 10am to 6pm. 7400 Las Vegas Blvd. S. (at Warm Springs Rd.). ✆ 702/896-5599. www.belz.com/factory/locations/lasvegas/index.html.

Fashion Outlet at Primm   Dedicated bargain hunters may want to make the roughly 40-minute drive along I-15 (there's also a $13 shuttle from New York–New York or MGM Grand) to this big outlet complex, right on the border of California and Nevada. On your left is a large factory outlet with some designer names prominent enough to make that drive well worthwhile—Kenneth Cole, Donna Karan, Gap, Banana Republic, Old Navy, even Williams-Sonoma, among several others. Why so far out of town? Our guess is because all these designers have full-price boutiques in various hotels, and they don't want you ignoring those in favor of discounted items. Open Monday through Saturday from 10am to 9pm and Sunday from 10am to 8pm. 32100 Las Vegas Blvd. S. ✆ 888/424-6898. www.fashion outletlasvegas.com.

3 Hotel Shopping Arcades

Just about every Las Vegas hotel offers some shopping opportunities. The following have the most extensive arcades. The physical spaces of these shopping arcades are always open, but individual stores keep unpredictable hours. For addresses and telephone numbers, see the hotels' listings in chapter 5.

Note: The Forum Shops at Caesars, the Grand Canal Shoppes at The Venetian, and the Desert Passage at Aladdin—as much sightseeing attractions as shopping arcades—are in the must-see category.

ALADDIN   The most recent Vegas "dazzle the tourists out of their money" shopping experience (the others being over at Caesars and The Venetian), the Desert Passage uses the mystical and romantic architecture (or re-creations thereof) of the Middle East (Egypt, Morocco, Turkey) as its theme, and the results are pretty swell. Even the ceiling overhead is painted to replicate sultry days and nights, with occasional thunderstorms hitting. There is a lot to look at beyond the shops, even more than usual, since, at this writing, they have frequent live entertainers—acrobats, jugglers, belly dancers—to add to the visuals. And it's not just visual but odiferous: They pipe in spices and other evocative scents appropriate to those regions. The whole thing allows you to have that Middle Eastern souk-shopping experience without all the pesky touts trying to drag you into their stall for hours of haggling. You can even take a pedicab (that would be a bicycle-powered vehicle pedaled by some comely worker) for a tour of Morocco, kinda. The stores are the assortment of mid- and high-end name brands one would expect (so the gouging happens in a different way than in the souks!). It's one of our favorite shopping areas in Vegas, for sure. The thing that worries us the most about the purchase of the Aladdin by Planet Hollywood— and the expected shift of the hotel's thematic focus—is how that might affect this mall and its appearance.

BALLY'S   Bally's **Avenue Shoppes** consist of around 20 emporia offering, you know, stuff (kitschy card-shop knickknacks and the like). In addition, there are several gift shops, art galleries, and a pool-wear shop. There are blackjack tables and slot and video-poker machines right in the mall, as well as a race and sports book. You can dispatch the kids to a video arcade here while you shop (or gamble). A recent addition of a walkway to neighboring hotel Paris features more stores and restaurants.

BELLAGIO   The Via Bellagio collection of stores isn't as big as some of the other megahotel shopping arcades, but here it's definitely quality over quantity. It's a veritable roll call of glossy magazine ads: Armani, Prada, Chanel, Tiffany, Hermès, Fred Leighton, Gucci, and Moschino. That's it. You need anything else? Well, yes—money. If you can afford this stuff, good for you, you lucky dog. (Actually, we've discovered affordable, good-taste items in every store here, from Tiffany's $30 silver key chains to $100 Prada business-card holders.) A nice touch is a parking lot by the far entrance to Via Bellagio, so you need not navigate the great distance from Bellagio's main parking structure; instead, you can simply pop in and pick up a little something.

CAESARS PALACE   Since 1978, Caesars has had an impressive arcade of shops called the **Appian Way,** highlighted by an immense white Carrara-marble replica of Michelangelo's *David* standing more than 18 feet high. All in all, a respectable grouping of hotel shops, and an expansion is in the works.

But in the hotel's tradition of constantly surpassing itself, in 1992 Caesars inaugurated the fabulous **Forum Shops** ⚔, an independently operated 250,000-square-foot Rodeo-Drive-meets-the-Roman-Empire affair complete with a 48-foot triumphal arch entranceway, a painted Mediterranean sky that changes as the day progresses from rosy-tinted dawn to twinkling evening stars, acres of marble, lofty Corinthian columns with gold capitals, and a welcoming goddess of fortune under a central dome. The architecture and sculpture span a period from 300 B.C. to A.D. 1700, so you've got all your ancient Italian cityscape clichés. Then there is the Festival Fountain, where some seemingly immovable "marble" Animatronic statues of Bacchus (slightly in his cups), a lyre-playing Apollo, Plutus, and Venus come to life for a 7-minute revel with dancing waters and high-tech laser-light effects. The shows take place every hour on the hour. The whole thing is pretty incredible, but also very Vegas—particularly the Bacchus show, which is truly frightening and bizarre. Even if you don't like shopping, it's worth the stroll just to giggle.

There are more than 70 prestigious emporia here, including Louis Vuitton, Plaza Escada, Bernini, Christian Dior, A/X Armani Exchange, bebe, Caché, Gucci, Ann Taylor, and Gianni Versace, along with many other clothing, shoe, and jewelry stores.

In 1998 the Forum Shops added an extension. The centerpiece is a giant **Roman Hall,** featuring a 50,000-gallon circular aquarium and another fountain that also comes to life with a show involving fire (don't stand too close—it gets really hot), dancing waters, and Animatronic figures, as the mythical continent of Atlantis rises and falls every hour. The production values are much higher than those of the Bacchus extravaganza, but this "performance" takes itself more seriously, so the giggle factor remains. The hall is also the entrance to the **Race for Atlantis IMAX 3-D ride** (p. 183).

In this shopping area, you'll find a number of significant stores, including a DKNY, Emporio Armani, Niketown, Fendi, Polo for Ralph Lauren, Guess, Virgin Megastore, and FAO Schwarz. Do go see the latter, as it is fronted by a gigantic Trojan horse, in which you can clamber around, while its head moves and smoke comes out its nostrils. We love it. Also in the shops are Wolfgang Puck's Chinois, a Cheesecake Factory, and a Caviartorium, where you can sample all kinds of varieties of high-priced fish eggs. As if that weren't enough, by fall 2004, yet another expansion will be open, with a three-story glass-walled entrance right on the Strip (phew, that walk was really getting on our nerves), and an additional 175,000 feet of retail space.

The majority of Caesars Palace's shops are open Sunday to Thursday from 10am to 11pm, Friday and Saturday from 10am to midnight.

CIRCUS CIRCUS   There are about 15 shops between the casino and the Adventuredome (p. 195), offering a wide selection of gifts and sundries, logo items, toys and games, jewelry, liquor, resort apparel for the entire family, T-shirts, homemade fudge/candy/soft ice cream, and, fittingly, clown dolls and puppets. Adjacent to the Adventuredome, there's a newer shopping arcade (with the usual souvenir stores and such) themed as a European village, with cobblestone walkways, fake woods, and so forth, decorated with replicas of vintage circus posters.

EXCALIBUR   For the most part, the shops of **"the Realm"** reflect the hotel's medieval theme. Dragon's Lair, for example, features items ranging from pewter swords and shields to full suits of armor, and Merlin's Mystic Shop carries crystals, luck charms, and gargoyles. Other shops carry more conventional wares— gifts, candy, jewelry, women's clothing, and Excalibur logo items. At Fantasy Faire, you can have your photo taken in Renaissance attire. And most important, they have a branch of that medieval staple—Krispy Kreme donuts!

THE FLAMINGO LAS VEGAS   The **Crystal Court** shopping promenade here accommodates men's and women's clothing/accessories stores, gift shops, and a variety of other emporia selling jewelry, beachwear, Southwestern crafts, fresh-baked goods, logo items, children's gifts, toys, and games.

HARRAH'S   Harrah's has a small outdoor shopping promenade called **Carnaval Court.** Among the store highlights is a Ghirardelli chocolate store, a branch of the famous San Francisco–based chocolate company. This store is remarkably like a smaller version of the one in San Francisco (alas, without the vats of liquid chocolate being mixed up), and in addition to candy, you can get a variety of delicious sundaes and other ice-cream treats. Other stores include the Carnaval Market and Wine and Spirits shops, perfect for creating your own outdoor picnic feast.

LUXOR   The **Giza Galleria** is a 20,000-square-foot shopping arcade with eight full shops. Most of the stores emphasize clothing. Adjacent is the Cairo Bazaar, a trinket shop.

MGM GRAND   The hotel's **Star Lane Shops** include more than a dozen upscale emporia lining the corridors en route from the monorail entrance. And it's here that you can still find the semi-banished figures from the hotel's original *Wizard of Oz* diorama. **Studio Walk** is another shopping area adjacent to the main casino, featuring some upscale boutiques and several restaurants.

MONTE CARLO   An arcade of retail shops here includes several upscale clothing, timepiece, eyewear, and gift boutiques plus a Lance Burton magic-paraphernalia shop. Of course if that's not enough for you, this is where you can catch the 24-hour tram to Bellagio and really get your shopping action going.

RIO   The 60,000-square-foot **Masquerade Village** is a nicely executed shopping arcade at Rio. It's done as a European village, and is two stories tall, featuring a wide variety of shops including the nation's largest Nicole Miller, Speedo, and the N'awlins store, which includes "authentic" voodoo items, Mardi Gras masks, and so forth.

THE RIVIERA   The Riviera has a fairly extensive shopping arcade comprising art galleries, jewelers, and shops specializing in women's shoes and handbags, clothing for the entire family, furs, gifts, logo items, toys, phones and electronic gadgets, and chocolates.

STRATOSPHERE   The internationally themed (though in a high-school production kind of way, compared to what's over at Aladdin and The Venetian) second-floor **Tower Shops** promenade, housing more than 40 stores, is entered via an escalator from the casino. Some shops are in "Paris," along the Rue Lafayette and Avenue de l'Opéra (there are replicas of the Eiffel Tower and Arc de Triomphe in this section). Others occupy Hong Kong and New York City streetscapes.

TREASURE ISLAND   Treasure Island's shopping promenade—doubling as a portrait gallery of famed buccaneers—has wooden ship figureheads and battling pirates suspended from its ceiling. Emporia here include the Treasure Island Store (your basic hotel gift/sundry shop, also offering much pirate-themed merchandise). The Crow's Nest, en route to the Mirage monorail, carries Cirque du Soleil logo items. Cirque du Soleil and *Mystère* logo wares are also sold in a shop near the ticket office in the hotel.

THE VENETIAN ⍟   The **Grand Canal Shoppes** are a direct challenge to Caesars Palace's shopping eminence. As in the Forum Shops, you stroll through a re-created Italian village—in this case, more or less Renaissance-era Venice, complete with a painted, cloud-studded blue sky overhead, and a canal right down the center on which gondoliers float and sing. Pay them ($12) and you can take a lazy float down and back, serenaded by your boatman (actors hired especially for this purpose and with accents perfect enough to fool Roberto Benigni). As you pass by, under and over bridges, flower girls will serenade you and courtesans will flirt with you, and you may have an encounter with a famous Venetian or two, as Marco Polo discusses his travels, and Casanova exerts his famous charm. The stroll (or float) ends at a miniature (though not by all that much) version of St. Mark's Square, the central landmark of Venice. Here, you'll find opera singers, strolling musicians, glass blowers, and other bustling marketplace activity. It's all most ambitious and beats the heck out of Animatronic statues.

The Shoppes are accessible directly from outside (so you don't have to navigate miles of casino and other clutter), via a grand staircase whose ceiling features more of those impressive hand-painted art re-creations. It's quite smashing. The Venetian's "Phase Two" hotel addition will eventually adjoin the Shoppes at the far end of St. Mark's Square.

Oh, the shops themselves? The usual high- and medium-end brand names: Jimmy Choo, Mikimoto, Movado, Davidoff, Lana Marks, Kieselstein-Cord, Donna Karan, Oliver & Col, Ludwig Reiter, Kenneth Cole, Ann Taylor, BCBG, bebe, Banana Republic, Rockport, and more, plus Venetian glass and paper shops. Madame Tussaud's waxworks (p. 182) is also located here, and so is the Canyon Ranch Spa Club.

4 Vintage Clothing

The Attic   The Attic shares a large space with Cafe Neon, a coffeehouse that serves Greek-influenced cafe food (so you can raise your blood sugar after a long stretch of shopping), and a comedy-club stage; it's also upstairs from an attempt at a weekly club (as of this writing, the Sat-night Underworld). The store itself, former star of a Visa commercial, offers plenty of clothing choices on many racks. During a recent visit, a man came in asking for a poodle skirt for his 8-year-old. They had one. Open Monday through Thursday from 10am until 5pm, Friday from 10am until 6pm, Saturday from 11am until 6pm, and closed Sunday. 1018 S. Main St. © 702/388-4088. www.theatticlasvegas.com.

Buffalo Exchange   This is actually a branch of a chain of stores spread out across the western United States. If the chain part worries you, don't let it—this merchandise doesn't feel processed. Staffed by plenty of incredibly hip alt-culture kids (ask them what's happening in town during your visit), it is stuffed with dresses, shirts, pants, and so forth. You can easily go in one day and come out with 12 fabulous new outfits, but you can just as easily go in and come up dry. But it's still probably the most reliable of the local vintage shops. The store is open Monday through Saturday from 11am to 8pm and Sunday from noon until 7pm. 4110 S. Maryland Pkwy. (at Flamingo Rd.). © 702/791-3960. www.buffaloexchange.com/loc_lasvegas.htm.

5 Souvenirs

The **Arts Factory Complex,** 103 E. Charleston Blvd. (© 702/382-3886), has a gift shop full of pink flamingos and Vegas-specific items. There should be something here for every camp fancy.

If you prefer your souvenirs to be less deliberately ironic, head over to the **Bonanza Gift and Souvenir Shop,** 2460 Las Vegas Blvd. S. (© 702/384-0005). We looked, and we felt the tackiest item available was the pair of earrings made out of poker chips.

For reverent camp, encrusted with sequins, do take a peek at the **Liberace Museum gift store,** 1775 E. Tropicana Ave. (© 702/798-5595). Encourage them to get even more out there (don't you think they should add Liberace mouse pads and screensavers?).

If you like your souvenirs with more style (spoilsports), **Cirque de Soleil's O** has a gift shop in Bellagio, 3600 Las Vegas Blvd. S. (© 702/693-7444), with Cirque-specific articles, but also fanciful pottery, masks, and other curiosities.

6 Reading Material: Used Books, Comics & Gambler Books

USED BOOKS

Albion Books *Value*   Six thousand square feet of used books, including first editions, vintage children's books, pop and sci-fi, pulp fiction, and bestsellers, both hard and paperback. You're welcome to take a seat and browse through your finds before purchasing. Open daily from 10am until 6pm. 2466 E. Desert Inn Dr. 702/792-9554.

Dead Poet Books *Finds*   The dead poet in question was the man from whose estate the owners bought their start-up stock. He had such good taste in books that they "fell in love with him" and wanted to name the store in his memory. Just one problem—they never did get his name. So they just called him "the dead poet." His legacy continues at this book-lover's haven. Open Monday through Saturday from 10am until 6pm and Sunday from noon to 5pm. 3874 W. Sahara Ave. (corner of Valley View, near Raley's Supermarket). © 702/227-4070.

LAS VEGAS SPECIALTY BOOKSTORES

Gambler's Book Shop   Here you can buy a book on any system ever devised to beat casino odds. Owner Edna Luckman carries more than 4,000 gambling-related titles, including many out-of-print books, computer software, and videotapes. She describes her store as a place where "gamblers, writers, researchers, statisticians, and computer specialists can meet and exchange information." On request, knowledgeable clerks provide on-the-spot expert advice on handicapping the ponies and other aspects of sports betting. The store's motto is "knowledge is protection." Open Monday through Saturday from 9am until 5pm; closed Sunday. 630 S. 11th St. (just off Charleston Blvd.). © 800/522-1777 or 702/382-7555. www.gamblersbook.com.

Gamblers General Store   A gambler's paradise stocked with a massive book collection, both antique and current slot machines, gaming tables (blackjack, craps, and so on), roulette wheels, collectible chips, casino dice, classic Vegas photos, and a ton of gaming-related souvenirs. Open daily from 9am to 5pm. 800 S. Main St. (Downtown). © 800/322-2447 or 702/382-9903. www.gamblersgeneralstore.com.

COMIC BOOKS

Alternate Reality Comics   The best place in Vegas for all your comic-book needs. They have a nearly comprehensive selection, with a heavy emphasis on underground comics. But don't worry—the superheroes are here too. Open Monday through Saturday from 11am until 7pm, Sunday from noon to 6pm. 4800 S. Maryland Pkwy. © 702/736-3673. http://altrealitycomics.com/NewFiles/home.html.

7 Candy

M&M World *(Kids)*   What can one do when faced with a wall of M&Ms in colors never before seen by man or woman (black! white! gray!)? Overpriced? Yeah! Who cares? There are doodads galore, replete with the M&M logo, and a surprisingly enjoyable short film and comedy routine, ostensibly about the "history" of the candy, but really just a cute little adventure with a decent budget behind it. Open Sunday through Thursday from 9am until midnight, Friday and Saturday from 9am until 1am. In the Showcase Mall, 3785 Las Vegas Blvd. S. (just north of the MGM Grand Hotel). © 702/736-7611.

8 Antiques

Antiques in Vegas? You mean really old slot machines, or the people playing the really old slot machines?

Actually, Vegas has quite a few antiques stores—nearly two dozen—of consistent quality and price, nearly all located within a few blocks of each other. We have one friend, someone who takes interior design very seriously, who comes straight to Vegas for most of her best finds (you should see her antique chandelier collection!).

To get to this antiquing mecca, start in the middle of the **1600 block of East Charleston Boulevard** and keep driving east. The little stores, nearly all in old houses dating from the '30s, line each side of the street. Or you can stop in at **Silver Horse Antiques,** 1651 E. Charleston Blvd. (© 702/385-2700), and pick up a map to almost all of the locations, with phone numbers and hours of operation.

Antique Sampler Shoppes   Head here for everything under one roof. More than 200 small antiques shops sell their wares in this mall, which offers a diversity of antiques ranging from exquisite Indian bird cages to *Star Wars* memorabilia (let's not call those sorts of items "antiques" but rather "nostalgia"). Changing selections mean they can never guarantee what will be available, but you can probably count on antique clothing and shoes, lamps, silver, decorative plates and china, old sewing machines, antique furniture, and '50s prom dresses. The displays are well labeled and well laid out, making it easy to take in all the antiques. The oldest antiques are from the mid-1800s and range in price from $100 to $4,000. Open

Monday through Saturday from 10am until 7pm, Sunday from noon until 7pm. 6115 W. Tropicana Ave. © **702/368-1170**. www.antiquesampler.com.

Antiques at the Market   A brand-new antiques minimall (for lack of a better phrase) with a number of individuals operating stalls under one roof. Open Monday through Saturday from 10am until 6pm, Sunday from noon until 5pm. 6663 S. Eastern Ave. (between Sunset and Warm Springs Rd.). © **702/307-3960**. www.antiquesatthe market.com.

Antique Square   A cruddy-looking collection of stores in several remodeled houses arranged in a square. But every good antiques shopper knows that these kinds of crammed junk stores are the places to find real treasures, and to do real antiques hunting (because once they've been really picked through and prettily displayed by pros, you can kiss bargains and real finds goodbye). Individual store hours vary but most are closed on Sunday and Monday. 2014–2034 Charleston Blvd. (at Eastern Ave.). © **702/471-6500**.

Red Rooster Antique Mall   Sort of a combination of the two preceding entries; older and battered, but also featuring those individual stalls. But with nearby highway construction ongoing (for years now!), it's very hard to get to, so bear that in mind if work is still going on. Individual store hours vary. 307 W. Charleston Blvd. (at I-15). © **702/382-5253**.

9 Wigs

Serge's Showgirl Wigs   Oh, you probably thought all those showgirls just naturally had bountiful thick manes. Sorry to burst your bubble. Actually, we aren't—if you don't know it's all illusion, you ought to. Meanwhile, if you have a desire to look like a showgirl yourself (and why not?), come to Serge's, which for 23 years has been supplying Vegas's wiggy needs, with more than 2,000 wigs to choose from. This, by the way, is not just for showgirls or the similarly delusional. Not only can wigs be fun for everyone (we treasure our own turquoise number) but at least one sassy gal we know with thinning hair issues recently bought two natural-looking models, and reports that the sales staff was as nice and helpful as could be. Wigs range in price from $130 to over $1,500, depending on quality and realness, and you can pick from Dolly Parton's wig line or get something custom-made. They also make hairpieces and toupees and carry hair-care products. Open Monday through Saturday from 10am until 5:30pm.

And, if the prices at Serge's are too rich to bring your fantasy alive, right across the way is **Serge's Showgirl Wigs outlet,** with prices running from a more reasonable $60 to $70. 953 E. Sahara Ave. no. A-2. © **702/732-1015**. www.showgirlwigs.com.

10

Las Vegas After Dark

You will not lack for things to do at night in Vegas. This is a town that truly comes alive only after dark. Don't believe us? Just look at the difference between the Strip during the day, when it's kind of dingy and nothing special, and at night, when the lights hit and the place glows in all its glory. Night is when it's happening in this 24-hour town. In fact, most bars and clubs don't even get going until close to midnight. That's because it's only around then that all the restaurant workers and people connected with the shows get off the clock and can go out and play themselves. It's extraordinary. Just sit down in a bar at 11pm; it's empty. You might well conclude it's dead. Return in 2 hours and you'll find it completely full and jumping.

But you also won't lack for things to do before 11pm. There are shows all over town, ranging from traditional magic shows to cutting-edge acts such as *Mystère*. The showgirls remain, topless and otherwise; Las Vegas revues are what happened to vaudeville, by the way, as chorus girls do their thing in between jugglers, comics, magicians, singers, and specialty acts of dubious category. Even the topless shows are tame; all that changes is that the already scantily clad showgirls are even more so.

Every hotel has at least one lounge, usually offering live music. But the days of fabulous Vegas lounge entertainment, when the lounge acts were sometimes of better quality than the headliners (and headliners like Sinatra would join the lounge acts on stage between their own sets), are gone.

Most of what remains is homogeneous and bland, and serves best as a brief respite or background noise. On the other hand, finding the most awful lounge act in town can be a rewarding pursuit of its own.

Vegas still does attract some dazzling headliner entertainment in its showrooms and arenas. Madonna's 2001 show commanded the top prices on her tour, Bruce Springsteen played his first Vegas show ever in early 2000, while Bette Midler did an HBO special from the MGM Grand in early 1997 (and her Millennium show at Mandalay Bay), U2 started their Pop-Mart tour at UNLV's stadium, the Rolling Stones played both the MGM Grand and the Hard Rock Hotel's The Joint, Pavarotti inaugurated Mandalay Bay's Arena, with Bob Dylan doing the same for the House of Blues, and Cher opened up The Venetian with a rare live performance. It is still a badge of honor for comedians to play Vegas, and there is almost always someone of marquee value playing one showroom or the other.

Admission to shows runs the gamut, from about $28 for *An Evening at La Cage* (a female-impersonator show at The Riviera) to $90 and more for top headliners or *Siegfried & Roy.* Prices occasionally include two drinks or, in rare instances, dinner.

To find out who'll be performing during your stay and for up-to-date listings of shows (prices change, shows close), you can call the various hotels, using their toll-free numbers. Or call the **Las Vegas Convention and Visitors Authority** (© 877/VISIT-LV)

Moments Lounge Lizard Supreme

All those faux-hipster artists doing woeful lounge-act characters in Hollywood and New York only wish they could be Mr. Cook E. Jarr, whose sincerity and obvious drive to entertain puts mere performance artists to shame. With George Hamilton's tan, Cher's first shag haircut (it's certainly not his factory-original coif), and a bottomless, borderless catalog of rock, pop, soul, swing, and standard favorites, he's more Vegas than Wayne Newton.

Cook has a cult following of blue-collar casino denizens and the youthful cocktail set, who listen enraptured as he plays human jukebox, complete with karaoke-style backing recordings, terrible jokes, an array of disco-era lights, and (his favorite) a smoke machine. He's actually a solid, throaty singer, with a gift for vocal mimicry as he moves from Ben E. King to Bee Gees to Tony Bennett turf. And his tribute the night Sinatra died—a version of "My Way" in which he voiced, alternately, Sammy, Dino, and Elvis welcoming Ol' Blue Eyes to Heaven—was priceless.

He moves around a lot but lately you can often catch him on Friday and Saturday nights, late, at **Harrah's Carnaval Court Lounge** at 3475 Las Vegas Blvd. S. (© **702/369-5222**). Don't miss him! (And if he has left there by the time you read this, try to track him down.)

and ask them to send you a free copy of *Showguide* or *What's On in Las Vegas* (one or both of which will probably be in your hotel room). You can also check out what's playing at **www.vegas freedom.com**. It's best to plan well ahead if you have your heart set on seeing one of the most popular shows, or catching a major headliner.

The hotel entertainment options described below include information on ticket prices, what's included in that price (drinks, dinner, taxes, and/or gratuities), showroom policies (whether it's preassigned or maitre d' seating, and smoking policies), and how to make reservations. Whenever possible, reserve in advance, especially on weekends and holidays. If the showroom has **maitre d' seating** (as opposed to preassigned seats), you may want to tip him to upgrade your seat. A tip of $15 to $20 per couple will usually do the trick at a major show, less at a small showroom. An alternative to tipping the maitre d' is to wait until the captain shows you to

your seat. Perhaps it will be adequate, in which case you've saved some money. If not, you can offer the captain a tip for a better seat. If you do plan to tip, have the money ready; maitre d's and captains tend to get annoyed if you fumble around for it. They have other people to seat. You can also tip with casino chips (from the hotel casino where the show is taking place only) in lieu of cash. Whatever you tip, the proper etiquette is to do it rather subtly—a kind of palm-to-palm action. There's really no reason for this, since everyone knows what's going on, but being blatant is in poor taste. Arrive early at maitre d' shows to get the best choice of seats.

If you buy tickets for an assigned-seat show in person, you can look over a seating chart. Avoid sitting right up by the stage if possible, especially for big-production shows. Dance numbers are better viewed from the middle of the theater. With headliners, you might like to sit up close.

Note: All of these caveats and instructions aside, most casino-hotel showrooms offer good visibility from just about every seat in the house.

If you prefer alternative or real rock music, your choices used to be limited, but that's all changing. More rock bands are coming to town, attracted to the House of Blues or the Hard Rock Hotel's The Joint, so that means you can actually see folks like Marilyn Manson and Beck in Vegas. But otherwise, the alternative club scene in town is no great shakes. Check out the listings below for bars and coffeehouses, several of which offer live alternative or blues music. If you want to know what's playing during your stay, consult the local free alternative papers: the *Las Vegas Weekly,* formerly *Scope* magazine (biweekly, with great club and bar descriptions in their listings) and *City Life* (weekly, with no descriptions but comprehensive listings of what's playing where all over town). Both can be picked up at restaurants, bars, record and music stores, and hip retail stores. Or you can call *Las Vegas Weekly* directly; act nice and they just might give you a tip on the spot. If you're looking for good alt-culture tips, try asking the cool staff at the **Buffalo Exchange** vintage-clothing store (© **702/791-3960**); they have their fingers right on the pulse of the underground.

In addition to the listings below, consider the **Fremont Street Experience,** described on p. 179.

Be aware that there is a curfew law in Vegas: anyone under 18 is forbidden from being on the Strip without a parent after 9pm on weekends and holidays. In the rest of the county, minors cannot be out without parents after 10pm on school nights, and midnight on weekends.

1 What's Playing Where

It used to be that a show was an essential part of the Vegas experience. Back in those days, a show was pretty simple: A bunch of scantily (and we mean scantily) clad showgirls paraded around while a comedian engaged in some raunchy patter. The showgirls are still here and still scantily clad (though not as often topless; guess cable TV has taken some of that thrill away), but the productions around them have gotten impossibly elaborate. And they have to be, because they have to compete with a free dancing water fountains show held several times nightly right on the Strip. Not to mention a volcano, a Mardi Gras parade in the sky, lounge acts galore, and the occasional imploding building. All for free.

The big resort hotels, in keeping with their general over-the-top tendencies, are pouring mountains of money into high-spectacle extravaganzas, luring big-name acts into decades-long residencies and surrounding them with special effects that would put some Hollywood movies to shame. Which is not to say the results are Broadway quality—they're big, cheesy fun. Still, with the exception of the astonishing work done by the Cirque du Soleil productions, most of what passes for a "show" in Vegas is just a flashier revue, with a predictable lineup of production number/magic act/production number/acrobatics/production number.

Unfortunately, along with big budgets and big goals come big-ticket prices. Sure, you can still take the whole family of four to a show for under $100, but you're not going to get the same production values that you'd get by splurging on a Cirque du Soleil show. Which is not to say you always get what you pay for: There are some reasonably priced shows that are considerably better values than their more expensive counterparts.

Note: Although every effort has been made to keep up with the volatile Las Vegas show scene, keep in mind that the following reviews may not be indicative of the actual show you'll see, but the basic concept and idea will be the same. What's more, the show itself may have closed, so it's a good idea to always call the venue and check.

The following section will describe each of the major production shows currently playing in Las Vegas, arranged alphabetically by the title of the production. But first, here's a handy list arranged by hotel:

- **Bally's:** *Jubilee!* (Las Vegas–style revue)
- **Bellagio:** Cirque du Soleil's *O* (unique circus-meets-performance-art theatrical experience)
- **Caesars Palace:** *Celine Dion* (music and variety)
- **Excalibur:** *Tournament of Kings* (medieval-themed revue)
- **The Flamingo Las Vegas:** *Second City Improv* (improvisational comedy)
- **Harrah's:** *Clint Holmes* (music and variety)
- **Imperial Palace:** *Legends in Concert* (musical impersonators)
- **Luxor:** Blue Man Group: *Live at Luxor* (hilarious performance art)
- **Mandalay Bay:** *Mamma Mia!* (a musical that features ABBA songs and was a great hit in London and on Broadway)
- **The Mirage:** *Siegfried & Roy* (magical extravaganza); *Danny Gans* (impressions)
- **Monte Carlo:** Lance Burton: *Master Magician* (magic show and revue)
- **New York–New York:** Cirque du Soleil's *Zumanity* (adults-only provocative revue)
- **The Riviera:** *An Evening at La Cage* (female impersonators), *Crazy Girls* (sexy Las Vegas–style revue), and *Splash* (aquatic revue)
- **Stratosphere Casino Hotel & Tower:** *American Superstars* (an impression-filled production show) and *Viva Las Vegas* (Las Vegas–style revue)
- **Treasure Island:** Cirque du Soleil's *Mystère* (unique circus performance)
- **Tropicana:** *Folies Bergère* (Las Vegas–style revue)

2 The Major Production Shows

This category covers all of the major Las Vegas production shows and a few of the minor ones as well. In addition to the following, we also recommend **Rita Rudner**'s stand-up comedy at New York–New York, and we urge you to stay away from the musical family the **Scintas** at the Rio; a fossilized Vegas act full of near-parody-level lounge singing and jokes at the expense of every ethnicity, handicap, and sexual orientation out there.

Note: Shows can close without warning, even ones that have been running just shy of forever, so please call first. Note also that some ticket prices may not include tax or drinks, so you might also check for those potential hidden costs.

> ⌒ *Value* **HOT TIP!**
>
> **Tickets2Nite** is a new-ish daily service that puts any unsold seats for that evening on sale, starting at 2pm, for—get this!—*half price.* Hot diggity! Of course, there are some drawbacks. It's rare and downright unlikely that really ultra-super-duper shows are ever going to have unsold seats (because the hotel will just sell them to the always-waiting-and-happy-to-pay-full-price stand-by line), but you'd be shocked at the range otherwise, from basic crap to stuff that we would recommend even at full price (they aren't allowed to say on the record which shows' tickets often come up for sale). Alas, the very nature of the service means you can't plan; you have to stand in line and take your chances starting at 2pm (we advise getting in line even earlier than that). So if you have your heart set on white tigers, don't rely on Tickets2Nite, but, if like a good gambler, you like taking chances, head for 3785 Las Vegas Blvd. S. (in the Showcase Mall Booth).

American Superstars   One of a number of celebrity-impersonator shows (well, it's cheaper than getting the real headliners), *American Superstars* is one of the few shows where the impersonators actually sing live. Five performers do their thing; the celebs impersonated vary depending on the evening.

A typical Friday night featured Gloria Estefan, Charlie Daniels, Madonna, Michael Jackson, and Diana Ross and the Supremes. (And they recently added Christina Aguilera and Ricky Martin.) The performers won't be putting the originals out of work any time soon, but they aren't bad. Actually, they were closer in voice than in looks to the celeb in question (half the black performers were played by white actors), which is an unusual switch for Vegas impersonators. The "Charlie Daniels" actually proved to be a fine fiddler in his own right and was the hands-down crowd favorite. The live band actually had a look-alike of their own: Kato Kaelin on drums (it's good that he's getting work). The youngish crowd (by Vegas standards) included a healthy smattering of children and seemed to find no faults with the production. The action is also shown on two large, and completely unnecessary, video screens flanking the stage, so you don't have to miss a moment. In the Stratosphere Casino Hotel & Tower, 2000 Las Vegas Blvd. S. (ℂ) **800/99-TOWER** or 702/380-7711. Tickets $36 adults, $25 children 5–12, show and buffet package $44. Sun–Tues at 7pm; Wed and Fri–Sat at 7 and 10pm; dark Thurs.

Blue Man Group: *Live at Luxor*   Are they blue? Indeed they are—three hairless, nonspeaking men dipped in azure paint, doing decidedly odd stunts with marshmallows, art supplies, audience members, tons of paper, and an amazing array of percussion instruments fashioned fancifully from PVC piping. If that doesn't sound very Vegas, well, it's not. It's the latest franchise of a New York–born performance-art troupe that seems to have slipped into town through a side door opened by Cirque de Soleil's groundbreaking successes. Don't get the wrong idea: This is no Cirque clone. There are no acrobatics or flowing choreography, no attempt to create an alternate universe, just a series of surreal, unconnected bits. But even if the whole is no greater than the sum of the parts, the parts are pretty great themselves. It's funny in the weirdest and most unexpected ways and the crowd is usually roaring by the end. Fans of typical Vegas shows may leave scratching their heads, but we are glad there is another color in the Vegas entertainment spectrum. In Luxor Las Vegas, 3900 Las Vegas Blvd. S. (ℂ) **702/262-4000.** Tickets $88–$94. Tues at 7pm; Sun, Mon, and Wed–Fri 7 and 10pm; Sat 4, 7, and 10pm.

Celine Dion   Here's the hottest ticket in town, and no wonder: It's genuinely unprecedented for a star of this magnitude to take up a 3-year residency in a Vegas show—not to mention a Vegas show designed, theater and all, just for her, and a show with a subsequent $150 million price tag, and ticket prices that seem nearly that high. For those of you with (understandable) sticker shock, you can take some comfort in the fact that the money is all on the stage here. Some of that cost is represented by Our Star's salary, certainly, but the rest is present in one magnificent theater (battling it out with *O*'s home at the Bellagio for finest in town), where, thanks to steep stadium seating, no seat is less than 150 feet from the stage. (Though in some cases, that means straight up, so you decide if that's really a good thing.) And the rest is quite evident in stunning staging, including a heralded enormous LED screen that allows for the most extraordinary special effects in town. Along with the sweeping landscapes, storms, and occasional video close-ups of the action brought to you on the screen, you can add the usual Cirque du Soleil touches (the show's director/producer is Franco Dragone, who previously brought this town *O* and *Mystère*), which means dancers (the finest of any show in Vegas) moving enigmatically, plus blooming trees, flying pianos, giant chandeliers, and other artistic touches straight out of Chagall or Magritte.

None of it even remotely relates to whichever song they occur during, but no matter. The Diva herself silences early negative predictions by appearing on stage at least 90% of the time, and generally working her tail off when she's there. Her pearly tones are right on the money. Are they live? Probably not always, but such issues are no longer relevant in the context of modern pop concerts where so many of today's performers rely on tape. More to the point is that no matter how visually stunning or remarkably staged, this is nonetheless a Celine Dion concert, and nothing else. That's great news if you are a fan, but not if you aren't. (It's worth noting that in an effort to make this appeal to audience members beyond her fan base, she's included covers ranging from Sinatra to Stevie Wonder, and that these songs are the least successfully performed.) This won't convert anyone, probably, despite her genuine best efforts—she's got a heck of a voice and she is a true entertainer, in the best sense of the tradition, if not the most charismatic one. And perhaps also not the most thoughtful one; did she notice that the Wonder song begins "Looking back on when I was a little nappy headed boy?" In Caesars Palace, 3570 Las Vegas Blvd. S. ℂ **877/CELINE-4.** Tickets $88–$200 (excluding tax). Wed–Sun 8:30pm.

Cirque du Soleil's *Mystère* *Kids*   The in-house ads for *Mystère* (say miss-*tair*) say "Words don't do it justice," and for once, that's not just hype. The show is so visual that trying to describe it is a losing proposition. And simply calling it

---

⌒*Tips*   Coolest House in Town?

The Ice House, a new $5 million, two-story, 12,800-square-foot restaurant, bar, and gaming facility, is the latest sign of Downtown's upswing. Scheduled to open in summer 2003, the Art Deco–inspired building will evoke images of South Beach rather than a Downtown dive, with an interior accented by retrospective photos of old Vegas and '60s-style furniture. Both of the Ice House's two lounges will sport frozen bar-tops made of solid ice to keep drinks cold. Down a drink, grab a bite, and then play video poker or watch one of the 13 42-inch HDTV plasma screen televisions.

> **Kids Family-Friendly Shows**
>
> Appropriate shows for kids, all described in this chapter, include the following:
>
> - *Tournament of Kings* at Excalibur (p. 256)
> - *Siegfried & Roy* at The Mirage (p. 255)
> - **Lance Burton** at the Monte Carlo (p. 253)
> - **Cirque du Soleil's** *Mystère* at Treasure Island (p. 248)

a circus is like calling the Hope Diamond a gem, or the Taj Mahal a building. It's accurate but, as the ad says, doesn't begin to do it justice.

Cirque du Soleil began in Montreal as a unique circus experience, not only shunning traditional animal acts in favor of gorgeous feats of human strength and agility, but also adding elements of the surreal and the absurd. The result seems like a collaboration between Salvador Dalí and Luis Buñuel, with a few touches by Magritte and choreography by Twyla Tharp. MGM MIRAGE has built the troupe its own theater, an incredible space with an enormous dome and super-hydraulics that allow for the Cirque performers to fly in space. Or so it seems.

While part of the fun of the early Cirque was seeing what amazing stuff they could do on a shoestring, seeing what they can do with virtually unlimited funds is spectacular. Cirque took full advantage of MGM MIRAGE's largesse, and their art only rose with their budget. The show features one simply unbelievable act after another (seemingly boneless contortionists and acrobats, breathtakingly beautiful aerial maneuvers), interspersed with Dadaist/commedia dell'arte clowns, and everyone clad in costumes like nothing you've ever seen before. All this and a giant snail!

The show is dreamlike, suspenseful, funny, erotic, mesmerizing, and just lovely. At times, you might even find yourself moved to tears. For some children, however, it might be a bit too sophisticated and arty. Even if you've seen Cirque before, it's worth coming to check out, thanks to the large production values. It's a world-class show, no matter where it's playing. That this arty and intellectual show is playing in Vegas is astonishing. In Treasure Island, 3300 Las Vegas Blvd. S. (C) **800/288-7206** or 702/894-7722. www.cirquedusoleil.com. Tickets $80 (excluding tax). Fri–Tues 7:30 and 10:30pm.

Cirque du Soleil's *O* *(Finds)*   How to describe the seemingly indescribable wonder and artistry of Cirque du Soleil's latest and most dazzling display? An Esther Williams–Busby Berkeley spectacular on peyote? A Salvador Dalí painting come to life? A stage show by Fellini? The French troupe has topped itself with this production—and not simply because it's situated its breathtaking acrobatics in, on, around, and above a 1.5-million-gallon pool (*eau*—pronounced *O*—is French for "water"). Even without those impossible feats, this might be worth the price just to see the presentation, a constantly shifting dreamscape tableau that's a marvel of imagination and staging. If you've seen *Mystère* at Treasure Island or other Cirque productions, you'll be amazed that they've once again raised the bar to new heights without losing any of the humor or stylistic trademarks, including the sensuous music. If you've never seen a Cirque show, prepare to have your brain turned inside out. We know—those ticket prices— *ouch*. We want to say that we can guarantee it's worth it, but that's a decision only you can make. (Though no one we've personally sent has come back regretting that they went.) But we can say this: Watch this show, and you know where a good chunk of the money is going (in other words, they spend a bundle nightly to mount this thing). Note that no tank tops, shorts, or sneakers are allowed. In Bellagio, 3600 Las Vegas Blvd. S. ℭ 888/488-7111 or 702/693-7722. Tickets $90–$136 (excluding tax). Wed–Sun 7:30 and 10:30pm.

Cirque du Soleil's *Zumanity*   Surely by now you've gotten the message—*Vegas is not for families anymore.* Need further proof? New York–New York, the hotel most like a theme park, is offering up this, yet another Cirque de Soleil (which started, let's remember, as a circus) show, with all the artistic imagery and astonishing human feats we've come to expect, but this one is . . . topless. Occasionally. We think. It won't open until after we go to press, and in typical Vegas fashion, everyone is being cagey about exactly what is going to take place and how much of it will be bare, but the words "provocative," "arousing," "sensuality," "desire," and best of all, "created for adults over 18" are being thrown around. Also, there is some cabaret stool seating, and, even more tellingly, "Love Seats" and "Duo Sofas." You do the math. While you are doing that, we are getting in line, because anything Cirque does is all right by us. We think. 3790 Las Vegas Blvd. S. (in New York–New York). ℭ 702/740-6969. www.zumanity.com. Tickets $190 (for sofas), $150 (love seats), $75 (theater seats), $55 (cabaret stools), all including tax. Tues–Sat 7:30 and 10:30pm.

Crazy Girls   *Crazy Girls*, presented in an intimate theater, is probably the raciest revue on the Strip. It features sexy showgirls with perfect bodies in erotic song-and-dance numbers enhanced by innovative lighting effects. Think of *Penthouse* poses coming to life. Perhaps it was best summed up by one older man from Kentucky: "It's okay if you like boobs and butt. But most of the girls can't even dance." In The Riviera Hotel & Casino, 2901 Las Vegas Blvd. S. ℭ 877/892-7469 or 702/794-9433. Tickets $33 (excluding tax). Fri–Wed 8 and 9:30pm.

Clint Holmes   Who? "My name is Michael, I've got a nickel." Oh, right. So why should you go? Because you miss, or simply still long for, the days of pure Vegas *entertainers,* you know, guys who sang (competently), told jokes and self-deprecating stories (competently), and dared the audience to love him with great confidence and, well, competence. No tigers, no magic, just a strong band and a strong sense of self—which is interesting as it's been hard to market this guy, because he doesn't offer magic, tigers, or any other kind of flashy gimmick, and has a bit of talent to back up his confident and competent stage manner. You will hear some originals, some covers ("Banana Boat Song," "What Kind of Fool Am I?"), in addition to stories of how Holmes was influenced by Sammy Davis Jr., which explains a lot, and we mean that in a positive way. He's good, but you need to want to see this kind of retro entertainment, and we mean that in a positive way as well. In Harrah's, 3475 Las Vegas Blvd. S. ℭ 800/392-9002. Tickets $60 (excluding tax). Mon–Sat 7:30pm.

Danny Gans: *The Man of Many Voices*   In a town where the consistent sell-outs are costly, elaborate extravaganzas, it's a tribute to Danny Gans's charisma and appeal that his one-man variety act can draw the same crowds with nothing more than a back-up band and a few props. Gans is "the man of many voices"—more than 400 of them—and his show features impressions of 80 different celebrities, usually a different mix each night depending on audience demographics.

The emphasis is on musical impressions (everyone from Sinatra to Springsteen), with some movie scenes (Hepburn and Fonda from *On Golden Pond,* Tom Hanks in *Forrest Gump*) thrown in. A standout (though he doesn't always do it) is "The Twelve Months of Christmas" sung by 12 different celebrities (Paul Lynde, Clint Eastwood, Woody Allen, and so on). Gans's vocal flexibility is impressive, though his impersonations are hit or miss (his Springsteen needs work). That said, when we last saw him, he did a dead-on impression of comedian Jeff Foxworthy that had the crowd rolling, a hilarious bit involving George Burns imitating MC Hammer, and a somewhat freaky, but totally on-target impression of Macy Gray. Truth be told, he's better than his current material (particularly if the mood strikes and he improvises), which is padded with obvious jokes and mawkish sentimentality. Still, he's a consistent crowd-pleaser, and the lack of bombast can be a refreshing change of pace. In The Mirage, 3400 Las Vegas Blvd. S. ℂ 800/963-9634 or 702/792-7777. Tickets $100 (including tax). Tues–Thurs and Sat–Sun 8pm.

An Evening at La Cage   No, it wasn't inspired by the French movie or the recent American remake, or even the Broadway musical. Actually, it's more like the stage show derived from the movie *Priscilla, Queen of the Desert*. Female impersonators dress up as various entertainers (with varying degrees of success) to lip-synch to those celebrity entertainers' greatest hits (with varying degrees of success). The celebs lampooned can include Cher, Bette Midler, Judy Garland, Whitney Houston, Dionne Warwick, and, intriguingly, Michael Jackson. A Joan Rivers impersonator, looking not unlike the original but sounding not at all like her (even with the aid of an odd constant echo), is the hostess, delivering scatological phrases and stale jokes. They do make the most of a tiny stage with some pretty stunning lighting, though the choreography is bland. Still, it's a crowd-pleaser—one couple was back for their fourth visit (all comped, but still). In The Riviera Hotel & Casino, 2901 Las Vegas Blvd. S. ℂ 877/892-7469 or 702/794-9433. Tickets $38 (excluding tax). Wed–Mon 7 and 9pm.

Folies Bergère   The longest-running production show in town has recently undergone a "sexier than ever" face-lift, but the result is far from that. It's more like tamed-down burlesque, as done by a college drama department. Bare breasts pop up (sorry) at odd moments (late shows only): not during the cancan line, but rather during a fashion show and an en-pointe ballet sequence. The effect is neither erotic nor titillating, suggesting only that absent-minded dancers simply forgot to put their shirts on. The dance sequences (more acrobatics than true dance) range from the aforementioned ballet and cancan to jazz and hoedown, and are only occasionally well costumed. A coyly cute '50s striptease number on a *Hollywood Squares*–type set is more successful, as is a clever and funny juggling act (don't miss his finale with the vest and hat). In Tropicana Resort & Casino, 3801 Las Vegas Blvd. S. ℂ 800/829-9034 or 702/739-2411. Tickets $45–$55 (excluding tax). Fri–Wed 7:30 and 10pm.

Jubilee!   A classic Vegas spectacular, crammed with singing, dancing, magic, acrobats, elaborate costumes and sets, and, of course, bare breasts. It's a basic revue, with production numbers featuring homogenized versions of standards (Gershwin, Cole Porter, some Fred Astaire numbers) sometimes sung live, sometimes

---

⟮ *Tips* **Heading Backstage**

If you'd like to take a backstage tour of the *Folies* set, they are scheduled Sunday to Thursday at 12:30, 1:30, and 2:30pm. Tickets cost $2; call the above phone number for details.

12 Inaccuracies in the Movie *Showgirls*

By the showgirls in *Jubilee!*

1. Nomi Malone wouldn't be in a Las Vegas production because she can't sing (or act).
2. Showgirls do not live in trailers.
3. Showgirls aren't discovered in strip bars.
4. Showgirls do not pimp themselves at conventions or trade shows.
5. Hotel owners do not throw lavish cast parties.
6. A lead dancer does not become a celebrity.
7. No one learns a show in a day.
8. Pushing someone down the stairs doesn't get you a lead role—it gets you fired.
9. Ice is used backstage to treat injuries, not to erect nipples.
10. Leaving rehearsal to go to Spago to drink champagne is generally frowned upon.
11. Showgirls are not coke-sniffing, champagne-drinking lesbians.
12. Anyway, showgirls do not drink champagne backstage—we prefer Jack Daniel's!

lip-synched, and always accompanied by lavishly costumed and frequently topless showgirls. Humorous set pieces about Samson and Delilah and the sinking of the *Titanic* (!) show off some pretty awesome sets. (They were doing the *Titanic* long before a certain movie, and recent attendees claimed the ship-sinking effect on stage here was better than the one in the movie.) The finale features aerodynamically impossible feathered and bejeweled costumes and headpieces designed by Bob Mackie. So what if the dancers are occasionally out of step, and the action sometimes veers into the dubious (a Vegas-style revue about a disaster that took more than 1,000 lives?) or even the inexplicable (a finale praising beautiful and bare-breasted girls suddenly stops for three lines of "Somewhere Over the Rainbow"?). In Bally's Las Vegas, 3645 Las Vegas Blvd. S. ✆ **800/237-7469** or 702/739-4567. Tickets $54–$64 (excluding tax). Sat–Thurs 7:30 and 10:30pm.

La Femme!   Further proof that Vegas is trying to distance itself from the "Vegas is for Families" image, Classy Adult Entertainment are the new watchwords in several hotels, with *La Femme!* leading the pack. Allegedly the same show that has been running for years in a famous racy French nightclub, this show is just a bunch of pretty girls taking their clothes off. Except that the girls are smashingly pretty, with the kind of bodies just not found on real live human beings, and they take their clothes off in curious and yes, artistic ways, gyrating on pointe shoes while holding on to ropes or hoops, falling over sofas while lip syncing to French torch songs—in short, it's what striptease ought to be, and by gosh, if strip clubs were this well staged, we'd go to them all the time. But $60 a ticket is a great deal to pay for arty nudie fun, especially when the routines, no matter how clever or how naked (the girls get down to a postage-stamp-size triangle soul patch covering the naughtiest of their bits, so they aren't "nude," but talk about a technicality), start to seem alike after awhile. In the MGM Grand, 3799 Las Vegas Blvd. S. ✆ **800/929-1111** or 702/891-7777. Tickets $59 (excluding tax). Wed–Mon 8:30 and 10:30pm.

Lance Burton: *Master Magician* *(Kids)* *(Value)*   Magic acts are a dime a dozen in Vegas of late. Along with impersonator acts, they seem to have largely replaced the topless showgirls of yore. Most magic shows seem more than a little influenced by the immeasurable success of Siegfried & Roy. So when someone pops up who is original—not to mention charming and, yes, actually good at his job—it comes as a relief. Handsome and folksy (he hails from Lexington, Kentucky), Burton is talented and engaging, for the most part shunning the big-ticket special effects that seem to have swamped most other shows in town. Instead, he offers an extremely appealing production that starts small, with "close-up" magic. These rather lovely tricks, he tells us, are what won him a number of prestigious magic competitions. They are truly extraordinary. (We swear that he tossed a bird up in the air, and the darn thing turned into confetti in front of our eyes. Really.) Burton doesn't have patter, per se, but his dry, laconic, low-key delivery is plenty amusing and contrasts nicely to other performers in town, who seem as if they have been spending way too much time at Starbucks. He does eventually move to bigger illusions, but his manner follows him—he knows the stuff is good, but he also knows the whole thing is a bit silly, so why not have fun with it? His long-time support act is comedian/juggler Michael Goudeau, who is not only perhaps the only genuinely funny and talented support act on the Strip, but he can also juggle a bean bag chair, a chainsaw, and a peanut M&M all at once. His presence is just further proof of how right Burton's show is overall.

All this and extremely comfortable movie-theater-style plush seats with cup holders. And for a most reasonable price. In the Monte Carlo Resort & Casino, 3770 Las Vegas Blvd. S. (C) 877/386-8224 or 702/730-7160. Tickets $55–$60 (excluding tax). Tues and Sat 7 and 10pm, Wed–Fri 7pm.

Legends in Concert   This is a crowd-pleaser, which is probably why it's been running since May 1983. Arguably the best of the Vegas impersonator shows (though it's hard to quantify such things), *Legends* features performers singing live rather than lip-synching. And the performers look remarkably like the originals; free use of video cutting between action on stage and the real performer generally shows what a good simulation the former is. Acts vary from night to night (in a showroom that could use a face-lift) on a nice, large stage with modern hydraulics but twinkle lighting that is stuck in a *Flip Wilson Show* time warp. The personal touches here include scantily clad (but well-choreographed) male and female dancers, and an utterly useless green laser. When we went, the performers included a carbon copy (at least in looks) of the early Little Richard, a crowd-pleasing Shania Twain, an energetic Prince, an appropriately flamboyant Liberace, a striking Bette Midler, and one helluva Elvis impersonator. In Imperial Palace, 3535 Las Vegas Blvd. S. (C) 888/777-7664. Tickets $40 adults (includes 1 drink, tax, and gratuity), $25 children 12 and under. Mon–Sat 7:30 and 10:30pm.

Mac King *(Value)*   One of the best entertainment values in Vegas, this is an afternoon comedy-magic show—and note order of precedence in that introduction. King does magic; thankfully, as far as we are concerned, emphasizing the only kind that's really mind-blowing these days—those close-up tricks that defy your eyes and mind. But he surrounds his tricks with whimsy and wit, and sometimes gut-busting guffaws, which makes you wonder how someone else can still perform stunts with a straight face. (Check out how he takes a $100 bill and—wait, we don't want to give it away, but suffice to say, it involves an old shoe and a Fig Newton and several other unexpected props.) Perfect for the kids, perfect for the budget, perfect timing if you need something in the afternoon before an evening of gambling, dining, and cavorting. Then again, we are rather surprised he's still just an afternoon gig. One day, someone is going to wise up and move him to the big time, and his ticket prices will move up too. So catch him while he's still a bargain. 3475 Las Vegas Blvd. S (in Harrah's). ℂ **800/427-7247**. Tickets $17 (plus tax). Tues–Sat 1 and 3pm.

Mamma Mia! We applaud Mandalay Bay for continuing to try to offer genuine theater options for Vegas patrons. Their first attempt was a production of the revival of *Chicago* (we can only imagine the business it would have done post-2003 Oscars!), and this charming and fluffy show is their second. It seems even better suited for Vegas audiences, since it's all-ages, innocuous, and promotes much clapping and dancing. There is little of substance in the story, a loose narrative created solely for the purposes of bringing the many, many hit songs of the Swedish '70s wonder group ABBA to the stage. Don't get us wrong; it's quite cute, as a young woman on the eve of her wedding, longing for the father she never knew to be a part of her present happiness, brings the three men who are the most likely biological daddy to her Greek island home, forcing her long independent mother to face up to her past and make choices for the future. Some of the songs fit better than others, but all are sung with the appropriate breezy joy. We want to shake the director when we witness all too many broad gestures and pointless scamperings during the rare moments of dialogue, but the cast is earnest and those darn Swedes wrote songs that we have to admit, 30 years on, are still mighty infectious. 3950 Las Vegas Blvd. S. (in Mandalay Bay). ℂ **702/632-7777**. www.mandalaybay.com. Tickets $65 and $85 plus tax. Mon, Wed, Thurs 7pm; Fri 8pm; Sat 7 and 10:30pm; Sun 5 and 9:30pm.

Penn & Teller *(Moments* The most intelligent show in Vegas, as these two—magicians? Illusionists? Truth-tellers? BS artists? Tell you what, let's settle on geniuses—put on 90 minutes of, yes, magic and juggling, but also acerbic comedy, mean stunts, and great quiet beauty. Looking like two characters out of Dr. Seuss, big loud Penn and smaller quiet Teller (to reduce them to their basic characteristics) perform magic, reveal the secrets behind a few major magic tricks, discuss why magic is nothing but a bunch of lies, and then turn around and show why magic is as lovely an art form as any other. We won't tell you much about the various tricks and acts, for fear of ruining punch lines, but watching Teller fish money out of an empty glass aquarium or play with shadows is to belie Penn's earlier caveats about learning how tricks are done—it doesn't ruin the wonder of it, not at all, nor the serenity that settles in your Vegas-sensory-overload brain. 3700 W. Flamingo (in the Rio Hotel). ℂ **888/746-7784**. Tickets $65. Wed–Mon 9pm.

Second City Improv Second City is the Chicago-based comedy group that spawned not only *SCTV* but some of the best modern-day comics (such as Gilda Radner, John Belushi, Martin Short, and Mike Myers). This is an improv and sketch-comedy show, with cast members performing stunts similar to those you might have seen on *Whose Line Is It Anyway?*—you know, taking suggestions from the audience and creating bizarre little skits and such out of them, all of it done at lightning speed with wit and a wink. Some of it can turn R-rated, so be careful bringing the kids, but do not hesitate to see it yourself. And join in—any improv group is only as good as the material fed it (so remember, there's only so much a group can do with jokes about sex and vomiting, especially if every single audience thinks that would be funny material with which to work). One of the best values and highest-quality shows in Vegas. In The Flamingo Las Vegas, 3555 Las Vegas Blvd. S. ℂ **800/732-2111**. Tickets $30 (excluding tax). Sun–Mon 8pm; Tues and Thurs–Sat 8 and 10:30pm.

Siegfried & Roy (Overrated   A Vegas institution for more than 2 decades, illusionists Siegfried and Roy started as an opening act, became headliners at the Frontier, and finally were given their own $30 million show and $25 million theater in The Mirage. They (and their extensive exotic animal menagerie) have amply repaid this enormous investment by selling out every show since. No wonder The Mirage has them booked "until the end of time."

But while the spectacle is undeniable (and the money is all right up there on the stage), the result is overproduced. From the get-go, there's too much light, sound, smoke, and fire; too many dancing girls, fire-breathing dragons, robots, and other often completely superfluous effects, not to mention an original (and forgettable) Michael Jackson song. It almost overwhelms the point of the whole thing. Or maybe it's *become* the point of the whole thing. The magic, which was the Austrian duo's original act, after all, seems to have gotten lost. Sometimes literally. The tricks are at a minimum, allowing the flashpots, lasers, and whatnot to fill out the nearly 2-hour show. More often than not, when a trick was actually being performed, our attention was elsewhere, gawking at an effect, a showgirl, or

 Penn & Teller's Top 10 Things One Should NEVER Do in a Vegas Magic Show

Penn & Teller have been exercising their acerbic wit and magical talents in numerous forums together for more than 25 years, and their show at the Rio is one of Vegas's best and most intelligent. We must confess that we couldn't get the quieter half of the duo, Teller, to cough up a few words, but the more verbose Penn Jillette was happy to share.

1. Costume yourself in gray business suits totally lacking in rhinestones, animal patterns, Mylar, capes, bell-bottoms, shoulder pads, and top hats.
2. Wear your hair in any style that could NOT be described as "feathered," or "spiked."
3. Use really good live jazz music instead of canned sound-alike cheesy rip-off fake pop "music."
4. Cruelly (but truthfully) make fun of your siblings in the magic brotherhood.
5. Do the dangerous tricks on each other instead of anonymous show women with aftermarket breasts, and/or endangered species.
6. Toss a cute little magic bunny into a cute little chipper shredder.
7. Open your show by explaining *and* demonstrating how other magicians on The Strip do their most amazing tricks, then do that venerable classic of magic, "The Cups and Balls," with transparent plastic cups.
8. Treat the audience as if they had a brain in their collective head.
9. Allow audience members to sign real bullets, load them into real guns, and fire those bullets into your face.
10. Bleed

(You will find **all 10** of these "don'ts" in the *Penn & Teller* show at the Rio All-Suite Hotel and Casino.)

something. Only the gasps from the audience members who actually happened to be looking in the right place let us know we missed something really neat.

Tellingly, the best part of the show is when all that stuff is switched off, and Siegfried & Roy take the stage to perform smaller magic and chat with the audience. The charm that helped get them so far shines through, and spontaneity is allowed to sneak in. The white tigers are certainly magnificent, but they don't do much other than get cuddled (charmingly) by Roy and badly lip-synch to pretaped roars. The duo is clearly doing something right, judging from the heartfelt standing ovations they receive night after night. But more than one couple was heard to say it was not the best show they had seen, and also to express a feeling that it was overpriced. And those ticket prices (over $100 *per person!*) are indeed sky-high. Go if you can't live without seeing a true, modern Vegas legend, but you can find better entertainment values in town. In The Mirage, 3400 Las Vegas Blvd. S. ℂ **800/963-9634** or 702/792-7777. Tickets $111 (includes souvenir program, 2 drinks, tax, and gratuity). Sun–Tues 7:30pm; Fri–Sat 7:30 and 11pm.

Splash They took out the mermaids and water tank that gave this show its name, froze the water, and added ice skaters and some increased production values. If the show is now the one in town that most closely resembles the guffaw-inducing extravaganza in *Showgirls*, it's nonetheless a considerable improvement over its previous incarnations. That may be because we are partial to ice skaters in any form, even if they are performing to the music from *Titanic* while topless dancers preen on a small version of the deck of the boat. The weird lip-synching numbers, including a long tribute to Madonna that reenacts portions of *Evita,* even as clips from the real thing are shown on video screens, still remain, though improved and more ambitious choreography has been added. Expect up-close looks at bare breasts as the flashy and not-terribly-competent dancers parade through the crowd (sometimes in see-through filmy net cat suits that show less and are thus considerably more sexy—more topless shows should go this teasing route). Some "comedy gauchos" crack whips and insensitive jokes, and there's a truly talented trio of juggling brothers. Pass the time wondering if it's uncomfortable skating in a butt thong, and pondering the philosophical implications of a country's wretched political problems providing fodder for first the Andrew Lloyd Webber mill and now a Vegas topless revue. *Seating warnings:* Seats on the sides are so bad that fully three-quarters of the stage might be obscured. In The Riviera Hotel & Casino, 2901 Las Vegas Blvd. S. ℂ **877/892-7469** or 702/734-9301. Tickets $57 (excluding tax). Sat–Thurs 8 and 10:30pm.

Tournament of Kings (Kids) If you've seen the Jim Carrey movie *The Cable Guy,* you probably laughed at the scene in which the two protagonists went to a medieval dinner and tournament. Perhaps you thought it was satire, created just for the movie. You would be wrong. It's actually part of a chain, and something very like it can be found right here in Vegas, though in a new and improved version. Those of us who shuddered at the former incarnation find this new one to be at worst highly tolerable, and at times downright entertaining.

For a fixed price, you get a dinner that's better than you might expect (Cornish game hen, very fine baked potato, and more), which you eat with your hands (in keeping with the theme), while Merlin (or someone like him) spends too much time trying to work the crowd up with a singalong. This gives way to a competition between the kings of various medieval countries, competing for titles in knightly contests (jousting, horse races, and such) that are every bit as unrehearsed and spontaneous as a professional wrestling match. Eventually, good triumphs over evil and all that.

Afternoon Delight?

By now, it will not have escaped your attention that most of the night-time shows in Vegas, at least the ones of any quality, cost a lot. Except for the ones that cost a whole heck of a lot. And that we tend to pre-fer the latter. "Isn't there *any* cheap entertainment in this town?" you may have begun to wonder, and trust us, even if we are awfully liberal with the contents of your wallets, we feel your pain.

So, barring the possibility that you might be the kind of gambler we wish to be, the sort who gets comped free tickets to expensive shows (that you could probably afford anyway, in typical Vegas irony), there are some alternatives. Several Vegas hotels offer afternoon shows, at much more reasonable prices—that, of course, being a relative term. Here are a couple of the better offerings (note that Mac King, because he's quite a bit better, gets his own full review above).

Rick Thomas (Tropicana Resort & Casino, 3801 Las Vegas Blvd. S., ℂ **800/634-4000** or 702/739-2411; Sat–Thurs 2 and 4pm; $17) is an entertaining magician, though one wonders why he merits his own afternoon show, but not his own nighttime show, or a part of one of the big nighttime production revues. *Viva Las Vegas* (in the Stratos-phere Casino Hotel & Tower, 2000 Las Vegas Blvd. S., ℂ **800/99-TOWER** or 702/380-7777; Mon–Sat 2 and 4pm; $12, excluding tax), an every-thing-but-the-kitchen-sink Vegas variety show, is good only if you really need an hour's respite from the slots in the afternoon.

Note: Discount coupons are often found in those free magazines in your hotel room for the afternoon shows. Sometimes the discount gets you in free, with just the price of a drink.

Each section of the arena is given a king to be the subjects of and to root for, and the audience is encouraged to hoot, holler, and pound on the tables, which kids love, but teens will be too jaded for (though we know some from whom a spontaneous "way cool" slipped out a few times unchecked). Many adults might find it tiresome, particularly when they insist you shout "huzzah!" and other period slang. Acrobatics are terrific, and certain buff performers make for a differ-ent sort of enjoyment. In Excalibur, 3850 Las Vegas Blvd. S. ℂ **800/933-1334** or 702/597-7600. Tickets $42. Daily 6 and 8:30pm.

3 Headliner Showrooms

Vegas entertainment made its name with its showrooms, though its glory days are somewhat behind it, gone with the Rat Pack themselves. For a long time, Vegas headliners were something of a joke; only those on the downhill side of fame were thought to play here. But with all the new performance spaces—and high fees—offered by the new hotels, Vegas suddenly has some respect again, especially, on (of all things) the rock scene. Both the Hard Rock Hotel's The Joint and the House of Blues are attracting very current and very popular acts who find it hip, rather than humiliating, to play Sin City. However, the classic Vegas showroom itself does seem headed the way of the dinosaurs; many of the hotels have shuttered theirs. As for the remainder, one is pretty much like the other, with the exception of the Hard Rock and HOB (hence their detailed descriptions), and in any case, audiences go based on the performer rather than the space itself. Check with your hotel, or those free magazines in your room, to see who is in town when you are.

Note also that **Mr. Wayne Newton,** who really *is* Vegas, is currently playing the Stardust on a regular basis, about 40 weeks out of the year.

Hard Rock Hotel's The Joint   Formerly just about the only game in town in terms of good rock bookings, The Joint, with its 1,400-seat capacity, now faces some stiff competition from the House of Blues. For example, when Alanis Morrisette came to town, she played the Hard Rock, but her opening act, Garbage, played the House of Blues. On the other hand, it was here the Rolling Stones chose to do a show during their arena tour—this was the smallest venue the band had played in years, and, as you can imagine, it was one hot ticket. When the Hard Rock Hotel opened in 1995, the Eagles were the first act to appear. Since then the facility has presented Bob Dylan, Ziggy Marley, Marilyn Manson, Hootie and the Blowfish, the Black Crowes, Donna Summer, Stephen Stills, Jimmy Cliff, Tears for Fears, Johnny Cash, Lyle Lovett, and James Brown.

The venue is not a preferred one, however; it's only worth going if a favorite performer is playing or if it's an opportunity to see a big artist play a smaller-than-usual room. Though there's sometimes table seating, it's usually festival style, making personal space at a premium during a crowded show; and though the floor is slightly raked, this still makes for poor sightlines. The balconies upstairs, if you can get to them, aren't much better, as once the bodies are packed in about two deep, the stage is completely obscured. Unless you want to brave the crush at the very front (sure, you should—it's a rock show!), we suggest standing at the rail toward the back, which not only elevates you slightly above

---

Fun Fact **Wayne Newton's Top 10 Favorite Lounge Songs**

Wayne Newton is the consummate entertainer. He has performed more than 25,000 concerts in Las Vegas alone, and in front of more than 25 million people worldwide. Wayne has received more standing ovations than any other entertainer in history. Along with his singing credits, his acting credits are soaring—one of his more recent credits is *Vegas Vacation*. Make sure you catch him playing at the Stardust. No trip to Vegas is complete without seeing the "King of Las Vegas."

1. "You're Nobody, Til Somebody Loves You" (You don't have a body unless somebody loves you!)
2. "Up a Lazy River" (or "Up Your Lazy River!")
3. "Don't Go Changing (Just the Way You Are)" (The clothes will last another week!)
4. "Having My Baby" (Oh God!)
5. "The Windmills of My Mind" (A mind is a terrible thing to waste!)
6. "The Wind Beneath My Wings" (Soft and Dry usually helps!)
7. "Copacabana"
8. "When the Saints Go Marching In"
9. "I Am, I Said" (Huh?!)
10. "The Theme from the Love Boat" (or "Would a Dinghy Do?")

Headliner Stadiums

Three arenas are worth a special mention since they often feature major entertainers. **Sam Boyd Stadium,** the outdoor stadium at the University of Nevada, Las Vegas (UNLV), has been host to such major acts as Paul McCartney, U2, the Eagles, and Metallica. **Thomas and Mack Center,** the university's indoor arena, has a more comprehensive concert schedule, including such names as Van Halen, Michael Bolton, and Celine Dion, as well as such shows as Disney on Ice and Ringling Bros. Circus. Both are located on the **UNLV campus** at Boulder Highway and Russell Road (℃ **702/895-3900**). **Ticketmaster** (℃ **702/474-4000**) handles ticketing for both arenas.

the crowd (improving those sightlines), but at least protects one side of your body from the crowd.

Showroom Policies: Smoking permitted for some shows; seating is either preassigned or general, depending on the performer. **Price:** $20 to $250, depending on the performer (tax and drinks extra). **Show Times:** 8:30pm (nights of performance vary). **Reservations:** You can reserve up to 30 days in advance. In the Hard Rock Hotel & Casino, 4455 Paradise Rd. ℃ 800/693-7625 or 702/693-5000.

House of Blues   With its entry into Las Vegas, the House of Blues is going head-to-head with The Joint at the Hard Rock Hotel, and the prospects for some great bookings due to competition are high. On its own merits, the House of Blues is a good, intimate room with a cozy floor surrounded by a bar area, and an upstairs balcony area that has actual theater seating. (The balcony might actually be a better place to see a show since the sightlines are unobscured, unlike down below, where posts and such can obstruct the view.) It's probably the most comfortable and user-friendly place to see a rock show in Vegas.

The heavy theme decor (a constant evocation of the Delta region and New Orleans) is a bit too Disneyland-meets-Hearst-Castle, with corrugated-tin this and weathered-wood that, plus walls covered in outsider/primitive/folk art from various Southern artists. But it annoys us less in Vegas than it does in New Orleans; here it's sort of a welcome touch of the genuine amid the artificial, while in the actual Big Easy, it comes off as pre-fab.

The House of Blues has rock and blues shows just about every night, and, as mentioned, nationally recognized acts are already flocking to the place, starting with Bob Dylan on opening night and continuing with shows by Seal, X, Garbage, Taylor Dane, Al Green, James Brown, the Go-Go's, the Neville Brothers, and even spoken word by Henry Rollins.

Showroom Policies: Smoking permitted; seating is either preassigned or general, depending on the performer (some shows are all general admission, with everyone standing on the floor). **Price:** $18 to $250, depending on the performer. **Show Times:** Vary, but usually 8pm. **Reservations:** You can buy tickets as soon as shows are announced; lead time varies with each artist. In Mandalay Bay, 3950 Las Vegas Blvd. S. ℃ 877/632-7400 or 702/632-7600.

The other major headliner showrooms in Vegas include the following:

- **Aladdin Center for the Performing Arts**   In the Aladdin Resort & Casino, 3667 Las Vegas Blvd. S. (℃ **877/333-WISH** [333-9474] or 702/785-5555)
- **Las Vegas Hilton Showroom**   In the Las Vegas Hilton, 3000 Paradise Rd. (℃ **800/222-5361** or 702/732-5755)

- **Mandalay Bay Events Center**   In Mandalay Bay, 3950 Las Vegas Blvd. S. (© **877/632-7400** or 702/632-7580)
- **MGM Grand Garden Events Arena**   In the MGM Grand Hotel/Casino, 3799 Las Vegas Blvd. S. (© **800/929-1111** or 702/891-7777)
- **MGM Grand Hollywood Theatre**   In the MGM Grand Hotel/Casino, 3799 Las Vegas Blvd. S. (© **800/929-1111** or 702/891-7777)
- **Orleans Showroom**   In the Orleans, 4500 W. Tropicana Ave. (© **800/ ORLEANS**)

4 Comedy Clubs

Catch a Rising Star   The world-famous Catch a Rising Star returns to Vegas with a new venue at Excalibur. Expect two comedians nightly; although you probably won't know them by name, this comedy club is widely known for bringing in top-notch talent. In the Excalibur, 3850 Las Vegas Blvd. S. © **800-937-7777**. Tickets $19 (includes tax). Daily 10pm, additional 7:30pm show Thurs only.

Comedy Club   The Riviera's comedy club, on the second floor of the Mardi Gras Plaza, showcases four comedians nightly. Once a month, usually on the last weekend, the club hosts a late-night *XXXTREME Comedy Showcase* for shock and X-rated comedians. Other special events include the *All Gay Comedy Revue* and R-rated hypnotist Frank Santos. In The Riviera Hotel & Casino, 2901 Las Vegas Blvd. S. © **800/634-6753** or 702/734-9301. Tickets $20. Daily 8 and 10pm, with occasional Fri–Sat late-night shows at 11:45pm.

Comedy Stop   Similar to the other comedy clubs in town, the Comedy Stop features three nationally known comedy headliners nightly. In Tropicana Resort & Casino, 3801 Las Vegas Blvd. S. © **800/468-9494** or 702/739-2411. Tickets $20 (includes tax, tip, and 2 drinks). Daily 8 and 10:30pm.

The Improv   This offshoot of Budd Friedman's famed comedy club (the 1st one opened in 1963 in New York City) presents about four comedians per show in a 400-seat showroom. These are talented performers—the top comics on the circuit, who you're likely to see on Leno and Letterman. You can be sure of an entertaining evening. In Harrah's Las Vegas, 3475 Las Vegas Blvd. S. © **800/392-9002** or 702/369-5111. Tickets $25. Tues–Sun 8:30 and 10:30pm.

5 Coffeehouses

Coffeehouses are buzzing both day- and nighttime; so far, not too many stay open past midnight. They can either be pretentious or the center of youth culture, depending on your demographic group. They can also be an oasis for those seeking alternative culture or just a respite from the usual Vegas hangouts. Many also offer live music and/or poetry readings; check the listings in *Las Vegas Weekly* and *City Life* for details (or just call the place in question).

Cafe Espresso Roma   Despite the vintage-sofa look, the truth is told by the clean tile counter—this is an artificially manufactured attempt at the coffeehouse scene and, arguably, a successful one. Most of the patrons are UNLV students. They do have poetry and live music on certain nights, but they close too early. Open daily from 7am to 10pm or later depending on events. 4440 S. Maryland Pkwy. (near Harmon Ave.). © **702/369-1540**.

Jazzed Cafe & Vinoteca *(Finds*   This genuine European-style (well, by way of California) cafe is owned and operated by the charming and friendly Kirk, a choreographer who lived in Italy for 10 years. Originally just an itty-bitty location on

Flamingo, it's now a larger, but still intimate (seating only 40) venue on Sahara, an even farther drive for the average tourist, but well worth it if you want something less Vegas. Featuring candlelight and cool jazz most nights, with hot art on the walls, they try to serve eclectic and unusual wines, along with multiple coffee drinks (be sure to try the terrific Illy, a renowned Italian brand). There's a small but satisfying food menu featuring inexpensive authentic Italian specialties—simple pastas, focaccia bread, and so forth, all made by Kirk on the spot. It's a great respite from the maddening crowds (and a cheap place to eat well), though it fills up with the owner's show-and-dance pals after the shows let out. A sign warns you not to order lemon peel with your espresso—if you do, be prepared to be sworn at (sweetly) in Italian. Open Tuesday to Thursday and Sunday from 5 to 10pm and Friday and Saturday from 5pm to 3am. 8615 W. Sahara (at Durango). ⓒ **702/233-2859.**

6 Piano Bars

In addition to the establishments listed below, **Cafe Nicolle** (p. 158) has a small but agreeable genuine piano bar.

The Bar at Times Square   If you're looking for a quiet piano bar, this is not the place for you. It's smack in the middle of the Central Park part of the New York–New York casino. Two pianos are going strong every night, and the young hipster, cigar-smoking crowd overflows out the doors. It always seems to be packed with a singing, swaying, drinking throng of camaraderie and good cheer—or at least, full of booze. Hugely fun, provided you can get a foot in the door. And yes, every night, right outside, the ball on top drops at midnight, for a little *Auld Lang Syne.* Shows daily from 8pm to 2:15am. In New York–New York, 3790 Las Vegas Blvd. S. ⓒ **702/740-6969.** Cover Fri–Sat $10.

Club Monaco   This low-key, sophisticated piano bar—its walls lined with oil paintings of icons such as Elvis, Bogart, James Dean, and Marilyn Monroe (not to mention Rodney Dangerfield, finally getting respect)—is a romantic setting for cocktails and classic piano-bar entertainment. There's a small dance floor. On Friday and Saturday a talented vocalist is on hand as well. Club Monaco is far from a meat market, but it's a relaxed atmosphere in which to meet people, with an over-30 crowd. A menu offers salads, burgers, steak sandwiches, pastas, and gourmet appetizers such as oysters Rockefeller and escargot-stuffed mushrooms. Open 24 hours. 1487 E. Flamingo Rd. (between Maryland Pkwy. and Tamarus St.; on your right as you come from the Strip; look for the La-Z-Boy Furniture Gallery). ⓒ **702/737-6212.**

7 Gay Bars

Hip and happening Vegas locals know that some of the best scenes and dance action can be found in the city's gay bars. And no, they don't ask for sexuality ID at the door. All are welcome at any of the following establishments—as long as you don't have a problem with the people inside, they aren't going to have a problem with you. For women, this can be a fun way to dance and not get hassled by overeager Lotharios. (Lesbians, by the way, are just as welcome at any of the gay bars.)

If you want to know what's going on in gay Las Vegas during your visit, pick up a copy of the ***Las Vegas Bugle,*** a free gay-oriented newspaper that's available at any of the places described below. Or call them at ⓒ **702/369-6260.** You can also find gay nightlife listings on the Web at **http://gayvegas.tripod.com.**

The Buffalo   Close to both Icon (formerly Angles) and Gipsy, this is a leather/Levi's bar popular with motorcycle clubs. It features beer busts (all the beer you can drink for $5) Friday night from 9pm to midnight. There are pool tables and darts, and music videos play in this not-striking environment. It's very cheap, however, with longnecks going for $2, and it gets very, very busy, very late (3 or 4am). Open 24 hours. 4640 Paradise Rd. (at Naples St.). ℂ 702/733-8355.

The Eagle Off the beaten track in just about every sense of the phrase, The Eagle is the place to go if well-lit bars make you nervous. It's dark and slightly seedy, but in that great '70s gay bar kind of way. All in all, it's a refreshing change from the overprocessed slickness that is Las Vegas. The crowd, tending toward middle age, is mostly male and of the Levi's/leather group. There is a small dance area (calling it a dance floor would be generous), a pool table, video poker, and a nice-size bar. Drinks are inexpensive, and special events make them even more so. For instance, The Eagle is rapidly becoming famous for its twice-weekly underwear parties (if you check your pants, you receive draft beer and drinks for free—that's right: free). The 20-minute drive from the Strip makes it a questionable option, but try it out if you've got a sense of adventure. Open 24 hours. 3430 E. Tropicana Ave. (at Pecos Rd.). ℂ 702/458-8662.

Gipsy For years, Gipsy reigned supreme as the best gay dance place in the city, and for good reason: great location (Paradise Rd. near the Hard Rock), excellent layout (sunken dance floor and two bars), and very little competition. A few years ago, some fierce competition stole some of its spotlight, along with a good portion of the clientele, and so the Gipsy fought back with a $750,000 renovation that seemed to recapture past glories. The drink specials, along with special events, shows, male dancers, and theme nights make this place a good party bar. Open daily from 10pm to 6am. 4605 Paradise Rd. (at Naples St.). ℂ 702/731-1919. Cover varies, but is usually $5 and up on weekends, less or even free on weekdays.

Good Times This quiet neighborhood bar is located (for those of you with a taste for subtle irony) in the same complex as the Liberace Museum, a few miles due east of the MGM Grand. There's a small dance floor, but on a recent Friday night, nobody was using it, the crowd preferring instead to take advantage of the cozy bar area. A small conversation pit is a perfect spot for an intimate chat. Of course, there's the omnipresent pool and video poker if you're not interested in witty repartee. We remember this place as being a lot more crowded than it was during our most recent visit (but perhaps we were there on an off night). It makes a nice respite after the Liberace Museum (after which you may very well need a stiff drink). Open 24 hours. In the Liberace Plaza, 1775 E. Tropicana Ave. (at Spencer St.). ℂ 702/736-9494.

Icon This 24-hour gay bar received a new name (it used to be Angles) and not a whole heck of a lot else. It's still a casual neighborhood hangout compared to gay bars in other cities. The clientele is mostly local, about 85% men (including drag queens) in their mid-20s to early 30s. There are special promotions that vary from week to week, including occasional drag shows and go-go boys. There's a dance floor (the music's pretty loud), a small outdoor courtyard, and a game area with pool tables and darts, plus the requisite video poker at the bar. 4633 Paradise Rd. (at Naples St.). ℂ 702/791-0100.

8 Other Bars

In addition to the venues listed below, consider hanging out, as the locals quickly began doing, at **Aureole, Red Square,** and the **House of Blues,** all in **Mandalay Bay** (see chapter 6). There's a separate bar at Aureole facing the wine tower, where your wish for wine sends comely lasses flying up four stories, courtesy of *Peter Pan*–style harnesses, to fetch your desired bottle. At Red Square, keep your drink nicely chilled all night long on the ice bar, created by water that's freshly poured and frozen daily. Or hang out and feel the blues at the small bottle-cap-bedecked bar in the corner of the House of Blues restaurant, which gets quite lively with off-duty locals after midnight.

You might also check out the incredible nighttime view at the bar atop the **Stratosphere Casino Hotel & Tower**—nothing beats it.

There's also the **Viva Las Vegas Lounge** at the Hard Rock Hotel, which every rock-connected person in Vegas will eventually pass through.

And the **Petrossian Bar** in Bellagio offers class along with its cocktails (to say nothing of caviar and other delicacies)—but come for the cocktails, as those in the know claim it's not only the best bar in Vegas for such matters, but maybe the best bar in the West.

Caramel   It's small, but worlds away from the Bellagio-business-as-usual just outside its doors. How happy the 20-somethings are that there is this hip-hop spinning, glowing, caramel-and-chocolate-coated drink glasses, glowing bar, nonthreatening (and non-Euro-stodgy), scene-intensive hangout in the middle of Bellagio. How much does this prove Bellagio is trying to lure the Ghost Bar crowd away from the Palms? Not that this will do it, but if you are here and young, it's where you should be. 3600 Las Vegas Blvd. S. (in the Bellagio Hotel). ✆ 702/693-7111.

Champagnes Cafe   Wonder where old Vegas went? It ossified right here. Red-and gold-flocked wallpaper and other such trappings of "glamour" never die—in fact, with this ultralow lighting, they will never even fade. A seedy old bar with seedy old scary men leering away. They even serve ice-cream shakes spiked with booze—two indulgences wrapped into one frothy package, and quite a double addiction delight. Some might run screaming from the place, while others will think they've died and gone to heaven. Just remember—this is the kind of place director Quentin Tarantino, or this year's alt-cult hit movie, will make famous. It can't be long. And then it will be overrun with hipsters. Beat the rush, go there now, and brag that you knew about it back before it was so cool it became passé. Again. 3557 S. Maryland Pkwy. (between Twain Ave. and Desert Inn Rd.). ✆ 702/737-1699.

Coyote Ugly   You've seen the movie, now go have some of that prepackaged fun for yourself. Oh, come on—you don't think those bartender girls really dance on the bar and hose down the crowd just because they are so full of spontaneous rowdy high sprits, now do you? Not when the original locale built a reputation (and inspired a bad movie) on just such behavior, creating a success strong enough to start a whole chain of such frat-boy fun places? By the way, sarcastic and cynical as we are, can we say, totally fun place? In New York–New York, 3790 Las Vegas Blvd. S. (at Tropicana Ave.). ✆ 702/740-6969. Cover varies, usually $10 and up on weekends.

The Dispensary   Stuck in a '70s time warp (the waterwheel and the ferns are the tip-off, though the Muzak songs confirm it), this is a fine place for a nice, long, quiet drink. One that lasts decades, perhaps. It's very quiet, low-key, and often on the empty side. Things pick up on weekends, but it still isn't the sort of place that attracts raucous drunks. (Of course, if it were on the Strip instead of being tucked away, it probably would.) "We leave you alone if you don't want to be bothered," says the proprietor. (We still worry about what happens if you sit here long enough.) If you are a hepcat, but one on the mild side, you'll love it. 2451 E. Tropicana Ave. (at Eastern Ave.). ✆ 702/458-6343.

Double Down Saloon *(Finds)* "House rule: You puke, you clean." Okay, that about sums up the Double Down. Well, no, it doesn't really do the place justice. This is a big local hangout, with management quoting an old *Scope* magazine description of its clientele: "Hipsters, blue collars, the well-heeled lunatic fringe." Rumored to have been spotted here: director Tim Burton and Dr. Timothy Leary. Need to know more? Okay, trippy hallucinogenic graffiti covers the walls, the ceiling, the tables, and possibly you if you sit there long enough. Decor includes Abby Rents–type chairs, thrift-store battered armchairs and sofa, a couple of pool tables, and a jukebox that holds everything from the Germs and Frank Zappa to Link Wray, Dick Dale, and the Rev. Horton Heat. On Wednesday night, they have a live blues band, while other nights might find local alternative, punk, or ska groups performing. On some Sundays, the Blue Man Group plays, but under another name, as a percussion band. Call about that, for sure. There's no cover unless they have some out-of-town band that actually has a label deal. 4640 Paradise Rd. (at Naples St.). 𝄞 702/791-5775. www.doubledownsaloon.com.

Drop Bar Smack in the middle of the Green Valley Resort Casino, with '60s-inspired go-go girls dancing away. In the Green Valley Ranch Resort, 2300 Paseo Verde Pkwy., Henderson. 𝄞 702/221-6560. Cover varies, usually $10 and up.

Eiffel Tower Bar From this chic and elegant room, in the restaurant on the 11th floor of the Eiffel Tower, you can look down on everyone (in Vegas)—just like a real Parisian! (Just kidding, Francophiles.) But really, this is a date-impressing bar, and, since there's no cover or minimum, it's a cost-effective alternative to the overly inflated food prices at the restaurant. Drop by for a drink, but try to look sophisticated. And then you can cop an attitude and dismiss everything as gauche—or droit, depending on which way you are seated. In Paris Las Vegas, 3655 Las Vegas Blvd. S. 𝄞 702/948-6937.

Ghost Bar Probably the most interesting aspect of this desperate-to-get-into-the-gossip-pages-as-the-trendy-bar-of-the-moment place (decorated with a '60s Mod/futuristic silver-gleam look) is that though much is made of the fact that it's on the 55th floor, it's really on the 42nd. Something about the number 4 being bad luck in Asian cultures. Whatever. The view still is fabulous, which is the main reason to come here, that and to peer at those tousled-hair beauties copping an attitude on the couches and see if any of them have the kind of names that will make tomorrow's gossip pages. This may be the hot bar of the moment by the time you get there (dress up), or everyone may have moved on. Who knows? In the Palms Resort & Casino, 4321 W. Flamingo Rd. (just west of the Strip). 𝄞 702/942-7778. Cover varies, usually $10 and up.

Gordon-Biersch Brewing Company This is part of a chain, and while it does feel like it, it's better than the average lounge chain. The interior is both contemporary and rustic, and warmer than its semi-industrial look sounds like it would be. It's roomy, so you don't feel stacked up on top of other customers. The house lager (they specialize in German brews) was tasty and the noise level acceptable. A good place to go hoist a few. 3987 Paradise Rd. (just north of Flamingo Rd.). 𝄞 702/312-5247.

Peppermill's Fireside Lounge *(Finds)* Walk through the classic Peppermill's coffee shop (not a bad place to eat, by the way) on the Strip, and you land in its dark, plush, cozy 24-hour lounge. A fabulously dated view of hip, it has low, circular banquette seats, fake floral foliage, low neon, and electric candles. But best of all is the water and fire pit as the room's centerpiece—a piece of kitsch thought to be long vanished from the earth, and attracting nostalgia buffs like moths to a flame. It all adds up to a cozy, womblike place, perfect for unwinding a bit after some time spent on the hectic Strip. The enormous, exotic froufrou tropical drinks (including the signature bathtub-size margaritas) will ensure that you sink into a level of comfortable stupor. 2985 Las Vegas Blvd. S. © 702/735-7635.

Pink E's   Sick of the attitude at Club Rio? Escape directly across the street to Pink E's, where the theme is pink. (You were expecting maybe seafoam?) Anyway, at least one regular described this as "the only place to go if you are over 25 and have a brain." And like pink. Because everything at this 24-hour joint is: the many pool tables, the Ping-Pong tables, the booths, the lighting, the lava lamp on the bar, and even the people. In its own way, it's as gimmick-ridden as The Beach dance club (see below), but surely no one would put out a pink pool table in all seriousness? Yeah, it's a ludicrous heresy, but don't you want to play on one? Pink E's offers retro diner food and a DJ on weekends. The dress code basically translates to "no gangsta-wannabe wear." Go, but wear all black (and no pink) just to be ornery. 3695 W. Flamingo Rd. © 702/252-4666.

Risque   Ready to put the *ooh la la* back in Vegas (like it needed it, but never mind), this is Paris Las Vegas's most recent lounge (a bar with a dance floor, in this case), which has '80s lingerie, as reconceived in the Cirque du Soleil world, clad girls practicing lurid versions of their yoga poses, with a detached and yet erotic attitude, perched on a ledge for you to gawk at as soon as you walk in the door. More scantily dressed gals work the top of the bar, while a DJ spins discs in this industrial-nightclub-meets-modern-day-strip-bar. Fancy constructed desserts are for sale, and there are dark nooks everywhere (including balconies that fit no more than four), where the desserts can be consumed and we don't want to know what else could go on. Of course, for every dipped-in-black club kid beauty there is a denim-wearing tourist, but still, you can get your jollies. 3655 Las Vegas Blvd. S. (in the Paris Hotel). © 702/946-7000. Cover: Men $20, women $10.

Sand Dollar Blues Lounge   The kind of funky, no-decor (think posters and beer signs), atmosphere-intensive, slightly grimy, friendly bar you either wish your town had or wish it had something other than. Just up the road from Treasure Island, this is a great antidote to artificial Vegas. Attracting a solid mix of locals and tourists (employees claim the former includes everything from bikers to chamber of commerce members), the Sand Dollar features live blues (both electric and acoustic, with a little Cajun and zydeco thrown in) every night. We wondered how Vegas had enough blues bands to fill out a whole weekly bill. The answer? All the musicians play in multiple bands in different configurations. The dance floor is tiny and often full. The minimal cover always goes to the band. Depending on your desires, it's either refreshingly not Las Vegas, or just the kind of place you came to Vegas to escape. Go before someone has the idea

---

Impressions

"It's a wonderful town all right!" a stick man at the Thunderbird told me. "Where else can a fellow gamble all day, get drunk, go to sleep, get up at four in the morning and find plenty of company when he walks into the lobby?"

—Daniel Lang, *Blackjack and Flashes*

Tips Bathroom Break

When you gotta go, you gotta go, particularly if you've tried drinking at every bar listed here, and so when you do, do try to do so in the unisex, freestanding, Space Age pods at **Mandalay Bay's China Grill**.

---

to build a theme hotel based on it. Open 24 hours. 3355 Spring Mountain Rd. (at Polaris Ave.). ✆ **702/871-6651**. Cover varies but is usually no more than a few bucks.

Sky Lounge   It may not be the view offered by the Stratosphere's bar, but it's pretty darn good and a lot easier to get to. You don't see quite enough of the MGM Grand to the left, but otherwise there are no complaints. The decor is too modern (heavy on '80s black and purple), but overall the place is quiet (especially during the day) and civil. A jazz vocal/piano act performs at night, when the views are, naturally, the best. The atmosphere produced by all this is classic Vegas in the best sense (with only a slight touch of necessary kitsch). Worth a trip for an escape from the mob, though you won't be the only tourist fighting for window seats. Open 8am until whenever they feel like closing. At the Polo Towers, 3745 Las Vegas Blvd. S. ✆ **702/261-1000**.

Tommy Rocker's   Tommy Rocker is the owner—surely he wasn't born with that name—and he plays his club every Friday and Saturday night, mixing bar-band standards with '80s and '90s hits. It's a one-man show, with Strip musicians dropping by after their own shifts are done. (Occasionally, local bands are permitted to play as well.) Sort of like the inside of a Quonset hut painted black, his vaguely beach-frat-party-themed club has become the home for local and out-of-town Parrot Heads (Jimmy Buffet fans, for those not in the know), with the result that the crowd is 5 to 10 years past their heavy college-drinking days. A large bar dominates the middle of the room; there are two pool tables and a grill for ordering food, plus an espresso machine. 4275 Industrial Blvd. (at Flamingo Rd.). ✆ **702/ 261-6688**.

Triple 7 Brew Pub *Finds*   Yet another of the many things the new(ish) Main Street Station hotel has done right. Stepping into its microbrew pub feels like stepping out of Vegas. Well, except for the dueling-piano entertainment. The place has a partial modern warehouse look (exposed pipes, microbrew fixtures visible through exposed glass at the back, and a very high ceiling), but a hammered-tin ceiling continues the hotel's Victorian decor; the overall effect seems straight out of San Francisco's North Beach. It's a bit on the yuppified side but escapes being pretentious. And frankly, it's a much-needed modern space for the Downtown area. This place has its own brew master, a number of microbrews ready to try, and if you want a quick bite, there's also an oyster-and-sushi bar, plus fancy burgers and pizzas. It can get noisy during the aforementioned piano-duel act, but otherwise casino noise stays out. Since all of Downtown is too heavy on the old Las Vegas side (which is fine, but not *all* the time), this is good for a suitable breather. In Main St. Station, 200 Main St. ✆ **702/387-1896**.

Whiskey Sky   Probably your best bet for a trendy place that might actually have either beautiful locals or out-of-town celebs looking for a cool time but wanting a lower profile. This cool, low-key vibe is due to the bar's off-the-Strip location, and also its creator, hip-bar-master Rande Gerber (Cindy Crawford's hubby). Think beds instead of couches, and you've got a sense of the gestalt. In the Green Valley Ranch Resort, 2300 Paseo Verde Pkwy., Henderson. ✆ **702/221-6560**. Cover varies, usually $10 and up.

A KARAOKE BAR

Ellis Island Casino—Karaoke   Admit it. You sing in the shower. And when the acoustics are just right, you fancy you could give a Vegas lounge singer a run for his money. Here's your chance to test this theory without the comfort of tile acoustics. In this small, smoky den filled with leather and candles, any number of people from all walks of life get up and act out their lounge-singer fantasies. You can join them. With over 6,000 titles, including multiple Englebert Humperdinck, Mac Davis, and Tom Jones selections, there are plenty of cheesy numbers just perfect for this kind of environment. And if you stay here long enough, you'll hear them all.

The bar is decked out with video-poker machines, and if you're planning on singing, there is a two-drink minimum. For $10, you can videotape your moment of glory. All you have to do to strut your stuff is choose a song and walk it up to the host. You may have to wait a while for your tune, but part of the fun is watching other people make fools out of them—er, singing. Karaoke is offered daily from 9pm to 3am. 4178 Koval Lane (off Flamingo Rd., behind Bally's). © 702/733-8901.

9 Dance Clubs

In addition to the options listed below, country-music fans might want to wander on over to **Dylan's,** 4660 Boulder Hwy. (© 702/451-4006). They offer country music (live and otherwise) and line dancing, with free dance lessons. Dylan's is more casual and basic, with a definite roadhouse vibe.

Note: As far as a dress code is concerned, you are going to go farther with more obviously expensive clothes, but you may not have the budget or fashion sense for that (and who travels with really good clothes, anyway?). When in doubt, all black should do it, and showing skin helps. Otherwise, just dress as nicely as you can. But do avoid sports team–affiliated jerseys and baseball hats, baggy pants, and other things that might fall under the heading "gangster-wear," because that's one sure way of not getting past the velvet rope.

Baby's   This place is so cool, tears in your eyes freeze as you enter. That is not necessarily a good thing. It means a velvet-rope policy that will probably keep out the uncool (most of us), and futuristically hip drinks that require a bank loan to afford, and a magazine-cover appearance is required to not feel really lame. If that sounds cranky, it's only because we're kinda jealous; this is a cool scene and it's not its fault we're wallflowers. This is *the* Vegas party bar and if you can handle the pressure, by all means go, and have a good time for us. (Note that Baby's was closed for a renovation when we went to press, but the interior changes won't make a difference—none of us will still be able to go.) Baby's is open Thursday through Saturday from 11pm until 4:30am. In the Hard Rock, 4455 Paradise Rd. © 702/693-5555. Cover $10–$20.

The Beach   If you're a fan of loud, crowded, 24-hour party bars filled with tons of good-looking fun-seekers, then bow in this direction, for you have found Mecca. This huge tropical-themed (hence the whole "Beach" thing) nightclub is right across the street from the Convention Center and is, according to just about anyone you ask, the hottest club in the city. It's a two-story affair with five separate bars downstairs and another three up.

Just in case walking the 20 feet to the closest bar is too much of an effort, they also have bikini-clad women serving beer out of steel tubs full of ice (they also roam the floor with shot belts). The drinks are on the pricey side ($4.25 for an 8-oz. domestic beer), but the unfailingly gorgeous, 4% body-fat bartenders (both men and women) are friendly and offer rotating drink specials that might keep you from busting your budget.

Downstairs is the large two-story dance floor, which dominates the center of the room and is built around a full-service bar at one end. The sound system is top-of-the-line, as is the lighting design (but the wash from the rest of the bar made it a little too bright on the floor to appreciate). Nobody really seemed to care though—there wasn't 1 square inch of space available on a recent Friday night. Upstairs, there are balconies overlooking the dance floor, pool tables, darts, foosball, pinball, and various other arcade games plus slot machines, video poker, and a sports book. Other neat touches include tarot-card readings by the stairs and hot-pizza vendors. And let's not forget those Jell-O-shot contests where club-goers try to eat shaky cubes of alcohol-spiked gelatin off each other's partially bared bodies.

The crowd is aggressively young and pretty, more men than women (70/30 split), and about 60% tourist, which is probably why the place can get away with charging a $10 cover. Party people look no further: There's free valet parking, and if you've driven here and become intoxicated, they'll drive you back home at no charge. Open daily from 10pm until the wee hours. 365 S. Convention Center Dr. (at Paradise Rd.). ⓒ 702/731-1925. www.beachlv.com. Cover $5 and up.

Bikinis   By now, you should be getting the format for the most recent trend in clubs and lounges in Vegas: liberal use of dancing girls who wear very, very little. What makes this different from an honest strip bar, we don't know (but you can read some thoughts on the matter below in our review of Sapphire), but it does show how mainstream strip bars have become. How else to explain the go-go dancers here, who wear thong bikinis and little wisps of gauze as they dance, with various degrees of enthusiasm and talent, on stages with strippers' poles, and then sometimes get into tanks of water to gyrate? How else to explain the gaggle of male customers who watch them with studied blank expressions, and how the female customers end up congregating towards the back, studiously ignoring the floor show, except to say things like "I wish I had her legs?" Expect also occasional pillow fights and lingerie shows. In between this is a dance floor for you to shake your thang to hip-hop and house, while the interior Lava Lounge plays old-school funk. Open Thursday to Sunday from 10pm to late into the night. 3700 W. Flamingo Rd. (in the Rio). ⓒ 702/777-7777. Cover varies.

Cleopatra's Barge Nightclub   This is a small, unique nightclub set in part on a floating barge—you can feel it rocking. The bandstand, a small dance floor, and a few (usually reserved) tables are here, while others are set around the boat on "land." It's a gimmick, but one that makes this far more fun than other, more pedestrian, hotel bars. Plenty of dark makes for romance, but blaring volume levels mean you will have to scream those sweet nothings. Check out the bare-breasted figurehead on the ship's prow, who juts out over the hallway going past the entrance. She could put someone's eye out. Open nightly from 10:30pm until 4am. In Caesars Palace, 3570 Las Vegas Blvd. S. ⓒ 702/731-7110. No cover; 2-drink minimum.

Club Rio   This is one of the hottest nightspots in Vegas as of this writing, but apparently made so by people who don't mind long lines, restrictive dress codes, attitudinal door people, hefty cover charges, and bland dance music. Waits can be interminable and admittance denied thanks to the wrong footwear or shirt. The dress code (no sneakers, and shirts must have a collar) is supposed to make the clientele look more sophisticated than grungy; the effect is the opposite, as most of the men end up in combinations of chinos and button-down shirts. Of course, it's so dark you can't tell if someone is wearing sneakers.

Once inside, you find a large, circular room, with a spacious dance floor taking up much of the space. Giant video screens line the upper parts of the walls, showing anything from shots of the action down below to catwalk footage. Comfy circular booths fill out the next couple of concentric circles; these seem mostly reserved, and when empty, they leave the impression that the place isn't very full—so why the wait? Music on a recent visit included a Madonna medley and the perennial "Celebration," not the most *au courant* of tunes. The total effect is of a grown-up, not terribly drunken, frat and sorority mixer. The club opens at 11:30pm on Wednesday and 10:30pm Thursday through Saturday, and stays open until about 4am each of these nights. In the Rio All-Suite Hotel & Casino, 3700 W. Flamingo Rd. © **702/252-7777.** Advertised cover $10 for men, local women free, out-of-state women $5 (but frequently when we went by on a weekend night, the cover was $20 for everyone).

Drai's After Hours   Young Hollywood film execs and record-company types are likely to be found here, schmoozing and dancing it up to house, techno, and tribal music. Open Wednesday through Saturday from midnight until 9am. In Barbary Coast, 3595 Las Vegas Blvd. S. © **702/737-0555.** Cover varies, usually $20.

Light   In contrast to the metallic high gloss that characterizes most trendy nightspots, this is a grown-up nightclub (sister to an establishment in NYC)—fitting, since it's in the grown-up Bellagio—all wood and velvet and polite attitudes from the staff. Music tends toward both modern and old-school hip-hop and pop, with dancers (real ones) clad in rather modest costumes. Sometimes there are other touches, such as a live sax player jamming along to the music. Guests are probably all tourists, but tourists of the heir-to-the-hotel-fortune sort; yet the club doesn't feel exclusive, but rather like one big open party—a nifty and tricky feat to pull off. Open Thursday through Sunday from 9:30pm until 4am. In Bellagio, 3600 Las Vegas Blvd. S. © **702/693-8300.** Cover varies, usually $20.

Monte Carlo Pub & Brewery *Finds*   After 9pm nightly, this immense warehouselike pub and working microbrewery (details on p. 134) turns from a casual restaurant into something of a dance club. Rock videos blare forth from a large screen and 40 TV monitors around the room, while on stage, dueling pianos provide music and audience-participation entertainment. The pub is cigar-friendly and maintains a humidor. There's a full bar, and, of course, the house microbrews are featured. You can also order pizza. Open until 2am Sunday to Thursday, until 4am Friday and Saturday. In the Monte Carlo Resort & Casino, 3770 Las Vegas Blvd. S. © **702/730-7777.**

Ra   The futuristic Egyptian-themed Ra is part of the new generation of Vegas hot spots. It has that Vegas "we're a show and an attraction" vibe, but is still not overly pretentious. The staff is friendly, which is a rare thing for a hot club. It might be worth it to go just to gawk at the heavy gilt decor. You'll also find a major light show, cigar lounges off the disco, draped VIP booths, and plenty of little nooks and crannies. Current dance music (mostly techno) is on the soundtrack. The later you go, the more likely the mid-to-upper-20s clientele will be entirely local. Open Wednesday through Saturday from 10pm until 4am. In Luxor Las Vegas, 3900 Las Vegas Blvd. S. © **702/262-4000.** Cover $5–$15.

Rain   At press time, this was the hottest nightclub in Vegas. Which means you (and us—don't think we aren't standing there with you, shoulder to shoulder in solidarity) probably will spend most of your time trying to convince someone, anyone, to let you in. You and a couple of thousand of Size-2 Juicy Couture jeans-clad 20-somethings who feel they will simply cease to exist if they don't get inside. We smirk and snicker at their desperation, because it makes us feel superior. But we also have to be honest; if you can brave the wait, the crowds, and the attitude, you will be inside a club that has done everything right, from the multilevel lay-out that allows them to pack the crowds in and allows those crowds to peer up and down at their brethren, to DJs who play the right house and techno cuts (at a pulse-thumping tempo, so don't expect for your good pickup lines to be over-heard), to the scaffolding that holds pyrotechnic and other mood-revvers, to the ubiquitous-of-late go-go girls dressed like strippers. You will have more fun here than at, say, Bikinis (see above), because this is bigger and more crowded, but then again, you can get in there more readily, so you decide what's more impor-tant to you. If this is your choice, then note that they start lining up way before the 11pm opening time. Open Thursday to Saturday from 11pm until dawn. 4321 W. Flamingo Rd. ℂ **702/940-7246.** Cover $20.

rumjungle　Now, normally our delicate sensibilities wince at such overkill, and we tend to write off such efforts as just trying a bit too hard. But surpris-ingly, rumjungle really delivers the great fun it promises. The fire-wall entrance gives way to a wall of water; the two-story bar is full of the largest collection of rum varieties anywhere, each bottle illuminated with a laser beam of light; go-go girls dance and prance between bottles of wine to dueling congas; and the food all comes skewered on swords. It's all a bit much, but it works, it really does. A great deal of thought went into the various clever designs and schemes, and it's paid off. Almost instantly, rumjungle became the hottest club in Vegas, with lines of partiers out the door every night, ready to dance to live world-beat music. Get there early (before 10pm) to avoid lines/guest lists/the cover charge, and consider having dinner (served till 11pm); it's costly, but it's a multicourse, all-you-can-eat feast of flame-pit-cooked Brazilian food. For the amount of food and the waiving of the cover charge, dinner is a good deal. Then dance it all off all night long (the club is open 'til 2am on weeknights, 'til 4am Thurs–Sat night). In Mandalay Bay, 3950 Las Vegas Blvd. S. ℂ **702/632-7408.** Cover $10–$20.

Seven　This is a former restaurant converted to a club by the addition of a whole lot of marble, and the effect is cold and cavernous. No cover charge, which is nice (though a long line, which is not), but that means that just about anyone can get in; while we aren't trying to be snobs, we can do without homo-phobic pretend cowboys and other beer-guzzling jerks. We just wanna dance, you know? Open Monday through Wednesday from 11pm until 2am, Thursday through Saturday until 4am. 3724 Las Vegas Blvd. S. (at Harmon). ℂ **702/739-7744.**

Studio 54　The legendary Studio 54 has been resurrected here in Las Vegas, but with all the bad elements and none of the good ones. Forget Truman, Hal-ston, and Liza doing illegal (or at least immoral) things in the bathroom stalls; that part of Studio 54 remains but a fond memory. The snooty, exclusive door attitude has been retained, however. Hooray. Red-rope policies are all well and good if you're trying to build mystique in a regular club, but for a tourist attrac-tion, where guests are likely to be one-time-only (or at best, once a year), it's obnoxious. Oddly, this doesn't lead to a high-class clientele; of all the new clubs, this is the trashiest (though apparently the hot night for locals is Tues, so if you do go, go then). The large dance floor has a balcony overlooking it, the decor is industrial (exposed piping and the like), the music is hip-hop and electronic, and there is nothing to do other than dance. If the real Studio 54 were this bor-ing, no one would remember it today. Open Tuesday through Saturday from 10pm until 3am or later. In the MGM Grand, 3799 Las Vegas Blvd. S. ℂ **702/891-1111.** Cover $10 for men Tues–Thurs, $20 Fri–Sat; free for women.

Utopia   According to the old *Scope* magazine, Utopia was "less a discotheque and more a revolution"—which is an apt description, considering that in Las Vegas, underground once-a-week nightclubs usually disappear in a matter of weeks. (And for that matter, the underground itself is a shaky, hard-to-find thing.) Utopia is still going strong, despite the death (in a car accident) of its founder, Aaron Britt. The music is progressive house, tribal, trance, techno, and rave. The atmosphere is industrial, foggy, and heavy with lasers and other dazzling visuals. A cool and outrageous crowd fills three rooms with fun, peace, and love, in a heart-pounding, techno way. It's for the tragically hip, but isn't it good to know they are out there in Vegas? Internationally known deejays spin, and live rave acts play. It's open Friday and Saturday from 10:30pm until the sun comes up. 3765 Las Vegas Blvd. S. ℂ 702/736-3105. Cover $20.

Voodoo Lounge   Occupying, along with the Voodoo Cafe, two floors in the new addition to the Rio, the Lounge almost successfully combines Haitian voodoo and New Orleans Creole in its decor and theme. There are two main rooms: one with a large dance floor and stage for live music, and a disco room, which is filled with large video screens and serious light action. Big club chairs in groups form conversation pits, where you might actually be able to have a conversation. The big seller? The bartenders put on a show, a la Tom Cruise in *Cocktail.* They shake, jiggle, and light stuff on fire. Supposedly the live music includes Cajun acts, but when it comes down to it, rock seems to rule the day. The mid- to late-20s crowd is more heavily local than you might expect; the dress code calls for "business casual," with no shorts, jeans, or shirts without collars for men. It's open nightly from 8pm to 3am. In the Rio All-Suite Hotel & Casino, 3700 Las Vegas Blvd. S. ℂ 702/252-7777. Cover $10 and up.

10 Strip Clubs

No, we don't mean entertainment establishments on Las Vegas Boulevard South. We mean the other kind of "strip." Yes, people come to town for the gambling and the wedding chapels, but the lure of Vegas doesn't stop there. Though prostitution is not legal within the city, the sex industry is an active and obvious force in town. Every other cab carries a placard for a strip club, and a walk down the Strip at night will have dozens of men thrusting flyers at you for clubs, escort services, phone-sex lines, and more. And some of you are going to want to check it out.

And why not? An essential part of the Vegas allure is decadence, and naked flesh would certainly qualify, as does the thrill of trying something new and daring. Of course, by and large, the nicer bars aren't particularly daring, and if you go to more than one in an evening, the thrill wears off, and the breasts don't look quite so bare.

In the finest of Vegas traditions, the "something for everyone" mentality extends to strip clubs. Here is a guide to the most prominent and heavily advertised; there are plenty more, of increasing seediness, out there. You don't have to look too hard. The most crowded and zoolike times are after midnight, especially on Friday and Saturday nights. Should you want a "meaningful" experience, you might wish to avoid the rush and choose an off-hour for a visit.

Cheetah's   This is the strip club used as the set in the movie *Showgirls,* but thanks to the magic of Hollywood and later renovations by the club, only the main stage will look vaguely familiar to those few looking for Nomi Malone. There's also a smaller stage, plus three tiny "tip stages" so that you can really get close to (and give much money to) the woman of your choice. Eight TVs line the walls; the club does a brisk business during major sporting events. The management believes, "If you treat people right, they will keep coming back," so the atmosphere is friendlier than at other clubs. They "encourage couples—people who want to party—to come here. We get a 21- to 40-aged party kind of crowd," the manager told us. And indeed there is a sporty, frat-bar feel to the place. (Though on a crowded Sat night, some unescorted women were turned away, despite policy.) Lap dances are $20. Open 24 hours. 2112 Western Ave. © 702/384-0074. Topless. Cover $10.

Club Paradise Until the new behemoths moved into town, this was the nicest of the strip clubs. Which isn't to say it isn't still nice, it's just got competition. The outside looks a lot like the Golden Nugget; the interior and atmosphere are rather like that of a hot nightclub where most of the women happen to be topless. The glitzy stage looks like something from a miniature showroom: The lights flash and the dance music pounds, there are two big video screens (one featuring soft porn, the other showing sports!), the chairs are plush and comfortable, the place is relatively bright by strip-club standards, and they offer champagne and cigars. Not too surprisingly, they get a very white-collar crowd here. The result is not terribly sleazy, which may please some and turn others off. The women ("actual centerfolds") are heavy (and we do mean heavy) on the silicone. They don't so much dance as pose and prance, after which they don skimpy evening dresses and come down to solicit lap dances, which eventually fills the place up with writhing females in thongs. The club says it is "women-friendly," and indeed there were a few couples, including one woman who was receiving a lap dance herself—and didn't seem too uncomfortable. Occasionally the action stops for a minirevue, which ends up being more like semi-naked cheerleading than a show. Lap dances are $20. Open Monday to Friday from 4pm to 6am and Saturday and Sunday from 6pm to 6am. 4416 Paradise Rd. © 702/734-7990. $10 cover, 2-drink minimum (drinks are $4.50 and up). Unescorted women allowed. Topless. Cover $10.

Crazy Horse, Two *(Overrated)* We've omitted the address of this place on purpose. It's full of so much obnoxious jerk attitude, with overly aggressive girls soliciting lap dances, that even the other clubs in town sneer at them. There are plenty of strip bars—pass this one by.

Déjà vu Showgirls Owned by the same people as Little Darlings (see below), this place both deeply perturbs us and amuses the heck out of us. The latter because it's one of the rare strip clubs where the women actually perform numbers. Instead of just coming out and taking off an article or two of clothing and then parading around in a desultory manner before collecting a few tips and running off to solicit lap dances, each stripper comes out and does an actual routine—well, okay, maybe not so much, but she does remove her clothes to personally chosen music, shedding an outfit tailored to her music selection. And so it happened that we have now seen a punk rock chick strip to "Anarchy in the UK" and a Ramones tune. But it also distresses us because it's the kind of place where guys bring their buds the night before their wedding to make sure they get photographed with a naked girl (yes, the girls get totally naked here) performing something raunchy with a sex toy—that's the kind of fun that leaves a bad taste in the mouth. Open daily from 11am to 6am. 3247 Industrial Rd. © 702/894-4167. $20 cover. $20–$30 lap dances. Totally nude. Unescorted women allowed.

> ### *Tips* Two Strippers Give Nine Strip-Bar Etiquette Tips
>
> Brittany and Kitty each have several years' experience working in strip bars, so they know what they're talking about. And they both really are sweet girls, honest.
>
> 1. Bathe.
> 2. Don't lie and say you never go in these places.
> 3. Don't take off your wedding ring. We can still see the mark it leaves.
> 4. Don't ask if we take credit cards. Bring cash!
> 5. Don't fall asleep. Just because we are open 24 hours, we aren't a hotel.
> 6. Don't wear wool pants. They scratch.
> 7. Don't ask for our phone numbers.
> 8. Don't lick us. We're not Popsicles.
> 9. Don't forget: We aren't dumb strippers. We are a lot smarter than you think.

Glitter Gulch   Right there in the middle of the Fremont Street Experience, Glitter Gulch is either an eyesore or the last bastion of Old Las Vegas, depending on your point of view. The inside is modern enough: black light and bubble fountains, arranged around a runway strip. The shows are basic—the women take off sequined gowns to reveal G-strings. Customers sit in comfortable booths, and the dancers then come around and offer up-close and personal table dances, often chatting merrily away while they expose themselves. As you enter, you are assigned your own (overly clothed) waitress who escorts you to your table. They also offer limo service to the hotels and even a line of souvenir clothing. Given such services and its convenient location, this is the perfect place for the merely curious—you can easily pop in, check things out, goggle and ogle, and then hit the road. Table dances are $20. Open daily from noon to 4am. 20 Fremont St. © 702/385-4774. Topless. No cover, 2-drink minimum (drinks $7.75 and up).

Little Darlings   They call themselves the "Pornocopia of Sex," and given the number of services they offer, you can see why. In addition to a fully stocked adult store, they have private nude dances in booths (dancers must stay 6 in. from the customer at all times). This is one of the few clubs where the women are not allowed any physical contact with the customers. There are also rooms where you can watch a nude woman take a shower (in theory doing erotic things with soap), and "Fantasy Rooms" where a glass pane separates you from a woman performing still more erotic stunts. The women are all healthy and athletic, including some who do impressive work with the poles on stage (using their legs to climb all the way to the rafters). Despite all the nude offerings, the resultant atmosphere is not especially dirty, just rowdy. (Tellingly, they do promotions with a local radio station.) That's not surprising when you consider that alcohol is not served on the premises. At least one late-20s customer felt it was all too much like high school and that the cover was prohibitively expensive. Totally nude private dance in booth $20, Fantasy Rooms $30. Open Monday to Saturday from 11am to 6am, Sunday from 6pm to 4am. 1514 Western Ave. © 702/366-0145. No unescorted women. Totally nude. Cover $20.

Jaguar's These guys were totally going to be the largest strip club in town—25,000 square feet—and then someone built something twice as big. So they had to settle for being perhaps the prettiest. They are also sort of the Bellagio of strip clubs, by which we mean, two-story over-the-top marble Italian palace style (think the glory days of Caesars Palace), with high-tech gizmos (such as fingerprint identification for certain VIP rooms) for the well-heeled (and willing to spend it on semi-naked girls). There are three stages with four bars (interesting ratio), and each stage holds four performers, and really is more a series of poles, so this is the place to go if pole work is your particular thing (though weirdly, the stages can be so dark you can't actually see the girls work). Forty percent of the clientele is women, the rest mid-30s guys with money. Lap dances are $20. Open 24 hours. 3355 S. Procyon.© 702/732-1116. Unescorted women allowed. Topless. Cover $10.

Olympic Gardens Topless Cabaret Once the largest of the strip clubs, this almost feels like a family operation, thanks to the middle-aged women handling the door. They also have a boutique selling lingerie and naughty outfits. (Because they get a lot of couples coming in, perhaps this is in case someone gets inspired and wants to try out what they learned here at home.) There are two rooms: one with large padded tables for the women to dance on, the other featuring a more classic strip runway. The girls all seemed really cute—perhaps the best-looking of the major clubs. The crowd is a mix of 20s to 30s blue-collar guys and techno geeks. As the place fills up and the chairs are crammed in next to each other, it's hard to see how enjoyable, or intimate, a lap dance can be when the guy next to you is getting one as well. That didn't seem to stop all the guys there, who seemed appropriately blissed out. Lap dances are $20, more in the VIP room. Open 24 hours. 1531 Las Vegas Blvd. S. © 702/385-8987. Unescorted women allowed. Topless. Cover $20.

The Palomino This used to be a classy, proper strip bar, the way perhaps some of you, who haven't experienced them lately, imagine such establishments to be. Now, however, it edges into the seedy end of things. It's also a bit out of the way. On the other hand, it does offer total nudity in a classic red-walled setting. And its location outside of the Vegas city limits means that it's one of the only clubs that offers both total nudity *and* alcohol. It's two levels, with the downstairs consisting of a large stage where featured dancers ("all have appeared in *Playboy* or *Penthouse* or some kind of publication") do themed dances with specific music, costumes, and props (one healthy blonde surfer gal used a big, white bed and satin nightie in her set), which can result in some incongruous sights, like an essentially interpretive dance with pauses for gynecological shots. Upstairs has two or three small stages with dancers doing their thing up close and personal. There is also a large room off to the side where they take you for lap dances, ensuring a small measure of privacy. Topless lap dances are $20, totally nude dances are $40. Open 24 hours. 1848 Las Vegas Blvd. N. © 702/642-2984. Totally nude. Cover $24.

Sapphires Ladies and Gentlemen, particularly the latter, Las Vegas, home of the largest everything else, now brings you—drum roll—the largest strip club *in the world!* That's right, 71,000 square feet of nakedidity. Of course, you have to see it—and of course, that's what they are counting on. But let's say this: While really, it's nothing you haven't seen before strip-club wise, if you haven't seen a strip club, this is the place to start (though the size and looks are atypical, to say the least; it's all downhill from here), because it's modern and clean and, frankly, it's not all that different, looks-wise, from Rain, the super hot nightclub over at the Rio, except that here you can actually hear yourself think, and also, the girls sometimes wear more clothes than at Rain. And it's also more friendly and less attitudinal. Expect three stages in a bridge shape (including one where gawkers who paid for the privilege can watch the action from below, thanks to a glass floor), and a fourth in a separate, and still large, room, with several poles and strippers all working it at the same time. Giant video screens occasionally act as a Jumbotron for the action on the other side of the cavernous room. Upstairs are incredibly posh and incredibly expensive rooms for wealthy sports and movie figures to utilize. Lap dances are $20. Open 24 hours. 3025 S. Industrial ✆ 702/796-0000. Topless. Cover $20 after 6pm.

Spearmint Rhino   Did you know that even strip bars come in chains? They do, and this is a familiar brand to those in the know, or who read billboards close to airports. The runway (where some of the dancers get a little personal with each other) is actually in a separate back area, so it is possible to have a drink at the front (where there are many TVs and other manly accoutrements) and never see a naked girl (save for the smaller stage and pole nearby). On a busy night, it's crammed with grown-up frat boys enjoying a clubby space. There can be a veritable factory assembly line of lap dances during these busy periods, which frankly, seems the opposite of a turn-on to us. Unescorted women should also note that while nominally they are permitted, lately it seems that they might also be taken for hookers and turned away from the door (lest they come inside and lure customers away). Lap dances are $20. Open 24 hours. 3444 Highland Dr. ✆ 702/796-3600. Unescorted women allowed. Topless. Cover $10.

Strip Tease Cabaret   This club has been redone to eliminate the rather disturbing "fantasy rooms" (where lap dances could occur in private), replacing them with a generic "classy" gentlemen's-club look, all shiny runways and stages (three total, plus the "shower" stage, where periodically two girls will soap each other up). One of the bouncers was in the recent *Ocean's Eleven* as a thug menacing George Clooney. With live deejays and girls far more interested in working the lap-dance angle than dancing, it's a fine safe first-time strip-bar experience, but not one to make you see what all the fuss is about. Lap dances are $20 and up. Courtesy limo pickup. Open daily from 11am to 6am. 3750 S. Valley View Blvd. ✆ 702/253-1555. Unescorted women allowed, couples encouraged. Topless. Cover $7–$12.

11

Side Trips from Las Vegas

Though all of Vegas is designed to make you forget that there is an outside world, it might do you and your pocketbook much good to reacquaint yourself with the non-Vegas realm. Actually, if you're spending more than 3 days in Vegas, this may become a necessity; 2 days with kids and it absolutely will.

Plus, there is such a stark, startling contrast between the artificial wonders of Sin City and the natural wonders that in some cases lie just a few miles away. Few places are as developed and modern as Vegas; few places are as untouched as some of the canyons, desert, and mountains that surround it. The electrical and design marvel that is the Strip couldn't exist without the extraordinary structural feat that is Hoover Dam. Need some fresh air? (My heavens, don't you!) There are plenty of opportunities for outdoor recreation, all in a landscape like no other.

The excursions covered in this chapter, with the exception of Area 51 and the Grand Canyon trips mentioned below, will take you from 20 to 60 miles out of town. Every one of them offers a memorable travel experience.

GRAND CANYON TOURS

Generally, tourists visiting Las Vegas don't drive 300 miles to Arizona to see the Grand Canyon, but there are dozens of sightseeing tours departing from the city daily. In addition to the Coach USA tours described in chapter 7, a major operator, **Scenic Airlines** (© **800/634-6801** or 702/638-3300; www.scenic.com), runs several tours, including their most popular, a deluxe, full-day guided air-ground tour for $219 per person ($189 for children 2–11); the price includes a bus excursion through the national park, a flight over the canyon, and lunch. All scenic tours include flightseeing. The company also offers both full-day and overnight tours with hiking.

Scenic Airlines also offers tours to other points of interest and national parks, including Bryce Canyon and Monument Valley. Ask for details when you call.

1 Hoover Dam & Lake Mead

30 miles SE of Las Vegas

This is one of the most popular excursions from Las Vegas. Hoover Dam is visited by 2,000 to 3,000 people daily. Why should you join them? Because it's an engineering and architectural marvel and it changed the Southwest forever. Without it, you wouldn't even be going to Vegas. Kids may be bored, unless they like machinery or just plain big things, but expose them to it anyway, for their own good. (Buy them ice cream and a Hoover Dam snow globe as a bribe.) Obviously, if you are staying at Lake Mead, it's a must.

The tour itself is a bit cursory, but you do get up close and personal with the dam. Wear comfortable shoes; the tour involves quite a bit of walking. Try to take the tour in the morning to beat the desert heat and the really big crowds.

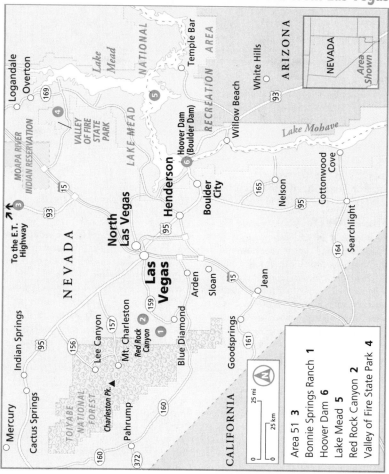

You can have lunch out in Boulder City, and then perhaps drive back through the **Valley of Fire State Park** (a landscape of wind and water-hewn formations of red sandstone), which is about 60 magnificently scenic miles from Lake Mead (purchase gas before you start!). Or you can spend the afternoon on Lake Mead–centered pursuits such as hiking, boating, even scuba diving in season, or perhaps a rafting trip down the Colorado River.

GETTING THERE

Drive east on Flamingo or Tropicana to U.S. 515 south, which automatically turns into I-93 south and takes you right to the dam. This will involve a rather dramatic drive as you go through Boulder City, come over a rise, and Lake Mead suddenly appears spread out before you. It's a beautiful sight. At about this point, the road narrows down to two lanes and traffic can slow considerably. On busy tourist days, this means the drive can take an hour or more.

Impressions
Everybody knows Las Vegas is the best town by a dam site.
    —Masthead slogan of the *Las Vegas Review-Journal*

Go past the turnoff to Lake Mead. As you near the dam, you'll see a five-story parking structure tucked into the canyon wall on your left. Park here ($5 charge) and take the elevators or stairs to the walkway leading to the new visitor center. If you would rather go on an **organized tour,** Coach USA (© **800/ 828-6699;** www.coachusa.com) offers a Hoover Dam package that includes admission and a tour of the dam. When you're in Las Vegas, look for discount coupons in the numerous free publications available at hotels. The 4-hour **Hoover Dam Shuttle Tour** departs daily at 1:30pm and includes pickup and drop-off at your hotel; the price is $44 for adults, $35 for children 2 to 12.

THE HOOVER DAM ★★★

There would be no Las Vegas as we know it without the Hoover Dam. Certainly the neon and glitz that we know and love would not exist. In fact, the growth of the entire Southwest can be tied directly to the electricity that comes from the dam.

Until the Hoover Dam was built, much of the southwestern United States was plagued by two natural problems: parched, sandy terrain that lacked irrigation for most of the year, and extensive flooding in spring and early summer when the mighty Colorado River, fed by melting snow from its source in the Rocky Mountains, overflowed its banks and destroyed crops, lives, and property. On the positive side, raging unchecked over eons, the river's turbulent, rushing waters carved the Grand Canyon.

In 1928, prodded by the seven states through which the river runs during the course of its 1,400-mile journey to the Gulf of California, Congress authorized construction of a dam at Boulder Canyon (later moved to Black Canyon). The Senate's declaration of intention was that "A mighty river, now a source of destruction, is to be curbed and put to work in the interests of society." Construction began in 1931. Because of its vast scope, and the unprecedented problems posed in its realization, the project generated significant advances in many areas of machinery production, engineering, and construction. An army of more than 5,200 laborers was assembled, and work proceeded 24 hours a day. Completed in 1936, 2 years ahead of schedule and $15 million under budget (it is, no doubt, a Wonder of the Modern Fiscal World), the dam stopped the annual floods and conserved water for irrigation, industrial, and domestic use. Equally important, it became one of the world's major electrical generating plants, providing low-cost, pollution-free hydroelectric power to a score of surrounding communities. Hoover Dam's $165 million cost has been repaid with interest by the sale of inexpensive power to a number of California cities and the states of Arizona and Nevada. The dam is a government project that paid for itself—a feat almost as awe-inspiring as its engineering.

The dam itself is a massive curved wall, 660 feet thick at the bottom, tapering to 45 feet where the road crosses it at the top. It towers 726 feet above bedrock (about the height of a 60-story skyscraper) and acts as a plug between the canyon walls to hold back up to 9.2 trillion gallons of water in Lake Mead, the reservoir created by its construction. Four concrete intake towers on the lake side drop the water down about 600 feet to drive turbines and create power, after which the water spills out into the river and continues south.

All the architecture is on a grand scale, and the design has beautiful Art Deco elements, unusual in an engineering project. Note, for instance, the monumental 30-foot bronze sculpture, *Winged Figures of the Republic,* flanking a 142-foot flagpole at the Nevada entrance. According to its creator, Oskar Hansen, the sculpture symbolizes "the immutable calm of intellectual resolution, and the enormous power of trained physical strength, equally enthroned in placid triumph of scientific achievement."

The dam has become a major sightseeing attraction along with Lake Mead, America's largest artificial reservoir and a major Nevada recreation area.

Seven miles northwest of the dam on U.S. 93, you'll pass through **Boulder City,** which was built to house managerial and construction workers. Sweltering summer heat (many days it is 125°F/52°C) ruled out a campsite by the dam. The higher elevation of Boulder City offered lower temperatures. The city emerged within a single year, turning a desert wasteland into a community of 6,000. By 1934 it was Nevada's third-largest town.

TOURING THE DAM

The very nice **Hoover Dam Visitor Center,** a vast three-level circular concrete structure with a rooftop overlook, opened in 1995. You'll enter the Reception Lobby (bags were not allowed inside after the Sept. 11 terrorist attacks, but ask about current security measures as they may have changed), where you can buy tickets; peruse informational exhibits, photographs, and memorabilia; and view three 12-minute video presentations (about the importance of water to life, the events leading up to the construction of Hoover Dam, and the construction itself, as well as the many benefits it confers). Exhibits on the Plaza Level include interactive displays on the environment, habitation, and development of the Southwest, the people who built the dam, and related topics.

Yet another floor up, galleries on the Overlook Level demonstrate, via sculpted bronze panels, the benefits of Hoover Dam and Lake Mead to the states of Arizona, Nevada, and California. The Overlook Level additionally provides an unobstructed view of Lake Mead, the dam, the power plant, the Colorado River, and Black Canyon. (There are multiple photo opportunities throughout this trip.)

You can visit an exhibit center across the street where a 10-minute presentation in a small theater focuses on a topographical map of the 1,400-mile Colorado River. It also has a cafeteria. Notice, by the way, how the restrooms in the exhibition center only have electric dryers, no paper towels. A tribute?

Thirty-minute tours of the dam depart from the Reception Lobby every 15 minutes or so daily, except Thanksgiving and Christmas. The visitor center opens at 9am, and the first tour departs soon after. The last tour leaves at 4:30pm, and the center closes at 5pm. Admission is $10 for adults, $8 for senior citizens and military personnel and their dependents, $4 for children 7 to 16, and free for children under 7. There is no need to call ahead to reserve a place on the tour but for more information, call © **866/291-TOUR** or 702/597-5970.

Note: At this writing, because of post–September 11 security measures, tours of the dam are highly restricted. Groups go to the center, see a movie, and, best of all, get to walk on top of the dam, meeting with six different tour guides (each with their own informative spiel) along the way. Guests should also get to descend, via elevator, partly into the bowels of the thing. Obviously, those measures could at any moment be lifted, or further tightened. We include a description of the usual tour to illustrate what you would get if the restrictions are ever lifted. You may want to call in advance to find out about current restrictions; but apparently, even with the new measures, the tour is still pretty informative.

The usual tour begins with a 561-foot elevator descent into the dam's interior, where an access tunnel leads to the Nevada wing of the power plant. In the three stops on the regular tour, you see the massive turbines that generate the electricity using the water flow, go outside on the downriver side of the dam looking up at the towering structure (which is pretty awesome), and then go into one of the tunnels that contains a steel water-diversion pipe that feeds the turbines. (It's one of the largest steel water pipes ever made—its interior could accommodate two lanes of automobile traffic.)

Some fun facts you might hear along the way: It took 6½ years to fill the lake. Though 96 workers were killed during the construction, contrary to popular myth, none were accidentally buried as the concrete was poured (it was poured only at a level of 8 in. at a time). Look for a monument outside, dedicated to the workers who were killed—"they died to make the desert bloom"—along with a tombstone for their doggy mascot who was also killed, albeit after the dam was completed. Compare their wages of 50¢ an hour to their Depression-era peers, who made 5¢ to 30¢.

For more information on the dam, surf over to its website at **www.usbr.gov/lc/hooverdam**.

LAKE MEAD NATIONAL RECREATION AREA ★★

Under the auspices of the National Park Service, 1.5-million-acre Lake Mead National Recreation Area was created in 1936 around Lake Mead (the reservoir lake that is the result of the construction of Hoover Dam) and later Lake Mohave to the south (formed by the construction of Davis Dam). Before the lakes emerged, this desert region was brutally hot, dry, and rugged—unfit for human habitation. Today, it's one of the nation's most popular playgrounds, attracting about nine million visitors annually. The two lakes comprise 291 square miles. At an elevation of 1,221 feet, Lake Mead itself extends some 110 miles upstream toward the Grand Canyon. Its 550-mile shoreline, backed by spectacular cliff and canyon scenery, forms a perfect setting for a wide variety of watersports and desert hiking.

The **Alan Bible Visitor Center,** 4 miles northeast of Boulder City on U.S. 93 at Nev. 166 (© **702/293-8990**), can provide information on all area activities and services. You can pick up trail maps and brochures here, view informative films, and find out about scenic drives, accommodations, ranger-guided hikes, naturalist programs and lectures, bird-watching, canoeing, camping, lakeside RV parks, and picnic facilities. The center also sells books and videotapes about the area. It's open daily from 8:30am to 4:30pm except Thanksgiving, Christmas, and New Year's Day.

For information on accommodations, boat rentals, and fishing, call **Seven Crown Resorts** (© **800/752-9669**; www.sevencrown.com).

You can also find info on the Web at **www.nps.gov/lame**.

In May 2000 the park service began to charge **entry fees** for the first time. Fees are $5 per vehicle, and this covers all passengers.

OUTDOOR ACTIVITIES

This is a lovely area for scenic drives amidst the dramatic desert scenery. One popular route follows the Lakeshore and Northshore Scenic drives along the edge of Lake Mead. From these roads there are panoramic views of the blue lake set against a backdrop of the browns, blacks, reds, and grays that make up the

desert mountains. Northshore Scenic Drive also leads through areas of brilliant red boulders and rock formations, and you'll find a picnic area along the way.

BOATING & FISHING A store at **Lake Mead Resort and Marina,** under the auspices of Seven Crown Resorts (© **800/752-9669** or 702/293-3484), rents fishing boats, ski boats, personal watercraft, and patio boats. It also carries groceries, clothing, marine supplies, sporting goods, water-skiing gear, fishing equipment, and bait and tackle. You can get a fishing license here ($51 for a year, $20 for 3 days, $48 for 10 days; discounts for children under 15 are available; additional fees apply for special fishing classifications). The staff is knowledgeable and can apprise you of good fishing spots. Largemouth bass, striped bass, channel catfish, crappie, and bluegill are found in Lake Mead; rainbow trout, largemouth bass, and striped bass in Lake Mohave. You can also arrange here to rent a fully equipped houseboat at **Echo Bay,** 40 miles north.

Other convenient Lake Mead marinas offering similar rentals and equipment are **Las Vegas Bay** (© **702/565-9111**), which is even closer to Las Vegas, and **Callville Bay** (© **702/565-8958**), which is the least crowded of the five on the Nevada Shore.

CAMPING Lake Mead's shoreline is dotted with campsites, all of them equipped with running water, picnic tables, and grills. Available on a first-come, first-served basis, they are administered by the **National Park Service** (© **702/293-8990;** www.nps.gov). There's a charge of $10 per night at each campsite.

CANOEING The **Alan Bible Visitor Center** (see above) can provide a list of outfitters who rent canoes for trips on the Colorado River. There's one catch, however: A canoeing permit ($5 per person) is required in advance for certain areas near the dam and is available from the **Bureau of Reclamation** (Attn.: Canoe Launch Permits), Box 60400, Boulder City, NV 89006-0400 (© **702/293-8204**). You can apply for and receive the permit on the same day that you plan to canoe.

HIKING The best season for hiking is November to March (it's too hot the rest of the year). Some ranger-guided hikes are offered via the **Alan Bible Visitor Center** (see above), which also stocks detailed trail maps. Three trails, ranging in length from ¾ mile to 6 miles, originate at the visitor center. The 6-mile trail goes past remains of the railroad built for the dam project. Be sure to take all necessary desert-hiking precautions (see details in chapter 7).

LAKE CRUISES A delightful way to enjoy Lake Mead is on a cruise aboard **Lake Mead Cruises'** *Desert Princess* ✦ (© **702/293-6180;** www.lakemead cruises.com), a Mississippi-style paddle-wheeler. Cruises depart year-round from a terminal near **Lake Mead Lodge** (see below). It's a relaxing, scenic trip (enjoyed from an open promenade deck or one of two fully enclosed, climate-controlled decks) through Black Canyon and past colorful rock formations known as the "Arizona Paint Pots" en route to Hoover Dam, which is lit at night. Options include buffet breakfast cruises ($29 adults, $15 children under 12), narrated midday cruises ($19 adults, $9 children), cocktail/dinner cruises ($40 adults, $21 children), and sunset dinner/dance cruises with live music ($51 adults; children not permitted). Dinner is served in a pleasant, windowed, air-conditioned dining room. There's a full bar onboard. Call for departure times.

SCUBA DIVING October to April, there's good visibility, lessened in summer months when algae flourishes. A list of good dive locations, authorized instructors, and nearby dive shops is available at **Alan Bible Visitor Center** (see above). There's an underwater, designated diving area near Lake Mead Marina.

BOULDER CITY

You might want to consider poking around Boulder City on your way back to Vegas. Literally the company town for those building Hoover Dam, it was created by the wives who came with their husbands and turned a temporary site into a real community, since aided by the recreational attractions and attendant businesses of Lake Mead. It doesn't look like much as you first approach it, but once you are in the heart, you'll discover that it's quite charming. There are some antiques and curio shops, and a number of family-style restaurants and burger and Mexican joints, including **Totos,** a reasonably priced Mexican restaurant at 806 Buchanan Blvd. (© **702/293-1744**); it's in the Von's shopping center. Or you could try the **Happy Days Diner,** 512 Nevada Hwy. (© **702/293-4637**), which is right on the road to and from the dam. A '50s diner in looks and menu, it has the usual burgers, shakes, and fries, plus complete breakfasts, and is quite inexpensive ($3 for a turkey burger on a recent visit), friendly, and a good place to take the kids.

ACCOMMODATIONS

In addition to the hotel below (the only place to stay right on Lake Mead itself, aside from campsites), there are a number of little hotels in Boulder City.

Lake Mead Lodge *Value* If camping isn't your bag, spend your night or nights at this rustic and comfortable bungalow-style lodge. It's an easy drive from Hoover Dam and is right on the lake, but also right on the desert, so don't picture it as a wooded resort. The rooms are pleasant, with wood-paneled ceilings and walls of white-painted brick or rough-hewn pine. All offer full private bathrooms. There is a suite with three rooms and a small kitchen, which might be good for families staying a few days. (There are plans to add a second suite.) The pool is rudimentary, but you might want to relax with a good book in one of the gazebos on the property. About ½-mile down the road is the marina, where you can while away a few hours over cocktails on a lakeside patio. The marina (the Lake Mead Resort and Marina) is the headquarters for boating, fishing, and watersports; it also houses a large shop (see marina details above, under "Boating & Fishing").

There's a nautically themed restaurant called **Tale of the Whale** (🕿 **702/293-3484**) at the marina, its rough-hewn pine interior embellished with various seafaring iconography. It's open from 7am to 8pm Sunday to Thursday, and until 9pm Friday and Saturday (it closes an hour later during the summer). The restaurant serves hearty breakfasts; sandwiches, salads, and burgers at lunch; and steak-and-seafood dinners. And Boulder Beach, also an easy walk from the lodge, has waterfront picnic tables and barbecue grills.

322 Lakeshore Rd., Boulder City, NV 89005. 🕿 **800/752-9669** or 702/293-2074. www.lakemeadmarina. com/lodge.html. 42 units. Apr–Oct $85 and up double; the rest of the year $70 and up double. Extra person $10. Children under 5 stay free in parent's room. Pets accepted, $10 per pet. DISC, MC, V. **Amenities:** Restaurant; outdoor pool; watersports equipment; picnic area with barbecue pit. *In room:* A/C, TV w/basic cable.

2 Valley of Fire State Park ★ ★

60 miles NE of Las Vegas

Most people visualize the desert as a vast expanse of undulating sands punctuated by the occasional cactus or palm-fringed oasis. But the desert of America's Southwest bears little relation to this Lawrence of Arabia image. Stretching for hundreds of miles around Las Vegas in every direction is a seemingly lifeless tundra of vivid reddish earth, shaped by time, climate, and subterranean upheavals into majestic canyons, cliffs, and ridges.

The 36,000-acre Valley of Fire State Park typifies the mountainous red Mojave Desert. It derives its name from the brilliant sandstone formations that were created 150 million years ago by a great shifting of sand and that continue to be shaped by the geologic processes of wind and water erosion. These are rock formations like you'll never see anywhere else. There is nothing green, just fiery flaming red rocks, swirling unrelieved as far as the eye can see. No wonder various sci-fi movies have used this as a stand-in for another planet—it has a most otherworldly look. The whole place is very mysterious, loaded with petroglyphs, and totally inhospitable. It's not hard to believe that for the Indians it was a sacred place, where men came as a test of their manhood. It is a natural wonder that must be seen to be appreciated.

Although it's hard to imagine in the sweltering Nevada heat, for billions of years these rocks were under hundreds of feet of ocean. This ocean floor began to rise some 200 million years ago, and the waters became more and more shallow. Eventually the sea made a complete retreat, leaving a muddy terrain traversed by ever-diminishing streams. A great sandy desert covered much of the southwestern part of the American continent until about 140 million years ago. Over eons, winds, massive fault action, and water erosion sculpted fantastic formations of sand and limestone. Oxidation of iron in the sands and mud—and the effect of groundwater leaching the oxidized iron—turned the rocks the many hues of red, pink, russet, lavender, and white that can be seen today. Logs of ancient forests washed down from faraway highlands and became petrified fossils, which can be seen along two interpretive trails.

Human beings occupied the region—a wetter and cooler one—as far back as 4,000 years ago. They didn't live in the Valley of Fire, but during the Gypsum period (2000 B.C.–300 B.C.), men hunted bighorn sheep (a source of food, clothing, blankets, and hut coverings) here with a notched stick called an *atlatl* that is depicted in the park's petroglyphs. Women and children caught rabbits, tortoises, and other small game. In the next phase, from 300 B.C. to A.D. 700, the climate became warmer and dryer. Bows and arrows replaced the atlatl, and the hunters and gatherers discovered farming. The Anasazi people began cultivating corn, squash, and beans, and communities began replacing small nomadic family groups. These ancient people wove watertight baskets, mats, hunting nets, and clothing. Around A.D. 300, they learned how to make sun-dried ceramic pottery. Other tribes, notably the Paiutes, migrated to the area. By A.D. 1150, they had become the dominant group. Unlike the Anasazi, the Paiutes were still nomadic and used the Valley of Fire region seasonally. These were the inhabitants whom white settlers found when they entered the area in the early to mid-1800s. The newcomers diverted river and spring waters to irrigate their farmlands, destroying the nature-based Paiute way of life. About 300 descendants of those Paiute tribespeople still live on the Moapa Indian Reservation (about 20 miles northwest) that was established along the Muddy River in 1872.

GETTING THERE

From Las Vegas, take I-15 north to exit 75 (Valley of Fire turnoff). However, the more scenic route is to take I-15 north, then travel Lake Mead Boulevard east to Northshore Road (Nev. 167), and proceed north to the Valley of Fire exit. The first route takes about an hour, the second 1½ hours.

There is a $5 per vehicle admission charge to the park, regardless of how many people you cram inside.

Plan on spending a minimum of an hour in the park, though you can spend a great deal of time more. It can get very hot in there (there is nothing to relieve the sun beating down on all that red and reflecting off it) and there is no water, so be certain to bring a liter, maybe two, with you in the summer. Without a guide, you must stay on paved roads, but don't worry if they end, you can always turn around and come back to the main road again. You can see a great deal from the car, but there are also hiking trails.

Numerous **sightseeing tours** go to the Valley of Fire. **Coach USA** (© **800/828-6699;** www.coachusa.com) offers a 6-hour tour from Las Vegas, including Lake Mead in the morning and the Valley of Fire in the afternoon, plus lunch. Cost is $100 for adults, $96 for children 2 to 12. Inquire at your hotel tour desk. Char Cruze of **Creative Adventures** (p. 197) also offers a fantastic tour.

The Valley of Fire can also be visited in conjunction with Lake Mead. From **Lake Mead Lodge** (see above), take Nev. 166 (Lakeshore Scenic Dr.) north, make a right turn on Nev. 167 (Northshore Scenic Dr.), turn left on Nev. 169 (Moapa Valley Blvd.) west—a spectacularly scenic drive—and follow the signs. Valley of Fire is about 65 miles from Hoover Dam.

WHAT TO SEE & DO

There are no food concessions or gas stations in the park; however, you can obtain meals or gas on Nev. 167 or in nearby **Overton** (15 miles northwest on Nev. 169). Overton is a fertile valley town replete with trees, agricultural crops, horses, and herds of cattle—quite a change in scenery. On your way in or out of the teeming metropolis, do stop off at **Inside Scoop** ⭐, 395 S. Moapa Valley Blvd. (℃ **702/ 397-2055**), open daily from 11am to 6pm. It's a sweet, old-fashioned ice-cream parlor run by extremely friendly people, with a proper menu that, in addition to classic sandwiches and the like, features some surprising choices—a vegetarian sandwich and a fish salad with crab and shrimp, for example. Everything is quite tasty and fresh. They also do box lunches, perfect for picnicking inside the park. We strongly recommend coming by here on your way in for a box lunch, and then coming by afterward for a much-needed cooling ice cream.

At the southern edge of town is the **Lost City Museum** ⭐, 721 S. Moapa Valley Blvd. (℃ **702/397-2193**), a sweet little museum, very nicely done, commemorating an ancient Anasazi village that was discovered in the region in 1924. Artifacts dating back 12,000 years are on display, as are clay jars, dried corn and beans, arrowheads, seashell necklaces, and willow baskets from the ancient Pueblo culture that inhabited this region between A.D. 300 and 1150. Other exhibits document the Mormon farmers who settled the valley in the 1860s. A large collection of local rocks—petrified wood, fern fossils, iron pyrite, green copper, and red iron oxide—along with manganese blown bottles turned purple by the ultraviolet rays of the sun are also displayed here. The museum is surrounded by reconstructed wattle-and-daub pueblos. Admission is $2, free for children under 18. The museum is open daily from 8:30am to 4:30pm. Closed Thanksgiving, December 25, and January 1.

Information headquarters for Valley of Fire is the **visitor center** on Nev. 169, 6 miles west of Northshore Road (℃ **702/397-2088**). It's open daily from 8:30am to 4:30pm and is worth a quick stop for information and a bit of history before entering the park. Exhibits on the premises explain the origin and geologic history of the park's colorful sandstone formations, describe the ancient peoples who carved their rock art on canyon walls, and identify the plants and wildlife you're likely to see. Postcards, books, slides, and films are on sale here, and you can pick up hiking maps and brochures. Rangers can answer your park-related questions. For Web information on the park, surf over to **http://parks.nv.gov/vf.htm**.

There are **hiking trails, shaded picnic sites,** and **two campgrounds** in the park. Most sites are equipped with tables, grills, water, and restrooms. A $12-per-vehicle, per-night camping fee is charged for use of the campground; if you're not camping, it costs $5 per vehicle to enter the park.

Some of the notable formations in the park have been named for the shapes they vaguely resemble—a duck, an elephant, seven sisters, domes, beehives, and so on. Mouse's Tank is a natural basin that collects rainwater, so named for a fugitive Paiute called Mouse who hid there in the late 1890s. And Native American petroglyphs etched into the rock walls and boulders—some dating from as early as 3,000 years ago—can be observed on self-guided trails. **Petroglyphs** at Atlatl Rock and Petroglyph Canyon are both easily accessible. In summer, when temperatures are usually over 100°F (38°C), you may have to settle for driving through the park in an air-conditioned car.

3 Red Rock Canyon ⭐⭐⭐

19 miles W of Las Vegas

If you need a break from the casinos of Vegas, with their windowless, claustrophobic, noisy interiors, Red Rock Canyon is balm for your overstimulated soul. Less than 20 miles away—but a world apart—this is a magnificent unspoiled vista that should cleanse and refresh you (and if you must, a morning visit should leave you enough time for an afternoon's gambling). You can drive the panoramic 13-mile **Scenic Drive** (open daily 7am–dusk) or explore it in more depth on foot, making it perfect for both athletes and armchair types. There are many interesting sights and trail heads along the drive itself. The wider **National Conservation Area** offers hiking trails and internationally acclaimed rock-climbing opportunities. Especially notable is 7,068-foot Mount Wilson, the highest sandstone peak among the bluffs; for information on climbing, contact the **Red Rock Canyon Visitor Center** at ℂ **702/363-1921.** There are picnic areas along the drive and in nearby **Spring Mountain Ranch State Park,** 5 miles south, which also offers plays in an outdoor theater during the summer. Since Bonnie Springs Ranch (see the next section) is just a few miles away, it makes a great base for exploring Red Rock Canyon.

GETTING THERE

Just drive west on Charleston Boulevard, which becomes Nev. 159. As soon as you leave the city, the red rocks will begin to loom around you. The visitor center will appear on your right.

You can also go on an **organized tour.** Coach USA (ℂ **800/828-6699;** www.coachusa.com), among other companies, runs bus tours to Red Rock Canyon. Inquire at your hotel tour desk.

Finally, you can go **by bike.** Not very far out of town (at Rainbow Blvd.), Charleston Boulevard is flanked by a bike path that continues for about 11 miles to the visitor center/scenic drive. The path is hilly but not difficult if you're in reasonable shape. However, exploring Red Rock Canyon by bike should be attempted only by exceptionally fit and experienced bikers.

Just off Nev. 159, you'll see the **Red Rock Canyon Visitor Center** (ℂ **702/ 363-1921;** www.redrockcanyon.blm.gov), which marks the actual entrance to the park. There, you can pick up information on trails and view history exhibits on the canyon. The center is open daily from 8:30am to 4:30pm. Red Rock Canyon can be combined with a visit to Bonnie Springs Ranch.

ABOUT RED ROCK CANYON

The geological history of these ancient stones goes back some 600 million years. Over eons, the forces of nature have formed Red Rock's sandstone monoliths into arches, natural bridges, and massive sculptures painted in a stunning palette of gray-white limestone and dolomite, black mineral deposits, and oxidized minerals in earth-toned sienna hues ranging from pink to crimson and burgundy. Orange and green lichens add further contrast, as do spring-fed areas of lush foliage. And formations like Calico Hill are brilliantly white where groundwater has leached out oxidized iron. Cliffs cut by deep canyons tower 2,000 feet above the valley floor.

During most of its history, Red Rock Canyon was below a warm, shallow sea. Massive fault action and volcanic eruptions caused this seabed to begin rising some 225 million years ago. As the waters receded, sea creatures died and the calcium in their bodies combined with sea minerals to form limestone cliffs studded with ancient fossils. Some 45 million years later, the region was buried beneath thousands of feet of windblown sand. The landscape was as arid as the Sahara. As time progressed, iron oxide and calcium carbonate infiltrated the sand, consolidating it into cross-bedded rock.

Shallow streams began carving the Red Rock landscape, and logs that washed down from ancient highland forests fossilized, their molecules gradually replaced by quartz and other minerals. These petrified stone logs, which the Paiute Indians believed were weapons of the wolf god Shinarav, can be viewed in the **Chinle Formation** at the base of the Red Rock Cliffs. About 100 million years ago, massive fault action began dramatically shifting the rock landscape here, forming spectacular limestone and sandstone cliffs and rugged canyons punctuated by waterfalls, shallow streams, and serene oasis pools. Especially notable is the **Keystone Thrust Fault,** dating back about 65 million years when two of the earth's crustal plates collided, forcing older limestone and dolomite plates from the ancient seas over younger red and white sandstones. Over the years, water and wind have been ever-creative sculptors, continuing to redefine this strikingly beautiful landscape.

Red Rock's valley is home to more than 45 species of mammals, about 100 species of birds, 30 reptiles and amphibians, and an abundance of plant life. Ascending the slopes from the valley, you'll see cactus and creosote bushes, aromatic purple sage, yellow-flowering blackbrush, yucca and Joshua trees, and, at higher elevations, clusters of forest-green piñon, juniper, and ponderosa pines. In spring, the desert blooms with extraordinary wildflowers.

Archaeological studies of Red Rock have turned up pottery fragments, stone tools, pictographs (rock drawings), and petroglyphs (rock etchings), along with other ancient artifacts. They show that humans have been in this region since about 3000 B.C. (some experts say as early as 10,000 B.C.). You can still see remains of early inhabitants on hiking expeditions in the park. (As for habitation of Red Rock, the same Anasazi-to-Paiutes-to-white-settlers progression related in the Valley of Fire section above occurred here.)

In the latter part of the 19th century, Red Rock was a mining site and later a sandstone quarry that provided materials for many buildings in Los Angeles, San Francisco, and early Las Vegas. By the end of World War II, as Las Vegas developed, many people became aware of the importance of preserving the canyon. In 1967 the Secretary of the Interior designated 62,000 acres as Red Rock Canyon Recreation Lands under the auspices of the Bureau of Land Management, and later legislation banned all development except hiking trails and limited recreational facilities. In 1990, Red Rock Canyon became a National Conservation Area, further elevating its protected status. Its current acreage is 197,000.

WHAT TO SEE & DO

Begin with a stop at the **visitor center;** not only is there a $5 per-vehicle fee to pay, but you can pick up a variety of helpful literature: history, guides, hiking trail maps, and lists of local flora and fauna. You can also view exhibits that tell the history of the canyon and depict its plant and animal life. You'll see a fascinating video here about Nevada's thousands of wild horses and burros, protected by an act of Congress since 1971. Furthermore, you can obtain permits for hiking and backpacking. Call ahead to find out about ranger-guided tours as well as informative guided hikes offered by groups like the Sierra Club and the Audubon Society. And, if you're traveling with children, ask about the free *Junior Ranger Discovery Book* filled with fun family activities. Books and videotapes are on sale here, including a guidebook identifying more than 100 top-rated climbing sites.

The easiest thing to do is to **drive the 13-mile scenic loop** ★★. It really is a loop and it only goes one way, so once you start you are committed to driving the whole thing. You can stop the car to admire any number of fabulous views and sights along the way, or have a picnic, or take a walk or hike. As you drive, observe how dramatically the milky-white limestone alternates with iron-rich red rocks. Farther along, the mountains become solid limestone, with canyons running between them, which lead to an evergreen forest—a surprising sight in the desert.

If you're up to it, however, we can't stress enough that the way to really see the canyon is by **hiking.** Every trail is incredible—glance over your options and decide what you might be looking for. You can begin from the visitor center or drive into the loop, park your car, and start from points therein. Hiking trails range from a 7/10-mile-loop stroll to a waterfall (its flow varying seasonally) at Lost Creek to much longer and more strenuous treks. Actually, all the hikes involve a certain amount of effort, as you have to scramble over rocks on even the shortest hikes. Unfit or undexterous people should beware. Be sure to wear good shoes, as the rocks can be slippery. You must have a map; you won't get lost forever (there usually are other hikers around to help you out, eventually), but you can get lost. It is often tough to find a landmark, and once deep into the rocks, everything looks the same, even with the map. Consequently, give yourself extra time for each hike (at least an additional hour), regardless of its billed length, to allow for the lack of paths, getting disoriented, and simply to slow down and admire the scenery.

A popular 2-mile round-trip hike leads to **Pine Creek Canyon** and the creekside ruins of a historic homesite surrounded by ponderosa pine trees. Our hiking trail of choice is the **Calico Basin,** which is accessed along the loop. After an hour walk up the rocks (which is not that well marked), you end up at an oasis surrounded by sheer walls of limestone (which makes the oasis itself inaccessible, alas). In the summer, flowers and deciduous trees grow out of the walls.

As you hike, keep your eyes peeled for lizards, the occasional desert tortoise, herds of bighorn sheep, birds, and other critters. But the rocks themselves are the most fun, with many minicaves to explore and rock formations to climb on. (Relive childhood with a politically incorrect game of Cowboys and Indians!) On trails along Calico Hills and the escarpment, look for "Indian marbles," a local name for small, rounded sandstone rocks that have eroded off larger sandstone formations. Petroglyphs are also tucked away in various locales.

Biking is another option; riding a bicycle would be a tremendous way to travel the loop. There are also terrific off-road mountain-biking trails, with levels from amateur to expert.

After you tour the canyon, drive over to Bonnie Springs Ranch (details in the next section) for lunch or dinner. See chapter 7 for further details on biking and climbing.

4 Bonnie Springs Ranch/Old Nevada ⟨★⟩⟨★

About 24 miles W of Las Vegas, 5 miles past Red Rock Canyon

Bonnie Springs Ranch/Old Nevada is a kind of Wild West theme park with accommodations and a restaurant. If you're traveling with kids, a day or overnight trip to Bonnie Springs is recommended, but it is surprisingly appealing for adults too. It could even be a romantic getaway, as it offers horseback riding, gorgeous mountain vistas, proximity to Red Rock Canyon, and temperatures 5°F to 10°F (−15°C to−12°C) cooler than on the Strip.

For additional information, you can call **Bonnie Springs Ranch/Old Nevada** at ℂ **702/875-4191** or visit them on the Web at **www.bonniesprings.com.**

If you're **driving,** a trip to Bonnie Springs Ranch can be combined easily with a day trip to Red Rock Canyon; it is about 5 miles farther on. But you can also stay overnight.

For those without transportation, there are jeep tours to and from Las Vegas available through **Action Tours** (© **702/796-9355;** http://actiontours.com).

WHAT TO SEE & DO IN OLD NEVADA

Old Nevada ⭐⭐ (© **702/875-4191**) is a re-creation of an 1880s frontier town, built on the site of a very old ranch. As tourist sights go, this is a good one; it's a bit cheesy, but knowingly, perhaps even deliberately, so. It's terrific for kids up to about the age of 12 or so (before teenage cynicism kicks in) but not all that bad for adults fondly remembering similar places from their own childhoods. Many go expecting a tourist trap, only to come away saying that it really was rather cute and charming.

Certainly, Old Nevada looks authentic, with rustic buildings made entirely of weathered wood. And the setting, right in front of beautiful mountains with layered red rock, couldn't be more perfect for a Western film fantasy. You can wander the town (it's only about a block long), taking peeps into well-replicated places of business, such as a blacksmith shop, a working mill, a saloon, and an old-fashioned general store (cum gift shop) and museum that has a potpourri of items from the Old West and Old Las Vegas: antique gaming tables and slot machines, typewriters, and a great display of old shoes including lace-up boots. There is also a rather lame wax museum; the less said about it, the better.

Country music is played in the saloon during the day, except when **stage melodramas** take place (at frequent intervals between 11:30am and 5pm). These are entirely tongue-in-cheek—the actors are goofy and know it, and the plot is hokey and fully intended to be that way. Somehow, it just heightens the fun factor. It's interactive with the audience, which, in response to cue cards held up by the players, boos and hisses the mustache-twirling villain, sobs in sympathy with the distressed heroine, and laughs, cheers, and applauds. It's hugely silly and hugely fun, provided you all play along. Kids love it, though younger ones might be scared by the occasional gunshot.

Following each melodrama, a **Western drama** is presented outside the saloon, involving a bank robbery, a shootout, and the trial of the bad guy. A judge, prosecuting attorney, and defense attorney are chosen from the audience, the remainder of whom act as the jury. The action always culminates in a hanging. None of this is a particularly polished act, but the dialogue is quite funny and the whole thing is performed with enthusiasm and affection.

Throughout the area, cowboys continually interact with visiting kids, who, on the weekends, are given badges so that they can join a posse hunting for bad guys. There are also ongoing **stunt shootouts** (maybe not at the level found at, say, Universal Studios) in this wild frontier town, and some rather unsavory characters occasionally languish in the town jail.

In the **Old Nevada Photograph Shoppe** you can have a tintype picture taken in 1890s Wild West costume (they have a fairly large selection) with a 120-year-old camera. There are replicas of a turn-of-the-century church and stamp mill; the latter, which has original 1902 machinery, was used for crushing rocks to separate gold and silver from the earth. Movies (one about nearby Red Rock Canyon, one a silent film) are shown in the **Old Movie House** throughout the day from 10:30am to 5pm. You can tour the remains of the **old Comstock lode silver mine,** though there isn't much to see there. You can also shop for a variety of "Western" souvenirs (though to us, that's when the tourist trap part kicks in). Eateries in Old Nevada are discussed below. There's plenty of parking; weekends and holidays a free shuttle train takes visitors from the parking lot to the entrance.

Admission to Old Nevada is charged by vehicle—$5 per car weekdays, for up to six people in the car, and $7 per car on the weekend. The park is open daily from 10:30am to 5pm November to April, and until 6pm the rest of the year.

WHAT TO SEE & DO AT BONNIE SPRINGS RANCH

There are several things to do here free of charge, and it's right next door to Old Nevada. It's quite a pretty place, in a funky, Western kind of way, and in season, there are tons of flowers everywhere, including honeysuckle and roses. The main attraction is the small **zoo** 🌟 on the premises. Now, when we say "zoo," unfortunately, we mean in addition to a petting zoo with the usual suspects (deer, sheep, goats, and rabbits) and some unusual animals (potbelly pigs and snooty, beautiful llamas) to caress and feed, there is also a mazelike enclosure of a series of wire-mesh pens that contain a variety of livestock, some of whom should not be penned up (though they are well taken care of), including wolves and bobcats. Still, it's more than diverting for kids.

Less politically and ecologically distressing is the aviary, which houses peacocks, Polish chickens, peachface and blackmask lovebirds, finches, parakeets, ravens, ducks, pheasants, and geese. Keep your eyes peeled for the peacocks roaming free; with luck, they will spread their tails for a photo-op. With greater luck, some of the angelic, rare white peacocks will do the same. It may be worth dropping by just in the hopes of spotting one in full fan-tailed glory. (And the ranch also sells peacocks, for $25. Now *there's* a souvenir!)

Riding stables offer guided trail rides into the mountain area on a continuous basis throughout the day (9am–3:15pm spring to fall, until 5:45pm in summer). Children must be at least 6 years old to participate. Cost is $25 per person. For more information, call ☎ **702/875-4191.**

Scenic 20-minute **stagecoach rides,** offered weekends and holidays, cost $5 for adults, $3 for children under 12.

ACCOMMODATIONS & DINING

In Old Nevada, the **Miner's Restaurant** is a snack bar located in quite a large room that looks great thanks to Western-motif accessories. Inexpensive fare (sandwiches, decent burgers, pizza, and hot dogs) is served, along with fresh-baked desserts. There are tables out on the porch. In summer you can also get beer and soft drinks in a similarly old-fashioned **Beer Parlor.**

Bonnie Springs Motel 🌟   This is really a hoot; a funky, friendly little place in the middle of nowhere—except that nowhere is a gorgeous setting. The motel is in two double-story buildings and offers regular rooms, "Western" rooms, "specialty theme" rooms, and kitchen suites.

Where to begin? Here, the theme is expressed mostly through the use of fabrics, personally decorated by the owner, who did a pretty nice job. The "gay 1890s" room is done in black and pink, with a lace canopy over the bed, an old-fashioned commode, and liberal use of velvet. The American Indian room uses skins, feathers, and has a burl-wood chair covered in bearskin. You get the idea. The "Western" rooms have more burl-wood furniture and electric-log fireplaces that blow heat into the room.

All special theme rooms (aka fantasy suites) have mirrors over the beds and big whirlpool tubs in the middle of the room (not in the bathrooms) and come with bottles of champagne (the empties of which you can see littering the road on your way out). All the rooms are quite large, though long and narrow, and have private balconies or patios, and mountain views. There are also large family suites with fully equipped kitchens, bedrooms, living rooms (with convertible sofas), and dressing areas; these are equipped with two phones and two TVs and are available for long-term rentals (many of the people who work at Old Nevada actually rent these as apartments). Videotapes and players are available for rental, and there is even a tiny train that takes you around the grounds and on a short tour of the desert.

The **Bonnie Springs Ranch Restaurant** has a lot of character and is a perfect family place. It's heavily rustic (stone floors, log beams, raw wooden chairs made from tree branches, lanterns, a roaring fire in winter, and plenty of dead animals adorning the walls). It's a bit touristy, but small-town touristy. The food is basic—steak, ribs, chicken, burgers, and potato skins; pancakes and eggs for breakfast; it's all greasy but good. There is a cozy bar attached to the restaurant, its walls covered with thousands of dollar bills with messages on them—a classic neighborhood bar, if it were actually in a neighborhood.

1 Gunfighter Lane, Old Nevada, NV 89004. ℂ 702/875-4400. Fax 702/875-4424. www.bonniesprings. com/motel.html. 50 units. Sun–Thurs $60–$70 double, Fri–Sat $70–$80 double; Sun–Thurs $120 fantasy suite, Fri–Sat $135 fantasy suite; Sun–Thurs $95 family suite, Fri–Sat $100 family suite. Extra person $5. AE, MC, V. **Amenities:** Restaurant; outdoor pool; nonsmoking rooms. *In room:* A/C, TV w/pay movies, coffeemakers.

5 A Close Encounter with Area 51 ⟨⋆

150 miles N of Las Vegas

Want to feel like an extra on the *X-Files?* Just want to get an idea of the kind of spots the government picks when it needs a place in which to do secret things? Take the drive from Vegas out to the **"E.T. Highway,"** where folks were spotting aliens years before it became fashionable. This is about a 150-mile trip one-way, so it's probably not something to do on a whim, but even for non–alien buffs, it can be a long, strange—and oddly illuminating—trip indeed.

Area 51 is a secret military facility, containing a large air base that the government will not discuss. The site was selected in the mid-1950s for the testing of the U2 spy plane, and is supposedly the current testing ground for "black budget" aircraft before their public acknowledgment. (Oh, heck, who are they trying to kid? *Of course* that's where they are testing high-tech gadgets.) But its real fame comes with the stories of aliens, whose bodies and ships were supposedly taken there when they "crashed" at Roswell.

Mind you, the only thing alien you are guaranteed to see is the landscape. Only fans of desert topography will find the scenery attractive. It's a desolate area, but that's part of the inexplicable charm. There is absolutely a weird vibe in the air; something is going on out here. And one thing's for sure: If you need a place for covert, or at least private, activities, you couldn't find a better location for it. Alien bodies? Shoot, you could hide an entire alien fleet.

But don't come looking for monuments, historical markers, or good shopping—with a few exceptions, there's a whole lot of nothing out there. You'd think the tourist possibilities would have led to more development, but even in Vegas, despite the presence of plenty of alien merchandise in the gift shops and an entire Area 51–themed shopping area at the new airport expansion, there is not as much awareness as you might think. One waitress, when asked if she'd been there, responded, "Not since they remodeled."

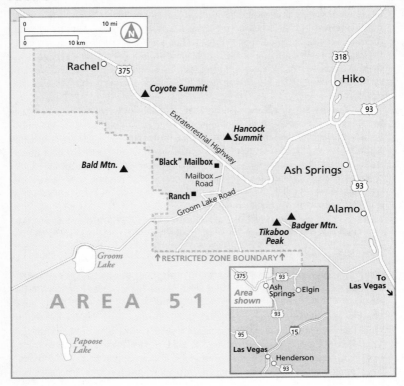

All we know for sure is that you turn down one of the most well-maintained dirt roads you will ever encounter, drive a few miles, and come upon a fence with a sign that warns you against going any farther in the utmost of strict terms (though the language has been toned down from "use of deadly force authorized" to threats of fines and jail time). Along the way down that road, notice how there is absolutely no wildlife other than grasshoppers, that the Joshua trees suddenly turn to an enormous size and monstrous shape, and that the few cattle grazing around don't seem like any cattle you've seen before. Then notice those blasted-out craters in the earth, with the core sample holes in the center. When you realize you are looking at nuclear test sites, the desolation and mutations suddenly make sense. Wave hi at the guys in the military vehicles who are making damn sure you don't go through that gate, and hightail it out of there.

The other hot spot is the "town" of **Rachel (www.rachel.dreamlandresort. com),** really just a collection of trailer homes. Here's where you'll find the **Little A'Le'Inn** diner and gift shop ("Earthlings Welcome")—where a very funny *X-Files* episode was filmed—and in theory, chat with fellow E.T.-spotters, who often gather at night to search the skies. The owners don't play along as much as one would like, though they do feel they were "called there for a special purpose," but their gift shop makes up for it with fine humorous souvenirs (we liked the alien-head-shaped guitar pick). Plus, they serve up satisfying diner food. You can also drop in at the **Area 51 Research Center** (just look for the big yellow trailer), which was opened after its founder (Glenn Campbell, who is largely responsible for Area 51's recent cultural icon status, and who wrote the definitive book, *Area 51 Viewer's Guide*) got kicked out of the Little A'Le'Inn. Their headquarters is now in Las Vegas, and their store is open only during spring and summer but stocks all manner of Area 51 logo items and a number of related books.

There is no place to stay out here, so unless you want to camp (which could be fun; aliens usually show up at night), plan this as a lengthy day trip. Be sure to fill your tank before you head out, as there are few opportunities to do so once you leave Vegas. If you'll be doing this drive in the heat of the summer, bring water, for your car and yourself. Along the way, keep your eyes peeled for little green men (or weather balloons, jackrabbits, tumbleweeds, broken-down cars . . .), and should you spot one, don't forget to write us all about it.

By the way, word is starting to spread of a *really* mysterious, secret base even farther out in the desert. Just mention Area 58 and watch people go nuts.

To start, you take I-15 north to U.S. 93 north (paying close attention—it's an easy exit to miss; if you do, you can take State Rte. 168 at Moapa, and take that west back to U.S. 93), and then get off at the E.T. Highway, a 98-mile stretch of State Route 375. The town of Rachel is approximately 43 miles away; the "black mailbox" (it's now white) road, which leads you to Area 51, actually comes first, about 17 miles down the highway. (We strongly suggest going to Rachel first, to get your bearings, chat with knowledgeable locals and other alien-spotters, and pick up some literature, including a good local map.) Turn left, and keep driving; any of the dirt roads that lead off of it will get you to the Area 51 fence and gates. Veer right at the fork in the road (not the ranch turnoff, which you come to first) if you want to go to the most commonly talked-about entrance, the one at Groom Lake (though you can't see the lake from where you are forced to stop.)

For more information, call the **Nevada Commission on Tourism** (ⓒ **800/ NEVADA-8**), and ask them to send you their *Pioneer Territory* brochure and a list of E.T. Highway services (gas stations, chambers of commerce, restaurants, and more). On the Internet, check out **www.ufomind.com** (this is a huge site maintained by the Area 51 Research folks, and contains countless links and all sorts of information) and **www.ufo-hyway.com**.

Appendix:
Las Vegas in Depth

There has rarely been a time in Vegas's post-Bugsy history when the city wasn't booming, but it seems on a particular roll right now. A new megaresort seems to go up every other week, and each brings something new to the party, sometimes things hitherto never invited: great works of art, five-star world-renowned chefs, rock clubs and arenas that attract significant and still-current acts—you get the idea. In other words, everything old is new again, and Vegas glamour is back.

1 A Look at the Past

THE EIGHTH WONDER OF THE WORLD

For many years after its creation, Las Vegas was a mere whistle-stop town. That all changed in 1928 when Congress authorized the building of nearby Boulder Dam (later renamed Hoover Dam), bringing thousands of workers to the area. In 1931, gambling once again became legal in Nevada, and Fremont Street's gaming emporiums and speak-easies attracted dam workers. Upon the dam's completion, the Las Vegas Chamber of Commerce worked hard to lure the hordes of tourists who came to see the engineering marvel (it was called "the Eighth Wonder of the World") to its casinos. But it wasn't until the early years of World War II that visionary entrepreneurs began to plan for the city's glittering future.

LAS VEGAS GOES SOUTH

Contrary to popular lore, developer Bugsy Siegel didn't actually stake a claim in the middle of nowhere—he just built a few blocks south of already-existing properties.

And in 1941, El Rancho Vegas, ultraluxurious for its time, was built on the same remote stretch of highway (across the street from where the Sahara now stands). Scores of Hollywood stars were invited to the grand opening, and El Rancho Vegas soon became the hotel of choice for visiting film stars.

Beginning a trend that continues today, each new property tried to outdo existing hotels in luxurious amenities and thematic splendor. Las Vegas was on its way to becoming the entertainment capital of the world.

Las Vegas promoted itself in the 1940s as a town that combined Wild West frontier friendliness with glamour and excitement. As Chamber of Commerce president Maxwell Kelch put it in a 1947 speech, "Las Vegas has the impact of a Wild West show, the friendliness of a country store, and the sophistication of Monte Carlo." Throughout the decade, the city was Hollywood's celebrity playground. The Hollywood connection gave the town glamour in the public's mind. So did the mob connection (something Las Vegas has spent decades trying to live down), which became clear when notorious underworld gangster Bugsy Siegel built the fabulous Flamingo, a tropical paradise and "a real class joint."

A steady stream of name entertainers came to Las Vegas. In 1947, Jimmy Durante opened the showroom at The Flamingo. Other headliners of the 1940s included Dean Martin and Jerry Lewis, tap-dancing legend Bill "Bojangles" Robinson, the Mills Brothers, skater Sonja Henie, and Frankie Laine. Future Las Vegas legend Sammy Davis Jr. debuted at El Rancho Vegas in 1945.

While the Strip was expanding, Downtown kept pace with new hotels such as the El Cortez and the Golden Nugget. By the end of the decade, Fremont Street was known as "Glitter Gulch," its profusion of neon signs proclaiming round-the-clock gaming and entertainment.

THE 1950S: BUILDING BOOMS & A-BOMBS

Las Vegas entered the new decade as a city (no longer a frontier town) with a population of about 50,000. Hotel growth was phenomenal. The Desert Inn, which opened in 1950 with headliners Edgar Bergen and Charlie McCarthy, brought country-club elegance (including an 18-hole golf course and tennis courts) to the Strip.

In 1951 the Eldorado Club Downtown became Benny Binion's Horseshoe Club, which would gain fame as the home of the annual World Series of Poker. In 1954 the Showboat sailed into a new area east of Downtown. The Showboat not only introduced buffet meals, but it also offered round-the-clock bingo and a bowling alley (106 lanes to date).

In 1955 the Côte d'Azur–themed Riviera became the ninth big hotel to open on the Strip. Breaking the ranch-style mode, it was, at nine stories, the Strip's first high-rise. Liberace, one of the hottest names in show business, was paid the unprecedented sum of $50,000 a week to dazzle audiences in The Riviera's posh Clover Room.

Elvis appeared at the New Frontier in 1956 but wasn't a huge success; his fans were too young to fit the Las Vegas tourist mold. In 1958 the $10 million, 1,065-room Stardust upped the spectacular stakes by importing the famed *Lido de Paris* spectacle from the French capital. It became one of the longest-running shows ever to play Las Vegas.

Throughout the 1950s, most of the Vegas hotels competed for performers whose followers spent freely in the casinos. The advent of big-name Strip entertainment tolled a death knell for glamorous nightclubs in America; owners simply could not compete with the astronomical salaries paid to Las Vegas headliners. Two performers whose names have been linked to Las Vegas ever since—Frank Sinatra and Wayne Newton—made their debuts there. Mae West not only performed in Las Vegas, but also cleverly bought up ½ mile of desolate Strip frontage between the Dunes and the Tropicana.

Competition for the tourist dollar also brought nationally televised sporting events such as the PGA's Tournament of Champions. In the 1950s the wedding industry helped make Las Vegas one of the nation's most popular venues for "goin' to the chapel." Celebrity weddings of the 1950s that sparked the trend included singer Dick Haymes and Rita Hayworth, Joan Crawford and Pepsi chairman Alfred Steele, Carol Channing and TV exec Charles Lowe, and Paul Newman and Joanne Woodward.

On a grimmer note, the '50s also heralded the atomic age in Nevada, with nuclear testing taking place just 65 miles northwest of Las Vegas. A chilling 1951 photograph shows a mushroom-shaped cloud from an atomic bomb test visible over the Fremont Street horizon. Throughout the decade, about one bomb a month was detonated in the nearby desert (an event, interestingly enough, that often attracted loads of tourists).

THE 1960S: THE RAT PACK & A PACK RAT

The very first month of the new decade made entertainment history when the Sands hosted a 3-week "Summit Meeting" in the Copa Room that was presided over by "Chairman of the Board" Frank Sinatra with Rat Pack cronies Dean

Martin, Sammy Davis Jr., Peter Lawford, and Joey Bishop (all of whom happened to be in town filming *Ocean's Eleven*).

The building boom of the '50s took a brief respite. Most of the Strip's first property, the El Rancho Vegas, burned down in 1960. And the first new hotel of the decade, the first to be built in 9 years, was the exotic Aladdin in 1966.

During the '60s, negative attention focused on mob influence in Las Vegas. Of the 11 major casino hotels that had opened in the previous decade, 10 were believed to have been financed with mob money. Then, like a knight in shining armor, Howard Hughes rode into town and embarked on a $300 million hotel- and property-buying spree, which included the Desert Inn itself (in 1967). Hughes was as "bugsy" as Benjamin Siegel any day, but his pristine reputation helped bring respectability to the desert city and lessen its gangland stigma.

Las Vegas became a family destination in 1968, when Circus Circus burst onto the scene with the world's largest permanent circus and a "junior casino" featuring dozens of carnival midway games on its mezzanine level. In 1969, Elvis made a triumphant return to Las Vegas at the International's showroom and went on to become one of the city's all-time legendary performers. His fans had come of age.

Hoping to establish Las Vegas as "the Broadway of the West," the Thunderbird Hotel presented Rodgers and Hammerstein's *Flower Drum Song*. It was a smash hit. Soon The Riviera picked up *Bye, Bye, Birdie*, and, as the decade progressed, *Mame* and *The Odd Couple* played at Caesars Palace. While Broadway played the Strip, production shows such as the Dunes's *Casino de Paris* became ever more lavish, expensive, and technically innovative.

THE 1970S: MERV & MAGIC

In 1971 the 500-room Union Plaza opened at the head of Fremont Street on the site of the old Union Pacific Station. It had what was, at the time, the world's largest casino, and its showroom specialized in Broadway productions. The same year, talk-show host Merv Griffin began taping at Caesars Palace, taking advantage of a ready supply of local headliner guests. He helped popularize Las Vegas even more by bringing it into America's living rooms every afternoon.

The year 1973 was eventful: Over at the Tropicana, illusionists extraordinaire Siegfried & Roy began turning women into tigers and themselves into legends in the *Folies Bergère*.

Two major disasters hit Las Vegas in the 1970s. First, a flash flood devastated the Strip, causing more than $1 million in damage. Second, gambling was legalized in Atlantic City. Las Vegas's hotel business slumped as fickle tourists decided to check out the new East Coast gambling mecca.

As the decade drew to a close, an international arrivals building opened at McCarran International Airport, and dollar slot machines caused a sensation in the casinos.

THE 1980S: THE CITY ERUPTS

As the '80s began, Las Vegas was booming once again. McCarran Airport began a 20-year, $785-million expansion program.

Siegfried & Roy were no longer just the star segment of various stage spectaculars. Their own show, *Beyond Belief*, ran for 6 years at the Frontier, playing a record-breaking 3,538 performances to sellout audiences every night. It became the most successful attraction in the city's history.

In 1989, Steve Wynn made Las Vegas sit up and take notice. His gleaming white-and-gold The Mirage was fronted by five-story waterfalls, lagoons, and lush tropical foliage—not to mention a 50-foot volcano that dramatically erupted regularly! Wynn gave world-renowned illusionists Siegfried & Roy carte blanche (and more than $30 million) to create the most spellbinding show Las Vegas had ever seen.

THE 1990S THROUGH TODAY: KING ARTHUR MEETS KING TUT

The 1990s began with a blare of trumpets heralding the rise of a turreted medieval castle fronted by a moated drawbridge and staffed by jousting knights and fair damsels. Excalibur reflected the '90s marketing trend to promote Las Vegas as a family-vacation destination.

More sensational megahotels followed on the Strip, including the *new* MGM Grand hotel, backed by a full theme park (it ended Excalibur's brief reign as the world's largest resort), Luxor Las Vegas, and Steve Wynn's Treasure Island.

In 1993 a unique pink-domed 5-acre indoor amusement park, Grand Slam Canyon, became part of the Circus Circus hotel. In 1995 the Fremont Street Experience was completed, revitalizing downtown Las Vegas. Closer to the Strip, rock restaurant magnate Peter Morton opened the Hard Rock Hotel, billed as "the world's first rock 'n' roll hotel and casino." The year 1996 saw the advent of the French Riviera–themed Monte Carlo and the Stratosphere Casino Hotel & Tower, its 1,149-foot tower the highest building west of the Mississippi. The unbelievable New York–New York arrived in 1997.

But it all paled compared with 1998–99. As Vegas hastily repositioned itself from "family destination" to "luxury resort," several new hotels, once again eclipsing anything that had come before, opened. Bellagio was the latest from Vegas visionary Steve Wynn, an attempt to bring grand European style to the desert, while at the far southern end of the Strip, Mandalay Bay charmed. As if this weren't enough, The Venetian's ambitious detailed re-creation of everyone's favorite Italian city came along in May 1999, and was followed in short order by the opening of Paris Las Vegas in the fall of 1999.

The 21st century opened up with a bang as the Aladdin blew itself up and gave itself a from-the-ground-up makeover, while Steve Wynn blew up the Desert Inn, with plans to open a new showstopper, Le Reve, by 2005. Along the way, everyone has expanded, with first the Luxor, then Caesars, and lately, Mandalay Bay, Venetian, and Bellagio all adding new towers and hundreds more rooms each. Clearly, no one can rest on their laurels in Vegas, for this is not only a city that never sleeps, but one in which progress never stops moving, even for a heartbeat.

For the latest shake-ups on the Strip, see "What's New in Las Vegas," at the beginning of this guide.

Index

See also Accommodations and Restaurant indexes, below.

Frommer's Portable Guides

Complete Guides for the
Short-Term Traveler

Portable Acapulco, Ixtapa & Zihuatanejo
Portable Amsterdam
Portable Aruba
Portable Australia's Great Barrier Reef
Portable Bahamas
Portable Berlin
Portable Big Island of Hawaii
Portable Boston
Portable California Wine Country
Portable Cancún
Portable Charleston & Savannah
Portable Chicago
Portable Disneyland®
Portable Dublin
Portable Florence
Portable Frankfurt
Portable Hong Kong
Portable Houston
Portable Las Vegas
Portable London
Portable Los Angeles
Portable Los Cabos & Baja

Portable Maine Coast
Portable Maui
Portable Miami
Portable New Orleans
Portable New York City
Portable Paris
Portable Phoenix & Scottsdale
Portable Portland
Portable Puerto Rico
Portable Puerto Vallarta, Manzanillo &
  Guadalajara
Portable Rio de Janeiro
Portable San Diego
Portable San Francisco
Portable Seattle
Portable Sydney
Portable Tampa & St. Petersburg
Portable Vancouver
Portable Venice
Portable Virgin Islands
Portable Washington, D.C.

Available at bookstores everywhere.

Wickedly honest guides for sophisticated travelers—and those who want to be.

Irreverent Guide to Amsterdam
Irreverent Guide to Boston
Irreverent Guide to Chicago
Irreverent Guide to Las Vegas
Irreverent Guide to London
Irreverent Guide to Los Angeles
Irreverent Guide to Manhattan
Irreverent Guide to New Orleans
Irreverent Guide to Paris
Irreverent Guide to Rome
Irreverent Guide to San Francisco
Irreverent Guide to Seattle & Portland
Irreverent Guide to Vancouver
Irreverent Guide to Walt Disney World®
Irreverent Guide to Washington, D.C.

Available at bookstores everywhere.

FROMMER'S® COMPLETE TRAVEL GUIDES

FROMMER'S® DOLLAR-A-DAY GUIDES

FROMMER'S® PORTABLE GUIDES

FROMMER'S® NATIONAL PARK GUIDES

FROMMER'S® MEMORABLE WALKS

Chicago
London

New York
Paris

San Francisco

FROMMER'S® WITH KIDS GUIDES

Chicago
Las Vegas
New York City

Ottawa
San Francisco
Toronto

Vancouver
Washington, D.C.

SUZY GERSHMAN'S BORN TO SHOP GUIDES

Born to Shop: France
Born to Shop: Hong Kong,
  Shanghai & Beijing

Born to Shop: Italy
Born to Shop: London

Born to Shop: New York
Born to Shop: Paris

FROMMER'S® IRREVERENT GUIDES

Amsterdam
Boston
Chicago
Las Vegas
London

Los Angeles
Manhattan
New Orleans
Paris
Rome

San Francisco
Seattle & Portland
Vancouver
Walt Disney World®
Washington, D.C.

FROMMER'S® BEST-LOVED DRIVING TOURS

Britain
California
Florida
France

Germany
Ireland
Italy
New England

Northern Italy
Scotland
Spain
Tuscany & Umbria

HANGING OUT™ GUIDES

Hanging Out in England
Hanging Out in Europe

Hanging Out in France
Hanging Out in Ireland

Hanging Out in Italy
Hanging Out in Spain

THE UNOFFICIAL GUIDES®

Bed & Breakfasts and Country
  Inns in:
  California
  Great Lakes States
  Mid-Atlantic
  New England
  Northwest
  Rockies
  Southeast
  Southwest
Best RV & Tent Campgrounds in:
  California & the West
  Florida & the Southeast
  Great Lakes States
  Mid-Atlantic
  Northeast
  Northwest & Central Plains

Southwest & South Central
  Plains
  U.S.A.
Beyond Disney
Branson, Missouri
California with Kids
Central Italy
Chicago
Cruises
Disneyland®
Florida with Kids
Golf Vacations in the Eastern U.S.
Great Smoky & Blue Ridge Region
Inside Disney
Hawaii
Las Vegas
London
Maui

Mexio's Best Beach Resorts
Mid-Atlantic with Kids
Mini Las Vegas
Mini-Mickey
New England & New York with
  Kids
New Orleans
New York City
Paris
San Francisco
Skiing & Snowboarding in the West
Southeast with Kids
Walt Disney World®
Walt Disney World® for
  Grown-ups
Walt Disney World® with Kids
Washington, D.C.
World's Best Diving Vacations

SPECIAL-INTEREST TITLES

Frommer's Adventure Guide to Australia &
  New Zealand
Frommer's Adventure Guide to Central America
Frommer's Adventure Guide to India & Pakistan
Frommer's Adventure Guide to South America
Frommer's Adventure Guide to Southeast Asia
Frommer's Adventure Guide to Southern Africa
Frommer's Britain's Best Bed & Breakfasts and
  Country Inns
Frommer's Caribbean Hideaways
Frommer's Exploring America by RV
Frommer's Fly Safe, Fly Smart

Frommer's France's Best Bed & Breakfasts and
  Country Inns
Frommer's Gay & Lesbian Europe
Frommer's Italy's Best Bed & Breakfasts and
  Country Inns
Frommer's Road Atlas Britain
Frommer's Road Atlas Europe
Frommer's Road Atlas France
The New York Times' Guide to Unforgettable
  Weekends
Places Rated Almanac
Retirement Places Rated
Rome Past & Present